The Proceedings of The Conference
on Biblical Inerrancy
1987

THE PROCEEDINGS OF THE CONFERENCE ON BIBLICAL INERRANCY 1987

BROADMAN PRESS
Nashville, Tennessee

© Copyright 1987 • Broadman Press
All rights reserved
4260-04
ISBN: 0-8054-6004-7
Printed in the United States of America

EDITORIAL PREFACE

This book contains the papers presented at The Conference on Biblical Inerrancy, May 4-7, 1987, at Ridgecrest Baptist Conference Center in Ridgecrest, North Carolina. The conference was sponsored and coordinated by the six seminaries of the Southern Baptist Convention. We appreciate the cooperation of the presidents of the seminaries in this project—William Crews (Golden Gate); Milton Ferguson (Midwestern); Landrum P. Leavell II (New Orleans); W. Randall Lolley (Southeastern); Roy L. Honeycutt (Southern); and Russell H. Dilday (Southwestern). Over 1,000 persons gathered to hear the papers read, participate in seminars, and engage in dialogue on the subject of biblical inerrancy.

The papers in this collection have been edited with a light and hasty hand in order to move the materials through the process quickly. No effort was made to edit in such a way as to bring the papers into conformity with one standard of style or grammar; rather, we have chosen to let each author's work stand substantially as it was written. Of course, we have corrected errors of spelling and sometimes altered the order of words when clarity was at stake. A few of the authors had bibliographies attached to their presentations; most did not. Since the bibliographies were not part of the actual presentations at the conference, we have not included them with the papers. Bibliographies are included at the end of this volume. Also, readers will find ample suggestions for reading and research in the well-documented notes that appear throughout the book.

Two sets of papers require further explanation. First, Joel Gregory's task at the conference was to preach a sermon on the Scripture as part of the opening worship service. Dr. Gregory did not preach from a prepared manuscript. The paper contained in this book was produced by editing a typescript taken from an audiotape of the service. Because of this, readers may note that the paper has a different sound to it than the other papers in the book. This is as it should be since Gregory's task and method of presentation differed from that of the other speakers.

Second, J. I. Packer's three papers—"Inerrancy and the Divinity and Humanity of the Bible," "Problem Areas Related to Biblical Inerrancy," and "Implications of Biblical Inerrancy for the Christian Mission"—presented some difficulties in the course of the book's preparation. Because he accepted the invitation to address the conference on very short notice and was already heavily committed to similar duties elsewhere, Dr. Packer was unable to prepare formal papers. Instead, he spoke from rather detailed and extended notes. Typescripts were made from the audiotapes of his addresses, and it was the editor's task to develop manuscripts for inclusion in this volume by carefully comparing the typescripts with the notes. It is hoped that the results accord with both the views and the high standards of J. I. Packer, though of course only the editor is responsible for any miscommunications as a result of this process.

The Proceedings of The Conference on Biblical Inerrancy is divided into two sections. Part I contains the major addresses and responses given during the plenary sessions. Part II contains papers presented in the various seminars offered during the afternoon.

ABOUT THE AUTHORS

Morris Ashcraft is professor of theology and academic dean at Southeastern Theological Seminary in Wake Forest, North Carolina.

L. Russ Bush is associate professor of philosophy of religion at Southwestern Baptist Theological Seminary in Fort Worth, Texas.

James E. Carter is pastor of University Baptist Church in Fort Worth, Texas.

Robert L. Cate is dean of academic affairs at Golden Gate Baptist Theological Seminary in Mill Valley, California.

Bruce Corley is associate professor of New Testament at Southwestern Baptist Theological Seminary in Fort Worth, Texas.

Joe H. Cothen is vice president for academic affairs and professor of pastoral work at New Orleans Baptist Theological Seminary in New Orleans, Louisiana.

M. Vernon Davis is associate professor of Christian Theology and dean at Midwestern Baptist Theological Seminary in Kansas City, Missouri.

Lewis A. Drummond holds the Billy Graham Chair of Evangelism at Southern Baptist Theological Seminary in Louisville, Kentucky.

J. Kenneth Eakins is professor of archaeology and Old Testament interpretation at Golden Gate Baptist Theological Seminary in Mill Valley, California.

E. Earle Ellis is research professor of theology at Southwestern Baptist Theological Seminary in Fort Worth, Texas.

Millard J. Erickson is dean at Bethel Theological Seminary in St. Paul, Minnesota.

James Flamming is pastor of First Baptist Church in Richmond, Virginia.

James Leo Garrett is professor of theology at Southwestern Baptist Theological Seminary in Fort Worth, Texas.

Joel Gregory is pastor of Travis Avenue Baptist Church in Fort Worth, Texas.

William L. Hendricks is professor of Christian theology, director of seminary graduate studies, and director for the Center of Religion and the Arts at Southern Baptist Theological Seminary in Louisville, Kentucky.

William E. Hull is provost at Samford University in Birmingham, Alabama.

Fisher Humphreys is professor of theology at New Orleans Baptist Theological Seminary in New Orleans, Louisiana.

Peter Rhea Jones is pastor of First Baptist Church in Decatur, Georgia.

Kenneth Kantzer is dean of the Christianity Today Institute and professor at Trinity Evangelical Divinity School.

Richard Land is vice-president for academic affairs and professor of theology and church history at Criswell College in Dallas, Texas. He is currently on leave in order to serve as a special counsel on church and state relations to the governor of Texas.

John Lewis is pastor of First Baptist Church in Raleigh, North Carolina.

Richard R. Melick is professor of Greek and New Testament at Mid-America Seminary in Memphis, Tennessee.

David L. Mueller is professor of Christian theology at Southern Baptist Theological Seminary in Louisville, Kentucky.

Alan Neely is professor of missions at Southeastern Baptist Theological Seminary in Wake Forest, North Carolina.

Mark Noll is professor of historical and systematic theology at Regent College at Vancouver, Canada, and is a senior editor of *Christianity Today*.

J. I. Packer is professor of systematic and historical theology at Regent College, Vancouver, Canada.

Paige Patterson is president of the Criswell Center for Biblical Studies in Dallas, Texas.

Clark H. Pinnock is professor of systematic theology at McMaster Divinity College in Hamilton, Ontario, Canada.

Frank Pollard is pastor of First Baptist Church in Jackson, Mississippi.

Robert Preus is president of Concordia Theological Seminary in Fort Wayne, Indiana.

Adrian Rogers is pastor of Bellevue Baptist Church in Memphis, Tennessee.

G. Hugh Wamble is professor of church history at Midwestern Baptist Theological Seminary in Kansas City, Missouri.

Wayne Ward is the Joseph Emerson Brown professor of Christian theology at Southern Baptist Theological Seminary in Louisville, Kentucky.

Gene M. Williams is president of Luther Rice Seminary in Jacksonville, Florida.

H. Edwin Young is pastor of Second Baptist Church in Houston, Texas.

J. Terry Young is professor of theology at New Orleans Baptist Theological Seminary in New Orleans, Louisiana.

CONTENTS

1

GOD'S INDESTRUCTIBLE WORD

Joel Gregory

The theme of our conference is the word of God. We may start in a very literal way by asking just how many Bibles are being made every year. Gathering some statistics on that, I found that a single Bible publishing company, Thomas Nelson, last year used 15 tons of paper, 2 million square inches of gold leaf, 100,000 zippers, and a million square feet of leather. As I reflected on that last statistic I wondered how different this conference might be if the cattle of the nation could gather here. Whereas we may make a contribution they have made a sacrifice!

We have gathered to extol and to exalt the word of God which does not err. In its inspiration and in its preservation, surely the wonder of the whole world is the word of God. A secondary source states that 1,500 years after Heroditus recorded his history there was one manuscript remaining. Twelve hundred years after Plato had recorded his *Apology*, the zenith of philosophical idealism, there was said to be a single manuscript of that masterpiece of classical greek antiquity.

Yet all of us know that the wonder of the world is the word of God. Two thousand years after the autographs were written we have more than 4,000 manuscripts or parts of manuscripts of the Greek New Testament. We have 15 to 30 thousand Latin manuscripts and thousands of manuscripts in other versions. Both in its inspiration and in its preservation the wonder of the world is indeed God's word.

My favorite Old Testament prophet is that remarkably faithful man, Jeremiah. When you consider the depression that he suffered, the rejection that his message faced, the frustrations, the retardants, the impediments to his ministry, Jeremiah may stand tallest among all of them in his call to faithfulness as a prophet of God. In this longest prophetic book, I would invite your attention to the 36th chapter this evening as we look together *at* the word of God in this conference *on* the word of God. It is a chapter which surely touches on both the inspiration and the preservation of sacred scripture. We believe our *Baptist Faith and Message* confesses both the unity and the canonicity of the word of God. We believe that by implication what Jeremiah said about inspiration and preservation of Scripture likewise belongs to those other books that are part of that unified and organic whole of canonical Scripture. When you look at this passage, you examine the words of a book that faced both political and religious rejection, both spiritual disregard and physical destruction from within and without the community of faith. You look at a man and his message that

1

faced derogation and a book that faced destruction. Nevertheless, it stands as part of God's indestructible word.

> In the fourth year of Jehoiakim son of Josiah king of Judah, this word came to Jeremiah from the Lord: "Take a scroll and write on it all the words I have spoken to you concerning Israel, Judah and all the other nations from the time I began speaking to you in the reign of Josiah till now. Perhaps when the people of Judah hear about every disaster I plan to inflict on them, each of them will turn from his wicked way; then I will forgive their wickedness and their sin."

In the following paragraphs we read of a remarkable and striking three-fold reading of the then extant words of Jeremiah. They were read to the *majority* who proved to be indifferent. They were read to the *minority*, a select group of those who's blood ran rich with spiritual renewal. The minority were reverent toward it. It was read to the *magistrate,* or Jehoiakim and his court circle. They rejected that word. That brings us to one of the unforgettable scenes of Jeremiah's life and times in Jeremiah 36:23.

> It was the ninth month and the king was sitting in the winter apartment, with the fire burning in the firepot in front of him. Whenever Jehudi had read three or four columns of the scroll, the king cut them off with a scribe's knife and threw them into the firepot, until the entire scroll was burned in the fire. The king and all his attendants who heard all these words showed no fear, nor did they tear their clothes. Even though Elnathan, Delaiah and Gemariah urged the king not to burn the scroll, he would not listen to them. Instead the king commanded Jerahmeel, a son of the king, Seraiah son of Azriel and Shelemiah son of Abdeel to arrest Baruch the scribe and Jeremiah the prophet. But the Lord had hidden them. After the king burned the scroll containing the words that Baruch had written at Jeremiah's dictation, the word of the Lord came to Jeremiah: "Take another scroll and write on it all the words that were on the first scroll which Jehoiakim king of Judah burned up."

The indestructible word of God. Why can we say that? *I. It is as the word of God a revelation.* The 36th chapter of Jeremiah states as explicitly, as exactly, as precisely what happened in the production of a biblical book as anywhere I can find in sacred Scripture. Indeed, someone made the remark that this is the only record of the production of part of a book of sacred Scripture. In the second verse the words fairly leap off of the page. "Take a scroll and write on it all the words I have spoken to you." For approximately 23 years Jeremiah had been the recipient of the oracles of God—a lonely, rejected, depressed prophet who always preached and whose invitation no one ever answered. He had treasured all of the words that God had spoken to him. It is as if the Spirit of God in order to underscore this repeated it four times in this passage: "Take a scroll and write on it all of the words that I have spoken to you."

Sometimes in our discussions we have said, "Let us use concerning the Bible only the language that the Bible uses concerning itself." Indeed, that being the case, the words from Jeremiah written on that scroll were nothing but veritably

2

the words of God himself. It was an oracle recorded by Jeremiah. Augustine of Hippo in North Africa stands with three or four others as casting the longest shadow in the history of the Christian church. His *Confessions* 13:29 spoke as if God were speaking: "O man, what my scripture says, I say." Veritably, God's word.

As I weigh the words of Jeremiah, I weigh them against other understandings of the word of God. Was Jeremiah simply reacting to the mighty acts of God as an illuminated Hebrew genius, recording his thoughts concerning God's great interventions in history? If so, we have some difficulty with Jeremiah because Jeremiah was a man who conspicuously looked up to high heaven above and asked God, "Why don't you act?" He was a man for whom the mighty acts of God belonged to that which was yet to come. The book we hold must be more than simply a reverent reflection of the mighty acts of God.

What else might it be? It might be a mysterious, speechless encounter with a transcendent God—something of an afterglow, something of a crater that was left after the bomb went off in the encounter with God. But we are told that the Lord spoke to Jeremiah and said, "Take a scroll and write on it *the words that I have spoken to you.*"

Most certainly when speaking of Jeremiah it is difficult to say that this word is a revelation only if it is an existential revelation of God to those who first read it. If that were the case, there would be no revelation at all. That generation heard the words of Jeremiah and almost to a person rejected them. As clearly as could be stated here God said, "Take a scroll and write on it the words that I have spoken to you." It is veritably the words of God.

It has always been a difficulty for me in my own reflection to separate the great revelation of God from the words that God himself spoke. One of the durable problems in psychiatry, psychology, philosophy and epistemology is the difference between mind and brain. Our brain is the physical mechanism which in some way is the vehicle for the spiritual reality that we call the human mind. Just as it is impossible for me to conceive of mind apart from brain, it is also difficult for me to conceive that God can reveal and disclose himself apart from speaking words.

When you turn to the New Testament, you find evidence for that. On Tuesday of Passion Week our Lord Jesus was in the temple debating with the rationalistic Sadducees concerning the doctrine of the resurrection of the dead. They had asked him a supercilious question, a silly question. He responded to them by saying, "You err; you do not know the power of God or scripture." He quoted that mighty word when God had encountered Moses and said "I am the God of Abraham, the God of Isaac, and the God of Jacob." Our Lord's comment on that was, "He is the God not of the dead but of the living." As our Lord handled Exodus 3:6 He was willing to hang upon the tense of a verb from the Hebrew Old Testament His argument for the resurrection of the body of the believer at the last day. He did *not* say "I *was* the God of Abraham," for that would mean that Abraham no longer existed. But in that blessed present tense He said, "I *am* the God of Abraham." I have read a reaction to that that would say Jesus was simply a prisoner of first century rabbinical exegesis. I hope I am

3

not an obscurantist, I hope that I am not someone who is uninformed. You know and I know that the overwhelming number of Southern Baptists do not believe that Jesus Christ was simply prisoner of first century rabbinic exegesis. He was the Son of God speaking God's word.

In Galatians 3 the apostle Paul confronted the same question. He was dealing with the covenant promises of God to Abraham and us. In Galatians 3 he took the promise in Genesis 12, 13, and 24 and brought it to focus upon the Lord Jesus Christ. Paul said it was not to seeds (plural) but to a seed (singular) of Abraham that the promise was made. So in this instance, the apostle Paul drew from a single Word of the Word his covenant theology.

I remember confronting this when I was a freshman in the basement of Kokernot Hall at Baylor University. I had an experience that many of you have had. I was sitting there in the middle of the night memorizing the paradigm of the Greek verb *luo*. I subsequently became a major in Greek at the university level and went on to study through doctoral level work. In the midst of the night, working on the plu-perfect passive of *luo*, it suddenly dawned on me as it must have on many of you: "Why are you doing this, Gregory?" If it was an indifferent matter, if Paul could have used an imperfect passive or an aorist passive or a perfect passive, if it was simply up for grabs as the whim struck him, why on the earth was I sitting there memorizing that paradigm? It came to me that evening in an experience that was 22 years ago now. "You are doing this because these words are *theopneustos*, "God breathed."

It is the word of God not only because it is remarkable in its indestructible revelation. *2. It is remarkable in its prediction of the reaction to word.* In this passage we find the spectrum of human reaction to the word of God. You find that the *majority* was indifferent, the *minority* was reverent, and the *establishment* rejected that word. Jeremiah told Baruch, his faithful emanuences and secretary, "Go, I am debarred from the temple." I think we would say today that Jeremiah had been churched. He could not go. He was circumscribed. So Baruch went and in a prominent place he persistently read the accumulation of 23 years of the words of God to Jeremiah in days of peril.

I need not rehearse to this group the significance of the battle of Carcemish. That defeat of pharaoh by Nebuchadrezzar was one of those times in world history that the tide of empire flowed another way and the map of history was changed. And 23 years of prophecy was literally burning in fulfillment before the eyes of that generation, ringing in their ears with the verity of the word of God. In those circumstances, Baruch read the words of Jeremiah.

I suppose it must have been a saddening and heart breaking thing. That rugged prophet somewhere huddling in Jerusalem heard the ringing voice of Baruch speaking of that which was in the process of being fulfilled before their eyes. The reaction of that generation was one of indifference. For the masses, the mob, the multitude, the *hoi polloi* there was no reaction. No response. No conviction. No confession. Even as the words of Baruch ricocheted off the stones of the temple on that icy winter day, they met an icy reception from the multitude of people.

One reason I believe in the indestructible verity of the word of God is how accurately it predicts the reaction that people will have to it through the ages. As I stood to preach at Travis Avenue yesterday, where were most of the people? As I looked out there at about 2500 people, the thought crossed my mind, *Where are the 900,000 people in Tarrant County? More than 820,000 of them were in nobody's church. They were in their boats and polishing their cars and on the fairways and in the bowling alleys and in front of their T.V.'s. They were jogging and bicycling. They were everywhere but where the word of God was being proclaimed.* But I want you to understand that both in the days of Jeremiah and now that regardless of reaction it is *still* the indestructible word of God.

From the *minority* there was reverence. Michaiah, the son of Gemariah, son of Shaphan and others heard it with reverence. "When they heard the word of God," the Hebrew says literally, "they trembled toward one another." They trembled with a sense of personal sin. They trembled with the sense of national sin. They trembled for the fate of Jeremiah and Baruch. They trembled when they considered the rage of Jehoiakim. The minority of people met it with an awesome reverence.

What is this but a presaging of our Lord's "Parable of the Soils"? He spoke of the same reception that the word of God would get: minority reverent and a majority indifferent.

3. *The indestructible word of God is revealed even in the rejection of that word of God.* We find that here as if in a schematic, if we were looking at all of history collectively, in advance.

The rejection of the word of God has been in *physical destruction* of the book, in *spiritual disregard* for its message, and *in destruction of its messengers.*

As they sat there in the winter apartment of Jehoiakim, there was first of all an effort for *the physical destruction of the book.* It is one of the vivid pictures of the Old Testament. There is the king sitting with a brazier in an indentation in the floor of the palace. Archeologists have found such indentations full of coals from burned out fires. There to dull the winter winds blowing through his palace, he had built a fire. Jehudi, some court official, was ordered to read the scroll. As Jehoiakim heard it, he took a scribe's knife and cynically, silently, intermittently he would cut off every three of four columns and throw them into the brazier. A lifetime of the revelation of God in words to Jeremiah was physically destroyed by the king.

It is interesting in this regard to contrast another episode. The father of Jehoiakim, Josiah, had likewise had the word of God brought to him. When that word was brought—the rediscovered scroll of Deuteronomy—Josiah had instituted national repentance. His son, Jehoiakim, instituted a man hunt for the messengers. Josiah had torn his clothes. His son, Jehoiakim, had torn the word of God. Attitudes toward the word of God can drastically change in a single generation. We are not made of angel dust or finer stuff than those were. In a single generation the attitude had so changed that whereas a father tore his garments, a son tore the scroll.

But it was not successful. It is interesting that in the aftermath of this physical

5

destruction of the word of God, the word came again to Jeremiah: "Take another scroll and write on it all the words that were on the first scroll." In recent years we've heard a great deal about the word "autograph." Well, this autograph was certainly lost! It was consumed in the fire. But even in its absence, the same Lord of inspiration and providence said, "Take another scroll and write on it all the words that were on the first scroll." Even in the light of the physical destruction of his word, God intervenes in preservation. Antiochus Epiphanes in his attack upon the temple wanted to burn all the scrolls of the Old Testament. Three years later he died in disgrace. At that same time the great Maccabean dynasty lifted up, exalted, extolled and honored the word of God. In A.D. 303 Diocletian Emperor of Rome at its zenith of political power and influence unleashed what must have one of the greatest acts of persecution against a book in history. In spite of that, only 22 years later at the Council of Nicea in A.D. 325 there was so much reverence for the written word of God that the contending parties of the theological debate weighed every word of the Nicea Creed against the written word of God.

God can preserve his word. It can survive *spiritual disregard*. In verse 24, "The king and all his attendants who heard all these words showed no fear nor did they tear their clothes." Proud, ossified in his spirit, unbending and unheeding, Jehoiakim showed no reverence toward this word. It is reminiscent to me of the fact that the word of God has repeatedly withstood that kind of disregard. You are familiar with the name Voltaire. One of the striking illustrations I have ever read about the word of God was a statement Voltaire made. He died in 1788 and he made the pathetic prediction that within a century the word of God would be a forgotten object. Someone noted that approximately a century later in the bookstalls near the Seine close to the Il de France a copy of Voltaire's most famous words sold for 11 cents. In that same year the British government through the British museum spent 500,000 dollars to buy a single copy of the word of God. It is able to withstand spiritual disregard.

When President Ronald W. Reagan named 1983 "The Year of the Bible," the American Civil Liberties Union and a group of others filed a lawsuit. There were ministers, humanists, an athiest, agnostics who sued the President for proclaiming "The Year of the Bible." Someone noted in a rather droll way the year of the Bible went on anyway! Finally, the Book is able to withstand the rejection and the *destruction of its messengers*. We read that the final reaction of the King was to send his son and another to arrest Baruch the scribe and Jeremiah the prophet. But the Lord had hidden them. In the providence of God He was not through with Jeremiah. They never knew what to do with that old prophet. When we see him last they are dragging him off to Egypt. They couldn't live with him and they couldn't live without him. They didn't know what to do with him I suppose. For if you cannot get the book you can get those who carry the book and preach the book and proclaim the book. It was Wycliffe of England whose poor priests went about the country speaking the word of God in the venacular. Wycliffe died in 1384, his death date certain even though his birthdate was uncertain. He died where he had lived and worked and translated the Bible into the venacular, the idiom of the English

6

speaking people. As such he was one of the harbingers of the coming Reformation. You are familiar with the story of how it was sometime later as an act of spite English officials exhumed the moldering bones of Wycliffe and consumed them with fire. Someone wrote a little verse of poetry. The ashes of Wycliffe were thrown into the Swift, and the Swift flows into the Avon and the Avon into the Severn and the Severn into the sea. So the ashes of Wycliffe touched every continent on the planet.

Some might say that was just a preacher's poem. An event in 1981 made it more than that.

There was a boy who grew up in Lancaster, Pennsylvania named Chester Bitterman and he had a dream, a dream that one day he would go somewhere and translate the word of God into a language where there was no language. And so he took upon himself the role of a Wycliffe Bible translator. Chet Bitterman was trained along with his wife, Brenda. With his 3 year old daughter, Ruth Ann and 1 and a half year old daughter, Hester, he went to the interior of Colombia. With a tribe he would invent a language and then give them the word of God. But as in the days of Jehoiakim, a terrorist group—the M19— unable to destroy the message sought to destroy the messenger. They held him, terrorized him and traumatized his family for 48 days and then his beaten, bruised and bleeding body was found dead on a bus in Bogata. But you know the impact of that? It took the work of Wycliffe off the bottom of the church page and put it on the front page of newspapers all over the world. For "the grass withers and the flowers fade but the word of God will *stand up* forever." Smite the fire and the embers spread. If you destroy the Book, God causes it to stand again. If you destroy the messengers, God spreads the message.

2
A BRIEF HISTORY OF INERRANCY, MOSTLY IN AMERICA

Mark Noll

It is an honor and a privilege for me to speak to you tonight. The Southern Baptists make up a great American denomination, but I like many other supposedly knowledgeable folk have given it far too little attention. Although I grew up a Baptist, it was in Iowa where at that time, which to the eye of memory now seems like the middle ages, we did not see many Southern Baptists. And although I studied for two years in Tennessee, I had by that time become a Presbyterian, and so missed a chance to learn about Southern Baptists first hand. As a historian, however, I have grown increasingly aware of how important the Southern Baptists are for the story of Christianity in America and for the spread of the gospel around the world. You are a large, diverse, and vital denomination with capable leaders and faithful followers. Given your stature and diversity and my culpable ignorance about your ways, it would be foolish to think that I could tell you what to do in your current discussions about the Bible.

It may be almost as foolish to think that I could tell you something about the history of biblical inerrancy, for that is a topic spanning the centuries and engaging some of the sharpest minds in the history of Christianity. Yet the attempt is still worthwhile. History does not reveal the future, but at least it shows the path by which the past has led to the present.

Tonight I would like to offer a short sketch of how the question of biblical inerrancy emerged within the Christian churches, especially Protestant churches, and more particularly Protestant churches in America. Then at somewhat greater length, I would like to explore four closely related positions that were articulated in the late nineteenth century against those who attacked the Bible's integrity. These positions, it soon will become apparent, continue with us to this day. My conclusion will attempt several generalizations on the subject.[1]

The Emergence of the Question

Most Christians in most churches since the founding of Christianity have believed in the inerrancy of the Bible. Or at least they have believed that the Scriptures are inspired by God, and so are the words of eternal life. The term *inerrancy* was not common until the nineteenth century. But the conviction that God communicates in Scripture a revelation of himself and of his deeds, and that this revelation is entirely truthful, has always been the common belief of

9

most Catholics, most Protestants, most Orthodox, and even most of the sects of the fringe of Christianity.[2]

Questions about possible errors in the Bible arose in Europe only fairly recently, at least when considering the lengthy history of the church. In a vast oversimplification, we can pick out one circumstance each from the sixteenth, seventeenth, and eighteenth centuries that paved the way for objections to the conviction that the Bible was perfectly true. The Protestant Reformation is the first of these, and it involves an irony. As is well known, the earliest Protestants rested their case for reform on the authority of Scripture, in fact *scriptura sola*—whatever other authorities a Christian might heed, it was the Bible alone that must be authoritative over all the rest. To be sure, it was not this Protestant reliance on the Bible that opened the door for the questioning on inerrancy. Luther, Calvin, and Menno Simons would have been appalled at the lineage, but when they broke up the religious hegemony of the Roman Catholic church, they nonetheless introduced a principle of criticism which, centuries later, was used to undermine confidence in Scripture. That principle led to reasoning of this sort: If there was some kind of innate human right to pose the individual's understanding of Scripture over against the magisterium of the Catholic Church, might there not also be an innate right to pose the individual's conception of Scripture over against the traditional Christian view of its entire truthfulness.[3] The irony is that the early Protestants would have detested that move as much as they abhorred the perversions of late-medieval Catholicism.

The contribution of the next two centuries to doubts about the Bible's truthfulness were much more direct.[4] The seventeenth century saw the birth of modern science. With modern science came a great confidence in knowledge gained by experience and a corresponding suspicion of knowledge held on the basis of tradition. When knowledge supposedly gained on the basis of scientific experience—such as knowledge about how the Bible was thought to be composed—was set against knowledge relying on religious tradition, the preference of the age was for science. In the eighteenth century the issue was not so much science as human progress. A growing number of educated elite came to think that traditional religion, especially traditional faith in the Scriptures, actually restrained the human race from reaching its potential for peace, prosperity, and happiness.

These very general shifts in cultural orientation, much more than specific discoveries concerning the texts of Scripture or ancient biblical history, established the foundation for the later "higher criticism" of Scripture. When in the late seventeenth century, public voices for the first time began to question whether Moses wrote the Pentateuch, when in the eighteenth century skepticism grew about the miracle stories of Scripture, when in the nineteenth century learned Europeans overturned almost all traditional opinions concerning the ancient Hebrews, the life of Jesus, and the ministry of Paul—the reasons were theological and philosophical as much as they were historical and exegetical. John Dillenberger and Claude Welch caught the sequence very well in their book on the development of Protestantism. "This does not mean," they

10

wrote, "that the new conception of the Bible which came to characterize Protestant liberalism originated simply as a reaction to the discoveries of historical criticism. In fact, the situation was more nearly the reverse. It was new conceptions of religious authority and of the meaning of revelation which made possible the development of biblical criticism."[5]

The newer critical views, with their doubts about the truthfulness of Scripture, caught on more slowly in England and America than in the Continent. In 1860 seven ministers of the Church of England published a volume entitled *Essays and Reviews* which was meant, among other things, to promote the newer Continental views on Scripture in Great Britain. One of the essayists, Benjamin Jowett, Regius Professor of Greek at Oxford, asserted that in "the meaning of words, the connexion of sentences, the settlement of the text, the evidence of facts, the same rules apply to the Old and New Testaments as to other books."[6] That is, just as classical scholars regularly overturned traditional interpretations of Greek and Latin writers, so too biblical scholars should not be afraid to follow the criticism of the Continent in accepting new views of Scripture.

The most notable thing about *Essays and Reviews* was not its arguments, for they were fairly placid by comparison to what was available on the Continent, but the storm of protest that greeted the book from both Anglicans and members of Britain's dissenting churches. Hundreds of printed responses, judicial complaints in the Church of England, national agitation that eventually resulted in a decision by the privy council—all reflected widespread dismay at the book and its effort to question the truthfulness of Scripture as traditionally understood.

After 1860 newer critical views did make some headway in England, but always against considerable opposition. Among the most successful defenders of traditional opinions, were three great New Testament scholars—Fenton A. J. Hort, B. F. Westcott, and J. B. Lightfoot—who worked in concert with each other.[7] Although Hort did not consider himself an advocate of the Bible's strict inerrancy, he joined Westcott and Lightfoot in painstakingly careful scholarship that usually had the effect of increasing confidence in the historical accuracy and textual credibility of the New Testament. For a number of reasons, the story concerning the Old Testament was different, and English academics more readily assumed Continental views on the nature of the Hebrew Scriptures. The situation by around 1900 in Great Britain remained therefore quite conservative on the New Testament: it was widely held that the Bible's record of Jesus' words and deeds was accurate, and that the church was entitled to the same confidence in the veracity of the New Testament as heretofore. It was somewhat different for the Old Testament. Leading Old Testament scholars still felt that God had revealed himself through the Hebrew Scriptures, but they also tended to be evolutionary in perspective (ancient Israelite faith was similar to the primitive religions of the Canaanites) and critical in detail (the books of Moses were written as late as the exilic or post-exilic periods; most of the purported history of the Old Testament was legend or myth). Towards the end of the nineteenth century, Britain, in short, was a half-way house between the Continent, where critical views had triumphed, and America, where they had only begun to be heard.[8]

Scholars and pastors in America were even more skeptical than their colleagues in Britain concerning any effort to question the detailed accuracy of Scripture. Most ordinary believers throughout the United States, and most scholars not associated with the country's leading universities, maintained traditional views well into the twentieth century. But again, large changes in the culture made way for specific shifts on the Bible. The most important of these was the professionalization of academic life and the rise of the modern university. As a further chapter in the story of intellectual inferiority that Americans have always felt toward Europe, the new universities defined their superiority to the old colleges by imitating the form and substance of European education. The founding of the Society of Biblical Literature in 1880 was only the most obvious sign of professionalization for students of Scripture. When the Johns Hopkins University opened its doors in 1876 as a graduate school for specialized study on the Germanic model and when Charles Eliot transformed Harvard into a research university shortly thereafter, a new and influential conception of academic life began to assert its sway in America.[9]

Leaders of the new academy self-consciously set themselves apart from the pious but parochial mentors who had directed higher education in America. The grail of science beckoned invitingly. To attain it, the sacrifice of traditional opinions was a small price to pay. As Andrew D. White put it in his vision for Cornell, the university would "afford an asylum for Science—where truth shall be sought for truth's sake, where it shall not be the main purpose of the Faculty to stretch or cut sciences exactly to fit 'Revealed Religion'."[10] Received dogma was suspect in every field, not least for the Bible.

Most importantly, the new universities embodied a new attitude toward history. The Germans seemed to have demonstrated conclusively that facts were always relative to historical context, each stage of history was always the product of what had gone before, minds were always a function of cultures, and the divine was always immanent in human experience. Historical consciousness of this sort had revolutionary implications when applied to Scripture. The Bible might retain its status as a revered document, but only because it was a unique expression of religious experience, not because it was a word from God.

The challenge of biblical higher criticism as represented most clearly in the new universities was troubling to conservative defenders of the traditional view that the Bible was truthful in common sensical terms. These conservatives continued to believe that events described in the Bible as historical were historical, that its statements about matters of fact were matters of fact. Soon they were galvanized into action, but not so much by agnostics, skeptics, or even liberals who questioned the Bible's veracity. Rather the conservatives began carefully to formulate what had previously been largely an intuitive confidence in the Bible only when other Christians, and often Christians of a fairly conservative theology, accepted the new views. Assertions by figures like the American Presbyterian Charles Briggs or the Anglican S. R. Driver were the important

12

ones for stimulating a conservative defense of biblical inerrancy. Briggs wrote in 1881, for example, that "theories of text and author, date, style, and integrity of writings" can never by themselves establish or undercut confidence in the Scriptures. This was true even if criticism revealed minor errors in the biblical record: "The doctrine of Inspiration . . . will maintain its integrity in spite of any circumstantial errors that may be admitted or proved in the Scriptures, so long as these errors do not directly or indirectly disturb the infallibility of its matters, of faith or of the historic events and institutions with which they are inseparably united."[11] In a similar way, Driver contended in 1897 that "critical conclusions" are not "in conflict either with the Christian creeds or with the articles of the Christian faith. Those conclusions affect not the *fact* of revelation, but only its *form*."[12] A formal, self-conscious defense of inerrancy in the face of higher criticism was a reaction, in other words, to the claim by other evangelicals that no harm came to Christianity in giving up earlier formulations of the Bible's truthful character.

The Defense of a Fully Truthful Bible

The claim of the conservatives, on the contrary, was that deviation from the traditional concept of the Bible as an inerrant book detracted, and detracted very much, from Scripture in particular and the Christian faith in general. As conservatives prepared their defenses, however, they did so in different ways. Again to simplify a more complicated picture, four different American and British positions emerged. Each sought to repudiate the assumptions and results of modern criticism, each attempted to defend a conception of the Bible's perfect truthfulness.

Princeton Presbyterians

The first, most visible, and best known effort was by Presbyterians associated with the Princeton Theological Seminary. The "Princeton Theology" which had developed under Archibald Alexander and Charles Hodge during the middle decades of the nineteenth century had always held tenaciously to the Bible as the supreme authority for faith and practice, for truth and life. Now toward the end of the century, Princeton conservatives led by Hodge's son, Archibald Alexander Hodge, and Hodge's best pupil, Benjamin Breckinridge Warfield, took the measure of higher criticism and found it wanting.

The occasion for refining a Princeton view of inerrancy from the seminary's earlier, more general trust in the Bible was an extensive literary discussion of the early 1880s. The *Presbyterian Review,* under the dual editorship of Charles Briggs, who was open to higher criticism, and A. A. Hodge, who opposed it, published eight long articles on the subject. It was a remarkable exchange, with dense arguments and miles of footnotes on both sides. It arose from the feeling shared by all concerned that since a great deal of publicity was being given to new views on the Bible from Europe, the American churches should consider them seriously. In the debate Briggs and like-minded scholars developed the argument that, within limits, the higher criticism aided the church in its effort to understand and apply the Scriptures.

13

The Princeton conservatives dissented vigorously. They were not, in general, greatly impressed with the new claims to knowledge about the Bible. While they felt it was always appropriate to acknowledge new facts about Scripture—providing they really were facts—they did not feel that the modern question dealt primarily with facts. It seemed rather that the struggle lay between a set of modern assumptions about human progress, on the one hand, and the nearly universal Christian testimony of the Scriptures, on the other. They conceded that their view of the church's traditional understanding of Scripture made it very difficult to accept the new critical conclusions. Hodge and Warfield stated this most clearly in their first contribution to the exchange in 1881, entitled simply "Inspiration": "The historical faith of the Church has always been, that all the affirmations of Scripture of all kinds, whether of spiritual doctrine or duty, or of physical or historical fact, or of psychological or philosophical principle, are without any error when the *ipsissima verba* of the original autographs are ascertained and interpreted in their natural and intended sense."[13]

As these conservative Presbyterians explored the modern debate, moreover, they found a surprising absence of self-criticism among the supposedly critical scholars. The principal problem in their view was the large role assigned to presuppositions. It was, for example, "naturalistic postulates" that led scholars to discredit the Mosaic authorship of the Pentateuch. Evolutionary theories about religion prevailed because "the development theory is all the rage." In turn, the influence of such theories, rather than a careful perusal of facts, encouraged scholars to think that all religion reflects an evolutionary development from the primitive to the complex or to suppose that miraculous events are merely the fictions of primitive people.[14]

The conservatives came to the conclusion that neither the supposedly new facts nor the new historical consciousness justified either the ascription of error to any part of Scripture or any serious modifications of traditional views on authorship, composition, and origin of the biblical books. No apparent discrepancy in the Bible qualified as an error—that is, something affirmed in the original autograph, interpreted according to its intended sense, and actually contradicting "some certainly known fact of history, or truth of science, or some other statement of Scripture certainly ascertained and interpreted."[15]

Several qualities characterized this defense of inerrancy in the early 1880s, qualities which continued at Princeton Seminary until its reorganization in 1929 as a pluralistic, less conservative institution. First, the conservative Presbyterians were scholars. They matched their opponents Hebrew phrase for Hebrew phrase, footnote for footnote, learned disquisition from the German for learned disquisition from the German. They did not take intellectual shortcuts nor allow the certainties of piety to replace the practice of research.

Second, they were sharply aware of presuppositions in scholarship. They were as willing to acknowledge that they relied upon the tradition of the church and the work of the Spirit in their interpretation of Scripture as to attack their opponents for accepting the intellectual conventions of the modern European scene.

14

Third, they felt that questions about the use of higher criticism touched matters of greatest consequence. If the Bible perpetrated errors of fact in history, science, or the accounts of its literary origins, it could not be relied upon to describe the relationship between God and humanity, the way of salvation, or the finality of divine law. As Hodge and Warfield put it in 1881, since "no organism can be stronger than its weakest part, that if error be found in any one element, or in any class of statements, certainty as to any portion could rise no higher than belongs to that exercise of human reason to which it will be left to discriminate the infallible from the fallible."[16] The choice, in other words, was between the infallible words of God or the volatile opinions of men and women.

Fourth, although the Princetonians were definitely conservatives, they were not necessarily hidebound conservatives. They could conceive, in other words, that it was possible to discover new truths about the Bible or to change older interpretations of Scripture on the basis of new understandings. Again, Hodge and Warfield said it best in their essay on "Inspiration": The key in understanding the nature of the Bible and its teaching lay in the texts "in all their real affirmations." They stressed that the books of the Bible "were not designed to teach philosophy, science, or human history as such," and that the writers depended on "sources and methods in themselves fallible." This does not mean the Bible errs when its writers speak on history or its own literary origins. It simply means that "the affirmations of Scripture of all kinds" are true when "ascertained and interpreted in their natural and intended sense."[17] As we will see below, these opinions about the possibility of new interpretations from the inerrant Bible led the Princeton theologians to conclusions that not all other defenders of inerrancy accepted.

The Princeton view of biblical inerrancy was the first American contribution to the subject in the late nineteenth century. Arguments and opinions descending from that view have probably remained the most visible way of accounting for biblical inerrancy since that day. At the same time, however, other ways of defending the Bible's full truthfulness also appeared at the end of last century. They shared with the conservative Presbyterians a full confidence that the Scriptures were the true word of God and that higher criticism was fundamentally flawed. But they developed their defenses along other lines.

Dispensational/Fundamentalist

A second way of describing the Bible's perfect truthfulness could be called the dispensational or the fundamentalist. This view shared an emphasis on the divine character of Scripture, and so has often been regarded as a variation of the Princeton conviction. There is truth to that assessment, even if dispensationalists and fundamentalists also differed from the scholars at Princeton in significant ways.

Dispensationalism grew out of the work of John Nelson Darby (1800-1882), a clergyman in the Church of Ireland who became disenchanted with the compromises of that body and went on to help found the Plymouth Brethren. Darby stressed a division of history into a number of discrete epochs or dispensations, during which God was thought to offer salvation under different methods. The basis for this view was a strict literalism in the interpretation of the Bible, especially its prophetic passages. The Darbyite system first gained popularity in the United States during major conferences on prophecy which were held in the 1880s and 1890s. In 1909 the American branch of the Oxford University Press published an edition of the Bible edited by C. I. Scofield (1843-1921) whose annotations set out a dispensational interpretation of the text. The Scofield Bible sold in great numbers and remains a mainstay of dispensational biblical interpretation.[18]

Dispensationalists were uniformly defenders of biblical inerrancy against advocates of biblical higher criticism. Their views of Scripture emphasized the Bible's supernatural character, even to the extent of downplaying its character as a book written by humans. As a consequence, dispensationalists had very little patience with professional scholars who concentrated on the human characteristics of Scripture. The key to dispensational interpretation was the ability to connect different portions from the entire Scripture into a coherent picture of prophecy and fulfillment. To do this, it was necessary to emphasize the repetition of words in different biblical books, to discriminate fine shades of meaning in phrases referring to the divine Kingdom, and to trace a literal fulfillment of even the most imaginative apocalyptic passages. As the historian George Marsden put it in his book, *Fundamentalism and American Culture,* "In this view Scripture was an encyclopedic puzzle. It was a dictionary of facts that had been progressively revealed in various historical circumstances and literary genres and still needed to be sorted out and arranged."[19] The key thing for our purposes is that this view of the Bible rested on a complete and entire confidence in the specific accuracy of Scripture to the last detail.

Unlike the Princeton defense of inerrancy, however, the dispensational view was not scholarly as that word had come to be defined in the modern university. Most of dispensationalism's major proponents made a point of steering clear of technical learning. Darby was well educated and versed in the major European languages, yet he devoted his energies to itinerant evangelism and popular writing. Scofield was a lawyer turned lay annotator. Lewis Sperry Chafer, who published a multivolume systematic theology from a dispensational viewpoint in 1947, attended Oberlin College for three years before beginning a pastoral career. To Chafer and other dispensationalists it was a positive advantage not to be contaminated by the learning purveyed in the universities. He once was quoted as saying, "The very fact that I did not study a prescribed course in theology made it possible for me to approach the subject with an unprejudiced mind to be concerned only with what the Bible actually teaches."[20] The modern university was a place of danger. Not only its promotion of naturalism, but even its methods of scholarship were suspect.

The dispensational conception of biblical inerrancy made a large contribution to the fundamentalist movement which developed in the North among Baptists, Presbyterians, and independents during the 1920s. Before that time, the dispensational attitude had also been present in *The Fundamentals,* a series of booklets published between 1910 and 1915. Many of the contributors to *The*

Fundamentals were not dispensationalists, but the booklets shared the dispensationalist antagonism to critical ways of interpreting the Bible. The problem with higher criticism was not the misapplication of scholarship but the perverse perspective of the critics. "The whole movement with its conclusions," said one contributor, "was the result of the adoption of the hypothesis of evolution." Wrote another, "the fundamental postulates" which grounded a belief in the plural authorship of Isaiah were "unsound." A third claimed that "modern objections to the Book of Daniel were started by German scholars who were prejudiced against the supernatural." Yet another warned that "the assumptions" of "the agnostic scientist, and the rationalistic Hebraist" must "be watched with the utmost vigilance and jealousy."[21] The view of biblical inerrancy in *The Fundamentals* was thus often a view that had almost no place for modern scholarship on Scripture.

To this second defense of biblical inerrancy, the entire enterprise of modern academic study of the Scriptures was suspect. Those who held to it objected to modern assumptions, to modern methods, to modern conclusions. In their opinion, virtually all attempts to modify traditional views of the Bible's composition, dating, prophetic validity, and historicity were anathema.

"Baptist"

A third defense of biblical truthfulness in the face of modern higher criticism could be called the Baptist way. Baptists in the North and South had remained staunchly conservative in theology when liberal influences began to change other major denominations. The conclusions of modern biblical criticism had made only slight headway in the North by 1930, and almost none in the South. Yet Baptists tended to present the case for the perfect truthfulness of Scripture differently than either the conservative Presbyterians at Princeton or the anti-academic dispensationalists.

Intellectual leaders among Baptists in this critical period made less of detailed apologetical argument and more of subjective inner experience, faith. Early in the twentieth century many Northern Baptists disassociated themselves from liberals at the University of Chicago which had been founded as a Baptist institution. The founding of Northern Baptist Seminary in Chicago in 1913 as a conservative alternative to that University testified to the denomination's support for those who would uphold the inerrancy of Scripture. Yet the Baptist turn from modernism did not rest so much upon technical arguments in Bible scholarship as it did upon an intuitive sense that the new critical conclusions compromised important aspects of Christian faith. Baptists had produced outstanding Bible scholars at the end of the nineteenth century, of whom John Broadus and A. T. Robertson were the most notable. But before the turn of the century, at least some influential Baptists were giving subjective Christian feeling a higher place in the defense of the faith than logical arguments for traditional positions. E. H. Johnson of Crozer Seminary phrased this spirit well in 1884 at that year's Baptist Congress: "If your only ground for believing the doctrines of Christianity is that they are in the book, every question of the higher or lower criticism shakes your faith, and you are alarmed at such ques-

17

tions. . . . But, brethren, take courage from your fear. It is because we have found the doctrines of the Bible true, inwardly true, because we have tested them through and through, that we have no reason to fear."[22]

A. H. Strong (1836-1921), the president of Rochester Seminary and author of a widely used *Systematic Theology* came to exemplify an approach which joined doctrinal traditionalism with theological subjectivity. Although Strong made his peace with a few proposals of the higher criticism, he also grew increasingly perturbed at the overall implications of the new views. For him it was axiomatic that "the Bible is a revelation of Christ" and that this fact undergirded "the unity, the sufficiency, and the authority of Scripture."[23] Critical conclusions that undermined these convictions were suspect.

Strong's response to attacks on biblical inerrancy was not, however, a detailed set of arguments for the Bible. Strong was a theological idealist who had been influenced by the "personalism" taught at Boston University. To Strong, the development, expression, and realization of personhood was the key to truth and life. With this perspective, Strong placed less reliance on technical arguments for the Bible. His confidence in Scripture rested rather on the Spirit of Christ as it undergirded and suffused the processes of history.[24] Strong wanted to maintain an infallible Bible, but he hoped to do so on the basis of spiritual rather than intellectual foundations.

Baptists in the South had less contact with the higher criticism of the Bible than did Baptists in the North. In 1901 less than five percent of the Society of Biblical Literature's 198 members lived in points south of Washington, D.C., less than ten percent as late as 1921.[25] The professionalization of academic life was also proceeding at a slower pace. Shortly after the Civil War, Crawford Toy had attempted to import some of the new critical views into Southern Seminary, but he was forced to resign from that institution in 1879. From that time little interest in biblical higher criticism remained among the Southern Baptists. Southern Baptist efforts to defend the truthfulness of the Bible, moreover, paralleled those of Strong's in seeking support from inner spirituality more than from academic scholarship.

The dominant Southern Baptist theologian during the first third of the century was E. Y. Mullins, president of the Southern Baptist Seminary in Louisville from 1899 to his death in 1928. Mullins's importance for Southern Baptist attitudes toward Scripture is suggested by a recent symposium on biblical scholarship in *Baptist History and Heritage*. Three different authors examined liberal, moderate, and fundamentalist approaches to Scripture among the Southern Baptists; each cited Mullins as contributing something essential to the stream he described.[26] Mullins's own views on the Bible were traditional, though he supported a broad liberality of approach. Like Strong, Mullins played down the objective, scientific approach to apologetics. Mullins was probably the most significant American conservative advocate of a subjectivist philosophy in the early twentieth century. He expressed his point of view succinctly in a contribution to *The Fundamentals:* "Christian experience sheds light on all the unique claims of Christianity. . . . Christ acts upon the soul in experience as God and manifests all the power of God. . . . Christian experience transforms the whole problem of Christian evidences to the sphere of practical life."[27]

When Mullins made these assertions, he was not denying traditional views of the Bible's entire truthfulness. In 1925 he was a major figure in the move to enlist an old description of the Bible for the Southern Baptist Statement of Faith and Mission of 1925. Scripture, as the Statement put it, "has God for its author, salvation for its end,, and truth, without any mixture of error, for its matter."[28] Rather, Mullins was asserting that technical arguments about the Scriptures, while important, were not as significant for faith as the experience of Christ. This point of view, when combined with the academic isolation of the South, meant that little attention would be given to questions of biblical inerrancy among Southern Baptists until well after World War II.

Almost the same thing could be said about several other evangelical denominations. Holiness, Wesleyan, and Pentecostal churches also held conservative views on the Bible. But as with the Baptists, a belief in the Bible's truthfulness among such groups rested more on spiritual than on intellectual grounds. Very few in these groups, as also very few among the Baptists, questioned the inerrancy of Scripture. At the same time, the language of inerrancy as developed by the conservative Presbyterians and northern dispensational-fundamentalists remained a somewhat foreign dialect, at least until recent decades.

British Evangelical

One final response to biblical higher criticism must be mentioned. It was a viewpoint held by a few evangelicals in America and by a much larger group in England. These conservatives accepted a trifle more from the modern study of the Bible, even while they condemned the naturalistic presuppositions which so often underlay critical study of Scripture. They argued for the truthfulness of the Bible even while they raised a question or two about the language of biblical inerrancy. Two well-known representatives of this position were the Scottish theologians James Denney (1856-1917) and James Orr (1844-1913) whose works have had a wide circulation in the United States.

Denney is best known for defending the substitionary atonement of Christ against Albert Ritschl's view of atonement through subjective influence. The skill with which Denney advanced this and other conservative doctrines set him apart as one of the weightier evangelical voices at the turn of the century. On Scripture, however, Denney was able to make some adjustments in light of modern scholarship. His experience with opponents of higher criticism during a trip to the United States left him unsettled, for he found them manifesting an unhealthy interest in "the millennium, premillennial notions, and in general the fads of the uneducated and half-educated men."[29] For Denney, Scripture was "*the* means through which God communicates with man. . . . No Christian questions . . . that God actually speaks to man through the Scriptures, and that man hears the voice and knows it to be God's." But once this truth-telling character of the Bible is established, and so long as no anti-supernaturalism intrudes, biblical "criticism is free to do its appropriate work." Denney conceded that "the evangelists may make mistakes in dates, in the orders of events, in

19

reporting the occasion of a word of Jesus, possibly in the application of a parable . . . ; we may differ—Christian men do differ—about numberless questions of this kind; but . . . even through in any number of cases of this kind the *gospels* should be proved in error, the *gospel* is untouched."[30]

The views of James Orr were similar, although somewhat more conservative. Orr was also unusual in that he brought both evangelical convictions and technical expertise to bear on study of the Old Testament. In *The Problem of the Old Testament,* published in 1906, Orr argued, with careful attention to recent literature and sophisticated use of exegetical tools, that criticism based on an unsupported evolutionism or the arbitrary rejection of the miraculous must be rejected. Traditional views were far sounder than academic fashion indicated. Yet Orr also found modest concepts of development helpful in describing the growth of doctrine for both the ancient Hebrews and in the Christian church.

Orr commended the biblical theories of A. A. Hodge and B. B. Warfield, yet he did not share their exact response to modern criticism. In his 1910 book, *Revelation and Inspiration,* Orr set forth a chain of conservative assertions. For instance, the words of Jesus on the Old Testament meant for modern Christians that "the truths of God's revelation were not in the air. They became the possession of mankind through *real* events and *real* acts of God. Revelation, in a word, was *historical.*" At the same time, Orr could also say "that when Jesus used popular language about 'Moses' or 'Isaiah,' He did nothing more than designate certain books, and need not be understood as giving *ex cathedra* judgments on the intricate critical questions which the contents of these books raise." Similarly, Orr held that the American defenders of biblical inerrancy were correct "in affirming that *the sweeping assertions* of error and discrepancy in the Bible often made cannot be sustantiated." He agreed that a theory of inerrancy yielded a positive view of Scripture as "supernaturally inspired to be an infallible guide in the great matters for which it was given." At the same time, however, he accepted moderate results of modern criticism which called details of the historical record into question. The presumption, he wrote, that "unless we can demonstrate what is called the 'inerrancy' of the Biblical record, down even to its munutest details, the whole edifice of belief in revealed religion falls to the ground," was a "suicidal position."[31]

In sum, Orr, Denney, and a fair number of especially British evangelicals joined American conservatives in repudiating destructive higher criticism and in defending the truthfulness of the Bible. But for these British evangelicals, it was sufficient to affirm the basic veracity of Scripture without going on to a detailed conception of inerrancy.

The four positions I have outlined are not the only conservative responses to the rise of biblical higher criticism, but they represent important strands of opinion. They also suggest the range of possibilities that can be found today among conservative Protestants on the question of Scripture. Like the dispensationalists and fundamentalists at the start of the twentieth century, there are those today who defend a strict view of inerrancy, who are deeply suspicious of academic biblical study, and who frown on attempted reinterpretations of traditional views. Like the Princeton conservatives, there are those today who argue with full academic resources for inerrancy and yet who do not rule out the possibility of new ways to interpret the inerrant Scriptures. Like A. H. Strong and E. Y. Mullins, there are those today who trust implicitly in the truthfulness and the authority of the Bible, but who rest that trust more on the force of spiritual life than on the skill of apologetical argument. And there are those like James Orr, who today defend conservative views on the Bible but who do not think it necessary to expand those views into a full advocacy of biblical inerrancy.

Without knowing the recent history of the Southern Baptists very well, it would seem that representatives of all four positions, and perhaps of even more, have been active among you in recent years. It solves no problems to know that these positions have existed for the better part of a century or more. But at least it makes possible a longer view concerning current debates.

Conclusions

At least four conclusions follow from this sketchy account of the recent history of biblical inerrancy. First, a historical examination would seem to suggest that the doctrine of biblical inerrancy is not by itself the key to understanding theological development or the general history of Christianity. In every case, those who attacked inerrancy had committed themselves to larger worldviews which undergirded their opinions. Belief in the inevitability of human progress and the evolutionary character of religious development was the womb from which biblical higher criticism came forth. The same thing may be said for the defenders of the view that the Bible was a thoroughly truthful book. The defense of inerrancy, or of other conservative views, did not rest primarily on conclusions about literary authorship or recent archaeological discoveries. It rested rather on the time-honored Christian belief that the Bible portrayed the human condition with perfect accuracy and that it set out the means for humans to be reconciled with God. From these more basic commitments arose the desire to defend Scripture from its detractors, and so preserve the Bible's message of eternal life.

A second conclusion follows immediately, however. If the stance of an individual or a group on the truthfulness of the Bible did not determine its general position, views on the Bible still have been extremely important. Given the intellectual climate of Europe for the past three centuries and of America for the last century and a half, opinions on the Bible have been barometers faithfully reflecting change or stability in the theological firmament. In addition, views on the Bible have been crucial focal points for discussion. Although these discussions have often involved other matters beneath the surface, the consideration of Scripture has often been the thing that draws more general opinions into the open, that allows for the fullest development of assumptions and presuppositions.

A modern history of Scripture does not, in my opinion, justify the famous slippery slope argument. That is, I do not feel that it is accurate to conclude that giving up traditional views of Scripture is the first mark of a slide into liberalism and unbelief. On the other hand, I do feel that attitudes toward Scripture have been very important. It simply is beyond dispute that denominations or other Christian institutions which have denied the full truthfulness of the Bible also have become less concerned about spreading the gospel to the lost, have wavered on the application of God's law to contemporary life, and have temporized on the nature of God, the nature of Christ, and the nature of salvation. The relationship is not necessarily a cause and effect relationship. But decline in orthodoxy and willingness to give up on the truthfulness of Scripture do go hand and hand.

The reverse, it should be noted, is not always the case. Stricter views of the Bible's truthfulness do not inevitably go along with more sensitive evangelism, more faithful theology, and more fruitful Christian influence on society. Yet in general, where denominations and Christian institutions reflect, however imperfectly, the spirit of Christ and are active, however incompletely, in the work of the Kingdom, among those groups we regularly find great deference to the Scriptures.

A third conclusion is that the question of the Bible's inerrancy is a somewhat different question than the interpretation of Scripture. An example helps to make this point. Theologically conservative Protestants in America have long regarded B. B. Warfield as a champion of biblical inerrancy. Warfield's 1881 essay with A. A. Hodge on "Inspiration" may in fact still be the single best statement of biblical inerrancy. In more than one hundred works after 1881, Warfield expanded, refined, and developed that defense. His opposition to the conclusions of modern higher criticism was implacable. It was an opposition worked out in lengthy encyclopedia articles, expert examination of historical questions, lengthy theological discourses, and countless reviews (many of them painstakingly detailed) of scores of books written in English and several European languages. In short, there has not been a more determined advocate of the view that "all the affirmations of Scripture of all kinds . . . are without error when . . . the original autographs are ascertained and interpreted in their natural and intended sense."[32]

Warfield's credentials as an inerrantist are beyond dispute. At the same time, however, Warfield advocated several interpretations of Scripture that many other biblical inerrantists have not shared. For him, the complete truthfulness of Scripture was the bedrock. But on the basis of his own study of the text and the influence of his theological tradition, Warfield was an amillennialist who considered premillennialism an aberrant conclusion arising from sloppy treatment of Scripture. On the basis of an avocational reading of scientific literature and special attention to Reformation commentaries on the Pentateuch, he came to the conclusion that theistic evolution was compatible with the inerrancy of the book of Genesis. The Bible, Warfield held, taught that God by a special direct act created the original "world stuff" and also the human soul. For everything else in the world, Warfield concluded that God could have exerted his creative power through evolutionary processes.[33] The point here is not whether Warfield was right or wrong on these matters. The point is that this unquestioned

22

inerrantist interpreted the Bible differently than others who also held to the inerrancy of Scripture.

The issue should not need to be belabored. The whole history of Protestantism since the Reformation shows that inerrantist Lutherans have interpreted certain Scriptures differently than inerrantist Presbyterians, who in turn have interpreted some passages differently than inerrantist Baptists. What is new in the last one hundred and fifty years or so is that differences of interpretation among biblical conservatives also pertain to some aspects of the Scriptures themselves. To note the difference between convictions about the Bible and interpretations of the Bible does not solve problems of interpretation. It does, however, suggest the wisdom in recognizing that questions about Scripture itself and about its interpretation should not be confused with each other.

Finally, a history of inerrancy shows that the question has been worked out differently among different groups of Christians. In 1925 convictions about the Bible were more strategically important for Baptists in the North than they were for Baptists in the South. Today they are probably more momentous in the South than in the North. Similarly, debates over the Bible mean something different in groups defined as "no creed but the Bible" denominations than for groups with historic confessions. Likewise they have meant something different in England and Scotland, with their state churches, than in America, with our separation between church and state. The point of this observation is that discussion over the truthfulness of Scripture occupies different places for the various denominations and at various periods of their histories. I will hazard examples: When America's Northern Presbyterians turned as a denomination in the 1920s and 1930s from the Princeton view of inerrancy, it went along with a general move toward less conservative theology. In subsequent decades fuzziness on Scripture has gone hand in hand with indecisiveness on a whole range of theological and moral issues. We see a different story on the other side of the Atlantic. When British evangelicals failed to match their American counterparts around the turn of the century and did not define a sharply-edged concept of inerrancy, it seems not to have affected their general vitality. In fact, while continuing somewhat fuzzy on biblical inerrancy, British evangelicals experienced a renewal beginning in the 1930s, and this renewal finally led in the 1950s and 1960s to sharper, more decisive statements concerning the Bible's complete truthfulness.[34]

In the end, the differences we see in different denominations can mean only one thing. As each Christian community, with inherited confidence in the Bible, confronts the intellectual and social realities of the modern world, it must meet the challenge for itself. But in meeting the challenge, that church or denomination does not have to struggle on its own. Others have been there before. Their history can in fact guide those who now traverse similar terrain. When all is said and done, that history discloses two realities. The secondary reality is that not all truly Christian efforts to preserve the full authority of the Bible have looked exactly the same. The primary reality, however, is that Christianity worthy of the name cannot be preserved without fullest confidence in the truth of that God-inspired book.

Notes

1. Much of the material in this address is from my book, *Between Faith and Criticism: Evangelicals, Scholarship, and the Bible in America* (San Francisco, 1986), which also includes a bibliography of relevant sources.

2. See especially John D. Woodbridge, *Biblical Authority: A Critique of the Rodgers-McKim Proposal* (Grand Rapids, 1982).

3. On the development of the critical principle, see Rupert E. Davies, *The Problem of Authority in the Continental Reformation* (London, 1946); and on the use of sixteenth-century precedent for later attacks on conservative theology, see the sections on the seventeenth and eighteenth centuries in A. G. Dickens and John M. Tonkin, *The Reformation in Historical Thought* (Cambridge, Mass., 1985).

4. The fullest account is Henning Graf Reventlow, *The Authority of the Bible and the Rise of the Modern World* (Eng. tr., Philadelphia, 1984).

5. John Dillenberger and Claude Welch, *Protestant Christianity Interpreted Through Its Development* (New York, 1954), 197.

6. Benjamin Jowett, "On the Interpretation of Scripture," in *Essays and Reviews* (London, 1860), 337.

7. For the general picture, see Stephen Neill, *The Interpretation of the New Testament 1861-1961* (Oxford, 1964).

8. See Willis B. Glover, *Evangelical Nonconformists and Higher Criticism in the Nineteenth Century* (London, 1954).

9. On the implications of these developments for theological conservatives, see George M. Marsden, "The Collapse of Evangelical Academia," in *Faith and Rationality: Reason and Belief in God,* eds. Alvin Plantinga and Nicholas Wolterstorff (Notre Dame, 1983).

10. Quoted in Carl Becker, *Cornell University: Founders and Founding* (Ithaca, N.Y., 1943), 156.

11. Charles Briggs, "Critical Theories of the Sacred Scriptures in Relation to Their Inspiration," *Presbyterian Journal, 2* (July 1881), 555, 552.

12. S. R. Driver, *An Introduction to the Literature of the Old Testament* (London, 1897), vii.

13. A. A. Hodge and B. B. Warfield, "Inspiration," *Presbyterian Journal, 2* (Apr. 1881), 238.

14. Francis L. Patton, "The Dogmatic Aspects of Pentateuchal Criticism," *ibid.*, 4 (Apr. 1883), 379; William Henry Green, "Professor W. Robertson Smith on the Pentateuch," *ibid.*, 3 (Jan. 1882), 122; Willis J. Beecher, "The Logical Metyhods of Professor Kuenen," *ibid.*, 3 (Oct. 1882), 707, 729-30.

15. Hodge and Warfield, "Inspiration," 242.

16. *Ibid.*

17. *Ibid.*, 237-38.

18. For overviews of dispensationalism, see Clarence B. Bass, *Backgrounds to Dispensationalism: Its Historical Genesis and Ecclesiastical Implications* (Grand Rapids, 1960); and C. C. Ryrie, *Dispensationalism Today* (Chicago, 1965); and for the influence of these views in the late nineteenth century, Ernest R. Sandeen, *The Roots of Fundamentalism: British and American Millenarianism, 1800-1930* (Chicago, 1970).

19. George M. Marsden, *Fundamentalism and American Culture: The Shaping of Twentieth Century Evangelicalism 1870-1925* (New York, 1980), 58.

20. F. Lincoln, "Biographical Sketch," prefaced to Lewis Sperry Chafer, *Systematic Theology, Vol. VIII* (Dallas, 1948), 5-6.

21. These comments are from the first volume of *The Fundamentals* (Grand Rapids, 1972; a reprint of the 4-volume edition issued by the Bible Institute of Los Angeles, 1917): J. J. Reeve, "My Personal Experience with the Higher Criticism," 349; George L. Robinson, "One Isaiah," 248; Joseph D. Wilson, "The Book of Daniel," 259; and Dyson Hague, "The Doctrinal Value of the First Chapter of Genesis," 275.

22. Quoted in Norman H. Maring, "Baptists and Changing Views of the Bible, 1865-1918 (Part I)," *Foundations*, 1 (July 1958), 68.

23. Quoted in Maring, "Baptists and Changing Views of the Bible, 1865-1918 (Part II)," *Foundations*, 1 (Oct. 1958), 56.

24. For background, see Carl F. H. Henry, *Personal Idealism and Strong's Theology* (Wheaton, 1951); and Grant Wacker, *Augustus H. Strong and the Dilemma of Historical Consciousness* (Macon, 1985).

25. *Journal of Biblical Literature*, 20 (1901), xv-xix; 40 (1921), xi-xix.

26. E. Glenn Hinson, "Southern Baptists and the Liberal Tradition in Biblical Interpretation, 1845-1945"; Claude L. Howe, Jr., "Southern Baptists and the Moderate Tradition in Biblical Interpretation, 1945-1945"; and Richard D. Land, "Southern Baptists and the Fundamentalist Tradition in Biblical Interpretation 1845-1945," *Baptist History and Heritage*, 19 (July 1984), 17, 25-26, 30. For a general account, see William E. Ellis, *"A Man of Books and a Man of the People": E. Y. Mullins and the Crisis of Moderate Southern Baptist Leadership* (Macon, 1985).

27. E. Y. Mullins, "The Testimony of Christian Experience," in *The Fundamentals*, 4:319-22.

28. John H. Leith, ed., *Creeds of the Churches* (3rd ed., Atlanta, 1982), 345-46.

29. Quoted by David Wells, "Introduction," to James Denney, *Studies in Theology*, first published 1895 (Grand Rapids, 1976), xv.

30. Denney, *ibid.*, 202, 204, 207, 209.

31. James Orr, *Revelation and Inspiration* (New York, 1910), 154, 153, 215, 217, 198.

32. Hodge and Warfield, "Inspiration," 238.

33. Warfield developed this view most fully in an essay, "Calvin's Doctrine of Creation," *Princeton Theological Review*, 13 (Apr. 1915), reprinted in *The Works of Benjamin B. Warfield, Vol. V* (New York, 1931).

34. The outstanding example was J. I. Packer, *"Fundamentalism" and the Word of God* (Grand Rapids, 1958).

RESPONSE: James E. Carter

In the olden days many of us remember going to Vacation Bible School. Along with the pledge of allegiance to the American flag and the Christian flag, we pledged allegiance to the Bible. Following that pledge we sang a little song: "The B-I-B-L-E, / Yes, that's the book for me. / I stand alone on the Word of God, / The B-I-B-L-E."[1]

And that pretty well expressed our position as Southern Baptists. We have pledged allegiance to the Bible as the Word of God. We stand on the Bible alone as our authority on all matters of faith and practice. The Bible, rather

25

than councils, creeds, or decrees has guided us in our understanding of God, Jesus Christ and the Christian faith.

But for some that simple statement is no longer sufficient. It is not enough to affirm belief in the Bible as the inspired, trustworthy, authoritative, reliable Word of God to us. That statement must be qualified even more. The term *inerrant* has become for many the operative word.

Mark Noll has given to us an excellent history of the doctrine of biblical inerrancy. In fact, for many of us Mark Noll has guided us in our historical understanding of the development of belief in inerrancy already through his writing on that topic. He has continued to teach us tonight through this fine presentation.

There would be little that I could add to a history of inerrancy by Mark Noll. From his paper I want to draw attention to a few emphases, then to make some observations from the viewpoint of Baptist history, theology, and pastoral care as seen by a conservative, mainstream, traditional Baptist pastor.

The first emphasis from Noll's paper that I think significant is the cultural context out of which the doctrine of biblical inerrancy arose. This belief, too, is culturally conditioned, especially as the culture of the late nineteenth and early twentieth century impacted the study of the Bible. Noll stated correctly ". . . the conservatives began carefully to formulate what had previously been largely an intuitive confidence in the Bible only when other Christians, and often Christians of a fairly conservative theology, accepted the new views." In the first volume of his projected four volume comprehensive history of twentieth century American Christianity, Martin Marty cited how inerrancy developed as a cultural reaction. He wrote:

> Since the modernists were relativists about authority, their critics had to be absolutists. Because the liberals favored dynamic and fluid views of history, the anti-progressives needed a stable and rigid superstructure. They found this in an assertion of the infallibility, or more scrupulously, the inerrancy of the canonical Bible. . . . in reaction to the erosions they felt precisely when modern biblical criticism reached American foundations, they fabricated a more articulated view of inerrancy than before.[2]

What met one cultural need cannot be made the standard expression for all time.

A second significant emphasis has to do with the theological and exegetical divergencies of the leading proponents of inerrancy themselves. They were not altogether agreed on all matters of biblical interpretation and application. As Dr. Noll stated with reference to the four major responses to biblical criticism that he outlined: "They . . . suggest the range of possibilities that can be found today among conservative Protestants on the question of Scripture." And in showing how B. B. Warfield in particular differed from other leading inerrantist scholars, Mark Noll said: "To note the difference between convictions about the Bible and interpretations of the Bible does not solve problems of interpretation. It does, however, suggest the wisdom in recognizing that questions about Scripture itself and about its interpretation should not be confused with each other". The Baptist strength has been the ability to accept one another as brothers and as persons of integrity while differing on some matters of interpretation. This must never be surrendered!

With reference to the final statements in Mark Noll's presentation, let me take the last one first, what he called the primary reality: that "Christianity worthy of the name cannot be preserved without fullest confidence in the truth of that God-inspired book." With that I agree whole-heartedly.

What he called the secondary reality—that "not all truly Christian efforts to preserve the full authority of the Bible have looked exactly the same"—is what I now want to address.

That not all truly Christian efforts to preserve the full authority of the Bible have looked exactly the same is precisely where I and other serious Baptists of my persuasion stand. And our conviction is that they do not have to look exactly the same to be either truly Christian or truly Baptist. In another survey of the belief in inerrancy, Jack Rogers of Fuller Theological Seminary said,

> It is . . . irresponsible to claim that the old Princeton theology of Alexander, Hodge, and Warfield is the only legitimate evangelical, or Reformed, theological tradition in America. The old Princeton tradition clearly had its roots in the scholasticism of Turretin and Thomas Aquinas. This tradition is a reactionary one developed to refute attacks on the Bible, especially by the science of biblical criticism. The demand for reasons prior to faith in the authority of the Bible seems wedded to a prior commitment to Aristotelian philosophy.[3]

And in the Foreword of that same book, *Biblical Authority,* edited by Jack Rogers, well-known evangelical leader Paul Rees wrote: "It is historically obvious, when the records are studied in depth, that the Christian church, through its confessions and in its leadership, has been exceedingly cautious about formalizing a commitment to inerrancy."[4] And that is where I stand—with a caution about a commitment to inerrancy while holding to a firm commitment to both the authority and the reliability of the Bible.

One of the cautions concerning inerrancy is from a *biblical perspective*. Inerrancy is not itself a Bible word. The Bible talks about the inspiration of the scriptures by God and the leading to eternal life through faith in Jesus Christ. We must be very careful about claiming more for the Bible than the Bible claims for itself. In his recent book, *The Scripture Principle,* Clark Pinnock (another program personality in this conference) wrote:

> It is not just that the term *inerrancy* is not used in the Bible. That would not settle anything. The point to remember is that the category of inerrancy as used today is quite a technical one and difficult to define exactly. It is postulated of the original texts of Scripture not now extant; it is held to apply to round numbers, grammatical structures, incidental details in texts; it is held to be unfalsifiable except by some indisputable argument. Once we recall how complex a hypothesis inerrancy in, it is obvious that the Bible teaches no such thing explicitly.[5]

27

Inerrancy is based on reason more than on revelation. If we accept the Bible as our authority for matters of faith, then our expressions of biblical faith should be based on biblical witness. Inerrancy starts with the proposition that God is without error and that anything that comes from God must be fully without error of any kind. While stating that, those of us who preach should remember that we preach with the assumption that the word of God can be delivered by instruments that are much less than perfect. Dr. Noll has given us a quotation from James Denney that is also helpful at this point:

> ". . . the evangelists may make mistakes in dates, in the order of events, in reporting the occasion of a word of Jesus, possibly in the application of a parable . . . ; we may differ—Christian men do differ—about numberless questions of this kind; but . . . even though in any number of cases of this kind the *gospels* should be proved in error, the *gospel* is untouched."

The famed "slippery slope" and "domino theory" arguments for inerrancy are based on reason. They reason that if one steps out on a slippery slope by admitting any error of any kind in the Bible the slide could carry that person to the bottom of the slippery slope with a complete denial of Christ. Or if error is found in any one statement of the Bible it creates a domino effect knocking down every belief until even the witness to the virgin birth or the bodily resurrection of Jesus could be doubted.

These are based on a fortress mentality. They feed on the fear that the Bible may be less than what we had thought it to be or that Southern Baptists' strength and vitality in the Christian world might be eroded.

Hear Clark Pinnock again: "In the last analysis, the inerrancy theory is a logical deduction not well supported exegetically. Those who press it hard are elevating reason over Scripture at that point."[6] Simply from a biblical perspective with the acceptance of the Bible as the revealed word of God, I have caution about using the term "inerrancy" to express my belief in the Bible.

Another of my cautions concerning inerrancy is from a *Baptist perspective*. The major Baptist confession of faith have not included biblical inerrancy as an article of faith. The Baptist confessions of faith were more concerned with inspiration and authority than with inerrancy. It is not until the Second London Confession, which was adopted in 1677 and reissued in 1689, that the article on the scriptures became the first article in the confession of faith. And they followed the order of the Westminster Confession of Faith in that. In the Second London Confession the word "infallible" is used when the article began by stating "The Holy Scripture is the only sufficient, certain, and infallible rule of all saving Knowledge, Faith, and Obedience. . . ."[7] Notice that it asserts infallibility in *saving* knowledge, faith and obedience—the Bible's intent. This was followed in the Philadelphia Confession adopted in 1742.

The New Hampshire Confession of Faith which is usually dated 1833 began with the article on scripture. It is that poetic expression of belief in the scriptures that is so familiar to us.

> We believe that the Holy Bible was written by men divinely inspired, and is a perfect treasure of heavenly instruction; that it has God for its author, salvation for its end, and truth, without any mixture of error, for its matter; that it reveals the principles by which God will judge us; and, therefore is, and shall remain to the end of the world, the true centre of Christian union, and the supreme standard by which all human conduct, creeds, and opinions shall be tried.[8]

When the Southern Baptist Convention was formed in 1845 no doctrinal statement was adopted. Not until 1925 did the Southern Baptist Convention adopt a confession of faith. The Statement on Baptist Faith and Message was a revision of the popular New Hampshire Confession of Faith. The article on "The Scriptures" was unchanged except for one addition. The word "religious" was added before "opinions." That was a significant addition because it indicated that the Bible was authoritative for religious opinions only and not all opinions. The 1963 Baptist Faith and Message was a revision of the 1925 statement. The article on "The Scriptures" was again put first in the statement. The earlier addition to the New Hampshire article was retained and two additional statements were added. After the words "divinely inspired" were added the words "and is the record of God's revelation of Himself to man" which followed some of the earlier English Baptist statements of faith. A final sentence was also added to the statement which read: "The criterion by which the Bible is to be interpreted is Jesus Christ."[9] This statement established a standard for the interpretation of the scripture.

For over 150 years this statement on the Bible has served Baptists well. It is exclusive in its insistence on the divine origin of the Bible, yet it is inclusive. Persons who believe that "truth, without any mixture of error" means biblical inerrancy can feel comfortable with that statement as well as those who feel that "truth, without any mixture of error" refers to the Bible's religious and spiritual intent. The Bible is not going to lead anyone into religious error.

I also find it instructive as well as interesting that the confessions of faith of the Landmark American Baptist Association and North American Baptist Association do not call the Bible "inerrant," even though they do use the words "infallible" and "verbal inspiration."[10] And the confession of faith adopted by the Fundamental Fellowship of the Northern Baptist Convention and later adopted by both the General Association of Regular Baptists and the Conservative Baptist Association does not mention inerrancy but acknowledges the Bible as divinely inspired and the "supreme authority in all matters of faith and practice."[11]

The point of all this is that in their confessions of faith Baptists historically have held out for the inspiration of the Bible and the authority of the Scriptures but have not insisted on inerrancy.

It only begs the question to say that earlier Baptists meant inerrancy even if they did not say it. I agree with Jack Rogers who said: ". . . it is historically irresponsible to claim for two thousand years Christians have believed that the authority of the Bible entails a modern concept of inerrancy in scientific and historical details."[12] We cannot read modern concepts back into earlier times.

The Princeton Theology, and the Evangelicalism that grew out of it, with its insistence on inerrancy came from different roots than Baptist theology generally. Dr. Noll indicated this when he said:

> . . . Baptists tended to present the case of the perfect truthfulness of Scripture differently than either the conservative Presbyterians at Princeton or the anti-academic dispensationalists. . . . the Baptist turn from modernism did not rest so much upon technical arguments in Bible scholarship as it did upon an intuitive sense that the new critical conclusions compromised important aspects of Christian faith.

The Princeton Theology and Evangelicalism generally have come directly from the Reformed tradition in Europe, especially the Protestant Scholastics. While it would be inaccurate to deny Reformed influence on Baptist life and thought, it is a part of what Walter Shurden called "The Southern Baptist Synthesis," Baptists are not lineal descendants either denominationally or theologically from those Reformation roots.[13] Baptists are evangelical but not Evangelical, as for the most part they are fundamental without being Fundamentalists. It was not until 1881 that A. A. Hodge and B. B. Warfield advanced the assertion that inerrancy referred only to the original autographs of the Scriptures.[14] So the concept of biblical inerrancy in the original autographs has grown out of a tightly reasoned, rational system that is rather modern.

From the perspective of the historic statement and development of Baptist theology there is a hesitation about both the acceptance of and insistence on the inerrancy of the Bible in the original autographs as the concept is currently understood.

A third caution about inerrancy comes from a *pastoral perspective*. Inerrantists insist on inerrancy in the original autographs only. But we do not have the original autographs, have never had them, and probably never will have them. What we are concerned with pastorally is the authority and responsible uses of the Bible that we have in our hands.

What the people in the pew want to know is whether the Bible is reliable to show them their need before God and to lead them to faith in Jesus Christ as Savior and Lord. We affirm that it is. And we do not have to resort to an assertion of inerrancy, especially with the qualification of the original autographs, to make that affirmation and to teach our people. I agree with Clark Pinnock when he answers his question "Is inerrancy meaningful?" with these words:

> A term is meaningful when it conveys the sense intended without too many qualifications being required. Some evangelicals have trouble with inerrancy on these grounds. It is not that they disagree with the thought behind the word. The word itself has become a liability because of the misunderstandings it creates. Inerrancy, as applied by many of its scholarly exponents, is actually hedged about by numerous exceptions.[15]

There is a problem with any word that takes twenty-five articles of affirmation and denial to explain its meaning as in the Chicago Statement of the International Council on Biblical Inerrancy.

It is bordering on intellectual dishonesty, if not religious demagoguery, for a person on a platform to hold up a Bible and proclaim "I believe in an inerrant Bible!" with the mental reservation of an inerrant Bible in the original autographs, knowing that the person in the pew thinks he is talking about the King James Version in his hand. It is the Bible that we hold in our hands that we have to take seriously and interpret honestly.

In the end, it is not really what you say that you believe about the Bible but how you handle the Bible that counts. For a person to affirm an inerrant Bible and then fall into allegory, eisegesis, proof-texting and the spiritualization of texts is *not* to treat the Bible either responsibly or reverently. Believing the Bible to be trustworthy we must handle it in a trustworthy manner.

In my first pastorate in an open country church on the Cane River in Louisiana there was an old, illiterate woman whom everyone called Aunt Sweet. Active in church and regular in attendance in earlier days, Aunt Sweet was practically bed-ridden by the time I became pastor of that church. As a twenty-year-old college student pastor, I would often go by her small house located in her son-in-law's goatyard on a Sunday afternoon to visit her. I thought I would just read a passage of scripture, pray with her, then be on my way. But every time I would read a passage of scripture to that bed-ridden, illiterate woman she would respond by saying, "That's a good 'un, ain't it?" And I would say, "Yes, ma'am, Aunt Sweet, that's a good 'un" and read another passage of scripture. I would end up spending half an afternoon reading the Bible to that Christian woman who could not read it for herself.

What really matters in our statements of belief in the reliability, authority and trustworthiness of the Bible is whether after studying, interpreting and applying a passage of scripture we can say, "That's a good 'un . . . ."

Ain't it?

Notes

1. Anonymous and H. D. Loes, "The B-I-B-L-E," *Singable Songs for Children No. II* (Winona Lake, Ind.: Rodeheaver, Hall-Mack Co., 1962), p. 12.

2. Martin E. Marty, *Modern American Religion: Volume 1, The Irony of It All, 1893-1919* (Chicago and London: The University of Chicago Press, 1986), p. 232.

3. Jack Rogers, "The Church Doctrine of Biblical Authority" in *Biblical Authority,* ed. Jack Rogers (Waco: Word Books, 1977), p. 45.

4. Paul Rees, "Embattlement or Understanding?" in *Biblical Authority,* ed. Jack Rogers (Waco: Word Books, 1977), p. 12.

5. Clark Pinnock, *The Scripture Principle* (San Francisco: Harper and Row Publishers, 1984), p. 58.

6. Ibid.

7. In W. L. Lumpkin, *Baptist Confessions of Faith* (Philadelphia: The Judson Press, 1959), p. 248.

8 Ibid., pp. 361-62.

9. "The Baptist Faith and Message" (Nashville: The Sunday School Board of the Southern Baptist Convention, Adopted May 9, 1963), p. 7.

10. In Lumpkin, pp. 378, 380.

11. In Lumpkin, p. 383.

12. *Biblical Authority*, p. 44.

13. A full discussion of this question can be found in James Leo Garrett, Jr., E. Glenn Hinson and James E. Tull, *Are Southern Baptists "Evangelicals"?* (Macon, GA: Mercer University Press, 1983).

14. See A. A. Hodge and B. B. Warfield, "Inspiration" in *The Princeton Theology,* ed. and compiler Mark A. Noll (Grand Rapids: Baker Book House, 1983), p. 221.

15. In Rogers, *Biblical Authority,* p. 64.

RESPONSE: Richard Land

Dr. Noll's paper, "A Brief History of Inerrancy, Mostly in America" is a model of succinct historical survey. A comparison, however, between his paper and the book upon which the address is based, *Between Faith and Criticism,*[1] is both instructive and illustrative. People interested in the subject will find the paper instructive, but they will discover that the book is even far more illuminating.

A comparison of the two provides an arresting case study of the difficulties of brevity and simplification, which are but two of modernity's burdens.[2] All too often brevity weakens clarification and emphasis sacrifices nuance. It is to be hoped that this will be remembered and that the subjects discussed here, under the tyranny imposed by time restraints, by people who have most often spent years researching these subjects will be examined in more depth in the months to come. Where the reading of referenced and cited works is needed, may it be done, and where inquiry and clarification is needed, may it be requested.[3]

I share Dr. Noll's love for history and his appreciation for its importance as being that which illuminates "the path by which the past has led to the present."[4] As an undergraduate history major I developed a firm conviction that it was impossible to understand fully anyone or anything without understanding the historical development and context. As my Oxford mentor B. R. White has so aptly noted, Baptists have often assumed inaccurately that since they are not bound by their tradition, they do not have one. Baptists have a proud heritage and it is vital that they understand their tradition and its history. To be led to disagreement with one's tradition is one thing, to ignore or misunderstand it is quite another.

Noll addresses the question forthrightly of inerrancy's prevalence within the Christian tradition when he concludes, "Most Christians in most churches since the founding of Christianity have believed in the inerrancy of the Bible."[5] His position is supported impressively by the evidence. Brunner acknowledged that the "doctrine of Verbal Inspiration was already known to pre-Christian Judaism and was probably also taken over by Paul and the rest of the Apostles."[6]

The early post-apostolic and patristic period achieved almost total unanimity on the subject of inspiration.[7] Augustine concluded:

> I have learned to yield such respect and honour only to the canonical books of Scripture; of these do I most firmly believe that the authors were completely free from error. And if in these writings I am perplexed by anything which appears to me opposed to truth, I do not hesitate to suppose that either the *manuscript is faulty*, or the translator has not caught the meaning of what was said, or I myself have failed to understand it.[8]

Even Karl Barth acknowledged the early church's position on inspiration, admitting that it "extended to the individual phraseology used . . . in the grammatical sense of the concept," and acquiesced to the fact that the Reformation leaders advocated the same understanding of verbal inspiration.[9] Luther, Calvin and the other Reformers seem to have been remarkably consistent in accepting and articulating a clear doctrine of Scripture's verbal inspiration and complete accuracy and veracity.[10]

There has been considerable effort put forth in recent years to revive earlier attempts to drive a wedge between the Reformers and the nineteenth century and to make that century's "Princeton theologians" the creators of a far more elaborate doctrine of "inerrancy."[11] It must be said at this point in time that these efforts have been investigated in light of the available data and found wanting. John Woodbridge has examined the "Rogers/McKim Proposal" exhaustively and has revealed grave difficulties with it evidentially and methodologically.[12] I agree with Noll's assessment that Woodbridge's "more conservative position seems clearly stronger in the exact matter under consideration."[13]

By this he means that we must separate the issue into two questions. First, did the forebears of our Christian tradition believe the Bible to be "inerrant?" Second, if they believed in the inerrancy of the Bible, were they correct in their beliefs in the light of modern research? The discipline of history is far better equipped to answer the first question than the second.

For Baptists and others who stand in the free church tradition, however, to answer the first question affirmatively does not provide an automatic affirmative answer to the second. It must be noted additionally that to answer the second question negatively does not allow one to revise history, only to disagree with our forebears conclusions.[14] Kirsop Lake, noted Harvard professor, concluded just that in the third decade of the present century.

> It is a mistake often made by educated persons who happen to have but little knowledge of historical theology to suppose that fundamentalism is a new and strange form of thought. It is nothing of the kind; it is a partial and uneducated survival of a theology which was once universally held by all Christians. How many were there, for instance, in Christian churches in the

eighteenth century, who doubted the infallible inspiration of all Scripture? A few perhaps, but very few.

No, the fundamentalist may be wrong; I think that he is. But it is we who have departed from the tradition not he, and I am sorry for the fate of anyone who tries to argue with a fundamentalist on the basis of authority. The Bible and the *corpus theologicum* of the Church is on the fundamentalist side.[15]

The "fundamentalism" which Lake both compliments for its faithfulness and caricatures as "uneducated" arose as a culmination of attempts to respond to the collapse of "the great evangelical consensus" in the post-Civil War era in America, a collapse more complete, and thus more keenly felt, in the North than in the South.[16] As I attempted to explain in an earlier article, Fundamentalism as a movement was forged by a coalition of Princeton theology and dispensationalism that "while allowing for numerous interpretive differences, united in the defense of inerrancy."[17]

The fundamentalist coalition's agreement on the Scripture's inerrancy clearly illustrates that inerrancy was concerned with the origin and the nature of Scripture, not its interpretation. B. B. Warfield and C. I. Scofield, exemplifying divergent segments of the fundamentalist's coalition, disagreed acrimoniously and vehemently concerning what they understood the Bible to say about many things, but they agreed that it was God's inerrant and infallible Word.

This coalition was composed of Americans who were disturbed "by the decline of the old-time religion with its accent on conversion; . . . their bonds were chiefly doctrinal. Whether rich or poor, educated or illiterate, rural or urban, Baptist or Presbyterian, they were troubled by the advance of theological liberalism . . ."[18] These folks easily and accurately fit into one of the three American categories outlined by Noll as "Princeton Presbyterians," "Dispensational/ Fundamentalist," and "Baptist."[19]

It should be noted at this point that I believe that each of Noll's three traditions coalesced into the broader Fundamentalist movement. Further, I would find less distinction between the Princeton theology and *The Fundamentals* than does Noll, and I would agree with Sydney Ahlstrom that the pamphlets represented "a focal point" or culmination of a Fundamentalism which "was launched . . . with dignity, breadth of subject matter, rhetorical moderation . . . and considerable intellectual power."[20]

Noll's three categories are symbolized by men like B. B. Warfield, C. I. Scofield, and A. H. Strong. Baptists in the South found their counterparts to these categories in J. P. Boyce, J. R. Graves, and E. Y. Mullins, respectively. It would be difficult to find any substantive non-ecclesiological divergence between Warfield and Boyce (Princeton tradition) or Scofield and Graves (Dispensational tradition). In the case of Strong and Mullins (Baptist tradition), their doctrinal differences were confined largely to non-ecclesiological matters and were largely a matter of degree rather than divergence.[21]

J. P. Boyce, a graduate of Brown and destined to become perhaps Southern Baptists' most influential nineteenth century theologian through his service as professor of theology at Furman University and later as "chairman" and guiding spirit of Southern Baptist Theological Seminary in its formative years, was deeply influenced by his studies at Princeton Theological Seminary. Boyce "was more powerfully impressed by Dr. Hodge than by any other Princeton professor."[22] Boyce's *Abstract of Systematic Theology* bears the indelible imprint of Hodge and the Princeton tradition throughout its pages.[23]

Basil Manly, Jr., destined to write Southern Baptist Theological Seminary's *Abstract of Principles* at the request of Boyce, also stated "that he learned more from Hodge" than anyone else on the Princeton faculty.[24] John A. Broadus, another of the founding faculty at Southern Seminary, was moved to comment on the Princeton experience of Boyce and Manly:

> It was a great privilege to be directed and upborne by such a teacher in studying that exalted system of Pauline truth which is technically called Calvinism, which compels an earnest student to profound thinking . . .[25]

The Southern Baptist tradition has never been as monolithically Calvinist as the Princeton tradition, thus the affinity of Boyce, Manly and Broadus for the Princeton system's Calvinism is yet another indication of its influence upon them.[26]

It should be noted that even if it were granted that "inerrancy" as an elaborated doctrine of inspiration was developed in a new way by the Princeton theologians, its acceptance by Boyce, Manly and Broadus would place it at the foundation of at least Southern Baptist "Convention" life in the South. Before attention is focused on Boyce's, Manly's, and Broadus' view of inspiration, it should be noted that the commanding figure of J. R. Graves and his influence in mid and latter nineteenth century Southern Baptist life is sufficient to trace the dispensational traditional back to the foundations of the Convention's life in the South.[27]

A. H. Strong and E. Y. Mullins, as noted earlier, shared much in common theologically, including being the outstanding late nineteenth and early twentieth century representatives of what Noll describes as the "Baptist" or "fideist" position of validating Scripture authority. While Strong and Mullins both sought to maintain a very high view of Scripture, Strong "made his peace with a few proposals of the higher criticism"[28] in a way which Mullins did not. They were in agreement, however, in epistemological approach. They both wanted to defend the Bible's authenticity and veracity on a spiritual, experiential, and fideistic base.

Dr. Noll has perceptively noted that E. Y. Mullins cast such a shadow across Southern Baptist life and was so illustrative of the "Baptist" tradition that at "a recent symposium on biblical scholarship . . . three different authors examined liberal, moderate, and fundamentalist approaches to Scripture among Southern Baptists; each cited Mullins as contributing something essential to the stream he described."[29]

The intriguing thing is that Hinson, Howe, and I were all correct. Noll understands that Mullins never abandoned a "traditional view of the Bible's entire truthfulness."[30] He cited the work of Mullins as the leading figure in employing

35

the old New Hampshire Confession of Faith's language to describe the accuracy of Scripture in the *Baptist Faith and Message* Confession adopted by the Convention in 1925 which states:

> We believe that the Holy Bible was written by men divinely inspired, and is a perfect treasure of heavenly instruction, that it has God for its author, salvation for its end, and truth, without any mixture of error, for its matter; . . .[31]

When we return to the views of the founders of Southern Seminary we find unanimity in ascribing infallibility to the entirety of Scripture. Boyce's views are clearly in accordance with "verbal inspiration" in the Princeton tradition's understanding of that concept. He further argued for the adoption of "a declaration of doctrine" for professors who would teach at a projected Southern Baptist theological institution.[32]

When the Southern Baptist Theological Seminary was founded a short time later, an *Abstract of Principles,* drafted by Basil Manly, Jr., was adopted. The *Abstract* saw that "The Scriptures of the Old and New Testament were given by inspiration of God, and are the only sufficient, certain and authoritative rule of all saving knowledge, faith and obedience."[33] In the wake of the Crawford Toy controversy in 1879, Basil Manly, Jr. responded to a letter inquiring as to the seminary's view of the Bible's accuracy. He quoted the statement of the *Abstract* and then commented as follows:

> This language must be understood in accordance with the well-known convictions and views of the founders of the Seminary, and of the Baptist denomination generally. While I am accustomed to insist on no *theory* of the manner in which inspiration was effected, I hold and teach the fact, that the Scriptures are so inspired as to possess infallibility and divine authority, and fairly interpreted, to be an adequate guide in all matters of saving knowledge and of practice. This is what I understand by the expression, "the *only sufficient, certain,* and *authoritative* rule," etc. In brief, then, the points are the Infallibility, Divine Authority, and the Sufficiency of the Scriptures, as the Word of God.[34]

It should be noted that Manly here separates the infallibility of the Scripture as a whole from its role as a guide for matters of doctrine. Manly's position certainly seems at odds with those who argue for infallibility of purpose only.[35] In light of the fact that Manly used "infallibility" in more public records such as his *The Bible Doctrine of Inspiration*[36] to describe Scripture's accuracy, it is difficult to explain the recent assertion that since 1677 "'mainline' Baptists in our heritage have generally avoided the word *infallible.*"[37] Broadus affirmed his belief in the infallibility of the Scripture as well.[38]

Noll concludes his discussion of his "Baptist" position by saying that "very few among the Baptists questioned the inerrancy of Scripture. At the same time, the language of inerrancy as developed by the conservative Presbyterians and northern dispensational-fundamentalists remained a somewhat foreign dialect, at least until recent decades."[39] I certainly accept the accuracy of his first conclusion, but I am afraid the evidence will not support his second conclusion. Yes, leading Southern Baptists did use the term and concept of "infallibility." But were they using "inerrancy" to describe their view? Yes, they were. Not only were a number of leaders doing so, but they were often among the most influential leaders in the Southern Baptist Zion.

No Southern Baptist scholar has ever achieved greater influence both within and beyond Southern Baptist ranks than did A. T. Robertson. Robertson traveled to New York early in his career to present an address to the Baptist Congress in May, 1892.[40] In this address, "The Relative Authority of Scripture and Reason," Robertson made it clear he was intimately familiar with the heated Warfield-Briggs debate then swirling through Presbyterianism and which would end with C. A. Briggs's suspension from the Presbyterian ministry and the loss of Union Seminary from direct denominational control.[41]

Robertson began by stating his belief that authority resided in God alone. The question was, "Where does God speak to us with infallible authority? . . . . Is there a Greenwich anywhere in the religious world for us to set our time by?"[42] After rejecting ecclesiastical and experiential authority, he addressed Briggs's assertion "that the Bible, the church, and the reason are all sources of divine authority."[43] He quoted Briggs's assertion "that 'higher criticism has forced its way into the Bible, and has brought us face to face with its holy contents, so that we may see and know whether they are divine or not.'"[44] He then commented,

> The modesty of that assertion is astonishing, for he means not so much the exercise of the reasoning faculties as modern higher criticism in the form we have it now. If that be true, the people who lived before modern higher criticism came along must have had a pretty hard time of it since the Bible was a closed book to them. He claims that higher criticism can tell us whether it is divine or not. Perhaps Christendom ought to wait with bated breath till the "holy contents" of the Bible have been sifted out of the rubbish. Let us wait till it tells us finally what is divine and what is not, if it has a sort of second sight for seeing the divine in the human. He says also that it is a sin even to prop up divine authority of any kind. And he proceeds immediately to prop it up with the authority of reason and the church.[45]

Robertson then proceeds to argue for the total and final authority of the Scriptures. Speaking of the Bible, he asserted that if it is recognized "as God's revelation, 'Ours not to make reply, ours not to reason why, ours but to do or die,' when God has commanded."[46] Robertson then argued for the "inerrancy of God's original Scriptures" and argued that the "whole question is whether there were any errors in the original manuscript."[47]

Robertson then boldly sought to ascribe motives to those who attacked the "inerrancy of the original Scriptures."[48] He believed it was because they wanted to be free "to shift and change the order of the Word to suit themselves."[49] He acknowledged the human setting of God's revelation, but asserted that it did not involve error.[50]

Lastly, Robertson noted that "when Scripture has spoken" on something,

37

"that is the end of the matter."[51] For Robertson "Scripture is not inconsistent with sound reason. It is inconsistent with the rapid reasonings of vain and wicked men."[52]

Nor was Robertson alone. J. M. Frost, founder of the Convention's Sunday School Board, at the outset of the present century stated his understanding of Southern Baptists' position clearly:

> We accept the Scriptures as an all-sufficient and infallible rule of faith and practice, and insist upon the absolute inerrancy and sole authority of the Word of God.
> We recognize at this point no room for division, either of practice or belief, or even sentiment. More and more we must come to feel as the deepest and mightiest power of our conviction that a "thus saith the Lord" is the end of all controversy. With this definitely settled and fixed all else comes into line as regards belief and practice.[53]

John R. Sampey, long-time doyen of Old Testament studies at Southern Seminary, stated in his *Syllabus for Old Testament Study* a position that was inerrancy in everything but label.

> Conservatives hold that the writers were preserved from all error by the enbreathed Spirit guiding them. Radicals reject such a theory with scorn. Some Liberals believe in a sort of inspiration which heightened the spiritual perceptions of the Scriptural writers, but did not preserve them from error.[54]

If we turn to the great Southwest, we find the great founder of Southwestern Baptist Theological Seminary, B. H. Carroll, arguing against the "errancy" of the Bible in the context of its lack of contradiction with science.[55]

In the light of the preceding, it isn't surprising that L. L. Gwaltney, long-time Alabama pastor, editor of the *Alabama Baptist* from 1919 to 1950, and president of the Alabama Baptist State Convention, 1935-37, could estimate "that in the twenties fewer than one per cent of the South's Baptists had questioned the Christian fundamentals of biblical inspiration."[56] Indeed, as late as 1979 one Southern Baptist historian could lament that "the majority" of the Southern Baptists were "still biblical literalists or near-literalists" and that as late as 1953 "historical critical interpretation had barely gotten started even in Southern Baptist seminaries."[57]

Most Southern Baptists, in most places, at most times in our history have believed,

> that the Bible is fully inspired; it is "God-breathed" (II Tim. 3:16), utterly unique. No other book or collection of books can justify that claim. The sixty-six books of the Bible are not errant in any area of reality. We hold to their infallible power and binding authority.[58]

Few if any Southern Baptists espousing inerrancy have any problem with that statement, or with the wording of the *Baptist Faith and Message,* 1925 or 1963.

We have, however, in the post-World War II era become a more divergent people.[59] The vital question, then, is do other Southern Baptists have a problem with affirming that the Bible is "not errant in any area of reality" and if so, how is that problem to be resolved?

In the few moments that remain, I want to address briefly Noll's observation concerning the premise that abandonment of the full authority and infallibility of Scripture inevitably leads to more liberal views doctrinally. Noll notes that often it is less a "cause and effect" relationship, but rather a symptom of having been subverted by prevailing cultural presuppositions at variance with the authority of Scripture. Noll has provided several superb examples from the sixteenth, seventeenth, eighteenth, and nineteenth centuries respectively in which biblical authority was questioned for cultural and philosophical, as much as for academic, reasons.[60]

Abandonment of high views of Scripture may be as much a symptom as a cause for many. Were some Southern Baptists convinced of inerrancy's lack of truth for objective academic reasons, or were they subverted by the "siren song" of modernity, choosing trend over tradition, culture over confession, and popularity over piety? Perhaps some, raised within a Southern Baptist heritage of only a Mullins-type fideistic affirmation of Scripture's veracity, never having had exposure to the Princeton-Boyce tradition, or worse yet, having been repelled by an ossified, hardened and bitter anti-intellectualism, were seduced by appeals to be intellectual, academic and "educated." It is easy to see how one could step gradually from a Mullins-type fideism into neo-orthodoxy and not fully realize what one had lost until much later.

Pressure to conform to a rather narrow definition of "academic respectability" has certainly been present in recent decades in Southern Baptist life.[61] Indeed, one Southern Baptist seminary president recently asserted, "It's never been an agenda item to underrepresent (inerrantists) on the faculty" and then added, "But there are few people well-trained enough to qualify for the faculty who hold that position."[62]

Three tragic examples of faith damaged, or lost, in Southern Baptist educational life have recently appeared. John Jewell's aptly entitled *The Long Way Home* describes his painful pilgrimage in response to the pressures of academic respectability.[63] Clayton Sullivan's *Called to Preach, Condemned to Survive* is an even more pathos-filled account of partial, and evidently more permanent, loss of faith than Jewell's while a student at Southern Baptist Seminary.[64] Third, Joe Barnhart's *The Southern Baptist Holy War,* an attempt to explain our Southern Baptist conflicts which has gained some popularity, is written by a Southern Baptist Theological Seminary graduate with a Ph.D. in philosophy who is currently an agnostically inclined member of a Unitarian church.[65]

We have heard that abandonment of inerrancy may be a cause and effect and it may be a symptom of acquiessence to culture pressures. At the very least there is a "correlation" between one's view of Scripture and doctrinal diversity. Recently, a prominent Southern Baptist historian has called for a "divorce" in our Southern Baptist family:

We have a marriage that is broken down irretrievably, and I'm now convinced it would be more Christian and serve Christ's kingdom better if we got a divorce.[66]

I do not know which distresses me more, his diagnosis of the Convention or his doctrine of marriage. I do know that as a Southern Baptist and as an inerrantist, I reject both. I know few Southern Baptists who believe our difficulties are that severe, and I know of even fewer who believe any marriage, or any relationship, is irretrievably beyond the grace of God. I pray we will all affirm that this conference is a giant first step away from both such diagnosis and such doctrine among us.

Notes

1. Mark A. Noll, *Between Faith and Criticism: Evangelicals, Scholarship, and the Bible in America.* (San Francisco: Harper & Row, 1986).

2. Fortunately, Dr. Noll has facilitated matters by narrowing the subject's scope from "Biblical Inerrancy in Historical Perspective" to a focus on the subject "mostly in America."

3. All of the conference's presenters and their responders labor under these burdens, and I know they all would welcome detailed examination of their sources and incisive inquiry on their subjects.

4. Noll, *A Brief History.*

5. Ibid. He acknowledges that "the phrase 'inerrancy' was not common until the nineteenth century," which is "entirely truthful . . . has always been the common belief" of most of Christendom.

6. Emil Brunner, *The Christian Doctrine of God,* Vol. 1 of *Dogmatics,* trans. by Olive Wyon (Philadelphia: Westminster Press, 1950), p. 107.

7. Richard Lovelace, "Inerrancy: Some Historical Perspectives," in *Inerrancy and Common Sense.* eds. Roger R. Nicole and J. Ramsey Michaels (Grand Rapids: Baker Book House, 1980), pp. 20-21.

8. Ibid., p. 20.

9. Karl Barth, *Church Dogmatics.* ed. by G. W. Bromiley and T. F. Torrance (Edinburgh: T. & T. Clark, 1936-1969), I/2, p. 517, 520.

10. Cf. John Warwick Montgomery, "Lessons from Luther on the Inerrancy of Holy Writ," and J. I. Packer, "Calvin's View of Scripture," in *God's Inerrant Word,* ed. by John Warwick Montgomery (Minneapolis: Bethany Fellowship, 1974), pp. 63-94 and 95-114 respectively. Cf. also Carl F. H. Henry, *God, Revelation and Authority* (Waco: Word Books, 1979-), pp. 368-384.

11. The most notable, extensive and popular is Jack Rogers and Donald McKim, *The Authority and Interpretation of the Bible: An Historical Approach* (New York: Harper & Row, 1979).

12. John D. Woodbridge, *Biblical Authority: A Critique of the Rogers/McKim Proposal* (Grand Rapids: Zondervan, 1982). Cf. Noll, *Between Faith and Criticism,* pp. 16ff. and pp. 217-218 for a review of the earlier debate and its "uncanny reprise" in the Rogers/McKim-Woodbridge debate.

13. Noll, *Between Faith and Criticism,* p. 218.

14. It should serve as a warning that those who answer the second question nega-

tively (i.e. Rogers/McKim) are the ones who argue against answering the first question affirmatively and those inclined to answer the second question affirmatively conclude that evidence supports answering the first question affirmatively (i.e., Montgomery, Packer, Henry, Woodbridge, etc.). The evidence of Woodbridge's research and critique is of such a strong nature, however, that those who continue to support the Rogers/McKim view would be well-advised not to proceed in the future as though it did not exist. Cf. Russel H. Dilday, Jr., *The Doctrine of Biblical Authority* (Nashville: Convention Press, 1982) and Claude L. Howe, Jr., "Southern Baptists and the Moderate Tradition in Biblical Interpretation, 1845-1945," *Baptist History and Heritage* Vol. XIX (July, 1984), pp. 21-28.

15. Kirsop Lake, *The Religion of Yesterday and Tomorrow* (Boston: Houghton, 1926), p. 61.

16. Sydney E. Ahlstrom, *A Religious History of the American People* (New Haven: Yale University Press, 1972), p. 815.

17. Richard D. Land, "Southern Baptists and the Fundamentalist Tradition in Biblical Interpretation, 1845-1945," in *Baptist History and Heritage,* Vol. XIX (July, 1984), pp. 29. Cf. Ibid, pp. 29-30 for an attempt to trace briefly the rise and development of Fundamentalism as a movement.

18. Ahlstrom, p. 816.

19. Noll, *A Brief History.* I have omitted further consideration of Noll's fourth category, "British Evangelical," because of time and space constraints and because others, such as J. I. Packer, are infinitely more qualified than I to analyze it.

20. Ahlstrom, p. 816.

21. Cf. L. Russ Bush and Tom J. Nettles, *Baptists and the Bible* (Chicago: Moody Press, 1980), pp. 261-273 and pp. 285-300 for a survey of Strong's and Mullins' views of Scripture respectively.

22. John A. Broadus, *Memoir of James Pettigru Boyce* (New York: A. C. Armstrong and Son, 1893), p. 73. Dr. Charles Hodge is described as being "at the height of his powers" (ibid., p. 72) during Boyce's tenure in Princeton. Cf. Mark A. Noll, ed., *The Princeton Theology 1812-1921* (Grand Rapids: Baker Book House, 1983), pp. 107-207 for an excellent introduction to Hodge, selection of his writings, and analysis of his enormous influence.

23. J. P. Boyce, *Abstract of Systematic Theology* (Philadelphia: American Baptist Publication Society, 1887). Boyce's *Abstract* was first printed privately for use in Boyce's seminary classes in 1882. Cf. L. Russ Bush and Tom J. Nettles, *op. cit.,* p. 207.

24. Broadus, *Memoir,* p. 73. Cf. Robert A. Baker, *A Baptist Source Book* (Nashville: Broadman Press, 1966), pp. 137-139 for the most accessible copy of the *Abstract of Principles.* Cf. Bush and Nettles, *op. cit.,* p. 211 for the background of the *Abstract.*

25. Ibid.

26. As an unreconstructed Separate Baptist, I personally would agree more with a different aspect of our Southern Baptist soteriological heritage, illustrated by John Leland's comment in 1791. "I conclude that the *eternal purposes* of God, and the freedom of the human will, are both truths; and it is a matter of fact, that the preaching that has been most blessed of God, and most profitable to men, is *the doctrine of sovereign grace in the salvation of souls, mixed with a little of what is called Arminianism.* These two propositions can be tolerably well reconciled together, but the modern misfortune is, that men often spend too much time in explaining away one or the other, or in fixing the lock-link to join the others together; and by such means, have but little time in a sermon to insist on those two great thing which God blesses." "A Letter of Valediction on Leaving Virginia, 1791", in *The Writings of the Elder John Leland,* ed. Louise F.

Green (New York, 1945), p. 172, quoted in Ahlstrom, p. 322. Leland is a superb example of that "providential element in the mingling of the Separate Baptist distinctives with those of the older General and Particular Baptists in the South" which prepared the way for the "remarkable development that followed." Cf. Robert A. Baker, *The Southern Baptist Convention and Its People 1706-1972* (Nashville: Broadman, 1974), p. 55.

27. Norman Wade Cox, managing editor, *Encylopedia of Southern Baptists* (Nashville: Broadman, 1958) Vol. I, pp. 576-585 and Vol. II, p. 757 for Graves's life, influence and theology.

28. Noll, *A Brief History,* p. 17. Mullins wrote in 1924 that "It is my view that ultimately we must accept the record of the supernatural in the New Testament substantially as it stands, or else reject it as a whole." He concluded, "As a matter of fact men usually proceed to total rejection or practically full acceptance. One or the other of these results seem to be inevitable." (E. Y. Mullins, *Christianity at the Cross Roads.* Nashville: Sunday School Board of the Southern Baptist Convention, 1924, p. 30).

29. Ibid., citing E. Glenn Hinson, "Southern Baptists and the Liberal Tradition in Biblical Interpretation, 1845-1945," Howe, *op. cit.,* and Land, *op. cit.,* in *Baptist History and Heritage,* Vol. 19 (July, 1984), pp. 17, 25-26, 30.

30. Ibid. Since Mullins never abandoned his own theological stance as to the Scripture's accuracy, I was correct in claiming him as part of the fundamentalist tradition doctrinally. Since, as Noll notes, Mullins "supported a broad liberality of approach" in apologetic, Howe was correct in terms of Mullins' epistemological presuppositions. And, as I noted at the time, Mullins can easily be perceived, as a "transitional" figure "on the road to the more pluralistic post-World War II years" (Land, *op. cit.,* p. 31). Consequently, in terms of end result Hinson was correct in claiming him for the "liberal" tradition as well.

31. Cf. Baker, *A Baptist Source Book,* pp. 200-211 for the 1925 and 1963 *Baptist Faith and Message* confessions. Cf. William L. Lumpkin, *Baptist Confessions of Faith* (Valley Forge: The Judson Press, 1969 rev. ed.), pp. 360-367 for the New Hampshire Confession of 1833. Recent attempts to read complicated post-critical distinctions between "form" and "matter" back into the minds of mid-nineteenth century Baptists remain unconvincing. (Cf. Roy L. Honeycutt, "Biblical Authority: A Treasured Heritage!" *Review and Expositor,* Vol. LXXXIII (Fall, 1986), pp. 605-622. As noted earlier, it is one thing to argue that our forebearers were wrong. It is quite another to seek to enlist them in support of positions they did not hold.

32. Baker, *A Baptist Source Book,* p. 135. Boyce adds, in his "Three Changes in Theological Institutions" inaugural address as a professor of theology at Furman, "It is, therefore, gentlemen, in perfect consistency with the position of Baptists, as well as of Bible Christians, that the test of doctrine I have suggested to you, should be adopted. It is based upon principles and practices sanctioned by the authority of Scripture, and by the usage of our people. In so doing, you will be acting simply in accordance with propriety and righteousness. You will infringe the rights of no man, and you will secure the rights of those who have established here an instrumentality for the production of a sound ministry. It is no hardship to those who teach here, to be called upon to sign the declaration of their principles, for there are fields of usefulness open elsewhere to every man, and none need accept your call who cannot conscientiously sign your formulary. And while all this is true, you will receive by this an assurance that the trust committed to you by the founders is fulfilling in accordance with their wishes, that the ministry that go forth have here learned to distinguish truth from error and to embrace the former, and that the same precious truths of the Bible which were so dear to the hearts of its founders, and which I trust are equally dear to yours will be propagated in our churches,

giving to them vigor and strength, and causing them to flourish by the godly sentiments and emotions they will awaken within them." (Ibid., pp. 136-137).

33. Ibid., pp. 137-38.

34. Letter to Basil Manly to Norman Fox, January 4, 1882, (*LCB*, XIII) in Joseph Powhatan Cox, "A Study of the Life and Work of Basil Manley, Jr." Unpublished Th.D. dissertation, The Southern Baptist Theological Seminary, 1954, p. 321.

35. Also, if William E. Hull can use "infallibility" as a virtual synonym for inerrancy as late as 1970, then surely the burden of proof should be on those who would assert that Manly, Broadus, Robertson, and others meant something different by it than inerrancy earlier. Cf. William E. Hull, "Shall We Call the Bible Infallible?" Crescent Hill Sermons, Crescent Hill Baptist Church, Louisville, Kentucky, August 16, 1970. Cf. also Honeycutt, "Biblical Authority," pp. 605 ff. for a more recent interchangeable usage. Indeed when I first entered seminary it was still possible to affirm belief in "verbal, plenary inspiration" or "plenary inspiration" to use Basil Manly, Jr.'s phrase, and to be understood as believing in the complete truthfulness and accuracy of scripture. Soon one had to start using "infallibility" to be understood properly. Somewhat later, one had to use "inerrancy" as "infallibility" was co-opted by others. Now it seems one increasingly has to use the phrase "full inerrancy" to mean the same thing that was meant by "verbal, plenary inspiration" a generation ago. I have found myself experiencing this process by which I now have to use "inerrancy" or "full inerrancy" to describe my view and my view hasn't changed since it was called "verbal, plenary inspiration."

36. Basil Manly, Jr., *The Bible Doctrine of Inspiration* (New York: A. C. Armstrong & Son, 1888), pp. 29-30. Cf. also Joel F. Drinkard, Jr. and Page H. Kelley, "125 Years of Old Testament Study at Southern," *Review and Expositor,* Vol. LXXXII (Winter, 1985), pp. 7-19 which seems to lament that Manly's affirmation of belief "in the plenary inspiration of the Scriptures" (p. 14) triumphed over Toy's "genius" and that "Manly's traditionalism had the more lasting impact. Rather than being on the cutting edge of Old Testament scholarship, Southern Seminary would remain a citidel of unashamed orthodoxy" (p. 13).

37. Honeycutt, "Biblical Authority," p. 613.

38. John A. Broadus, *Three Questions As to the Bible* (Philadelphia: American Baptist Publication Society, n.d.), "an Address to the Southern Baptist Convention in Waco, Texas, May 9th, 1883."

39. Noll, *A Brief History*.

40. Everett Gill, *A. T. Robertson* (New York: MacMillan, 1943), pp. 71 ff.

41. A. T. Robertson, "The Relative Authority of Scripture and Reason," (n.p., n.d.), bound copy in The Southern Baptist Theological Seminary Library. Cf. also *Proceedings of the Tenth Baptist Congress*, pp. 186-193, hereafter cited as Robertson, "Authority."

42. Robertson, "Authority," p. 1-2.

43. Ibid., pp. 2-3.

44. Ibid., p. 3 quoting *The Authority of the Holy Scripture*.

45. Ibid., p. 3.

46. Ibid., p. 5.

47. Ibid., p. 6. In light of attempts of some within our ranks in recent years to belittle this position of the inerrancy of the original manuscripts it is instructive to note that Robertson argued that that was the "whole question" (Ibid., p. 6).

48. Ibid.

49. Ibid., p. 7.

50. Ibid., p. 7.

51. Ibid., p. 7.

52. Ibid., Robertson, "was stigmatized as hyper-orthodox" in contemporary accounts (Gill, *A. T. Robertson,* p. 71). Some things, it seems, seldom change. If you read his subsequent work, certainly Robertson did not.

53. J. M. Frost, (ed.) *Baptist—Why and Why Not* (Nashville: Sunday School Board of the Southern Baptist Convention, 1900), p. 12. Cf. also William Dudley Nowlin, *Fundamentals of the Faith* (Nashville, Sunday School Board of the Southern Baptist Convention, 1912), p. 26. Nowlin, noted Southern Baptist author, graduate of Southern Seminary, graduate student at the University of Chicago, prominent pastor in Kentucky, Tennessee and Florida, editor of the *Florida Baptist Witness* and associate editor of the *Western Recorder,* president of both the Kentucky and Florida Baptist Conventions, and vice-president of the Southern Baptist Convention, 1922-23, argued for "the divinely inspired and inerrant Word of God."

54. John R. Sampey, *Syllabus for Old Testament Study* (Nashville: Sunday School Board of the Southern Baptist Convention, 1924), p. 59.

55. B. H. Carroll, *Inspiration of the Bible,* comp. and ed. by J. B. Cranfill (Nashville: Thomas Nelson, 1980), Introduction and notes to 1980 edition by Paige Patterson. pp. 23, 27, 116, 123. Orig. publ. 1930.

56. Leslie L. Gwaltney, *Forty of the Twentieth or the First Forty Years of the Twentieth Century* (Birmingham: pub. by the author, 1940) p. 134, quoted in James J. Thompson, Jr. *Tried as by Fire. Southern Baptists and the Controversies of the 1920's* (Macon: Mercer University Press, 1982), p. 77. Figures like William L. Poteat served as reminders, as had Toy earlier, that there was dissent from this view, but it was notable for its weakness in numbers.

57. E. Glenn Hinson, "Eric Charles Rust, Apostle to an Age of Science and Technology," in *Science, Faith and Revelation, An Approach to Christian Philosophy* ed. Bob E. Patterson (Nashville: Broadman Press, 1979), p. 24.

58. "Glorietta Statement," presented to the Southern Baptist Convention Peace Committee by the six Southern Baptist seminary presidents, October 22, 1986.

59. Richard Land, "The Nation of 28 Million Ducks," *Baptist Times,* July 1, 1976, in which I concluded that a "debate is even now in progress concerning the extent to which theological inclusiveness and diversity is to be desired, or tolerated, in Southern Baptist life." (p. 3.)

60. Cf. Owen Chadwick, *The Secularization of the European Mind in the Nineteenth Century* (Cambridge: Cambridge University Press, 1975) and Gary Scott Smith, *The Seeds of Secularization. Calvinism, Culture and Pluralism in America, 1870-1915* (Grand Rapids: Christian University Press, 1985) for two in-depth examples of how broad cultural shifts influenced views of Scripture's authority.

61. Paul Vitz has presented a provocative proposal for a "psychology of atheism: which could easily be adapted to a "psychology of liberalism." Cf. Paul C. Vitz, "The Psychology of Atheism" in *Truth. An International, Interdisciplinary Journal of Christian Thought* ed. Roy Abraham Varghese, Vol. I (1985) pp. 29-36. The following episode is illustrative. Clark Pinnock, a major presenter at this conference was a popular and controversial professor at New Orleans Baptist Theological Seminary in the late 1960s. After his departure, a friend of mine (then and now a professor at the seminary) and I were sailing. During our sail he related that in a recent discussion with several of his colleagues he had said, "Well, Clark Pinnock at least proved one thing while he was here. He proved you could be a conservative and be smart." His colleagues stiffened and one replied, "I don't know what you mean by smart." I suspect many who have rejected inerrancy, especially if that rejection was in part determined by such cultural

pressures, have found their recent estimates of Pinnock's intellegence rising in direct proportion to the adjustment of his views away from inerrancy. I have had him favorably cited to me by an astonishing array of Southern Baptists of moderate and the liberal persuasion, some of them people who felt quite differently about him during his previous sojourn among us.

It should be added that Pinnock, if true to form, will say things in this conference which will challenge all and exasperate some. However, his brilliance should have been, and should remain, unquestioned.

62. Kevin Jones, quoting President Honeycutt, *Jackson Daily News*, December 12, 1984.

63. John P. Jewell, Jr., *The Long Way Home* (Nashville: Thomas Nelson, 1982).

64. Clayton Sllivan, *Called to Preach, Condemned to Survive* (Macon: Mercer University Press, 1985).

65. Joe Edward Barnhart, *The Southern Baptist Holy War* (Austin: Texas Monthly Press, 1986). While Barnhart is on the whole kind to me, I must state that he misquotes me and misunderstands my positions as well as those of many others.

66. *Baptist Standard*, April 15, 1987, p. 7 quoting E. Glenn Hinson.

THE INERRANCY OF SCRIPTURE

Robert Preus

This study is an approach to the problem of the inerrancy of Scripture as it concerns the church today. The attempt is to present a position that agrees with Scripture's testimony concerning itself and with the historic position of the Christian church. At the same time the attempt is made to be timely and to take into account contemporary issues raised by modern Biblical theology. I shall try to delineate and clarify what is meant by the inerrancy of Scripture, what is the basis of this doctrine, and what are its implications. It is not our purpose to become involved in the technicalities that have often obscured the doctrine or to traverse the labyrinth of intricate discussion that frequently belabors studies of this basic theological truth.

Indeed, a brief treatment such as we are about to give cannot possibly solve the many hermeneutical and isagogical problems that touch upon the inerrancy of Scripture. Yet hermeneutical and isagogical concerns cannot be avoided in a study of this nature. Therefore we have endeavored to lay down general principles concerning these matters which will comport with the inerrancy and sole authority of Scripture. Our procedure will be as follows: we shall begin with a very general definition (thesis) of inerrancy, a definition that will express the conviction of the orthodox church from her beginning to the present time. We shall next explain and justify our definition with a series of subtheses or corollaries. Finally, we shall with a series of adjunct comments attempt to relate the inerrancy of Scripture to hermeneutical principles and other concerns so as to clarify just what is included in the inerrancy of Scripture and what is not.

Thesis

In calling the sacred Scriptures inerrant we recognize in them (A), as words taught by the Holy Spirit (B), that quality which makes them overwhelmingly (C) reliable witnesses (D-E) to the words and deeds of the God who has in His inspired spokesmen and in His incarnate Son disclosed Himself to men for their salvation (F).

This definition is very general, seeking as it does to fit all the Biblical data (for example, the bold language of prophecy and of adoration, the promises concerning the world to come for which human experience offers only imperfect and insufficient analogies, the expressive and indispensable anthropomorphisms and anthropopathisms used of God, the symbolic use of numbers and other referents in books like Daniel and Revelation, etc.). The definition also agrees, however, with what the church catholic has believed and confessed through her entire history. We offer a few typical examples to bring out this fact.

Augustine, *Epist. 82*, to Jerome: "Only to those books which are called canonical have I learned to give honor so that I believe most firmly that no author in these books made any error in writing . . . I read other authors not with the thought that what they have thought and written is true just because they have manifested holiness and learning!"

Thomas Aquinas, *In Ioh. 13, lect. 1:* "It is heretical to say that any falsehood whatsoever is contained either in the Gospels or in any canonical Scripture."

Luther (W² 15, 1481): "The Scriptures have never erred." (W² 9, 356): "It is impossible that Scripture should contradict itself; it only appears so to senseless and obstinate hypocrites."

Turrettin, *Instituio Theologiae Elencticae* (Genevae, 1688), I, 79: "We deny that there are any true and real contradictions in Scripture. Our reasons are as follows: namely, that Scripture is God-breathed (2 Tim. 3:16), that the Word of God cannot lie or be ignorant of what has happened (Ps. 19:8-9; Heb. 6:18) and cannot be set aside (Matt. 5:18), that it shall remain forever (1 Peter 1:25), and that it is the Word of truth (John 17:17). Now how could such things be predicated of Scripture if it were not free of contradictions, or if God were to allow the holy writers to err and lose their memory or were to allow hopeless blunders to enter into Scriptures?"

Brief Statement: "Since the Holy Scriptures are the Word of God, it goes without saying that they contain no errors or contradictions, but that they are in all their parts and words the infallible truth, also in those parts which treat of historical, geographical, and other secular matters. (John 10:35)"

Dei Verbum of Vatican II (See *Verbum Domini*, 44, 1 [1966], p. 8; also *The Documents of Vatican II*, ed. by Walter M. Abbott, S.J. [New York, 1966], p. 119): "Therefore, since everything asserted by the inspired authors or sacred writers must be held to be asserted by the Holy Spirit, it follows that the books of Scripture must be acknowledged as teaching firmly, faithfully and without error the truth which God wanted to put into the Sacred Writings for the sake of our salvation."

Harold Lindsell's book, *The Battle for the Bible,* p. 107: Board of Trustees of Fuller Seminary: "The books which form the canon of the Old and New Testaments as originally given are plenarily inspired and free from all error in the whole and in the part. These books constitute the written Word of God, the only infallible rule of faith and practice."

Such statements written under different circumstances and at different times evince the remarkable unanimity on this matter which obtained in the church throughout her history. The statements also indicate or infer the following six corollaries which will serve to delineate and further explain our definition.

Corollary A

Our "recognition" of the truthfulness of the written Word of God is not primarily intellectual: it takes place in the obedience of faith. The truthfulness and reliability of the Scriptures is an article of faith.

Corollary B

The basis of inerrancy rests on the nature of Scripture as God's Word. Inerrancy is an inextricable concomitant of inspiration. Our conviction is that since Scripture is truly and properly speaking God's Word, it will not deceive nor err. Admittedly this is an inference here (as in the case of the doctrine of the Trinity or the two natures of Christ), but it is a necessary inference, which both Christ and the apostles drew. (See not only John 10:34; Mark 12:24; Matt. 5:18-19 but also Christ's and the apostles' use of the Old Testament; they simply cite it as unconditionally true and unassailable.)

Corollary C

Our recognition of the reliability of the witness of Scripture is graciously *imposed* on us by the Spirit of God and this through the power of Scripture itself.

Corollary D

The nature of inerrancy is essentially twofold. First, Scripture does not contradict itself (formal inerrancy). Second, Scripture does not lie or deceive or err in any assertion it makes (material inerrancy). In other words, the holy writers, moved by the Spirit of God, infallibly achieve the intent of their writing. This is what is meant when we say that Scripture is a reliable witness to the words and deeds of God. Of His people God demands in the Second and Eighth Commandments that they tell the truth; of His prophets and apostles, that they do not lie. God will not countenance lying and prevarication (Prov. 14:5; 19:22; Ps. 63:11; Jer. 23:25 ff.; Zeph. 3:13; Acts 5:3; 1 John 2:21, 27). And God Himself will not lie or deceive (Prov. 30:6-7; Num. 23:19; Ps. 89:35; Heb. 6:18). In His written Word He will not break or suspend that standard of truth which He demands of His children. Thus we hear frequently from God's inspired witnesses the claim that they do not deceive, that they are not mistaken, that they tell the truth (Rom. 9:1; 2 Cor. 11:31; Gal. 1:20; 1 Tim. 2:7). The whole impact of entire books of the Bible depends on the authoritative and truthful witness of the writer. (John 21:24; 1 John 1:1-5a; 2 Peter 1:15-18)

It is obvious that such a position on the nature of Biblical inerrancy is predicated on a correspondence idea of truth which in part means this: declarative statements (at least in those Biblical genres, or literary forms, which purport to be dealing with fact or history) of Scripture are, according to their intention, true in that they correspond to what has taken place (for example, historical statements), to what obtains (for example, theological affirmations and other affirmations concerning fact), or to what will take place (for example, predictive prophecy). It really ought to go without saying that with all its different genres and figures of speech, Scripture, like all cognitive discourse, operates under the rubrics of a correspondence idea of truth. (See John 8:46; Eph. 4:25; 1 Kings 8:26, 22:16,22 ff.; Gen. 42:16,20; Deut. 18:22; Ps. 119:163; Dan. 2:9; Prov. 14:25; Zech. 8:16; John 5:21-32ff.; Acts 24:8,11; 1 Tim. 1:15; note, too, the forensic picture which haunts all of Scripture—for example, such concepts as witness, testimony, judge, the Eighth Commandment, etc.; John 21:24.)

49

To speak of inerrancy of purpose (that God achieves His purpose in Scripture) or of Christological inerrancy of Scripture is indeed relevant to the general question of inerrancy, but may at the same time be misleading if such a construct is understood as constituting the nature of inerrancy—for then we might speak of the inerrancy of Luther's Small Catechism or of a hymn of John Wesley, since they successfully achieve their author's purpose.

The first purpose of Scripture is to bring us to faith in Christ (John 20:31; 2 Tim. 3:15). Involved with this prime purpose of Scripture is the doctrine of the Christocentricity of Scripture (Old Testament as well as New Testament). Such Christocentricity has a soteriological purpose. Only when I understand that Scripture and Christ are for me will I understand the Scriptures themselves (or the inerrancy thereof). But to say that Scripture is inerrant only to the extent that it achieves its soteriological purpose is a misleading position if it is made to be identical with inerrancy or confused with it. How does Scripture achieve its saving purpose? By cognitive language, among other things. By presenting *facts,* by telling a history (Old Testament as well as New Testament). To say that there is a purpose in Scripture but no intentionality (that is, intent to give meaning) in the individual books or sections or verses, or to maintain that Scripture is inerrant in its eschatological purpose but not in the intentionality of its individual parts and pericopes would not only be nonsense, reducing all Scripture to the level of some sort of mystical utterances, but would be quite un-Scriptural (Luke 1:1-4, etc.). The eschatological purpose of Scripture does not mitigate or vitiate or render trivial and unimportant the cognitive and factual content of assertions (and the truth of assertions) throughout the Scripture, but requires all this (Rom. 15:4). And on the other hand, formal and material inerrancy does not threaten or eclipse the Christological purpose of Scripture but supports it. Nor does such a position (formal and material inerrancy) become tantamount to reading Scripture atomistically. Language is a primary structure of lived experience and cannot be studied in isolation from it. Because the language of imagery in Scripture may not always be adequately analyzed or ever completely exhausted implies neither that it is meaningless (positivism) nor that it is errant ("Christian" positivism). Not orthodoxy but neoorthodoxy has a positivistic, wooden theory of language.

Corollary E

Inerrancy is plenary or absolute. 1) It pertains not only to the substance of the doctrines and narratives in Scripture, but also to those things which are nonessential, adjunct, *obiter dicta,* or things clearly assumed by the author. 2) It covers not only the primary intent of the various pericopes and verses but also the secondary intent (for example, a passing historical reference within the framework of narrative, such as that Christ was crucified between two thieves, that wise men visited Him at His birth, that Joshua led the Children of Israel into Canaan, that Ruth was a Moabitess, Nimrod a hunter, etc.), not only soteriological, eschatological, and religious intent and content of Scripture but also all declarative statements touching history and the realm of nature.

There are various reasons for this strict position. 1) The New Testament cites

50

what might often be considered to be passing statements or negligible items from the Old Testament, accepting them as true and authoritative (Matt. 6:29; Matt. 12:42; John 10:35). Jesus accepts the basic framework of the Old Testament history, even those aspects of that history which seem unimportant to many today, for example, Sodom and Gomorrah (Luke 17:27), Lot's wife turning to salt, the murder of Abel (Luke 11:51), Naaman (Luke 4:27). The New Testament does not recognize *levicula* (minor details) in the Old Testament (Rom. 15:4; 2 Tim. 3:16). 2) The primary intent of a passage or pericope is often dependent on the secondary intent(s). For instance, the Exodus as a deliverance of God depends on the miraculous events connected with it. 3) If errors of fact or contradictions are admitted in minor matters recorded in Scripture (matters that do not matter [?]), by what right may one then assume that there is no error in important or doctrinal concerns? How does one determine what matters are important? And does not, after all, everything pertain at least indirectly to doctrine (2 Tim. 3:16)? In other words, to maintain that "things which do matter" in Scripture (doctrinal matters) are inerrant and "things which do not matter" (nondoctrinal matters) are errant is both arbitrary and impossible to apply.

Corollary F

There is great comfort and practical importance to the doctrine of Biblical inerrancy. Because God is true and faithful, the reader of Scripture can have the assurance that he will not be deceived or led astray by anything he reads in God's Word, Holy Scripture. Such a practical concern must also be emphasized in our day. Any approach to Scripture or method of interpretation which would make of Scripture something less than trustworthy is sub-Christian and does not take Scripture at its own terms. It must also be borne in mind that the truthfulness of Scripture is never an end in itself, but serves the saving purpose of Scripture.

Adjuncts To The Doctrine
of Biblical Inerrancy

1. Inerrancy does not imply verbal exactness of quotations (for example, the words of institution, the words on Jesus' cross). The New Testament ordinarily quotes the Old Testament according to its sense only, sometimes it only alludes to a pericope or verse in the Old Testament, sometimes there are conflations. In the case of extra-Biblical citations we ought to assume that the holy writer stands behind and accepts the truth of his quotation unless the context would indicate otherwise (see 2 Chron. 5:9, 8:8 where there are citations from documents which say that a situation obtains "to this day," that is, when the original document was written).

2. Inerrancy does not imply verbal or intentional agreement in parallel accounts of the same event. For instance, the portrayal of creation in Gen. 1 and in Job 38 are radically different because of a radical difference in the aim of the author. Again, the different evangelists write about our Lord from different vantage points and out of different concerns: therefore their accounts will differ

51

not only in details (as in the case of any two or three witnesses of the same event) but in aim. Moreover, it must be clearly recognized that incomplete history or an incomplete presentation of doctrine in a given pericope is not false history or a false presentation.

3. Scripture is replete with figures of speech, for example, metonymy (Luke 16:29), metaphor (Ps. 18:20), personification (Matt. 6:4), synecdoche (Luke 2:1), apostrophe, hyperbole (Matt. 2:3). It should go without saying that figurative language is not errant language. To assert that Scripture, by rounding numbers and employing hyperbole, metaphors, and so forth, is not concerned about precision of fact (and is therefore subject to error) is to misunderstand the intention of Biblical language. Figurative language (and not modern scientifically "precise" language) is precisely the mode of expression which the sacred writers' purposes demand. To imply that figurative language is *ex hypothesi* meaningless or that it cannot convey information—truthful and, from its own point of view, precise information—is the position of positivism, not the result of sensitive exegesis (for example, "Yanks slaughter Indians" is a meaningful and precise statement). How else does one speak of a transcendent God, of His epiphanies and revelations, than in metaphors and figures of speech? De-metaphorize, deanthropomorphize, and you are often not getting closer to the meaning of such expressions, but losing their meaning. Figurative language, then, meets all the canons necessary for inerrancy: (1) that statements perfectly represent the author's meaning; (2) that statements do not mislead the reader or lead him into error of any kind; and (3) that statements correspond to fact when they purport to deal with fact, and this is the case of poetry as well as in the case of straight narrative.

It must be added at this point that when we interpret or read Scripture we identify ourselves with the writers, not only with their *Sitz im Leben* and their use of language but with their entire spirit and their faith (which is more important, 1 Cor. 2:14-16). We not only understand them cognitively, but we feel and live and experience with them; we commit ourselves to what they teach and say; we become totally involved. To stand back dispassionately and assess and criticize as a modern man would criticize Shelley or Shakespeare or Homer is to fail to interpret Scripture.

4. Scripture uses popular phrases and expressions of its day, for example, bowels of mercy; four corners of the earth; Joseph is called the father of Christ. No error is involved in the use of such popular expressions. See Ps. 7:9, 22:10.

5. In describing the things of nature Scripture does not employ scientifically precise language, but describes and alludes to things phenomenally as they appear to our senses: for example, the fixity of stellar constellations and the magnitude of the stars (Is. 13:10; Judg. 5:20; Job 38:31; Amos 5:8; Job 9:9); the sun and moon as lights and the implication that the moon is larger than the stars (Gen. 1:16) [It *is* larger from our vantage point]; the earth as motionless in a fixed position (Eccl. 1:4; Ps. 93:1); the sun as going around the fixed earth (Eccl. 1:5; Matt. 13:6; Eph. 4:26); note that in the Hebrew Bible there is even

52

a phrase for the rising of the sun: *mizrach shemesh*, which means "east," Ps. 50:1). Phenomenal language also explains why the bat is classified with birds (Lev. 11:19; see Lev. 11:6; Ps. 135:6). Such a classification offers no attempt to be scientific.

Many things in the realm of nature are spoken of in poetic language: the spreading out of the heavens (Is. 40:22; Job 9:8), the foundations of the earth (Job 38:6), the pillars of the earth (Job 9:6) and of heaven (Job 26:11), the ends of the earth (Ps. 67:7, 72:8). Note that there is much apostrophe and hyperbole (Mark 4:31) when Scripture speaks of the things of nature.

In none of the above instances is inerrancy threatened or vitiated. The intention of the passages cited above is not to establish or vouch for a particular world view or scientific explanation of things. Because the language is not scientific does not imply that it is not true descriptively.

6. Certain alleged literary forms are not compatible either with the purpose of Scripture or with its inerrancy. For instance, in principle, strictly scientific, strictly historical, or salacious literary forms cannot be reconciled with the serious, practical theological purpose of Scripture. Specifically, any literary genre that would in itself be immoral or involve deceit or error is not compatible with Biblical inerrancy and is not to be found in Scripture, for example, myth, etiological tale, midrash, legend or saga according to the usual designation of these forms. None of these genres fits the serious theological purpose of Scripture. Thus, we do not find Scripture presenting material as factual or historical when in truth it is only mythical. (2 Peter 1:16ff.; 1 Tim. 1:4, 4:7; 2 Tim. 2:4)

Apart from the above strictures any form of ancient literature is hypothetically compatible with Biblical inerrancy, for example, allegory (Gal. 4) and fable (Judg. 9:8-15), provided the genre is indicated directly or indirectly. At the same time it does no violence to inerrancy if the language of folklore or mythical elements serves as a means to clothe a Biblical author's presentation of doctrine (for example, "helpers of Rahab" in Job 9:13; "Leviathan" in Job 3:8 and in Ps. 74:12-15; Idumea as inhabited by centaurs, satyrs, and other strange creatures [Is. 34:14], meaning that Idumea will be devastated so that only such animals can live there). We do the same today if in a sermon a pastor refers to a "dog in a manger." As for the midrash, there is no reason to maintain that Scripture cannot employ midrashim any more than other literary forms. In many cases midrash approaches parable in form and purpose. However, the fanciful examples of midrash with the indiscriminate admixture of truth and error and the production of pure fiction to stress a certain lesson is not compatible with the historical character and the inerrancy of Scripture.

7. Biblical historiography. (1) Some Biblical writers use and cite sources for their history. We must assume that the Biblical author by the way in which he cites sources believes that these sources speak the truth, that they are reliable sources; and therefore he follows them. The contrary contention is certainly possible, but it must be proved in individual cases (implicit citations, see 2 Sam.). In the case of explicit citations (the words of a character in a history) we assume the truth of the matter cited, but this again depends on the intention

53

of the historical writer. We can assume the truth of the matter cited only if the holy writer formally or implicitly asserts that he approved it and judges to be true what he asserts in the citation. (See Acts 17:29.)

(2) Historical events are not described phenomenally as are the data of nature.

(3) The historical genre employed by Scripture is apparently a unique form. As it cannot be judged according to the canons (whatever they may be) of modern scientific historiography, it cannot be judged by the mythological and legendary or even historical forms of ancient contemporary civilizations; for example, we take the ancient Babylonian and Ugaritic accounts of creation as pure myth, but quite clearly the Biblical account cannot be taken as such.

(4) Chronology and genealogies are not presented in Scripture in the full and orderly manner in which we might present a chronicle or family tree today. Scripture often spreads out time for the sake of symmetry or harmony, *hysteron proteron* is often employed, and also prolepsis (John 17:4, 13:31). Again, genealogies often omit many generations. (See 1 Chron. 26:24, where Moses, Gershom, Shebuel are given, covering a period of perhaps more than 400 years; or Heb. 7:9-10, where Levi is said to be in the loins of Abraham, his father, when Melchisedec met him; thus any ancestor is the father of all his descendants.)

8. We must grant that there is often a *sensus plenior* in Scripture pericopes in the sense of 1 Peter 1:10-12. That is to say, the writer of Scripture is not in every respect a child of his time, conditioned by his own cultural milieu, but he often writes for a later age. However, we cannot countenance the Roman Catholic notion of *sensus plenior* which finds in passages of Scriptures fuller meanings which are disparate and different from the intended sense of the passages. We hold only to a profounder and sometimes more distinct sense than the writer may have perceived as he expressed himself. This has serious implications relative to the New Testament use and interpretation of the Old Testament; the New Testament does not misinterpret or do violence to the Old Testament when it interprets. *Sensus litteralis Scripturae unus est* does not imply that the sacred writer understands the full divine implication of all his words.

9. Pseudepigrapha. Pseudonymity in the sense of one writer pretending to be another in order to secure acceptance of his own work is illicit and not compatible with inerrancy. That the motives for such action may be construed as good does not alter the fact that fraud or forgery has been perpetrated. The fact that such a practice was carried on in ancient times does not justify it nor indicate that the practice was considered moral. When in ancient times a pious fraud was found out and the authenticity of a work disproved, the work itself was suspect. (See *Fragmentum Muratorianum*, 5, where the *finctae* letters of Paul to the Laodiceans and the Alexandrians were not accepted by the church for that very reason.)

Pseudonymity must be carefully delimited. Pseudonymity is deliberate fraud (for any reason whatsoever). It has nothing to do with anonymity. Nor would it be pseudonymity if a later writer culled under inspiration all the wisdom sayings

54

of Solomon, gathering them into a volume and presenting them for what they are, Solomon's wisdom. His contemporaries know that Solomon has not written the book, but understand the sayings and the wisdom to be Solomon's (similar to this, we have the words of Christ in the Gospels). In such a case no deception is involved. In the case of the pastoral epistles such a conclusion could not be assumed by any stretch of the imagination. The letters were written to give the impression that they come directly from Paul, claiming his authority. If they were not in fact Pauline, a deception has taken place, a successful deception until lately.

10. Etymologies in Scripture are often according to sound and not (obviously) according to modern linguistic analysis. This fact does not affect inerrancy. The ancients are not thinking of etymologies in the modern sense.

11. The inerrancy and the authority of Scripture are inseparably related. This fact has been consistently recognized by orthodox theologians, who have often included inerrancy and authority under the rubric of infallibility. Without inerrancy the *sola scriptura* principle cannot be maintained or practiced. An erring authority for all Christian doctrine (like an erring Word of God) is an impossible and impracticable contradiction in terms.

12. In approaching the Scripture as children of God who stand under the Scriptures, we shall do well to recall and observe two basic principles of our Fathers: (1) Scripture is *autopistos*, that is to say, we are to believe its utterances simply because Scripture, the Word of God, makes these utterances (inerrancy is always to be accepted on faith!), and we are to believe without the need of any corroborating evidence. This applies to statements about God, but also to statements about events in history. (2) Scripture is *anapodeiktos*, that is, self-authenticating. It brings its own demonstration, the demonstration of the Spirit and of power. Again no corroborating evidence for Biblical assertions is necessary or sought for. Now *sola scriptura* means all this; and it means as well that there are no outside criteria for judging the truthfulness or factual content of Scriptural assertions (for example, neither a modern scientific world view nor modern "scientific historiography"). We accept the assertions of the Scripture on faith. For instance, the fact that the creation story or the flood or the story of Babel has some parallels in other Semitic and ancient lore gives no right to conclude that these accounts in Scripture are mythical (any more than we have the right to conclude that Christ's resurrection is not historical because there are mythical resurrections in history). Such an interpretation would involve a violation of the *sola scriptura* principle. At the same time it is possible that a changed world view (for example, our modern view as opposed to the Newtonian view of absolute space and time) will open for consideration a new interpretation of a Biblical pericope, although it can never determine our interpretation of Scripture.

It is particularly important to maintain the above principles in our day in view of the tendency to allow extra-Biblical data (particularly historical and archaeological data and opinions) to encroach on the absolute authority of Scripture.

55

The Trojan Horse: Historical Critical Method

The most important theological issue facing the evangelical Christians today as they seek to uphold the full inerrancy of Scripture centers in the use of the historical-critical method. The question is: May a genuine Christian, who believes that the Sacred Scriptures are the very Word of God and who is committed totally to the divine authority and inerrancy of Scripture, use the historical-critical method to understand, interpret, and apply the Scriptures? This crucial question can be answered only when we know two things. First, we must know what the historical-critical method is. And to know what any method is we must have a clear picture of its goals and its presuppositions. Second, we must determine whether the method as such denies or undermines the authority and inerrancy of Scripture.

So we ask, what is the historical-critical method? As far as I have been able to determine by examining the works of scores of scholars using the method a brief definition might run as follows. The historical-critical method is a way of studying Scripture by using all the criteria of scientific historical investigation. The method analyzes the text of Scripture in terms of language, literary form, redaction criticism, as well as historical, archeological, and other relevant data. The purpose of the method is not merely philological, or linguistic: to learn the intended meaning of texts and verses of Scripture. The over-arching purpose is historical: to discover the history and background of the form and content of any given portion or unit in Scripture and to trace that history of the given unit through every step of its development until it finds its way into the text of Scripture as we have it. This procedure, essential to the method, would apply to any story recorded in the Old Testament, any parable or discourse of Jesus, any action or miracle of our Lord, to any pericope in all of Scripture. The over-arching purpose, the ultimate goal, of the method is therefore to assess the historicity or factuality or truthfulness of the text of Scripture itself, to find the word or event behind the text, to find out what *really happened*, or to discover the historical origin of what is recorded in Scripture.

It is easy, I believe, to see some of the assumptions underlying this method of approaching Scripture. Assumptions regarding revelation, regarding Scripture, and regarding history. The method was first conceived and worked out in the eighteenth century by scholars who either denied that Scripture was such a divine revelation and so also its authority and inerrancy, as had been understood by historic Christianity.[1] They furthermore believed that all history has lived out according to principles of universal correspondence, analogy, uniformity within history; and all historical records including Scripture must be criticized according to such principles. Far reaching changes have taken place in the method over the past two hundred years—e.g., form criticism, redaction criticism, etc. have been invented—but the same assumptions underlie the use of the method today by all reputable and consistent practitioners of it.

Perhaps it is necessary at this point only to mention the devastating results of this method. Exegetes using the method have denied the historicity of all God's activities recounted in Scripture until the time of Abraham, they have denied the authenticity of many of Christ's sermons and discourses, they have denied His deity and every miracle performed by Him. Regin Prenter, a relatively conservative dogmatician, who uses the method, frankly says, "That it is the Creator himself who is present in Jesus' humanity has always been an impossible idea of historical-criticism. Therefore historical-criticism necessarily collides with everything in the tradition concerning Jesus which ascribes to him such divine majesty."[2]

Now why does the historical-critical method of interpreting Scripture come to such diverse, contradictory conclusions, and to conclusions so totally destructive of our Christian faith? Because it is a bad method. Because its assumptions regarding revelation, Biblical authority, and history are wrong and contrary to Scripture. Because it has set wrong goals for itself. And because, ultimately, it does not understand the nature of what it is dealing with, the sacred Scriptures themselves.

Any method of doing anything is determined by the subject with which the method deals. That is always true, whether we think of a method of managing a corporation, a method of cutting meat, a method of researching historical data, or a method of reading a book. If this is true, then the nature of Scripture as God's revelation of Himself and His will cannot be ignored or discounted at any point by any method seeking to deal with Scripture in terms of its *form* or *content*. Scripture's form is its revelatory character as God's Word. Scripture's content is God Himself—He is the one spoken of everywhere in Scripture—God, His will and actions of judgment and grace among people. In the nature of the case one cannot use the same method for reading, understanding, and applying Scripture that one uses for understanding any other human book which recounts merely human events and ideas. For instance, a historical-critical method is quite adequate and proper for understanding and analysing Caesar's *Gallic Wars*. The historian will immediately recognize, according to his principles of universal correspondence and analogy within history, that Caesar is a responsible and serious witness to events and a good historian in terms of his day. The critic will therefore accept Caesar's statement that his army built an elaborate and complicated bridge and crossed the River Rhine. But the critic will recognize Caesar's limitations as he comments on the flora and fauna of Britain and Caesar's *tendenz* as he speaks of his great victories over the barbarians.

But Scripture, though written by inspired men and reflecting their style of writing, thought forms, and convictions, is not a human book or record like Caesar's *Gallic Wars*. The Spirit of God is the author of Scripture, and the Spirit does not have *tendenz* which may be corrected according to any theory concerning continuity and analogy within history. Furthermore, unlike Caesar's *Gallic Wars*, which deals with the activities of Caesar, a man, the Scriptures witness to the mighty acts of God, acts which transcend space, time, secondary causes, historical analogy, and everything else within our created order. The reader of Scripture, as he confronts the content of Scripture, God Himself and

57

His mighty acts, can only accept the witness of the Spirit who testified through the writings of prophets and apostles to these revelations of God's judgment and grace.

Does the historical-critical method deny Christian theology? It most certainly does. Specifically it undermines the organic, cognitive foundation of all our theology, the sacred Scriptures, and as a result is at odds with every specific Biblical rule of interpretation. Let me illustrate with a few points.

1. We Christians believe in the unity of Scripture, in the analogy of Scripture. Scripture agrees with itself in its witness to Christ and the Gospel and in all its doctrine. But listen now to the historical critic on this matter. "The assertion of a doctrinal unity of the Biblical witnesses has been made impossible by the work of critical historical research."[3]

2. We Christians believe in the divine origin of Scripture. But listen to the historical critic on this matter. "The advent of modern natural science and historical research showed that the Bible is not inerrant in the sense of the doctrine of verbal inspiration. The historical-critical and later the history of religions methods of research investigated even the Biblical writings and showed that they originated in the same manner as other source documents of religion. These new research methods showed also that there are a great many points of similarity between Biblical religion and the other religions, similarities which are most naturally explained by the assumption that Biblical religion has been influenced by non-Biblical religions. All of this was a fatal blow to the orthodox conception of the Bible."[4]

3. We Christians believe that Scriptures are absolutely reliable and authoritative. But listen to the historical critic on the matter. "In the Bible we know there is no unity of doctrine, no one theology, no single line of interpretation, not even agreement on what the facts are . . . The historical-critical method . . . opened our eyes to pluralism, divergent trends, historical conditionedness and relativity, and also theological contradictions in the Bible."[5]

Who are these men I quoted? Radicals? Modernists? Not at all. Well respected Lutheran theologians who use the *historical-critical method*. And their root error in every case is that they insist *on principle* that Scripture *must be approached like any other purely human, historically conditioned book*. Listen to another Lutheran historical critic make this position crystal clear. "The historicality of the Bible, that is, the conditioned character of its contents, a conditioned-ness which makes them dependent upon all kinds of human limitations and situations in precisely the same way as the legacies of all sorts of historical traditions, *is an assumption of modern criticism throughout*."[6]

What arguments are used by those in evangelical circles who favor the use of historical-critical methodology? Let me mention a few and reply to them.

1. The historical-critical method is better than our older approach to Scripture because it makes the fullest use of all the tools available to the scholarly exegete. This argument is simply contrary to the facts. Conservative exegetes today, who reject the historical-critical method, use all the scholarly tools helpful to their work, lexicons, archeological finds, extra-Biblical historical data, and

the like. What they object to is not scholarship, but an unscholarly, sub-Christian method of using the tools of scholarship.

2. Another argument. "In and of itself so-called 'historical-critical' methodology is neutral."[7] This argument sounds humble and innocuous, but it is utterly false. The presuppositions underlying the method which I mentioned earlier make the historical-critical method anything but neutral. I might add that almost all historical-critical scholars agree with me on this point. Gerhard Ebeling says, "It leads only to obscuring the nature of the problem when the critical historical method is held to be a purely formal scientific technique, entirely free of presuppositions."[8]

But we are told we can use the method with evangelical presuppositions. This is not possible. Take away the radical, sub-Christian presuppositions of the method and replace them with the evangelical Biblical presuppositions regarding Law and Gospel, the Christocentricity of Scripture, the power of the Word, the divine origin and authority and inerrancy of Scripture, and you have destroyed the historical-critical method entirely.

3. Third, it is argued that the historical-critical method enables us to understand better what God says to us through Scripture. This argument is unclear because one does not know what it *means* to say that God speaks *through* Scripture. Does it mean that the very words of Scripture are the very words of God? Or does it mean that God somehow speaks to us through Scripture as He speaks through other media, e.g. Law, Gospel, history, nature, culture? But apart from its ambiguity the claim is false and incredible. At best the historical-critical method *ignores* the fact that the Bible is the utterly truthful and authoritative Word of God. How then can such a method help us to understand what God says to us in Scripture?

4. Finally, it is argued that the historical-critical method is used in the service of the Gospel and somehow helps us better to find the Gospel in Scripture and use it. This claim is absurd on many counts. Surely we do not *need* the method to find the Gospel in Scripture and apply it. For the Gospel message, which was proclaimed before the New Testament was written, existed and was well understood also before the advent of historical criticism. Furthermore, how can a method which ignores or rejects the divine origin and authority of Scripture, which is our only source of the Gospel, help us better to understand the Gospel as God's Word of reconciliation and pardon to us? I would insist that in fact the historical-critical method does the very opposite of what champions claim for it. It hinders us from getting to the Gospel of Scripture and undermines the Gospel itself by undermining confidence in the only divinely authoritative source we have for the Gospel today, the sacred Scripture.

Let there be no mistake about this. A method which at any point can cast doubt on the authenticity of the words and discourses and even the miracles and saving acts of our Lord will never enhance the preaching of the Gospel in the church.

It is for the sake of the Gospel therefore that I would urge every evangelical teacher, pastor, and layman to avoid the historical-critical method as such as the great heresy of our day. For the Gospel itself is at stake. The heart of the Gospel is Christ, our prophet, priest, and king. And He was no higher critic. He bowed to the written Word. Through His ministry the inerrant Scriptures ruled supreme. He in whom dwelt all the fulness of the Godhead drew all His doctrine from Scripture alone. And when He taught or quoted or applied Scripture there is never evasion, hesitation, or qualification. He says, "It is written." And what follows is unconditionally true and authoritative. We honor our Savior today by emulating His confidence in the divine origin and message of Scripture, not by using a method which assumes that Scriptures are merely human writings which teach contradictory theologies and contain errors. And as followers of Christ, saved by Him and committed utterly to His Gospel of reconciliation as revealed in Scripture, we will never, never tamper with that divine and saving Word of Scripture.

Notes

1. This is an a priori. Listen to C. H. Dodd, a conservative practitioner of the method, on the subject of the "Time-Relativity of Prophecy" (*The Authority of the Bible,* London: Nisbet & Co. Ltd., 1955, 127-8), "This inseparable interweaving of the eternal and the temporary in an historical revelation has important corrollaries in the philosophy of religion, which we must not here consider. All this means further that we must always allow for limitation and error in the prophets. It should hardly be necessary to state so obvious a proposition, but the doctrine of inspiration has been so confused by the demand for inerrancy that it is necessary. No one not blinded by a superstitious bibliolarty could possibly accept for truth, as they stand, many elements in Old Testament prophecy . . . It is unnecessary to multiply examples. Any theory of the inspiration of the Bible which suggests that we should recognize such utterances as authoritative for us stands self-condemned. They are relative to their age. But I think we should say more. They are false and they are wrong." cf. also Edgar Krentz (*The Historical-Critical Method,* Philadelphia: Fortress Press, 1975, p. 30.) "It is difficult to overestimate the significance the nineteenth century has for biblical interpretation. It made historical criticism *the* approved method of interpretation. The result was a revolution of viewpoint in evaluating the Bible. The Scriptures were, so to speak, secularized. The biblical books became historical documents to be studied and questioned like any other ancient source. The Bible was no longer the criterion for the writing of history; rather history had become the criterion for understanding the Bible."

2. Regin Prenter, *Creation and Redemption* (Philadelphia: Fortress Press, 1967) p. 433.

3. Wolfhard Pannenberg, *Basic Questions in Theology* (London: SCM Press, 1970) I, 194.

4. Prenter, *op. cit.*, p. 90.

5. Carl Braaten, *Dialog.* 1973, Oct. p. 180.

6. Walter E. Rast, *Tradition, History and the Old Testament* (Philadelphia: Fortress Press, 1972) Forward ix. cf. Hans-Joachim Krauss, *Geschichte der historisch-kritischen Erforschung des Alten Testaments* (Neukirchen: Verlag der Buchlandlung des Erziehungsvereins, 1969) p. 249 *passim.*

7. *Faithful to Our Calling, Faithful to Our Lord.* An Affirmation in two Parts by the Faculty of Concordia Seminary, St. Louis, Missouri. St. Louis, 1973, I, p. 41.

8. Gerhard Ebeling, *Word and Faith* (Philadelphia: Fortress, 1963) p. 22ff.

RESPONSE: William E. Hull

Pondering the address by Robert Preus, "The Inerrancy of Scripture," prompts comment in three areas.

I.

The first concerns the "two natures" of Scripture, or what might be called the divinity and the humanity of the Bible. Note how Preus, in the first major section of his paper, addresses almost entirely the Godward side of Holy Writ. To him, the sacred Scriptures are "words taught by the Holy Spirit" whose inerrancy is "plenary or absolute," extending both to formal consistency and to material content, both to the substance of doctrine and to nonessential assumptions, both to the primary intent of the authors and to the secondary intent of passing references. Preus rightly calls this a "strict position," one which permits him to affirm a total or unqualified view of inerrancy that recognizes no minor details. One finishes the first major section of his presentation with the strong impression that, for our author, reading the Bible is tantamount to a direct, unmediated encounter with the very Word of God.

While such an emphasis, in and of itself, may be salutary, the question which we must ask is whether it conveys in balanced fashion a comprehensive view of the reality of Scripture. One would hardly know from this presentation that the Bible is full of obscure terminology that lexicographers are still struggling to decipher. Or that the most exalted epistles of Paul contain passages of tortured syntax that almost defy translation even by skilled grammarians. Or that our best available manuscripts of the Bible have a host of variants that no method of textual criticism, however conservative, has been able to resolve. Or that many key parts of the Bible, such as the synoptic Gospels, reflect countless divergences in parallel accounts which the most devout inerrantist scholars cannot fully harmonize. In short, Preus has a great deal to say in his major thesis and six corollaries about those features of the bible regarding which one may make absolute affimations, but almost nothing to say about those features of the Bible which permit only ambiguous approximations.

What has happened here, I suggest, is that Preus has chosen to magnify the divine nature of the Bible, what he will later describe as its autonomous, self-authenticating character. But in so doing, he has neglected to emphasize its human nature as a witness to God's Word earthly language. There is much in Preus about the surpassing "treasure" given in Scripture, and rightly so, but little about the "earthen vessels" in which God was pleased to accommodate His self-disclosure (II Cor. 4:7). His presentation does not prepare us for the spiritual frailty of the inspired writers confessed so poignantly, for example, in the Psalms of Lament. Nor does it prepare us for the confession of the Apostle

61

Paul that he both knew in part and prophesied in part (I Cor. 13:9, 12).

My primary problem with this imbalance is theological. Christianity arose as an incredible exception to the dominant religions of its day. It offered a fresh alternative especially to the other-worldliness that had infected both Jewish apocalypticism and Hellenistic gnosticism. The scandal that became the glory of Christianity was its deep descent into historical contingency. The incarnation by which "the Word became flesh" (Jn. 1:14) was a radical condescension or "emptying" (kenosis) described so eloquently by Paul in Philippians 2:5-11. I find little kenosis in Preus' doctrine of Scripture. In his Bible, God seems to be speaking primarily from the heights rather than from the depths, out of the pure transcendence so coveted by apocalypticists and gnostics rather than out of lowly ambiguity so celebrated by the earliest Christian evangels. For Preus, divine revelation seems always to be clear, unmistakable, and self-evident, which, to a point, is well and good. But, in this paper at least, it seems to lack the anguish, the pathos, the irony that characterized the preaching of the apostles.

I would express concern at this point because ours is a day ripe for other-worldly understandings of religion. Living in an atmosphere of meaninglessness nourished by everything from cultural banality to the threat of nuclear holocaust, many are eager to embrace a modern version of apocalypticism or gnosticism, especially if it is offered in Christian garb. Without intending to do so, is it possible that the "strict" view of inerrancy presented by Preus plays unwittingly into the hands of those who frantically seek an immediate experience of transcendence, and that it does so by implying that such may be had merely by opening the pages of Scripture? One way to avoid that unintended distortion is to develop a doctrine of Scripture which emphasizes that, in the Bible, divine revelation entered deeply into the human situation rather than escaping from it, participating gladly in the limitations of our humanity without thereby becoming captive to them.

II.

By developing an absolutist premise in the first section of his paper, Preus is forced to devote the second major section to a number of "adjuncts" which qualify his strict view of inerrancy. I count at least ten characteristics of the Bible which he would exclude from the totalist claims made earlier: (1) verbal exactness of quotations; (2) verbal or intentional agreement in parallel accounts; (3) the rounding of numbers; (4) the employment of hyperbole, metaphor, and other figures of speech; (5) the use of popular phrases and expressions of the day; (6) the absence of scientifically precise language; (7) the use of the language of folklore or mythical elements; (8) the non-use of the canons of modern scientific historiography; (9) the presentation of chronology and geneologies in ways that expand or compress time; (10) the derivation of etymologies not in accordance with modern linguistic analysis.

This decalogue of disclaimers could, of course, be expanded by Preus or by anyone familiar with the standard literature in this field. But rather than try to build an even higher wall to hedge the theory of inerrancy, we may turn immediately to the practical problem of utilizing a doctrine which requires so much elaborate effort to explain its many exceptions. A pastor in the pulpit or on an outreach visit has no time to enter into such nuanced discussion, nor does Preus imply that such should be done. But without making allowance for such complex qualifications, does not the doctrine of inerrancy appear to claim more than its own advocates espouse? Again, how many dedicated, Bible-believing laypersons, not to say ministers, are competent to understand for themselves, and to interpret for others, these "adjuncts" to Preus' theory? My own suspicion is that a seminary education is required to grasp the intricacies of this part of his paper.

Lurking behind this practical problem is a theoretical issue of even greater moment. Historians of the doctrine of Scripture are aware that the classic view of inerrancy contained far fewer concessions than those enumerated here by Preus. Indeed, in a famous passage Dean Burgon insisted that the perfection of Scripture must extend to every word, every syllable, every letter down to the Hebrew vowel points! Only a century ago, it was common for inerrantists to defend the historicity of the creation accounts in Genesis by using Bishop Ussher's chronology, or to explain the language of the Bible by a theory of "Holy Ghost Greek," or to champion the late Byzantine "Textus receptus" of Robert Stephanus (1550) as the standard for all translation. As we might expect, such discredited notions are nowhere to be found in the paper by Preus. Which is to say that the doctrine of inerrancy is not some simple, timeless conviction occupying high ground above the vicissitudes of history. Rather, it is a complex, fluid theory that has changed significantly throughout the course of its development, perhaps never more so than in recent years.

But we must press this point one step further. Whence cometh the changes that make President Preus' position on inerrancy in the twentieth century so different from that of Dean Burgon's in the nineteenth century? Almost without exception they have come, not at the initiative of inerrantists themselves, but as reluctant concessions by inerrantists to the findings of scholars using the historical-critical method; e.g., the work of Deissmann and Robertson on Koine Greek, or the work of Westcott and Hort on textual recensions. Taken as a whole, the history of inerrancy is flawed by a fall-back psychology. Nor can holders of this view ever know when some fresh concession may be required in the future similar to those which have been made in the past. Surely we need a doctrine of Scripture that is on the offensive rather than on the defensive, one that welcomes rather than begrudges the assured findings of modern Biblical scholarship.

III.

The final section of Preus' paper, consisting of a spirited attack on the "historical/critical method," raises for us afresh the age-old question of the relation of faith and reason. Throughout its long history of missionary expansion, Christianity has been forced to respond repeatedly to fundamentally new ways of thinking. This was true in all four of the great eras of church history, and in the first three of these periods the theologians cited with approval by Preus led

63

in reformulating orthodox doctrine to accommodate fresh modes of under-standing. (1) In the Patristic Period (A. D. 200-500), Augustine led in the shift from Jewish to Hellenistic thought. (2) In the Medieval Period (A. D. 500-1500), Aquinas led in the shift from Platonic to Aristotelian thought. (3) In the Reformation Period (A. D. 1500-1700), Luther led in the shift from traditional to existential thought.

Before going farther, let us note that in every one of these cases the emerg-ing epistemology was condemned as unfit for Christian use. The Judaizers bitterly opposed the Hellenization of the Gospel as early as the ministry of Paul. Thomas Aquinas was roundly criticized by the Dominicans for tampering with the Augustinian theology that had dominated the church for centuries and was condemned as a heretic by the archbishops of both Paris and Canterbury shortly after his death. Luther, of course, was excommunicated from the church for daring to set his solitary convictions against the massive structures of established authority in a way that redefined the meaning of individualism. But in every case change was not only inevitable, it eventually came to be accepted as a gift of God by which to give fresh expression to orthodox doctrine. The church finally learned that faith could be put in new forms without diluting its substance. History suggests that it is the responsibility of the church to take the initiative in responding to new ways of knowing so that unbelievers will not have to first adopt alien or outdated ways of thinking in order to grasp the meaning of Christ.

Which brings us to the Modern Period, born in the Enlightenment of the eighteenth century. Here the great shift in epistemology was from classical to critical modes of thought, from deductive to inductive reasoning, from theoreti-cal to empirical assumptions. Many theologians have arisen in this era, espe-cially in the period from Schleiermacher to Barth, who have attempted to do for Kant and Hegel and other tutors of the modern mind what Augustine and Aquinas did for Plato and Aristotle. But Preus, if I understand him alright, will have none of it. For him, there is simply not any Christian way to think critically about the faith as moderns have learned to do about everything else, hence there is no way to utilize the historical-critical method as a tool for studying the Bible. Apparently, scientific historiography as a means of doing Christian theology is as foreign to Preus as the Platonism of Augustine was to Tertullian or the Aristotelianism of Aquinas was to Bonaventura, or the existentialism of Luther was to Eck.

Perhaps the broader issue here is that of Christ and culture, a debate made familiar in our day by H. Richard Niebuhr. In the church's witness to the world, are we to set Christ *above* culture, *in* culture, or *against* culture (defining "cul-ture" here to encompass the great intellectual traditions of Western civilization)? The inerrantist position espoused by Preus seems to favor the "Christ against culture" stance, especially in its insistence that one of the dominant modes of modern inquiry cannot be used to investigate the Bible. In times past, the "Church against culture" stance has sometimes proved useful as a corrective position but seldom enduring as a normative position. Preus will have to judge for himself whether he is correctly defining the scandal of the Gospel by demanding that moderns trained to think about reality in a critical/scientific/objective fashion lay aside that mindset if they would come to faith in Christ through the Scriptures.

For myself, I am prepared to discharge the theological task accepted by the church in earlier ages, that of taking the initiative to fashion an eternal yet contemporary Gospel out of the thought forms of this age, so that those who confront Christ may take offense only in His cross and not in the anachronistic categories by which He is presented. After thirty-five years of working daily with the historical/critical method as one tool in the reverent study of Scripture, I am convinced that it can be made a servant of Christ as much as a Platonism or Aristotelianism in ages past. At the same time, I respect and honor those who refuse to use it because they feel that it competes with the unhindered ministry of the Holy Spirit in their hearts.

In strange ways the use of this "secular" method, developed in part by unbelievers, is similar to the equally controversial issue in the time of Paul of eating meat that had first been offered to idols. Can we not all heed the admonition of the Apostle in addressing that issue and apply his wisdom to this issue which now divides us?

> The faith that you have, keep between yourself and God; happy is he who has no reason to judge himself for what he approves. But he who has doubts is condemned, if he eats [i.e., practices Biblical criticism], because he does not act from faith; for whatever does not proceed from faith is sin. (Romans 14:22-23).

RESPONSE: Paige Patterson

Dr. Robert Preus has made a monumental contribution to the evangelical cause through both scholarship and statesmanship. Therefore, I count myself fortunate to be able to respond to his excellent presentation. Since I find myself in agreement with his position, the nature of my response will be to anticipate possible objections to his paper.

The Bible and Inerrancy

First, there is the question as to whether or not the Bible itself teaches its own inerrancy. Dr. Preus has presented the case for believing that the Bible does suggest its own perfections. This is true both in principle (the commandments for truthfulness among God's people) and in the assertions of its writers regarding the truthfulness of their respective messages. Others are convinced that the Bible does not teach its own inerrancy and that inerrantists have used poor logic and weak hermeneutics in alleging that it does.

As I have suggested elsewhere (see response to Pinnock), inerrantists need not be "bullied" from their confidence on this issue. While all readily admit that the word "inerrancy" does not appear in the Bible, it is also true that this proves nothing at all. The creeds of Chalcedon and Nicea are not found in the Bible in the precise verbiage of the councils. This is not to say, however, that the essential elements of Nicean and Chalcedonian christology are absent from the Scriptures. To state that the Chalcedonian or Nicean formulations and the Chicago Statement On Biblical Inerrancy are not found in the Bible is hardly a striking insight. To conclude further that Nicean and Chalcedonian christology or inerrancy is, therefore, not taught in Scripture is a non-sequitur. The Bible does teach that Jessica is *homoousia* with the Father and with us even though it employs different language to do so. Nicean and Chalcedonian formulating are useful summarizations for biblical christology. And the Bible does teach its own inerrancy in its own wonderfully variegated language. Our definitions of inerrancy are attempts to summarize briefly, or sometimes at greater length to systematize what the Bible says about itself. In any case, we do not argue for use of the *word* "inerrancy" but rather for the concept that God spoke in Scripture, superintending the human authors in such a fashion that the latter wrote the word of God without error. Only the most determined hermeneutical gymnastics can distort *The Baptist Faith and Message* statement on the Scriptures to mean anything else. "It [The Holy Bible] has God for its author, salvation for its end, and truth, without any mixture of error, for its matter."

Recent attempts have been made to argue that the authors of the New Hampshire Confession of 1833, which serves as the foundational document for *The Baptist Faith and Message*, were making a philosophical distinction between "form" and "matter." It is alleged that

> The "matter" of the Bible is its saving content or substance. The "form" of the Bible is the literary verbal construction of its message of salvation.[1]

The problems with such a thesis are manifold. First, this definition of "form" and "matter" reverses the definitions of the Greek philosophers who popularized the terms. Second, no evidence is provided to show that this is, in fact, what the framers of the New Hampshire Confession were thinking. Attributing to them indulgence in this kind of philosophical subtlety without providing supporting evidence is unconvincing, especially since they were preparing a confession for the common people in the churches. Third, every reason exists for believing that "matter" to those early Baptists meant "content," not in part, but in whole.

If my thesis is accurate, then the question arises: Where did our forefathers get such an idea? While not denying the impact of previous confessions, it seems clear that they arrived at such a conclusion exegetically, i.e., they believed that the Bible taught that the Word of God was "truth without mixture of error."

This is precisely the position of inerrantists today. Not only are they convinced that the Bible teaches its own inerrancy, but they also note the example of the way in which Jesus responded to the Old Testament. They further note the way other biblical authors allow themselves to be bound by the authority of acknowledged Scripture.

For example, Peter argues that no prophecy of Scripture is of private origin. Instead, holy men of God were moved to speak God's word (2 Peter 1:20-21). Then in the third chapter of 2 Peter, he admits that Paul has written some difficult passages. However, Peter laments that some had "distorted" Paul's writings just as they had "the other Scriptures." This attitude presents a high view of Scripture similar to the inerrancy view.

By both example and sufficient declaration, the authors of Scripture do seem to hold a view of Scripture virtually identical to the view of modern inerrantists. This is not just an "inerrancy of purpose," which Preus identified as an inadequate perspective, but an inerrancy of word as Jesus Himself seems to indicate in Matthew 22:41-44.

> While the Pharisees were gathered together, Jesus asked them,
> Saying, What think ye of Christ? whose son is he? They say unto him, The son of David.
> He saith unto them, How then doth David in spirit call him Lord, saying,
> The Lord said unto my Lord, Sit thou on my right hand, till I make thine enemies thy footstool?

The point here is the inspiration of one word, the word "Lord." Note also the confluent nature of revelation. David said the word "Lord" but it was *en pneumati,* by means of the Spirit that David is able to say this.

The Problem of Qualifications

Dr. Preus has defined inerrancy. He has then proceed to qualify precisely what he means by inerrancy with a series of affirmations and denials. Common reaction of non-inerrantists is to object to the "complicated" nature of the "theory of inerrancy." Some allege that the whole idea dies the death of a thousand qualifications. Once inerrancy has been qualified it comes to mean nothing at all or at least to be indistinguishable from other "high views" of the Bible.

In answer to the charge that the definition is too complicated, inerrantists reply that the fault for most of the complications of the subject lies with non-inerrantists. Most inerrantists in the Southern Baptist context are perfectly content with the statement on the Bible as it stands in *The Baptist Faith and Message.* The problem arises when theologians begin alleging "error" in the Bible. In reaction, evangelicals say the Bible is "inerrant." The matter becomes more complicated still when a series of questions is asked of inerrantists concerning such things as phenomenal language in the Bible. Inerrantists then respond with full statements such as The Chicago Statement on Biblical Inerrancy. Finally, having utterly failed to dislodge inerrantists from their confidence in Scripture, non-inerrantists dismiss the whole storm as a "tempest in a tea pot" and walk away saying that the idea of inerrancy "died the death of a thousand qualifications."[2]

Strangely, this is the same argument which arose concerning theism in John

67

Wisdom's now famous parable of the divine gardener. Or take the case of the famous rabbit which was once the focus of Oxford philosophical discussion. This special rabbit was invisible, intangible, inaudible, weightless, and odorless. Qualified in such a way, does the rabbit have any real existence?[3] All of this terminates in Anthony Flew's question, "What would have to occur or to have occurred to constitute for you a disproof of the love of, or the existence of, God?"[4]

My point is this. Christian non-inerrantists do not admit such reasoning as valid evidence for dismissing God from the universe or from our faith. They do not, as a result of such assaults on theism, cease to argue for God's existence. Neither do they beg the question saying, "Well, God is a lion. Do not try to defend Him; just turn Him loose!" They argue for God not in order to protect Him but in order to demonstrate to unbelievers that no breach of intellectual honesty must occur in order to believe. The same is true of the Bible.

If theists in general are not persuaded by such positivistic arguments about God, then it will not do for them to marshall the same arguments against the idea of inerrancy. Of course, we must qualify what we mean by "inerrancy" and what we mean by "God." That does not eliminate either idea. Neither does it unduly complicate the perspicuity of the idea.

Pseudonymity

Dr. Preus provides us with a fine discussion of the question of the pseudonymity of the books of the Bible. He notes carefully that pseudonymity must be carefully distinguished from anonymity. He obviously rejects the modern idea that pseudonymity was a perfectly acceptable literary stratagem in the first century. One can add that Paul himself objected to this practice, obviously knowing that the attachment of a man's name to some document when, in fact, he was not involved at all, was immoral. Evidently, a pseudonymous letter purporting to be from Paul had arrived at Thessalonica. Paul clearly does not approve.

> Now we beseech you, brethren, by the coming of our Lord Jesus Christ, and by our gathering together unto him. That ye be not soon shaken in mind, or be troubled, neither by spirit, nor by word, nor by letter as from us, as that the day of Christ is at hand. 2 Thessalonians 2:1-2.

Misrepresentation is always wrong. Letters purporting to be from Paul, if pseudonymous, cannot be received as the word of God. This does not, however, rule out the use of amanuenses. Beginning with untruth, one seldom arrives at truth.

The Historical-Critical Method

Dr. Preus also addresses himself to the alleged "neutrality" of the historical-critical method. Gerhard Ebeling's testimony cited by Preus should be sufficient evidence to alert us to the lack of neutrality in this approach. To this warning we must add the admission of the early historical-critical scholars. Gerhard Maier quotes Johann Semler as follows.

> The root of the evil (in theology) is the interchangeable use of the terms "Scripture" and "Word of God."[5]

Here there is no disguise. The purpose of the historical-critical method is to discern the canon within the canon. The Scriptures are not God's word; they only contain God's word. The task of the interpreter is to do precisely as Bultmann suggested. He must jettison the mythological husk and savor the kernel of God's word. How can this formidable task be achieved? Gerhard Maier again cites W. G. Kuemmel in an answer which is typical of historical-critical scholars.

> The more a text points to the historical revelation of Christ, and the less it has been changed by thoughts from outside of Christianity or through later Christian questioning, the more surely it must be counted as belonging to the normative canon.[6]

This search for a canon within the canon, for the *true* words of Jesus, for the reconstruction of what *actually* happened, for the kernel of truth hidden in the trappings of mythological husks, is anything but the assured result of scientific research. One can use scientific methodology at some points while still arriving at the desired result if a sufficient number of presuppositions are allowed to intrude. This is precisely what has transpired among most practitioners of an historical-critical method.

Conclusion

In July of 1976, Noel Wesley Hollyfield, Jr., presented to the faculty of Southern Baptist Theological Seminary a Master's thesis entitled *A Sociological Analysis of the Degrees of "Christian Orthodoxy" Among Selected Students in the Southern Baptist Theological Seminary*. The thesis was approved by G. Willis Bennett, E. Glenn Hinson, and Henlee Barnett on August 26, 1976. The results of Hollyfield's research are alarming, and his thesis should be read by every interested Southern Baptist. For example, among Ph.D. students thirty-six percent were not able to say "Jesus is the Divine Son of God and I have no doubts about it." Only fifty-two percent could say that the devil definitely or at least probably exists. Many other questions of Baptist faith received similarly disturbing responses.[7] Maybe the questions were not prepared properly. Perhaps the survey was skewed. Or maybe it was just a bad year. Perhaps all of the above is true, though the three competent readers did not refer to any such problems. Even so, the results of this analysis ought to send us scurring to our prayer closets for direction and forgiveness. The thesis clearly reveals a serious loss of confidence in the veracity of the Bible.

My purpose here is not to assault our mother seminary with its wonderful heritage and able faculty. My purpose here is just to say that something has gone wrong with Southern Baptists and its symptoms popped to the surface in Hollyfield's thesis. I find it hard to believe that even non-inerrantists on the faculty at Southern greeted the results of Hollyfield's research with anything other than grave concern. The question then is this: Where did we go wrong? My contention is that we opened the door for this situation when we dismissed the perspectives of James P. Boyce and A. T. Robertson regarding the Sacred Scripture. We erred when we embraced uncritically the presuppositons of higher criticism.

On November 25, 1887, Charles Spurgeon wrote a tragic letter from Menton where he was recuperating. The letter said in part,

> Many do not believe that this "new theology" exists to any degree worthy of notice. I know that it does, and cannot but wonder that any should question it. Of course those who think all is well think me a needless alarmist. Another section is first of all for peace and unity, and hopes that the erring ones will come right; and therefore they are grieved to see the matter ventilated.
>
> Others hope to purge and save the Union. All my best desires go with these; but I have no hope of it. Essentially there is no doctrinal basis to begin with, and many believe this to be a great beauty. "Down with all creeds" seems to be their watchword.
>
> Protests failing, I left; and this has caused more enquiry than a thousand papers would have done. I do not see that I could have done else. Others might not lie under such a compulsion till they have tried to mend matters and have failed as I have done. With no confession of faith, or avowal of principles, there is nothing to work upon; and I do not see the use of repairing a house which is built on the air.

Spuregon's fears for the Baptist Union were not without foundation. The effectiveness of the Union was choked by the noxious fumes of unbelief. Spurgeon's description of affairs within the Baptist Union and the various proposed solutions has a contemporary ring. However, we have not gone that far as Southern Baptists. But the evidences all say that we are on that same road. God help us to stop, turn around, return to the faith of our fathers and hear Isaiah as he says, "here is the way, walk ye in it."

Notes

1. Roy Honeycutt. "Biblical Authority: A Treasured Heritage!" *Review and Expositor*. vol. 83, no. 4, (Louisvile: Economy Printing Concern, Inc., Fall, 1986), p. 616.

2. Roy Honeycutt. "Biblical Authority: A Treasured Heritage!" *Review and Expositor*. vol. 83, no. 4, (Fall, 1986), p. 608.

3. John Hick. *Philosophy of Religion*. (Englewood Cliffs, NJ: Prentice-Hall, Inc., 1963), pp. 95-96.

4. Anthony Flew. *New Essays in Philosophical Theology*, p. 79.

5. Gerhard Maier. *The End of The Historical-Critical Method*. (St. Louis: Concordia Publishing House, 1974), p. 15.

6. Gerhard Maier. *The End of the Historical-Critical method*. (St. Louis: Concordia Publishing House, 1974), p. 18.

7. Noel Wesley Hollyfield, Jr. *A Sociological Analysis of the Degrees of "Christian Orthodozy" Among Selected Students in the Southern Baptist Theological Seminary*, Unpublished Master's Thesis presented to the faculty of Southern Baptist Theological Seminary, July 1976, p. 70.

4

WHAT IS BIBLICAL INERRANCY?

Clark H. Pinnock

Introduction

Of the six main presenters at this conference, I alone had significant Southern Baptist connections (during the 1960's). This means that I bring to my presentations a greater awareness of the difficult struggle that has been going on in relation to the doctrine of Scripture. I hope this will enable me to sharpen the focus, and not result in a divisive influence.

In 1965 I arrived in New Orleans to teach at the Southern Baptist theological seminary there and found myself burdened by the fear that the Christian witness even among Baptists could be jeoparized by the influx of liberal theology seeping into the ranks of the educated elites of the Convention slowly but surely. I was glad to join with other conservatives at that time to blow the whistle on this dangerous folly which we perceived. I do not apologize for doing so to this day—it had to be done. The danger of religious liberalism in the 20th century is never a merely imaginary threat, and it has affected Baptist ranks in North America as deeply as any other deonmination. Southern Baptists should not suppose they are immune from theological infection. I may have behaved crudely during the New Orleans years and hurt some innocent people (for which I sincerely apologize), but I do think that very point had to be made at that very moment.

However, as I return now in 1987 to this conference, I see a somewhat different danger. I see a great evangelical denomination dangerously divided, not this time between a few liberal leaders and the Baptist majority, but between large numbers of evangelicals and fundamentalists in conflict with each other. I see the possibility of a "holy war" tearing the Convention apart and threatening to divide the forces of world mission. I see people divided, not over the good news of salvation which is the Word of God (1 Peter 1:25) but over the theory they hold about how to understand the inspiration and authority of the Bible. I see the possible fragmentation of believers which could have disastrous consequences for world evangelisation. At the very hours when we are seeing an unprecedent harvest on the mission fields and face the distinct possiblity of the first world-wide revival ever, I am fearful lest we snatch defeat from the jaws of victory and cripple our tremendously successful cooperative efforts which God has so signally used. The Lutheran Church-Missouri Synod split over biblical inerrancy a decade ago, and I am not aware of much good that was done to her mission and life. I am aware of a good deal of hurt.

If you listened to my warning in the 60's about the dangers of liberal

73

theology, I hope you will listen to me now. Besides other things, I want to tell you that having a "correct" view of the Bible (as some define correctness) will not guarantee soundness in theology or spiritual vitality or missionary zeal automatically. Some of the strictest churches in history have been spiritual dead and resistant to both revival and missions. Mere orthodoxy will not bring God's blessing if you bite and devour one another. God will not bless if you fight and claw at one another over what amounts to a difference of human opinion about which theory of inerrancy to employ. By all means let us discuss these matters as we are doing in this conference, but for the sake of the gospel let us not jeoparize the work of God or injure our fellow evangelical believers who love our Lord and believe his Word. I, too, desire to see the Convention unmistakably evangelical in theology and do not believe those who deny essential gospel truth have any place in its leadership. I have not changed my mind about this. However, I did not in the 60's and do not in the 80's want to see fundamentalists driving evangelicals out, when both groups are standing on the one foundation which is laid, Jesus Christ.

But some will say, Pinnock, you are piping a different tune to us now. We hear you have changed your mind on these matters. We are not sure we should listen to you now. Yes, it is true that I have come to new insights in this area of difficult doctrinal definition. I hope we all have and that none of us are standing still. There is no one even among our presenters who can honestly say he has all the answers and has nothing more to learn. But let me assure you in no uncertain terms that I have not changed one whit in the matter of holding to the Bible as the inspired Word of God written and as the absolutely trustworthy norm of the church, and whatever changes I may have undergone were in the way of points of clarification as to what it means to belive that. Therefore, I would appeal to those who listened to me before with approval to listen to me now with open mind.

I believe you can have peace without compromise in the Southern Baptist Convention if you would recognise that there is room within true evangelicalism for those with a very strict theory of Scripture and for those with a more open and moderate approach to the Bible, providing both acknowledge its divine inspiration and final authority. In my book *Biblical Revelation* (Presbyterian and Reformed, 1971), I mentioned how the strict inerrantist Warfield respected and supported the moderate evangelical James Orr and did not find it necessary to attack him even though Orr actually called his view suicidal (p. 81). In my own life experience, too, I did not see my colleague at L'Abri the strict inerrantist Francis Schaeffer spending his time seeking to drive out my doctoral mentor the moderate F. F. Bruce from the evangelical coalition just because of a difference of opinion over a theological theory and not the gospel. I commend to you the Lausanne formula which says the Bible is "inerrant in all it affirms" and the Chicago Statement with its solidity coupled to openness and generosity in recognizing the delicacy of precisely working out inerrancy in relation to the actual text of the Bible. The key issue is to maintain the right amount of form and freedom. These are matters for brothers and sisters to talk over, not the just cause for holy war. He who has ears to hear let him hear.

What is Biblical Inerrancy?

There are at least two ways to answer this question. One could attempt to duplicate what the Chicago Statement did in its lengthy series of propositions and qualifications, affirmations and denials. Obviously the question, though simple sounding, is not at all easy to answer briefly and simply along these lines. You ought to be aware, if you are not, how litle agreement there is among inerrantists about what biblical inerrancy actually means in practice. Besides I have written several books of this type trying to define inerrancy, the latest being *The Scripture Principle* (Harper & Row, 1984). But there is a second way to answer the question, one which involves dealing with it from a more historical perspective, and it is the approach I now wish to use. It involves our going back to the origin of the inerrancy category, and asking how it came to be the important category it has now become for us. By taking this slant on our subject maybe we can throw fresh light upon the problems we wrestle with, and perhaps even achieve a little healing and peace as well.

What we are really arguing about here, I believe, is whether it is prudent to insist upon a position of great elaboration and strictness with regard to the presuppositions with which we come to Scripture, or whether to adopt a simpler more spontaneous biblicism which also trusts the Bible without reservation but does not believe it is good to burden the Bible reader with too much human theory lest he or she miss what God is saying in the text. After all, presuppositions can distract us from seeing what lies before our eyes. We are dealing with an honest difference of opinion and one which is essentially prudential.

Simple Bibilicism

There is an evangelical view of the Bible which most evangelicals and Baptists hold, whether scholars or not, because the Spirit teaches it to them and which views the Scriptures as the only place to go to if you want to find the words of everlasting life. The Bible is, it believes, the God-given documentation which preserves for all time the gospel of our salvation, and so ordinary believers know instinctively from the Spirit their teacher to go there to be nourished in their faith. They are drawn to it as a baby is drawn to mother's milk. They love the Bible because they love the Lord. They repair naturally to it because there is nowhere else to go if you want to encounter the Savior of the world. They would scarcely understand it if you told them they needed an elaborate theory of the Bible first. Does a baby need an elaborate theory of mother's milk before it can suck? Ordinary believers have a Spirit-engendered inclination to love and trust the Scriptures. They are not intellectuals; they do not have and they do not need an elaborate defintion or defense of their inward certainty. They go to the Bible to find bread to nourish their souls, and they find it there in plenty. This is the simple uncomplicated approach to the Bible which the Christian faith has always had. It seems to me that 98% of Southern Baptists are simple bibilicists, pietists rather than doctrinalists in their orientation, what Mark Noll calls the Baptist way of inerrancy.

Simple biblicism preserves the essence of inerrancy as Packer and Erickson have explained it to us. It approaches the Bible determined to trust it without any reservation. It does not even make the reservation of trusting Scripture in saving matters but not in all matters. It lets Scripture itself create its own impression and make its own claims, and then bows to them. It certainly does not pick and choose what to believe. I fear that the moderates have brought trouble upon themselves by talking loosely about the macro-purpose of the Bible and by giving the impression that they refused biblical teaching on certain other subjects a priori, as though the Bible were just true in matters of faith but not of history etc. But it also lets Scripture and not modernity define for us what "error" is.

Elaborate Biblicism

But the doctrine of Scripture cannot always remain at the simple level. In the face of alien doctrine and unbelief, leaders of the church historically have seen the need from time to time to tighten up the theory of the Bible and not leave so many loose ends which could be misused by the enemies of Christ. No evangelical should deny the pastoral necessity involved here, to act on behalf of the well-being of the church facing spiritual and doctrinal danger. But the question arises, how far shall we go in elaborating the theory of Scripture? How many subtleties do we want to introduce? Do we want to say that the Bible is like the Koran is said to be—untouched by any human or historical factors at all, but produced entirely by God in a mechanical way? Or should we recognise a human element, an incarnate quality in the Bible which is one dimension of its uniqueness in contrast with a Koran? So as I said, it really boils down to the prudential question: would it better for the church if we imposed a tightly drawn theory of inspiration of God's people, or would it be better not to do so, but rather to let the Bible itself have more freedom to impress on the readers what kind of Word it actually is?

So "what is biblical inerrancy" historical speaking? It is a term belonging to the grammar and vocabulary of strict orthodoxy. It was adopted by those who sincerely believed that the strongest possible language must be employed to protect the Scriptures from any kind of suspicion or doubt. Robert Preus has given us a fine example of elaborate inerrancy in this conference. First in the face of Roman Catholic theology after the Reformation and then in the face of religious liberalism in the past two centuries, orthodox Protestants have often resorted to the strictest possible definitions of biblical inerrancy, for example, in the belief that the church required them in order to fight off the onslaughts of error and unbelief. It was hoped that by framing their theory of inspiration on a high level of technical precision that these dangers could be averted and the truth be preserved. They even went to incredible lengths to achieve this, arguing for example that God inspired the Hebrew vowel points which we know now were added much later by the rabbis and that God used a special sacred grammar in the New Testament which explains the oddities of the Greek in it. Quaint you say, but they were sincere in their desire to preserve the Bible and to guard the flock of God, and it lead them to take strict measures. I respect that. The danger is not imaginary.

The point to notice is this: that biblical inerrancy properly belongs to a rather complicated scholarly structure, created by intelligent and well-meaning Christian leaders for the good of the church. So what we are really asking here at this conference is whether it is wise to follow them into the realm of high theory or better to stay a little closer to a simpler biblicism and to the actual text. Therefore, it is not a question of inerrancy or not inerrancy, but of strict and elaborate theory versus simpler and more practical categories.

The Question of Prudence

I wish that Southern Baptists would see that within evangelicalism outside their context we have been able to maintain some peace and cooperative effort between those who think it is very important to hold a strict defintion of inerrancy and those who prefer a more open attitude to the text of Scripture. We have been going back and forth on this for forty years in the Evangelical Theological Society and the National Association of Evangelicals and even longer in other bodies and groups. We have not found it necessary to drive out believers who differ with us on this point. Both camps believe the Bible completely and work alongside one another in a complimentary way. (Let me recommend Mark Noll's book *Between Faith and Criticism*, 1986 for a historical account of this relationship.) So why can't Southern Baptists do this, too? Surely there is room for those who sincerely believe that a strict approach is wise and also for those who feel that a less defined and more open approach to the text of the Bible is the right one. They can even compliment one another. Is it that you are so numerically large that you feel you have the luxury of fighting with one another without any thought of the scandal you are causing for the Baptists and others watching from other parts of the world, or of the dangerous possibility that the Baptist work may suffer among you, too?

Appearances can be deceiving. It looks as if you have a fight over biblical inerrancy in the Convention, but you really do not. What you have is a fight over how inerrancy is to be defined: whether in an elaborate tight manner or in a more open permissive way. The irony of it is that the Chicago Statement, which the militants say they endorse, encompasses both your positions. Like the militants it speaks of complete errorlessness but like the moderates it also speaks of the lack of technical precision and the topical arrangment of material and such like. From the standpoint of your conflict then it speaks with a forked tongue. The reason for this is that the Statement wants to keep together these very groups within evangelicalism. It wants to prevent the very acrimony you are now suffering. So why don't the militants and the modrates among you just affirm the Chicago definition of inerrancy, which includes both their positions, and then get down to the real business of the day, which is to interpret the Word of God with power and relevence for our time? I commend the six seminary presidents for adopting inerrancy lanuage in the Glorietta statment because it promises to shift the discussion from a difficult-to-define slogan and even shibboleth to the really important issues of our Christian mission and interpretation.

Two Necessary Condtions

But if this historical compromise is to work here as it has worked elsewhere, two things have to be true or become true. First, the Southern Baptist moderates must make it much clearer than they have wanted to in the past that they are in fact biblical conservatives and evangelical Christians. It is not enough for them to say they are not fundamentalists if at the same time they do not make it even clearer that they are not religious liberals either. They are surely as aware as I am that out there in the wider theological world are those who deny the incarnation, the resurrection, the atonement, and the coming of our Lord. They cannot afford to draw lines between themselves and fundamentalists if at the same time they do not draw equally clear lines between themselves and liberals. I understand why in the context of the SBC, which is a conservative group by any standard, they may have felt this to be unnecessary, but they are mistaken about that. So long as they refuse to identify themselves in contradistinctions from the unbelieving theologians of our time on the left, the fundamentalists will be able unfairly to portray them or even sincerely perceive them as liberals, and there will never be peace. I urge the moderates to confess the faith clearly, distinguishing it as forcefully from the errors on the left as they presently do from errors on the right, because if they refuse to do so, or (God forbid) cannot do so, they will be unable to free themselves from the box the militants are putting them in, which does not distinguish between moderates and heretics. Let the moderates say loudly with Leo Garrett, "Southern Baptists *are* evangelicals!" (Mercer University Press, 1983) It is unreasonable to require all Baptist leaders to be fundamentalists, but it not unreasonable to expect them all to be soundly evangelical. On the matter of Scripture this means to declare their trust in the Bible without any mental reservations. It is urgent both theologically and prudentially to act on this matter.

The second condition which has to be met relates to the militants. They have to stop behaving as if they were Roman Catholics. We have to remember something about the logic of orthodoxy which gave us inerrancy in the first place. Behind inerrancy lies the desire to secure God's truth invincibly so it cannot be lost or distorted. It was hoped that by calling the Bible inerrant we will have an absolutely sure Word to go by. But what happened in the early church was that people began to realise that they could hardly stop there. What if people failed to read the Bible correctly? All would be in danger once again, and so they adopted creeds and confessions which they treated as infallible to place a fence around the Bible. But even that was not sufficient. After all, people might even misunderstand or twist the creed. Obviously we need a pope too, an authoritative leader who can drive out those who read neither the Bible or the creeds aright. Thus it is in a nutshell that the logic of orthodoxy taken to its full extent can lead one right to Rome. I am worried lest Southern Baptists will accept a theory the full implications of which they do not fully understand.

Now it would be an exaggeration to say that this is what the Southern Baptists now have, but it would not be without some truth. It seems to me as an outsider, if I may dare say so, that you have a party wielding the power of the presidency to impose its creed upon everyone else, something like the papacy. For more than inerrancy is involved it seems in this political takeover. Inerrancy commits one to a high view of the Scriptures but it does not establish any exegtical conclusions in advance. So how is it then that a whole set of beliefs relating to items such as women in ministry, or the method of creation, or captial punishment, or charismatic renewal seem to be entering the picture under the category of inerrancy with which they have no necessary connection? I do not believe that conservatives with integrity actually want to confuse inerrancy and hermeneutics in this way or drive out all those whose reading of the Scriptures differs on some points from theirs. But if they don't, perhaps they could make that clearer in their actions.

But how can peace break out when so many Baptists appear to think that true Christianity and elaborate inerrancy are crucially connected? If they refuse my premise that the moderate and the strict view are both evangelical and complimentary? Let me sketch in an answer to this important question. First, I think the moderates have to make a number of concessions to the miltants. (1) They must admit that the strict view of the Bible is not a fundamentalist invention but is at least as old as Augustine. It is not implausible that true Christianity is linked to it. The point the militants are making is not ridiculous. (2) The denial of a small biblical truth (eg. Paul's view of homosexuality) can be a slippery slope which leads to much deeper concessions. The militants are not making this up. It happens, let me assure you, I have seen it. (3) It is not preposterous to believe that, as evangelicals have become more numerous and diverse, the category "evangelical" means less and less, and the possibility exists that so-called evangelicalism may even become the seedbed of a new liberalism. Moderates should not laugh off this possibility. It is a real one. Most liberals historically were once evangelicals after all. The militants' anxiety is not unfounded. (4) We must admit that God has used the strict inerrantists in this day of shifting theolotical sands to stand up boldly for the truth of God's Word. The Council of Biblical Inerrancy movement has, let us admit it, borne some good fruit.

Having stated some of the concessions which moderates must make, let me go on to address the other side. The militants need to be aware of the danger of tying the evangelical faith and elaborate inerrancy theory too tightly together. (1) Warfield himself stated that a person could be a fully orthodox Christian by believing the gospel even if he thought no more of the Bible than that it was a merely human witness. The test of a true Christian after all is his faith in Christ not his views on inerrancy. I fear that some of Warfield's disciples have forgotten his moderation. (2) It is obvoius from a glance at modern theologians like Forsyth, Denney, Orr, Thielicke, and I would add Barth, Oden, Wainwright, Fackre, that one can have a vivid sense of the gospel without having a conservative view of the Bible. Do we want to drive away people who stand tall for Christ just because they do not see eye to eye with us on inerrancy theory? I hope we do not, because if we do, we may drive away leaders we need whom God has blessed and annointed. (3) Let us not forget that the Jehovahs Witnesses combine strict inerrancy with heretical doctrine, and the the orthodox Lutheran churches of Germany after the Reformation combined strict inerrancy with vehement resistance to the fires of evangelical revivals which were breaking out among the Moravians and pietists. Strict inerrancy guarantees neither orthodoxy or spiritual life and power. Let us not fool ourselves about that. Inerrancy is not a cure-all. (4) It is not historically true that liberalism always grew out of slippage on the doctrine of Scripture. The early liberals were mostly biblicists who interpreted the Bible over against the traditions of the churches. They were a sort of biblical reaction to the alleged hellenziation of dogma in Catholicism. Add to that the fact that many a liberal has been produced by having suffered from an overly tight conservative upbringing which choked his cirtical senses. There is more than one slippery slope in this world!

Before concluding, let me voice a possible objection. Someone might easily say, Pinnock, you have been taken for a ride by the so-called moderates. You have been hoodwinked by people whose critical stances on the Bible and unevangelical positions would appal you if you knew them. You simply do not know the facts. You think the problem of theological liberalism has diminished since 1969 when it has actually increased. If moderates were like F. F. Bruce or James Orr things would be great, but they are not. What should I say to this criticism?

First, it reminds me of the enormous hurt and anger felt by the militants which has resulted in deep suspicion on this scale. No doubt they have been excluded and looked down upon for decades by the moderates when they were in control, and they cannot forget the pain. Indeed I am impressed by the hurt on all sides. Perhaps this mutual hurt will drive us to our senses and lead to healing. Second, it makes me want to emphasise my point earlier. The ball is in the moderates' court. They must take definite steps to clear the air of suspicion. It can no longer be business as usual. The Glorieta Statement and this series of annual conferences are a good start. But more will have to be done. Some apologies, explanations, and even some retractions are in order. Courageous appointments to faculties and some cretive retirements have to happen. But above all, the theological lines must be drawn to the left. The moderates must make it absolutely unmistakable that they are sound on the evangelical essentials. There is no time to dawdle—it is the time to act, and act decisevely.

Being evangelical certainly involves loving and respecting the Bible, and I am certain that means that 99% of Southern Baptists are evangelicals. But whether it also implies taking the strict inerrancy positon rather than the simpler biblicist standpoint is surely open for discussion and debate and not already a closed question. May God grant you wisdom as you process it.

Nehemiah or Sanballat?

Nehemiah's plan was to get all the Israelites to work together in the rebulding of the wall of Jerusalem. Sanballat's strategy was to frustrate the effort by getting the Jews to quarrel among themselves. My hope and prayer for the SBC is that the great majority of Baptists will heed Nehemiah and unite together behind their global mission in the power of God, and will not listen to Sanballat who wants them to fight among themselves and accomplish nothing.

RESPONSE: William E. Hull

The paper by Clark Pinnock on "What Is Biblical Inerrancy?" offers striking contrasts to one on the same subject by Robert Preus which preceded it. These differences stimulate reflection in three areas.

I.

At the outset, comment is almost unavoidable on the depth of diversity that exists within the inerrancy camp. Although presumably writing without any awareness of Preus' paper, Pinnock likens the differences between them to those that divided his mentor, F. F. Bruce, and Francis Shaeffer within the modern inerrancy movement. His prototype of such divergencies is represented by the "stricter views" of the "militant" B. B. Warfield and the "more lenient views" of the "moderate" James Orr. For Southern Baptists, an even more pertinent example would be the sharp tensions that surfaced between the moderate E. Y. Mullins and the militant Gresham Machen just at the time (1924-25) when the former was guiding the development of our denomination's first confessional statement on the Bible.

These are not isolated instances of disagreement within the same theological family, nor are the issues that divide inerrantists superficial. Our speaker of last evening, Mark Noll, in a fine history of evangelical Biblical scholarship in America during the past century entitled *Between Faith and Criticism,* has detailed just how deep the differences run. On the watershed issue of the historical/critical method, British inerrantists have long differed from American inerrantists in their more positive attitude toward, and extensive use of, this controversial discipline. In our country, the depth of the conflict is reflected in the recent history of Fuller Theological Seminary as interpreted by Harold Lindsell and David Hubbard. Or in the badly divided vote of the Evangelical Theological Society, a strict inerrantist group, over Robert Gundry's understanding of *midrash* in the Gospel of Matthew.

Such illustrations could be multiplied indefinitely, but we may concentrate on one example of profound cleavage within the inerrancy camp which has special relevance for Southern Baptists, that of Dispensationalism. It is very clear that virtually all Dispensationalists are strict inerrantists, but it is equally clear that many inerrantists are far from being Dispensationalists. And yet, this is not some peripheral theological point on which differences are inconsequential. Rather, Dispensationalism offers a comprehensive framework for interpreting the entire Bible. This is the one doctrine more than any other which is unique to the inerrancy movement, and yet inerrantists are bitterly divided, not over certain of its details, but over whether to accept it at all as a key to Scriptural understanding! Some might reply that this impasse merely illustrates the dis-

81

tinction which must be maintained between Biblical authority and Biblical hermeneutics. But that solution fails in the face of the claim by many inerrantists that they believe in Dispensationalism, unlike those who do not, precisely because they are inerrantists (i.e. because they take the entire Bible as literally and totally true without "spiritualizing" away any of its prophecies).

An inherent part of the inerrantist outlook is the conviction that the Bible is self-evident and, with the help of the Holy Spirit, self-explanatory if only the reader will accept it for what it really is and not distort its plain truth by superimposing on it modern presuppositions and methods. But that claim carries with it the corollary that committed inerrantists should be able to reach a general consensus regarding the basic meaning of Scripture, a result that is conspicuously absent in the case of Dispensationalism. Inerrantists constantly urge us to "accept the assertions of the Scripture on faith." But those who bring a Dispensationalism faith to such assertions will come out with a drastically different understanding of Scripture from those who bring a non-Dispensationalist faith to the same assertions. The question with which we are left, obviously, is whether the inerrantist mindset carries within it a sufficient emphasis on self-criticism to deal responsibly with the doctrinal contradictions that surface among its own adherents, or whether its absolutist emphasis actually dulls its adherents' powers of self-criticism to the point that they are unable or unwilling to deal in responsible fashion with their own internal differences.

II.

Reflection on the great diversity *within* the inerrancy movement, and not just *between* it and other positions, prompts us to ponder next its potential as a cohesive basis for denominational cooperation, a concern which is uppermost in the presentation by Pinnock. Some might suppose from the first section of this response that the only problem to be solved is the diverse views of inerrantists regarding various Bible doctrines. But the problem of diversity is actually more serious than that because inerrantists also hold widely differing convictions regarding the very nature of inerrancy itself. Robert K. Johnston, in a book aptly entitled *Evangelicals at an Impasse,* describes four such positions: (1) detailed inerrancy, (2) partial infallibility, (3) irenic inerrancy, and (4) complete infallibility. David S. Dockery of Criswell College expands the alternatives to seven: (1) mechanical dictation (John R. Rice), (2) absolute inerrancy (Harold Lindsell), (3) critical inerrancy (D. A. Carson and John Woodbridge), (4) limited inerrancy (I. Howard Marshall), (5) qualified inerrancy (Donald Bloesch), (6) nuanced inerrancy (Clark Pinnock), and (7) functional inerrancy (Jack Rogers and Donald McKim). Actually, a number of subdivisions are possible within these categories which would double or triple the list of distinctions. The fact is that the many viewpoints which gather under the umbrella called inerrancy constitute not a single position but a wide spectrum.

Perhaps it is this need to make so many distinctions between varying viewpoints that accounts in part for the controversial nature of the inerrancy movement. Pinnock has just alluded in his oral presentation to the fact that in the sixties he must have hurt or angered half of the people in this room, whereas now, in the eighties, he has probably succeeded in hurting or angering the other half! The prior question, of course, is whether a doctrine is really useful which, when used as sincerely and as knowledgeably as Pinnock has done, should cut so many of his fellow Christians with a double-edged blade. Again, why should Pinnock be castigated so vehemently by fellow-inerrantists as his views on that doctrine mature? When one Christian changes his mind about a doctrine, another Christian has the perfect right to disagree, hopefully in a spirit of charity and respect. Then what is there about inerrancy which often causes polite disagreement to degenerate into charges of treachery and betrayal?

That question is probably beyond my competence to answer. But as I ponder the long history of inerrancy, I remember how it functioned in eighteenth century Protestant scholasticism as a rigid defense against Romanism. Later, in the nineteenth century, it was deployed as a bulwark against the enroachments of continental Biblical criticism. Then, in the twentieth century, it became almost synonymous with the Fundamentalist assault on Modernism. In a word, inerrancy offers us a legacy that is controversy-laden. All of its key concepts are battle scarred. Most of its great exemplars have been pugnacious defenders of the faith. To use a biological analogy, it is almost as if controversy is a dominant part of the "genetic material" which inerrancy bequeaths to those in whom it is reborn in each new generation. If history is any guide, here is a doctrine that seems almost destined to be divisive—even among its adherents!—whenever it is given center stage.

Such observations make me skeptical that inerrancy is able to provide the unifying force around which our Baptist folk can rally in building a voluntaristic denomination. To test that suspicion, I made a brief study of the Baptist groups listed in the *Encyclopedia of Southern Baptists* which were established with inerrancy as the central theological criterion of their organization. To my dismay, I discovered a sad history of instability and schism in all three cases. (1) The Baptist Missionary Association (1900) spawned by the Hayden-Cranfill controversy endured years of bitter tension between Ben M. Bogard and D. N. Jackson, finally falling apart in 1950. (2) The Baptist Bible Union (1923) led by the triumverate of W. B. Riley, T. T. Shields, and J. Frank Norris, rallied inerrantists for seven years but then collapsed. (3) In the South, Norris launched his own denomination under various names, such as the World Fundamentalist Baptist Missionary Fellowship (1936), only to see it split asunder in 1950 after a prolonged struggle with dissidents, led by G. Beauchamp Vick, who founded the Baptist Bible Fellowship.

I applaud the effort of Pinnock to redefine inerrancy as an irenic force in Baptist life, but I find it hard to believe that history is on his side. There is abroad in our denomination a supposition that if only we could all agree to become inerrantists, peace would somehow follow. Would that it were so! Unfortunatley, the biographies and memoirs of leading inerrantists in the past tell another story. We may think that we have seen controversy between the so-called "conservatives" and "moderates" in our midst, but I can assure you that such skirmishes are mild indeed compared to the struggles between fellow-

83

inerrantists in Baptist denominations dedicated to that cause. Perhaps we should ponder the witness of that staunch Southern Baptist inerrantist Jasper Massee who left the movement in 1926 because he feared that its insatiable appetite for controversy would finally sully his spirit.

III.

In offering these cautions to my colleague, Clark Pinnock, I realize that I am responding to one which is already well along on his pilgrimage from a combative to an irenic doctrine of Scripture. I hope that it will not appear unseemly to lay aside for a moment the formalities of scholarly discourse and deal in somewhat pastoral fashion with the spiritual dimensions of this changing stance which has attracted so much attention in connection with this conference.

Twenty years ago it was my assignment to bring Bible studies opening each session of the Louisiana Baptist Convention. One afternoon, just after I finished my exposition and sat down on the front pew, a visitor from New Orleans unwound his lanky frame, peered over the pulpit, and proceeded to unleash a withering attack on my most cherished friends in Southern Baptist theological education. That harsh jeremiad was my first encounter with the spirit and strategy of "strict inerrancy," but it was the harbinger of things to come a decade later. Now, that same speaker has just delivered an equally impassioned speech on the same subject, but this time his presentation is marked by prudence, charity, and forebearance. Furthermore, lying behind his remarks here is a truly fine book, *The Scripture Principle,* which eschews extremism, sympathetically understands other viewpoints, offers helpful concessions, not in order to compromise but in order to work for consensus among all who love the Bible and seek to exalt it as the Word of God.

I am not well acquainted with Clark Pinnock, nor have I had any meaningful contact with him in the twenty years between our two encounters just mentioned, therefore I am certainly not qualified to offer any pscho-biographical observations which might explain the "old" and the "new" Pinnock. But the differences are so striking, and are so significant for the deeper agenda of this conference, that I would like to attempt an interpretation of this transformation as I understand it in the light of the central issue looming behind our debate over inerrancy. In my view, Pinnock is on pilgrimage searching for the shape of authentic Christian authority, a task into which we all must enter.

The classic formulation of Christian authority is what might be called Constantinian. In simplest form it may be described as authority "from above." Traditionally, in its European expression, it was from the king of civil affairs, from the pope in religious affairs, and from the father in domestic affairs. In all three cases, authority was handed down from the head who ruled either on the throne, at the altar, or in the home. Obviously this understanding of authority could be institutionalized in laws decreed by those with power to enact them, in councils established by those with power to convene them, and in sacred Scriptures canonized and controlled by those with power to interpret them. Lest we forget, this was the shape of authority in the church for well over half of its two thousand year history. In a phrase, it was a system of submission to "the powers that be."

But in recent centuries, first in America and then spreading to the Third World, there has arisen a fundamentally different understanding of authority: "from below," as it were, rather than "from above." This post-Constantinian approach reverses the flow of authority by perceiving power as moving upward from the people to their chosen leaders. Inalienable rights belong, not to governments, but to its citizens, hence its laws are to be expressions of their will and for their common good. In the religious realm, likewise, power proceeds from the individual and the congregation to denominations that exist as servants of their need. Neither the Bible nor its interpretation belongs to the clergy but to a priesthood of all believers. In this system of authority, the people do not submit to the will of their leaders; rather, freely chosen leaders submit to the will of the people. To borrow a word made rich by the American experience, power is "democratized."

From their beginnings in the seventeenth century, Baptists were in the vanguard of this revolution in the way authority functioned. At first, of course, they were reviled and even persecuted both in Europe and in America for as long as the Constantinian mindset prevailed. But once the new approach to authority took root among the masses, Baptists began to flourish because they offered in their churches a spiritual counterpart to the civil liberties being claimed by the people. The greatest Baptist growth today is in Second World countries such as Russia and China, and in Third World settings such as Africa, Latin America, and Asia where a yearning for self-determination is seeking to find grass-roots expression. There are denominations, such as Roman Catholicism, which are historically conditioned to function comfortably in the Constantinian world of authority "from above." But Baptists clearly function best in the post-Constantinian world of authority "from below."

My guess is that Pinnock is trying valiantly to recast the concept of inerrancy so as to move beyond its Constantian rootage and equip it for usefulness in a post-Constantinian era. There is still in his makeup, I think, a residue of the old authority "from above," as when he wants to revert to thundering at Baptist "liberals," should one every turn up, but be gentle with Baptist "conservatives" even if they differ with him on details. Like Pinnock, all of us are torn between models of authority. Does the Gospel of a rejected and crucified Christ best reach the human heart "from above" or "from below?" With ringing shout or still small voice? With the clenched fist of unnegotiable conviction or the open-handed plea of confessed humility? May God give Clark Pinnock guidance as he struggles with these questions, for in their answer lies his peace—and ours as well!

RESPONSE: Paige Patterson

As my beloved mentor has stated, this is a critical time in the life of Southern Baptists. Dr. Pinnock's plea for peace is one which only the unwary souls who have never been under fire could possible fail to embrace. However, the passion of our Lord calls attention to the enormous cost involved in the purchase of our peace. Therefore, a peace arranged at the price of truth is unthinkable and is, I suspect, a peace that would prove too fragile for this period of testing.

The twenty-minute limitation for response prevents adequate reply to the multiple misconceptions which characterize Pinnock's presentation. Selectivity is thus necessary. Unfortunately, Pinnock's paper is less concerned with the assigned topic "What is Biblical Inerrancy" than it is with the professor's feelings, emotions, and forecasts about the political ramifications of the struggle among Southern Baptists. This leaves little alternative for me other than to reply to the issues which he has raised. Additionally, there is the problem of possessing only his draft and not the final paper. One cannot, therefore, be certain about the nature of the proposals to which he must reply. Nevertheless, an attempt must be ventured.

First Major Concern: Peace Among Brethren

Dr. Pinnock's first major concern is a divisiveness allegedly spawned by those supporting the doctrine of inerrancy. He expresses concern that this divisiveness threatens the future of the union of Southern Baptists. He admits to having once had a part in what he calls "militancy" and even admits that he was "preoccupied with driving out any liberals from the SBC where they really do not belong." But Pinnock has moderated his views and now views the mutual tolerance of a Warfield-Orr or a Schaeffer-Bruce model as the appropriate one for Southern Baptists. This presumably is because the two groups in the Baptist discussion are essentially representative of the same kinds of differences which characterized Bruce and Schaeffer. But is all of this an accurate assessment or just sentimentalism mixed together with a dose of hysteria? (1) Is a major split imminent? (2) Are inerrantists really the culprits in the present impasse? (3) Are inerrantists committed to Pinnock's old agenda of "driving out the liberals?" (4) Is the Schaeffer-Bruce analogy really applicable to Southern Baptists?

The first question may be answered by calling attention to the fact that inerrantists have tolerated for twenty-five years the propagation of liberalism and neoorthodoxy to say nothing at all of exclusion, misrepresentation, and discrimination. Why would inerrantists suddenly leave now? The only noise of an exodus has been the recent divorce proposal of Dr. Glenn Hinson of Southern Seminary. I doubt that many inerrantists, denominationalists, or even moderates would join his caravan. Southern Baptists are a loyal people. They have walked through tribulation before; they are not strangers to trial; they will only emerge stronger in the morning.

Furthermore, inerrantists are not the culprits who caused this ferment. Inerrantists have simply followed the death-bed instructions of B. H. Carroll to L. R. Scarborough. They have taken the matter to the people.[1] Inerrantists did not write books calling into question the historicity of biblical narratives. Neither did they arrange to leave themselves with virtually no voice on the faculties of some seminaries and with parity in none. Neither did they preside over the loss of the University of Richmond or Wake Forest. Inerrantists did not discriminate against and ridicule Bible-believing students in the institutions. Neither did they carefully exclude vocal inerrantists from major leadership roles in the denomination. Furthermore, inerrantists have not challenged incumbent presidents of the convention. Inerrantists are responsible only for responding in ways made possible by our forefathers to a situation in Southern Baptist life which to them was unconscionable.

Neither are inerrantists committed to Pinnock's old agenda of driving liberals from the denomination. We are a people of the local church. Anyone admitted to a local Southern Baptist church as a member is beyond the jurisdiction of the convention. The convention has a right to determine whose messengers it will seat but has no authority over the membership rolls of its cooperating churches. On the other hand, Southern Baptists do have every right and responsibility to decide what criteria will be used for determining who will be employed at their institutions and agencies. As the early Pinnock said:

> There is no reason why the money of God's people should be squandered on an unorthodox and ineffective student movement, on Baptist colleges which show very little mark of standing for biblical principles, on seminaries which indoctrinate students in the latest theological fads while ignoring historic evangelical thought, on a press and book stores which manifest considerable haziness about what a truly good Christian book is, on Sunday School materials which specialize in dilution, and on agencies which seem to prefer the antics of the radical left in the NCC to the mundane duty of preaching regeneration as the cure of social ills.[2]

But more important, is the Warfield-Orr/Schaeffer-Bruce analogy applicable? Here Pinnock must be ill-informed. Would Orr or Bruce be content with the following avowals? Speaking of the actual origin of the Rahab pericope, one Southern Baptist says,

> Israel has taken up a popular story centering around the ability of a prostitute to trick a king and gain freedom for two men. Israel has transformed this into a story preparing for the conquest of Jericho. The two men are spies sent out by Israel to conquer the land, that is the city-state ruled by the king of Jericho. The story has then been placed at the front of the conquest narratives as a whole to introduce the theology of conquest. The Deuteronomist has then made the story the basis for his theological creed. The growth of the story thus represents a manifold theological interpretation. Each generation

87

of Israelites has learned something new about itself and its God through telling and retelling the story of Jericho's favorite prostitute.[3]

Another Southern Baptist professor addresses the question of the historicity of Genesis,

> The disparity between Genesis and Darwin, if it comes down to it, has really been decided for all of us in Darwin's favor. If the Scriptures are not then reliable in matters scientific, how can they be trusted in other matters? Furthermore, scientific ('critical') study of the Scriptures has made clear the very human quality of the Bible itself, and has shown the rather surprising variety of outlook, witness, opinion and theology to be found in the Bible. What does this say about its authority? If indeed this book is shot-through with humanity, how can it be relied on as a testimony to faith and a source of doctrine?[4]

Another Southern Baptist supposes that the Bible misleads us about the time of the building of the tabernacle.

> In all probability the tabernacle should be traced to the period of the twelve-tribe federation at Shechem, and probably nearer the period immediately prior to the monarchy, if not the era of David himself.[5]

One Southern Baptist scholar even thinks that Jesus erred.

> Indeed, it is difficult to avoid the conclusion that Jesus expected the return of the Son of Man and the consummation to occur within his own lifetime (Mark 13:30). His 'error' was due to prophetic foreshortening.[6]

Or, consider the same author's incredible conclusion about revelation itself.

> Today, it would appear, the covenant and thus the mission of the church could be defined with a greater measure of tolerance. This would not necessitate an abandonment of monotheism nor of the conviction that some sort of special revelation occurred through Israel and Christ and the church. It might necessitate, however, the acknowledgement that the one God has disclosed himself in particular ways through other cultures and religions besides these.[7]

Would either Orr or Bruce settle for a theology in which one believed only that "some sort of special revelation" occurred through Christ? The controversy in Southern Baptist life today is not merely between conflicting theories of inspiration. It is not a question of an "elaborate" theory versus a more "spontaneous biblicism." Rather, Southern Baptists are being asked to decide between the orthodox faith of the apostles, prophets, and their own forefathers and the neoorthodoxy prevalent in an age of doubt and unbelief. A far better model for Southern Baptist discussions would be a Warfield-Briggs model. Pinnock admits in his paper that he does not really know the Southern Baptist situation. Why then make a proposal for therapy when the illness has not been adequately diagnosed?

Second Major Concern: Theories Of Inspiration

Dr. Pinnock supposes that the quarrel is between a complicated, rationalistic doctrine of the Bible held by "self-styled advocates of orthodoxy," and those who hold a "simpler and more spontaneous biblicism." He alleges that this latter approach is (1) spontaneous, (2) simple, and (3) practical. According to Pinnock both positions (4) love and (5) respect the Bible totally. But is this really the case? Consider the following recent observations from Southern Baptist authors and publications.

> When the J source and the Miriam couplet (Ex. 15:21) are juxtaposed, a probably event unfolds. The Hebrews fleeing Egypt were pursued by the Egyptians using chariots. When the Hebrews confronted a shallow body of water, a strong east wind blew back the water in a reedy, shallow area, permitting the Hebrews to cross. When the Egyptians sought to follow, their chariots were too heavy and bogged down. As the horses attempted to pull free, some of the Egyptians were thrown into the shallow water and mud. In the confusion some Egyptians died.[8]

Is this simple? Is it spontaneous? Is it practical? Is it faithful to the witness of the Scriptures? Does it suggest love or respect for the Scriptures?

Or, consider this explanation of the origins of Joshua.

> Word of God did not begin as a book. It began as a story told my men reacting in faith to actions they interpreted as the work of God. Such stories took various forms: spy stories, stories of Holy War, cultic catechism, divine call and testing, sacral judgment, tribal etiology, and so on. It did not remain as a simple story. Instead the stories were adopted and adapted by the Israelite cult, particularly the cult at Gilgal. Story of divine action became the center of cultic celebration. As such it received a new form and function, but continued to give dynamic life and faith to the people of God through many generations. Here each new generation learned of the faith of the fathers and was incorporated into the people of God. Finally, after Israel developed its own political cultural organizations, liturgy became literature, used to give identity and hope to the people of God. Still, it was not complete. Each new generation read, listened, and applied the word of God to its own situation. In so doing it incorporated its own experience with the word of God and with the continued leadership of God in daily life into the text.[9]

Can anyone believe that this is spontaneous biblicism? Is this simple? Is it practical? Do these positions evince a love and respect for the Bible equal to that of the inerrantists? If a particular theory of inspiration is "well beyond the capacity of ordinary Christians even to understand," what can be said of such hermeneutical gymnastics as these? Pinnock may well be able to justify the use of the historical-critical methodology which is predominant in theology today, but to pass if off as "spontaneous," "simple," or "practical" staggers the imagination.

Pinnock's suggestion that the SBC "battle" is between two types of inerran-

89

tists, 'permissive inerrantists" and "strict inerrantists" is one with which moderates and neoorthodox theologians of integrity should take serious exception. For example, a popular Southern Baptist who recently united with the Episcopalians stated the matter succinctly in a Broadman publication.

> The ultimate authority in a living religion can never be something as static as a book or an institution or even a human being. It must be none other than God himself, authenticating his truth in his own freedom and in the most personal of ways. This is why it borders on the heretical to speak of the Bible as the final authority in all matters religious. [10]

Is this permissive inerrancy? Is this inerrancy of any variety? Or again, in a widely acclaimed sermon, a well-known Southern Baptist said,

> We are now in a position to answer the specific question with which we began. The cumulative force of the evidence is overwhelming: No. It is not wise to call the Bible 'infallible.' That term is subject to too many problems to become a controlling concept in our witness to Scripture. Let us say, kindly but firmly, that here is not the decisive place for our denomination to take a stand, nor is this an issue worthy of splitting our ranks. There are many wonderfully unambiguous affirmations that we may all make about the Scriptures, but this is not one of them. [11]

Does this author who does not want to call the Bible infallible wish to be labeled a "permissive inerrantist?" Why not simple face the truth that this is not a question of two views of inerrancy, but of some who believe the Bible to be flawed with errors and others who believe that the Bible is "not errant in any area of reality," and who hold to the "infallible power and binding authority of the Bible." [12] Furthermore, for everyone to use the word "inerrancy" to describe his view of the Bible as Pinnock suggested at Southern Seminary will not do as long as that is capitulation rather than conviction.

Third Major Concern: Similarity To Catholicism

Dr. Pinnock next argues that an affinity exists between advocates of inerrancy on the one hand and Roman Catholicism on the other. He suggests that one really needs to go on and declare the infallibility of church declarations so that incorrect interpretations of the Bible will not arise. He then suggests that the Chicago statement on inerrancy would become our creed and the president of the convention our pope.

Such emotive and misleading rhetoric may make good preaching but does so at the cost of accuracy. Southern Baptists are nowhere close to making the Chicago statement or any other document to serve as its creed. As a matter of fact, the whole point about Baptists being non-creedal arose out of the cognizance that no human formulation could ever improve on the Bible since the Scriptures, unlike human creeds, were not subject to error or mistake.

Furthermore, all ecclesiastical declarations are of limited value for the same reason. Baptists have always insisted that there is more than just a semantic difference between the "illuminated mind" of the Bible reader and the "inspired mind" of the Bible author. The latter spoke the word of God flawlessly under the superintendence of the Holy Spirit. But Pinnock apparently does not understand this distinction. He suggests that his view provides more openness to the Holy Spirit. But what Pinnock has given the Holy Spirit with one hand, he has taken away with the other. Illumination without adequate revelation leaves us with no sure standard against which to "test the spirits." No decree of prelate, council, convention or other ecclesiastical body is perfect. Therefore, all ecclesiastical dicta must be judged by the Scriptures, which alone are absolutely trustworthy.

Finally, it should be noted that the danger most evangelicals face is the possibility of losing the opportunity to read and to interpret the Bible not to ecclesiastical officials but to an elitist priesthood of scholars whose historical-critical methodologies often rob the Bible reader of his confidence in the God-breathed word. Further, it is not the "scholastic inerrantist" that is likely to despise the simple, spontaneous, and practically-minded believer who comes to the Bible and hears God in every word. The same figures who have been purveyors of such condescension toward inerrantist students who were under their tutelage will be the most likely to belittle the simple, spontaneous, and practical common Christian in his literalistic reading of the Scriptures.

Fourth Concern: The Bible And Inerrancy

The objection that the Bible does not teach "inerrancy" ought not to be embraced too quickly. First, the Bible certainly does not teach "errancy." Nowhere can one find any hint of one biblical author questioning the veracity of another's contribution. Nowhere is there any indication of an approach to the hermeneutical task utilizing the kinds of presuppositions employed by modern historical-critical methodologists.

Furthermore, the Bible may not use the word "inerrancy," but, of course, neither does it employ the term "Trinity." It does not follow, however, that the concept of the "Trinity" is absent from the Scriptures. Neither do we cease to employ the word *Trinity* just because it has to be extensively explained or because it is a difficult concept. If one does approach the Scriptures from a "simple," "spontaneous," and "practical" perspective, just exactly how does he interpret the following:

(1) And he gave unto Moses, when he had made an end of communing with him upon mount Sinai, two tables of testimony, tables of stone, written with the finger of God. Exodus 31:18.

(2) The law of the Lord is perfect, converting the soul: the testimony of the Lord is sure, making wise the simple. Psalm 19:7.

(3) For ever, O Lord, thy word is settled in heaven. Psalm 119:89.

(4) For verily I say unto you, Till heaven and earth pass, one jot or one tittle shall in no wise pass from the law, till all be fulfilled. Matthew 5:18.

(5) But as touching the resurrection of the dead, have you not read that which was spoken unto you by God, saying, I am the God of Abraham, and

the God of Isaac, and the God of Jacob? God is not the God of the dead, but of the living. Matthew 22:31-32.

(6) Then he said unto them, O fools, and slow of heart to believe all that the prophets have spoken. Luke 24:25.

(7) For had ye believed Moses, ye would have believed me: for he wrote of me. But if you believe not his writings, how shall ye believe my words? John 5:46-47.

(8) Knowing this first, that no prophecy of the scripture is of any private interpretation. For the prophecy came not in old time by the will of man: but holy men of God spake as they were moved by the Holy Ghost. 2 Peter 1:20-21.

But we are informed that the "theory" of inerrancy is the problem and we are assured that "no two inerrantists agree on the definition of inerrancy," which incidentally is not really the case at all.[13] Then one may ask which two historical-critical methodologists agree about which passages capture the word of God and which passages show the flawed and error-inclined hand of man? At least when inerrantists disagree they disagree among themselves. But with Pinnock, one never knows which Pinnock we are hearing. Do we listen to "early Pinnock," "middle Pinnock," "late Pinnock," or just the "contradictory Pinnock" of his latest book on this subject *The Scripture Principle?*[14]

Obviously, part of the difficulty with any approach other than one of total confidence in the Scriptures is that *men* do not agree. And it is precisely in the forum of anthropocentric judgment where all non-inerrantist theories deposit us. We are thus set adrift in existential subjectivism. No longer is the problem that inerrantists must know everything for certain, as Pinnock imagines. Now the problem becomes how do we know anything for certain? If it be answered, "I know for certain because I experienced something to be true," then it is man's experience and not God's word that becomes the criterion for adjudication. We have elevated anthropocentric authority—man's authority over God's authority. On the other hand, if I know because "God said it," then what God said He must have said inerrantly. A perfect God could hardly be said to speak errantly. But suppose one replies that "some of the Bible is God's inerrant word but that some of it is unreliable due to man's involvement." Then who decides what is from God and what is from man? And with that we are back to subjectivism and to the authority of man over the word of God. With Adolf Schlatter I reply that we must stand "under the word!"

If one then objects, as Pinnock does, that inerrantists put an interpretive grid over the Scriptures through which the Bible must be understood, the answer is that everyone has such a grid. Historical-critical scholars impose their presuppositions of error upon the Bible. Pinnock, himself, approaches the Bible with presuppositions. There is no such thing as absolutely pure, presuppositionless hermeneutics. The difference is, inerrantists are predisposed to believe that *every* word is true until something is *proven* false whereas non-inerrantists are often predisposed to believe that the Bible contains mistakes. Further, inerrantists admit a predisposition toward belief but cite evidences from the Bible which seem to demand such a conclusion.

Neither is it the case that inerrantists spend inordinate amounts of time with "theory" instead of interpreting the texts. Does anyone really want to suggest that historical-critical scholars pursue more "simple," "spontaneous," and "practical" interpretation than inerrantist pastors and teachers? Is it not a much greater waste of time to invent endless theories about how things came about than to do careful textual and historical homework, including efforts which have frequently led to successful harmonization of apparently contradictory materials? After all, where is most of the expository preaching done? Is it in non-inerrantist or inerrantist pulpits?

Conclusion

My distinguished and greatly loved professor wants peace in the Southern Baptist Convention. So do I. In fact, I probably desire peace more than he does since I, unlike my professor, still labor within the Southern Baptist context and endure the misunderstandings and misrepresentations associated with the questions I have raised. Unlike Pinnock, the convention has been my life from the time I was a Sunbeam, Royal Ambassador, Baptist college student, Southern Baptist seminary student, Southern Baptist pastor, until this moment. Pinnock grieves over the state of disarray. But I probably grieve more than he. Not only must I grieve over the confusion, but also I must lament the plight of biblical inerrantists who endure discrimination, misrepresentation, and isolation. I must sorrow over the long history of denominational apostasy which rendered other Baptist federations impotent and now impinges upon our Southern Baptist Zion. I must bemoan the fate of millions of lost persons around the globe who remain oblivious to the message of Christ due to the inroads of universalism, liberation theology, and anemic evangelism which rests on a shifting foundation of historical-critical hypothesizing. Last of all I must grieve over my professor who has forsaken the prophetic pulpit of Luther for the indecisive desk of Erasmus and the certainty of Paul for the vacillation of the Athenians who must always "hear some new thing."

But Pinnock's price for peace is too high. He would have us to support those who teach the exact opposite of what we hold to be sacred. He would have us stand at the judgment seat of Christ and try to explain to the enthroned Christ that in the interest of peace in the convention we supported either by silence or by resources those who say that His word errs. This we cannot and will not do!

Notes

1. L. R. Scarborough, the second president of Southwestern Baptist Theological Seminary spoke of his last conference with B. H. Carroll. "B. H. Carroll, the greatest man I ever knew, as he was about to die, a few days before he died, expecting me, as he wanted me, to succeed him as president of the seminary. I went in his room one day and he pulled himself up by my chair with his hands and looked me in the face. There were times when he looked like he was forty feet high. And he looked into my face and said, 'My boy, on this Hill orthodoxy, the old truth is making one of its last stands and I want to deliver to you a charge and I do it in the blood of Jesus Christ.' He said, 'You will be

93

elected president of the seminary. I want you, if there ever comes heresy in your faculty, to take it to your faculty. If they won't hear you, take it to the trustees. If they won't hear you take it to the conventions that appointed them. If they won't hear you, take it to the common Baptists. They will hear you. And,' he said, 'I charge you in the name of Jesus Christ to keep it lashed to the old Gospel of Jesus Christ.' As long as I have influence in that institution, by the grace of God I will stand by the old Book." L. R. Scarborough. *Gospel Messages*. (Nashville: Sunday School Board of the Southern Baptist Convention, 1922), pp. 227-228.

2. Clark Pinnock. *A New Reformation*. (Tigerville, SC, Jewel Books, 1968), p. 18.

3. Trent Butler. *Word Biblical Commentary,* "Joshua." (Waco, TX: Word Books), p. 34. Butler currently serves on the staff of the Sunday School Board.

4. C. W. Christian. *Shaping Your Faith — A Guide To A Personal Theology*. (Waco, TX: Word Books, Inc., 1973), pp. 67-81. Christian currently serves as a professor at Baylor University.

5. Roy Lee Honeycutt. "Exodus." *The Broadman Bible Commentary*. vol. 1, ed. Clifton J. Allen, (Nashville: Broadman Press, rev. 1973), p. 448. Honeycutt currently serves as president of Southern Seminary.

6. E. Glenn Hinson. *Jesus Christ*. (Wilmington, NC: McGrath Publishing Co., 1977), p. 76. Hinson is currently a professor at Southern Seminary.

7. E. Glenn Hinson. *The Evangelization of the Roman Empire*. (Macon, GA: Mercer University Press, 1981), p. 287.

8. Frank Eakin, Jr. "The Plagues and the Crossing of the Sea," *Review and Expositor* 74 (Fall 1977): 478.

9. Trent C. Butler. *Word Biblical Commentary,* "Joshua." (Waco, TX: Word Books), p. 1.

10. John Claypool. "The Humanity of God" in *Is The Bible A Human Book?* ed. Joseph Green and Wayne Ward. (Nashville: Broadman Press, 1970), p. 28.

11. William E. Hull. "Shall We Call The Bible Infallible?" (Louisville: Crescent Hill Sermons, 1970). Hull is Provost at Samford University, Birmingham, Alabama.

12. Glorieta Statement of the six presidents of Southern Baptist Seminaries released to the Peace Committee of the Southern Baptist Convention earlier this year.

13. See, for example, the statement on inerrancy issued by a large group of evangelical scholars working with the International Council on Biblical Inerrancy. Most inerrantists would agree with a simple definition like that of Paul Feinberg. "Inerrancy means that when all facts are known, the Scriptures in their original autographs and properly interpreted will be shown to be wholly true in everything that they affirm, whether that has to do with doctrine or morality or with the social, physical, or life sciences." Paul D. Feinberg. "The Meaning of Inerrancy," *Inerrancy*. ed. Norman L. Geisler, (Grand Rapids: Zondervan, 1979), p. 294.

14. For example, Pinnock says, "We must be forthright and admit that contradiction is not something that we can consistently allow and that if contradiction exists our doctrine of Scripture is overthrown." Clark Pinnock. *The Scripture Principle*. (San Francisco: Harper & Row, 1984), p. 147. But on page 124 the same author says, "But being open to legend as a possible literary form does not open the door to this improbable and destructive thesis. There is no mythology to speak of in the New Testament. At most, there are fragments and suggestions of myth: for example, the strange allusion to the bodies of the saints being raised on Good Friday (Matt. 27:52) and the sick being healed through contact with pieces of cloth that had touched Paul's body (Acts 10:11-12)." No wonder that Bill Hendricks referred to Pinnock as a "tortured soul."

5

PARAMETERS OF BIBLICAL INERRANCY

Clark H. Pinnock

Introduction

The parameters of biblical inerrancy vary depending on which inerrantists you consult. Everybody attaches to the term their own set of qualifications and exceptions. In my case the parameters are much the same as those suggested by other terms such as trustworthy or inspired or infallible. Compared to them the term inerrancy enjoys no particular advantage. All of them do essentially the same job, which is to testify to our complete openness to God speaking to us through the Scriptures. None of them standing alone can begin to ennunciate an adequate understanding of the Bible. Each stands in need of explanation.

I think that, given my own history in Southern Baptist life which was marked by a certain militancy on the topic of inerrancy during the 60's when I was professor at New Orleans, I owe it to the present generation and this audience to explain why my convictions about biblical inerrancy changed and moved in a moderate direction. I think I have given enough aid and comfort to the militants in the past so that it is time now for me to balance this influence with reflections of another kind. Not only will this answer some questions which people may have about my own theological pilgrimage, but much more importantly it will also serve this conference well by indicating emphatically that inerrancy is far from a settled issue outside the SBC in evangelicalism and not the automatic cure-all militants within the denomination seem to think it is. If Southern Baptists want to use inerrancy language, then it is important that they do so responsibly and not merely rhetorically. One quick way to bring realism to our discussions this week will be for me to share candidly with you some of the things I have learned about biblical inerrancy in the past few years.

The Appeal of Strict Inerrancy

Unless we understand the appeal which an elaborate theory of the Bible offers to people, we will never comprehend why they cling to it so tenaciously despite enormous difficulties. What it does is to promise them the kind of absolute rational certainty which human beings have always wanted to possess but have never been able to secure. People want to be able to believe that there is no cause for doubt or hesitation in their religion. This is why people cling to the Watchtower Society, to the pope of Rome, to the Koran, to the book of Mormon—because they desparately hope they can walk by sight and not by faith. This is true everywhere in the world, and especially in North America

95

where the scientific ideal of objectivity and certainty is so influential. Surely it must be possible, we dream, to present our convictions in black and white, with unobscured clarity and absolute non-relativity. What a marvelous possibility! It is exactly what fuels the faith of Muslim fundamentalists as well. Just think of it—a Koran, written by God in heaven, a divine book, pure revelation untouched by the human and the historical. Assuming you can bring yourself to believe there is such a thing how could you resist it? Anyone would give his right arm for so divine a certainty. No price would be too high to pay for it.

Of course the Muslim has a certain advantage over us in that his culture never did go through a critical enlightenment and never has to this day looked squarely and honestly at that all too human book of his, so obviously written not by God but by a mere mortal. Whereas we, however conservative, know that we cannot fool ourselves into thinking that the Bible lacks human and historical dimension. Nevertheless, by the same token that very critical awareness however undeveloped in us gives us great fright. The ground seems to be shifting under us. The relativity of all things human has begun to touch us. The South is not the stable zone it once was. Secularism has brought with it a deconstruction of all meaning and a vacuum you can almost feel. And in this context of ours it is hardly any wonder that Christians would reach out for the absolute certainty which seems to be available to them in a perfectly errorless Bible.

I ask no one else to admit what I am about to say but it is important: the deep reason I defended the strict view of inerrancy in my earlier years was because I desperately wanted it to be true. I wanted it to be true so badly that I passed over the obvious problems in the theory and put the best face on them that I could. What helped me most to become more honest in the face of the realities of Scripture was simply the realization that absolute rational certainty was not something which I could have or even needed to have. The witness of the Spirit to the saving gospel of God was all I really needed then and now.

The Truth Question

Although my desire to prove the strict inerrancy theory was strong, gradually the truth dawned on me that it was burdened by a great many difficulties. Its appeal notwithstanding, there were factors which gave me pause and lessened my enthusiasm for the position. Let me share some of them with you now.

First, strict inerrantists make a good deal out of the claim that Jesus himself and the Bible itself teach the elaborate doctrine they hold. Being Protestants they are compelled to do so—there is nowhere else for them to turn for proof. I have attempted to argue along these lines myself. However, when you consider how complicated the modern theory of inerrancy is, involving as it does distinctions such as the one between autographs and copies, between what is intended and what is said, and between apparent and real errors, you are almost forced to admit that this doctrinal construction is a human contrivance which must be viewed on that level. It is an exaggeration to say Jesus and the apostles "teach" it. It is even clearer if you add in the fact that whatever they teach on this subject, they do not have the New Testament in mind since it did not yet exist, and therefore do not teach its inerrancy which is surely the most important for Christians. Furthermore, in any assessment of their teaching about biblical inerrancy one would need to weigh the significance of their actual use of the Hebrew scriptures and not just their so-called claims for it, which inerrantists seldom do. They seldom do it because it reveals a greater liberty in handling the text than these people wish to allow.

My point is not that Jesus and the apostles do not teach us about biblical inspiration and authority. Obviously they do so. But rather that in their teaching they present a far more practical and open concept than the high Protestant one. Just take 2 Timothy 3:15-17, for example, which says nothing about inerrancy, or autographs, or original intention. It is content to tell us that Scripture is inspired and very profitable to the believing community and to the life of faith. It supports simple biblicism, and not elaborate biblicism. If Southern Baptists would be content to say what Paul says here, and not fight over elaborate human theories of inspiration, there would be no holy war today.

The most painful change I have had to undergo in this area of doctrine has been the need to recognize that the Bible does not teach the elaborate inerrancy theory we have erected. It is an influential human tradition developed by well-meaning church leaders in response to serious dangers to the church. On this level, and on no higher level, ought its merits to be discussed. it is not immune from criticism or exalted above discussion.

Second, the problem of definition began to bother me. Why was it, if inerrancy is such a crucial and indispensable term, that there is so little agreement on what it means? Some people take it to great extremes and feel they have to reconcile the smallest discrepency (Archer, Lindsell, Preus), while others can live with enormous concessions (Erickson, Kantzer, Packer). We should note in passing, too, that no strict inerrantists today is as strict as Protestant scholastics used to be (eg. in their zeal for the inerrancy of the Hebrew vowel points). The Chicago Statement papers over this disagreement by compromise wording as virtually all creeds do. There is lots of rhetoric to satisfy the fundamentalists, and then there is article XIII for the liberal inerrantists to flee to. Do not forget Robert Gundry's convincing argument that his own theory that Matthew invented many of his stories was perfectly congruent with the Chicago Statement (see the appendix in his 1982 commentary). Indeed, it was, and therefore he had to be ejected from the Evangelical Theological Society for coming to the wrong exegetical conclusions instead! In my view the Southern Baptist moderates, if they wanted to avoid trouble with the militants, could do much worse than to declare themselves "Article Thirteen Inerrantists" and be done with it. The great majority could do so in my judgment without any insincerity. Seminary presidents then would find it much easier to appoint inerrantists because there would suddenly be a new crop of them. My point is deadly serious and not a joke.

The point here is that biblical inerrancy is not the firm and clear category we are being told that it is. It is supposed to be the answer to all our problems, and yet the inerrantists themselves cannot agree on what it signifies. I was given two topics: what is biblical inerrancy? and what are its parameters? The honest answer is, nobody can be sure. The reason for this is simply due to the fact that the biblical writers did not compose their work with the elaborate theory of inerrancy to guide them. Not having it at hand, they wrote hundreds of things which are hard for us who do have it to reconcile with it. This is the price one pays when he or she wishes to impose on the Scriptures a human theory not itself scriptural. It's the same problem as if you approached the Bible with the idea that Mary is the mediatrix. It just does not work. The text will resist it.

But the frightening thing is this: even though honest inerrantists surely must know that their favorite category is not clear or firm, some of them are intent upon ramming the strict version of it down the throats of others. This is unfair and disturbing. Obviously some people are spoiling for a fight and inerrancy is not the real reason but only the occasion. To put it the other way around, since according to the Chicago Statement biblical inerrancy is an open and flexible category, closely ressembling the simpler biblicism of the moderates, what are you fighting over? Why not just declare peace? Chicago declares almost all of us inerrantists.

Third, another thing about elaborate inerrancy theory that bothers me is its extreme difficulty. It is beyond the ability of at least 95% of evangelicals to deal with the set of hard questions which it stirs up. If you want to defend the actual inerrancy of the Bibles people actually use today, for example (and what other Bible is there to deal with?), then you have to face questions of this magnitude: the inspiration of the New Testament which is not really addressed in the Bible, the validity of the choice of books in the canons of the Hebrew and Christian Scriptures, the question of which form of the text if errorless and which translation of that text is correct, and then the hundreds of difficulties of every kind which are created for the Bible reader if he comes to the text with the elaborate theory in hand. Difficulties far more numeous than those included in Gleason Archer's "encyclopedia" of Bible difficulties.

I am not saying there are no helpful answers to such questions. Obviously there are, and evangelical scholars are responsible to help believers with them. However, to suggest that, unless and until we are able to answer these questions satisfactorily, we are not going to be able to trust the Bible in our hands is pastoral folly for the 95% of believers unable to do so, and also for the rest. Surely our confidance in Scripture rests on a better foundation than the ability of a few of our scholars to satisfy our intellectual questions! And why is it that strict inerrantists have produced so little by way of profound biblical interpretation, except for the fact that they have been exhausted, depleted, and sapped of time and energy by their self-imposed burden of having to defend strict inerrancy. Hard to define, this theory is much harder to defend and will quickly use up all of the time the Bible scholar has for his work. Isn't that a bit ridiculous? What a waste of good talent! Indeed Tony Thiselton once told me that he did not pay much attention to the debates over biblical inerrancy because he wanted to make progress in his studies of biblical and philosophical hermeneutics. I'm glad that he did. Inerrancy theory can be very distracting if you take it seriously.

Most "Bible" difficulties are not biblical at all anyway, but are created by readers who see something in the text which does not appeal to them or does not fit their presuppositions. Most of these alleged difficulties are created by the strict inerrancy theory itself. For example, the strict inerrantist will not like it that Matthew fiddles with the facts and abbreviates his genealogy to create a nice rounded impression (Matt. 1:1-17). They may have been told by some theologian that the Bible would not do such things. So they have a "problem." But it is a problem in their own minds and of their own making, one created by the theory they are hoping to impose upon the Bible. Ironically the solution to such cases is to be less modern and more biblical, to stop telling the Bible what to say and what not to say—exactly what we tell religious liberals to be and do.

The trouble with strict inerrancy theory is that it creates a mountain of problems we do not need and which requires a herculean effort to remove even assuming that they can be. This is why James Orr judged it "suicidal" to make Christian certainty depend upon this theory. To put it more gently, why do we want to have our hands tied and our possibilities limited when we come with faith and expectation to the Bible? Why can't we just let it inform us what it wants to say and be?

Fourth, another thing that worries me is the way elaborate biblicism attracts plain bad arguments the way honey attracts flies. I mean the way people quote verses to prove what they do not prove. Jesus says "thy Word is truth"—that settles the inspiration of the sixty six biblical books for some inerrantists. I mean the way they refer to the slippery slope which the non-fundamentalist is supposed to be on, and neglect the slippery slope of fundamentalism itself which has produced an impressive number of ex-Christians. I mean the way they tell us by way of deduction what God must do in the Bible totally disregarding what in fact God does do. (See a candid article in the *Journal of the Evangelical Theological Society,* Sept. 1986).

It seems to me that a theory which attracts irresponsible and unconvincing arguments so regularly, and not only from the uneducated but even from the scholars (I admit to having used most of them myself), is a theory in deep trouble. You do not employ bad arguments if there are good ones. It suggests fear and insecurity, and is a recipe for disillusionment. How many of our finest minds have we lost to religious liberalism because in promising them absolute certainty we actually gave them fallacious arguments and no certainty at all? No wonder there is a group called Fundamentatlist Anonymous. Can you blame them?

Fifth, you will remember how the Pharisees in Jesus's day had their interpretive protocols which they placed over the Old Testament text, preventing them from really hearing God's Word (Mark 7:1-13). This happens whenever we put an interpretive grid over the Scriptures whether doctrinal or ethical. It prevents us listening to God speaking in the Bible. Now the strict theory of inerrancy can function in exactly this way. Here too a complex presupposition is placed above the text, and the reader is commanded to read the Bible only in fidelity to it rather than the other way around. Thus we read the Bible in the light of human construction instead of judging that theory in the light of Scripture. Lindsell gives us an amusing and possibly harmless example of this when he says, because of his need to harmonize the gospel accounts, that the poor cock must have crowed six times at Peter's betrayal of Jesus even though no actual gospel text says so! What this implies is that in order to save the reliability of the Bible, Lindsell has to conclude that no gospel writer got the facts right. And even more seriously, it established the principle that it is alright for us to restrict and limit the Bible to our traditions, to deny the Bible in order to save the Bible. Surely this is the way to miss what God is saying to us. Surely we are not entitled to twist the Scriptures to make them fit our theories. This is no "high view" of the Bible!

Sixth, I have become increasingly nervous that this whole inerrancy debate is not what it seems. Inerrancy seems to be being used as a password into a certain right-wing hermeneutical community rather than the straightforward category I thought it was for years. It tends to distract us from the real challenge here, which is an attempt to impose upon the SBC a whole set of beliefs by force and not really a debate over inerrancy at all. Beliefs about women in ministry, the charismatic renewal, creationism, theories of eschatology and atonement. Beliefs which ought to be discussed by us all on the basis of the biblical text but which instead are being imposed without discussion under the inerrancy banner. Needless to say, this strikes me as an outsider and a well-wisher as devious and unacceptable. Just as the earlier fundamentalists would use the virgin birth (at least a scriptural doctrine) as a litmus test and a handy shortcut which they knew would exclude the liberals without having to discuss their real concerns, so today's fundamentalists are using inerrancy (not a scriptural term, though in a loose sense a biblical idea) as the shibboleth guarding the entrance to their fortress. If they have any integrity, I call upon them to disentangle inerrancy from hermeneutics, and political power grabbing from both, and to behave like Christian people.

As I have worked over the years with the inerrancy category, these are some of the difficulties which have come to light and compelled me to reconsider its strict rendition. Gradually I have come to see that elaborate biblicism which claims to offer such certainty, offers much less, and in reality appeals not to the mind but to basic instinct and the irrational desire for absolute certainty. If inerrantists would just be more candid about such matters, their followers would be prevented from being so harsh and judgmental of others and the church would be spared much harm.

Evangelical Certainty

Let us return in closing to the original appeal which strict inerrancy makes whether in Christianity or in Islam, the promise of rational certainty. It is necessary here to understand and to sort out the certainty which the gospel gives and the certainty it does not give. Paul uses a very strong word in 1 Cor. 2:4. He speaks about a certainty which does not result from the wisdom of human words, but arises from "a demonstration of the Spirit and power" which places believers' confidence in God's action. This kind of certainty, born of the Spirit's witness to our hearts, is a different thing from the kind of rational certainty the human theory or errorlessness attempts (and fails) to engender. I am not denying the value of apologetics to help us with our questions, but I am denying that it can deliver the kind of certainty we need in life and in death. To offer people absolute certainty on the basis of a theory of the Bible and apart from the witness of the Spirit, is a deeply flawed appeal, and Southern Baptists should know that instinctively. Our Baptist heritage is pietist not doctrinalist. We have valued a vital experience of Christ above any rationalistic theory or dogma. Therefore, we should not be easily taken in by those who offer us certainty on a purely intellectual basis, which they cannot even produce.

Furthermore, our belief in the Incarnation of Christ should tell us that we do not depend upon a pure divine revelation untouched by the human and the historical. We want neither a Savior or a Bible which has not been made flesh. Our delight is in a God who reveals himself to us in history and in our human-ity, where we are. This Jewish carpenter is the Son of God; this human Scrip-ture is the Word of God! This is where we stake our claim and take our stand. As Paul put is so beautifully: "We have this treasure in earthen vessels that the excellency of the power may be of God." (2. Cor. 4:7).

It is carnal to tell people to expect super-human divine certainty in this life. They have to walk by faith and not by sight, and we do them no service by telling them it is not so. Because we are creatures and not gods we cannot have a cerainty lifted up above all history and relativity. LIke Paul, we can only know "in part" (1. Cor. 13:12). The blessed certainty and assurance we can have arises not out of human argument and theory but from the light of the glory of God which shines from the face of Jesus. We don't need more than that.

The Preacher tells us, "There is a time for peace and a time for war." (Eccles 3:8) In the 60's I believed it was time to say that the SBC was threatened by religious liberalism. It was and it is to a certain extent. But in the 80's I believe I must say the threat has been turned back and the new danger is one of going too far in mopping up. It is not necessary to injure and maim godly evangelical pastors, professors and church workers just because we have the political power to do so. It saddens me to see men and women who have given their whole lives to the faithful preaching of the gospel now being labelled "liberals" and defamed when they deserve to be honored and praised. The battle against real liberalism has been won in the SBC if not yet elsewhere. Therefore, let us declare the peace, and not run the risk of fragmenting one of God's choicest agencies of global mission.

RESPONSE: Adrian Rogers

It is always a rather sad thing to confront a brother as a theological opponent who was once a valued ally. Who can forget the brilliant young New Orleans seminary professor who so ably and eloquently defended the cause of Chris-tian orthodoxy and Biblical inerrancy in the Southern Baptist Convention? One can only wonder at the influences of current theological thought which brought about this sad change. I pray it is only temporary. One can also only wonder— and only eternity will tell—how many Southern Baptists have been discouraged and disillusioned by that change. But life goes on. People change. Theologians change. Theological fads change. But—thank God—"the word of the Lord endureth forever" (I Pet 1:25).

In order to conserve the limited time available to me, I would like to go immediately to the principal points raised by Dr. Pinnock and address each one briefly—but not necessarily in the same sequence.

1. Dr. Pinnock argues that inerrancy is invalid partly because inerrantists can't define it and can't even agree among themselves as to what it is. This is simply not true. A century ago, B. B. Warfield, in his classic *The Inspiration and Authority of the Bible,* defined the inerrancy position rather precisely, and few, if any, inerrantists today would find much to differ with there. More recently, some 300 evangelical theologians from almost every Protestant denomination hammered out the "Chicago Statement on Biblical Inerrancy," which was adopted with very little dissent. Inerrancy *can* be defined. It *has* been defined. Every doctrine—the Trinity, the hypostatic union, the atonement—will produce some differing nuances of interpretation, but these nuances do not invalidate the doctrine. This is a false issue. Every participant at this conference knows what inerrancy is. The real issue is *acceptance*—not *definition.*

2. Dr. Pinnock questions whether inerrancy is actually taught by Scripture itself. In this regard, he states that *none* of the Biblical claims regarding inspiration have anything to do with the New Testament. This is a curious point. Even if it were true (which it is *not*), what would it prove? Are there any Christians anywhere who would contend that the New Testament is less inspired than the Old Testament? Even if the statements originally applied only to the Old Testament, would not the New Testament Scriptures fall under the same rubric when they were recognized as canonical?

But the statement is *not* true. In the same epistle in which he says that "holy men of God spoke as they were borne along by the Holy Spirit," Peter says that Paul's epistles are being twisted by the unlearned and unstable" as they do also *the other scriptures*" (II Pet 1:21; 3:16). Paul says (in I Tim 5:18)," . . . the scripture saith, Thou shalt not muzzle the ox that treadeth out the corn. And, The laborer is worthy of his reward." The first quotation is from Deuteronomy 25:4. The second is from Luke 10:7. Paul groups them together and calls them both "Scripture"—without distinction.

Virtually every *liberal* New Testament scholar in modern times, from Adolph Harnack to F. C. Grant and John Knox, have admitted that Jesus believed in the absolute inerrancy of the Scriptures—consistent with the Jewish rabbis of His day. These theologians thought that Jesus was *wrong* in His belief, but the nature of His position was virtually unquestioned until the recent advent of the "evangelical errantists" who wish to call Jesus "Lord"—but who are unwilling to accept our Lord's view of Scripture. This is a serious contradiction and has spawned the current aberration that Jesus did not believe in inerrancy.

102

3. Dr. Pinnock argues that inerrancy is invalid because the Biblical data do not sustain the position. He maintains that it is better to admit the Bible's "infelicities" than to waste our time trying to harmonize the difficulties. In response, several things need to be said:

a. Because of the advances in Biblical philology, archaeology, textual criticism, etc. in recent generations, there are considerably *fewer* Biblical difficulties to deal with today than in the past. Yet, modern theologians have moved farther *away* from Biblical authority, raising the rather obvious question as to whether such difficulties actually play a very important role in the whole matter. It is apparent to many of us that philosophical trends are the real problem—not the data of the text.

b. Most of the difficulties have been known for centuries and have been dealt with plausibly by competent scholars. Is it not more reverent to withhold judgment on those matters which are still uncertain until further information is available than to assume the worst immediately—as liberal theologians always do? Even if the Lord returns before we reconcile all the difficulties (and this is virtually certain to be the case), should we not embrace His own endorsement of the Scriptures by faith, even as we accept such doctrines as the Trinity by faith, despite the fact that unexplained mysteries remain? As Dr. Pinnock himself once said, "After all, there were similar problems facing the Fathers and the Reformers just as perplexing as those facing us, and yet they did not feel moved to jettison their belief in Biblical infallibility. Is is really the pressure of criticism which has lifted theology from its only mooring, or is it a shift in the philosophical presuppositions behind theology that has caused the radical change?" A very good question, Dr. Pinnock!

c. Dr. Pinnock suggests that we must prove "why these sixty-six books in precisely this text type and translated in this way are God's inerrant word." Perhaps, Dr. Pinnock, you could profit by re-reading some of your own earlier books. (1) Are you suggesting that canonicity is now in question also? Do not you also accept these sixty-six books? (2) Few if any inerrantists have ever argued that a particular text type is inerrant. We do not regard Nestle-Aland— or Westcott and Hort—or the Majority Text—as inerrant. And certainly few genuine inerrantists regard any translation as inerrant. We hold that status only for the autographs.

4. Dr. Pinnock suggests that inerrancy spawns fallacious arguments, such as the slippery slope theory—or the false in one, false in all possibility. But are these concepts so fallacious after all? Inerrantists do indeed fear that the existence of multiple inaccuracies and pagan mythological concepts in Scripture (if such were the case) would ultimately destroy Biblical credibility altogether. I might add that "evangelical errantists" have been singularly unconvincing in arguing against such a possibility. We have heard for years of "the canon within the canon," that scripture is accurate in matters of faith and practice but not in scientific or historical matters, etc. But who has yet demonstrated that the Biblical truth claims are thus limited? Who has yet given us that key for recognizing this elusive "canon within the canon"? Rather, we are asked to trade our iner-

103

rantist birthright for a mess of existential pottage! The Bible (in part), we are told, is true if the Holy Spirit (subjectively) bears witness to us of some "truth." Otherwise, we are free to disagree, reinterpret or ignore—at our option.

All of this, as Dr. Pinnock must know, is simply existential, neo-orthodox theology. For example, Dr. Pinnock, in his paper, urges us all to enjoy the certainty of our justification "on the basis of the shed blood of Jesus Christ." I am gratified that he still believes that, but where is the *certainty*? Many existential theologians today and in the recent past have concluded that the whole concept of blood atonement is repugnant to modern civilized man and that the Biblical materials on blood atonement represent unfortunate syncretistic accretions from Israel's pagan neighbors. How do you know as an evangelical certainty that they are not correct, Dr. Pinnock? I suggest that your belief in blood atonement is more a function of your conservative past than of your current philosophical and theological methodologies. In short, you believe it because you *want* to believe it, not because there is anything in your present Bibliology which *mandates* that you believe it. Apparently the Holy Spirit has borne witness (existentially) to you concerning this doctrine, but what about other theologians on these conference grounds this week who apparently have experienced no such witness and who regard the doctrine as foolish and even blasphemous? Is all doctrine, then, relative? Are there *no* absolutes?

Few have stated the matter more *succinctly than Dr. Pinnock,* in earlier days.

> There is no way of distinguishing an experience or an intuition about God from a sheer illusion unless we possess valid concepts and criteria from his self-disclosure. The wider we allow the gap to grow between the existential or theological "truth" of the Bible and the historical, factual, and doctrinal truth of it, the more vulnerable our theology becomes to the charge of meaninglessness. Inspiration and errancy are unequally yoked together in modern theology. The two are incompatible. If the historical material is inaccurate, the theological statement are uncertain too, and inspiration has not meaning.[2]

In existential theology, you believe what you want to believe and you reject whatever fails to fit the parameters of your own world view. The human mind becomes your ultimate authority, rather than "the eternal and inviolable word of God," as Luther described it. Luther also said, "My conscience is subject to the Word of God," meaning that what Luther *thought* had to be adjusted to bring it into conformity with the *Word of God*—not *vice versa.*

All of this has to do directly with Dr. Pinnock's suggestion that "rational certainty" is not the same as "evangelical certainty." When stripped of its philosophical trappings, this statement means that the content of the Christian faith does not arise wholly from scripture. From whence, then, does this so-called "certainty" come? Pinnock answers that question—"Our certainty comes from the light of our knowledge of the glory of God in the face of Jesus Christ." But how do we obtain this knowledge? How do we behold the face of Jesus Christ? Apart from scripture, are we not cast upon the uncertain seas of existential subjectivism or some type of medieval mysticism? What has happened to the *sola scriptura* of the Protestant reformation?

5. Dr. Pinnock assures us that his purpose in his paper was not to refute inerrancy or even to be unduly critical of inerrantists. I suppose that we can be grateful for that, because it boggles the mind to think what he might have said if he had intended to be critical! As it is, he accuses inerrantists of

a. Opting naively and uncritically for a "rational certainty" which more sophisticated people know doesn't exist.

b. Inferring a parallel between Christian inerrantists and the mind set of militant Muslims, Mormons, Jehovah's Witnesses, and Roman Catholics.

c "Cheating"—in pretending that the Bible claims to be the inerrant Word of God.

d. Attempting a desperate defense of a theory which is intellectually and Biblically indefensible.

e. Demonstrating fear and insecurity—and disillusioning bright young evangelicals.

f. Being modern Pharisees in twisting the scriptures to conform to their own preset traditions.

g. Abandoning serious Biblical exegesis so that they can dedicate themselves wholly to the hopeless task of defending inerrancy.

h. Maintaining a hidden agenda of brutal political coercion under the dishonest guise of a concern for Biblical orthodoxy.

In light of this kind of rhetoric, is it any wonder that inerrantists are a bit skeptical when Pinnock and his friends call for peace, love, tolerance and mutual respect?

6. Dr. Pinnock asks us to accept the "evangelical errantist" view of Scripture as an equally legitimate way "to express full confidence in the divine authority of the Bible." But we must consider where this kind of "divine authority" leads us. What kind of "divine authority" is reflected in the use of a primitive pagan cosmology by a series of rather clumsy redactors in an attempt to describe the origin of the universe and the life forms on this planet? What sort of "divine authority" is reflected in a dramatic story of a universal flood which never actually occurred? What sort of "divine authority" is reflected in the recorded sequence of plagues in Egypt as divine miracles when it is now known that the events either had perfectly natural causes or perhaps had no historical validity whatever and were simply recorded as saga and legend? What sort of "divine authority" is reflected in the amazing story of the floating axe head in the light of our contemporary certainty that Elisha simply fished the thing out with a pole? Where is the "divine authority" in countless sayings and deeds in the gospels attributed to Jesus which He actually neither said nor did? Where is the "divine authority" in the teachings of Paul which were so "culturally conditioned" that they have no authority at all for us today?

If all of this represents a "full confidence in the divine authority of the Bible," God help us all!

In closing, let me return to my opening comments. Conservative Southern

105

Baptists are sad that Dr. Pinnock has forsaken his former commitment to strict Biblical inerrancy. And most recently, they are saddened that he has renounced his belief in eternal punishment. One can only wonder just what the next port of call may be in the curious theological odyssey of Clark Pinnock. All the while, Southern Baptists need to turn away from ephemeral theological oddities and anchor themselves in the God-breathed book, "which liveth and abideth forever (I Pet 1:23)." As Dr. Pinnock himself has said,

> We have so long become accustomed to the powerful domination of fuzzy-minded liberal theologians that we have come to accept it as a fact of life.. . .
> It is time to break the status quo. Every year the problem of theological ambiguity grows larger. It is action, not slogans that we need, not the profession, but the practice of the truth. God is bypassing many of the great denominations today because they refused to maintain a pure testimony to the truth. If we do not wish to see our schools, presses, and buildings, fall into the hands of men who bow to the spirit of our age, then we need to act now.[3]

Amen, Dr. Pinnock—AMEN!

Notes

1. Clark Pinnock, *A Defense of Biblical Infallibility,* Presbyterian and Reformed Publishing Co., 1967, p. 3.
2. *Ibid.*, pp. 8-9.
3. Clark Pinnock, *A New Reformation—A Challenge to Southern Baptists,* Jewel Books, 1968, pp. 18-19.

RESPONSE: John Lewis

First of all let me express my genuine appreciation for the intellectual honesty with which you have bared your soul in your pilgrimage of faith which has brought you to your present position.

You have exhibited a spirit of understanding, openness, integrity and conciliation that is both winsome and contagious. Your terminology has been free from personal prejudices about individuals with whom you now disagree. You have dealt with issues and not persons. You have consistently stressed the central matters of the faith that bind us together while dealing with loving candor where we have honest difference of opinion on the main issue before us. You have kept yourself free from "partisan rhetoric" while making your case most persuasively.

I applaud your appeal for us to maintain the diversity that has characterized

Baptists and to recognize that we can hold differing views out of "genuine concern" and "honest motives," without breaking fellowship.

While noting the "absolute certainty" which "elaborate biblicism" promises, you quite properly raise the question as to whether or not "orthodox logic" with it's "coercive power" promises too much. It makes claims for the Scriptures which they do not make explicitly for themselves. This raises the whole question as to the true nature of faith itself. Is belief to be imposed from without, or can Scripture be trusted, as the Word of God, to speak directly to our own hearts? Is it to be imposed from without, or is it one's own free response to the hearing of the gospel?

Strict inerrancy changes faith from an "I/Thou" encounter with the living Christ to an "I/It" relationship to a man-made dogmatic theory. Inerrancy downgrades Christ as the "WORD of God," leading into "propositional theology," doctrine as the saving object of faith, which is a form of radical rationalism. Christ is no longer the key to biblical interpretation. A certain dogma— "inerrancy"—becomes the norm of Scripture: one must first believe in "inerrancy" before one can believe in Christ. Salvation by faith in Christ is moved off center, a certain view of the technical accuracy of the human words of the Bible is put in its place.

Rational certainty is radically different from Evangelical certainty as traditionally proclaimed by the church through the ages and by Baptist particularly.

The first and main parameter of strict inerrancy is to restrict the term as applying only to the autographs: an unassailable line of defense first proclaimed by the Post-Reformation theologians a hundred years after Luther and Calvin. Since the autographs no longer exist, "inerrancy" is a theory about the originals and is a moot question. It is a tacit admission that the copies we have do contain problems which inerrancy does not address. Since no biblical writer makes reference to the autographs, and does not deal directly with the questions raised by modern exponents of the theory of inerrancy, it is difficult to see why this theory should be made a cardinal doctrine of Scripture. The term *inerrancy* simply cannot be applied to the copies of copies with which we have to deal. Nowhere does the Bible appeal to a concept of technical inerrancy to substantiate its clear claim to be the authoritative Word of God sufficient for saving faith and practice. Strictly speaking, if only the autographs were inerrant, then only the autographs can be called the "written Word of God." Jesus and the writers of the New Testament refer to the copies from which they quote as the Word of God, and most New Testament writers refer more frequently to the Septuagint than to a Hebrew text. Augustine referred to a Latin translation as the Word of God. Belief in inerrant autographs is not essential for accepting our copies and modern translations as the written word of God! One of the marvels of the Scripture is that it can be translated in all the languages of mankind and still be considered the authentic record of the divine revelation of God and the authoritative Word of God leading us infallibly to a saving knowledge of Jesus Christ. One can hold to a high view of Scriptural authority without holding to inerrant copies or for that matter inerrant autographs. The manner in which strict inerrantists drastically qualify the term when dealing with our present copies is proof of the point made.

You are very perceptive to remind us that it is the theory of inerrancy itself that is inadvertantly compelled to recognize certain problems in the text as so-called "errors"! Hence the need to qualify the application of the theory to our present copies. From this observation you correctly raise the question as to the wisdom of letting ourselves get bogged down with incidental matters that have naught to do with the clear biblically stated function "to make us wise unto salvation in Jesus Christ." Inerrancy tends to major on minor details that take attention away from "actually interpreting the Bible instead of apologizing for its infelicities." Putting the unprovable assertion of the autographs aside, the more pressing question to face is, on what basis can our copies and translations be called the Word of God.

With all of us standing on the ridge of a high view of the Bible, we must recognize that the "slippery slope theory" requires us to recognize that one can slide down either side! It is fair game for each side of the issue to warn his brother and sister on the other side to beware. Inerrantists are properly alarmed, as we all should be, that the discipline of biblical criticism improperly handled can lead one astray from the cardinal doctrines of saving faith, that over-emphasis on the clearly apparent human element in the Scripture can denigrate the clearly discernable divine element in the Bible, that a purely natu-ralistic approach to the Scripture invalidates true biblical faith and waters down our commitment to evangelism.

On the other hand, inerrantists must be cautioned about sliding down the other side into bibliolatry and a new form of Medieval Scholasticism and Ratio-nalism. Inerrantists must also be warned about unwarrented use of the "dom-ino theory."

Such a misunderstanding of the Scriptures caused the church at first to reject the rise of modern science at the time of the Copernican Revolution. Coperni-cus, a Polish astronomer born in 1473, set forth the revolutionary idea that the earth moved around the sun. The church, accepting the limited science of the biblical writers as true science, rejected the new idea. The reasoning of the church went something like this, "If Copernicus is right, Joshua could not have commanded the sun to stand still. The Bible would be in error and therefore is not to be trusted any place. It cannot even be accepted as true when it speaks of Christ as God's Son and our Savior." Such a bad argument does not under-gird the biblical authority on matters of salvation. Galileo with his improved telescope proved Copernicus correct. Church leaders refused to look through the telescope and both men were condemned by the church!

While, on the one hand, it is correct to say the biblical writer accurately re-ports what was believed at that time and was phenomenologically so described, it is not permissible, on the other hand, to turn around and insist that any scientific allusion in the Scripture must be accepted as "fact" over against the assured findings of modern science. That is a form of obscuranticism that takes our minds off of the purpose and function which Scripture claims for itself. To make a claim for Scripture which it does not make explicitly for itself denigrates the true nature of the Bible and may well lead us into heresy.

The time consumed in "keeping the theory afloat" indeed distracts us from the more important matter of hermeneutics. The traditional and historic Baptist approach to Scripture has always been to concentrate on the stated claim of Scripture itself: "to make us wise unto salvation in Jesus Christ." Historically, Baptists, in their various confessions of faith, have stated their doctrine of Scripture on a broad and sound enough basis to allow freedom under "the competency of the soul in religion" for diversity of interpretation on matters not essential to salvation.

Up until the present time Baptists have never used a single word, insubstantially supported by scripture, as a test of fellowship and faith, and a term for eligibility for serving the denomination. One of the most serious problems we now face is the avowed effort of certain self-appointed watchdogs of the faith to use the word inerrancy as a "quasi-creedal weapon" to coerce conformity contrary to Baptist practice heretofore. It is like inverting a pyramid to make it stand on its pinnacle, abandoning the accepted inclusive doctrine of Scripture for a narrow, creedal, exclusive parameter. The narrow inerrantist base is too small to support the full weight of Biblical truth, Baptist theology, and Baptist history.

We have moved beyond the theological and political issue. The issue now is one of koinonia—fellowship. Through emphasis on "the competency of the soul in religion" we must accept each other, recognizing responsible diversity on matters not essential to salvation to be a strength not a weakness. Inasmuch as the Evangelical community is seriously divided on a generally accepted definition of the term inerrancy, diversity will prevail in applying the term. The strained and drastic qualifications used to conform our present text to fit some kind of definition so waters down its meaning that it serves no practical purpose in getting at the abiding and authoritative message so plainly set forth in Scripture.

Such qualifications mark out the parameters of the term as related only to matters not related to other clear message of salvation. That there is no error in that message we can all agree. The complex and involved qualifications become, therefore, a self-contradictory effort to force our copies into compliance with the theoretically assumed inerrancy of the autographs.

The most serious parameter set by the theory of inerrancy is to use it as a test word of faith, fellowship, and eligibility for service in the denomination. There is an ironic contradiction in such use of the term; one must surrender part of his Baptist heritage in order to serve in the denomination! In short one must be less a Baptist to hold such a position! One must conform to a narrow creedal dogma externally imposed, and one is no longer free to follow the Holy Spirit but must submit to a scholasticism wherein all doctrines are predefined by someone else, externally enforced on the conscience.

In the light of the statement of a staunch defender of inerrancy that, "Belief in an infallible Scripture is not essential to salvation," a view also held by Warfield, it is difficult to see why inerrancy must be considered a cardinal doctrine of the

109

Christian faith. If the term is to be used at all, it seems most appropriate to apply it to the function the Scripture claims for itself, "to make us wise unto salvation through faith in Jesus Christ," which scholars, theologians and ordinary believers have unanimously attested through the ages, despite varying views on the inspiration and nature of Scripture.

No where did Jesus say, or imply, "that by this sign shall all men know you are my disciples, that you all believe in inerrancy." Inerrancy sets a false parameter when it is used as a shibboleth or test-word of faith and eligibility.

Stable yet flexible, theologically conservative but progressive in viewpoint, Baptists are held together by a common commitment to Christ as Lord and Savior, with Scripture as the all-sufficient guide for faith and practice. With each Baptist body free and autonomous in its own right, we have always held "there is yet more light to break forth from God's word."

In our best moments, and in the light of our best theology and history, Baptists have been able to accept a great deal of diversity, as all seek the leadership of the Spirit in our individual lives and the life of the denomination. As a people of the Book, believing in Scripture as sufficient authority for faith and practice, the Bible is an indispensable, irreplaceable "perfect treasure of divine instruction." But we have always looked "beyond the sacred page" to its living Lord, Jesus Christ, as the sole and all sufficient criterion by which it is to be interpreted. "Inerrancy" may be a heresy because it insists on the man-made dogma of a narrow, restricted view of inspiration and authority as a criterion for interpreting the Christ!

Again let me thank you for opening up the discussion on inerrancy in such an honest and straight forward manner. You have raised for us the serious flaws in the theory that need more thorough examination. You have "spoken the truth in love," and made us all aware of the inadequacy of the term to deliver all it promises, a kind of rational certainty which the Scripture does not claim to supply. You have called us back to affirm again the central evangelical principles of *sola Scriptura,* the infallible authority of the Bible for faith and practice, salvation by grace in Christ alone, and the competency of the soul in religion. You have contributed most significantly to our dialogue and for that we are genuinely grateful.

6
PARAMETERS OF BIBLICAL INERRANCY
Kenneth Kantzer

Thank you very much for inviting me to share with you in your endeavor to thresh out an appropriate stance for your great denomination on a matter that has troubled the whole of the Christian world through the past century and a half. I am immensely honored by this privilege. Thank you.

What you do, may I remind you, is not just your own affair, and it is not done in a corner. You are not only the largest protestant denomination in America, you are the pace-setter for all evangelical bodies in the United States and, perhaps, in the world.[1] What you do sets the direction in which millions of others will go. It will determine the role of conservative evangelicals in many denominations, in our nation, and in many parts of the world for at least a generation to come. I am awed at the magnitude of your responsibility. I have covenanted with God to pray daily for you as a denomination because of all you mean to me, to my children, and to evangelicals everywhere.

My topic tonight, "Parameters of Biblical Inerrancy," could be taken several ways. In the light of my instructions, I have understood it as the boundaries or limits of Biblical inerrancy. When we say the Bible is inerrant, what sort of things are we ruling out as incompatible or inconsistent with Biblical inerrancy? Or, on the other hand, what range of viewpoints are within its bounds, that is, compatible with or consistent with an affirmation of Biblical inerrancy? In short, what are the boundaries indicated by this view of Holy Scripture?[2]

If Biblical inerrancy is defined to mean the Bible tells only the truth and never says what is not so, then in one sense there are no limits to Biblical inerrancy. In this sense the parameters or boundaries of Biblical inerrancy are determined by the term itself. It includes the whole Bible, that is, the sixty-six canonical books of scripture. All that these writings state to be so is the truth and nothing but the truth.[3]

Support for this doctrine is found in the teaching of our Lord as recorded in the gospels. In Luke 24, for example, Jesus rebuked his disciples for not believing all contained in the Scripture. In the Sermon on the Mount he reassured the multitudes that, though he did not accept the Pharisees' interpretations and additions to Scripture, he did accept the very least teaching of what was contained in Holy Scripture. And what is inspired is the *graphé*—that is, the written text of Scripture.[4]

For Christ as well as for the ancient Jews, moreover, inspired Scripture included just twenty-two canonical writings according to a common Jewish way

111

of combining and counting their sacred books; and these make up exactly the thirty-nine books we call our Old Testament.[5]

For us today, Holy Scripture includes not only the twenty-two or thirty-nine Old Testament books, but in addition, the twenty-seven books of the New Testament. Our Lord, himself, commissioned the apostles to speak with binding authority over his church, he certified them by miracle power; and the early church accepted their authority in the documents we call the New Testament.[6]

The whole process of the formation and reception of the canonical writings is not a simple one. Yet for the Christian, the key to this problem lies in the authority of Jesus Christ. He placed his imprimatur upon the Old Testament canon of the Jews. The processes involved in the formation and reception of the New Testament duplicate those he approved in the Old Testament. Therefore his imprimatur stands over both testaments guaranteeing to us the boundaries of what we dare call Holy Scripture or the Bible and, therefore, also the boundaries of what we can confidently accept as the inerrantly inspired word of God binding on our minds and hearts and conscience.[7]

In one legitimate sense, therefore, Biblical inerrancy has no limit except that designated by the phrase itself. The Bible never wanders from the truth in all that it says. It never says or means or teaches or affirms what is not so. And what it says comes with the authority of Christ behind it.[8]

Of course, not every word in every copy of the Bible is inerrantly true. Christ did not guarantee that everyone who copied the Bible would always copy it perfectly. The divine guarantee of the complete trustworthiness of Scripture and of its inerrant authority applies to the canonical scriptures inspired of God. The mistakes of the copyist are not inspired by God, and we have no right to accept them as infallible. We say, therefore, inspiration applies only to the original autographs of Scripture.[9]

This is not some sly trick in order to avoid difficulties in the Biblical text.[10] In all other books this is something we take for granted when we endeavor to ascertain what a particular author taught as truth. The inspiration of the autographs was well understood by the ancient Jews who destroyed defective copies of the text just because, for them too, only correct texts were divinely inspired. In the ancient world Augustine and Jerome argued over the correct text of the Biblical manuscripts available for them.[11]

Recognizing that inerrancy applies only to original autographs, poses two questions. First, what autographs were inspired? What about books of the Bible in which the author refers to sources? For example, our book of Kings refers to the book of the Chronicles of the Kings of Judah fifteen times[12] and cites the Chronicles of the Kings of Israel 18 times.[13] Must we reckon every source thus cited to be divinely inspired by God and, therefore, inerrant? Not at all! In some cases clearly the source cited is not inspired—like, for example, the heathen Greek poet cited by the Apostle Paul. In other cases we really do not know whether or not the source referred to was inspired by God and we do not need to know.[14] Our Lord guaranteed for us the divine authority of the writings in their canonical form—the prophetic writings that God chose to preserve in the church for its guidance. In some cases we do not even know the name of the author of the inspired book. We only know the Old Testament writings, certified by Christ, were preserved because they were reckoned prophetic and, therefore, divinely authoritative for the people of God. And the New Testament writings were reckoned apostolic and, therefore, commissioned by Christ to speak with authority for his church.[15]

It is the canonical form of these writings—the Old Testament books given to the Jews and the New Testament books given to the church—that provide for us the Bible we can be confident was divinely inspired and, therefore, of inerrant authority.

But granted that God gave to us a Bible inerrant in its original text, a second question is posed: Of what value can such an inerrant autograph possibly be to you and me? Emil Brunner pokes fun at those who get all hot and bothered about the inerrancy of a Bible "x"—the great unknown. Nobody has ever seen this inerrant autograph and, to tell the truth, no one really ever expects to see it. We are arguing for the inerrancy of a Bible we have never seen and certainly cannot use. The only Bible we have is a Bible that is generally true. Hence, why not be satisfied with defending the general truth of Scripture, for we actually do not possess today the original manuscripts whose inerrancy we are defending. At best we have in our hands only generally true texts.[16]

Evangelicals have always responded that the fact of an inerrant original, even though we may not have that original in our hand, is the means by which we are delivered from much subjectivism in our endeavor to arrive at the truth of God. This can best be seen if we trace through alternative approaches to the Scriptures: One based on the conviction that the originals were inerrant; and the other that they may be generally true but, in fact, represent a mixture of truth and error. If we know that the originals were inerrant, then to discover the truth we have two tasks. First, the task of textual criticism; and second, the task of historical and grammatical exegesis.

In determining what is the correct text, we base our decision on an examination of the history of the text. We do not say, "I do not like this text" or "This text makes me feel better." Rather, we draw our conclusion on the basis of objective textual data available to everybody. If someone disagrees, we do not make faces at him. We respond, "But what do you do with these textual data?"

Our next step is to exegate the passage to see what this written text really means. In so doing, we point to the data of language, grammar, and syntax. And again, if we disagree, we do not make a face at the person; nor do we say, "This interpretation makes me feel better." We say, "Here are the grammatical and historical data on the basis of which we believe this is the right meaning."

Then, when we have finished with the task of textual criticism and of historical and grammatical exegesis, we have arrived at truth, and truth possessing complete divine authority. The degree of probability that we have the correct text and the correct meaning of the text is precisely the degree of certainty that we have truth—truth from God, binding on our conscience.

Such is not the case if we are convinced that the originals are errant. Then these objective sciences of textual criticism and historical and grammatical exegesis give us something quite different. At the end of the road we can only say

113

that we have ideas taught by the author in his original autographs, but these are only the judgments of human authors, fallible like ourselves. They may contain truth coming to us with the authority of God, but they also may contain merely human errors that would be quite wrong to accept as coming from God. To separate out the truth of God from the errors of the human writer then demands an extra step or, perhaps, several extra steps. The great difficulty for those believing in an errant Bible is that they always have to put the Bible through a sieve in order to find the truth of God. This sieve almost invariably involves some subjective principle for the selection of the truth.[17] In addition, we need to justify whatever particular sieve we have chosen to use. Clearly the Bible itself and, certainly, our Lord never gives us any principle by which we could sieve out of an errant Bible what we did not need to believe. On the contrary, our Lord urged his disciples to believe all of the written text of Scripture, even its jot and tittle.[18]

It is reassuring to note that the application of textual criticism to the Bible does not leave us in a sea of doubt. Liberals and conservatives are in amazing agreement as to the best text. In the conservative school where I teach, we use as our standard Greek text the 24th edition of Nestle or the United Bible Society's text—texts prepared for the most part by liberal scholars. Yet liberals and conservatives are in pretty much agreement because both have to deal with the same objective data of textual criticism.[19]

Similarly, liberals and conservatives usually agree on the meaning of the text. The RSV, known as a liberal translation, is on the whole quite accurate. Those objecting to it usually did so on the basis of only a very few texts. In fact, the worst objections focused on the footnotes contained in it rather than on the actual text itself. The most negative criticism leveled by liberals against the conservative NIV translation is that it is altogether too much like the RSV. And Emil Brunner who objects to the doctrine of inerrant autographs as no help to Christians because we do not have the originals, still never objects to the virgin birth on the grounds that it is not in the text. He accepts the same text as do conservatives, and he interprets it exactly the same way. But he doubts the virgin birth and suspects that it is mythology, not true to the facts, because he has failed to come to terms with the Bible as an authoritative word from God. Belief in the inerrancy of Scripture would have helped Brunner come to a better conclusion with respect to the virgin birth of Christ. And if the erudite scholar, Emil Brunner, was left uncertain because he would not depend on a completely trustworthy Bible to settle such doctrinal points, how will the poor unlearned layman in the pew find assurance as to what he can believe?[20]

We conclude that whatever may be said for or against the doctrine of Biblical inerrancy, it should be abundantly clear that it is a most significant help in enabling us to arrive with assurance at the truth of God.[21]

No doubt Biblical inerrancy has suffered most—sometimes from its foes, sometimes, alas, from its friends—by identification of inerrancy with an artificial hermeneutic that denies its true nature as language. They conceive inerrancy as demanding a Bible written in a language of heavenly perfection as though its language were perfect, the most precise, most accurate, in the clearest and least ambiguous language possible. Of course, no human writing ever achieved that sort of standard. And when they find that this is not at all the way the gospels were written, they then assume that the gospels cannot be inerrant. The point is, we must not foist upon the Bible an *a priori* speculative view as to what inerrancy means. Our Lord commanded us to believe what Scripture says and to obey it when it applies to us. He did not say it would come to us in any perfection of literary style or in the precisely exact language on which we so greatly pride ourselves in this twentieth century.[22]

The Biblical doctrine of inerrancy is simply that every word of the Bible is God-given in the sense that it was produced under the control and care of the Spirit of God and states the ideas that God wished to convey to us humans. Therefore, it is all true—that is, all the concepts or judgments set forth by the words of Scripture are really true.[23]

The fact that Scripture is not written in a language of perfection is not at all to be understood as a limitation on the inerrancy of Scripture. All human statements are set forth in less than heavenly perfection. Yet in ordinary language we call some of these human statements true. In this same fashion, the inerrantist maintains that all Biblical statements are true.

In fact, Biblical inerrancy makes sense only when we interpret the Bible fairly and in conformity with the normal use of human language. Biblical illustrations of this are legion. For example, we must allow the Biblical writer to cite viewpoints with which he is not in total agreement. The Psalmist quotes the fool who says: "There is no God."[24] Ecclesiastes calls our attention to a false materialistic philosophy of life that holds when a man dies he is no better than a dog.[25] Job's character is defended, but that does not mean he is right in every point. Bildad may say many beautiful things but he is dead wrong on the main point he makes.[26] The proverb is true generally as a proverb is supposed to be in the statement: "Whoso findeth a wife findeth a good thing;"[27] but not every bride is a good wife. If inerrancy is to make sense, we must not foist on the Scriptural writer what he has no intention of saying and then find fault with it.

Similarly, we must allow the Biblical author to speak in a way appropriate to him and to his own culture. The Biblical authors were not scientists and they did not write primarily for modern scientists. They wrote for all humans. Accordingly the Bible does not give us scientific truth in technical or scientific language.[28] For the most part it is written in the language of common people. But it does give us the truth; and when it writes on truth lying in the area of history or of science, it is still telling us the truth.

Often the Biblical author does not state his truth in words that would be appropriate for us today. For example, Biblical references to time in the gospels are often in three-hour blocks. That is almost unthinkable for us, but we live in the era of wrist watches where minutes can be counted accurately and, therefore, become more important to us. No one in the Bible ever said: "I will meet you at the central square in Hebron at ten after three," presumably because no one would ever have known exactly when ten after three arrived. The Biblical equivalent of our phrase "last split second" is the eleventh hour. We must learn to judge the Biblical writings by the standards of what they meant to say, not by

115

the standard of what we who live in the twentieth century would have said were we in their shoes.[29]

Sometimes we even place more exact standards on the Biblical authors than we follow ourselves. In most cases the words of Jesus cited in the gospels are not to be thought of as direct quotes. They usually give us not the exact equivalent of his Greek or Aramaic words but the sense of what he said. This is often true even when the words are in the form of direct quotation. This is much like what we do when we report on a rapid conversation. We summarize the conversation and put it in the form of direct quotes to communicate the liveliness of the interchange. No one charges us with saying what is not so, and neither should we make such charges against the gospel writers.[30] A Biblical quotation may be both direct or indirect, partial, full, or a summary.

Similarly, inerrancy does not guarantee that New Testament citation of an Old Testament passage settles for us the correct text. When we quote the Bible, we do not always see the need of quoting it with exact precision. We ought not to base a doctrine on that part of the text that is incorrect, but neither do we find it necessary to correct every aspect of a text or translation when citing it, so long as the right text correctly understood actually does support the point we are making. Inerrancy only demands that the key idea for which the passage was cited be authentic in the sense that it was really a point made by the original author in the context from which it was taken.[31]

In this same way we often in prayer or in a sermon use Biblical words from a particular passage of Scripture not as a proof text but rather to state what we wish to say—knowing that the words we are using say what is true even though they may not reflect what the Scriptural writer meant in the context in which he first used those words. And we must allow the same freedom to the writers of the New Testament.[32]

The problem of variant reports in the gospels or discordant accounts in any passages of scripture purporting to relate the same events is exceedingly troublesome. Sometimes the harmonization of the different accounts is fairly simple. For example, in Acts 7, we do not have Luke pitted against Genesis, but Luke relaying what the deacon Stephen said in a speech that diverged at some points from the Genesis account.[33] The Bible is reporting the truth so long as Stephen really said these things—whether they were true or not. On the other hand, Stephen himself may simply be employing the Septuagint text (or Jewish tradition) with no sense of any necessity for correcting any mistakes in it so long as it was adequate for his purposes in recounting the relationship between God and Israel through Old Testament history.

Two accounts sometimes conflict verbally not because either is incorrect but, rather, because each is discussing the same event from a different perspective. One eyewitness speaks of a sermon on the mount. Another refers to the same sermon as located on a plain or level spot. Closely related to this are the divergent settings for the speeches of our Lord.[34] These variations are sometimes due to the difference in the purpose of the gospel writer and the audience each has in mind. Sometimes still other factors are at stake. The same story may be told twice by our Lord and thus recorded in different forms, in different settings, and even to make quite different points. Every preacher, mindful of how he uses illustrations and adapts them in each case for his immediate purpose, should readily understand this.

Figures must be treated with special care. One number is exact, the other an approximation. Or, both may just be different approximations.[35] Numbers and personal names are specially liable to textual errors through faulty copying because neither is protected by its context.[36]

The most important matter in dealing with varying reports or alleged discrepancies in the Bible is to treat the text fairly as the word of friend. Each alleged contradiction must be examined on its own merit. Yet on occasion we run up against discrepancies for which no plausible harmonization is possible. The Bible believing Christian only makes himself ridiculous when he foists a harmony on such passages. In this case it is always better frankly to admit that we find no reasonable explanation of the problem rather than to propose conjectures that are inherently unreasonable. It is not necessary for us to be able to have a plausible solution to every alleged contradiction before committing ourselves to the inerrancy of Scripture. The far stronger position is to refuse to attempt such a harmony and to point out that it is utterly unreasonable for anyone to demand that we must be able to offer such a harmonization in every case.

We could argue regarding doctrinal matters that a revelation coming from an infinite mind to finite minds would naturally present difficulties for our limited earthbound intelligence. It is only prudently humble on our part to acknowledge that we are willing to receive revelation from God even though we do not fully understand the infinite God or the truth He seeks to communicate to us. This is not to admit that it is impossible for mortals to have *adequate* ideas about what God is revealing to us, even if only God can possess *comprehensive* knowledge. How otherwise could we accept the doctrine of the trinity or the unity of the divine and human in Christ, which Scripture itself tells us is a great mystery.[37]

When the question is one of historical data stemming from the history of ancient Israel or the life of Christ, we can rightfully point out how unreasonable it is for anyone to insist that independent accounts stemming from alien cultures extending back through two to three thousand years of history should fit together neatly without problems. In fact, problems of this sort, insoluble to those of us living today, are exactly what we should expect if the Bible is what inerrantists claim it to be. We live at least two thousand years too late to expect to construct a sensible harmony of all the historical data in Scripture.

Some time ago the mother of a dear friend of ours was killed. We first learned of her death through a trusted mutual friend who reported that our friend's mother had been standing on the street corner at a bus intersection waiting for a bus, had been hit by another bus passing by, was fatally injured, and died a few minutes thereafter. A few minutes later we learned from the grandson of the dead woman that she had been involved in a collision, was thrown from the car in which she was riding, and was killed instantly. The boy was quite certain of his facts, relayed them clearly, and stated that he had secured his information directly from his mother—the daughter of the woman who had been killed. No further information was forthcoming from either source. Now which would you believe? We trusted both our friends, but we certainly couldn't put the data together. Much later upon further inquiry, we were able to seat the mother and grandson in our living room. There quietly and leisurely we probed for a harmonization. We learned that the grandmother had been waiting for a bus, was hit by another bus, and was fatally injured. She had been picked up by a passing car and dashed to the hospital, but in this haste the car in which she was being transported to the hospital collided with another car. She was thrown from the car and died instantly. I submit that this story from my own experience presents no greater difficulty than that of any recorded in the gospels, not even excepting the two divergent accounts of the death of Judas. Such coincidences occur repeatedly. They are inherent in any independent accounts of events. The only significant difference between this story and the accounts of the four evangelists is the fact that we cannot cross examine the gospel witnessers. We live 2,000 years too late. We can't say: "Now see here, Matthew and Luke, what really happened at the death of Judas?"[38]

Within the framework of the doctrine of Biblical inerrancy, how then ought we to regard the Biblical phenomena of which we have been speaking?

First, certainly, there are problems. And it is not becoming on the part of those who hold the Bible to be the inerrant word of God to use that doctrine as an escape for overlooking these problems. Intellectual integrity and honest scholarship require that we face them seriously.

Second, the fact that there are problems ought not to surprise us. We find in the Bible just what we should expect if the Bible is really inerrant. The many cultures in which it was written, the divergent authors who composed it, the sheer extent of time covered by the Biblical narratives, the 2,000 to 3,500 years of repeated copying of the Biblical text—all make it unthinkable that Biblical data should be easily harmonizable by those of us living in our modern world so alien to the scenes of the Bible.

Third, belief in the inerrancy of the Bible is not jeopardized by one or more insoluble discrepancies in the Biblical material; and our own commitment to the doctrine is not embarrassed by our inability to show a plausible harmonization of every discordant passage.

Fourth, the *a priori* case for belief in the inerrancy of the Bible rests not at all upon our ability to see how all Biblical accounts can be neatly harmonized.

Fifth, we can safely commit our own ministry to this doctrine because our conviction ultimately rests on the testimony of Christ and our commitment to him as the Lord of our thought and life.[39]

The real Jesus, the only Jesus for whom we have any evidence whatever, believed that the Bible was true and that it was the very word of God. He commanded his disciples to believe it and obey it. He rebuked those who disregarded it or sought to interpret away its obvious instructions. And he held its teachings binding over himself. The real issue for us today is: Is Jesus Christ Lord? What think ye of Christ? Only when we have answered this question—

the most basic of all questions—are we prepared to answer the further question: Is the Bible the inerrant Word of God, the authoritative guide for my life and thought? And our answer to this second question is the way to become obedient and faithful and useful disciples of the Lord Christ.

Notes

1. Whether or not Southern Baptists are to be reckoned evangelicals depends, naturally, on how one defines evangelicalism. In twentieth century English, the word is used in a number of ways. In this context I use the term *evangelical* for those who adhere to both the material and formative principles of Protestantism. The material principle is that human salvation is solely by God's grace through faith or personal commitment to Jesus Christ as our divine-human Lord and Savior. The formal or formative principle of Protestantism is that the Bible is our final guide for Christian thought and life. Not all evangelicals hold to inerrancy, but inerrancy (whether the word is employed or not) is an essential mark of consistent evangelicalism.

2 The word inerrant derives from two Latin words meaning "not wandering" with "from the truth" to be supplied. The basic meaning in English and in its cognates in other western European languages is "not wandering from the truth" or "truth without any mixture of error."

In the history of Christian doctrine, therefore, the word has had wide usage to mean that the Biblical statements never depart from what is true in the sense that they never affirm what, as a matter of fact, is false. During the last decade, however, the term has come to be appropriated for various and sundry views of inspiration that negate the original sense of the term. For example, Donald Bloesch employs the word to describe his own view, but notes that this allows for error in the historical and scientific data set forth in Scripture (*Essentials of Evangelical Theology*: Volume One, *God, Authority, and Salvation* [San Francisco; Harper and Row, c. 1978] pp. 82-84 and elsewhere). Daniel Fuller opts for verbal inerrancy but limits Biblical inerrancy to revelational matters ("The Nature of Biblical Inerrancy," *Journal of the American Scientific Affiliation*, June, 1972, pp. 47-51). What the author could observe on his own without special divine help, God does not miraculously provide. He leaves the Biblical author to his own natural abilities and, therefore, on occasions, because of a very natural human propensity to err, the Bible makes mistakes. David Hubbard prefers the word infallible to describe Biblical inspiration, but as applied to the Bible, that term always must be understood as limited to faith and practice. In other matters, the Biblical author can and may well err at many points ("The Current Tensions: Is There a Way Out?" pp. 149-181 in Jack B. Rogers, ed., *Biblical Authority* [Waco, Texas: Word Books, c. 1977]).

Karl Barth rejects the older view of an objectively given text inspired in the past and opts for a contemporary verbal inspiration in which the Spirit employs the very words of the text to speak to men today (*The Doctrine of the Word of God*; Vol. One Church Dogmatics, eds. G. W. Bromiley and T. F. Torrance (Edinburgh: T. and T. Clark, 1956) 1, 2, pp. 529-534.

Most of these limitations or restrictions upon Biblical inerrancy are attributed to the purpose of the Bible. The Bible is inerrant in the area relating to its function as a moral and spiritual guide for the Christian life. In matters irrelevant to its function, the Bible may and does err. There is, in truth, no serious objection to the use of the term in these ways so long as the exception is signaled to the reader when the term is used. To affirm a universal with stated exceptions is a perfectly legitimate and meaningful way to employ language. Unfortunately, many who use the term inerrant with such limitations, do not always indicate the exception. In such instances the use of the term inerrant becomes deceptive. Those who hold that statements not corresponding with the facts really do exist in the Bible should in the interest of clear communication avoid the term in describing their view of Biblical inspiration. Barth carefully avoided the term; and James Orr, writing nearly a century ago, reflected the common usage of his day when he rejected the term on the grounds that in areas outside the purpose of the Bible, inspiration did not guarantee inerrancy (*Revelation and Inspiration* [New York: Charles Scribner's Sons, 1910], pp. 197-218).

3. That this is the common use of the term can scarcely be denied. Whether this was also the standard doctrine of the church is hotly debated. A recent book defending the view that it was not is *The Authority and Interpretation of the Bible: An Historical Approach* by Jack B. Rogers and Donald K. McKim (San Francisco: Harper and Row, c. 1979). The volume is seriously flawed by a too easy equating of the full humanity of Scripture with its espousal of error. The subsequent volume edited by D. A. Carson and John D. Woodbridge (*Scripture and Truth*, [Grand Rapids: Zondervan, c. 1983], especially pp. 173-279) provides the altogether adequate antidote to the Rogers and McKim volume. See also the older work by John F. Walvoord, ed., *Inspiration and Interpretation* (Grand Rapids: Eerdmans, 1957).

4. See John W. Wenham, *Christ and the Bible* (Downers Grove, IL.: Intervarsity Press, c. 1972). The apologetic methodology by which evangelical scholars defend the doctrine of inerrancy is as diverse as that of their non-inerrantist counterparts. Many, following Karl Barth, would appeal exclusively to the inner witness of the Holy Spirit and label all rational defense of the truth of Christianity and of the authority of the Bible as mere rationalization. See Donald Bloesch, *op. cit.* Others hold to a more inductive and evidential approach to apologetics. See, for example, Benjamin Breckenridge Warfield, *The Inspiration and Authority of the Bible*, ed. Samuel G. Craig (Philadelphia: Presbyterian and Reformed Publishing Company, 1948) and James Oliver Buswell, *A Systematic Theology of the Christian Religion*, 4 Vols. (Grand Rapids: Zondervan, c. 1962), especially Volume One, Chapter six. I would hold to the crucial role of the witness of the Spirit as the decisive factor in creating certainty in Jesus Christ and the gospel. This is then confirmed by rational evidences. What ties these various apologetics together is not their varied methodology but their conclusion—the commitment to Scriptural inerrancy.

5. The study of the canon is, to say the least, not one on which present defenders of inerrancy have written widely. The monumental work on the New Testament canon by Brooks Foss Westcott, (*A General Survey of the History of the Canon of the New Testament*, [6th ed., Cambridge: MacMillan, 1889]) is now seriously outdated. The older, popular works by Louis Gaussen, (*The Canon of Holy Scriptures Examined in the Light of History* [trans. Edward N. Kirk. Boston: American Tract Society, c. 1912]) and William Henry Green (*General Introduction to the Old Testament: The Canon* [New York: C. Scribner's Sons, 1898]) leave much to be desired. The short treatment by R. Laird Harris (*Inspiration and Canonicity of the Bible* [Grand Rapids: Zondervan, c. 1957]) has not received the recognition it deserves. The same could be said for the more recent chapter by David G. Dunbar ("The Biblical Canon" in D. A. Carson and John D. Woodbridge, eds. *Hermeneutics, Authority, and Canon* [Grand Rapids: Zondervan, c. 1986]. A thorough study of the canon by a competent and contemporary evangelical scholar is a *desideratum* of the highest order.

6. This explains the strong claims of Paul to be an apostle as in II Cor. chapters 10-13 and II Cor. 14:37. And whatever may be said for or against the genuine apostolic authority of the New Testament books, the fathers of the ancient church clearly indicate

120

that in their view these books were apostolic written not necessarily by one of the original twelve but by a member of the apostolic circle of those commissioned by Christ, and whose authority for that reason must be accepted. Irenaeus is typical: "For the Lord of all gave to his apostles the power of the gospel through whom also we have known the truth, that is, the doctrine of the Son of God." Irenaeus, *Against Heresies* in *Ante Nicene Fathers*, iii, p. 414.

7. Evangelicals acknowledge that the apostles were the witnesses to the Jesus Christ, the living Word of God. But they are more than just the first and most reliable witnesses. They are *normative* witnesses whose witness we accept as normative because of the commission of Christ that in turn parallels the commission of the Old Testament prophets by Jahweh. In spite of his emphasis upon the present work of the Spirit, Karl Barth also recognizes this divine commission of the apostles to speak for and in behalf of Christ. (*Church Dogmatics*, 1, 2, pp. 487 *et passim*)

8. Inerrantists employ various verbs to indicate their understanding of the sense in which the Bible is understood as always telling the truth. They speak of inerrancy as covering all the Bible says or means or teaches or affirms. The Evangelical Theological Society in its basic platform employs the words: "The Holy Scripture in the Old and New Testament is the Word of God written and, therefore, inerrant in the autographs." The Lausanne Covenant (1976) employs the word "affirms."

On the contrary, some draw large distinctions by the variation in these verbs. They use terms like "teach" to limit inerrancy to formally didactive passages, and hold that the Bible is not necessarily inerrant when it merely asserts a certain idea. This is really to say that the Bible does in fact err, and it would seem wise in the interests of clarity for those who take this view to avoid the term. In any case, inerrantists use all four words interchangeably, and do not by any means limit the Bible's inerrancy to didactic passages. By employing the word affirm or teach, they merely wish to point out that words out of their Biblical context might easily suggest what is not true, but what the Biblical author really states to be the truth always is the truth. Of course, the Biblical writer does not say what his words taken out of their context might mean if those same words were used in a different situation. Inerrantists hold that what the Biblical writer really *says* or really *means* or really *affirms* is always true. Krister Stendahl provides a very profitable distinction between what the Bible *says* (the intended meaning of the author) and what it *means*. The latter is what provides for many the value of the Bible. But for them the Bible is not normative. It is not Holy Scripture. Its value is not what the Bible says or affirms or teaches to be true. That may be quite false. The Bible then becomes not normative Holy Scripture, but a piece of literature; and its value is found not in what the author intended to say, but what it means to the reader today (See Krister Stendahl, "The Bible as a Classic and the Bible as Holy Scripture" in *Journal of Biblical Literature*, 103 [1984], pp. 3-10; and his *Meanings: The Bible as Document and as Guide* [Philadelphia: Fortress Press, 1984]).

9. Note again the position on inerrancy held by the Evangelical Theological Society: "inerrant in the autographs" and the similar affirmation of the International Society for Biblical Inerrancy.

10. See, for example, the charge made by Charles Augustus Briggs (*The Bible, the Church and the Reason* [New York: Charles Scribner's & Sons, 1983] p. 114).

11. See the correspondence between Augustine and Jerome in *The Nicene and Post-Nicene Fathers*, Vol. 1, *The Confessions and Letters of St. Augustine* (New York: Christian Literature Company, 1872). Note especially Letter LXXV, pp. 333-343.

12. See 1 Kings 14:29 and elsewhere.

13. See 1 Kings 14:19 and elsewhere.

14. The Old Testament authors cite many sources; the New Testament a lesser number. We may safely presume that most were not inspired by the Spirit of God. Certainly there is no reason to hold that the Chronicles of the Kings of Israel or the Chronicles of the Kings of Judah were specially inspired by God. They were merely court records.

15. This raises the broader question of the relationship between inerrancy and so-called higher criticism. Inerrantists do not object to higher criticism in the sense of an investigation into the background, date, author, and similar matters with respect to the Biblical books. What they do object to is certain conclusions that are inconsistent with holding to Biblical inerrancy. For example. E. J. Young a staunch defender of inerrancy in an earlier book argued for the non-Solomonic authorship of the book of Ecclesiastes. Later he moderated his view. His general principle is that a consistent inerrantist cannot hold that a book is authored by a certain person if, as a matter of fact, it really stemmed from some quite different person. (*Introduction to the Old Testament* [Compare ed. of 1949 with rev. ed., Grand Rapids: Eerdmans, 1960], pp. 367 ff.).

16. Emil Brunner, *Revelation* and *Reason* (trans. Olive Wyon, Philadelphia: Westminster Press, c. 1946) pp. 274-275.

17. Barth is typical of those who reject inerrancy when he declares that he is bound by the "Christ" aspect of every word of Scripture. Yet for him the "Christ" aspect is something different from and less than what the Biblical author is saying and teaching. Emil Brunner uses the same sieve. Its very subjective nature can be observed from the fact that Barth deems the virgin birth to be an essential element of the Christ message of Scripture. Emil Brunner argues that the virgin birth as a biological fact is not at all pertinent to a right view of Christ.

Many other "sieves" are proposed such as the religious aspect of Scripture, moral truths, the material appropriate to the function of Scripture, the revelational truth and others. Most of these can be narrowly interpreted to include or exclude almost anything the person who uses the term wishes.

18. The value of inerrancy rests exactly on this point. When he has completed the task of textual criticism and the task of grammatical historical exegesis, the inerrantist is done. He has divine truth. By contrast, the errantist must not only put the Bible through additional sieves before he knows he has the truth, he must then be able to show why the particular sieve he has is the right one. Who said all Scripture is true and completely trustworthy except for what does not pertain to the religious and spiritual life? Who said its value and truth are limited to its revelational content? Why should one particular sieve be chosen over another?

19. It is true that some conservative evangelicals value the *Textus Receptus* above the more widely accepted texts of Westcott and Hort or Nestle or the United Bible Society. Even here, however, positions are defended on the basis of historical textual data not personal and subject preference.

20. Brunner's rejection of or reservations about the virgin birth is only one example of what could be multiplied many times over. Rudolf Bultmann's rejection of the bodily nature of the resurrection is another. For many, the doctrines of universal salvation and external punishment fall into the same category. Rational evidence fails us. Only if we know we can trust the Biblical text can we decide many of these questions with any assurance. The lay Christian in the pew is particularly vulnerable when he does not have a completely trustworthy Bible in his hand.

21. This is not an argument for the inerrancy of Scripture, but only for its value if true. Unfortunately, the argument that inerrant originals would be of no value is used frequently as an argument against inerrancy.

22. Karl Barth employed this argument to defend the errancy of Scripture. He has

essentially two basic reasons for arguing that the Scripture must be errant. First of all, revelation of God to man, because of the nature of human categories of thought, must necessarily distort the truth and introduce error when put in propositional form. Yet Barth wants to trust and to get us to trust his own statements—none of which is really true on his own theory. Therefore, in practice he divides between really false statements that ought not to be made and the good kind of false statements that Barth makes. In ordinary language we call this the analogical nature of all human truth. The inerrantist position is simply that all Biblical statements fall within the good kind of false statements that ought to be made (analogically true statements in ordinary language). The Bible never speaks in really false statements of the kind which Barth opposes.

Barth's second argument is that unless fallibility were necessarily involved in the human propositionalizing of truth, we would have to destroy the freedom and hence the humanity of the Biblical writers. Jack Rogers echoes the same thought again and again in his volume *Biblical Revelation*. But why must this be so? Only if God cannot get what he wants (i.e. those prophetic propositions that are true) would Barth's (and Rogers') case be valid. Romans 8:28 really should destroy this position for any theist. In short this is no objection against propositional revelation or the idea that a Biblical writer could speak or write what God wished spoken or written without God's dictation. This is really an objection against the Biblical view of the God of divine providence.

23. The word inerrancy as used by its defenders does not indicate a method of inspiration, but its extent. Inerrantists will vary in their understanding of the method by which the Biblical authors were guided by God to produce an inerrant text. Methodology involves the relationship between God's providential and special work on the human mind and the psychology of the human writer. Like the relationship between the divine and human in Christ, this, too, is mysterious. What inerrantists agree on is that, however the Spirit of God worked to attain the result, the end product—a book of Scripture—is inerrant.

24. Psalm 14:1.

25. Ecclesiastes 3:19 and 20.

26. The Biblical writer is certainly not responsible for the main position defended by Bildad and the other friends of Job. They argued against Job that his tragedies were due to the fact that he was an especially great sinner. They were wrong in this, but that does not mean that the author reckoned them to be wrong in everything he said. Just the reverse was true of Job. He was right on the main point. He was not specially guilty. Yet, that does not mean that he was correct in everything that they said.

27. Proverbs 18:22.

28. This is why any discussion of how exact the references to the "molten sea" in the ancient temple is not altogether relevant. It may be interesting to discover how close to pi an ancient writer comes, but it is irrelevant to the inerrancy of the text. The author is obviously not trying to give us an exact geometric analysis of the relationship between diameter and circumference. And since he is not trying to say that, he cannot be charged with saying what is not so if he misses it. You do not err in what you do not say. See Harold Lindsell, *The Battle for the Bible* (Grand Rapids: Zondervan, 1976), pp. 165-166.

29. This is simply to recognize the cultural differences between Biblical times and our own and to insist that Biblical translation must take account of these cross-cultural differences.

30. An excellent example of this occurs in the three reports of Jesus' instruction to his disciples to go in haste on their mission without delay for encumbrances unessential for the trip. See Matthew 10:9-11, Mark 6:8 & 99 Luke 9:3. Obviously, no one account

gives us our Lord's exact words. Each records vividly the thrust of the conversation. What at first sight looks like a flat contradiction is seen on careful analysis to be simply a vivid summary of complementary instructions: "Go in haste and take nothing that is not needed immediately for the journey."

31. Matthew's repeated formula, usually translated "That it might be fulfilled" represents a special case. This is frequently interpreted to mean that Matthew exegetes the Old Testament passage as predicting a specific future event and that the event Matthew is recording from the life of Christ is the specific future event that had been intended by the Old Testament author. This creates all sorts of problems, and the root difficulty is caused by insisting that "to be fulfilled" always carries this technical sense. It does not. It states, instead, that an idea is "filled out." It is general and ambiguous enough to include everything from simply "illustrate" to "This event in some interesting way is like the Old Testament event" to "The Old Testament passage states a general principle of which what Matthew refers to is simply one illustration or example" to "This specific historical event had been predicted to happen and was what was really in the mind of the Old Testament author."

32. So the quotation of words from the mouth of Eliphaz. In the Old Testament book of Job these words are not set forth as necessarily true but as what Eliphaz said in making his case for a position that was essentially false. The New Testament author employed them because that is what he wished to say in words that the Biblical author was very familiar with from his knowledge of the book of Job and that represented beautifully the thought he wished to get across. A slightly different situation may be found in James where the apostle refers to what is genuine scriptural teaching but is not found specifically stated in any one Old Testament passage.

33. According to the Book of Acts (7:14) Stephen said that seventy-five souls went down with Jacob into Egypt. The book of Genesis, obviously speaking of the same event, stated that seventy souls accompanied him into Egypt. Of course, no one really knows whether Genesis and Stephen were really talking about exactly the same individuals. Perhaps Stephen was referring to a slightly expanded group including wives. Since the figure comes from the Septuagint text, however, it seems much more likely that Stephen is simply referring to the Septuagint.

34. The problem of different perspectives and different settings is relevant to understanding the story of the healing of the nobleman's son/servant and the healing of Bartimaeus, in which one account has the healing of two men and the other only of one and in one it takes place as Jesus was leaving Jericho while in the other he was returning to Jericho. The order in which various events are lumped in the gospels is also important. One gospel writer prefers to pull together a number of parables and miracles. Another prefers a chronological order. Still another may allow events to flow on the basis of association in his own memory. One event gives rise to another as he reflects upon the life and ministry of Christ. No order is wrong unlesss the Biblical author specifically informs us as to what specific order he intends to give us, and that order simply does not fit the facts.

35. Typical of this are the chronological references to the life of Abraham and the sojourn of Israel in Egypt. When, for example, did the sojourn begin? At Ur? Or at Hebron? Or at Jacob's departure with his family to visit Joseph in Egypt? Each author may have had different points in mind. Accordingly, one author may base his total on a particular beginning point and thus give a different figure for the total. All would be equally correct.

36. Note how frequently we have to ask a name to be repeated when we are introduced to another person. We never need to ask what the one introducing is saying.

Context helps us get this immediately. But context really is little help in enabling us to know if the man's name is Jenson or Johnsen. Much the same is true regarding numbers, although if the context is of an army, we can usually infer that the number is not three but much more likely three hundred or even three thousand or thirty thousand.

37. See 1 Timothy 3:16.

38. See Matt. 27:6-10, Acts 1:15-20.

39. Some may reject this Christological defence of inerrancy on the grounds that we do not know that Jesus is the God-man. For such a person, inerrancy is really not a pertinent question and ought not to be. The issue he must face is not "Is the Bible inerrant?" but instead "What do you think of Jesus Christ? Is he Lord and Savior or is he not?" Only after this decisive question has been answered in the affirmative are we ready to determine whether or not the Bible is inerrant. Obviously if the Bible is wrong on its main point about Jesus Christ and the gospel, it would be useless to discuss whether or not it is really inerrant. The issue here is the Lordship of Jesus Christ.

RESPONSE: Adrian Rogers

Dr. Kantzer, I want to thank you for the brilliant work that you have given to us. I hope that it will be listened to by tape, watched on videotape, and read and studied and appreciated and appropriated into our hearts and into our lives. I am blessed and gratified to hear this clear, ringing testimony to the authenticity, inerrancy, infallibility and impeccability of the Word of God. I confess to you that the response that I give is not going to be the response of a scholar, which I certainly am not, but the response of a Baptist pastor.

We are talking about parameters of inerrancy, and a phrase from the Scripture came to my heart—the Word of God is not bound. God's favorite appellative, description, or name for the Bible is this—*The Word of God*. In Mark 7:13, Jesus warned of making the Word of God of none effect through tradition.

Other Scriptures come to mind. Luke 5:1: "And it came to pass, that, as the people pressed upon him to hear the word of God, He stood by the lake of Gennesaret."

Acts 4:31: "And when they had prayed, the place was shaken where they were assembled together; and they were all filled with the Holy Ghost, and they spake the word of God with boldness."

Acts 12:24: "But the word of God grew and multiplied."

Romans 10:17: "So then faith cometh by hearing, and hearing by the word of God."

Ephesians 6:17: "And take the helmet of salvation and the sword of the Spirit, which is the word of God."

Colossians 1:25: "Whereof I am made a minister, according to the dispensation of God which is given to me for you, to fulfill the word of God."

I Timothy 4:5: "For it is sanctified by the word of God and prayer."

Hebrews 4:12: "For the word of God is quick, and powerful, and sharper than any twoedged sword."

I Peter 1:23: "Being born again, not of corruptible seed, but of incorruptible, by the word of God which liveth and abideth forever."

2 Peter 3:5: "For this they willingly are ignorant of, that by the word of God the heavens were of old, and the earth standing out of the water and in the water."

Revelation 20:4: "And I saw thrones, and they sat upon them, and judgment was given unto them: and I saw the souls of them that were beheaded for the witness of Jesus, and for the word of God."

The more liberal man gets in his theology, the less he tends to call the Bible the Word of God. He likes to speak of the biblical materials, the record of God's revelation, or the Pauline Epistles. All of those phrases are correct and legitimate ways of speaking of the Bible. But over and over again, in the Bible, the Bible speaks of itself by divine inspiration as the Word of God. I know it came through men, but Paul reminds us in I Thessalonians 2:13, "For this cause also thank we God without ceasing, because, when ye received the word of God which ye heard of us, ye received it not as the word of men, but as it is in truth, the word of God, which effectually worketh also in you that believe." Now, with that in mind, as we are thinking of parameters of inerrancy, I want to mention three things that come to my mind as I think of the Word of God.

I. First of all it is absolute perfection.

II Timothy 3:16: "All Scripture is given by inspiration of God".

All of Scripture is inspired of God, and a God of truth cannot inspire error. All Scripture, every part, is given by inspiration of God. The instruments who penned the words make it no less the Word of God. Every word is the Word of God. Jesus said "Man shall not live by bread alone but by every word that proceedeth out of the mouth of God." And the Bible speaks of the Word of God, not so much in the sense of the writers being inspired, which they were, but as though the very writings were the breath of God. The Scripture itself is the breath of God. That speaks to me of its absolute perfection.

II. There is a second thing I think of when I think of the Bible being the Word of God. I think of the wonderful character of the Bible. The reason for this is that God not only has called His book the Word of God, but God has also called his Son the Word of God. John 1:1-3 says "In the beginning was the Word, and the Word was with God, and the Word was God. The same was in the beginning with God. All things were made by him; and without him was not anything made that was made." Revelation 19:13 says "his name is called The Word of God."

Now that is interesting to me because the Holy Spirit inspired the writers to call both the Lord Jesus Christ and the Bible the Word of God. The character of the Bible and the character of Jesus are linked together. The same name is used for the Word of the Lord and the Lord of the Word. As I study the Bible, I find out that the Living Word honored, impeccably, the written Word. As I read

126

the written Word, I find that the written word presents, unerringly, the Living Word. And I see a correspondence between the two. Their characters are linking and meshed together in the Word of God.

(1) Both have come from the Father. II Peter 1:21 says, "for the prophecy came not in old time by the will of man: but holy men of God spake as they were moved by the Holy Ghost." The action of the Holy Spirit gave us our wonderful book. But Galatians 4:4 says, "But when the fulness of the time was come, God sent forth His Son made of a woman, made under the law." God gave His son, the living Word; God gave His book, the written Word.

(2) Both the Lord Jesus and the Bible live forever. I Peter 1:25 says, "But the Word of the Lord endureth forever." I want to say that my faith does not depend upon the autographs, it goes beyond those. "Forever, oh Lord, thy Word is settled in heaven." Beyond the autographs, it is the eternal Word of God. Jesus said in Revelation 1:18, "I am he that liveth and was dead; and, behold, I am alive for evermore." The written Word and the living Word live forever.

(3) Both are unchanging. Matthew 5:18 says, "For verily I say unto you, till heaven and earth shall pass, one jot or one tittle shall in no wise pass from the law, till all be fulfilled." Hebrews 13:8 says, "Jesus Christ, the same yesterday, and today, and forever." The living Word and the written Word are unchanging.

(4) Both are a light for a dark world. Psalm 119:105 says, "Thy word is a lamp unto my feet, and a light unto my path." John 8:12 says, "Then spake Jesus again unto them, saying, I am the light of the world: he that follows me shalt not walk in darkness, but shall have the light of life."

(5) Both are absolute truth. John 17:17 says, "Thy word is truth." John 14:6 says, "Jesus saith unto him, I am the way, the truth, and the life."

(6) Both obviously include the human element. Question: How is it possible for a sinful woman, as Mary was, to give birth to one that was impeccably sinless? Likewise, I ask, how is it possible for sinful human beings to write a book which is God breathed and without error. The answer to both of these questions is that neither is possible apart from divine intervention and miracle, which is exactly what God did. The same Holy Spirit who protected the Lord Jesus Christ from sin and His humanity was the same Holy Spirit that kept the human writers of the Scripture from including error in what they wrote.

III. There is a third thing that comes to my mind. Not only, do I think of the absolute perfection and the wonderful character of the Word of God when it is called the Word of God, but there is the awesome power of this Word because it is the Word of God.

In I Thessalonians 2:13, Paul said again, "For this cause also thank we God without ceasing, because, when ye received the word of God which ye heard of us, ye received it not as the word of man, but as it is in truth, the word of God, which effectually worketh also in you that believe." Because it is the Word of God it works effectually. We are convicted by the Word. Consider Hebrews 4:12: "For the word of God is quick, and powerful, sharper than any two-edged sword, piercing even to the dividing asunder of soul and spirit, and of

127

the joins and marrow, and is a discerner of the thoughts and intents of the heart."

Anyone who has preached this Book knows the power of it. Not only are we convicted by the Word but we are converted by the Word. Note I Peter 1:23ff: "Being born again, not of corruptible seed but of incorruptible, by the word of God which liveth and abideth forever." Not only that, we are *cleansed* by the Word. John 15:3 says, "Now ye are clean through the word which I have spoken unto you." We are to be *controlled* by the Word. 2 Timothy 3:16-17 teaches that "All scripture is given by inspiration of God, and is profitable for doctrine, for reproof, for correction, for instruction in righteousness: that the man of God may be perfect." Finally, we are *confirmed* by the Word. John 5:24 says, "Verily, verily I say unto you, He that heareth my word, and believeth on him that sent me, hath everlasting life, and shall not come into condemnation: but is passed from death unto life."

It is the Word of God, and because of the Word of God, it is absolute perfection. What else could come from God? Because it is the Word of God, it is interwoven with the character of His son the Lord Jesus. I do not back up one inch to people who tell me that I love the Book too much. It is the Book that makes the Saviour more dear to me. Thank God that this book unerringly points me to the Lord Jesus Christ. I thank God for the power of His Word. It is His Word, and because it is His Word, it is power.

Now people tell us that it is the truth of the Bible which is true. That has always seemed to me to be silly. The truth of a lawnmower manual is true. The truth in anything is true. And I want to tell you, the Bible is truth. They say, well, you can accept the salvation truth, the faith and practice truth, but not necessarily the science and the history. I ask a question: Is the virgin birth of Jesus an historical event? Does that not deal with history? I ask another question: What does science have to say about a virgin birth. It says it is impossible. But, dear friend, if God said it, it happened. No, we are not to say that you can separate science and history from faith. They are inextricably interwoven. It is impossible to separate the two. When I get to heaven and face the Lord, He may say to me, "Adrian, you believed the Bible too much." I'll take my chances on that rather than having Him say, "Adrian, you explained it away and watered it down and substituted, thus saith the mind of man for thus saith the Word of God." Now some people say you want us to say your word. I don't care if you say my word. You can call it steamboat for all I care. It is not words about the Word, it is the Word itself and the Word is the Word of God.

Thank you Dr. Kantzer, for coming and giving such a clear Word about the Word.

RESPONSE: John Lewis

Dr. Kantzer, we are grateful for your splendid presentation of your clearly modified form of the theory of inerrancy. You have stated your position with clarity, precision and persuasive logic. Perhaps too logically. I'm not sure we deserve your characterization of Southern Baptists as "the pace-setter for all Evangelical bodies in the United States and, perhaps, in the world."

Inasmuch as Baptists have never heretofore depended on the theory of inerrancy to clarify their doctrine of Scripture, it comes as a painful surprise to all of us that we are now embroiled in a serious, and sometimes in too much of an acrimonious, debate over our beliefs in the Bible as God's authoritative Word sufficient for faith and practice.

One could devoutly wish that other Evangelicals had learned from us how to state a doctrine of Scripture that respected the competency of the soul in religion, leaving each reader under the guidance of the Holy Spirit to come to a saving knowledge of Christ, avoiding party-line labels not found in Scripture.

It seems, however, that the tables have been turned on us, and now we are having to deal with a foreign element being imported into our once sufficient confessions. The stream of theological discussion from Turretin through Warfield and the Princeton School on through the crystalized ambiguities of the Chicago Statement threaten to undo us precisely at the point where we have been fraternally and lovingly united for centuries. We, too, are awed at the responsibility before us, and we join you in prayer that our beloved denomination will not be rent asunder by the forces that would impose a coercive and authoritative conformity on us. Your paper makes a worthy contribution to our dialogue, and we thank you for it.

In your opening statements defining the term and its "boundaries," do I detech a slight difference between your view and the more restricted view stated by others? When you say, "all that these writings *state to be so* is the truth and nothing but the truth," you seem to be saying that the truth of Scripture is discerned in what the Bible directly and intentionally purposes to affirm as distinguished from the incidental statements of the biblical writers not having to do with essential matters of salvation.

In your article, "Evangelicals and Inerrancy, the Current Debate," in the April 21, 1978, edition of *Christianity Today,* you used the phrases "inerrant as to teaching," and "inerrant in all it affirms." That is indeed a legitimate "boundary" in the use of the term as many Evangelicals hold. How one defines the term, therefore, also defines the boundaries.

Stephen T. Davis in his book, *The Debate About the Bible,* describes the boundary in its widest aspect, when he says, "The word *inerrant* is a technical

129

theological term that claims that the Bible contains no errors at all—none in history, geography, botany, astronomy, sociology, psychiatry, economics, geology, logic, mathematics, or any area whatsoever." But no one can cite any passage wherein the Bible directly claims to be teaching divine truth in these various fields.

One cannot have it both ways. One cannot logically claim the "Bible is not a book on science" and then claim that whenever the Bible touches on any area of science the biblical statement must be taken for actual fact though it may contradict the assured results of modern science. Does not the strict definition require us to believe in a flat earth, that the sun actually moves around the earth, and that we indeed live in a three storied universe?

When the pre-scientific view of the biblical writer is thus made part of the divine revelation, we dishonor the true nature and purpose of Scripture and force people to a false choice. While it is correct to say the Bible accurately reports how the biblical writer viewed the phenomenon of nature in his limited pre-scientific age, such a qualification contradicts the extreme claim of inerrancy. It is a form of obscurantism that distracts us from giving attention to the stated claim the Scripture makes for itself.

In point of fact the whole elaborate scheme of qualifications so waters down the definition of extreme inerrancy that it no longer means what adherents claim for the theory. Extreme inerrancy leads straight to bibliolatry and a docetic view of Scripture. In this respect it comes dangerously close to heresy.

The appeal to Jesus in support of the theory of extreme inerrancy is fraught with many difficulties. That he accorded divine authority to the Old Testament is without dispute, of course. In citing the Lucan passage you say, he "rebuked his disciples for not believing all contained in the Scripture," but the context makes it clear that He dealt primarily with those passages "in all the scriptures concerning himself." Again when he refers to the jot and tittle, the context makes it clear that he was not talking about the technical accuracy of every word of the Old Testament but that no detail of the divine purpose will fail to be fulfilled. How Jesus interpreted the Old Testament is instructive for us in interpreting both testaments and needs more careful examination than our purpose requires here tonight. A case in point is his battle with the Evil One in the temptation experience when both quoted from the Old Testament, when the Devil was more literalistic while Jesus drew out the inner spiritual essence of the passages as they related to his mission as the Son of God sent to fulfill the mission of the Messiah. a clear instance where "the letter killeth but the Spirit giveth life."

Placing his imprimatur upon the Old Testament is not to be taken as a *prima facie* argument that he is endorsing the modern man-made theory of inerrancy. I believe that is stretching the matter unduly.

Again, the first and basic parameter of the extreme view of inerrancy is applied only to the autographs. This is a tacit admission that our present copies do contain problems to which the definition of inerrancy does not apply, including some "errors" as far as the technical accuracy of some words and ideas is concerned. Since we all agree that textual research gives us a Bible very close to

130

the original, some of these matters must have been contained in the originals as well. So all the qualifications applies to the copies we have must also be applied to the originals. To apply inerrancy only to the autographs is to affirm that we do not now inerrant copies. At this point it is important to confess what we all know to be true—that none of these problem passages affect the message of salvation and the stated claim of the Scripture themselves "to make us wise unto salvation in Jesus Christ."

Unfortunately the proponents of the theory are not telling our people the whole story in this regard. Hopefully material from this conference will help our people to become more knowledgeable of the issue before us.

I find it difficult to follow your reasoning why we must believe in inerrant originals in order to accept the authority of the copies with which we have to deal, since they have proved to be sufficient for the purpose of salvation. The authority you say Jesus attached to the Scriptures was to copies also. He never made any distinction between the autographs and the copies from which he quoted.

I also find it difficult to see why believing in inerrant originals delivers us from subjectivism. Are not all the qualifications applied to our copies also a subjective sieve in an effort to "rightly divide the word of truth" in our extant copies? There is simply no way to test the assertion about the autographs. It is a moot question and distracts us from a responsible treatment of our copies.

To reject the theory of inerrancy does not mean, therefore, that one believes in an "errant Bible," a phrase that is overloaded emotionally. Perhaps our difficulty is in using the word "error" to describe the kinds of problems we face in our copies. To say the Bible contains some minor errors (minor as far as the central message of salvation is concerned) sounds like one is holding God accountable for the human element in the Bible. Biblical man was certainly in error concerning the sun moving around the earth. Rejecting the theory of extreme inerrancy does not mean one believes the "Bible is full of such errors." The use of the term seems to suggest that one is morally at fault.

The extreme theory of inerrancy simply does not come to grips sufficiently with the human element in the Bible. The theory gives inadequate attention to the principle of accommodation as understood by Origen, Chrysostom, Augustine, Luther and Calvin. That God used fallible, imperfect men as his inspired spokesmen is apparent from reading the Scriptures. To use the phrase the Spirit gave Paul, "we have this treasure in earthen vessels, that the excellency of the power may be of God, and not of us." That is the glory of the Scripture, that God's WORD comes to us in the words of men. God was no ventriloquist! The main question of hermeneutics is not to determine what in the Bible we can believe or not believe, but to interpret the message of salvation.

The question of the autographs must be put aside—it is too distracting and unprofitable, impractical and misleading. We have to deal with our copies. The Bible itself provides us with the only sieve we need. As you yourself so clearly put it—we are to see the Bible through the eyes of Jesus. An old hymn puts it succicinctly for us:

Keep your eyes upon Jesus,
Look full in his wonderful face,
And the things of earth
Will grow strangely dim
In the light of his glory and grace.

The theory of inerrancy, and all the qualifications used to prop up its troubling weaknesses, by concentrating on matters not essential to salvation, "takes our eyes off of Jesus."

Donald Miller in his book, *The Authority of the Bible,* gives us another sieve, when he says, "We are making proper use of the Bible only when we are asking it questions about God, his will, his glory, and human salvation, faith and life."

The Bible itself also provides another sieve for getting at the essential truth of the revelation in Scripture. One might call it the "principle of promise and fulfillment." It deals primarily with the relationship of the New Testament to the Old Testament. There is much in the Old Testament we are no longer required to believe. It was a schoolmaster to bring us to Christ. Of course there is much in the Old Testament we are to believe, and especially we are to accept it as the record of the preparatory revelation leading up to Christ. Its moral and spiritual precepts are still binding. It is essential to accept it as the authoritative record of the divine revelation to God's people under the old covenant.

You do well to caution us that "we must not foist upon the Bible an *a priori* speculative view as to what inerrancy means." But is that not what we do when we insist that one must believe in the non-existing autographs in order to accept our copies as authoritative? The theory promises too much. By the time the intricate qualifications water it down it no longer means what its proponents define it supposedly to mean.

I find the following paragraph most fascinating:

> The Biblical doctrine of inerrancy is simply that every word of the Bible is God-given in the sense that it was produced under the control and care of the Spirit of God and states the *ideas* that God wished to convey to us humans. Therefore, it is all true—that is, all the *concepts* or *judgments* set forth by the words of Scripture are really true.

And you go on to say that "all human statements are set forth in less than heavenly perfection," and citing the fact that we may not even have in some instances the very words of Jesus though the essence of his thought has been preserved in the words of the writer. By what sieve do we determine this?

In the paragraph cited you speak of "ideas, concepts and judgments" which seems to lead us in the direction of "propositional theology" as the object of faith. Am I wrong to take this as another way of saying what you have said elsewhere, "that the Bible is true in all it affirms."

As you point out to us it is necessary to "allow the Biblical author to speak in a way appropriate to him and to his own culture," therefore, "the Bible does not give us scientific truth in technical or scientific language." With this *The Criswell Study Bible* agrees:

> The Bible is a book of redemption. It is that or nothing at all. It is not a book of history, science, anthropology, or cosmogony. It is a book of salvation and deliverance for lost mankind.

But then you go on to say the Bible "gives us the truth; and when it writes on truth lying in the area of history or of science, it is still telling us the truth."

You give us a number of instances to illustrate how allowance must be made for the quite human element in the Bible: paraphrasing the words of Jesus; inaccurate quotations from the Old Testament; variant readings on the same events; rounded-off numbers; differences in personal names, etc. Your able handling of these examples is an illustration of the point I made earlier: that by the time you qualify and harmonize such passages the theory of inerrancy has lost its practical meaning. Again it is important to remind ourselves that matters of this kind do not affect the message of salvation or the stated purpose Scripture claims for itself.

I appreciate the intellectual honesty with which you deal with the subject. However, I sense a struggle going on in your own mind to avoid the harsher extremes in which the theory of inerrancy is stated by some. The truth of the matter is one may hold to a high view of inspiration and the authority of the Bible without accepting the man-made dogma of a theory of extreme inerrancy. Ironically, the attempt to apply the theory to our copies itself makes the problems of Scripture stand out as supposed "errors." One simply does not need the theory to solve these problems. The wide range of definition and application of the theory in the large Evangelical community should give us pause before any attempt to impose it on others.

In your closing statements you call for responsible scholarship to face the problems that confront us in the copies with which we have to deal. However, you say that "if the Bible is really inerrant" we should expect to find such problems—a tacit admission that the theory itself highlights the problems as problems. The question is whether or not the theory is adequate to deal with the problems. The many qualifications used to justify the definition of extreme inerrancy suggests to me that the term is seriously flawed and really not adequate.

You yourself admit that some discrepancies are insoluable but do not invalidate belief in the theory, a view also held by Warfield. But is this not also an admission that the theory simply fails to deal adequately with all problem passages? Again we need to remind ourselves that such passages do not affect the message of salvation or the Bible's clear and direct statements as to its function in the divine scheme of revelation and redemption.

We heartily agree that we must look to Christ as the Lord of Scripture. The extreme inerrancy theory is fatally flawed because it presents itself as the norm of Scripture thus usurping Christ's Lordship.

133

We must return to the historic Baptist position that through soul-competency one is free to interpret the Scripture under the responsible tutelage of the Holy Spirit, believing with Luther that the clarity of Scripture is sufficient to authenticate itself to all who approach the Bible with an open mind, a prayerful heart and obedient will.

This one can affirm without being distracted by a flawed theory.

Again, sincere thanks for your timely and provocative presentation that helps us all to a clearer knowledge of the abiding truth of God's holy and authoritative WORD.

7

INERRANCY AND THE DIVINITY AND THE HUMANITY OF THE BIBLE

J. I. Packer

It will, I think, help you to assess what I say in this conference if you know a little more about where I come from, theologically and spiritually. Let me ask your indulgence in saying just a word or two more about myself. I was converted at age 18 through the Inter-Varsity people at Oxford University. They gave me my nurture, and one of the first things that became reality for me in the course of that nurture was what John Calvin some years later taught me to recognize as the inward witness of the Holy Spirit to the divinity of Holy Scripture. I can still remember the gathering at which I went in, not at all sure that the Bible was the Word of God, and came out absolutely certain that it was, though all that had happened was the one visionary chapter of the Book of Revelation had been reverently expounded. It was not, as I said, until long after that I found in Calvin the phrase that fits what had happened to me. Calvin said that this Spirit given certainty that the Bible is the Word of God is something that every Christian experiences. I rejoiced when I read that, for that was what I had experienced. The conviction that the Bible is as divine as it is human has been with me ever since, and has come out, I am sure, in all the speaking and writing that I have done over that past 35 years.

I come to you as one who identifies wholeheartedly with the evangelical heritage in Christendom. I claim it as my inheritance and I seek to learn from all its many varieties. I believe that in Christendom, values and insights are often divided and fragmented so that one needs to go around with one's eyes and ears open, drawing wisdom from every source where wisdom can be found. As a reformed and reforming Episcopalian, I am also, I hope, a learning Episcopalian and I have learned many things, may I say, from the Baptists. It will rejoice my heart if I can now share with my Baptist friends something worthwhile in return in this present in-house discussion about the nature and place of Scripture.

The *Review and Expositor* for winter, 1982, page 11, described me "as a well-known British fundamentalist." Where, I wonder, did they get that from? I suppose from the fact that in 1958, I published a response to a sustained two-year denunciation of British Evangelicals as fundamentalists. My defense of those evangelicals was entitled *"Fundamentalism" and the Word of God,* and there is nothing in it that I have ever wished to withdraw. If, now you want to tag me as a fundamentalist, you are free to do so. But let me say, my defense of what had been called fundamentalism was offered in the belief that the real issue here was and is the authority of the Bible. I do not take it on me to defend all the things that have been done in the name of fundamentalism, in Britain or anywhere else. Sometimes I have winced at the indifference of self-styled fundamentalists to issues of scholarship, and at their black and white way of reasoning about everything, as if uncertainty or suspended judgment is a great dishonor to God and a sign that your faith is failing. I have sometimes winced, too, at their public style and over their separatist tendancies. But for all that, you may call me a fundamentalist, if you wish. I stand with all those who maintain the full and absolute authority of the Bible. And since the historic fundamentalists maintain this I stand with them rather than apart from them, however little I like some particular things that they say and do.

Rather than identify myself as a fundamentalist, I would ask you to think of me as a Puritan: By which I mean, think of me as one who, like those great 17th century leaders on both sides of the Atlantic, seeks to combine in himself the roles of scholar, preacher, and pastor, and speaks to you out of that purpose. The word *Purtain,* like *fundamentalist,* is often used in an unfriendly way, but if I am to be given an unfriendly description this is the one I would prefer.

What, now, can I offer you in this biblical inerrancy conference? First, an exposition of what I believe to be true about the truth of the Bible and with it a warning out of my Anglican experience with the movement in England. When nowadays I see Christian folk teetering on the edge of what I call Biblical relativism, imagining that you can retain all of Christian life and vitality, all of Christian experience and devotion to Christ while yet sitting loose to the final authority of the Bible and the final truth of, for instance, the biblical doctrine of the atonement, I shudder, because observing the Liberal Evangelical Movement has taught me that this is not so.

It was in the first decade of this century that English Liberal Evangelicals came to birth. Its program and platform was as stated above. It took two generations for that movement to die. When I was converted, at the end of its first generation, it seemed that Liberal Evangelicalism was carrying all before it. The leaders of the church of England were saying that this was the only version of evangelicalism that could contribute anything to the Anglican future, and I was made to feel that in cleaving to the conservatives I was retreating into a backwater.

However, another generation has now gone by and during that generation, Liberal Evangelicalism, having killed a number of churches, has died itself. You will not find Liberal Evangelicals in England today; the breed is extinct for the position has no staying power. Over the years I have been involved in the task of reclaiming two congregations that had ruined by Liberal Evangelical ministries. In each case, the job took between five and ten years. It was totally tragic that previous ministries had detached these congregations so effectively from their biblical moorings, and it was a hard and painful enterprise to bring them back to their earlier anchorage.

It is with all that in my memory and in my heart that I speak to you. If I seem to be warning you against biblical relativism with more passion than you would have thought appropriate, remember, I am a burned child who dreads the fire.

I do not want to see that liberal evangelical scenario which did so much damage in England rerun in the Southern Baptist Convention, and I intend to say all I may to try and stop that from happening.

I should here explain what I mean when I speak of biblical relativism, lest there be any misunderstanding. Whenever the Bible is not allowed to have the last word on any matter of belief or behavior, there the Bible is being relativized to human opinion. That is what a certain type of biblical scholarship does all the time, and that is what I wish to warn you against.

The inerrancy of scripture is an overall theme in this conference, and my next step is to make some comments on both these terms. First, please note that the word *Scripture*, is a concertina word—that is to say, one that oscillates in use between broader and narrower meanings, like a concertina that is constantly being either extended or closed. When you speak of Scripture you may be using the word to refer simply to the 66 books of the Protestant Canon, as distinct from all other books; or to the original Hebrew and Greek and Aramaic text as distinct from any subsequent translations; or to the Bible in some vernacular translation as distinct from its original languages. Again, you may be using the term to refer to the Bible as historical tradition, the Bible as the historical tradition of the Judeo-Christian community of faith, honest narration, celebration and explanation of God's words and works in history, set forth for edificatory purposes by the various biblical writers. The academic discipline called biblical theology always approaches Scripture in this way.

Then, fifthly, you may be using the word *Scripture* to signifify universally applicable teaching about God and grace and godliness that emerges from these canonical books when you ask them the question, "What has God to say to us here and now about our life today?" And, sixthly, you may be using the word to articulate your own answer to that question.

None of these uses of *Scripture* is to be censured. All of them are perfectly proper and legitimate in their place. But if they get mixed up with each other, there can be a mental crossing of wires and a short circuiting of thought and consequent trouble for both mind and heart, as the distinction between the text that we must ascertain, translates and interpret and our own actual interpretation gets lost.

Now for a comment on the word *inerrancy*. Quite frankly, I recognize that it is in one way an awkward word, because it is negative in form. I have sympathy with those who say that they would rather not use a negative term to describe the Bible. But sometimes one has to use negative words in order to bar out mistakes. And that I believe is the position here. But in any case *inerrant* is only a negative way of saying "totally true and entirely trustworthy," and if that is the formula that you prefer to use, by all means do so. We are not tied to particular words as if they were magical. I find that in contemporary theological discussion, the older standard words like *revelation, inspiration, authority* and even *infallibility,* are taken and expounded by some in a way that explicitly allows, and indeed insists, that there are matters on which the Bible ought not to have the last word because what it says is wrong. In response to this, I want a word which nails my colors to the mast as one who holds that there is no point at which the Bible ought to be denied the last word because it's wrong. That is why I personally embrace the word *inerrancy* and make much of it in these days, for that reason.

Why is this assertion of inerrancy made? I make it to declare a methodological commitment that is perceived a part of a Christian's discipleship. The commitment is to (1) believing and obeying all the Scripture sets forth, (2) exegeting Scripture in a harmonious way, (3) letting Scripture judge and control one's thoughts, and (4) responding to everything said in Scripture as proceeding from God for the instruction of His people.

What does the assertion of inerrancy commit one to? It doesn't oblige one to agree with the domino theory that if inerrancy falls, everything will fall with it. That may or may not be true, but it is not implied by the use of the word *inerrancy*. Equally, using the word does not commit one to any exegetical *a priori* which would force one's understanding of Scripture into an unscriptural mold.

Belief in inerrancy does not commit me to belief in the inerrancy of any particular interpreter, not even myself. Nor does it commit me to disregarding any aspect of the humanness of Scripture. Acceptance of inerrancy does not commit one to arbitrary oscillations between literal and nonliteral interpretation.

On the positive side, asserting inerrancy does commit one to a radical and rigorous *a posterior* procedure whereby great pains are taken not to read into the text anything that cannot certainly be read out of it. Further, one is committed to robustly embracing all that the Scripture affirms when grammatically and historical exegeted. Finally, one is committed to a willingness to live with minor problems. I say minor problems because my testimony on the basis of 40 years of fairly detailed biblical study is that there are no major problems for the inerrantist. There are, indeed, problems for which satisfactory answers are not yet secured, but a commitment to inerrancy does not require, and has never required, that we solve them all. All that is required of us is that we be honest thinkers, striving to solve those problems that we can and admitting when we do not yet have the answer to this or that problem.

What is gained by asserting the inerrancy of Scripture? The assertion of inerrancy safeguards the Christian approach to Scripture as God's Word. Second, the assertion of inerrancy articulates the proper receptivity of faith, conscious of its own emptiness and ignorance and seeking to be taught by God. Further, the assertion of inerrancy establishes the Christian commitment to biblical authority in a clear way. It tells one that the Bible is always going to have the last word. And, finally, the inerrancy commitment brings the church's handling of Scripture under control, at least in principle.

The word *inerrancy* has a problematical status. Some people are frightened of it for reasons of their own. They fear that it will lead to bad apologetics, bad harmonizing, bad interpretation, or bad theology. Perhaps some inerrantists have dishonored the word by lapsing in those ways. But for all that, a commitment to biblical inerrancy, it seems to me, is not one which in itself can be anything other than good for the Christian and the church.

Turning to the subject of the divinity of the Bible, I give you a formula: Scripture, though human, is divine. This is where we must begin if we are ever to understand the matter. This is the mystery of Scripture, that is to say that here we face a divine reality that has in it more than we can understand, like the mystery of the Trinity or reincarnation. The mystery of Scripture focuses, first, in its marvelous integration of 66 different books, written over a span in excess of a thousand years in widely varied cultures, into a single organism of truth. The second part of the mystery is the way in which God has used, does use, and continually will use, the text of Scripture to communicate His message to His church and to the hearts of each of His people. We go to the Word of God and God speaks. Both of these aspects of the matter come into play as we celebrate the divinity of the Bible.

What is the meaning of the claim that the Bible is divine, that is, that it is the Word of God? The claim means three things together. It means, first, that holy Scripture has God for its source. This is its inspiration, the *theopneustia* to which Paul makes reference in 2 Timothy 3:16. God gave the documents through the human authors. Scripture is not only man's witness to God, it is God's own witness to Himself through what has been written. Scripture has God as its source.

The second thing that the claim of the divinity of Scripture means is that Scripture has God for its theme. This is one of the marvels of Scripture, the unity of the message in all of the 66 books concerning the Creator who becomes Redeemer and makes sinners His friend and establishes His kingdom. The third thing that the claim of the divinity of Scripture means is that Scripture has God as its user. Scripture mediates God's truth to His people; God communicates through it. The Barthian way is to explain the inspiration of Scripture in terms of its instrumentality as the means of communicating God's Word, thus collapsing the first of my points into the third. In my opinion, the Barthian approach does not do sufficient justice to the God-givenness of Scripture; therefore, I stress that the claim that Scripture is divine must give due account to all three points.

The crucial question, of course, is why one should claim that Scripture is divine. To be to the point, Christians make this claim because it is integral to the teaching of Jesus Christ and His disciples. The relevant evidence falls into three categories, essentially. First, there are the quotation formulae in which Jesus and His apostles cite Old Testament Scripture as coming from God or coming from the Holy Spirit. For example, Jesus, Himself quoted an observation by Moses from Genesis 2:24 as the word of the Creator, and I do not think He was forgetting the context; I think He was demonstrating that He understood all that He read in Scripture to have come from His heavenly Father. Jesus used this quotation on the occasion when his foes sought to ensnare him by means of a trick question on divorce: "Have you not read how He who made them at the beginning made them male and female and said, for this cause shall man leave father and mother and be joined to his wife, etc." When you look the passage up in Genesis 2:24, it is simply an explanatory comment by Moses. But Jesus cites it as the Word of the Creator because He read all of His Bible as the Word of His heavenly Father.

There is, secondly, a whole string of passages asserting the didactic function of Old Testament Scripture for Christians as something which God intended all along. Passages like Romans 15:4, where Paul wrote, "Whatever was written aforetime was written for our learning," are supportive of this idea. 2 Peter 3:15-17 says the same. Paul wrote to Timothy and said that the Holy Scriptures were able to to make one wise for salvation through faith in Christ Jesus; he added that all Scripture was breathed out by God. Because of its divine source, Scripture is profitable for teaching the Christian and the Church, so that spiritual maturity might be achieved.

Thirdly, there are explicit assertions that the Scripture, Old Testament Scripture, has authoritative force for Christians and, indeed, that first it had authoritative force for Christ, Himself, who fulfilled the law and the prophets and said that that was what he came to do. Consider Matthew 5:17, "Don't think I came to set aside, to destroy them but to fulfill them." And He did, fulfilling the law by His teaching and by His life, and the prophets by the enduring of the death that was predicted for the Messiah, because He knew, according to the Scriptures, that that was the path that the Father has appointed whereby the Messiah should enter into His kingdom.

After His resurrection, Jesus met two of His disciples on the Emmaus road and the rest of them in Jerusalem on resurrection day, and he spoke to them in exactly those terms. Even Jesus the son of God incarnate, lived under the authoritative force and direction of the Scriptures. If He set us that example, how dare we hesitate to follow it? As for the New Testament, it rests on the principle that the teaching of Jesus and His apostles is God-given and carries divine authority exactly as does the prophetic Old Testament. Apostolic teaching is to be received as given in the name of Christ, just as the Old Testament prophecies were to be received as given in the name of God. The apostolic testimony is written down in the New Testament, and what was true of the oral witness of the apostles applies equally to their written witness. Thus one works one's way to the point of setting the New Testament on the same level on which Christ and His apostles set the Old Testament. When this is done, we have the Christian Bible, the Old Testament and the New Testament, both divine for they both come from God.

The claim that the Bible is divine is an integral element in the doctrine of revelation. Revelation signifies the whole work of God in communicating with sinners redemptively to bring them to saving knowledge of himself. This revelation embraces three levels of activity. First, there is his self-revelation on the stage of history as He works redemption for the world. Revelation, at that level, finished when it reached its climax in the coming of Christ and the pouring out of the Spirit to give to the apostles the full understanding of Christ. Second, so that the knowledge of what God had done once and for all in history might be available for all the world, in every generation, God caused a written record, a celebration, a narration, and an explanation of it all, to be written, and that is the 66 books of our Bible. This might be called inscripturation. The third level of God's action can be called illumination, the work of His Hoy Spirit in helping persons understand and receive the message. God's revelatory action continues at this third level but not at either the first or second levels.

Obviously, it was and is necessary that the Bible should be a trustworthy record, adequately presenting the Redeemer and the redemption that are to be known. It will not do to trust the recording of historical events to oral tradition; the events will inevitably become distorted and misunderstood. If such had been the case, the third level of God's revelatory action, that is the work of His Spirit giving understanding of the message, would be frustrated. Think in terms of the three levels, the three stages of the revelatory process. Think of them together, and it becomes clear how vital it was that there should be a trustworthy record so that stage three might occur.

By way of balancing this discussion, let me address now the humanity of the Bible. Consider this formula: Scripture, though divine, is human. It is fully human. The divine method of inspiration involved all of the following items: accomodition to the personal qualities and cultural perspectives of the writers, including their literary styles; setting forth revelation in the form of the human story of how redemption was achieved and made known, and how individuals who were involved fared through their faithfulness or lack of faithfulness to God; using a variety of witnesses and a pluriformity of presentation to exhibit redemption from the many angles from which the human witnesses preceived it; using the creativity of the authors who consulted sources, gave their books careful literary shape, and used poetical and rhetorical forms designed to evoke specific responses from readers; incorporating all kinds of records (genealogies, liturgies, rubrics, census documents, and so forth) into the narrative. The combination of immediate revelation, enhanced insight, and providential overruling that constitutes inspiration added something to the factors that constitute fully human writing but in no way subtracted from them. God used the literary creativity which He had given these men; their humanity is part of the Bible, and it is to be celebrated and acknowledged. We don't honor God by minimizing the humanness of the Bible anymore than we honor Him by minimizing its divinity.

The divine authorship of Scripture entails the full truth (inerrancy) of all its teaching. The human authorship of Scripture necessitates care in determining what that teaching is. This, of course, leads to the question of exegesis. Exegesis should be grammatical, historical, culturally aware, empathetic, and self-critical. Cultural conventions of communication (e.g., with regard to numbers and narrative sequence), cultural boundaries of interest (e.g., innocence of the concerns of theoretical science), and the limited focus of each logical flow (e.g., the use of cosmological language without asserting their ontological validity) must be kept in view, lest teaching be read into texts that cannot be read out of them. In addition, the theological and religious purpose and the theocentric and doxological perspective of the biblical material must be kept in mind, for this helps us see the scope and limits of what is being taught.

The value of the brands of critical disciplines lies in the light they throw on the writers didactic purpose and scope of concerns. What they reveal can help

141

us in our quest to better understand the human writers so that we better understand Him. The critical disciplines and careful, scientific exegesis are developments in the modern church for which, in themselves, we should be grateful. Our concern should only be that they be not misused by being harnassed to a philosophy which already is resolved to set human judgment above what the Bible says. There is no necessary connection between any critical discipline and biblical relativism as a religious philosophy.

Finally, let me address the claim that an illuminating analogy exists between the inspiration of Scripture and the incarnation of the Son of God. In both cases, you have a mysterious union of divine and human. In both cases, you have perfection, as a result, in human form. Is that point valid? I believe that it is valid in at least these three ways. First, it is valid as a way of dispelling the suspicion that the humanness of Scripture in some way requires fallibility and error on the human side. It was not so with Jesus; why should we suppose that it has to be so with Scripture? Secondly, the analogy saves us from the temptation to relativize anything that we find the Bible teaching; after all, we most certainly would not allow ourselves to do that to anything that the Lord Jesus taught. Finally, the analogy serves to dispel the suspicion that the inerrantist view of the Bible is docetic. In these ways, the analogy between Christ and the Bible is real and true and helpful in our efforts to understand the things God wants to teach us through Holy Scripture.

RESPONSE: James Flamming

Let me begin by thanking Dr. Packer for his very excellent presentation. We appreciate him taking the time to be here.

Dr. Clark Pinnock said in an earlier session that we who are moderates should be more definitive. He suggested we should speak more precisely about what we mean and who we are. I will try to do this. By nature a moderate likes to leave room in which to move around just like our more strict brethren like to put truths in a tight corner. First, let me identify myself as an F. F. Bruce kind of conservative. He was my hero in Biblical studies long before I knew he thought of himself as an inerrantist, albeit a moderate one.

Second, my own definition of inerrancy, although I would much rather use the word inspiration, would be much like Dr. Packer's when he writes: "Scripture is inerrant, not in the sense of being absolutely precise by modern standards, but in the sense of making good its claims and achieving that measure of focused truth at which its authors aimed."[1] A definition of inerrancy even more specific is that of Millard Eriksen: "The Bible, when correctly interpreted in light of the level to which culture and the means of communication had developed at the time it was written, and in view of the purposes for which it was given, is fully truthful in all that it affirms."[2]

Let me also express appreciation for Ed Young's correction of an earlier article of mine. You were not aware he was quoting from me when he was giving his response. He was kind enough not to quote his source. It is from a chapter I wrote about 25 years ago in which I made the Nestorian error of identifying error with being human. I was at that time fresh from my graduate study, dealing with my own humanness, my own weaknesses, and that is reflected in that earlier viewpoint. Ed saw that error and corrected it in his talk. He handled it well.

My own bias, Dr. Packer, is to stay with the Biblical word *inspiration*. If the Bible is the authoritative word that I believe it is, then we ought to be able to stay within, indeed be obedient to, its God-appointed limits. I can appreciate Dr. Packer's concern that we offer assured support of what we believe in the midst of the rampant humanizing of the Bible in scholarly circles. But it seems inconsistent to me to affirm the Scripture's authority and then begin to use words and definitions never found therein.

Living within Biblical limits has become important and personal to me. About three years ago I was having a most enriching series of quiet times which had stretched on for several weeks. It was an enriching plateau, so to speak. I have learned through the years that when this happens, God often has something afoot. He is about to surface something with which I will need to deal and is firming me up for the inner challenge. This is indeed what happened. As I interpreted the Spirit's instruction at that time, I was asked to submit to the Scripture as the Holy Spirit's text book in his task of rebuking, developing, training, and equipping. Particularly I was to submit to what I could learn from those passages which were not my favorites. I suppose we all have favorite passages and less favorite passages. It is no trick to submit to those Scriptures we delight in. But to submit to others with an open willingness to be taught is quite another.

Now, the Holy Spirit is about the task of developing the soul (or spirit if you prefer). It is interesting that Paul late in his life mentions that he has not arrived spiritually. Soul-making is a lifelong journey, even for the noblest of minds and the most committed of saints. If that was true of Paul, how much more for the rest of us. The lesson, as I interpreted the Spirit's lesson for me then and now, was that I was to be submissive. I was to be obedient to whatever lessons the Holy Spirit would teach me as I opened my life to "the Word of God written." Doctrinally that is not difficult. Doctrine can be learned rather easily. It is when the Word impinges upon life that the shoe pinches. The Holy Spirit assured me I would not have to cut off my mind. He was not asking me to believe the unbelievable. He was about the business of trying to bring about a personal correction and wholeness through someone who saw things quite differently than I see them. He was teaching me the lesson of learning from someone with whom I disagree but of whom the Holy Spirit approves.

I confess I did not respond with enthusiasm to that directive. I do not like the word submission any more than most Americans do. I especially did not like the thought of submitting to some portions of the Scripture I did not particularly appreciate. I remember quibbling with God over Ecclesiastes, not one of my favorite books. I responded something like, "Lord, do you mean I have to submit to being taught by one who is close to what we might call in today's world a secularist? He organizes his life without you. He hardly mentions your name; he does not believe in the resurrection; and he is unbearably pessimistic. You know I have trouble with cynical negative people." The word I got in return was something like this, "You can learn from this preacher if you will listen." And I have. I have learned balance. I have learned some balance in my workaholism. Do you have that trouble? Never satisfied, always expecting more of yourself than you have any right to deliver? Well, the preacher in Ecclesiastes has taught me a lot about celebrating simply because something went well. Not perfectly, but adequately. He has taught me to live with my own limitations with joy, and to affirm a job well done. So you see, living in simple obedience with the Scripture and within Scriptural limits is not an academic matter with me.

My point in mentioning all of this is simply to ask, "If the Bible is the Holy Spirit's textbook, why do we need to improve upon it with our own words?" Is this not a reflection of our own need to be more precise than God intends?

I now turn quickly to Dr. Packer's topic on the Bible as divine and the Bible as human. I confess my viewpoint is more pastoral than academic, more practical than doctrinal. The place where the wheel of inspiration hits the road is where it meets life. It is where the divine and human within the Scripture meet up with the divine and human in us. This is crucially important because of the secular age in which we live, secular meaning the organization of life without God. This, to me, is our real enemy. This is where the real battle is. I have given my life to fighting the battle of secularism because of what it is doing to people, to families, to careers. If all we are is orphans in the vast cosmos then nothing fits. I'm not sure we ought to be wasting our energy fighting one another. We can become like firemen before a burning building, arguing about whether the water is pure.

Mark it well, things have changed in the last 100 years as to the credibility the Bible is given. First there was Darwin with the suggestion that everything later is better. Then came Comte pointing out how many influences go into making up of our perceptions. Then came Freud suggesting we are mere products of the inner pressures of our psyche. Add to that the scepticism of some irreverent higher criticism of the Bible. Put those in the salad bowl of our culture, and the average person is not apt to come out with a Scripture that has authority for modern life, everyday life. Our task is to bridge that gap. How do we do it?

Now we have bumped into why a human and divine Bible is so important. The authority of the Scripture is confirmed when in our human experiences we find the Holy Spirit ministering to our human need just as He did to the people of the Scripture. The authority of Scripture is not only a doctrine. It is an experience. When our experiences match Biblical experiences we say, "Eureka, that's for me." The humanness of the Bible is our bridge to the modern mind. This is why so many identify with Simon Peter. We say, "he was so human." We read David's Psalms and say, "He was where I am." We read some of Paul's letters and feel he has been reading our mail. Jesus' parables seem always to hook some human part of us and thus to set up a place for the divine to go to work.

To put it another way, the divine and the human in the Scripture serve as polarities for each other. Electricity may serve as an example here. As you know, what makes an electrical current are the two polarities creating the energy. Using the same metaphor, spiritual energy is created when the human side of us identifies with the human side of Scripture, and the Holy Spirit within us uses the inspired Scripture to create the energy necessary for redemption. When the human polarities meet the divine polarities, power develops: inner power, spiritual renewal.

So, how does one communicate Scripture to a humanistic culture that knows virtually nothing about the Bible to begin with? One way is to let God speak through the identification people make with the humanness within the Bible. From this can develop the act of redemption and renewal.

My fear is that we will treat the divine and human in the Scripture as academic rather than life-oriented. Let me illustrate. When I was in the Seminary I once preached a sermon on Psalm 23 to the small but wonderful congregation to which I had been called. In the seminary we had been doing some detailed exegetical work in the Psalms. (I had not learned then that sometimes the most important thing in a sermon is what you leave out!) So I took my thorough exegesis of Psalm 23 and dumped it on the congregation. One of my members was a great Bible teacher, Mrs. A. J. Blevins Sr. She is now past ninety. She was then and still is in my parthenon of saints. After the sermon was over she came to me and said, "Pastor, I don't know why you're having so much trouble with the twenty-third Psalm. I've always known what it meant." You see, my exegesis was correct, but it avoided the human and, consequently, was devoid of the divine.

Let me contrast that with an experience many years later, also with Psalm 23, when the result was quite different. In the providence of God I became pastor of the greatest teacher I ever had. He was also the brightest man I've ever known. I took everything he offered when I was in the University. He taught psychology. Years later, when I became his pastor, he was so supportive and fine. The years went by and one day I was called to the Intensive Care Unit where he had been taken. He said to me something like this, "Jim, in a former day I was your teacher. Now you must be mine. I know I am a Christian. But I have never died before. Teach me how to die." What would you have said? I did what I have learned to do in times like that, I started quoting Scripture. It was the twenty-third Psalm that made the connection. "Yea, though I walk through the valley of the shadow of death I will fear no evil for Thou art with me . . ." He squeezed my hand and smiled. The body relaxed. All was well, all was very well. The human and the divine in my teacher had connected with the human and the divine in the Scripture. It was enough.

My concern is that the human and the divine within the Scripture remain objects or subjects for our study. If so there will be no renewal there. Karl Olsson has a little book, *Meet Me on the Patio*.[3] In it he compares our lives with

145

towers. He says as we go along we climb the floors of our towers and talk to each other on the level we are at that particular time. That is fine. But the trouble is we expect to find renewal and healing there. It isn't there. It is down on the ground floor, where God is, on the basic level of human need. My fear is that we will talk to each other on the twentieth floor and never go back down to the patio level where God has always met us. It is only the basic level of our common human needs and our openness to God's answers that will ever bring us together.

Notes

1. J. I. Packer, *Beyond the Battle for the Bible* (Westchester, Illinois; Cornerstone Books, 1980), p. 58.
2. Millard J. Erickson, *Christian Theology, Vol. 1* (Grand Rapids, Michigan: Baker Book House, 1983), pp. 233, 4.
3. Karl Olsson, *Meet Me on the Patio* (Minneapolis: Augsburg, 1977).

RESPONSE: H. Edwin Young

From a practitioner's perspective, I wholeheartedly agree with Dr. Packer. His paper states clearly and succinctly the importance of understanding that the Bible is both divine and human. At the end of my response, Dr. Packer, with your permission, I do have one question I would like to ask.

In my opinion, there are only three viable positions to take on the Bible. Position number one: The Bible is the word of man only. Position number two: the Bible is a combination of the word of man and the Word of God. Position number three: the Bible is the Word of God.

The first view, that the Bible is the word of man only, represents the position of liberalism. Those in this camp stay away from words like "infallible" and "authoritative," and they laugh at the thought of inerrancy. I would put the neo-orthodox theologian in this category. (He is uncomfortable here, but this is where he belongs.) Barth and Brunner called the church back from rationalism and gave great attention to the Bible, but they denied that God actually speaks in human words. This school also emphasizes the transcendence of the divine and maintains that God reveals Himself in ways human beings cannot express. Therefore, the content of the Bible becomes nothing more than words from men who are expressing what they understand God to be conveying by non-verbal means. The Bible then becomes only a fallible witness to revelation, and it ceases to be revelation itself.

The second view of the nature of the Bible is that it contains both the word of man and the Word of God. In other words, it is a combination of the human and divine. Those in this camp talk about the human and the divine nature of the Bible, but in practice they start with and emphasize its human side.[1] For example, a prominent Southern Baptist deals with what he calls "error" in Mark's gospel being corrected by Matthew and Luke in their accounts. He goes on to state that, "Nothing man touches ever comes close to perfection."[2]

The thesis is that since God does not speak that which is untrue, then things in the Scripture that are perceived as untrue must necessarily come from human beings. When there is a combination of divine words and human words, the task of the interpreter is to distinguish between the two.

Man then must become the authority, and subjectivity becomes a part of the inevitable methodology. The scholar "plays" God and tells the people what is true and what is not true, what is God-breathed, and what is man's opinion. At this point we have abrogated the most cherished Baptist doctrine of the priesthood of every believer and substituted a new priesthood of the scholar using methods few laymen could ever comprehend. An eclectic view of the Scripture then evolves in which everybody "picks and chooses" what they think is from God and what they think is from man. "Thus sayeth the Lord. . ." is watered down to "maybe so, maybe not. . ." "It is written. . ." becomes, "It is my opinion. . ." I Corinthians 14:8 states it clearly: "For if the trumpet give an uncertain sound, who shall prepare himself to the battle."

The danger is obvious. All men (scholars included) tend to eliminate the things they do not want to hear. The portions of God's Word that are written to correct the church, to discipline our minds, and to form our lifestyles are usually the parts determined to be unreliable and not from God. It is a simple solution: get rid of the headache by cutting off the head.

Satan's question in Genesis 3:1 ". . . hath God said . . .?" virtually destroyed evangelism and the evangelical church in Europe and Great Britain in less than a generation. If we do not know we have a sure word from God, or if we believe the Bible is composed of truth mixed with error, the word will no longer cut. It will not convince or convict. It will not lead to repentance. It will not build up the body.

In the spiritual, as well as the physical world, growth is the sign of a healthy body! If that is true, and I believe it is, spiritual growth in a church can be measured by its reproductive growth; i.e., baptism of those being born into God's family, the church. Do you think it accidental that the churches who lead us in per capita baptisms and other churches who lead us in total baptisms are pastored by men who proclaim a Bible free from error? Is it coincidental that the churches which are dynamic, alive, exciting and involved in effective social ministries are pastored by men who hold a high view of Scripture?

The third view concerning the nature of Scripture states that the Bible is the Word of God. These words should be adequate, but, tragically, modern theologian have redefined this simple phrase. The uninitiated and the naive are impressed with the apparent conservatism of a theologian who says, "I believe the Bible is the Word of God," not realizing the same person can deny the bodily resurrection of Jesus Christ and totally repudiate the basic doctrine of the faith and still through "verbal gymnastics" say the Bible is the Word of God.

147

Now to say that the Bible is the Word of God is the classic evangelical posture. Even the heretics in church history used the Scripture (incorrectly, I might add) to prove their position. To say that the Bible is the Word of God does not deny the human side of Scripture. Non-inerrantists set up "straw men" and caricature the inerrantists as one who believes that the prophets and apostles were uninvolved, robot-like men who simply took dictation from the Almighty. It needs to be pointed out that, since the Reformation, no individual of any theological prominence has accepted this mechanical position.

The problem of style is really not theological; it is literary. There is no problem in trying to explain how the style of one book differs from the style of another book. The Word of God came to us through human authors whose distinctive phraseology and vocabulary were peculiar to their respective time and culture. Because of this factor, the Bible is also the word of men.

The point of departure is important. It seems to me we must begin with the fact that the Bible is a divine book, and then move to its humanness. From this perspective, it is easy to see how God superintended the writers as they were carried along by the Holy Spirit. This is how they could record His Word without error.

The Bible has a double authorship. The Word of God through the words of men is the Bible's own account of itself. The Old Testament law, for example, is sometimes called "The Law of Moses" and sometimes "The Law of the Lord." In Hebrews 1:1, we read that *God* spoke to the fathers through the prophets. In II Peter 1:21, however, we read that men spoke as they were moved by the Holy Spirit. God spoke and then man spoke. They spoke *from* Him, and He spoke *through* them. Both affirmations are true. What is the response then to the thesis that everything man handles is defiled or that to err is human?

The gospels of Luke and Mark are certainly human books. Luke used sophisticated Greek phrases and terminology. "Luke knew the rules of good Greek grammar and syntax and was accustomed to observing them."[3] Therefore, his is a scholarly gospel. In contrast, Mark wrote sermonic verbiage that were barely on a sixth-grade level. He combines bits and pieces of Old Testament Scripture and, as one commentary stated, "His style is not carefully wrought and polished. He tells a story as a child might tell it. He adds statement to statement connecting them simply with the word 'and'."[4]

For the sake of illustration I can image a sixth-grade dropout named Mark saying to a Jerusalem audience, "God don't like sin." Is that an error? Listen, "God does not like sin" proclaimed in Massachusetts is no truer than "God don't like sin" preached in Texas.

To apply modern historiographical methodology to biblical approximation, paraphrased Old Testament passages, and seeming contradictions and then shout "error" is, in my opinion, absurd.

Every weatherman in our modern world refers to the sunrise and the sunset. Now we know, cosmologically speaking, that the sun does not actually rise or set. So, is his unscientific usage inaccurate? Did he err? Absolutely not.

Biblical writers also described the world from their own perspective. The Bible is not man's word about God; it is God's Word about and to man. The

148

Bible does have a genuinely human element. When Peter wrote in II Peter 1:21, that "Men moved by the Holy Spirit spoke from God," he affirmed the human element in Scripture just as surely as he taught that the very words of those men were from God. It is imperative that we reject any attempt to make the Bible only divine and exclude the human, and it is just as imperative that we reject any effort to make it only human and exclude the divine. To say that it is a human book is not to say it consists of merely human thoughts about God.

The human traits of the biblical authors are not inconsistent with the doctrine of inerrancy. Certainly, the fact that to err is human does not mean that it is necessary for a person to err in every situation simply because he is human.

Consider the illustration of a printer. His assignment is to produce an instruction manual that explains how to operate a washing machine. He carefully describes how to load the machine, what temperature the water should be, how to hook up the washer, and what buttons to push to make it work. He puts all this information into a manual. It is quite possible that the manual produced is a totally inerrant document.

To push this illustration to the ridiculous misses my emphasis. Certainly all of us err. It is difficult to produce even a little instruction booklet that is without error. To produce an inerrant Scripture composed of sixty-six books by forty-plus authors over a period of fifteen hundred years on a wide variety of subjects is hard to imagine. Think about it.

There never was any order given to any man to plan the Bible. Nor was there any concerted plan on the part of man to write the Bible. The way in which the Bible gradually developed through the centuries is one of the mysteries of time. Little by little, part by part, century after century it came out in disconnected fragments and unrelated portions written by men without any intention of concerted agreement. But to deny the supernatural plan of the hand of God shaping it all is to deny something we know is a fact—the mystery of its unity!

The Bible was written on two continents in countries hundreds of miles apart. One man wrote one part of the Bible in Syria; another, in Arabia. Still others wrote other parts in Italy and in Greece. Other parts were written in the desert of Sinai, the wilderness of Judea, and the cave of Abdullam. Some of the Bible was written in the public prison of Rome, and other parts in solitary confinement on the Isle of Patmos. A variety of places and circumstances formed the backdrop for the creation of this unique mosaic. No literary phenomenon in the world can be compared with it. Some of the Bible was written during times of imminent danger and other portions of it were written in seasons of ecstatic joy. Not only do the authors who wrote the Word of God differ in background and in circumstance, but they also display in their writings examples of practically every kind of literary structure.[5]

What happened? God and man so cooperated that the Bible is God's Word in human language. The author's style and personality as well as the distinctive characteristics of the language in which he wrote are evident in the autographs. The very words are inspired. "There can be no inspiration of the book without the inspiration of the words of the book."[6]

How could this take place? The best answer is found in II Peter 1:21, and what took place was every bit as miraculous as the virgin birth. The Bible does have double authorship. As in the incarnate Word, so in the written word the divine and human come together without contradiction.

The analogy, of course, is not precise since Jesus was a person and the Bible is a book. Remembering this limitation, we should never speak of the deity of Jesus in a way that would question His humanity. Neither should we affirm His humanity to the lessening of His deity.

Scripture can be viewed in a like way. The Bible is the Word of God. God knew what He wanted to say, and, through prophets and apostles, He said it. On the other hand, the Bible is the word of man. Freely using their thought patterns, men spoke, but not in a way that would dilute or distort the truth of the divine message. I believe God molded the writers of Scripture into the men He wanted them to be. He guided the formation of their personalities and controlled their heredity and environment and supervised their lives, while He gave them freedom of choice and will. He made them into the individuals He needed to express His truth, and then He selected the words out of their personalities and their emotions. The words were the words of men whose lives had been so encompassed by God that their words became God's Words. "It is possible to say that Paul wrote the book of Romans, and to also say that God wrote it and to be right on both counts."[7]

Our Lord, though truly man, was completely free from sin. The Bible, though truly a human product, is completely free from error. If the non-inerrantists believe the Bible errs because of the human factor, then to be consistent they also must believe that Christ, as a man, sinned. The low view of Scripture ultimately leads to deep Christological problems. A low view of Scripture also leads to a diminished view of God. A low view of Scripture saps the spiritual vitality of any church. "Having a form of godliness but denying the power thereof" tells the tragic story of a diminished view of the Bible.

Recognition of the double authorship of the Bible will affect the way in which we read it. "Because it is the word of men, we shall study it like every other book, using our minds, investigating its words and synatx, its historical origins, and its literary composition. Because it is also the Word of God, we shall study it like no other book—on our knees, humbly crying to God for illumination and for the ministry of the Holy Spirit, without Whom we can never understand His word."[8]

My dear Doctor Packer, how desperately we need you in Southern Baptist life. Let me say, my Episcopalian brother, in light of your unapologetic and scholarly view of God's Word as totally inerrant, I must ask of you one question. But before I ask this question, it will be necessary for you to go with me following this session to Lake Ridgecrest. Together we will wade out into the water, and then I will ask you my question: "J. I. Packer, here is water. What prohibits you from being baptized?"

Notes

1. *Standing on the Rock*. James Montgomery Boice, pp. 46-47.
2. *Is The Bible A Human Book?* Edited by Wayne Ward and Joseph Green, Chapter entitled, Could God Trust Human Hands, James Flamming, p. 18.
3. *The Interpreter's Bible*. Volume 8, p. 3.
4. *God's Word for God's People*. John R. W. Stott, p. 19.
5. *Why I Preach That The Bible Is Literally True*. W. A. Criswell, pp. 70-71.
6. *Inspiration of the Bible*. B. H. Carroll, p. 20.
7. *Why Believe the Bible?* John MacArthur, pp. 36-37.
8. *God's Word for God's People*. John R. W. Stott, pp. 20-21.

8

INERRANCY AND THE HUMANITY AND DIVINITY OF THE BIBLE

Kenneth Kantzer

The Bible is a divine product. And it is a human product. In this it is like Jesus Christ, the God man. The unity of one person with two natures, divine and human, in Jesus Christ gives us, perhaps, our best analogy to the dual nature of Holy Scripture.

Of course, the analogy is not perfect. The Bible is not human. It is a human *product*. Neither is the Bible divine. It is a divine *product*. And because it is not *divine*, we do not worship the Bible. Yet as a divine *product*, we set great store by it. Psalm 19:1-6 lists the perfections of the Bible, and they are many: His law is perfect, his testimony is sure, his precepts are right, his commandments are pure, his judgments are true and righteous. More desirable are they than gold; Sweeter also than honey and the honey comb.

Yet, as a divine product, the Bible does not literally love us. Rather it conveys to us the love of God, who created it. The great Swiss theologian, Karl Barth, had it right when in response to the request, "Can you put your understanding of Biblical Christianity into a short simple statement?" responded: "Jesus loves me, this I know, for the Bible tells me so."[1]

As a divine product, the Bible is God's Word. In Mark 7:6-13 our Lord explicitly repudiates the tradition of the Jews and sets the Holy Scripture in sharp contrast to it. He then equates what Moses said with what God says. What Moses commanded is the Word of God.[2]

In similar fashion, our Lord and, following him, his apostles in the New Testament cite the Old Testament with the introduction, "God says,"[3] or "The Holy Spirit, by Isaiah the prophet, says,"[4] or "The Holy Spirit, by the mouth of David spake."[5] And then a passage of the Old Testament is introduced.[6]

Just because the Bible is God's word in written form it comes to us with infallible authority. Its authority stems from the God who stands behind the written words of Scripture and certifies that what it says is what he says to his church. It comes to us in the very human words of the prophets and apostles; but in condescending to speak to us in these human words, God tells us the truth and only the truth. He stoops to our humanity, but he does not stoop to our sinful humanity. And he does not stoop to our mistakes and error. He does not say what is not so.[7]

The Bible is the Word of God written. It is also a witness to the living Word of God—our Lord Jesus Christ. "These are they which testify of me," He said.[8] And 2 Timothy 3:14 through 17 spells out for us the dual purpose of Scripture: "But as for you, continue in what you have learned and have become con-

153

vinced of, because you know those from whom you learned it, and how from infancy you have known the Holy Scriptures, which are able to make you wise for salvation through faith in Christ Jesus."

The first purpose of Scripture is to bring us into personal acquaintance with Jesus Christ so we may come to know him as our Lord and Savior. The written word leads us to the Living Word.[9]

Then, once we have come to know the Savior, it also provides the instruction through which our living Lord by the power of his Holy Spirit, exerts his Lordship over our lives. In the 16th and 17th verses, therefore, the apostle sets forth the second purpose of Holy Scripture: "All Scripture is God-breathed and is useful for teaching, rebuking, correcting, and training in righteousness, so that the man of God may be thoroughly equipped for every good work." Scripture was spirated or breathed out by God so we would have a wholly trustworthy guide for the living of an obedient and useful Christian life.[10]

It is important to note that the relationship between the divine and the human in the Bible is analogous only to an orthodox doctrine of the person of Christ. All too often scholars begin with a preconceived idea of what the Bible is like and then draw the analogy between their faulty view of Scripture and equally faulty and even more dangerous view of Christ. This works out to the detriment of both—an unorthodox and unbiblical understanding of both Bible and Christ.

For example, the Bible is often compared to a docetic view of Christ in which Christ is fully divine but not really human. So, it is argued, the Bible is a fully divine product, but it is not in any legitimate sense a truly human product. The human element was involved simply as a transmitter of words that were not the choice of the human author and for which he took no responsibility.

This was a danger in the doctrine of Scripture frequently set forth by late Judaism—Philo,[11] for example—and in the first three centuries of the Christian church. Defenders of Scripture were too much influenced by the pattern of inspiration in the Greek oracles. The Biblical author was often portrayed as a set of lips and throat taken over by God and used by him to set forth the truth. The mind of the apostle was not in gear, and Scripture did not reflect the viewpoint of the Biblical author.[12] To their credit, both Philo and the early Christian fathers of the church also set forth right along side this Greek view of inspiration a much better and more thoroughly Biblical view of a Scripture that was truly divine but also genuinely human.[13]

In recent times a similar view has been advocated by a few Superfundamentalists, who insist that the method of Biblical inspiration was by dictation.[14] Do not misunderstand me. I do not say that God could not have dictated the whole Bible. In fact, I believe he did give us some revealed truth by dictation. The ten commandments represent an example of this.[15] Yet, other parts of Scripture are specifically said to be authored by humans. "Moses wrote,"[16] or "Moses commanded,"[17] or "David says"[18] are common ways by which the New Testament refers to Old Testament passages of Scripture. The prophets of the Old Testament and especially the Apostles of the New claim to be the author of their own works. Yet the Old Testament prophets delivered the message of the

Lord God. And the New Testament apostles spoke on the authority of Christ.[19]

Unfortunately even those who explicitly repudiate any dictation method of Biblical inspiration are sometimes wrongly charged with holding to a kind of dictation. It is argued that, in spite of their disclaimers, they are really logically and necessarily committed to a view of inspiration that demands a mechanical dictation. At the very least, they ought to hold to dictation in view of their defence of inerrancy or in defence of a verbal or plenary type of inspiration.[20]

Nevertheless, no theist can possibly object to the orthodox view of inspiration on this ground. It is true that, if one has a Greek view of man as absolutely free and a Biblical view of inspiration, his conclusions make no sense. If one adopts a Greek view of man, then one is, willy-nilly, forced logically to adopt a Delphic oracle dictation type of inspiration. But the Biblical view of man and of the providence of God is in complete harmony with the Biblical view of inspiration. Such a Biblical view of inspiration requires only that God can see to it that a human person says exactly the message he wishes to communicate. Certainly, the God of Romans 8:28 can secure through his use of a free human personality exactly what he wishes in the writings of Scripture even down to the jot and tittle of the text. A God who can use the free and sinful will of a Nebuchadnezzar to secure what he wanted for the blessing of his people, can surely so guide his chosen prophets and apostles as to lead them to say what he needed to have said for his people. This could be secured by God wholly through providential means even without any miracle at all if God had so desired.

The ordinary mechanical dictation method of inspiration is often objected to on the grounds that God would exercise too much control over man if he dictated Scripture. From a Biblical point of view, however, dictation is objectionable on exactly the opposite grounds. The mechanical or dictation view really allows far too little control by God. For example, as a boss dictates to his or her stenographer, there are many ways by which the words of the one who dictates may not get down exactly as intended. The boss is not sufficiently able to control the hearing, the writing, the coordinating, and the care of the stenographer so as to keep any slip from occurring.

This is a wholly wrong view of the psychology of inspiration as Biblically conceived. Rather, from the Biblical point of view, God can prepare a man who will produce entirely out of his own freedom just the kind of book He wants. In one sense, it is true, dictation speaks of too much control of God—that is, too much external control in hemming in man's freedom. But it is basically wrong in that that is not the way God secures Scripture. He produces the kind of man he wishes and prepares him through the experiences of life so that he will freely produce just such a book as God intends Scripture to be.

Those who object to an inerrantly inspired Bible on this ground really don't have a God big enough to run a peanut stand. They certainly do not have the God of the Apostle Paul. When God wanted Paul's book of Galatians written, he did not need to dictate it at the last minute. He began with Paul's grandparents and parents. He added his rearing in Tarsus, his education in the synagogue, his training under Gamaliel, his experiences as a Pharisee, his dramatic conversation on the road to Damascus; and then He brought Paul into contact with the troubles in the Galatian churches. In short, he prepared a man who would freely out of the burning zeal of his own heart and mind write the very message God wished to communicate to his church.

From quite a different viewpoint, the Holy Scripture is sometimes misunderstood by comparing it to the unorthodox Nestorian view of the person of Christ.[21] The Nestorians divided the divine and the human so that they were not the divine and human nature of the same person. According to this analogy the Spirit of God speaks through the written words of Scripture, but not through all of them. God did the best he could, but even he could not inspire a book of truth in human language and still leave it human. It is essential to our humanity to err. Therefore, the Bible, just because it is written in a human language and is a human book must be in error. To deny its error would be to deny its humanity. Therefore, what the Spirit speaks is separated from the written word. In this way, so it is argued, we save the divine Spirit from implication in the errors and mistakes of the written text that would be unworthy of ascription to God.[22]

But surely this is to misunderstand the nature of man created in the image of God. Man can know the truth, and he can tell the truth.

It is true, of course, that man's speech is imperfect. He cannot know all the truths that God knows. It is conceivable that he cannot know any truth exactly as God knows that same truth. No truly human statement can be identical with the truth as God sees it, but can at best approximate it. Philosophers call this the analogical nature of human thought forms and human language. Some argue that all human ideas are, by virtue of our finiteness, necessarily analogical and not identical with God's thoughts.[23] Certainly God has chosen to communicate to us in and through a written book that bears on every page of it its full humanity and the imperfections of its humanity.

Yet God distinguishes between true statements and false statements. He commands us never to bear false witness and always to tell the truth. He forbids the one and commands the other.[24] And in ordinary language, we make the same distinction. We commend one person for telling the truth; we punish another for perjury. Can man speak the truth but not God?

Inerrancy teaches us that God kept the Biblical writers from bearing false witness as they wrote the Bible. However inglorious human language may be, and therefore, however imperfect the human language of the Bible may be, it still always tells the truth. We cannot rule out *a priori* the ability of God to speak his truth through his inspired prophets and apostles. And Christ and the Biblical writers claim that he did just that: He gave us a Bible that tells the truth in human language. Their firm "It says" or "It is written" or "It stands written" simply will not allow any disjunction between what comes to us with divine authority and the written text of the Bible.[25]

Still another faulty analogy has been drawn between Scripture and an Ebionite view of Christ. According to the Ebionites, Jesus Christ was mere man. At a certain point in time the Spirit of God came upon him and adopted him into divinity. So the Bible is merely a human book containing all sorts of frailties including error. But now and again God sees fit to use it. Through its stumbling, faulty, and erroneous human language, the Spirit of God chooses to adopt it for his own message. The Bible is not God's message and it is not his written Word in itself. It is only potentially the Word of God at whatever time the Spirit chooses to use it and make it become for that moment the Word of God. If, it is asked, God sees fit to speak to us through the frail fallible human writings we call Scripture, what right have we to object?"[26]

But what is it that the Spirit says? Does God say something more or less than the Bible says? Does he say what is not true? Our Bible teaches us that God is a God of truth who never tells what is not so. And our Lord Jesus taught us that what the Bible says, God says. What it says conveys to us God's message with divine authority. And the Bible always tells the truth, even to its jot and tittle, and never teaches what is not so.

There is, indeed, a present on-going work of the Spirit of God here and now in the heart and mind of the believer. Scripture refers to this both as the witness of the Holy Spirit and as the illumination and present revelatory work of the Spirit of God.

The witness of the Spirit is discussed specifically in such passages of Scripture as Romans 8:14-16, Gal. 4:4-6, and 1 John 5:10-12. This last reads: "The one who believes in the Son of God has the witness in himself . . . and the witness is this, that God has given us eternal life, and this life is in his Son."[27] The Spirit of God opens the heart of the believer and seals on his mind the fact that we are sons in relationship to the Father. By this witness we know that we, in spite of our sin, are fully forgiven and accepted by a holy God as his dear children through personal faith in Jesus Christ as our Lord and Savior. Only in this way, through the direct and immediate work of the Spirit today, does the witness of the Bible to Jesus Christ take hold of us and become a living reality to us. The *objective* witness of the written Word to Christ must be complemented and completed by the *subjective* witness of the Holy Spirit or we will not profit from the objective witness of Scripture. Only by means of the objective written Word plus the subjective witness of the Holy Spirit do we enter into a personal and saving knowledge of the Living Word—Jesus Christ.[28]

Similarly, in 1 Cor. 2 the Apostle Paul treats of divine revelation from the mind of God coming to him (and other apostles). This revelation, received and appropriated by the Apostle Paul, he then hands over to others. He does so guided by the Holy Spirit as he states in 1 Cor. 2:13: "Which things we also speak not in words taught by human wisdom, but in those taught by the Spirit, combining spiritual thoughts with spiritual words."

This work we generally call inspiration. It would be more accurate to designate it as the spiration or productivity of the revelation by the Holy Spirit. The important thing in the mind of the Apostle Paul is that the revelation he gives forth to others he does so not merely as his own wisdom and in his own words, but rather as the divine wisdom that has been given to him and put into human words selected, guided, and controlled by the Spirit of God.

Unfortunately, we humans are finite sinners. We do not naturally on our own receive this divine revelation as from God. Again it takes the immediate work of

157

the Holy Spirit, working on our hearts and minds here and now, to enable us to appropriate this wisdom rightly and to receive it for what it is—the truth of God. This illumination of the Holy Spirit, or as it sometimes called, this internal revelation of the Spirit, takes what God revealed to the apostle and he, in turn, handed over to you and me as revelation available for us in Scripture, and makes it into your own and my own personal revelation.

This is a piece of truth in the often repeated statement that the Bible becomes the Word of God.[29] By this illuminating and revelatory work of the Spirit in me, the Bible does not become what it has never before been; it becomes personally and for me what I have never previously known or accepted it to be. The Bible, as it stands written, *is* the word of God, and by the work of the Spirit in my heart and mind, it *becomes* the word of God for me. The revelation to the prophet and apostle, shaped by the Holy Spirit into the written Word of God, by the power of that same Holy Spirit illuminating and revealing it to me, becomes the very word of God for me today.

In summary, the Biblical text is the product of both divine and human authors. In every word of it, it is fully a divine product as well as fully a human product. In this sense, Biblical inspiration is plenary and verbal. Verbal does not designate the method of inspiration and certainly does not mean that the Bible was dictated. Rather, verbal describes the extent of inspiration. The divine guidance of Scripture extends down to the very words—even the jot and tittle.[30]

Therefore, we do not need to go snooping through the Bible to discover what, above or below or behind its lines, is really the Word of God.[31] The Word of God is not something difficult to ferret out. We do not need to conjecture what would have made the Biblical writer say what we find in the text. Nor do we need to ask what this means to me today as opposed to what the Biblical author really said. But what the Biblical author really said in the light of his history and grammar and syntax and culture—that is precisely the truth that He is saying to me today.

At first sight, the divinity of the Bible seems more important to us than its humanity; and indeed, it is the crucial factor which gives it authority and makes its truth binding on our hearts and consciences. Nevertheless, the humanity of Scripture is just as important to a proper understanding and to a proper use of the Bible as is its divinity. Therefore, we need to recognize, and even emphasize, that in addition to its divine authority as the true Word of God, it is also a human Word. The books of the Bible flow out of the mind and heart of the Biblical author. That means all the characteristics essential to human writing are found in the Biblical writings. The Old Testament was written in the lip of Canaan, the language of one of the most corrupt and vile people who ever inhabited the face of the earth. The New Testament, too, was written in Hellenistic Greek and not in the language of heaven.

Being written in human languages, the Bible must necessarily partake of the capacities for good and evil inherent in such languages as languages. "Couldn't God transform and elevate this medium or instrument so as to free it from all difficulty?" it has been asked. Perhaps he could. I do not know. I am unacquainted with the language of heaven. And if God condescends to use human languages and not create a new one, then he must adapt himself to a human language with all its inherent inconveniences.

But this human aspect of revelational language is not merely negative. The positive side is that God may employ all the beauty and power and wonder of human language to reveal his truth to us. The thoughts of Aristotle, Augustine, Aquinas, and Kant, and the movement and life in the great dramatic power of Shakespeare's tragedies are all produced in human language. All of this and more lies within the capacity of human language and, therefore, is available to the divine hand for use in the production of Scripture. Yes, heavenly truth is clothed in mortal earthly language. But in the hand of our gracious God it brings to us immortal truth.

If we are to profit from the divinely inspired Word of Scripture, it is imperative that we understand also the thoroughly human aspects of the Bible. Theologically, the humanity of Scripture is an essential part of the historical view of the inspiration of the Bible held by the church. It is taught by the Bible about itself and by Christ about the Old Testament.

Far more important, it is crucial to our apologetic for receiving the Bible as God's Word. It alone makes a doctrine of inerrancy believable. The failure of some evangelicals to see and to delineate its clearly human aspect has had tragic consequences. It has fostered one of the prime arguments against a full acceptance of Biblical inerrancy on the part of other evangelicals who love the Scriptures and share with all evangelicals a high regard for the divine authority of the Bible.[32]

Finally, it is necessary in a practical way that we understand the humanity of the Bible in order for us to secure God's true Word. Only as we recognize and take its humanity thoroughly into account can we understand the Bible rightly and apply it rightly to our own lives and to our own day. Otherwise we do not have God's divine thoughts to guide us. We would have only our own poor human thoughts—thoughts suggested to us from the Bible. And that is precisely what we do not need. What this old world needs and what it cries out for from the depth of its suffering and despair is God's true thoughts clothed in human language that we can all understand. And that is just what we have in the book we call the Bible. The human and divine aspects of Holy Scripture, like the two natures of Christ, do not exist in isolation from each other or in conflict. They adhere to each other in one divine product, which is throughout a divine/human whole.[33] The divinity and the humanity of the Bible unite to give us God's Word in man's word—an inerrant Bible we can trust and trust completely.

Notes

1. Given by Karl Barth in answer to a student's query while he was visiting the United States in the sixties.
2. Jesus Christ is the primary "Word of God," but Holy Scripture is also the Word of

God and not in the sense that the Spirit of God sometimes uses it to reveal himself to us today, but because God so guided the authors that the ideas symbolized by their scriptural words are ideas God wished to communicate through his prophets and apostles. Note 1 Cor. 2:13.

3. See Matthew 19:3-9, especially 4 and 5; see also Mark 7:8, 9, and 13; Matt. 4:4, 7, and 10; and Luke 4:4 and 8. Similarly the apostles ascribed the Old Testament to God. See Eph. 4:8; and Hebrews 1:8.

4. Mark 12:36. See also Acts 1:16 and 4:25.

5. Acts 28:25.

6. Some passages ascribing the Biblical text to God also introduce the human author as well, thus indicating a dual authorship of the Biblical text. This is the point of "concurrence" as set forth by Benjamin Breckenridge Warfield, *The Inspiration and Authority of the Bible* (ed. Samuel G. Craig, Philadelphia: Presbyterian and Reformed, 1948), pp. 94 and 95.

7. While the Christian church has always recognized that the incarnate Christ experienced a self limitation in which he "grew in wisdom" and did not know the time of his own return, it has uniformly taught that he never sinned and always taught the truth. Even in his humiliation, he was our divine-human Lord and the One to whom we are called to make an ultimate commitment.

8. John 5:39.

9. In Scripture and in the teaching of our Lord, Christ is not presented as a sieve through which we can put Holy Scripture to discover what is worthwhile and what we can safely discard. Yet in spite of the high value Karl Barth places on the written text of Scripture, he still employs Christ as a sieve. While he is unwilling to discard any single word of Scripture and warns us against picking and choosing from SCRIPTURE what suits our fancy, he insists that we must search out the Christ aspect of every word of Scripture and reject the remainder. In this way he can speak of a verbal inspiration (an inspiration of every word) and yet also affirm that there are theological errors in Scripture (*Church Dogmatics* [eds. G. W. Bromiley and T. F. Torrance, Edinburgh: T. and T. Clark, 1956] 1, 2, pp. 507-509 and elsewhere). The inerrantist accepts the two-fold purpose of Scripture: Holy Scripture points us to Christ and leads us to him as our divine-human Lord and Savior from sin. It also gives us the instruction for daily life and thought that our Lord promised to us and commanded his apostles to give us. And they bring his instruction in a manner that is *entirely* trustworthy—that is inerrant.

10. The phrase translated "inspired of God" only occurs once in the New Testament and would better be translated "God-breathed" or "breathed out by God." The English word inspiration and the Latin word lying behind it do not readily convey the proper sense of the Greek. It is unfortunate that this word has become solidly entrenched in our vocabulary to describe the divine production of Scripture. See the excellent study of this word in B. B. Warfield's *Inspiration and Authority*, pp. 131-135 and 245-296.

11. Philo, for example, declares that "a prophet has no utterance of his own, but his utterance comes from somewhere else, the echoes of another voice." Again, "nothing of what he says will be his own . . . he serves as the channel for the insistent words of another's promptings." And "He is not pronouncing any command of his own, but is only the interpreter of another." Philo's chief objection to the parallel between Biblical prophets and bacchanalian frenzy or Dionysian ecstasy lies in the different sources. The source of Biblical prophetic frenzy is the grace of God instead of the "divine" possession or frenzy self-induced by the drinking of wine. Nevertheless, Philo also has quite a different view of Biblical prophecy according to which there is a divine suggestion to the mind of the Biblical author rather than a complete loss of self control. For a full discus-

160

sion of Philo's view see Henry Austyn Wolfson, *Philo: Foundations of Religious Philosophy*. (Cambridge,: Harvard University Press, 1962), Vol. II, pp. 3-72.

12. Justin Martyr, for example, declares: "We must not suppose that the language proceeds from the men who are inspired but from the divine Word which moves them" (*Apology* in *Ante-Nicene Fathers*. [eds. Alexander Roberts and James Donaldson] Buffalo: The Christian Literature Publishing Company, 1887), Vol. I, *Apology*, I, 36. Iranaeus, more careful than many, said Christ "availed himself of the prophets and declared his own matters through their instrumentality (*Against Heresies* in *Ante-Nicene Fathers*. vol. I, Book III, Chapter 10, Paragraph 2). And Athenagoras wrote: "While deprived of their natural powers of reason, by the influence of the divine Spirit, they uttered that which was wrought in them, the Spirit using them as his instruments, as a flute player might blow a flute." (*A Plea for the Christian* in *Ante-Nicene Fathers*, Vol. II, Chapter IX).

13. Yet, throughout, the ancient authors and especially Iranaeus gave credit also to the human authors and their preparation in knowledge and other ways to become instruments of Scripture. The near mechanical references by the ancient fathers must be understood as occurring in a culture that understood divine inspiration as ecstatic utterances. There was little need to protect the Biblical view from opposition on the grounds that it was too mechanical or too little human. For a balanced view of Irenaeus' understanding of inspiration, see J. Barton Payne, "The Biblical Interpretation of Irenaeus," pp. 11-66 in John F. Walvoord, ed., *Inspiration and Interpretation* (Grand Rapids: Eerdmans, c. 1957).

14. See, for example, John R. Rice, *Our God-Breathed Book — The Bible* (Murfreesboro, Tennessee: Sword of the Lord Publishers, c. 1969). Yet Rice carefully qualified his use of dictation as non-mechanical. He writes: "I do not know any reputable scholar of the past or present who could be properly accused of believing in mechanical dictation, that is, that the writers of the Bible were only machines and that their feelings and emotions, and their minds were not in gear when they were inspired to write down parts of the Bible" (p. 191).

15. See Ex. 24:12. In this case the commandments were not merely spoken but "written by the finger of God." (Ex. 31:18).

16. See, for example, Mark 10:4; 12:19; and dozens of times throughout the New Testament. Some of these, no doubt, can be explained as literally references to a document, but many could not. They refer to the human author.

17. Mark 1:14. Compare Mark 7:10 and 14 where Mark identifies what Moses said and commanded in the Old Testament as what God said and commanded.

18. Matt. 22:43 and 45; Mark 12:6; Luke 20:42; Acts 1:16, 2:25, 4:25; Rom. 4:6, 11:9 and throughout.

19. So Paul in 1 Cor. 12:11 and 13:9. Compare also Gal. 1:1 and his defence of his apostolate in that epistle.

20. This is really the point of Paul Rees in his foreword to the volume edited by Jack Rogers (Waco, Texas: Word Books, c. 1977), p. 10.

21. It must be noted again that this analogy is not perfect, and it is certainly no proof or even evidence of the inerrancy of Scripture. Our conviction that the Bible is inerrant flows from our conviction that Jesus Christ is our Lord and Savior. The relationship is one of trust in what our Lord has instructed us to believe, not a deduction from the nature of the divine and human in Christ. Still the orthodox doctrine of Christ *illustrates* beautifully the union of the divine and the human so that the whole person of Christ is both fully God and fully man. This is analogous to the Holy Scripture that is wholly (in all its parts) a product of the divine mind and therefore wholly (inerrantly) trustworthy as

161

well as wholly a human product and, therefore, exhibiting all that is essential to a human book written in human language.

22. So Karl Barth in *Das Christliche Verstaendnis der Offenbarung* (Muenchen: Chr. Kaiser Verlag, 1948) pp. 14ff; and John Baillie, *The Idea of Revelation in Recent Thought* (New York: Columbia University Press, c, 1956), pp. 116 ff.

23. So Cornelius VanTil, *A Christian Theory of Knowledge* (Grand Rapids: Baker Book House, c. 1969). See especially page 16.

24. Of course, in all human language there are necessarily various levels of exactness or preciseness. We understand this and interpret statements and commands accordingly. The point is that, while our statements and commands are less than exact. We do communicate meaningful ideas about reality and about what is right and wrong. Some of these ideas, in ordinary language, we label true and some false. Karl Barth's *Church Dogmatics* was not written in the perfect language of heaven as he himself will readily insist. Yet he considers his *Church Dogmatics* true in this ordinary way of speaking and reckons the language of Rudolph Bultmann to be wrong and false. Both may be inexact exemplifying their humanity and earth-bound imperfections throughout but one is true and the other false. The inerrant claims that the Bible, though written in language that is thoroughly human and, therefore, inexact and imperfect, exhibiting on every page and in every word its full humanity, is also throughout true and not false in the same ordinary way in which Barth claims his statements to be true by contrast with Bultmann's statements that are false.

25. The formula "it is written" is the simple formula by which appeal is made to Scripture. For our Lord that obviously represents the final authoritative word on the matter at hand. See luke 4:4, 6, 7, and 10; 24:46; Rom. 3:4 and 10; 1 Cor. 2:9; and elsewhere. Similarly, "Scripture says" has the same authoritative force. See Rom. 9:17 and elsewhere. Even the indefinite subject-less verb he/it says is frequently employed to introduce the authoritative text and one must supply "God" or "Scripture" as the subject of the verb. One cannot really interpret such passages in the sense "someone somewhere says" because of the final authoritative appeal in most of them. An excellent discussion of the New Testament usage of the Old Testament at this point is found in Warfield, *Inspiration and Authority*, pp. 299-348.

26. Karl Barth is representative of this view. The Bible is a human book, merely the word of man, until such time as the Spirit of God takes it and speaks it to the individual believer. Then what was a dead letter becomes the written Word of God that brings us into immediate contact with the Living Word by Jesus Christ.

The other side of Barth's view is that the Spirit of God prepared the Biblical writers so that their human word could appropriately and at the proper moment, by God's gracious action, *become* the true and living Word of God. Compare *The Doctrine of the Word of God* (trans. G. T. Thomson, Edinburgh: T. and T. Clark, 1936, pp. 126-133 and elsewhere with *Church Dogmatics*, 1, 2, pp. 487 ff.).

27. Note that the direct object of the Spirit's witness is our sonship, that is, our acceptance by God, in spite of our sin and guilt, as his dear sons through faith in the God-man, our Lord and Savior Jesus Christ. Holy Scripture is the indirect object of the witness—the Word promised and certified by Christ the Lord.

28. See. 1 Cor. 2:14 ff.

29. The Bible itself and our Lord do not speak of the Bible as becoming the Word of God. For them the Bible *is* the Word of God. It *became* that when God first spoke it to the prophet or apostle and enabled them to declare forth God's Word to you and me (1 Cor. 2:13). Yet there is a legitimate Biblical sense in which the Bible is not God's word

for me, until the Holy Spirit, here and now, makes it so. It is a matter not of what it is in itself—that does not change; but what it is *for me.* See below.

30. Inerrantists speak of a divine superintendance or guidance by God. How the Spirit of God worked in the human mind to convey to the prophet or apostle the truth is not spelled out exactly in Scripture. We know that Luke examined all sorts of previous witnesses. Some probably were written and one may have been our gospel of Mark. The Old Testament historical books used court records. Who knows what sources the authors of the Proverbs drew upon to write their sections of that book? In his epistle to the Galatians Paul certainly speaks out of his heart as he responds to the crisis in his beloved Galatian church. The point is not how God secured his written word; that we do not know exactly. Rather, using human instruments, he so guided the Biblical authors that their words in the canonical Scriptures represent what he wished to say to his people in an entirely trustworthy and, therefore, inerrant form.

31. As Barth puts it: No post-Biblical theologian is "a high school teacher authorized to look over their [the prophets and apostles] shoulder, benevolently or crossly, to correct their notebooks, or to give them good, average, or bad marks . . . [but] must agree to let *them* look over its *theology's* shoulder and correct its notebook." *An Introduction to Evangelical Theology* (New York: Holt, Rinehart and Winston, c. 1963). Yet Barth limits this to the Christ aspect of Scripture. Scripture itself presents Christ as the *focus* of Scripture, but never as a sieve to be applied to Scripture.

32. The full humanity of Scripture cannot be denied for it lies on the very surface of the Bible text. The Old Testament was written in the "lip of Canaan" and the New Testament in the common vernacular of the busy every day world of the eastern Mediterranean in the first century of the Christian era. To deny this, as Karl Barth admits for himself, would require a crucifixion of the intellect that he is simply unprepared to make. (*Christliche Verstaendnis*, p. 14). This is a crucifixion Christ does not ask us to make.

33. Just as the mystery of the two natures in one person does not have to be resolved in the case of Jesus Christ, so also it is not necessary to resolve the way in which God secured a thoroughly divine-human book. We can say Jesus is thoroughly divine yet without sin (though all other humans do sin) and that he, though human like us, is Lord (and there is only one Lord). So we can say the Bible is thoroughly human, exemplifying all that is essential to any human writing and yet is without error. It is not essential to humanity to say what is not so.

RESPONSE: James Flamming

Thank you, Dr. Kantzer. We appreciate so much your participation in our conference.

Before I make specific responses I would like to take the liberty to say a few words in behalf of the place of Christian doctrine in the life of faith. My reasons are two. The first is that my response to Dr. Packer earlier was so experiential I could be misunderstood. Second, when I was leaving last night I heard someone say, "Why do we have to have doctrine anyway. Why can't we just trust

Jesus?" What is the place of doctrine and the place of doctrinal discussion in the larger frame of the Christian faith? In answering that question let me use two analogies.

First, let me use the illustration of a mirror. The Scripture is like a mirror for us, and, like a mirror, can be used and studied in various ways. The most obvious use is to see what is mirrored therein. We can look in a mirror and see what is in the immediate vicinity. This is how we use the rear view mirror on our automobiles. We can look in a mirror and see the larger picture that is all around us, as for example those mirrors that are strategically placed in stores for the manager to see what is going on all over the store. Then, of course, we can look in the mirror to see ourselves. All of these reflective uses are important inasmuch as they allow us to see things our natural eyes cannot see. The Bible is a mirror for us in all three ways.

There is, however, one other way in which a mirror can be studied. We can examine the mirror to see if it is working right, if it is giving off a true reflection. You have doubtless looked at mirrors in certain amusement parks which made you look strange. They did not give off a true reflection. So a mirror is important only if it can be ascertained that it is giving off a true reflection. The doctrine of Scripture deals with the reliability of the reflection that is given off as it relates to the Word that comes from God. That is what this conference is all about. Does the Scripture mirror God at all times and in every place? Does it mirror God's truth in everything that it touches, even that which it did not originally intend to portray as God's Word? Since revelation is always given in a cultural situation, does that particular cultural point of view mirror God's Word, or is God's Word to be found within that cultural frame of reference?

All of us here believe the Scripture to be trustworthy in its affirmations of Christian truth. The question is whether the peripheral matters unrelated to the major truths are a reflection of God's Word or whether they are cultural reflections within which the Word is revealed. One group feels that if you can't trust every bit of it to be God's Word you can't trust any of it. The other group feels that the cultural milieu in which the Word was given is worthy of reverent scholarly study so that the Word of God may be "rightly divided" from the limited cultural situation in which it was given. Obviously this is an important question and worthy of our consideration. In doctrinal studies we look "at" the mirror rather than "in" the mirror. Both are important.

The second analogy is that of a map. When someone asks me about the importance of Christian doctrine I usually reply like this, "It depends upon how far you want to go." I used to fly a lot as a private pilot so let me use an illustration from the world of private aviation. For instance, suppose someone came to me and said, "I would like to fly to the outer banks of North Carolina where the Wright brothers made their first flight. There is an airport there isn't there?" I would nod my assent. "Well," they might then ask, "how do I get there? Do I need a map?" I might reply, "A map is always helpful, especially in knowing the restricted areas. But basically what you need to do is fly east to the first ocean and turn right." Contrast that with someone who came to me and said, "I would like to do something that few have done. I would like to take my small plane and fly down the eastern coast of the United States, across the Caribbean, down the eastern coast of South America, around the horn and back up the western coast of South America, back across the Caribbean, and then home." Would a map be essential? You bet it would. You would need to know where the airports were, languages, terrain, weather, and so forth. Christian doctrine is not the reality. It is only a map. But if you are going to go any distance in the faith, you had better pay attention to your maps. It is especially important not to let the secular world hand us our maps as they say, "These are the only maps there are."

Now I would like to respond to Dr. Kantzer's address by expressing concerns in three areas. The first has to do, Dr. Kantzer, with your statement about language. You said, "Being written in human languages, the Bible must necessarily partake of the capacities for good and evil inherent in such languages as languages." I'm not sure language is in itself good or evil. Is it not neutral? Obviously some languages are more limited than others, but limitation does not equate with evil. That is the Nestorian error you mentioned in your presentation. If you would comment on that please.

Second, let me ask you to address a question out of your wide experiences among evangelicals of all persuasions. Your experience and wisdom would be a real asset to us in the area I will mention. This has to do with responding to fellow Christians, fellow evangelicals, who differ from us. Some Christians need a great deal of apartness. Their verse might be "Come ye apart from among them and be ye separate." Others of us need a sense of togetherness, of unity, of relationship. Our verse might be "one Lord, one faith, one Baptism, one God and father of us all, who is over all and through all and in all."

Sometimes, it seems to me, those of us who want union and togetherness seem to drive away those who need apartness. What we get is similar to a marriage when the husband needs lots of space and the wife needs close relationship. The closer she moves toward him, the further he moves away from her. This is important to some of us who desire oneness. Sometimes it seems that the closer we move toward our more strict brethren, the further they move away from us. I see this happening with the inerrancy question. The more we seem willing to take inerrancy as a way of exalting a high view of Scripture, the more distressed our more strict brethren become. I have heard this statement lately from one of them: "The moderates are even taking our word from us." Out of your considerable wisdom and experience would you speak to this.

My final concern has to do with your coming close to equating Scripture with Christ. Scripture is an indispensible good. It is not God. We are redeemed not through the Scripture but through the Christ of the Scripture. I recognize you have carefully qualified your paralleling Scripture with Christ. But surely history teaches us that the subtle idolatries are the most dangerous. Idolatry is the most tempting when it is closest to the temple where holy words are used.

Is this not the error that the Roman Catholic church made when they equated the church with Christ. Actually there might be a more scriptural base for equating the church with Christ than equating the Bible with Christ. The church, the Scripture tells us, is the body of Christ. To equate tradition, church,

165

or Bible with Christ would seem quite dangerous, even though history gives witness to times when all three were placed in that position. Scripture itself gives this instruction. "In all things he must have the supremacy." (Col. 1:18)

Carlo Caretto speaks to the intimate of Christ to God's revelation of Himself.

> God presents himself to us little by little. The whole story of salvation is the story of God who comes . . .
>
> The hour of His coming is the Incarnation.
>
> The Incarnation brings the world his presence. It is a presence so complete that it overshadows every presence before it.
>
> God is made human in Christ. God makes himself present with us with such a special presence, such an obvious presence, as to overthrow all the complicated calculations made about him in the past.
>
> The invisible, intangible God has made himself visible and tangible in Christ.
>
> If Jesus is truly God, everything is clear; if I cannot believe this, everything darkens again.[1]

The uniqueness of the Christian faith is not primarily its Scripture. Most religions have scriptures of one kind or another. The eternal uniqueness of our faith is a Person, our Lord and Savior Jesus Christ. It is He who draws us to Himself, coming to us to heal our wounds and lay hold of our strengths. Should we not carefully and caringly guard this uniqueness?

On this past Easter a man responded to the invitation of our church. He is Professor at a nearby University. His journey the last two decades has been one of skepticism, even cynicism. In the midst of his recommitment to Christ he sent me a poem he wrote, a portion of which I share with you.

> I joined the church on Easter.
> I'm back in fellowship with kindred Christians . . .
>
> I'm David the Baptist again,
> After 20 years of agnosticism, skepticism, unbelief.
> It's interesting that my re-birth to faith in Christ
> Brought me back to the same name,
> But not to the same place . . .
> Acquiescence to the truth of creedal propositions
> Is not commitment to the Person who saves.
>
> The church had always been my way to acceptance
> And identity and community,
> But it was a place built on fables (I thought)
> And myths (a four-letter word to me then.)
> I never knew the Person
> Because I always believed the metaphor,
> "God the father," and my father was nothing like God.
> I guess I never knew the persons who knew that Person,
> Or never believed them if I did . . .

166

In my intelligence, trained in fine graduate schools,
Sharpened by twenty years of practice,
And defended by high walls erected against my feelings,
I knew I could not relate to God the Father,
Arising as He must from the propositions I had rejected.
The only way to meet the Father
Is in the Person of His Son.
For instance, I never saw God's love in sunsets,
Lovely as sunsets are.
Looking at it from my point of view,
It was too easy to buy into Einstein and Darwin.
"Sunsets are a subjective experience of responding emotionally
To the sun's light rays refracting through a polluted atmosphere,"
And we knew, for certain, we can't trust our subjective
    responses.
Didn't we?
I just enjoyed the sunset, and skipped the Artist part.

But now I can plainly see God's love in a Man on a Cross,
Looking at it from His point of view,
Whose words to me are always, "Fear not."
Whose willingness to die spells "Forgiveness."
Whose empty tomb legitimizes the promise of "Freedom."

So I joined the church on Easter.
I thrilled, and cried, to the Hallelujah Chorus.
I listened to the bell choir, heaven's music.
I looked at the Easter lillies banked across the stage.
I prayed with the congregation.
I reflected on the sermon: "In Him it is always Yes and Amen."
Once again, I walked the aisle,
And joined the church, by statement of my faith.

I am concerned that we lose the Person who sums up all things unto himself in the midst of our arguments about the Book that points to Him.

Note

1. Quoted in *A Guide to Prayer for Ministers & Other Servants* (The Upper Room, Nashville, Tenn.), p. 27, 28.

RESPONSE: H. Edwin Young

The word *inerrancy,* to me, is not a good word. I have noticed that most people are uncomfortable with it because of its negative connotation. Surely someone can come up with a positive word that carries the same weight and meaning. Perhaps the phrase "totally true" would be adequate. To state that the Bible is totally true and to illustrate that phrase with biblical examples would keep the term from being compromised. For example, "totally true" means that Adam and Eve were historical figures; there really was an ark and a great flood; two million plus Israelites were fed with manna in the wilderness, and Jonah was swallowed by a great fish. Actually, the Bible's statement about itself—that it is God-breathed *(theoneustos)*—is still the clearest word we have.

Inerrancy, in one sense, has been forced upon us. The inerrant view has always been a basic doctrine of the church, but the word inerrancy is relatively new. My grandmother never heard the word *inerrancy,* but there would have been no doubt in her mind that all Southern Baptists believe the Bible to be true. This word was propelled to the forefront of theological terminology because the underlying doctrine of the Scripture was under attack. This "crisis development" of a doctrine follows a historical pattern. For example, the early church had never defined a full-blown doctrine of the Trinity until the appearance of certain heretical elements requires a thorough-going staement about the three-in-one God.

Dr. Kantzer, writing in *Christianity Today,* said: "Evangelicals must show that they are not insisting upon a single word as a shibboleth, but rather are witnessing to the complete truthfulness and divine authority of Scripture. the words 'infallibilty,' 'trustworthiness,' 'plenary inspiration,' 'inerrancy as to teaching,' or, 'inerrant in all it affirms' are all adequate. But all can be and are being used with qualifications and limitations so as to mean the opposite of what ws originally intended. These qualified words are used to mean that some of what Scripture says or affirms or teaches is not true."[1]

Although the word *inerrancy* is by no means free from abuse and ambiguity, I have come to the conclusion that it is still necessary. We need to strip the word *inerrancy* of its political connotation and to give it a fair chance to prove its semantic worth. We cannot forget that any word can become a "weasel word" when its meaning has eroded or changed.

Exactly how the minds of the prophets and the apostles worked as they wrote, I cannot explain. The beginning point for me is an *a priori* assumption that the Holy Spirit fully utilized the reason, the memory, the intellect, the perspective, and the unique termperament of each writer of Scripture. I cannot explain this anymore than I can explain the union of two natures, God and man, in the person of our Lord Jesus Christ. I do know there is a divine and human element in the Bible, and I choose to express its nature by using the word *inerrant*.

I do not think we are dealing with a peripheral matter. We cannot forget that the inerrancy debate is, in fact, a debate about truth. Therefore, we are talking about foundations. A crisis over the Bible is unlike any other crisis.

Let's think of ourselves as occupants of an attractive building with many rooms, and in the rooms are various groups who might be wrangling over different issues. Although some would call these various disputes "crises," we are all in the same building and will remain so after the tussles and debates and hassles are over. Within the building, there is definitely unity. There is also diversity. Within the building, for example, the "general" and the "particular" Baptists are still identifiable among us, even though both groups are "dressed up" with new vocabularies. Within the building, we all seek to keep our distinctives intact, while giving ample room for the interpretation of Scripture. We have lived and will continue to live together in the same building and serve in His kingdom within given parameters. This has been our history. We have taken care to see that the building has always remained intact. But it must be understood that a debate about what the Bible is is different from a debate over interpretation or polity or program.

Now, while all this is going on, there is another group of folks who very subtly and very quietly have gone down to the basement and are hacking away at the very foundation of our building. Unless they are stopped, the whole building—rooms, walls, doors, windows—all of it will come crashing down. That is the inevitable result of an unresolved crisis over the inspiration and the authority of the Bible. We can never forget inerrancy has to do with our foundations. We are talking about *what the Bible is*.

The issue is not scaffolding, superstructure, or even the building. It is not theological minutia and no one is seeking to state a Baptist creed. "No creed but the Bible" is where we all stand. But to say that, it seems to me we have to decide what the Bible is. *The Baptist Faith and Message* says it clearly: ". . . truth without mixtue of error." The "Glorieta Statement" even improves on that statement, in my opinion.

But we need to understand clearly that the basic issue is that of the nature of Scripture. Is it primarily human or primarily divine? Those who emphasize man's ability to look beneath the fallible words of fallible men, hoping to discern the eternal truth of God, are errantists, not inerrantists. This approach, it seems to me, makes it impossible to guard Scripture as authoritative without question. What then becomes authoritative is not Scripture as it stands but Scripture as decided upon by a certain type of scholarship. In other words, human subjectivity becomes the methodology. Those who take this approach give lip service to the authority of Scripture, but their view of Scripture as having error contradicts their alleged acceptance of its authority. Such a contradiction negates the very authority they profess. Their treatment of the Bible as primarily a human book subject to historical and cosmological errors undermines the very foundations of our faith. If those historical facts and events are questioned, then so are the doctrines they teach. Once Adam and Eve are denied, then the fall of man

169

is questioned, and when the fall is denied, there is no reason for the cross.

Those in the neo-orthodox camp say that the debate over the Bible is small and petty. Using the analogy of the building, they would say this debate about inerrancy is only a little crack on an otherwise solid wall. But look closely. That crack is not superficial. It is actually a sign of a serious structural problem. The wall is cracked because it is not built on a sound foundation. The more we probe the differences between those who look at the Bible as being riddled with errors and those who subject themselves to an inerrant Bible, the deeper the cracks become. Finally, the surface cracks that were thought to be only minor are discovered to be evidence of deep fissures that run down to the very foundation, broadening as they go. J. I. Packer contends, "Nothing is gained just by trying to cement up the cracks. That would only encourage the collapse of the entire wall. Shammed unity is not worth working for. Real unity will come only as the sections of the wall rest on solid foundations."[2]

As the hymn writer said, "How firm a foundation, ye saints of the Lord, is laid for your faith in His excellent word." The psalmist asks, "When the foundations are being destroyed, what can the righteous do?" (Psalm 11:3)

Biblical inerrancy is not a dividing point. It is a rallying point. The high view of Scripture always rallies the brethren to new heights in evangelism and missions. I believe this with all my heart. Christianity is unique in that it is the only major religion in the world that has preachers. Judaism, Islam, Buddhism, and Hinduism have their rabbis, teachers, lecturers, and gurus, but preaching is uniquely Christian. Jesus came preaching! Something supernaturally happens when a man of God, under the power of the Holy Spirit, stands and preaches from a Bible that he knows is totally true. The thing that ties us together is a common experience of salvation through the Christ of the Bible. If we cannot agree that the written record of our faith is true, how can we go forward?

Without authority we will be like the Israelites who were described in the last verse of the book of Judges. "In those days there was no king (that is, authority) in Israel. Every man did that which was right in his own eyes." (Judges 21:25)

Without a sure word from God, the evangelical church will disintegrate just as the liberal church has. If evangelicals are being divided, it is by those who have departed from a high view and have embraced a low view of the Bible. They have emphasized the human at the expense of the divine. Errancy is the great divider. Inerrancy is the rallying point.

The Bible continues to be under attack. The greatest attack is from within the church, and it is very subtle. We all agree that the Bible is the Word of God and the only proper rule for faith and practice. There are those who maintain that it also contains errors.

The average Christian would just pass this by and say, "Well, when man's hand touches something, error is there. That's logical enough. A few errors here and there make no difference." Now, if a liberal denies the virgin birth, questions the miracles of Jesus, or even says that the Lord was only a man, most Christians recognize this for what it is: unbelief.

Someone might even use the right "catch" words, call himself an evangelical and preach or speak with a sense of unction, have a touch of poise, and maybe even a dose of piosity and say, "Sure, I believe the Bible. What difference does it make if there are a few errors in it? After all, the Bible is not a history book. It's not a science book, and it's there only to tell us about God and salvation." The uninitiated fail to see this as an attack on the Bible, and they have their belief undermined without even recognizing this first crack in the wall. When the Bible is established as a sure foundation for a life, a church, or a denomination, that sure foundation is a rallying point, not a dividing point.

Some believe that inerrancy reflects a lack of scholarship, and that only the unlettered could believe such a thing. In recent years, there has been a somewhat widely held impression that scientific investigation, archaeology, and linguisitic studies have disproved much of the Bible. Have biblical or secular scholars really uncovered errors that have been verified beyond a doubt? Nobody argues that there are problems in some places. There are many, many questions that are yet unanswered. Thank God we have wonderful Southern Baptist scholars in our universities and seminaries who are grappling in these areas. I applaud them, and I thank God for their erudition and their commitment. Virtually all of them are teaching at a great personal sacrifice and with a high sense of call.

I think these men, along with a host of other scholars who have studied the evidence, will join the rest of the evangelical world in rejoicing over the fact that instead of discrediting the Bible, modern scholarship increasingly supports its accuracy. It is not likely that all data will ever be in to totally verify inerrancy. But who knows?

Even a writer for *Time* magazine observed in a cover story, "After more than two centuries of facing the heaviest scientific guns that could be brought to bear, the Bible has survived—and is perhpas the better for the seige. Even on the critics' own terms—historical fact—the Scriptures seem more acceptable now than they did when the rationalists began the attack."[3] It is thrilling to me to see so many attacks on the truth of the Bible finally being laid to rest.

The question about inerrancy is not one of scholarship. Dr. Kantzer was right on target when he wrote, "Inerrrancy rests precisely where it has alawys rested: on the Lordship of Christ and His commision to the representatives, the prophets and the apostles. Just because it rests on Christ and Christ's authority, therefore, the question of inerrancy will remain a key doctrine of the evangelical church for as long as Christ is Lord. Evangelicals must remember however, that this basis must be set forth anew for every generation."[4]

Jesus taught that the Bible is reliable, and to all professing Christians, the authority of the Lord Jesus Christ is final. From Matthew to Revelation, the New Testament testifies to the deity of our Lord and Savior. All evangelicals agree on this point. Logically, then, whatever Jesus Christ believed about the truthfulness of Scripture must be accepted by every believer. Any objective examination of Christ's reference to the Old Testament makes it clear that He accepted as completely true some of the most difficult statements in the Hebrew Scripture pertaining to science and history. Let me say again, Adam and Eve were historical figures. There really was an ark and a great flood. Two million plus Israelites were fed with manna in the wilderness and Jonah was swallowed by a great fish. Why do I believe these historical facts are true? Because Jesus affirmed their historicity, and what Jesus affirmed, I affirm. Why? He is Lord! The question is not one of scholarship—it is one of Lordship. Gleason Archer states, "It is safe to say that in no recorded utterance of Jesus Himself, or any of His inspired apostles, is there the slightest suggestion that inaccuracy in matters of history or science ever occurs in the Old Testament."[5]

Do you remember what Jesus said in matthew 5:18? "Until heaven and earth disappear, not the smallest letter, not the least stroke of a pen will by any means disappear from the earth until everything is accomplished." In John 10:35 he reiterated, "The Scripture cannot be broken," and in Matthew 24:35, "Heaven and earth will pass away, but my words will never pass away."

The old adage is still true, my brethren. "If Jesus is Lord at all, He is Lord of all." Is it possible to believe the oldest of confessions, "Jesus is Lord," and to have a low view of Scripture? To proclaim His Lordship means to believe Him and to follow Him in all he says, including—and perhaps I would add, especially including—His teachings about the Bible. Jesus asked, "Why do you call me Lord, Lord and do not do what I say?" (Luke 6:46).

In the middle of this century a battle over the Bible was raging in America. Those who objected to inerrancy often used the following analogy to illustrate the error or the humanness of the Scriptures.

"As light that passes through the colored glass of a cathedral window, is light from heaven, but it is stained by the tints of the glass through which it passes, so any word of God which is passed through the mind and soul of a man must come out discolored by the personality through which it is given, and just to that degree ceases to be the pure Word of God."

Now that analogy might make sense after a cursory reading. It appeals to our rational minds. But, wait! Even in the natural world, light is unstainable and incorruptible. Light cannot be defiled by any medium through which it passes. Light is never made less pure, either by what it passes through or what passes through it. Light is not susceptible to contamination, either by infection or contagion. Whether it is sunlight, moonlight, starlight or lamplight; whether it is instense or pale, light is always nothing but light. So it is with the light of God. "Thy word is a lamp unto my feet and a light unto my path." (Psalm 119:105)

Just as it is incorrect to say that light which passes through colored glass is stained, it is also incorrect to say that God's Word is discolored or stained by the personalities through which it was transmitted.

If colored glass can be designed by an architect for the specific purpose of transmitting the light that floods a cathedral with exactly the tone and quality that is needed, certainly God's light which passes through men who have been molded by Him to record His Word floods the world with exactly the tone and quality He intended.

Inerrancy is not a peripheral matter. It has to do with the foundation. Inerrancy is not a dividing point. It is a rallying point. Inerrancy is not a question of scholarship. It is, it always has been, and it always will be a question of Lordship.

Notes

1. "Evangelicals and the Inerrancy Question," *Christianity Today,* April 29, 1978. Kenneth S. Kantzer, p. 20.

2. *"Fundamentalism" and the Word of God; Some Evangelical Principles.* J. I. Packer, p. 45.

3. *Time Magazine.* December, 1984.

4. "Evangelism and the Inerrancy Question." *Christianity Today.* Kenneth S. Kantzer, p. 19.

5. *Encyclopedia of Bible Difficulties.* Gleason L. Archer, p. 22.

9

PROBLEM AREAS RELATED TO BIBLICAL INERRANCY

Millard J. Erickson

In dealing with the topic of problems with inerrancy, I wish to make a basic division of the topic into two parts. The first is the problems which a doctrine of inerrancy must face. These constitute the agenda of unfinished business, the unresolved difficulties, which must be dealt with to maintain the doctrine of inerrancy. The other area relates to the dangers which may attach to a view of inerrancy. Here we are talking about the misconceptions or misinterpretations which may erroneously cause problems for the church.

I need to make two preliminary observations about the basis of the doctrine of biblical inerrancy. I do not believe that this view is taught explicitly in the Bible. It is, however, an inference from the teachings of the biblical writers about the Scripture and the way they treated the sacred writings which they had in their time. It is not merely a deduction from the nature of God, or what we think he must have done. In this respect, inerrancy is like the doctrine of the trinity, which, while not taught explicitly in the Bible, is a valid inference from a number of Bible texts.

The doctrine of Scripture is, according to my view, not based primarily upon an inductive examination of the phenomena of Scripture. I suggest here that the same method is to be followed in constructing this doctrine as in dealing with other doctrines, where primacy is given to the biblical teaching, rather than the phenomena.[1] So, for example, in the doctrine of sanctification, we use the biblical teachings on the subject to interpret the data from the study of the psychology of religious experience, rather than vice versa. In Christology, we settle the question of Jesus' sinlessness by giving greater weight to plain statements such as Hebrews 4:15, rather than to incidents from his life, such as the cursing of the fig tree (Matthew 21:19). In each area, we will use the phenomena to understand better what the teaching does or does not mean, but we give primary attention to God's explanation of what he has done, rather than our own understanding of it.

I also do not understand the doctrine of inerrancy to be a late development of Christian thought. While the issues clustering around this doctrine have been much more thoroughly delineated in the past 100 years than was true earlier in the history of the church, this is by no means a late creation. Statements by Augustine, Luther, Calvin, and others indicate a commitment to the full truthfulness of the Bible on the part of these classical theologians.[2]

175

Problems for Inerrancy

While the belief in inerrancy is primarily derived from the doctrinal teachings of the Bible or from inferences drawn from those rather than an induction of the phenomena, it must at some point correlate with the data if it is to be maintained.

The Problem of the Text

The value of an inerrant original is directly dependent upon the degree to which we actually have that text. We can speak of the "derivative inspiration" and "derivative inerrancy" of the text as we now have it, but unless we believe in some very powerful providential working of the Holy Spirit in relationship to the later copists who transmitted the text, we must settle for some such concept. The aim, then, of textual criticism, is to reduce as much as possible the gap between the text produced by the biblical authors under the inspiration of the Holy Spirit, and thus inerrant, and the text which we have before us.

The idea of inerrant autographs has been the object of a considerable amount of scorn, usually along the lines that "no one has ever seen the infallible originals." It should be noted, however, as Carl Henry has remarked, that no one has seen the fallible originals, either.[3] In reality, we are not faced with as severe a difficulty as is sometimes thought. The number of texts where variations among the manuscripts are signficiant is very small.

The problem here is not unique to the study of the Scripture. Science is always engaged in a closer approximation to its object. Its results are only as exact as the measuring devices which it employs. The weight of a sample is an approximation to the true weight, and actually is probably the average of the readings on several weighings. It is an average of several erroneous readings. The fact that the figure cited is only an approximation does not preclude the belief that the same actually has a definite weight.

The Problem of Lexical Research

The efficacy of the doctrine of biblical inerrancy depends upon knowing the meaning of the text, once we have determined the reading of that text. I recall my first Old Testament professor commenting on a footnote in an English translation which said, "The Hebrew is obscure," by saying, "The Hebrew is not obscure. We know exactly what the reading should be at that point. The problem is that the English is obscure. We don't know what words to use to translate the Hebrew, because we don't know the meaning of the Hebrew." The need is for further lexical work, in many cases. This might remove some of the difficulty which is posed for the belief in inerrancy.

Some real progress has been made in some of these areas in the past. The discovery of the Greek papyri was of particular help. These documents written in the common language of the time, dealt with many varied subjects, even including grocery lists in some cases. They have, however, supplied us with insights into the meaning of the Greek words which we would not otherwise have had.

One problem issue that has been alleviated is the question of the manner of Judas' death. Did he hang himself, as Matthew 27:5 asserts, or did he fall headlong, as Acts 1:18 would seem to say? The papyri gives us some help at this point, as we now learn that an alternative rendering of *prenes* in Acts 1:18, is "swelling up." Since swelling up as a result of the degeneration of the visceral organs would be the normal occurrence some hours and days after death, a much less difficult harmonization of the two passages now presents itself. I would theorize that what may well have happened was that Judas hanged himself, was not discovered for some time, so that he swelled up and his bowels gushed forth. There are probably a number of problem issues that could be resolved with better understanding of the lexical considerations. In the case of the Old Testament Hebrew, increased study of the cognate languages may produce this result.

The Problem of Definition of Error

A third major area is the need to offer a more precise specification of just what constitutes an error. Inerrantists have not always been as explicit in this matter as might be wished. Sometimes here has been what one of my doctoral professors, Eliseo Vivas of Northwestern University, termed, "the infinite coefficient of elasticity of words." A word can be stretched to cover more and more. The same idea was put in negative terms by Antony Flew, who spoke of a fine brash hypothesis "being killed in inches, by the death by a thousand qualifications."[4] Another of my doctoral professors, William Hordern, characterized the view of what he termed the "new conservatives" as "The Bible is inerrant, but of course this does not mean that it is without errors."[5]

Back in the heyday of the philosophical movement known as Logical Positivism, the leaders of that group insisted that the meaning of a synthetic statement (one in which the predicate contains something not found in the subject) is the set of sense data that would verify or falsify the proposition. We now recognize that this was too narrow a conception of meaning, restricting it to the realm of sense perception. Nonetheless, there was a basically valid point in all of this. It was that for something to count in favor of the truth of a proposition, there must also be something that counts against it, or counts for its falsity. If this is not the case, then we quite possibly are dealing with a meaningless statement, one that is compatible with almost any state of affairs. Then it becomes merely a label for "whatever is the case."

In actual practice, what frequently happens is equivocation upon the meaning of the word "inerrancy." There is both a narrow and a broad sense of the word. We might term these, respectively I_1 and I_2. I_1 deals with a very specific and precise type of meaning suggesting accuracy of a rather detailed sort. I_2, on the other hand, refers to a rather general type of meaning, in which detailed objections do not always present a real hindrance to maintenance of the view. Some inerrantists seem to hold to both views. In practice, they appear to be asserting something as bold as I_1. When pressed with difficulties, however, they defend I_2. But evidence for I_2 does not necessarily establish I_1.

It is important that inerrantists be prepared to state under what circumstances they would feel compelled to surrender the doctrine of biblical inerrancy. To put it more specifically, just what would cause us to acknowledge the presence of an error?

Note, however, that what we are talking about here is an "in principle" verification or falsification. The Logical Positivists did not insist that one actually be physically able to gather the pertinent data. The statement, "the other side of the moon is made of green cheese" was meaningful even before space travel made possible observation of the backside of the moon. Similarly, some data not currently available to us might clearly determine whether a given problem is an instance of an error, but for purposes of the issue of meaning, it is only necessary to be able to specify what sort of evidence that would be, not actually to have that evidence to inspect. It is important that in arguing for inerrancy this not be done at too great a cost, so that the doctrine is established, but is a meaningless doctrine.

The Problem of Parallel Accounts

The most obvious place where there are parallel accounts is in the synoptic gospels. One other place, however, is the historical books of Samuel, Kings, and Chronicles. There are, in addition, some parallels between poetic and prophetic books on the one hand and historical books, on the other.

The difficulties are of two kinds. One is the order or sequence of events, which may differ greatly from one account to the other. Here, at least in the synoptic gospels, there is less difficulty than was once thought to be the case, because we now recognize that it was not always the intention of the writer to give a chronological sequence. In many cases, material was grouped topically. Thus, for example, many scholars would hold that not everything included in Matthew's account of the Sermon on the Mount was spoken by Jesus on that occasion. Rather, according to this view, what Matthew did was to gather into this discourse sayings given by Jesus on more than one occasion.

More vexing, however, are the places were two accounts refer to the same matter, but in different fashion. These examples are numerous: did Jesus say "take a staff" or "don't take a staff?" Did the centurion speak to Jesus face to face or did he not? While much progress has been made at reconciling these differences, there are still problem passages which require continued attention.

Problems of Chronology

One frequently raised problem is the length of stay of the people of Israel in Egypt. Perhaps the most vexing one pertains to the reign of Pekah, who is reported to have reigned for twenty years, whereas dating of the reigns of his predecessor and successor only allow eight years for his reign. Edwin R. Thiele did a monumental work on the chronology of the kings of Israel and Judah and succeeded in unravelling the puzzles of virtually all of the other kings.[6] In this one case, however, the solution seems to be very difficult to determine. Since the other dates can be seen to be very accurate when understood in light of the two methods of reckoning, namely accession-year and nonaccession-year dating, it does appear that some historical accuracy was intended for the listing as a whole. It will not do, therefore, to regard this as a case in which more general references were intended.

The Problem of the Use of Non-Canonical Sources by Canonical Writers

This can be seen especially in two references by Jude. In verse 9, he cites the archangel Michael who, "contending with the devil, disputed about the body of Moses, he did not presume to pronounce a reviling judgment upon him, but said, 'The Lord rebuke you.'" This is not a quotation from any biblical book but according to tradition is a portion of the apocryphal Assumption of Moses which has been lost in the transmission of the book. In verse 14, Jude quotes from the pseudepigraphal book, I Enoch 1:9. The particular reference Jude makes is to Enoch as "in the seventh generation from Adam." He regards this as a prophecy which is being fulfilled in his time.

The problem with these quotations is that they seem to be made in just the same fashion as those from canonical books. If the presence of such quotations is regarded as establishing the inspiration and consequent authority of those latter books, then what is to be thought of these non-canonical works? Are we not forced either to abandon the argument for the authority of the Old Testament books on the basis of being quoted by canonical New Testament authors, or else to extend that same imputation of authority to these apocryphal books? Unless some credible basis is given for distinguishing the one type of quotation from the other, we either must conclude that too much or too little has been proved.

The Problem of Scientific Type Scripture References

A more general designation would be those elements in Scripture relating to other non-biblical or non-theological disciplines. This includes the secular disciplines of history and archaeology, where there has sometimes appeared to be conflict between Scripture and the record found in non-biblical historical records. It also has been focused to a considerable extent upon the "science and Scripture" issues, especially the relationship of Scripture to biological evolution, geology, and anthropology. Currently, however, the focus is not so much upon natural science as upon the various social sciences. This takes several forms. It may be in terms of the descriptive, where the Bible assumes divine causation or human freedom and consequent responsibility, whereas behavioral science may assert that these occurrences are determined by psychological or other forms of conditioning. It may also come in terms of the prescriptive, where the Bible may command types of behavior which behavioral science may claim to be detrimental, such as certain guilt-inducing teachings. Much more work still needs to be done in many of these areas.

Problems of Ethics

Some ethical teachings in the Bible appear at least to some persons to conflict with fairly widely accepted norms. At other times the Bible seems to report actions done or commanded by God that conflict with teachings that he has given to human beings.

One primary instance is those Old Testament passages where God commanded the slaughter of large numbers of persons, such as the neighboring nations surrounding Israel as they sought to enter the promised land. This seems to conflict with the prohibition of killing, as spelled out in Genesis 9:6 and elsewhere. Another is the apparent practice of lying by Rahab in Joshua 2:3-7, which seems to conflict with the commandment prohibiting bearing false witness against one's neighbor in Exodus 20:16. What further complicates this is that Rahab is commended for her part in God's redemptive working in Hebrews 11:13.

The difficulty here is not only with the relationship of these actions or commands to more generally accepted ethical standards and practices but also with the relationship between what God requires of us and what he himself does and condones. It is customary to relate ethical norms to the nature and the command of God. If, however, what he does is in conflict with what he expects from us, then we have a crisis in meaning. It is difficult to determine just what is good and right. There would appear to be no univocal meaning of such terms. Ethical discourse and discussion tends to break down under circumstances of this type.

Conclusion

In giving this brief survey of some of the problem areas which inerrantists must deal with, we should not overlook the progress that has occurred and continues to occur in resolving the difficulties. The work of archaeology has contributed to this. More careful analytical work on the definition of ethical terms and issues will help in other matters.

Rahab's telling of an untruth, for example, must be seen in view of the fact that not every species of untruth is lying. Lying is failure to give the truth to someone to whom the truth is due, and thus is immoral. There are, however, other species of untruth, including jokes, fairy tales, and more pertinently, ruses of war and trick plays in sports. These are social situations in which different rules apply than in a court testimony. One's enemy in war, or one's opponent in an athletic contest, is not someone to whom the truth is owed. Rahab's act and God's apparent use of it should probably be evaluated in the light of these considerations.

While there are still tensions for the holding of the doctrine of inerrancy, there is less basis for abandoning the doctrine now than there was one hundred years ago. One must always ask what is the alternative to any view. To abandon belief in biblical inerrancy is to entangle oneself in serious epistemological difficulties. If the fact that the Bible affirms a statement does not guarantee its truth, we may need to find an independent basis for tenets of our faith. We may hold to the truth of those biblical statements which are subject neither to verification nor falsification, while abandoning some which we believe have been disproved on empirical grounds. We must ask, however, what is the basis of this former belief. It would then appear to be a variation of a statement by one of Mark Twain's characters, Tom Sawyer, I believe, that "faith is believing what you know ain't so." Here faith would be, "believing what you don't know ain't so."

Problems Resulting from Misunderstandings of Inerrancy

We have noted the difficulties with which adherents of the doctrine of biblical inerrancy must deal. We wish now to observe some of the distortions to which it may be subjected, and the consequences resulting therefrom.

Overlooking the Variety of Materials in Scripture

Inerrancy, properly speaking, refers to a quality of statements which can be treated as being true or false. In other words, it applies to indicative sentences. Yet, there are many other types of sentences in the Bible. We will need to be certain that we do not overlook them and the imporatnt role which they play in our faith. Some of these types of sentences are the following:

1. *Interrogatives.* "Can we find anyone like this man, one in whom is the spirit of God?" was the question put by Pharoah to his officials (Gen. 41:36). As a question, it does not really admit of the question, true or false, and therefore cannot be considered to be either inerranct or errant. It simply is neither. In actuality, the statement to which the issue of inerrancy applies is the larger statement, "So Pharoah asked them 'Can we find anyone like this man, one in whom is the spirit of God?'" Less obvious, however, is a passage that is expressive in nature, such as Psalm 42:5, "Why are you downcast, O my soul? Why so disturbed within me?" Here the author is making a first person statement, rather than reporting what someone has said. The inerrant proposition would have to be something like, "The psalmist actually said this," or, "the psalmist actually felt this." In so doing, however, we are focusing our own attention away from the primary purpose of the passage, which is the expressive or even emotive nature of what the psalmist was feeling. The aim of the passage is not so much to inform us about the inner state of the psalmist as it is evoke from us the similar feeling, to enable us empathetically to experience what he (or she) was experiencing.

2. *Exclamations.* The same is true of some statements that seem on the surface to be simply declarative statements. These include statements about the goodness and faithfulness of God. These are indeed telling about the nature of God. More than that, however, they are expressing value judgments about the worth of God, as this is felt by the psalmist. They indicate that his knowledge of God had proceeded beyond cognition or recognition to valuing with consequent action based upon that estimation.

If we treat these exclamations simply in terms of their truth and falsity, we will miss much of the real significance of these expressions. They are both subjective and objective at the same time, and they accomplish God's full purpose only when they are the means by which we also enter into such an expeience.

3. *Imperatives*. Despite the considerable emphasis in recent years upon the indicative rather than the imperative mood with respect to Christian living, the Bible contains a large number of imperatives, both positive and negative (prohibitions). The Old Testament law and prophets are prominent examples. Jesus' Sermon on the Mount and other teachings call for a particular type of action. The writings of Paul and the other epistolary authors abound in directives regarding Christian action.

With action commands such as these, the appropriate response is not, "Is it true?" but "Is it binding upon me?" The reader is not so much called upon the believe the truth of the statement as to act in accordance with the prescribed behavior.

4. *Wishes*. These are frequently expressed in the subjunctive mood. They reflect the hope, the longing, the wish, of the person expressing them. Again, they are not the type of statement that is subject to verficiation, to true-false type considerations.

5. *Prayers*. A considerable amount of material in the Bible is prayers. Moses' intercession for his people (Exodus 32:32), Jesus' high priestly prayer (John 17), Paul's prayer for the Ephesians (Ephesians 3:14-20), are examples of these. Inerrancy merely tells us that these people indeed prayed such prayers. The significance of the prayer goes far beyond that.

6. *Exhortations*. These are milder invitations to action than are imperatives, because the author or speaker may not possess a relationship of authority sufficient to enable him to require compliance. It is, however, a request for the desired action, or an offer of benefits of which the speaker desires the hearer to avail himself or herself.

We are not depreciating the value of the doctrine of inerrancy in guaranteeing to us that these words were truly what the person to whom they are attributed spoke, wrote, thought, or felt. What we must be concerned about, however, is that we do not simply stop with the assurance that we have a faithful report of the message, but rather, that we go on to respond to the message in a fashion appropriate to the function which it serves, which was God's intention in giving it to us.

Failure to See the Statement in its Cultural Context

The various portions of the Bible were written at specific times and places, and in many cases to particular individuals or groups. This fact is not nullified or modified by our inability in some cases to identify and specify those circumstances and details. To be properly understood, they must be seen and interpreted in the light of that fact. Belief in inerrancy may cause us to forget that. Because we have assurance that we have a message whose truthfulness is guaranteed, we may too quickly make the transition from the statement as it is to our own situation.

In some cases this is not likely to happen, since the statement has no immediate meaning in our context which we are therefore liable to confuse with the biblical statements. We do not attempt to apply literally the statements about the Urim and Thummin, for example, since we do not have such today nor do we even understand with certainty just what the objects were like. Nor do we struggle with passages such as Jesus' statement, "Take a staff" or "Don't take a staff," although we have a rather accurate understanding of what staffs are like. We may be concerned over how to reconcile the apparently contradictory statements, as threatening to the doctrine of biblical inerrancy. We do not, however, engage in soul-searching as to whether we should bear such an instrument. We recognize the cultural difference between our situation and that in which the command was first given. The problem is more aggravated, however, when we ask about whether Jesus' command to turn the other cheek requires us to be pacifists, or whether we should exclude women from speaking in church because Paul forbade it. Because the situations appear to be the same, we may tend to make the transfer from one to the other without doing the hard work of asking whether they really are the same in the significant dimensions involved.

Here we encounter a problem with a largely lay-oriented approach to the Bible. As Baptists, we have stressed the authority of the Bible and the priesthood of the believer. Together these produced an important emphasis upon each person reading and studying the Bible for him/herself. This reading was largely devotional in nature, in which the reader sought to make immediate application of the material being read. But in so doing, the "obvious meaning" or face value rendering frequently was followed, without asking whether this was what the meaning today would be, or whether it might actually mean the exact opposite.

In this concern, we want to be careful to avoid creating a new priesthood, the exegete who alone is capable of understanding the Bible and upon whose every word of wisdom the lay person must wait. It would seem strange indeed if a God who removed the human intermediary from the reception of grace, would require a human intermediary for people to understand just how that grace is to be received. Thus, if the real meaning of the most basic concepts of belief is somehow radically different from the apparent meaning, there is a serious problem. If, however, this is extended to the point where the apparent surface meaning of passages can be taken and applied without asking what was really being said, we have serious problems.

Extending the Range of the Bible's Statements

It is good to believe that the Bible is truthful and authoritative on every subject on which it teaches. There is a tendency, however, to expand the domain of authoritativeness by maintaining that the Bible teaches on every subject which it mentions, or even beyond that, to subjects that it does not address. If we do this, we will find ourselves in rather considerable difficulty. Since the Bible is divinely inspired, there is a tendency to treat it as omniscient as well.

I recall one period during my first pastorate when I frequently drove back to our parsonage at the same time each evening. I would listen to a certain well-known radio broadcaster give his nightly program, which took the form of a commentary on the events in the news. At this particular time a major steel strike was in progress, and this radio personage would relate each day's developments in the strke to some portion of Scripture. I remember thinking, "Either

183

this must be the most important year in the history of the world—or our Bible should be much larger than it currently is." We have probably all heard messages of this type in which the speaker finds specific prophetic reference in the Bible to such modern devices as airplanes (Isaiah 31:5) or television (Revelation 11:3-12). In some cases, relatively little direct harm is done to the lives of believers, other than their time being wasted, and the church coming under ridicule. When these interpretations of Scripture are made normative for action, however, problems result. I know of one Baptist congregation that planned the construction of a new church bulding. The membership was attempting to choose between two proposed plans which differed in the amount of seating in the sanctuary. One member suggested the solution, when he discovered that the relationship between the seating capacity of the smaller plan to that of the larger plan was directly proportional to that between the number of times that King Jehoash struck the ground (II Kings 13:18-19) and the number of times that he was told he should have struck it.

Identifying Inerrancy and Interpretation

When Protestants have emphasized the inerrancy of the Bible, Roman Catholics have sometimes agreed but insisted that the argument was incomplete. If we have the truth objectively present, we still have the problem of understanding it. Otherwise, the message of the inerrant Bible may become corrupted by a fallible and erring interpreter. Consequently, the infallibility of the pope was the completion of the principle of biblical authority.

Some of us solve the problem, however, by creating a large one. We identify our interpretation of the Bible with its meaning. We, therefore, are prone to become more dogmatic about our views than we otherwise would be, because thinking them to be the meaning of Scripture, we conclude that they cannot be in error since the Bible is inerrant. Thus is lost the type of dialogue that might expose us to differing views, and hopefully to more accurate views.

Conversely, we may limit the extent of the inerrant word to our understanding. Sometimes we who hold to inerrancy may fall into an error similar to that of those liberals who held that the Bible was inspired because it was inspiring. Similarly, the locus of inerrancy may come to be the significance which the passage has for us or the application which the Holy Spirit makes to our lives of that truth, whereas it may be much more basic and capable of many more applications than that which we have made of it.

Overzealous Attempts to Demonstrate the Inerrancy of Scripture

There are some inerrantists whom I call "harmonists." Their intention is a commendable one. They attempt to remove the problems from the doctrine of inerrancy by solving the difficulties. This is especially the case where there are apparently conflicts between passages of Scripture that relate to the same issue. Some examples of these are where Cain got his wife (i.e., was his marriage incestuous?), whether Joseph was sold to the Ishmaelites or the Midianites, whether Jesus commanded the disciples to take staff or not to a

184

take a staff on one particular occasion, whether the people of Israel spent 215 or 430 years of bondage in Egypt, and the like. The harmonistic school believes that the doctrine of inerrancy requires us to answer these questions, and to do so now with the data currently available to us.[7]

In so doing, however, speculation often results. If the assumption is that we must actually see that the Bible is inerrant in this particular case, then we must assume that the explanation that will best relieve the tension is the best one, whether it best fits the data or not.

This endeavor frequently results in a new kind of speculative source criticism, not greatly unlike that of a hundred years ago. It does this by positing multiple tellings of the same story by Jesus in different settings. To be sure, this device draws upon the phenomenon, well known to all of us who do itinerant speaking, of repeating ermons. One colleague of mine referred to this phenomenon as "homiletical Darwinism," the survival of the fittest sermons, whereas the less effective ones died out after one telling. No doubt Jesus did not decline to retell a parable simply becuse he had once used it before at the other end of Palestine. But to construct such multiple tellings simply to remove the apparent contradiction can be a type of *deus ex machina*, especially where the other cirumstantces in the parallel accounts suggest that we are dealing with the same instance and incident. It becomes subject to the same criticism as was the older source criticism, that it violates the Law of Ockham's Razor, or as it is known in more scientific circles, the Law of Parsimony. It would probably be better in some of these cases simply to say, "We do not know the answer to the problem; perhaps we will never know the answer to the difficulty. But we rest confidently in the belief that the meaning of the passage is authoritative, infallible, and inerrant, because of our doctrine of Scripture, and because of the progress we have made in the resolution of other difficulties."

In this connection, one of the difficulties comes not from confusing what subject is being dealt with, but the degree of specificity with which it is handled. One such question pertains to the dimensions of the sea described in II Chronicles 4:2. It is said to have been round and to have had a diameter of ten cubits and a circumference of thirty cubits. That would mean a circumference three times the diameter. But, as any student of mathematics knows, the circumference of a circle is pi times the diameter, and the value of pi is approximately 3.1416. Do we not have a difficulty here?

There is a difficulty only if we assume that this account is given with such specificity as to make such comparisons possible. That would be the case if the description were given us for the purpose of enabling us to construct a replica of the object. Then we would need to know whether to make it 30 cubits (or about 45 feet) in circumference, or to make it 10 cubits in diameter. That is not the purpose of the account, however. It does not matter whether we have such an object. Rather, it appears that the description was given simply to inform us of roughly the magnitude of the object. In that case, an approximation of the two dimensions and of the relationship between them will be sufficient, and pi is approximately three. We must, therefore, be careful to avoid making the Bible say things that it is not intended to say.

The Problem of Ignoring the Scripture

Belief in the inerrancy of the Bible can produce such a level of security and satisfaction that we neglect the study of what it actually says. The end result of this practice is that the Bible has no further effect than it would have if it were studied and acted upon but were not inerrant. In fact, it may have even less. The problem stems from a type of complacency or false security based upon the bare or sheer doctrinal belief. It is one version of what I call "the fallacy of neglecting the minor premise." One can conceive of exegetical argumentation in a sort of syllogistic fashion as follows:

> Everything taught in the Bible is true and inerrant.
> This is taught in the Bible.
> Therefore, this is true and inerrant.

Without spending the time to determine what the Bible teaches (the minor premise), however, the belief in inerrancy (the major premise) is of no value to us, for it will not give us the conclusion.

There are errors or heresies of belief, which differ from correct belief or orthodoxy and therefore are referred to as heterodoxy. Similarly, there are errors of action or living, which depart from orthopraxy and therefore should be termed heteropraxy. If disbelief in the truth of the Bible is heterodoxy, then failure to study the Bible and to obey it is heteropraxy.

A young man left for college for a year, and was given a new Bible by his father, a deeply orthodox believer. He was urged to read it every day and to be careful that no ungodly or liberal professor undercut his belief in the Bible. When he returned at the end of the school term, his father questioned him about his faith by asking him about his continued belief in a number of the miracle accounts. When he came to the story of Jonah, the son indicated that he no longered believed in the literal historicity of the report that Jonah had been swallowed by a large fish. His father was devastated. The son, however, asked the father to open his own Bible to the book of Jonah, and the father found those pages taped shut, as they had been since the son taped them shortly before leaving for school in the fall. The father believed in the historicity of those pages, but had not read them for nine months.

Oversimplication of Ethical Issues

Much has been written about the difficulty of applying biblical teachings to complex contemporary social issues.[8] There are many reasons why this is so, including the brevity of the Bible, the complexity of present-day life, and the large cultural gap present in many cases between the biblical culture and ours. One of these, however, is too fragmentary an induction of the relevant biblical material.

While the Bible does not speak explicity or directly about a large number of the situations we now face, it does contain a great many principles that have ethical relevance. The danger, however, is that we will discover one of these principles and then stop the process of inquiry at that point, thus overlooking other potential relevant principles.

186

One of these principles is the value and even sacredness of human life, as found in passages such as Genesis 9:6. I may simply stop at this point, assuming that the application of this principle forbids participation in war and capital punishment. Actually, however, there may be other pertinent principles, such as protection of the defenseless and a view of justice which requires that wrongful actions be punished. Or one may assume that the principles of divine sovereignty and providence mean that no exceptional action should be taken to treat illness, whereas such principles as the value of life and the good of alleviating suffering might argue otherwise. Every part of the Bible is inspired, inerrant, and authoritative. In terms of arriving at a normatively authoritative action directive for today, however, we do not use any part of Scripture in isolation from the other parts.

Neglect of the General Revelation

The high value placed upon the Word of God may lead us to overlook the fact that God has given us not one but two revelations of himself, a special and a general revelation or the message of his Word and that of his world. The Bible itself (the special revelation) tells us of this other, more general revelation in passages such as Psalm 19 and Romans 1. We overlook part of what God wants us to know, if we neglect his self-manifestation in the world, history, and human nature.

An example can be drawn in the realm of ethics. We may well conclude that because the body is the temple of God (I Corinthians 3:16) or the Holy Spirit, (I Corinthians 6:19) we must treat it with care. Anything done as a sin against the body is ultimately a sin against God. This appears to be the point of Paul's condemnation of relations with a prostitute. From this we may then conclude that what is harmful to our physical health is wrong or sinful. But the Bible, except for a few specific matters, does not tell us what is helpful and what is harmful to our health. For that we must turn to medicine and allied sciences.

What we have here is another case of neglect of the minor premise. This time the argument goes as follows:

> What is harmful to physical health is wrong.
> This practice is harmful to physical health.
> Therefore, this practice is wrong.

But God's revelation of the minor premise is frequently through his general revelation, not his special revelation. Respect for the latter must not be allowed obliterate the former.

Failure to Distinguish the Bible from the Subject of its Teaching

We must always bear in mind that the Bible is not an end in itself. It does not exist merely to bring people into a relationship with it. The aim of faith is not belief in the Bible, per se, but rather, belief in the God who has revealed himself in its pages, and inspired its writing.

If this distinction is not kept clearly in mind, we may find ourselves substituting the Bible for God. In this fashion, people do not obey the personal and living God, but rather, the words of Scripture, which may become rather legalistically treated. Or there may be a type of veneration for the Bible which should be reserved for the author and object of its teachings. If the Bible is regarded as having virtually automatic effect, then it is possible that we are attributing intrinsic powers to the book.

This is seen in some evangelistic efforts. The printing of Scripture on billboards, or on tracts which are handed out or left to be picked up, in the expectation that "the Word" will bring about faith may verge on such conceptions. This may also appear in certain devotional practices, where the mere reading of a certain amount of Scripture each day is thought to have a special effect. This may approximate a spiritual version of the old adage, "An apple a day keeps the doctor away." Here, the message seems to be, "A chapter a day keeps the devil away."

The "higher" the view of the Bible, the more its divine characteristics are emphasized to the neglect of the human elements, the greater is the tendency and temptation to treat the Bible as only God should be treated. One song that I never select for congregational singing is "Holy Bible, Book Divine." The problem is that the words of the song are directed to the Bible itself. This, it appears to me, is in effect an act of worship. As such, it would be idolatry. The Bible's value lies in bringing us into relationship with God and conveying God's message to us. This instrumental role, rather than serving as the object of faith and worship, constitutes the real value of the Bible.

The Danger of Using the Domino Argument

One argument sometimes used in defense of the doctrine of biblical inerrancy is that abandonment of the doctrine leads logically to abandonment of other doctrines. This may well be true. Most uses of the so-called domino argument are based upon a considerable amount of validity. One might note, parenthetically, that labelling a view rather than refuting it is more a rhetorical than a logical device.

The problem, however, is that in attempting to show people the seriousness of such a step as abandoning belief in inerrancy, we have sometimes pushed them in the opposite direction. Some sincere young people, wrestling with difficulties connected with Scripture, have been told by well-meaning Christians, "If you don't believe in the inerrancy of the Bible, you don't logically have the basis for believing in the deity of Christ." Instead of moving them back to belief in inerrancy, however, this type of argumentation has sometimes tragically forced the person into abandonment of belief in the deity of Christ and other major doctrines. While inerrancy is part of a consistent evangelicalism, logical consistency is not an essential for membership in the Kingdom of God. Better an inconsistent faith than a logically consistent unbelief. We need to exercise real care in the use of argumentation of this type.[9]

Unnecessary Fragmentation of the Body of Christ

Biblical doctrine is given us for edification, growth in understanding, encouragement, and many other practical values. It is not given to us in order to provoke controversy. Sometimes, however, the latter results. Paul explained the second coming of Christ and the resurrection of believers to the Thessalonians so that they would not sorrow and might comfort one another (I Thessalonians 4:13, 18). This doctrine has sometimes, however, been used to divide Christian brothers and sisters who differed on some minute point of its interpretation, and did so in an uncharitable fashion.

There are undoubtedly differences of opinion among us here about the exact meaning of inerrancy. We may and should seek to engage in courteous and respectful dialogue, attempting to persuade one another of our own convictions. To short-circuit this process, either by acrimonious debate or by withdrawing from the dialogue and from fellowship entirely, may prematurely and unnecessarily fragment the body of Christ, which surely grieves our Lord, in view of the biblical statement about the value of unity in that body (e.g., Psalm 133:1; Acts 4:32; I Corinthians 11:17-22; Ephesians 4:3-4, 13; Philippians 1:27; 4:2). It is sometimes said that inerrancy is the "watershed" of evangelicalism. We want to make certain that it does not also become the occasion of its bloodshed.

Despite the difficulties of maintaining belief in biblical inerrancy, and the dangers that may befall those who misunderstand or misapply it, this is a doctrine of great value, and the effort of dealing with the problem areas will be well rewarded.

Notes

1. For a fuller statement of my view on this matter, see my *Christian Theology* (Grand Rapids: Baker Book House, 1986), pp. 207-10.

2. *Ibid*, pp. 225-26.

3. Everett F. Harrison, "The Phenomena of Scripture," *Revelation and the Bible*, ed. Carl F. H. Henry (Grand Rapids: Baker Book House, 1958), p. 239.

4. Antony Flew, "Theology and Falsification" *New Essays in Philosophical Theology*, ed. Antony Flew and Alsadair MacIntyre (New York: The Macmillan Co., 1955), p. 97.

5. William Hordern, *New Directions in Theology Today, Volume I Introduction* (Philadelphia: Westminster Press, 1966), p. 83.

6. Edwin R. Thiele, *The Mysterious Numbers of the Hebrew Kings* (Chicago: University of Chicago Press, 1951; rev. ed Grand Rapids: Eerdmans, 1965).

7. Louis Gaussen, for example, explains the death of Judas by saying the death of Judas was by hanging himself *and* falling headlong. He likens it to a story of a man in Lyons who committed suicide by sitting on a fourth story window and shooting himself in the mouth. *The Inspiration of the Holy Scriptures* (Chicago: Moody Press, 1949), p. 215.

8. Kenneth S. Kantzer, "Problems Inerrancy Doesn't Solve," *Christianity Today*, Vol. 31. No. 3 (February 20, 1987), p. 14-15.

9. For a helpful discussion on this and related problems, see Michael Bauman, "Why the Noninerrantists are not Listening: Six Tactical Errors Evangelicals Commit," *Journal of the Evangelical Theological Society*, Vol. 29, No. 3 (September, 1986), pp. 317-24.

RESPONSE: Peter Rhea Jones

I am benefitting from this conference. Those of us who differ are beginning to talk to one another. Rick Melick, professor at Mid-America, and I met for the first time last night and hit it off and talked from 9:30 to 1:30 a.m. And I want to say he is a fine scholar and a devoted Christian.

I have thoroughly enjoyed my earlier reading of this distinguished paper and then the hearing of this stimulating address by Dean Erickson. The paper is particularly well organized, and Dr. Erickson has set out his perspective in a clear manner both with his preliminary observations, which I found extremely clarifying, and then his attention to detail, rather than merely theories and analogies. I am glad we have finally reached the stage of Biblical passages. I find in this paper an inerrantist who is facing the facts rather than denying the difficulties. I want to register as well that it is easier to find fault with an hypothesis than to fashion one of your own and then defend it.

Dr. Erickson is a theologian. I want to take this public opportunity to commend Erickson's own published systematic theology.[1] I find the reading of it to be of great profit. Simply to look at the footnotes is to see how widely he has read. To read his theology is to discover how openminded he is to truth from any quarter, how measured and careful his own judgments, and how conservative his bottom line. His theological chapters make excellent background reading for sermons on doctrinal subjects.

I for my part spent many years working primarily in Biblical studies where the *inductive* method is very natural. I worked in what I like to call the basement of the temple. I was like a miner digging up raw materials. I was then and am now commmitted to the scripture principle as the foundation for systematic theology. I understand that, to follow my analogy of the temple, theologians are assigned a lofty post on or near the steeple of the temple. All a theologian has to know is everything and then to put it together coherently with a good strong Biblical base! Nowadays I serve as paster of a local church, so I enjoy standing in the sanctuary of the temple preaching. It was primarily exegesis before. My exegetical hero above all is Adolf Schlatter. Now it is primarily exposition. My expository hero is Alexander Maclaren. I have not forgotten the dedication and the hard work and the low salaries of the miners in the basement and the theologians on the roof.

In the first of Dean Erickson's two preliminary observations he admits his own opinion that the theory of inerrancy is not taught explicitly in the Bible. Nevertheless, he is prepared to defend inerrancy as Biblical in the sense of being an inference from the Biblical writers. He does not base his theory of inerrancy on the nature of God argument, which is necessarily more *a priori*. His second preliminary observation involves a major procedural approach for

190

building a Biblical theology. He gives priority to the doctrinal text as it relates to a given subject rather than to the actual phenomena of scripture. He instances Christology where we settle the question of the sinlessness of our Lord by a doctrinal text such as Hebrews 4:15 rather than by incidents in the life of Jesus such as the cursing of the fig tree. It is precisely at this point that I must begin to state some personal tension with this thesis, though not a rejection of it. To quibble first. Surely the Christian belief in the sinlessness of Jesus must not and cannot be supported merely by the doctrinal statements. Indeed, the belief must be related to the actual life of Jesus. Therefore, we must face such issues as the reason for his baptism, the nature of his temptations, his struggle in Gethsemane, his cleansing of the temple, and the cursing of the fig tree. It is my own judgment, as it is likely also of Dr. Erickson, that such a testing still results in a positive doctrine of the sinlessness of Jesus. Doctrinal statements though primarily must be supported by the phenomena.

Dr. Erickson's recommended procedure did remind me of a modest hermeneutical proposal of my own that I made in a graduate school paper years ago. I argued not very differently that the text that spoke directly to a theme should provide the direction for building New Testatment theology. It is possible that this approach has the danger of elevating certain portions of scripture to a higher role than others and could be too neat and rationalistic, but I confess that it does have appeal to me as well. It would further seem to me that Dr. Erickson's theory as applied could raise some embarrassing problems. At least I. Howard Marshall believes that some denominations have not appointed leaders called *bishops* in spite of a doctrinal passage like Titus 1:5-9.[2] What do we do if scripture differs with tradition and the tradition happens to be our own? As a Baptist I squirm.

I further call attention to what I would name a *logical strain* or circumstantial problem, though not a contradiction. Dean Erickson insists upon making the doctrinal text primary in his second observation, but in his first observation he admits there is no explicit doctrinal text for inerrancy. It must be inferred. He seems prepared to draw the doctrine of inerrancy from inferences but not willing to accept inferences from the phenomena. In his fuller statement in his theology[3] he does indicate that both the didactic text and the phenomena should be integrated, and later in his paper as well, but he rejects the fully inductive approach of someone like Dewey Beegle. Professor Ericson has far too much academic integrity to claim that of which he was not convinced. Had he found a text acceptable to him as teaching inerrancy explicitly, his case would have been easier logically. (What a tragedy if we split a great denomination over a word not in the Bible.)

I will follow now the two large sections of Dr. Erickson's paper but without an attempt in the time available to dialogue with all of his points. His first section outlines some of the *difficulties* for inerrancy. He raises the issue of the autographs as the very first problem because quite appropriately he takes up the problem of the original texts first. Let us be measured in response to this sensitive issue by making only two points. First of all, surely Clark Pinnock is right that II Timothy 3:16 affirms the plenary profitability of the scriptures, but Paul "does not present a theory about a perfect Bible given long ago but now lost, but declares the Bible in Timothy's possession to be alive with the breath of God and full of the transforming informa. . . ."[4] The Bible we have is inspired and trustworthy. However, possession of the authographs would surely solve at least some textual problems. I cannot think of a textual critic from a theological persuasion as different as Boers or Greenlee and Bruce Metzger who would not revel in the original of Luke's gospel and turn rapidly to the 23rd chapter to see if the 34th verse were present! Some current difficulties such as minor transcriptioinal problems might well be dispelled by possission of the autographs, such as whether to take a staff on mission, but wholesale appeal to the autographs is simply not convincing. Rather, hard work and research and exegesis are required. I can imagine devoted textual critics sitting in their assigned study carrel in the celestial library, where A. T. Robertson must already be working, studying the autographs available on the reserved reading list!

Secondly, I would single out the issue of *semantics*. Dr. Erickson faces the issue which hangs over this conference: *what constitutes an error?* In particular, is inexactness error? One of the reasons we differ with one another and have difficulty in communication is precisely because implicitly we are working with different concepts of error. Erickson does not beat around the bush about the fluidity in the use of the work inerrancy and indeed the presence of a certain equivocation. I suppose it is fair to say that the definition of error should correspond with the definition of inerrancy, but some inerrantists lessen the problems and difficulties at the expense of broadening the definition. The word inerrancy on the surface appears to be a rather absolute word, and certainly most laymen, when they hear the word inerrant advocated have no idea that the speaker may personally subscribe to a long list of exceptions. Howard Marshall, a conservative scholar himself, notes that the word inerrancy requires so much qualification that it is "in danger of dying the death of a thousand qualifications."[5] The advent of the category "limited inerrancy" is particularly perplexing semantically, though it appears to me that nearly every defender of inerrancy is actually somewhere on the spectrum of limited inerrancy. The thirteenth article in the Chicago Statement on Biblical Inerrancy is by its presence and scope an admission of some form of limited inerrancy. I personally could accept some form of limited inerrancy, but one wonders with Stephen Davis if we are not now dealing with a contradictory term.[6] The perspectives, however, of Bloesch, Pinnock, and Erickson are very attractive.

Dr. Erickson himself, who sees the doctrine of inerrancy as "the completion of the doctrine of scripture," offers a definition of inerrancy in his *Christian Theology* as follows:

> The Bible, when correctly interpreted in the light of the level to which culture
> and the means of communication had developed at the time it was written,
> and in view of the purposes for which it was given, is fully truthful in all that it
> affirms.[7]

What I understand is that Dr. Erickson is attempting to define inerrancy in terms of Biblical intentions rather than modern precision. We can recognize an integrity in his perspective and genuine consistency, and I have no difficulty with an inerrancy of this kind. In any event, it is my contention that your view of inspiration must correspond with the actual character of scripture.

In leaving the topic of definition and moving to the isssue of phenomena I tarry to register a memory. I was studying at Tyndale House Library at Cambridge, England, in the mid-seventies when Dr. Clark Pinnock published his article on limited inerrancy. I can still recall the tempest and the furor. Our coffee times that we called "elevenses"' and the English teatime in the afternoon became times for spirited debate. Though the feelings ran high, looking back I can see that it was an educational experience for scholars on break.

Dr. Erickson also faces the problem of difference in parallel accounts straight away. So he calls our attention to difficulties in the synoptic gospels and in the Old Testament historical books of Samuel, Kings, and Chronicles. If the rest of us want an independent opinion on this subject it will cost us as it has Dr. Erickson. Unless we are simple going to accept the opinion of admired professors and respected pastors, we must work on the issue directly by studying the Bible. Study comparatively the four Gospels in a parallel or harmony, preferably in the original language. It will take hours and hours, days and days, in the basement of the temple. We will then have a considered basis for our own judgments, whatever they may be. Among other chronological problems is one concerning Abraham in a comparison of Acts 7:4 and Genesis 11 and 12. Of course, there are two rather different genealogies for Jesus in Matthew and Luke, and even Francis Schaeffer recognizes that the genealogies in Scripture do not have perfect historical accuracy.[8] There is the famous problem of David's numbering of the people. In II Samuel 24:1-2, God was angry with Israel. The warriors were counted, and there were 800,000 warriors in Israel and 500,000 in Judah. In I Chronicles 21:1-2 Satan induced David to count the warriors. The count was 1,100,000 warriors in Israel and 470,000 in Judah. These are merely illustrative of other such problems.

Consider the whole issue of Old Testament quotations in the New Testatment. This is an area where *testability* is appropriate for at least some theories of inerrancy. Article 13 of the Chicago Statement does include in its exceptions "free citation." Again, for an individual believer to have independent judgment, that person needs to study extensively what has been called the substratum of the New Testatment. Center for a moment on the Old Testament quotations in the Epistle to the Hebrews, the New Testament book that uses the Old Testament more than any other. Many positive things can be learned. The Old Testament Scripture is seen and portrayed as alive, as speaking, as dynamic and relevant to the present. The major theme and purpose of the Epistle to the Hebrews can be derived from the quotations. It also becomes evident that Deuteronomy 1:1—4:40 is a prime basis for concerns of Hebrews. It is also very likely from the vast array of Old Testatment quotations that the recipients of Hebrews most likely were Jewish.

There are numerous minor divergencies, however. There is a variant wording of Habakkuk 2:4 cited in Hebrews 10:38 from the wording in Romans 1:17 or Galatians 3:11. There is the very unusual introductory formula to a quota-

193

tion, "Somewhere someone. . . . " Indeed, there are as many as 56 divergences from the Septuagint (A/B) found in the 29 direct quotations in the Epistle to the Hebrews.[9] Hebrews can even cite the same text with different wording. What these kinds of facts do as they are experienced personally and directly is to impact gradually upon your sense of the nature of Scripture as inspired. It certainly requires you to move to a less brittle and wooden understanding, but it does not require you to have a negative attitude. Some scholars have posited a pre-Massoretic Hebrew text, and others have resorted to the autographs. To resort to autographs here, it seems to me, is to invite more trouble because it then opens the possibility of as many difficulties in the doctrinal texts. Also note the problem of Matthew's quotations for ourselves in our own Bibles.

Dr. Erickson in his *Christian Theology* recognizes the validity of the historical critical method and makes a winsome case of what might be called believing criticism. There are a number of such New Testament scholars such as F. F. Bruce, Eldon Ladd, I. Howard Marshall, and E. Earle Ellis, to name a few with whom I gladly identify and in whom I have confidence as believing critics. Erickson explains that his own view of faith and reason will not allow him to settle historical matters by presumption without rigorous research.[10] He includes not only textual criticism, in the past called "lower criticism," but also source, form, redaction, and structural criticism. Erickson forcefully reminds us that form criticism in particular was applied to the Bible not only creatively but recklessly by certain liberal and radical scholars and can be open to misuse.[11] Bultmann, in particular, has been severe in his judgments about the authenticity of the sayings of Jesus. I noticed in my personal study of the parables a category I came to call "refusal parables." Three of them are in the M source and three in the L source. What is striking to be able to demonstrate is that though they are in the different sources they have a similar structure and reveal the same author.[12] Erickson is very conscious that some proponents of critical methods have assumptions against the supernatural and indulge in circular reasoning.[13] He also warns against arbitrariness and subjectivity, with which I would concur.

The results of Biblical criticism ("enlightened appreciation") can be positive if the interpreter is open to the possibility of the supernatural. The virginal conception is often rejected on the basis that the infancy narrative in Luke and in Matthew never corroborate one another by reporting the same story. This is a problem, but this also means that Luke and Matthew are independent of one another, and both affirm virginal conception.

I recall a semester when I was lecturing on the parables of Jesus. I was making some application of form critical analysis as we worked through the text. There was one student who sat high up in the theater room who was an older fellow who had just retired from military service. He was more mature than average. He knew his name what he intended to do with the second half of his life. After a few days he hung around at the lecture podium after the class was dismissed. He grinned at me and said, "I have caught on to you. What I have found out in your class is that you can use form criticism in a conservative way and actually make the Bible come alive and let us see the early church.'" I also recall an informal lesson Dr. Ray Summers taught me. He was standing at the end of a row of stacks in the library, and I was chatting with him. He commented to me that he was a conservative essentially. I was quizzical, and he explained himself: "I refuse to make my conclusions in advance of my research, but if the conclusions I reach after my research is finished are conservative I am pleased. It is in that sense I am a conservative." That has stuck with me ever since, and each of us needs to be conservative in this way. In the sixties I developed a simple hermeneutical thesis that the historical critical method is indispensable but inadequate, and asserted that God speaks as well as acts despite Wright, Bright, and Albright. Also I see as an acceptable alternative to speak instead of a "grammatico-historical" method, which puts more stress on the language.

It is encouraging to notice some of the favorable theological winds in Germany today. Martin Hengel in particular is providing much-needed corrective to the excesses of the Bultmann school. Peter Stuhlmacher is offering strong options from a thoughtful academic posture.[14] The problem with Bultmann, despite his contributions as related to the relevance to today's world, has to do with the fact that he accepted *positivism* and believed in a closed continuum of cause and effect.[15] In many ways this is no better than fideism. Even Pannenberg, broadly speaking, with his renewed emphasis on history is helping to turn things in a more constructive direction.

Dr. Raymond Brown, a beloved mentor of my theological generation, always gave two days of lecture to an assessment of Rudolf Bultmann. Student interest ran high. Viintage Brown, he made so many points that he went through the alphabet more than once in order to give Bultmann his due but also to show very clearly to students where and why and how Bultmann was misleading. Ernst Käsemann once said to me that "you Southern Baptists should not follow our school because it is radical. What we are doing is trying to follow it out to see where it will lead."

Dr. Glenn Hinson, in a controversial book some years ago, drew out some of the critical problems of chronology and possible polarities in the mind of Christ. The best and most Christian response to his book is not polemic but plausible problem-solving. Let graduate students and professors face up to the problems he isolated honestly, do thorough research, and seek to reach constructive results and solutions as an effective response.

The final section of Dr. Erickson's paper addresses what he calls the *dangers* of misunderstanding inerrancy. Each of his comments on dangers strikes a sympathetic chord, but let us focus just briefly on two issues. First of all consider what he calls the domino argument. Inerrantists sincerely express a concern that persons who give up the doctrine of Biblical inerrancy will also abandon other precious beliefs as well. It should be said forthrightly that some persons who lose a degree of their confidence in Scripture may sometimes in due course give up other segments of the faith as well. I recall a student who on his own began reading the radical results of Bultmann with great enthusiasm. Then after a time he began to have emotional problems. He was supported during his spiritual and emotional crisis by friends and faculty, but it was a damaging experience. If we accept too much of the reductionism of skeptical scholarship, we can be left with far too little. What do you do when it dawns on you that the rather exciting Christian message that Bultmann advocated simply has no basis in historical truth? Your tolerance for ambiguity then had best be enormous.

On the other hand, let us not forget that orthodoxy is not secured by inerrancy. Remember that the Jehovah's Witnesses believe in the total inerrancy of Scripture and so does the sect called the Christadelphians. In fact, they sometimes hold conferences in defense of Biblical Inerrancy. Also the Mormons and the Unitarian Pentecostals and the Seventh-Day Adventists contend for Biblical inerrancy.[16]

Let us also bear in mind great evangelicals who did not accept strict inerrancy but neither were victims of the domino theory. I refer to people like James Orr, Alexander Maclaren, and others. Today there are people like F. F. Bruce and Bruce Metzger and George Eldon Ladd who are somewhat less than full inerrantists but who uphold with vigor and vitality the faith.

I have seen some young people who appreared to be victims of too strict a view of inerrancy, who slipped down the other side of the slope. When they got into college they came to feel that their earlier doctrine of Scripture could not stand, and some spiritual damage occurred. Some feel because they find a few insoluble problems in the Bible that the whole structure has to cave in. One famous writer felt he had to reject the Christian faith when as an adult he found out that one gospel reports one man or angel at the empty tomb while another records two. So he concluded the the Bible itself was not true.

I am genuinely concerned about both sides of the slope. On both sides of this slippery slope there is a need for great pastoral sensitivity and care and an awareness of each person's individual pilgrimage. When the rhetoric has died down and no one is trying to prove anything, pastoral care will be needed on both sides of the slope.

Another area that Dr. Erickson presents has to do with the failure to see a Biblical text in its cultural context. He specifically asks whether we should exclude women from speaking in church today because Paul forbade it in his culture. I too raise this question. The issue is hermeneutical, and I believe that it is the unspoken and sometimes unconscious transition from exegesis to exposition that divides many Christians. Some Christians with integrity are convinced, from their handling of the text, that women should not speak in church. At least, in practical terms, they are opposed to women as deacons or pastors. I for one defend the full Christian citizenship of women in the body of Christ (Galatians 3:28), but I have refused to do so by the facile system of rejecting texts out of hand or by demeaning the Apostle Paul. Cultural conditions have changed, thanks in part to the influence of Christianity. Paul was not wrong in his restrictions in given, limited, temporary circumstances. But today hermeneutically we must ask for his intention.

In conclusion, it is my hope that Christians increasingly will be able to agree in general in their confidence in the Bible and move on to the primary thrust of

196

II Timothy 3:16, which is the profitability or the coping power of the Word of God. The Bible would give us directives to what we should be doing and proclaiming. Old Dr. Clyde Francisco knew what he was doing. It was my privilege sometimes to teach Biblical Preaching with him. He loved the Old Testament, and he preached it with so much conviction that it came alive and changed lives. He would sometimes cover critical theories or technical points in class just to show you that he knew them, but his genius was the practical knowledge that the Bible is a sharp, two-edged sword relevant for the church's mission.

For myself, my Cradle Roll certificate still hangs on the wall in my old bedroom in my hometown. I ate doughnuts in the youth group during revivals when Chester Swor was a young man but looked like he does now. I went to Camp Linden in Tennessee and to Ridgecrest and was deeply touched by the call of Christ. I experienced a rededication of my life in an Eddie Martin revival when I was a teenager. I was called to preach during the invitation "Whereever He Leads I'll Go." Believing the Bible is in my bones.

I thank Dr. Erickson for a resourceful presentation.

Notes

1. Millard Erickson, *Christian Theology* (Grand Rapids, Mich.: 1985).
2. I. Howard Marshall, *Biblical Inspiration* (Grand Rapids, Mich.: Eerdmans, 1982), p. 95.
3. Erickson, p. 208.
4. Clark Pinnock, *The Scripture Principle* (New York: Harper & Row, 1984), xviii and p. 75.
5. Marshall, p. 72.
6. Stephen Davis, *The Debate About the Bible* Philadelphia: Westminister, 1977).
7. Erickson, pp. 233-24.
8. Francis Schaeffer, *No Final Conflict* (Downer's Grove, Ill.: InterVasity, 1975), p. 40.
9. See Kenneth J. Thomas, "The Old Testament Citations in Hebrew," *New Testament Studies,* 11:303 (1964-65).
10. Erickson, p. 84.
11. *Ibid.,* pp. 90-94.
12. Peter Rhea Jones, *The Teaching of the Parables* (Nashville: Broadman, 1982), pp. 58-59
13. Erickson, pp. 102-103.
14. See Stuhlmacher, *Historical Criticism and Theological Interpretation of Scripture,* trans. by Roy A. Harrisville (Philadelphia: Fortress, 1977).
15. See Rudolf Bultman, "'Is Exegesis without Presuppositions Possible?" *Existence and Faith,* ed. by Schubert Ogden (London: Hodder and Stoughton, 1960), pp. 291-292.
16. So Donald Bloesch, *Essentials of Evangelical Theology* (San Francisco: Harper & Row, 1978), 1:20, 83.

RESPONSE: Richard R. Melick

Dean Erickson has written a thoughtful paper regarding the problems areas of inerrancy. He is to be commended for his honesty, candor, and willingness to face issues openly. Although the list of difficulties he proposes may seem extensive, no doubt some would add other areas. Of course, what is a difficulty in the mind of one is not necessarily a problem to another, and Dean Erickson's paper represents the kinds of difficulties encountered.

The two divisions of the paper suggest real areas of concern. His "dangers a doctrine must face" are real dangers. Likewise, his "problems resulting from misunderstandings of inerrancy" insightfully catalogues what each of us has observed. Dr. Erickson's heading correctly states, however, that they characterize those who *misunderstand* inerrancy.

Although the thesis is difficult to find, the paper does take a position. Dr. Erickson's conclusion is that "this is a doctrine of great value, and the effort of dealing with the problem areas will be well rewarded." It appears, therefore, that Erickson wants us to know that although there are problem areas in defining and maintaining inerrancy, these problems do not invalidate the concept or its usefulness in theological studies. In this, he aligns himself with the historic teaching of the church from the time of the apostles and the majority of orthodox theologians throughout the centuries.

Before turning to the substance of the paper, it will be helpful to make some introductory comments. These will include some general remarks, observations on the doctrine of inerrancy in Scripture, and a clarification of Dr. Erickson's categories.

Several general matters are worth noting, First, the list of problems come from an inerrantist! In this, Dr. Erickson represents a host of scholars throughout the Christian centuries who have been convinced of and committed to inerrancy even when there are complicated issues involved. Such informed conviction strikes at the heart of those who claim that inerrantists can only hold the doctrine in their ignorance. Second, the list of problem areas comes in a true spirit of dialogue and open acknowledgement of some difficulties. Again, this typifies true inerrantist scholarship which seeks truth, not only apologetics and polemics. Third, many of the problems are shared by non-inerrantists. (Unfortunately from a semantic perspective the word "non-inerrantist" is meaningless because of its double negative formation. However, the word "errantist" is problematic, and, inasmuch as "inerrancy" is a theological affirmation, the word "non-inerrantist" may be the best alternative. At least it does communicate.) Some, both of Erickson's dangers and the misunderstandings, are problematic to all serious inerrancy scholars. Fourth, the problems are not insurmountable, and the task of working through them has proven to be both necessary and a worthwhile exercise.

In addition to these general comments, it will be helpful to make some observations about the nature of the doctrine of inerrancy in Scripture. First, Dr. Erickson states that the doctrine is an inference about Scripture from the teaching of the biblical writers, rather than a direct and explicit teaching. Since he equated it to the doctrine of the Trinity, apparently he considers it an important, even self-evident doctrine. However, it is important to note that the biblical writers *assumed* the inerrancy of Scripture, and it thus was foundational to their belief and the construction of the theologies.

Second, many have protested the use of a word that has no occurrence in the Scriptures. This represents a naive understanding of theological categories. Many of the names of the traditional theological categories cannot be found in the Scriptures, yet they are accepted as adequate by most theologians. The use of the word Trinity for the Godhead functions in this fashion, and the concept of God as "person" falls into this category as well. Some, using this same kind of reasoning, claim that Jesus never taught inerrancy. But this suggestion requires engaging in a wooden, literal exegesis which is so decried by the opponents of inerrancy as well as responsible inerrantists. Naturally, the context greatly affects the nature of a teaching. If Jesus had been in a technical discussion of the Bible He *might* have included more—we simply cannot know.

Third, there is a tension between the phenomena and the dogma in Scripture. The tension, however, exists in several other areas of theology as well. This is apparent in such doctrines as the love of God in tension with His justice and the sovereignty of God in tension with the freedom of man. In these cases, one must construct a systematic statement of what the Bible teaches which may actually transcend the polarities of the phenomena. If one builds a theology on one of the poles, he will have a shortsighted and onesided understanding. Thus, the clear teaching of the text gives structure to the phenomena. This same pattern is followed in the doctrine of inerrancy. Ideally, the phenomena correlate with the doctrinal teaching so there is little difficulty, but Dr. Erickson correctly observes that the greater weight must be given to the dogma.

One final introductory matter is an important clarification. Dean Erickson's paper actually identified nineteen areas of concern when the two divisions are considered together. Thus, a cursory reading of the paper appears to make a doctrine of inerrancy more problematic than it actually is. While there are genuine problems, and some are complex, the wording of Erickson's second section should be remembered. He entitled it "Problems Resulting from Misunderstandings of Inerrancy." Apparently, he does not consider these areas as necessary to the doctrine, and, upon close examination, they are only problems which result when one *misunderstands* inerrancy. That subject will occupy the second section of this response.

The first section of Dr. Erickson's paper catalogues eight "Problems for Inerrancy." These have long been recognized and for that reason seminaries have addressed them in some detail. Although they are problems inerrantists face, it

199

will be shown that they are also problems for non-inerrantists, although in a slightly different way. Time constraints prohibit addressing each of these in detail. Most are handled smoothly by realizing that the Bible was written in language and style characteristic of the ancient Near East, and it must be studied with that understanding. Since Dr. Packer's paper will address most of these, particularly history, science, and ethics, this response singles out three crucial matters.

Dr. Erickson's first problem was the problem of the text. The value of the text depends upon the degree to which we actually have the text. Initially, it may be disconcerting to some to hear that the doctrine refers to the autographs. This has been often attacked unfairly. First, the logic of inerrancy is clear. Since there are variations due to copying of the manuscripts, we must live with the variations. But no one would affirm the correctness of multiple differing texts. Obviously one reading must be correct. Second, the autographs are not a mysterious and nebulous entity. Virtually all textual critics know where the problems are and can reconstruct a reliable Greek and Hebrew text which witnesses faithfully to the autograph. Third, no significant matter is at stake in the places of variation. Certainly no doctrine is affected.

Fourth, the argument against inerrancy because of the corrupted copies of the text we possess often involves a nonsequitor. The relatively minor areas of textual variants addresses the question of the written text and the transcriptional process. No inerrantist believes that if the autographs were found all problems of harmony and parallels, for example, would be solved. They would say little about the problems of a philosophical nature. They also would only clarify the text. On the other hand, recognizing that the copies we do have contain transcriptional discrepancies does not argue that the writers were wrong in areas of science, history, ethics, or thought. Variations due to the reproduction of the text are not the same as errors of thinking or concept. These are two different matters entirely. Even if the copies are considered normative, the problems of error and non-error would have just begun. Fifth, many who object to the autograph argument do so because they do not believe there was one. Many believe in a developing tradition incorporating ideas and stories from a variety of sources. The first time the text really reached a fixed form, they say, was late in its history.

Sixth, from a pastoral perspective, the argument against inerrancy and the autographs has been blown out of proportion. Few must engage in a statement of inerrancy in personal evangelism anyway, but on occasion it does arise. The inerrantist can assure an inquirer that he has a reliable text because of its nearness to the original. If he is asked, he can certainly explain his reasoning simply. If the criterion for our theology is whether or not the unbeliever can understand easily and simply, many doctrines will be excluded. Everyone engaging in personal evangelism has been asked "How do you explain the deity and humanity of Jesus?" and "How does the blood of Christ care for my sins?" Are we to abandon these tenets too? Of course not.

Some passing remarks on several other "danger" areas may be helpful. Lexical research is necessary from all scholars, but its primary focus is not the solving of problems. It is to understand the author's message correctly. Naturally, when the author is correctly understood, many problems are solved. The definition of error is indirectly a subject of the conference, and thus each presentation relates to that. The problem of parallel accounts remains a difficulty. No one should engage in sloppy exegesis that produces superficial and irresponsible harmonizations. The same could be said for the problems of chronology. When, for example, there is a problem in the biblical numbers four options present themselves.

First, one may declare there is an error incapable of harmonization. Second, one may look for a new manuscript that will correct the problem. With so many manuscripts available, however, this is unlikely to help. Third, he may hope to redefine the words of the text, particularly the numbers, as John Wenhem does with the census of Israel at the Exodus. Fourth, he may look for ancient methods of historiography which solve the problem. A premature judgment that the accounts are in error may actually inhibit exegesis and historical studies. Dr. Thiele has demonstrated the value of work in these areas. Finally, because science and ethics will be addressed by Dr. Packer, the question of the use of non-canonical literature by canonical writers remains. Dr. Erickson could have cited many places where this occurs. Since the criteria for canonicity were far more complicated that the fact that a book was quoted in the New Testament, this poses no substantive problem.

No one is suggesting that inerrantists have solved all the problems. That, in fact, was the point of Dr. Erickson's paper. What is being suggested is that more work must be done in these areas because of their problematic nature, but a supportive context has been developed by historical-grammatical work.

The second portion of Dr. Erickson's paper was devoted to "misunderstandings" and some comments are in order here. Frequently it is assumed that inerrancy is to be equated to a hyper fundamentalism which, at times, displays many of these characteristics. But, though inerrancy is held by Fundamentalism, it is also held by other movements as well. For example, considerable debate rages as to whether or not inerrancy is essential to defining modern Evangelicalism, since the leaders of the movement espoused the doctrine. On the other hand, a study of the fundamentals of American Fundamentalism from the Niagara Conferences reveals that the inerrancy of Scripture was not one of the original five fundamentals. Inerrancy was, however, a point of unity between the Princetonians and other groups—some Baptists included—because it protected the fundamentals.

The point of Dr. Erickson's section seems to be that inerrancy itself is not the cause of these attitudes. Too often its opponents have utilized the logical fallacies of "guilt by association" and improper "cause and effect" in concluding the doctrine was at fault. As was stated earlier, each of us has observed these attitudes, or "problems" as Dr. Erickson calls them. He is entirely correct that they prevail in inerrantist circles, and they should be corrected. It is equally true that complex psychological and theological factors contribute to these attitudes, and to single out inerrancy as the cause is extremely tenuous. It is like saying "all men who fight with their wives deny the existence of God. Therefore, atheism

201

is the cause of marital disharmony." In fact, these attitudes characterize non-inerrantists as well.

Several examples from the "misunderstandings" section of Dr. Erickson's paper will illustrate the point. One of his categories is "ignoring the Scripture." While it may be true that some inerrantists disregard certain passages or sections of Scripture, that practice is never encouraged by responsible inerrantists. The very nature of the doctrine prohibits this, since it says "every Scripture is inspired of God and is profitable . . ." On the other hand, many non-inerrantists dismiss areas of Scripture that conflict with their understanding or criteria for truth, and, thus, are guilty of the same charge. In addition, both groups are painfully aware of the many people who ignore the message of the Scriptures while sitting in the pews of churches every Sunday. The problem Erickson identifies is simply *not* a problem of inerrancy; it is a problem of specific kinds of personalities.

Another example occurs in Dr. Erickson's section "Overzealous Attempts to Demonstrate the Inerrancy of Scripture." Admittedly, these are many, and the history of Biblical studies is clouded with embarrassing interpretations which bear little similarity to the text. Yet these have been found among people holding many different Bibliologies. There are certainly overzealous attempts to demonstrate the *errancy* of Scripture as well. For example, a man was criticizing the "literal" interpretation of the Bible in the reference "the heavens are brass." He took great pains to demonstrate that the Bible was wrong in assuming a metal atmosphere. Of course that was not the intent of the biblical writer who obviously knew better, and this man's interpretation violated the plain sense of Scripture. Although it may be conceded that sometimes bizarre explanations have come from inerrantists, such abuse of the Bible is not limited to inerrantists, and is seldom encouraged by them. This, too, is a problem of specific personalities.

The list of illustrations from Dr. Erickson's paper could go on. Regarding the acknowledgement of general revelation, many non-inerrantists neglect a great mass of scientific, archaeological, and historical material which supports the integrity of the text. Regarding oversimplification of ethical issues, some reach simplistic conclusions by affirming one portion of the Bible's teaching and failing to consider the normative nature of a seemingly contradictory stream of teaching. Likewise, some non-inerrantists fail to see biblical statements in their cultural context and, therefore, interpret them according to their own understandings. In so doing they sometimes find "errors" which are not properly of the text, but are of specific interpretations of the text.

Again, the "domino theory" is overused by inerrantists, although it is a difficult point to argue because of the time it takes for the domino effect. Often it requires plotting more than one generation of scholars to note the trends and movements. On the other hand, the "slippery slope" charge brought by non-inerrantists which makes use of the "fundamentalists splinter groups" is normally fallacious. These groups generally agree on inerrancy, their inability to cooperate is due to other factors—at least *as well*. Non-inerrantists are also often guilty of "straw man" caricatures which belittle and misrepresent true inerrantists. Finally, on the matter of divisiveness, there are those who unnecessarily divide the church, but the church is equally divided by some non-inerrantists who instruct their students to disregard what their pastors at home taught them.

The point to be made is that these "problems arising from misunderstandings of inerrancy" are real concerns and should be addressed. They are, however, largely problems of temperament which may surface regardless of theological position. They may be accentuated among "emotional inerrantists," but the fact that some people who adhere to a position do not represent it well does not invalidate their position. Christianity would be in a sad sate if that were the case. As one man said, "the greatest evidence of the reality of Christianity is that it has survived the Church." In other words, these may be *tendencies* of some inerrantists, but they are not *tenets* of inerrancy. Hopefully, all these "misunderstandings" will be put in proper perspective and addressed with a view to correcting them.

At this point it will be helpful to insert a word abut the value of holding to inerrancy in the tasks of exegesis and hermeneutics. The inerrantist begins with an authoritative text which must be handled seriously and carefully. This means, in part, that the inerrantist must continue his study to find a satisfactory resolution to problems. While Erickson's warning about superficial harmonizations is well taken, it is also true that a responsible correlation of facts and theology with all pertinent texts has led, at times, to creative scholarship and deeper understanding. The consistent application of the principles espoused by inerrancy will not allow the text to become a proof text for prevailing philosophies!

One other area of Dr. Erickson's paper must be mentioned. It relates to orthopraxy, or proper behavior. He pointedly cautions against "distinguishing the Bible from the subject of its teaching," and his point should be well taken. Naturally, no one advocates substituting the Bible for God and for the personal encounter He brings. But no one has effectively explained why revelation cannot be both personal and propositional, or why the God-man relationship cannot be both objectively measured by the Bible and subjectively enjoyed. Why can't faith be structured in accord with the teaching of the Bible and measured by its dictates?

In all, Dr. Erickson has written a fine paper acknowledging many of the difficulties. This response has been sympathetic and supportive. Dr. Erickson's conclusion is also sound. In spite of these minor difficulties, the inerrancy of Scripture remains a helpful doctrine to exegesis, theology, and life.

10

PROBLEM AREAS RELATED TO BIBLICAL INERRANCY

J. I. Packer

I am to speak about problem areas relating to biblical inerrancy taking up the same subject on which Dr. Erickson has already spoken. There will be some overlap and there will be some points that I make going beyond anything that he said. You must be the judge as to how far we are together and how far there are interesting differences. I would like to begin with the question of whether inerrancy is an inference as distinct from some unexplicit teaching of Scripture. I am not happy simply to say it is an inference. I want to use the philosophical word *entailment*. An entailment is a necessary inference and biblical inerrancy is a necessary inference. I believe that the inerrancy of Scripture is an entailment from all that is said about Scripture having God as its origin and all that is said about the character of God as a teller of truth.

In regard to the problems related to biblical inerrancy, the concept of error must first be taken up. Let me tell you right at the start how I circumscribe the concept of error, and then I will be able to tell you what I mean by a problem. I circumscribe the concept of error thus, error is an affirmation, an assertion, which fails to be veridical when it seeks to be veridical—an affirmation in other words which is an attempt to tell the truth and fails. In assessing whether any statement constitutes an error, you first of all ask what the speaker intends to express, then you go on to ask does it succeed in being veridical or does it not? If it can be shown that the affirmation is limited in its scope well beyond that intended scope there can be no error. How do you tell? The simple way of telling is to see what follows from the affirmation in the speaker's own discourse, what he takes himself to be implying by what he says. Beyond that, it is hard to be sure.

This presentation is organized around a question: do the phenomena of Scripture force upon us biblical relativism after all. That is really the issue which arises when one speaks of problems relating to biblical inerrancy. Do the phenomena of Scripture present difficulties of such magnitude that one is forced out of an inerrancy position into a biblical relativism. I think the answer is *no*, but I have to give reasons for that, and the style of this presentation is deliberately confessional. I am an inerrantest asking whether the phenomena of Scripture oblige me to abandon my inerrancy position and take up some form of biblical relativism after all.

To whom do the problems related to biblical inerrancy belong? I have already said from one standpoint they are mine, but I think that they ought to be categorized in another way also. Let me say, therefore, in answer to my own question, they could be the problems of unbelievers, persons with an antiChristian commitment who wish to show Christianity as unreasonable, people like Celsus against whom Origin wrote or Tom Payne, that supercilious deist of the Eighteenth century. Or they could be the problems of believers, Bible believers, believers in Jesus Christ who have received the witness of God's Holy Spirit to the divinity and authority of the Scriptures, who yet find themselves puzzled either about questions of the coherence of this strand of Bible teaching or who have questions about the morality of God's commands and actions and the saints behavior which apparently is approved in Scripture. These are real problems and sometimes very painful ones for Bible believers.

I could concentrate exclusively on the problems of Christian academics. But then there are different sorts of Christian academics. And it is important again to distinguish. There are Christian academics who have an avowed liberal agenda before they begin exploring the problems of Holy Scripture, and their liberal agenda is a naturalistic belief that both truth and expediency require Christianity to accommodate itself in these days to some type of post-Christian, antisupernaturalist view of God and the world. It might be deistic. It might be pantheistic, panentheistic, or process type. In any case, it is a retreat from biblical theism and involves biblical relativism as a methodological necessity, and it is in the light of that prior commitment that the problems will be faced. To those who take such a relativist stance, I beg, think again. I am not going to address myself to your basic world view. Ask yourself whether there are not good reasons for maintaining the older line in which the Bible has the last word.

There are also, however, scholars who, while not identifying with the liberal agenda do embrace what I call a neoconservative agenda, an agenda based on maintaining biblical essentials while keeping at a distance from what these scholars perceive to be simplistic, rationalistic conservatism, fundamentalism in at least one sense of that word.

It seems to them much too simple and to take questions of integrity of thought much less seriously than they should be taken. They dislike the word inerrancy because it is embraced by those with whose theology they hesitate to identify, and they are heavily committed to the full involvement of the academic process of inquiry in relation to every matter of biblical interpretation and every question of Christian theology. With these folk, I have much sympathy. I think I have stood where they stand myself, but I say to them that their's is a reactionary stance; would they please think again? There is a danger of distancing one's self too much from those who theologically have the root of the matter in them. Whatever mistakes they may make in interpretation, they do in fact seek to give the Bible the last word on all matters as Christians should do.

Thirdly, there are scholars who have no particular leaning toward either the liberal or neoconservative way, but nonetheless, they experience a certain personal crisis of integrity regarding problems of scholarship. They hate being pressured into instant decisions, and they fear that that kind of pressure is being put upon them. They feel that surely one has no right to affirm all that Scripture says about God, events, and values when so many difficulties and questions of detail present themselves. To them a strategy of systematically dispelling difficulties is academically artificial and unconvincing, and they feel that challenging the noninerrantist's mainstream of critical scholarship cannot be an academically responsible thing to do. I recognize their sense of academic responsibility, and I affirm it. But will they not also think again? Think again about what is involved in challenging a century of critical scholarship. What you will be asked to challenge is an unbelieving, relativist, liberal post-Christian method. This is something different from challenging or simply jettisoning all the precise information about the historical background of texts, the lexical background of biblical words, the vast helps to exegesis which the critical scholarship of the last hundred years has made available to us. I am not asking them to jettison that, but only to jettison unbelieving presuppositions.

As for the suspicion that a strategy of systematically dispelling difficulties is academically artificial and unconvincing, remember or learn that there are many engaged in this task of seeking to show in these days that in fact there is nothing unconvincing, nothing artificial about this strategy, but rather the reverse. One can follow it in a way that is academically convincing. When I was a theological student there were not many literary resources to help me in my theological struggles. Today there are enormous evangelical academic resources of the highest quality to help in coping with these problems. The landscape has changed. Sound scholars will admit this to be the case and be open to reconsidering their inhibiting suspicion about evangelical efforts to clear the problem areas that arise in relation to the doctrine of biblical inerrancy.

Having dealt with the question of which sets of people might experience problems with biblical inerrancy, I want now to explore in principle all the main areas of felt factual and moral difficulty experienced by some believers and Christian academics. The discussion will assume three things which I have already attempted to justify in my earlier paper. It will assume first that by biblical inerrancy we mean that biblical teaching is to be treated as entirely true and trustworthy and on that basis given the last word. That view now becomes a working hypothesis to be put to the test. I presuppose, second, that no interpreter may claim personal inerrancy for his interpretations of Scripture on the ground that he believes that the Bible is inerrant. After all, anyone may misinterpret the Scriptures. And thirdly, I shall assume the propriety of leaving open questions of detail when the available solutions seem less than certain and when corroborative facts are unavailable. When, for instance, it is a matter of identifying Darius the Mede in Daniel, chapter 5, or Theudas referred to by Gamaliel in Acts, chapter 5, or the details of Quirinius' census referred to in Luke, chapter 2, we have to acknowledge, I think, that information is lacking and we cannot be too sure. That the Bible is true in what it says is not a matter of doubt, but what exactly we should be saying about the persons and events referred to in the Bible is not always clear for lack of supplementary information. I do not believe that the honor of God requires me to have an answer, and a complete answer, for everything.

Finally, I hope to demonstrate two rather important points. I want to show that belief in biblical inerrancy does not require unscholarly obscurantism with regard to any of the phenomena of Scripture and, secondly, that the alleged discrepancies and errors in the Bible, for the most part, dissolve away when one sees clearly that the biblical books are human products of their own time and stops expecting of them the perspective and precision of a modern laboratory report.

Let me clear the ground by making some preliminary points. First, the canonicity of Scripture should not be seen as a problem, rather it should be taken as a starting point. Confidence that all the books belonging to the divinely planned organism of Scripture are in the sixty-six books of the Protestant canon and confidence that there are no books in the canon that should not be there seems to be justified. There is no doubt that the Palestinian canon which Jesus implicitly endorsed, by his use of it, was identical with the Hebrew Old Testament as we have it. Further, there is no solid reason to doubt the authenticity or to posit the pseudonymity of any book in the New Testament canon. Finally, God has, as a matter of fact, authenticated the whole of the Protestant canon over and over again in the experience of His own people, generation by generation. God has confirmed that these books are, indeed, His word by the power that He has given in the lives of His people. That is a positive theological argument for the authenticity of the canon, an argument that gains weight in every generation as millions more Christians have this experience. That means that we have even less right in A. D. 1987 to suppose, for instance, that the Book of James is out of place in the canon than had Martin Luther in his time, because we have had more than 4½ centuries more than Luther had of God using the Letter of James to build up His own people.

Second, I do not think that the accessibility of Scripture ought to be regarded as a problem either. By accessibility, I mean the confidence that we have the canonical original text in such form that we may learn from it all that is needed for life and godliness. There is no objective reason for doubting the substantial accuracy of the text as we have it, thanks to the work of textual critics, or of our translations of the bible, thanks to the work of scholarly, careful translators. We have no reason to doubt that those translations bring us into direct touch with the substance of the biblical message.

There is a third matter that ought not be regarded as a problem: the rules for the interpretation of Scripture. There is, indeed, general agreement on these rules, and they serve to direct and safeguard the quest for the natural sense and flow of Scripture. Protestants have affirmed the clairity or perspicuity of Scripture for more than four centuries, that is that the theology that becomes clear as texts are studied reverently and with a dependence on the Holy Spirit and with the wise use of scholarly tools is the genuine teaching of God. The rules of interpretation turn out on inspection and reflection to be scarcely more than matters of common sense. The main rules of interpretation seem to me to be as follows.

Interpretation must be grammatical and historical. It must take account of philology, the study of the meaning of words as they developed historically, semantics, the study of how words carry meaning in various units and of how to determine that meaning, and logic, the study of the various kinds of meaning language may be used to convey. Language is used to do more than convey information. It is used to issue commands; it is used in order to create situations of commitment; it is used in order to evoke responses; it is used in order to illustrate; it is used in order to stir the imagination. Logicians distinguish all these functions. Grammatical study of the text of Scripture means that one asks of each sentence, each paragraph, and each unit of thought what sort of message it was written to convey. And one expounds accordingly. Historical interpretation takes account of the social, economic, religious, and political factors which formed the background of the text, shaping the situation out of which the text came. Historical interpretation also takes account of assumptions and conventions governing human association and communication in each era from which biblical material came. The way into the mind of God the Holy Spirit is *via* the expressed meaning of the human writers. Only as we understand what they were saying to those who they were initially addressing in their own historical situation, can we with certainty advance to an understanding of the mind of God. This is why allegorizing will not do. Allegorizing bypasses the meaning expressed by the human author, and that is not the way into God's thoughts at all.

Rule number two in interpretation is that one much interpret Scripture in a theocentric and doxological way. Remember that every part of Scripture was written to glorify God and to edify saints. Even the Book of Esther in which God's name is not mentioned or the Book of Job in which the sufferings of Job are highlighted with a vividness that can never be forgotten were written primarily to show the glorious works of God. This is so with all the other books of Scripture. If one forgets that this is so, then much of the point of specific things said in Scripture is bound to be missed.

Rule number three is that interpretation should be coherent and unitive. That follows from the fact that all Scripture proceeds from the mind and, we might say, the mouth of God. Because all Scripture proceeds from His mind passages supplementing each other will not contradict each other nor will their combined testimony to God be a mind-defying muddle. The interpreter's proper task is to seek to show that this is so and to explore the theological depths opened to him thereby.

The fourth rule is that the interpretation of Scripture must not stop short at discerning what was meant by the Bible writer, we must go on to ask what his meaning, his historical meaning, means for us. The Scripture was communicating truth about God, His world, and the human beings in it to these addressed in its original setting; that truth(s) must now be formulated and reapplied to persons and situations in the present. Interpretation becomes applicatory as we seek to bring it to bear on our own lives. Interpretation becomes dialogical as we recognize that God, when He says something to us through His word requires of us a response. It's as if the letters RSVP were attached to every bit of His teaching. It is in preaching and in private meditation that the applicatory and dialogical dimensions of interpretation come to be fully realized. Academic work in the classroom is a preparation for interpretation, but it stops short of discerning the text's meaning. It is the preacher and the believer in his meditation who go on to explore what it means. They then are the true and final interpreters of Scripture.

Fifth, interpretation should be covenantal and kingdom-oriented, for the covenant of God with His people and the kingdom that He sets up through Christ is, in very truth, the center of the biblical message. Finally, interpretation must be empathetic and self-critical, lest our own prejudices prevent us identifying with the Bible writers' concerns and thus hide from us some, perhaps even much of his meaning. Similarly, we must learn to identify with Bible characters, or lest we fail to appreciate the Scriptures record of their lives of faith or—in some cases—their lives of unbelief. Let us be quite clear that that is what Bible biography is meant to teach us, truth about the way of faith and the way of unbelief, what happens if you trust and obey God and what happens if you do not. Interpreters should be self-critical at any and every point where their own culture prejudices might hinder them from being empathetic. This is the needle of wisdom hidden in the haystack of Bultmannian dymythologisation, the Fuchs-Ebeling "new hermeneutic," and the Gadamerian image of intersecting horizons.

With those matters settled, I want now to consider the central question of possible problem areas for the biblical inerrantist in regard to history, science, and moral matters. In the first place, does Scripture misrepresent historical events? As an inerrantist, my working hypothesis is no. By way of substantiation, I offer the following points which ought always to be borne in mind. To begin with, our biblical narratives are celebratory and religious in character, evocative and often poetical in style and educative and edificatory in purpose. They are concerned with advancing personal knowledge of God through knowledge of His work in this world, rather than with advancing scientific knowledge of this world and processes that have occurred within it. The perspective and purpose of the biblical assertions set limits to their range, the range of what is being asserted and the degree of precision with which it is being asserted. Their range sets limits for their function as sources of historical information. Where assertions are intended, no error can be committed. Biblical history told from the standpoint of divine overruling, is by our standards sketchy. We want the inner links of the human process, and often we are not given them, but those ommissions should not be regarded as errors.

The second point about history is that the Bible does not have the modern concern for exact chronological sequence. Hopping backwards and forwards in disregard of chronology for topical reasons seems to us a defect of history writing, calculated to mislead. The only reason why we think that is because we do not do history that way, and we impose our own latter day expectations on the Scripture. For example, in the Synoptic gospels chronology is deliberately rearranged for topical purposes. This is no new insight. From the time of Augustine, Christian exegetes have discerned that the Bible writers were not particularly concerned with chronology but with something else.

A third point has to do with the conventions of reporting speech. All the historians of the ancient world reported what people said by a convention that is the exact opposite of ours. If they knew the substance of what was said, they felt free to construct a speech, sentences and paragraphs of direct speech, in which words were put into the mouth of the character. In the modern era, even when we know what the direct speech was, what words a person actually used, we prefer to report the substance of what that person said in what we call "reported speech." In the Bible, it is unwarranted to think that the accounts of speeches on spying are necessarily *ipsissima verba* and then to base problems on that supposition, for example, finding a problem in the Johannine style of Jesus' sermon as compared with the aphoristic wisdom style of His sermons in the Synoptics. Reportorial conventions are not errors. A closely related fourth point has to do with conventions of ommission in biblical genealogies of using round numbers, symbolic numbers, and large numbers particularly in the Old Testament. There conventions are often elusive, difficult to crystalize and formulate, but it seems certain that they are there. What confronts the interpreter, then, are conventions of understanding rather than errors of fact.

A fifth point about history must be advanced. Though harmonization is much decried today in academic circles as a misguided interest, it is in fact a proper and necessary course when facing for example, five accounts of events of Jesus resurrection, four accounts of the Last Supper and of Peter's denial, four accounts of the feeding of the five thousand, two or three accounts of many other episodes in the gospels, two accounts of Judas' death, two parallel accounts of the Hebrew monarchy and so on. To ask how we should fit these together is not only natural but necessary. If one believes that all Scripture proceeds ultimately from a single mind, the mind of the Holy Spirit, then the propriety of the questions cannot be doubted and the hope of success in the inquiry becomes strong. As a matter of fact, in every case where an apparent discrepancy has been found, a fairly natural harmonization has actually been suggested, and so the conclusion that the Bible contradicts itself is never unavoidable.

Finally, it is not necessary to disregard biblical evidence on such matters as the date of the Exodus, Zerah the Ethiopian of 2 Chronicles 14:9-15, the geography of the Garden of Eden, or the longevity of the patriarchs, simply because such literary, archaeological, and geographical evidence as we have at present does not confirm it. We may still take God's word about these things even if corroborative clarifying evidence is lacking.

A second major area of potential problem for the inerrantist has to do with science. Does Scripture misstate scientific fact? In my considered opinion, Scripture does not misrepresent scientific facts. This statement can be supported. First, in the strictest sense, the Bible contains no scientific statements at all. Scientific statements are tested generalizations or aetiological analyses that trace the internal relations of elements in this world, viewing this world as a "going concern" or working system. They are tested statements, tested by an induction from all the evidence that is available. Biblical statements about this world order, by contrast, are statements about God as "first cause" of all and say nothing directly about "second causes," that is links operating within the system. Biblical statements about natural processes explain them in terms of God's personal purpose but do not describe them scientifically. We say it rains;

Jesus in the Sermon on the Mount said God sends his rain. Note the difference between the two perspectives. We would explain the rain in terms of climatic conditions. Jesus explains the rain in terms of the will of God. Scientific statements are derived by induction through inspecting the workings of the system. Theological and scientific statements are complementary, the latter standing in a hierarchical, interpretative relation to the former. We must take care not to confuse the relative standing of first and second causes. The Christian ought to explain second causes in terms of the first cause. But since scientific statements are statements which operate entirely in the world of second causes, it is necessary for clarity to say there are no such statements in the Bible, and Bible statements about natural events are not scientific statements strictly speaking. the biblical descriptions of natural processes are "naive-observational," telling how things looked, and sometimes "poetic-theological," envisioning nature imaginatively as reflecting and reinforcing the perceptions of humans. Sometimes it is plain that God did order the cause of nature in a way as to underscore a significant event, as when the world went dark for three hours when Jesus was on the cross. But again, the statement in the gospels about this event is a naive observational statement. If is not a scientific statement about how that effect of darkness was produced. All we are told is what that God did it. We must be clear that statements about nature and natural processes in Scripture are never scientific in the technical, methodological sense, and they should not be treated as such.

This point about the nature of observational statements helps to clear away several oft-mentioned difficulties for the inerrantist. Statements, for instance, that present the sun rising and setting, or heaven as above us and sheol as below us, are not cosmological assertions. They are simply speech forms taken from the contemporary culture and used to express truths about relations between God and man. The use of such speech forms for theological purposes raises no question of scientific error. Another example might be the charge that the Bible is guilty of bad biology in Leviticus 11:5 where conies and rabbits are said to chew the cud. The language is that of naive-observation; therefore, we ought not to regard this as a scientific error. It would be perverse to do that. Where no attempt at a scientific specification is being made, no scientific error is being committed.

Again, what can we be sure of with regard to the creation narrative? What we can be sure of is that its prime purpose is to introduce not the creation but the Creator. Some questions about the creation narratives, it seems to me, have to be left open on hermeneutical grounds. One is not sure how the biblical writer meant his words to be interpreted, especially in relation to the questions that we ask. We cannot know what some ideal observer would have perceived had he been present at the start of things. It is certain that Genesis 1—2:4 celebrates the fact of creation and that Genesis 2:4—3:24 teaches about the ruined relationship between God and the man and the woman. What is less certain is whether all the physical details of the narrative are meant to inform us of what we would in fact have seen happen had we been there, or whether God means them to function as significant symbols only. Differences here do

212

not argue abandonment of inerrancy on anyone's part, and are in any case only matters of each person's present opinion on an obscure interpretative question. The exception to this rule is the historicity of Adam and Eve, which is evidently assumed and taught since they are linked by geneology to the rest of us.

On the question of miracle, I can only say that since miracles are exercises of God's power counteracting natural processes, natural science can only shelve them as anomalies. Christians, then, are on solid ground when they insist that affirming miracle does not contradict science.

One major potential problem for inerrantists remains: does Scripture ever represent evil as good? I must answer in the negative, that there is no difficulty here sufficient to push one into biblical relativism. Several points may be made in support of my position. First, God is the judge. In both Testaments, God is the judge and His judgment is regarded as morally glorious, not as morally embarrassing. Nothing that is said about the judgment of God on human sin can be regarded as presenting a moral problem. Second, in the Old Testament God often used his own people individually and corporately as the executioners of His judgment. In the New Testament Christians are not called to function in this way; this, though, is not due to ethical evolution but, rather, is a consequence of dispensational change.

Third, what Jesus teaches about divorce shows that God tolerated and regulated at least one mode of behavior which He never approved. It is possible, at least, that other modes of behavior may well have been tolerated by Him on the same basis. So we must not suppose that God approved, or that the biblical writers thought he approved, of all he tolerated. Finally, what about Rahab? Her lie was a lie. It was false witness for her neighbors rather than against them, but even so it was speaking untruth and so deceiving. It is, perhaps, best to think of her lie as tolerated by God because it was the least evil rather than to argue that her lie was a positive good. Again and again, we find ourselves today put in situations where to do right we have to do something that is regrettable, something that is from one standpoint wrong. It is very painful when it happens, but happen it does. In war situations, for example, believers cannot always avoid lying, and indeed do so on the basis that the lie is the least evil course of action available. But a "least-evil" ethic does not treat evil as good; it simply recognizes that some situations require that we do the best we can and hope for God's toleration. That was the case with Rahab.

My conclusion is that the nothing we have found convicts biblical inerrantists of factual or moral error, that no biblical phenomena invalidates the confession of inerrancy that the teaching of Jesus and the apostles has led us to make. In short, as a hypothesis biblical inerrancy stands up to testing; as an article of faith, one of the controls of exegesis and theology, it is stimulating. So I leave you with this question: could it be that those who dismiss inerrancy, believing that there were too many problems, and that they cannot in fact be solved, have simply not thought about the matter deeply enough.

RESPONSE: Peter Rhea Jones

Just the other day I was sharing with a doctoral student about our inerrancy conference and some of the distinguished participants giving major addresses at the plenary sessions. When I mentioned J. I. Packer he wondered if he were the theologian who had a book on the apostles creed. "Yes," I replied. "He certainly writes at an elevated level of discourse," he spontaneously responded.

I am honored to respond to Dr. Packer and wish to express my admiration for this famous conservative scholar. He has given as much consideration to our topic as anyone anywhere and has participated in far flung dialogues and conferences on inerrancy. Tonight he has given his bottom line opinion in condensed form without the benefit of space or time to develop fully. Some of the small sections out of his address could well be extended chapters. While I am not able to follow him at every point I venture the suggestion that Dr. Packer has a God-given *vocation* to defend the authority of Scripture, and he has been faithful. He has the gifts and commitments of a systematician and logician.

His book *Knowing God* is classic. In a recent conference with metro pastors one participant glowed as he talked about preaching out of some of the chapters of *Knowing God*. There Dr. Packer provides an illuminating revelation of human existence in one chapter from the truth of God's Word. He says in one place of the Bible's illumination that it "gives us a working definition of true humanity. It shows us what man was made to be, and teaches us how to be truly human, and warns us against moral self-destruction."[1] He offers help to the pastor as well as to academic discussion.

Dr. Packer is very highly regarded by the Tyndale Fellowship. My year of study in Tyndale House in Cambridge, England opened my eyes to the substantial contributions of very conservative scholars, which are often overlooked. Now I consult my *Dictionary of New Testament Theology* in addition to my *Theological Dictionary of the New Testament*. When I returned to seminary teaching I had my graduate assistant order Dick France's bibliographical guide for biblical research, which proved to be invaluable for doctoral students. I have just seen the first issue of *CTR,* and while differing with its dispensationalism I respect the quality of its book reviews and its topical articles on James.

In Dr. Packer's presentation we see not only high quality, conservative scholarship, but both the force and flexibility we have come to expect from him on the theme of inerrancy. He appears far more aware of the problems than many and demonstrates no design to ignore them or to make premature or inappropriate appeal to autographs. His concursive theory of inspiration, championed also by Benjamin Warfield,[2] attempts a bold, comprehensive position that allows him to take seriously both the human participation and the divine activity.

I am uneasy about pressing the analogy to the Incarnation too far, for an analogy is not a form of recognized logic, but the concursive theory can be a meeting place of different view points and can help avoid both the docetic and ebionitic excesses. So Packer can allow for long processes and the complex character of different parts of the Bible as well as for chastened critical methodologies. My own response to him will not be antithetical but dialogical.

In my own study in the basement of the temple working inductively I soon saw that in a sense each book or at least each type of biblical book required an individualized understanding of its inspiration. I have no difficulty accepting the claim of prophets to have seen dreams and visions and to have heard an inward voice. Apocalyptic inspiration in Ezekiel, Daniel, and Revelation (1:2, 10; 4:2; 17:3) is distinctive. Much of the prophecy of Jeremiah actually proclaims the words of God. Amen. On the other hand, Luke—Acts has a different evolution as the author sets it out in his preface (Luke 1:4-4). James Steward wrote that "Luke there makes it perfectly clear that the inspired writers were not miraculously freed from the necessity of hard historical research which other writers have to face."[3] While Dr. Packer's concursus theory may, like the Christological statement at Chalcedon, contribute parameters more than final explanations, it is worthy of fuller consideration.

Dr. Packer's presentation on problem areas is so condensed that I must single out only a few points for further interaction. One of his big categories is clearly *cultural conventions*. This takes us immediately beyond modern mathematical models and can be applied in numerous instances. The risk is to dissolve difficulties by definition or by "jesuistical casuistry." Out of my recent pastoral experience teaching James I met with a problem passage. I used Joel Gregory's fine book and a host of other commentaries, and our congregation eagerly responded to the purple passages, the inspiring moments, and the courageous warnings of James. Every paragraph was edifying and not a single sentence was presented as spurious. Then we reached James 4:5. There is a translation problem first of all and dependent upon translation the verse may be included with the first four verses or related to the following verses. More problematic is the apparent introduction of a forth-coming Old Testament citation $\grave{e}$ *graphè légei* rendered the Scripture or Writing says or speaks (v. 5a). This, incidentally, is similar to the formulas of introduction elsewhere in James (2:8, 11a,b; 2:23a; 4:6). The problem is finding the statement that follows (v. 5b) in the Old Testament. The daughter of Dr. Charles Williams is in our congregation, and one of our members reading the Williams translation noticed according to her footnotes that the verse was not in the Old Testament. Here is not the place to chase this rabbit far into the briarpatch. Many scholars deal with the problem by saying James was not so much quoting any single verse as giving a general sense from Old Testament teaching. Richard Longenecker makes the best case under the circumstances by calling it a proverbial maxim drawn from scattered Biblical material.[4] If so, this would be an example of what Dr. Packer calls a cultural convention, or the Chicago Statement deems a free citation. One nevertheless feels that some tension remains, or perhaps we still lack the answer.

Perhaps the Quirinius problem in Luke (2:2) qualifies as one that Dr. Packer

215

says we must live with. While an enrolment by Quirinius during the reign of Herod is not impossible, no current solution is free of difficulty.[5] When I taught the gospel of Luke I did the best I could with the facts, admitting it was a glaring chronological problem not yet resolved. I did go on to say to my class that this was the kind of problem that conceivably could be solved by future discoveries. We simply do not know, but we can live with problems.

In Dr. Packer's category of scientific problems, I think of the celebrated statement of the mustard seed as the smallest seed on the earth. Clark Pinnock offered the suggestion that the Greek form is the comparative form rather than the superlative,[6] but typically koiné Greek uses the comparative to cover the superlative. Harold Lindsell tries Matthew Henry's translation "one of the least of all seeds,"[7] but this is hardly the natural translation of Mark 4:31. The mustard seed was certainly referred to popularly for its smallness in the Mishnah, but modern botanists indicate that the smallest known seeds in the microspermous family are found in orchids, carnivorous plants, and total parasites.[8] If we are working with a modern scientific model, then we must reckon with a small error. Stephen Davis considers this an example of an insoluble problem.[9] However, if we simply recognize that Jesus was speaking proverbially, then it is no longer necessary to demand scientific accuracy. My argument is similar to Dr. Packer's category of cultural convention.

I am not willing to resolve every problem by resort to the category of convention, but it is often an illuminating angle of vision. Furthermore, I have no brief against all harmonizing, only against forced harmonization. You can harmonize Paul and James on faith and works, though suspecting that if you put the two men in a room they would have a spirited discussion. Perhaps you can harmonize the fall of Jerusalem and the coming of the Son of Man in Mark 13 by means of form criticixm. As a youngster, I once asked my mother whether we believed that you went to heaven when you died or did you sleep in the cemetery until the end of time. She responded, "I believe you had better ask the preacher." Later I understood as an adult you needed to correlate I Corinthians 15 and II Corinthians 5, and the assignment is tough but perhaps not impossible. The amazing coherences in the Scriptures are also impressive, such as Christ, agent of creation, in Colossians 1, Hebrews 1, and John 1, which I rather expected Dr. Packer to emphasize. Another obvious problem often cited is the two cleansings of the temple, one at the end of the ministry of Jesus in the Synoptics and one at the beginning in John. Some solve it by saying there were two cleansings, and this is not impossible; but there were not two crucifixions, and in four sources no single one reports two cleansings. However, if the Synoptics report the propher chronological moment, it may well be said that John placed the cleansing at the beginning of the ministry as part of his theological intention.

I note also that Dr. Packer himself is uneasy with the word inerrancy because of its negativity, though he is very committed to keeping it. As a modest proposal consider the alternative word *infallibility*. Inerrant and infallible are sometimes used interchangeably, but are often distinguished as in the Chicago Statement. It seems to me that some are claiming a greater degree of precision than God has seen fit to give us, and the word inerrancy certainly denotes on first hearing an absolute meaning without exceptions. My contention is that the actual character of the Bible corresponds to infallibility. Some, such as Dr. Erickson, will wish to complete their doctrine of inspiration with inerrancy,[10] but those who lean toward functional inerrancy or limited inerrancy or the dynamic theory of inspiration may find infallibility an appropriate term. The high view of Scripture position does lack specificity. I for one stand to the best of my knowledge in the Mullins-Conner-Dilday tradition. I cut my teeth on Conner's *Christian Doctrine* at Union University. Many in this tradition could use this stronger word to express a strong conviction about the Bible.

The meaning of infallibility as I am using it centers on the Bible's trustworthiness for the purpose God intended. The Bible is dependable and will not mislead. I. Howard Marshall put it succinctly, "The Bible is entirely trustworthy for the purposes for which God inspired it."[11] Hence for me it is not a compromise but turns on divine intent rather than modern models. Conservatives who are not necessarily absolute inerrantists could claim the word *infallible* to clarify where they stand, to discourage declension, and to encourage confidence in Scripture. The use of the word infallible creates appropriate distance from the liberal view of the Bible as "a fallible testament of human opinion" and communicates that we in the S.B.C. are not so far apart. We should accept *the Bible's tests of fellowship* found in I John, which are believing in Christ come in the flesh and loving one another (3:23). Strict inerrantists can utilize the word *infallible* to emphasize the dependability of the message and complete their doctrines of Scripture with inerrancy. I do note that E. Y. Mullins warned against allowing one single difficulty in science to invalidate the authority of the Bible[12] and recommended an understanding of infallibility to be determined by the Bible's purpose.[13] This is rather an inerrancy of purpose.

Some who do not use the word inerrancy normally because of rigid association with "absolute inerrancy" do not say the other expected thing—that the Bible is errant. I never told a class of mine that any passage of the New Testament was errant, nor have I ever heard Wayne Ward or Dale Moody or Bill Hull deny a passage or book genuine canonicity. Dr. Raymond Brown took me aside one day when I was a B.D. student to say that despite all the critical problems we can and should hang on to the doctrine of infallibility. The longer I live the better his wisdom sounds. The Bible should have the last word. I do believe the intention of the Holy Spirit was fully realized. Al McEachern is right when he says the Bible both contains the Word of God and is the Word of God.

I close these varied remarks by returning to the last sentence in my copy of Dr. Packer's paper. He, in effect, makes the challenge that some conservatives have just not thought enough about inerrancy. Though I have been studying the Bible for a quarter of a century my focus has been on the meaning and relevance of texts. My vocation is exegesis and exposition. I have recently preached on the great chapters of the Bible. That is my thing. Dr. Packer, on the other hand, has devoted some of his finest efforts to the defense of the authority of Scripture and the explication of the doctrine of inerrancy. His strong position makes radical theories look recklessly excessive. I covenant with him and others to continue to meditate upon and investigate the meaning of inspiration. I covenant to remain open.

In the meantime I enjoy a quiet certitude about my Bible. My Bible inspires me to preach. I have found God's spirit in its pages since I was a boy of seven battling with a deadly disease. And when I study the parables of Jesus I encounter not only the background and the life situation and the stages of the story, but delightfully I also meet the Teller of the tale and hear his invitation to respond.

I close with words from the Westminster Confession:

> our full persuasion and assurance of the infallible truth, and divine authority thereof, is from the inward work of the Holy Spirit, bearing witness by and with the Word in our hearts (1.5).

My Christian testimony is that I have known spiritually the inward work of the Holy Spirit. The Holy spirit bears witness by and with the Word in my heart.

Notes

1. Packer, *Knowing God* (Downers Grove, Ill,: Inter Varsity, 1973), p. 102.

2. See Benjamin Warfield, *The Inspiration and Authority of the Bible,* ed. Samuel Craig (Philadelphia: Presbyterian and Reformed, 1948), pp. 158,168.

3. Stewart, *The Life and Teaching of Jesus Christ* (Nashville: Abingdon), p. 9.

4. Longnecker, *Biblical Exegesis in the Apostolic Period* (Grand Rapids, Mich.: Eerdmans, 1975), p. 196n.

5. See Howard Marshall, *Commentary on Luke* (Grand Rapids, Mich.: Eerdmans, 1978), pp. 100ff.

6. Pinnock, *Biblical Revelation* (Chicago: Moody, 1971), p. 76.

7. Lindsell, *Battle for the Bible* (Grand Rapids, Mich.: Zondervan, 1976), p. 169.

8. See "Seed and Fruit," *Encyclopedia Britannica,* Vol. 16 of "Macropedia," (Chicago: Benton, 1976), 482.

9. Davis, *The Debate about the Bible* (Philadelphia: Westminster, 1977), p. 100.

10. Erickson, *Cristian Theology,* p. 221.

11. Marshall, *Biblical Inspiration* (Grand Rapids, Mich.: Eerdmans, 1982), p. 116.

12. Mullins, *Freedom and Authority in Religions* (Philadelphia: Griffith and Rowland, 1913), pp 342-43.

13. Mullins, *The Christian Religion in its Doctrinal Expression* (Nashville: Sunday School Board, 1917), pp. 152-53, quoting Marcus Dods.

RESPONSE: Richard R. Melick

Dr. Packer has written an excellent paper on the problem areas of Biblical inerrancy. He is to be commended for his precision of statement, clear logic, and command of the subject. Typical of his books and lectures, this paper exudes a vitality of Christian commitment, honesty, and depth of understanding that should characterize all Christian scholars.

At the outset, it will be helpful to determine the thesis of the paper. Although it was not stated directly, it appears that Dr. Packer was saying "when we let the author of Scripture set the rules for his communication, we will find that what he affirms and assumes is reliable." While this statement may lack sophistication and detail, it includes or anticipates most of the elements Dr. Packer has included in his paper. It also identifies crucial areas of conflict and disagreement in Biblical studies today. First, there is some major discussion about the author of Scripture. Some continue to argue over the identity of the various authors and over whether or not the authorial designations are accurate. Of course, various and complex theories of multiple authorships and community authorship prevail, and the problem of the author's meaning is proportionately complicated. The editor or community become the focus. Second, there is considerable discussion about allowing the author to set his own rules for communication. Many have opted for a hermeneutical principle that effectively disregards the author. Third, a great deal of study has been done and remains to be done about the area of our ability to understand the author's conventions. Finally, not everyone agrees that the outcome of all of this will produce an accurate, hence reliable, statement of truth. Nevertheless, Dr. Packer's thesis is responsible and sound.

The paper is developed in two major divisions. First, Dr. Packer "clears the ground" for problem areas by discussing canonicity, the accessibility of Scripture, and hermeneutics (the interpretation). He then undertakes a discussion of problem areas, dividing them into the three categories: are historical facts misrepresented, are scientific facts misstated, and is evil represented as good? Certainly most of the difficulties encountered from a Biblical and textual perspective may be found within these categories. Thus, Dr. Packer's paper beautifully addresses the crucial issues and creatively allows for other specific problems to be included. Even the titles of his three problem areas set the direction properly. The words "misrepresented," "misstated," and "represented" correctly frame the discussion. In principle he has anticipated and addressed the problems.

Not all interpreters agree with the first section, particularly the aspects of interpretation. There is, for example, a growing trend to diminish the importance of grammatical/historical exegesis. This is seen in the dropping of Biblical languages from the various curricula and in the embracing of existential herme-neutics. Again, the prominence of Biblical theology, a necessary and helpful study, has led some to deny the unity of Scripture and set one writer against another. Certainly there is less a tendency today to employ the analogy of Scripture and the analogy of faith principles which have helped to shape theology through the centuries. These are direct reflections of the divine as-pects of the Scriptures, but do not, of themselves, violate the human aspects.

Throughout the paper there is an underlying principle that the interpreter must understand an author's intent if he is to understand and appreciate the message. This means that the meaning of the author had and purpose for writing must be considered and accepted. Some, however, have taken it to mean that the author did not intend to deceive, or that he did not intend to be incorrect in his writings. In other words, he did the best he could, and this is what counts. This understanding, however, shifts the focus from the message, which is the product and location of inspiration, to the motivation or the inten-tion of the author. The discussion then becomes meaningless because, first, no person speaking with a sensitivity to God would intend to deceive, and, sec-ond, the Scriptures place the focus of their teaching on the product itself, al-though one can certainly argue that the men were temporarily inspired as well. In order to deal with the relationship of this to inerrancy, one must ask "what would this situation look like to ancient man," and, once that is understood, "Is that correct?" The serious interpreter cannot require that the text fit into con-temporary expectations.

The doctrine of inerrancy involves allowing the author to "set the ground rules" for his own writing, but it also means that the statement must be consid-ered as correct regardless of how they are interpreted. A clear distinction must be maintained between the text itself and a personal interpretation of it. An illustration will help to clarify this point. The Revelation of St. John, as it is called in our versions, is an unusual type of literature. It has been the subject of much abuse, and the interpreter has probably failed in his exegesis if, at the end of his study, he does not feel uncertain about many points of the text. The majority of Christians have seen a futuristic aspect to the book, although not all will agree that every point is predictive of specific future events. Many inerran-tists, however, are amillenial, and thus do not expect the events described to be forthcoming, except in the most general of sense (the second coming of Christ). But this does not violate inerrancy. In similar fashion, inerrantists dis-agree on the nature of the creation days. Some are 24 hour day advocates, some are day-age advocates. Inerrantists disagree on the date of the Exodus. Some are 15th century people; some are 13th century people. They do, how-ever, agree on the fact of the Exodus. There are inerrantists of many confes-sional groups and denominations. They differ on ecclesiology and other doctrines. Inerrancy does *not* argue for an interpretation. It argues that the message and its details are correct and, therefore, inerrant. Every interpreter must possess a humility appropriate to the task.

Inerrancy, however, does has a much greater restriction regarding what the Bible is. That opens the door to rampant subjectivity, and we must have an objective basis for faith. In a somewhat Wittgensteinian term, it opens up a new "language game." Another interpretive problem is the consistent application of these principles. Some of his details may provide fertile areas for dialogue. How and in what direction are they to be extended? Two suggestions may provide help. First, events which are regarded as historical by the author—or the Lord—must be considered historical. There must be clarity about which genre is being utilized. Second, extensions of ideas cannot contradict the basic essence of the teaching. For example, the vicarious suffering of Christ cannot become an example theory only, as European scholar Fuchs attempts to do.

Possibilities other than following the authors intent are problematic. One is to claim that the book *incorrectly* interpreted is authoritative. As bizarre as it appears, this is being done, in effect, by the "New Hermeneutic" school which argues that whatever it may mean to you that meaning has authority. Many literary critics, encouraged by philosophers like Gadamer, claim that there are as many interpretations as there are readers, and there is a growing movement away from the intent of the author. Some argue that once the Word is spoken or written, even the author cannot know the meaning. Such subjectivity regarding the text itself must be dismissed.

The other possibility if one denies the normative nature of the message is to claim that a text correctly interpreted is wrong. This, of course, is commonly done by many who study the Bible. The problem here is that one must choose which passage is authoritative, that is, contains truth, and that calls for some outside principle of authority. In Biblical studies, the "other principle" is normally some theological theme within the text to which all other texts are subordinated or disregarded. This is the search for a "canon within the canon," which has produced little agreement among those committed to it.

With these few comments, the evaluation of Dr. Packer's paper is over. In all, it is an excellent paper which well reflects sane, responsible, and pious inerrantist scholarship. Even though we might disagree with particulars, the guidelines are consistent with the principle of inerrancy.

One final area of the response seems pertinent. There are lingering questions which need answers. Perhaps it is good to consider some of them in dealing with the problem areas.

1. Why is it impossible for personal and propositional revelation to coexist and complement each other? Does it have to be Christ or the Bible, or can it be Christ through the Bible?

2. Why is it difficult for faith to have structure such as is provided in the Bible? The Biblical definition of faith assumes some content which points to the person of Christ. This is seen especially in the Gospel of John where Jesus presents works and words to bring commitment. The Johannine use of faith, pisteuo, is instructive. Three precise patterns are found. "Believe that" (pisteuo hoti), was always followed by content. The Greek verb was followed by the dative, which seems to have some specific word or words as object, and finally the verb was followed by the preposition "eis" (believe "into") which implies trust. They had an objective content to encourage faith. Was it necessary for them to have objectivity to bring them to faith but unnecessary for them to have

objectivity to bring them to faith but unnecessary for us? Objective parameters are not identical to "rational certainties." Faith always takes the believer beyond his securities, but it does not start in a sea of the unknown as some of the existentialists have suggested.

3. Why does human have to be errant? Is it a moral problem? The Bible reveals three persons who were human but not sinful, Adam and Eve before the fall, and Jesus. But even with sinfulness, no one argues that the writers of Scripture were without sin, they argue that the product of their writings was without error. None of us would argue that everything man does is errant. Even sinful humans can arrive at correct conclusions on occasion. A child can tell the parents "I love you" and be correct, or $2+2=4$ and be correct. Inerrancy argues that when the Bible was written it was the one certain time when men made correct statements because the Spirit of God supervised.

Is the reason humanness is equated to error ontological? Is it because man is less than God and to claim to have reached the divine level of understanding is arrogant? That appears to assume a "totally other" and "far removed" Deity. Besides, the Christian understanding is not that man reached the heights of understanding but that God came down to the depths of man's understanding in Christ and in revelation. Either option for the essential errancy of the Bible because it is human appears problematic.

4. How is it that errancy is not the alternative to inerrancy? Is it the literary nature of the Bible which frees it from normal analytical categories? Is it an epistemological orientation allowing for a sometimes ambivalent or diverse understanding of truth?

These issues are also involved in the discussion of inerrancy. In fact, it is impossible to discuss the topic without some orientation epistemologically (there have been these discussions under the surface) in the concept of revelation, and without addressing the nagging question of whether or not God expects man to reorient himself away from his own natural perspective to the perspective of the Bibilcal writers. This of course, leads to the questions of hermeneutic and hermeneutics, the subject for next year. Inasmuch, however, as Dr. Packer's paper introduced hermeneutics, these thoughts came to mind.

Dr. Packer is to be compliemented for his excellent discussion of problem areas. This response has been supportive and, hopefully, complementary.

222

11

IMPLICATIONS OF BIBLICAL INERRANCY FOR THE CHRISTIAN MISSION

Millard J. Erickson

Some years ago I took a course in which we were taught how to read critically. The course was applied more broadly than merely to written material as such. Two questions which we were taught to ask routinely of any claim that we heard presented were, "Please specify" and "So what?" It is important to ask both of these questions about any doctrinal or other teachings which we as Christians hold. The papers given in this conference have focused to a considerable extent upon the first of those questions, "Please specify." We now, however, need to press the question, "So what?" What real difference is there or should there be in our practice of the Christian life and of ministry if we hold to the inerrancy of Scripture? We need not be pragmatists to recognize that the pragmatic view of truth, if understood merely as a theory of meaning, makes a point of considerable significance. If the truth of a given conception does not actually make any discernible difference in what we do, then perhaps its truth is not too important.

To a considerable extent, these implications will be the same as those of views which hold to a high estimation of biblical inspiration and authority, but not necessarily inerrancy. This is because inerrancy is a strong form of the conservative view of inspiration. The difference is that inerrancy leads to more complete and more consistent forms of those implications.

1. A result of this belief in the inerrancy of Scripture will be the development of extensive literature of a scholarly nature unfolding the meaning of those Scriptures. This will mean particularly the development of commentaries of the highest quality and of positive expositions of Scripture. We Baptists have not always been known primarily for our scholarly activity. We have stressed personal spiritual experience, so that we have been known as born-again believers, and we have emphasized evangelism, so that others might also experience this new birth. We have been those who proclaimed the good news. This should, however, be accompanied by diligent scholarly study of the inerrant Word.

It would be surprising, however, if someone were to question the need for additional commentaries. Are there not enough works of this type, many of them recently published, and thus reflecting the latest in scholarship? Why need inerrantists add to the collection? Where we start goes a long way toward determining where we will end up. This is particularly true in interpretation of the Bible. If we believe in its inerrancy, then we will work intensively at developing our interpretations of its passages in a way that is consistent with that assumption. To some this may seem like beginning where one should end, or assuming what one should conclude, but the nature of presuppositions is such that one does not and indeed cannot prove them prior to using them. We will presently respond more fully to this concern.

Frequently we are urged to come to the Bible and simply let it speak for itself. This assumes a type of pure objectivity of the interpreter, however, which is not likely to be present, and especially so if the issue is not initially faced self-consciously. In the choice of exegetical and hermeneutical methods and even in the choice of commentaries to consult, we will want to ask whether these really are based upon the conception that the Bible we are studying is inerrant.

When I taught required introductory courses in theology on a regular basis, I always gave a lecture on the "pre-exegetical issues," the questions that one must deal with prior to being able to interpret the Bible. On one occasion, a student came to me after class and said, "It seems to me you are saying that we have to have a theology before we do the exegesis necessary to develop our theology." Although I would not use the term theology in the former case, I would agree with that statement. The question is not whether we are to have such pre-exegetical presuppositions, but whether we will scrutinize them.

Exegesis and hermeneutics are like navigation by dead reckoning, sometimes used on water and in the air, the latter of which I am more familiar with. Here a pilot calculates the true course to be flown from point of origin to destination, makes adjustments for the wind direction and velocity at the altitude at which he will be flying, adjusts again for the variation of the magnetic course from the true course at the longitude at which he is flying, and proceeds to fly that course at a throttle setting appropriate to produce the groundspeed calculated. At the end of the elapsed calculated time, our pilot should be able to look out the window of his cockpit and see his destination immediately below him, assuming that his calculations of wind direction and velocity and his groundspeed are accurate and he has accurately followed the prescribed heading and speed.

The statement, however, lacks one additional very important element: "and assuming that his compass is perfectly accurate." For all magnetic compasses contain a certain amount of deviation from the correct reading, and this deviation differs with various headings, so it is not possible to adjust it out. Consequently, the compass ordinarily has a card mounted near it indicating this deviation for different headings. If, for example, the pilot's heading after all the other compensations mentioned above is 215 degrees and the compass card indicates a deviation of plus two degrees for that heading, he must adjust his heading to 213 degrees. To fail to do so, or to have inaccurate compass information, will result in missing the destination, even if all the other compensations have been properly made. On a flight of 200 miles, an error of 2 degrees will result in a course error of 3.5 miles, sufficient to result in the pilot failing to spot the destination airport.

The assumptions made in interpreting the Bible are similar in their effect. The conclusions reached regarding the meaning of a given passage of Scripture are affected (not determined) by the assumptions underlying the method being used. Inerrantists will want to do three things: Scrutinize their own hermeneutical and exegetical methods to make sure that they are consistent with an inerrant Scripture; develop an abundance of commentary and other interpretational literature which starts from the assumption of the inerrancy of Scripture; ascertain the presuppositions of the author of any commentary being consulted, and evaluate what is being said therein in light of those assumptions.

This may sound as if I am advocating an obscurantist approach which only consults sources which agree with one's own viewpoints. Nothing could be further from the truth, and I believe my biography confirms that. I deliberately chose at least three of the academic institutions at which I studied so that I would be exposed to different viewpoints than I had previously experienced. Rather, what I am suggesting is that we be aware of the perspective from which an interpretative judgment is being made and compensate for it. I am further proposing that there be intensive literary production from an inerrantist standpoint, so that there is a genuine option for the student of Scripture to consult.

To see the reason for this, it is necessary for us to take yet another look at the nature of presuppositions and how they function. It is frequently possible to construct two or more mutually exclusive interpretations of a given event or set of data, each of which is completely internally consistent. For example, the Pharisees interpreted Jesus' actions and words as blasphemy. From their perspective this made perfect sense, for they assumed that he was merely a human, and he was doing and saying things which only God has the right to do and say. If, however, he was truly God, as he was implicitly claiming, then this was not blasphemy; it was merely appropriate behavior. There are other perfectly consistent interpretations of Jesus' conduct as well. A very good case can be made, for example, that he was a paranoid schizophrenic. Much of what he said and did would then reflect his delusions of grandeur and of persecution.

Each of these interpretations of a set of data may be quite consistent internally. When, however, the conclusions of one approach are interpreted from the standpoint of the assumptions of an alternative approach, contradictions result. A case in point from my own experience was my master of arts thesis at the University of Chicago. It concerned an analysis made by a contemporary philosopher of Plato's third man argument in the *Parmenides*. He concluded that there was an internal contradiction in Plato's thinking which Plato was unable to reconcile because he made two contradictory assumptions. In reality, however, the interpretation offered by the philosopher was being made from what was basically an Aristotelian framework (in a scheme in which one is either a Platonist or an Aristotelian). What he discovered was a contradiction between an assumption of Plato's and an assumption which an Aristotelian would make. The correct conclusion should have been that Plato was not a very good Aristotelian (which Plato would surely not deny) or that Platonism and Aristotelianism are mutually contradictory (which neither Plato nor Aristotle would deny).

To apply this more pointedly: from the perspective of a hermeneutic which does not accept the inerrancy of Scripture, certain inerrantist interpretations of

225

Scripture will seem contradictory. For example, in dealing with the differences between parallel accounts in the synoptic gospels, we may choose to look for ways in which they can be seen to agree or may anticipate finding contradictions. The underlying issue, however, may be the conception of the nature of truth or even of reality. If one holds a Kierkegaardian view of truth, in which faith is inversely proportional to the degree of objective certainty, and in which reality is essentially paradoxical, he will approach these questions quite differently than if he believes that at its core reality is rational and harmonious. As one of my New Testament colleagues puts it, "We interpret the 5% of the material on which there is disagreement in light of the 95% in which there is agreement, rather than vice versa."

This means careful scrutiny of the assumptions of the methodology being employed by the author of an interpretation which one is considering or of a methodology which one is considering adopting. If, for example, one holds that the development of the material which Luke used in writing the third gospel was restricted to the same patterns of development which govern the growth of all oral traditions, one will give a different interpretation to a passage of the Bible than he might give if he assumed that a special divine providence was operative in the preservation and shaping of that body of materials between the time of the occurrence of the event and Luke's reporting of it.

We must ask two additional questions, however. The first concerns whether there is absolutely no value in the interpretations authored by those who begin from differing presuppositions than those of the inerrantist. If this were the case, one should simply disregard a large percentage of the exegetical material which has been written. This is not the case, however. No commentator is completely consistent with his presuppositions, and the question of inerrancy does not enter into the interpretation of each and every passage. Inerrantists can derive much exegetical insight from the work of non-inerrantists. What does need to be done, however, is to ask whether the particular point involved in this interpretation under consideration rests upon an assumption that is incompatible with the inerrancy of the Bible.

One remaining question concerns how one decides between the presuppositions of methods and, therefore, between the interpretations that follow from the application of those methods. Since these are indeed presuppositions, it is not possible, as we pointed out earlier, to prove them prior to adopting them and putting them into use. How then does one prove them, if at all? "Prove" or "verify" are probably too strong a set of terms to use. It is possible, however, to vindicate the use of one particular presupposition over against another. Each presupposition or set of presuppositions, when applied, leads to a system or a synoptic pattern of interpretation. The appropriateness of such a scheme can be evaluated, and the superiority of one to a competitive scheme shown.

There are both internal and external criteria which can be applied to assess such a scheme. Here I find the set of criteria expounded by Frederick Ferre' in his book *Language, Logic and God* to be quite helpful.[1] The internal criteria are the ways of measuring the relationship of various ideas within a system to one another. One of these is consistency. Do the several tenets of the interpretive methodology conflict with one another, or is there basically harmony among them? While this criterion may be criticized by some as itself a presupposition, we should note that in practice anyone who attempts to communicate with anyone else makes such an assumption. If I tell you, "I am not now telling the truth," you will have great difficulty knowing what to do with that statement. Its truth implies its falsity, and its falsity its truth. One cannot really believe two or more contradictory propositions at the same time and in the same respect.

The second internal criterion is coherence. There may be many statements which are consistent with each other. They do not conflict simply because they are quite unrelated, dealing with different realms of experience. When, however, there is positive interrelationship and mutual support among propositions, that is a stronger vindication. Note, however, that both of these internal criteria are primarily negative criteria. The absence of them suggests falsehood, but the presence of them does not necessarily guarantee truth. They are necessary but not sufficient conditions of truth.

When we come to the external criteria, however, we are facing more definite positive evidences. Here we are speaking of the way in which a hermeneutical or exegetical method relates to the data to be interpreted, the material of Scripture. The first of these criteria is applicability: does this view ring true to the facts? To put it specifically, does this interpretation offer a credible explanation of the passage to which it is applied, or is there something artificial and strained about it? There should be the "ring of truth" to the interpretation which this method gives us.

More important yet, however, is the criterion of adequacy. Presumably every hermeneutic rings true to some part of the holy Scripture. Some methods, however, and some interpretations are able to account for a broader sweep of the phenomena than are others and to explain those features of the narrative or the story with less distortion than are others. In the final analysis, this greater inclusiveness and more natural rendering must be considered a mark of superiority of one view over another.

2. There will be a motivation to work intensively at determining the precise meaning of Scripture. Here we have in mind primarily those who preach and teach the Word of God, as contrasted with the scholars who prepare the resources and tools for this. The preacher who preaches from the inerrant Bible will want to be diligent in studying that Bible, knowing that when the meaning is identified, it will be a fully truthful message.

Let us suppose for a moment that the Bible is not inerrant. Perhaps God merely gave Paul some ideas, perhaps quite general or perhaps rather specific, but that Paul expressed these in his own words and that the inspiration of the Holy Spirit did not extend to guiding the way in which Paul explained and expressed that message. Does it matter whether we get at the exact meaning if all we then have is a more precise understanding of what Paul thought? Our interest in the study of the Bible is not merely historical or biographical. That is the work of the historians and the biographers, but they do not preach. The motivation in our study is because we believe that when we obtain the correct understanding of the writing, we are hearing God speak. This makes worth-

227

while all the effort invested in learning Greek and Hebrew, so that we may more precisely understand the meaning of what was said. How much difference does it make whether Paul said, "Stop doing" something or "Don't begin doing" something, if the choice of one expression rather than the other merely represents Paul's (possibly mistaken) opinion?

Study of the Scripture, intensive study of the Scripture, is hard work. It involves more than merely reading a secondary work or two, drawing up an outline, finding the central thought of the passage. Whether in our study of the Bible for our own personal edification or for teaching it to others, the pressure of time might be such as to cause us to settle for the first plausible, satisfying, and applicable interpretation we find. It is the belief that the end result of the diligent study is of special value that motivates our study. On one occasion, the small letter scale in the department office in which I worked was broken. A screw in the connecting mechanism between the pan of the scale and the indicating arrow had come loose. Because I enjoy repairing mechanical things, I took on the challenge. It proved to be a formidable task, but I pressed on, motivated by the same sense of desire that causes people to work at puzzles like the Rubik's cube. Finally, after about twenty minutes of work, I succeeded in reinstalling the screw. The secretary then took the scale down to the mailing room to check it against the precise postal scales for accuracy and returned to tell me that as a result of my diligent labors we now had a mechanically perfectly functioning but greatly inaccurate scale. Belief in biblical inerrancy means that the effort expended in interpretation of the Bible is not invested in vain.

3. Belief in biblical inerrancy will help give us the ability to preach with authority and confidence. One of the most interesting passages in the Bible is in Mark 1:22, where the people "were amazed at Jesus' teaching, because he taught them as one who had authority, not as the teachers of the law." There was a discernible difference between these two types of preaching. Just what it was about Jesus' preaching that caused the hearers to make this sort of judgment we do not know. We do know, however, that Jesus had the conviction that his teaching stood on the same level as the writings of the received Scriptures of his day, and even superceded them. At least in part, the authority of Jesus' teaching was because he knew that what he said was indeed a work from God, rather than merely his own opinion. Paul, similarly, spoke with emphasis and insistence because he was convinced that his message had come from the Lord. He was willing to risk his life on the basis of what he was preaching, for he was so certain of its divine origin.

Inerrancy provides the preacher today with the boldness to preach with authority. Preaching and teaching about spiritual matters is a sacred responsibility, and one which could cause hesitation. Jesus spoke of the responsibility upon those who cause one of the little ones who believe in him to sin (Mark 9:42). James also warned his hearers that not many of them should become teachers, since they would be judged the more severely (James 3:1). The underlying reason for this was that incorrect teaching would affect the relationship to God of the one taught, and could even determine that person's ultimate destiny. If one is not absolutely certain of the divine origin and authority of what is being preached, there will be a less than clearcut utterance of that message. Note the difference between the early preaching of John the Baptist, when he boldly proclaimed, "Look, the Lamb of God, who takes away the sin of the world!" (John 1:29) and his later question, "Are you he who should come, or should we look for another?" It is probably fortunate in a sense that at this latter time John was in prison, where he was neither able nor required to preach, for he certainly would not have been able to preach with authority or with effectiveness.

Suppose that the preacher today, in proclaiming the gospel, has questions about the inerrancy of the Scripture which he is using. He may be using as the text for an evangelistic sermon, Acts 16:31, where Paul is reported as replying to the Philippian jailor's question, "What must I do to be saved?" by saying, "Believe in the Lord Jesus, and you will be saved." Suppose, however, that Paul was mistaken in what he said at this point, that this was merely his opinion intruding upon the divine revelation. Or suppose that Luke did not give an inerrant report of what Paul said? Perhaps this statement of Paul's has been perverted in the retelling that was part of the transmission of the tradition. The spiritual condition of this hearer now depends upon whether this is indeed the correct answer, the answer that God would want given to the question, "What must I do to be saved?" If that is the case, then there will be an element of wavering in the words of the preacher. The tone of the message will to some extent be, in effect, "Believe in the Lord Jesus Christ, and you will be saved . . . I think." Inerrancy of the Scripture means that the preacher who has correctly interpreted the message and accurately represented it need not fear judgment for speaking falsely.

4. Belief in the inerrancy of the Bible also motivates us to preach on the whole of the Scripture. Inerrancy refutes the idea that some parts of the Bible may be merely erroneous, legendary, mythical, or antiquated. While inerrancy does not prescribe what type of literature is found in any given portion of the Bible, or what is to be the correct interpretation of any specific passage, it does mean that all of it is authoritative. It all has some spiritual value, and no part of it is therefore to be ignored.

It is helpful for those of us who preach regularly to keep a chart recording the sermons that we preach. One factor would be to identify the type of sermon or subject matter that we deal with, such as evangelistic, doctrinal, ethical, stewardship, etc. The other dimension would be the biblical material that we preach from, the various books of the Bible. Such a plotting of our preaching will sometimes reveal some interesting facts. We may find, for example, a heavy preponderance of preaching from the gospels, or from Paul's epistles, or the narrative portions of the Old Testament. Although certain books will surely be more applicable to a particular audience at a given time and, therefore, should be utilized more, some attention should be given to the less frequently treated portions. I must confess, for example, that my records reveal only two sermons from the book of Ecclesiastes and none from the Song of Solomon. Yet the inerrancy of Scripture applies to those books as well.

Even certain types of material sometimes neglected should be incorporated

229

into our teaching and preaching, if the inerrancy of Scripture is true. I tend, in my own devotional reading of the Bible, to skip rather quickly over the genealogies, and I have not preached on them per se. Yet, we should not overlook the spiritual truths that these contain, as well. Some of the abiding teachings of the genealogies are these: all of us have a human heritage from which we derive much of what we are; we have all, through the long process of descent, received our life from God; God is at work providentially in human history.

5. The belief in inerrancy contributes to the missionary impulse. This stems from two considerations. The first is the certification of the missionary commands and authorizations. Because the Bible is inerrant, we need not wonder whether Jesus' great commission, "Go and make disciples of all nations" is really the Lord's message and will for the church. Even any authorial interpretation or commentary upon the words of Jesus is inspired by the Holy Spirit so that we have without error the message that He intended for us to receive. We may, therefore, on the basis of this and many other missionary commands in Scripture, conclude with confidence that we are doing God's will and pleasing him by seeking to evangelize the entire populated world.

The second reason is that the basic teachings of Scripture upon which the missionary enterprise rests are also guaranteed to us. One of these is the universality of sin. Because some cultures are much more genteel than ours in the behavior that is acceptable for their members, we may not recognize sin, at least in the manifestations which it usually takes within our society. We might think that the members of a less competitive society, for example, lack the selfishness so frequently associated with sinfulness in American society. Belief in the inerrancy of such portions of Scripture as the opening chapters of Romans, for example, assures us that sin, whatever form of expression it takes, is indeed universal.

Similarly, the inerrancy of Scripture assures us that the salvation accomplished by Jesus Christ is of exclusive and universal value and applicability. When Peter said in Acts 4:12, "Salvation is found in no one else, for there is no other name under heaven given to men by which we must be saved," we can believe that this is indeed what God wanted to convey to those hearers and to us as well. Jesus' statement, "I am the way, and the truth and the life. No one comes to the Father except through me" (John 14:6), is also an authoritative word to us that Jesus and Jesus alone is the means by which we find salvation. We need not wonder whether there is some other possibility by which these people can obtain forgiveness of the sinfulness of which they, like all other humans, are guilty. There is only one way, and we must proclaim it. The inerrant word teaches us that there is universal need but that there is also a universal solution to that need.

6. There is a powerful motivation to work at contextualizing the biblical message. The revelation preserved in Scripture came into specific times and places, and the message is sometimes very much particularized to the circumstances of the first readers. The inerrancy of the Bible means that we have a dependable record of the message for those people to whom it was given. It is, therefore, historically authoritative for us, as a means of informing us of what

was normatively authoritative for them or what they were required by God to do. It is not necessarily, in that same form at least, normatively authoritative for us. We do not have to offer animal sacrifices, abstain from eating fish that have no scales or wearing clothing of two types of cloth, or prohibit women from speaking in public gatherings of the body of believers, simply because those actions were commanded or prohibited in the Bible. Yet, having said that, we must nonetheless ask what there is in those ancient teachings which is relevant for us today. This means distilling the essence of the teaching, the permanent or timeless factor, from the form in which that was first expressed and finding its appropriate application and expression for today. Thus, for example, the concern underlying the various dietary laws given to Israel was the preservation of physical health. That still is pertinent today. Were Leviticus written today, however, it might prescribe a certain amount of physical exercise or restrict the use of foods containing large amounts of fats and cholesterol. This desire to find the meaning of the Scriptures and apply it to our situations of today is heightened by the conviction of its inerrancy, which for our purposes here means that we are not merely dealing with antiquated or obsolete teachings in these portions of the Bible.

This dimension of contextualization pertains to translating the message from biblical times into the present. Traditionally, belief in the thorough authority and inerrancy of Scripture has served to motivate Bible translation, in the sense of producing ever more current renderings of the biblical text into contemporary language. What we are here talking about is a similar translation of biblical concepts into contemporary thought. Thus, for example, we need to ask what the parable of the Good Samaritan might mean today. The underlying truth of the parable would seem to be that we are to love our neighbors (as Jesus said) and that this involves caring for the needs of those who are deprived or suffering. We will then ask what that might mean in our situation today and apply it. This may dictate actions quite different in nature, but we will not ignore the parable simply because we do not encounter anyone who has been robbed, lying naked, and bleeding beside the road. It may instead affect how we vote in elections and what stand we take on moral issues, both locally and internationally.

The form of translation or contextualization we have just been discussing is what I have sometimes termed the dimension of length, bringing the message from a first-century (or earlier) setting into the present time. A second dimension, however, involves what might be termed breadth. That is the re-expression and re-application across differing cultures within the same time span. Here we are particularly talking about the missionary enterprise, both worldwide and within our own American culture. This type of translation involves discerning the basic underlying essence of the biblical doctrine of forgiveness, for example, as separated from the various forms of expression used in the biblical teaching and in basically western categories and finding ways to convey this to people whose culture may not have a concept quite like that. It will mean finding some starting point for building a bridge from where the person in the other culture is to where the biblical concept is and then back again.

231

This may not be restricted to foreign cultures, however. Within the many subcultures found in American society, we may encounter people whose culture does not really provide them with a strong father image or father concept. To translate the biblical doctrine of the fatherhood of God into a form that enables them to begin to grasp the rich biblical truth will be a difficult but very important and thus, worthwhile, endeavor. It also is an endeavor for which we have good biblical precedent. The gospel writers have a common purpose: to present the account of the life and teachings of Jesus in such a way as to elicit understanding and faith. Each of them is dealing with a slightly different audience, however, and so each interprets Jesus somewhat differently. Jesus no doubt usually spoke in Aramaic and each of the gospel writers wrote in Greek. Their translations varied as much as do the several translations into contemporary English that we have today. Each was trying to make it easier for his specific audience to grasp what Jesus was saying for and to them. In the case of the first beatitude, for example, Luke has probably given a more literal translation of what Jesus said, "Blessed are you who are poor" (Luke 6:20), while Matthew has given a bit of amplified translation of the meaning, "Blessed are the poor in spirit" (Matthew 5:3). Redaction criticism can be of great help to us in showing the nuances of interpretation made by each gospel writer, thus assisting us in doing the same thing in our presentation to our audience today.

Paul, too, did not always express his message in identical fashion each time he wrote or spoke. Note, for example, the differences between Romans and Galatians, which although dealing with rather similar subjects, involve small nuances of meaning in their expression. Other letters give slightly different expressions to concepts such as the greatness of Jesus Christ and the glory of divine grace. Note particularly the contextualization that Paul engaged in during his speech before the philosophers in Athens, in Acts 17. He began at a point of contact, their altar to the unknown god, and related his message to that. This was quite different than the approach that he typically made when addressing an audience made up predominantly of Jews.

Some inerrantists have mistakenly thought that the doctrine of biblical inerrancy prohibits this type of activity. Their understanding of inspiration is such that there virtually had to be identity and homogeneity between the several gospel author's writings. So when Merrill Tenney wrote his book, *The Genius of the Gospels,*[2] in 1951, one conservative evangelist attacked the book in his publication. This, however, was a case of excessive understanding of the signification of inerrancy. Inerrantists do not expect exact uniformity of expression of the biblical truth in all situations. Rather, they see the unity in the underlying essence of the biblical message, and take encouragement from the fact that it could be contextualized differently for different groups in biblical times, and thus can also be similarly customized today.

Finally, contextualization will take place along the dimension of height. Here we are referring to the adaptation of the message to different levels of complexity and sophistication. The person who believes in the inerrancy of Scripture will hold that there is an objective element in the basic core of the message which is unvaryingly true. The message of salvation is for all ages, all educational levels, all religious backgrounds, and all intelligence quotients. To adapt the message to all of these, regardless of whether they are college professors or manual laborers, first graders or adults, persons who have studied the Bible for thirty years or those who do not know whether Joel or John are located in the Old Testament or the New Testament—that is as much a part of the mission of the church as is taking the gospel to Orientals or Africans.

This last dimension of contextualization is particularly difficult. Whereas one's audience of hearers or readers may be fairly uniform in terms of the time period or the culture, they are not likely to be so when it comes to the level of intelligence, learning, age, or experience. One frequently finds wide variations in these matters within the same audience. This was very apparent to me the day I, as a young pastor in my first church, looked out and saw two persons sitting next to each other in the sanctuary. One was the teacher of the high school Sunday school class. A college graduate possessed of a keen mind, she was a public high school teacher. Next to her, however, sat a young man who probably had an I.Q. of about 80, was a school dropout, and could write his own name but not much more. He was a functional illiterate. I said to myself, "How am I supposed to preach to both of those people simultaneously?" That was not an easy question to answer, either then or now. It is, however, a very important task to work at.

The question needs to be raised, however, as to why inerrancy makes a difference in endeavors such as we have been describing under the general rubric of contextualization. Does not anyone who accepts the Bible as authoritative in some sense endeavor to do something of this type? The difference is that the inerrantist places a particularly high value upon retaining the basic content in the process of giving various expressions to that message or presenting it in various forms. At the core of the biblical message is an unvarying truth, and insofar as this is preserved in the process of contextualization, it will have the same results that God promised in Isaiah 55:11, "so is my Word that goes out from my mouth: It will not return to me empty, but will accomplish what I desire and achieve the purpose for which I sent it out."

7. There will also be conviction which enables one to speak out on the ethical issues of our time. Both in terms of individual behavior and of social political issues, there is need for taking of bold stands. Human lives are being destroyed and whether by a great and sudden nuclear destruction or a more progressive choking off of the means of life, the same potential exists for destruction of the entire human race. Many different answers are offered as the solution to these problems. One perplexity is how to determine which answer is correct. More troubling, however, is the suspicion that perhaps none of these answers is correct, that there really is no objective basis for ethical judgments. Perhaps all of these are human opinions. Unless truth and right are determined by a majority count or by force of power or persuasion, there may be no point in seeking solutions, for there may not really be any objective good. When ethical relativism prevails, each answer may be as good as any other. It is like a footrace, in which any runner may be judged to be ahead, since on a circular track one might be considered either ahead or behind any other, and after several laps

leadership may not be at all apparent to the casual observer. There must be some objective standard, a line from which progress is measured and toward which the race progresses.

This is the role which the Bible plays in the great moral issues. The standard of right and wrong and of good and bad is God's moral law and behind that the very nature of God himself. The Bible preserves for us God's self-revelation of his moral nature. The inerrancy of Scripture guarantees the accuracy of that record.

This is not to suggest that the Bible can be consulted in a simplistic or legalistic fashion on all or even most of the issues that we face. We cannot merely look in our topical Bible or concordance, for example, to find a biblical statement on the use of nuclear generated electricity or the determination of the proper recipient of an organ transplant. The Bible says nothing directly on those and similarly complex subjects. It does, however, give us principles (such as the value of human life and God's concern for the helpless and defenseless) which can give us guidance if the Bible is used principally. And the assurance that the Bible presents not merely human opinion basically similar to other human opinions on these matters but a divine standard encourages us in the ethical task.

Possession of the biblical revelation in these matters is like having a compass or seeing the North star or flying on instruments. Beyond all our subjective feelings there is an objective source and standard. This is illustrated in one pilot's account:

> I was alone in a storm in the middle of the night, and I was being tossed around until every strap on my harness was creaking. I had a feeling that my right wing was too low, and so I pulled it up some more. By and by I thought my shoulder straps were too tight. I made up my mind that I was going to loosen them as soon as I got a chance. Then suddenly I came to myself and looked at the instrument board. I was upside down and going in the wrong direction—the words of the instructor came ringing in my ear, "Fly by your instrument board; trust it and not your feelings."[3]

The inerrant word is that set of instruments pointing to the right, the good, and the true, in a world of confusing feelings and conflicting opinions.

8. Belief in the inerrant Word of God causes us to place our trust in truth rather than human personality. We live in a day in which glamour and style are very influential. What color of suit one wears, where one sits, how one speaks, affects people in ways that are not always consciously recognized. A young, handsome, perfectly dressed, charming preacher with charisma is frequently able to influence people in almost any direction he wishes, sometimes without even being aware of what he is doing. Such preachers may not always rely heavily upon the Bible in their ministry. Gripping stories, expertly told, may massage the feelings of listeners and even manipulate them. In popular Christian circles, there is virtually a group of prophets, persons who at a given time achieve great popularity, to the point that for many Christians whatever that person says is taken as in some sense absolute. "Disciples" are formed who

accept uncritically the teaching of the prophet without really putting it to the test of biblical support.

Recent developments in the realm of religious broadcasting in this country have demythologized somewhat the glamour syndrome that has tended to attach to certain media personalities, yet the temptation is still present to some degree. The preacher or the lay person, however, who believes in the inerrant word will want to make sure that it is biblical substance, not personal style, that is the focus of the experience of worship and commitment.

This applies as well to the fashion in which the biblical truth is presented. Sometimes this is done in an authoritarian fashion, with the preacher loudly and dogmatically proclaiming his message. For the inerrantist, however, the question will be whether this is indeed the correct rendering of the biblical passage. The only important issue is, "Does the Bible say this?" There is no other authority.

9. Finally, the preacher or other Christian servant will take encouragement and comfort from the fact that there is an authoritative and inerrant Scripture, and that the success of the ministry depends upon it and upon God's working, not upon human strength. This is, as it were, the positive point correlative to the negative one just made. While we must be careful not to place our trust in human skill, glamour, and method, the reverse is that the absence of such human strength does not preclude God's working.

Two cautions must be observed here. The first is that there is no excuse found in the Scripture for any sort of laxity, indifference, or neglect of our responsibilities in God's service. We must seek to do our very best, even though that alone will never be sufficient. The other caution is closely related to this. There is a danger of treating the Bible as having mechanical or "magical" efficacy. Some may feel that so long as people are presented with the truth of Scripture, it will have its effect. This overlooks the fact that the pattern of authority involves both an objective and a subjective component. The Bible with its message content is the objective factor. The subjective factor, however, is that the Holy Spirit illuminates the mind of the hearer or reader in terms of understanding, conviction, and decision. It is quite possible for someone to read or hear the Scripture, without any real effect.

When I was a seminary student, I somehow thought, at least in practice, that for God to use a sermon it had to be a perfect sermon. The exegesis had to be perfect, the outline precise, the vocabulary, the illustrations, the delivery all ideal, or nothing would happen. I have since learned better, and I am glad that is the case, for I have never preached a perfect sermon, and I doubt that I have ever heard one. Yet God is able to bless the preaching of the Word, for it is inerrantly his Word, and his Holy Spirit adds his blessing to that Word.

Sometimes God has to remind us of that, and in humbling ways. I recall one particularly vivid instance of that. I was serving as interim pastor of the Central Baptist Church of St. Paul. Of all of the sermons that I preached there in 10½ months, one clearly stands out as by far the worst. There was not even a close second. In fact, I would have to rate it with the very worst preaching performances of my entire career. It was not that the sermon was not based on Scripture. That it surely was. I had not really achieved clarity in my own understanding of what I had prepared to say, and the clarity did not emerge in the process of preaching the sermon. I struggled to communicate, but simply continued to flounder. As was the custom, I had to go to the door following the sermon and greet the worshippers. I would have preferred to slip out the back door, but that was not a socially acceptable procedure. I felt like saying to each person, "I'm sorry," rather than "Good morning," or "How are you?" I almost considered asking the ushers to bring the offering back and pass the plates again, so that people could take their money out if they felt they had been cheated. To make matters worse, that afternoon was the Sunday school picnic, and I had to face all of these people again. But during the afternoon, the man who ran the sound system that day said to me, "I thought you would be interested to know that we had more requests for tapes of this morning's message than any other service we've ever taped at Central." The inerrancy of Scripture means that the Bible is true and therefore can be used of God, even if I am having a bad day as a preacher.

The Bible has been given to us to guide our own personal lives and ministries and to supply the content of the message which we proclaim in word and deed. May the doctrine of the inerrancy of Scripture add urgency and effectiveness to the execution of our mission.

Notes

1. Frederick Ferre', *Language, Logic, and God* (New York: Harper and Row, 1961), pp. 162-63.
2. Merrill C. Tenney, *The Genius of the Gospels* (Grand Rapids: Eerdmans, 1951).
3. C. Roy Angell, *Baskets of Silver* (Nashville: Broadman, 1955), pp. 43-44.

RESPONSE: Gene M. Williams

Introduction to Response
    A. Appreciation to all Six Seminary Presidents
        1. I really love Landrum Leavell, Russell Dilday, Milton Ferguson.
        2. I surely appreciate all participants for being willing to come.
    B. Glad to take the Responsibility
        1. Saved (9) and Baptized (10) at First Baptist Church, Houston, Texas.
        2. Licensed and Ordained in a Southern Baptist Church, Houston, Texas.
        3. At Baylor I turned to personal witnessing through studying *With Christ After the Lost* by Dr. Lee Scarbrough; at New Orleans Bap-

tist Seminary Dr. Roland Leavell encouraged me in evangelism and in my Th.D. Program and I studied History of Preaching and Revivals.

4. I've spent thirty years in evangelism and missions.
5. My concern: Inerrancy as it related to the Christian Mission

C. All dealt with until now has been Theory! Now we deal with the *Practical*.
1. It is important to deal with the theory.
2. However, what the theories will do to the Christian Mission is what is really important

I. Introduction of Dr. Erickson's Academic Paper
A. He said that he is dealing with the "So What." That is important.
1. This is the reason the inerrancy question is so vitally important. I hear people say, "Let us quit quibbling."
2. If we fail to maintain the acceptance of Biblical Inerrancy, we will:
   a. Fail to fulfill the Christian Mission
   b. In a generation (after failure), we will have no one committed to the Great Commission
   c. For, if no one accepted Biblical inerrancy, how would we know Jesus really gave the Great Commission? Erickson said, ". . . inerrancy is a strong form of the conservative view of inspiration." It is not only a strong form because: (1) If our historical position as Southern Baptist has been that the Bible is "truth, without mixture of error," and (2) if the word "conservative" means one who does not move away for a traditional position (3) then inerrancy is the *only* form of the conservative view of inspiration.

II. Discussion of Erickson.
A. *Development of Literature*
1. Yes, we need literature produced by scholars who are inerrantists.
2. Erickson said: "Baptists have not always been known for our scholarly activity." I understand and agree.
   a. However, we have had scholars: E. Y. Mullins, John A. Broadus, A. T. Robertson, J. Wash Watts, W. T. Conners, B. H. Carroll, and J. B. Tidwell. I don't agree with everything these men said (that is interpretation), but they were scholars!
   b. It is true—we have emphasized evangelism, because we believed the Bible was correct as it recorded the Great Commission. Baptists have an inferiority complex about Biblical scholarship, but we are not inferior in scholarship simply because we succeed in evangelism.
   c. Some Southern Baptists have longed to be recognized as scholars by others outside of the Southern Baptist tradition. These others have redefined scholarship to mean something that agrees with them.
   d. These liberal theologians judge our scholars to be unscholarly, because we will not agree with them and their critical method.

237

e. If we will agree with the Historical Critical Method, which was developed in the first place by those who already rejected the truth of the Bible, then they will say that we are scholars. i.e. We have scholars, but liberal theologians won't agree with them.

3. Erickson said that: inerrancy is a pre-supposition.

   a. That is fine with some: (1) we must approach the Bible with some bias (either inerrancy or errancy). (2) Since it claims to be from God if we accept that, then it is up to the *non*-inerrantist to prove any error in the Bible.

   b. However, that is not acceptable to others; to them it is not merely a pre-supposition, but is logically derived, deductively, from allowing Scripture to testify concerning itself, then acting initially on that testimony. The real presupposition is that by faith God exists and is able and desires to reveal His will. Next: any work claiming to be the revelation of God must first be allowed to testify freely about itself; then be examined by normal laws of evidence to verify the veracity of its testimony. The Bereans (Acts 17:11) were more noble than those in Thessalonica in that they searched the Scriptures daily to find out whether these things were so. Once such veracity is established, then we accept inerrancy as the proven hypothesis upon which we can work, teach, and win.

4. Erickson said (I agree): "Ascertain the presuppositions of the author of any commentary . . . and evaluate what is being said . . . in light of those assumptions."

5. Erickson said (I agree): "I . . . propose intensive literary production from an inerrantist standpoint."

6. Erickson's Colleague said (I agree): "We interpret the 5% . . . on which there is disagreement in light of the 95% in which there is agreement. . . ." The 5% still needs examination, but that doesn't shake us. I have won men who questioned the Scripture until after they were saved. Then the questions were gone.

7. Erickson said that there is value in reading commentaries by errantists, if one keeps in mind his bias. That is true, yet, if I read them all the time, it dulls my faith and hurts my evangelistic zeal and performance.

8. Erickson rightly said, "If I tell you, 'I am not now telling the truth,' you will have great difficulty knowing what to do with that statement." If the Bible is not telling the truth at all times, how do we know it is telling the truth any of the time. Only by a "so-called" scholarship which becomes the authority instead of the Bible. Some non-inerrants seem to accept the writings of their colleagues as more authoritative than the Bible. Let me say that I cannot accept the view that authority comes from below, from the people, anymore than I can accept papal authority. That which is true *wisdom* comes from *above* (not below) Seem James 3:17. James 3:16

238

states: "Wisdom that doesn't descend from above is earthly, humanistic, of the devil, and results in bitter envyings and striff. . . ." After all, we accept the priesthood of the believer, because we believe that what the Bible says is true.

B. Erickson said that inerrancy assures preachers and teachers that they will have a fully-true message! (I agree.)
   1. Why study exact meanings of the Greek and Hebrew?
   2. Know the difference between *aorist* and *present* tenses?
   3. Why study textual criticism, if God didn't lead the writer to give us an inerrant text.

C. Dr. Erickson also said that belief in inerrancy will cause preachers to preach with authority and confidence. (I agree.)
   1. We must have this confidence in the Bible in order to drive for a conversion. We can't do this if we are not sure the Lord really inspired an inerrant Bible. This is the authority of the preacher.
   2. This is also an authority over the preacher! What is the authority over the preacher who doesn't accept the Bible as entirely true. What rules him? The answer is only his intellect, so-called scholarship (opinion of other men). He becomes a slave to his own background, culture, environment, and education.
   3. As Dr. Erickson says, correct and incorrect teaching affects not only the relationship to God of the one taught, but (according to James) also affects the relationship to God of the one who teaches.
   4. Erickson says, "Preaching is a sacred responsibility." True! How can a preacher merely speak his "own opinion."
   5. Erickson said (and I agree) that Paul's statement in Acts 16:31 "Believe on the Lord Jesus Christ and thou shalt be saved" may be wrong, if the Bible is not inerrant. Paul could be wrong. It could be merely Paul's opinion. Luke could be wrong in his record of what Paul said. Some answer, "My authority is Jesus!" How do we know if He is the Son of God, Virgin Born, Crucified, Raised, what He said or if He ever existed, if the Bible is not infallable?

D. I agree with his statements about the motivation to preach the whole Bible.

E. Contributes to the Missionary (Evangelism) Impulse: *Main Problem*
   1. Erickson said that belief in inerrancy gave us assurance of the truth of the Great Commission. I add: Did Jesus give it? When? Where is the imperative? What about the order? Could baptism come before "make disciples?"
   2. He mentions basic teachings that cause us to want to evangelize (I agree).
      1. Why send anyone if men are not lost?
      2. How do we know they are lost? Because we accept the veracity of the Bible
      3. How do we know He can save? Because we believe the Bible
      4. How do we know only He can save? Because the Bible says so

239

5. How do we know Hinduism ins't just as good, if the Bible is wrong in some places?
6. Let me be very pragmatic: Inerrancy leads one to obey the Great Commission.
   a. Those who are inerrantists are generally the ones who lead in the number of baptisms, in Sunday School attendance, growth of churches (Read *Why Conservative Churches are Growing* by Dean Kelley), leading in Personal Evangelism and Revival. These inerrantists are asked to give to missions. They do! Many are having trouble getting enough money to build buildings, because their churches are growing so rapidly, but they still give, even though it is difficult for part of these funds to go to some whom they believe cut the foundation from evangelism by casting a doubt on the Word of God. Since the common denominator of most churches which are growing is that they are led by inerrantists, surely we can see the importance of at least giving room for that teaching in our schools.

F. He talks about contextualizing the Biblical Message.
   1. Yes, we should make it relevant to our day.
   2. Yes, we must make it relevant to other cultures: The simple gospel is relevant, but we do need to contextualize it into their language and culture.
   3. However, in relation to contextualizing, we must be careful about a desire to re-write Scripture into a "relevant" application of today without seriously trying to discern the fullness of the revelation as originally given. *Example:* We did not understand, until the discovery of the Ugaritic texts, that Baal worship in Canaanite culture included seething a kid in its mother's milk. The admonition against this was to keep Israel separated from practices of Baal Worship and not merely for health purposes.
   4. Dr. Erickson said Jesus spoke in Aramaic. Yet the Holy Spirit led as the Gospel writers wrote in Greek and inspired them to write as He saw fit. I surely agree.
   5. However, let me say that Matthew did not change the words of Jesus. We can't agree with Gundry, who suggested that Matthew was a Midrashic expansion upon Luke, and that Jesus didn't say, "Blessed are the poor in Spirit" at all, but that Matthew amplified (the) translation of the meaning. I believe Luke reported about the Sermon on the Plain and that Matthew reported about the Sermon on the Mount. Jesus preached many times at many locations. He often preached the same sermon, but used different expressions and phrases in different places. I believe Matthew and Luke were writing about 2 different occasions.
   6. Redaction Criticism he says can help us. I agree that certain types can. Keep in mind, however, that there is a difference in a writer

240

editing his own work and a later writer (redactor) rewriting it so it will apply to a later church.

7. Inerrantists believe in honest, scholarly evaluation, but inerrancy cannot be a "watered down" higher criticism drawn from the liberal hypothesis concerning the nature of revelation. The doctrine of Biblical inerrancy does prohibit certain unwarranted methods and conclusions based on the liberal hypothesis.

G. I agree with all he says about ethical issues. Yet, how do we know what is ethical, what is the moral law, or what is the nature of God, if the Bible is not inerrant?

H. He rightly says inerrancy causes us to trust truth rather than human personality.

1. He speaks of Christians who uncritically accept what the prophet is teaching without really putting it to the test of biblical support.

2. This is what non-inerrants are asking loyalist members of churches to do by accepting what the professor is teaching without even finding out what they teach.

I. I agree that success in ministry depends on God's working through using the written Word.

Conclusion to Response

Dr. Erickson, I really appreciate your academic paper and I thank you for being here to deliver it. I am thankful that you believe in an inerrant Bible. I am sympathetic to your position.

I believe in five years we will see relative peace in our Southern Baptist Convention. These days will be history. I believe the Southern Baptist Convention is less fragile and more capable of surviving this test than some others do.

In the meanntime, let us keep on with the God-given commission of bringing the gospel to a lost world.

I believe we can deal with this theological problem and begin to understand it better and still carry out the Great Commission.

RESPONSE: Frank Pollard

It is now my job to respond to Dr. Erickson's paper. My response is: "Yes. Amen. I like it."

I could invite him to come to our church and share this message with our people. They would like it, agree with it, probably applaud it. There is only one possible word in the whole paper which might confuse them. The only concept here presented with which they might not be familiar is the word "inerrancy."

Many years ago, with great encouragement from my professors at Southwestern Seminary, I developed a conviction that this Bible is the Word of God. I have never even considered the notion that I was to study to see if it were true but only to understand what it is saying.

Lately I have learned that I am an inerrantist. This week I have learned a group cannot define clearly what an inerrantist is. To get a clear, concise definition on just about anything, you have to have only one source.

In his paper, Dr. Erickson makes much of presuppositions. He begins his paper by presupposing that by now we all understand what inerrancy is. I believe that is so, but it is apparent we don't all understand the same thing.

In this excellent study of "The Implications of Biblical Inerrancy for the Christian Mission," all the points made are well-stated and true. Since this is a practical paper studying the practical effects of inerrancy on our mission, I want to make a simple and practical reply.

The first observation is that the ideals of this paper are not being matched by the actual in our Convention's life. Many ministers claiming inerrancy do not fit the magnificent mold here presented. I do not speak in judgment, for I consider myself to be an inerrantist.

When the Volkswagon Bug made its appearance in the United States, most of us had never seen an automobile so small. Jokes were made about pedestrians being run under and accidents caused because a driver hiccuped and turned his car over. One such tale pictured a puzzled donkey in the middle of the road confronting a Volkswagon Bug, eyeball to headlight. "What in the world are you?" asked the animal. "I am an automobile," was the reply. To which the donkey responded: "Then I'm a racehorse." The old song rightly declares: "Everybody talking 'bout heaven ain't going there," has a strong message for us if we are to accept the implications of this paper as the natural outgrowth of inerrancy.

We should see Dr. Erickson's presentation as more of a challenge than merely an argument. I thank God for what He has said and I pray to our Father that it will be true of us. Let's try to match his implications with reality as observed in the Southern Baptist Convention.

I. Points one, two and three declare that an inerrant approach to interpreting Scriptures will allow us to develop a literature, will motivate us to work intensively at determining the precise meaning of Scripture and will equip us to preach with authority and confidence.

He makes a strong case for the need of proper presuppositions in approaching Scripture. Of course this is true but obviously fraught with danger. There seems to be a fine line, non-existent in some minds, between the presupposition that Scriptural matter is inerrant and that personal interpretations of scriptural matter are inerrant. The whole purpose of an inerrant, authoritative Word of God is that it dictate to us, not vice versa.

To approach the Holy Word of God believing it is an inerrant matter and must be accepted and understood as God's truth is one thing. Coming to the Scripture declaring: "I know what God's truth is and I'm going to let this Scripture tell me what I want to hear" is another.

Committed men who had devoted their lives to studying the Scripture, recognized by all to be experts in the law, were reprimanded by our Lord Christ. "You diligently study the Scriptures because you think that by them you possess eternal life" (bad presupposition). These are the Scriptures that testify about me. "Yet you refuse to come to me to have life" (John 5:39).

They had studied messianic Scripture for years but because of their faulty presuppositions they couldn't recognize Him when He looked them in the eyes.

Presuppositions are necessary. Perhaps the most necessary one of all is to approach Holy Writ saying: "This is God's Word even if it tells me I am wrong."

II. Points four and seven declare that inerrancy should motivate us to speak out on ethical issues of our times.

Most all of us share the conviction that all of the Bible is the Word of God, not just parts of it. Our Southern Baptist Convention president has rightly stated that ninety-five percent (a properly conservative estimate) of Southern Baptists believe the Bible is God's Word. In this family of faith it appears to me that most all of us believe the Bible, and some are given one or another label because of the Scriptures ignored and the Scriptures emphasized.

Perhaps it should be stated here that I do not believe inerrancy is the major issue among us or the cause of our current stress. A more critical issue is integrity, simply telling the truth about each other. I have not gotten involved in the political activity because I do not believe politics is the answer. Politics is our problem.

III. In point five, Dr. Erickson states that biblical inerrancy contributes to the missionary impulse. This is an obviously true implication of taking the Bible seriously. Certainly if we see God's Word as that which should be obeyed, we will do what it says. But if we begin to shift our energies from hearing and doing the Word to fighting over the Word and defending it, we thwart the missionary impulse. During a similar period of Baptist controversy, C. H. Spurgeon was criticized for not defending the Bible.

"Defend the Bible?" he said. "I would rather defend a lion. Unchain it and it will defend itself!"

While we can't make that statement crawl on all fours, we must say the Bible gives us a message to proclaim rather than to defend. If our major message is the Bible itself, then we are in danger of perverting its purpose.

An interesting phenomenon in our society is the emergence of churches who do little or no evangelism or mission, yet are almost totally committed to studying the Bible. They live off of other people's evangelism. They are a select society of Christian saints who simply gather and study the Bible.

Matthew 25 states that our Lord's "Well done, good and faithful servant" will not be for those who guessed right about how He was coming again, but for those who did what He said to do until He returns.

We study the Bible, yes. We study it as God's Word to us telling us what to do until He comes to take us with Him.

IV. In point eight, "Belief in the inerrant Word of God causes us to place our trust in truth rather than human personalities." This is another truth which is obviously true and amazingly absent in our fellowship.

243

It may be that the greatest heresy among us centers around the word "authority." Not the authority of the Word, but the authority of the self-proclaimed "man of God."

In the first Christian seminary, all twelve were present. The subject: leadership. Our Lord Christ spoke inerrant, infallible Words. "Then Jesus said to the crowds and to his disciples: 'The teachers of the law and the Pharisees sit in Moses' seat. So you must obey them and do everything they tell you. But do not do what they do, for they do not practice what they preach. They tie up heavy loads and put them on men's shoulders, but they themselves are not willing to lift a finger to move them. Everything they do is done for men to see: They make their phylacteries wide and the tassels of their prayer shawls long; they love the place of honor at banquets and the most important seats in the synagogues; they love to be greeted in the marketplaces and to have men call them 'Rabbi.' But you are not to be called 'Rabbi,' for you have only one Master and you are all brothers. And do not call anyone on earth 'father,' for you have one Father, and he is in heaven. Nor are you to be called 'teacher,' for you have one Teacher, the Christ. The greatest among you will be your servant.'" (Matthew 23:1-1 NIV).

Perhaps the most profane word among us is the first personal pronoun. May God help us to lead our people to place their trust in His Word rather than human personality.

We all handle the Word with soiled hands. We often smudge and mark the sacred pages with our own prejudices, preconceptions and sins. We must guard against seeing the smudges of our own making as part of the inerrant matter.

God deliver us from the spiritual egomania which assumes our people never get a truth from God unless it has been initialed by us.

12

IMPLICATIONS OF BIBLICAL INERRANCY FOR THE CHRISTIAN MISSION

J. I. Packer

Biblical inerrancy is a revealed truth. It is a revealed doctrine on the same footing as any other teaching given by the Lord Jesus and His apostles. It is as an entailment from the broader idea of inspiration. An entailment is an inference which is not just possible but necessary, because as an inference it makes explicit the implications of the original proposition from which the inference is drawn.

Inspiration entails inerrancy. *Inspiration* and *inerrancy* are both technical terms of theology constructed from a wide range of biblical data. *Inspiration* means that the Bible comes from God and His instruction to man. *Inerrancy* says all that the Bible tells us is true, for all that the Bible tells us is told by God, and it is God's nature to tell the truth and nothing else. So, Scripture is true and trustworthy. And, thus, faith receives its sold foundation.

If then one asks what are the grounds of belief in biblical inerrancy, the correct theological answer as I understand it will be this: Objectively the grounds are the teaching and testimony of Christ and His apostles set alongside, indeed, set against the background of the Old Testament faith in the God-givenness of Old Testament Scripture. Subjectively, the ground of belief in inerrancy is what Calvin called the inward witness of the Holy Spirit, which is not a feeling but a God-given state of mind in which one is enlightened to discern divinity. The inward witness of the Holy Spirit enlightening the eyes of the heart, to put it in biblical phraseology, is the subjective ground of faith in the divine Christ; we discern deity in Him and so learn to trust Him as our divine Savior. That same enlightening operation of the Holy Spirit upon the eyes of the heart brings us to recognition of divinity in Scripture. Of course, we do not worship the Bible; we recognize that it is the divine product and, in that sense, in quite a different category from Jesus the divine person. Nonetheless, divinity is there. And, the inward witness of the Holy Spirit is that enlightening operation which enables us to discern it.

The thesis of this final presentation builds on the assumption that belief in biblical inerrancy is intellectually viable as well as being spiritually proper, in the way that I have just described. Given that assumption, my thesis is that belief in the inerrancy of Scripture is a benefit, an enormous benefit, to the Christian and to the church. It stablizes the Christian and the church, for, trusting the Bible, we know the content of our faith. It strengthens and matures the Christian and the church, for, living by God's promises, which are now implicitly trusted, and working out of responsible obedience to His commands, which now we take as absolutes and refuse to relativize or diminish in any way, we are led by the Holy Spirit into that maturity and strength of Christian character which is our true Christlikeness. Thus, belief in the inerrancy of Scripture is enlivening and empowering.

Not for nothing did the Reformers insist, and four more generations of evangelical theologians after them, that God's way of communicating spiritual life to His people is through His Word and Spirit together. It is as we are led by the Word and Spirit together that we are kept close to Christ, and His life becomes more and more a demonstratable reality in our transformed way of living. The enlivening and the empowering come from the Spirit, come from the Savior through the Spirit via the Word, the Word which leads us to the Savior, the Word which keeps our vision of the Savior clear and thus keeps our fellowship with the Savior close. Without belief in the total trustworthiness of Scripture, we shall not be quite sure as to what we ought to believe or which statements, if any, are trustworthy promises from God. We shall not be quite sure which biblical imperatives, if any, bind us since our world is very different from the world of the first century. Our fellowship with him will not be unreal, but much of the time it will be fellowship through a fog. Consequently, the enlivening and empowering which would otherwise be present will be restricted and straitened and diminished. Thus, the loss of belief in inerrancy whenever and wherever it happens will inevitably be weakening and result in a pattern of Christian living and church existence which lacks stability, vision, and authority and is impotent, ultimately, in face of the challenge of a godless world.

Any drift or shift from a consistent Christian supernaturalism, which includes a robust and thorough going faith in a supernatural Bible, to a partly naturalistic Christianity, which includes a naturalistic view of the Bible, will hobble the individual Christian and the Church, and it will certainly lead, in a generation or two, to a quenching of the Holy Spirit. Only a consistent willingness to accept all the Bible's teachings as being from God will open one to the full work of the Holy Spirit in authenticating the Scripture and guiding in the task of interpretation and application. According to Johnathan Edwards in his book *The Distinguishing Marks of a Work of the Spirit of God,* one of the signs that the Spirit of God is at work among men is a raised estimate of Scripture as the Word (instruction, message) of God, and the history of revivals, down to the modern renewal movement, verifies Edward's thesis. The Christian who would know the full power of the Holy Spirit in life and ministry must learn to trust the Bible unreservedly.

Is it really credible that belief in biblical inerrancy can further and strengthen the Christian mission? Some very serious-minded people have posed this question. Often, the question reflects the assumption that "fundamentalism" represents all that Bible-believing Christianity has produced in the twentieth century. That, of course, is not the case, but because the question has been asked seriously, it deserves a serious answer.

Perhaps a good starting point would be to consider the work of James Barr who has argued that it is not credible that a doctrine of inerrancy can help the Christian mission and who is a scholarly critic of fundamentalism. While I find his major work *Fundamentalism* to be unconvincing because of its generalizations and narrow data base, and while his alternative to Bible-believing evangelicalism is not a good one, being actually only the rediscovery of an old-fashioned type of liberalism—I must confess that he has made several fair points in his critique which I think we ought to take as guidance for ourselves.

First, Barr says, and I have to agree with him, that regressiveism in biblical and theological study would be an evil thing. Regressiveism means choosing to ignore modern questions and challenges. That, says Barr, is the wrong thing to do, and I have to agree with him. God calls us to live in the present, to face present questions in the church as well as outside it, not to take refuge in any sort of vagueness or trite formulas, but to give our minds under God to think through our answers as Bible-believers to the questions of our own day. The questions being asked today are legitimate questions and must be faced. We must work to answer them.

Barr makes a second point that is also worthy of acceptance: sectarian isolationism in the ongoing life of the Christian church is evil. Sectarian isolation is always an expression of human pride; no single group within Christendom can ever be self-sufficient in its understanding of God's truth and ways or the spiritual life. In this sinful church, of which inerrantists, as a part, truths and values get divided and fragmented, and all of us need to learn from folk outside our own circle as well as folk inside it. Outside our circle we see mistakes being made and we note them. But, if we look again, we shall see a great deal of insight, a great deal of wisdom, outside our own circle, and that we must gratefully claim for ourselves, for our own enrichment. For example, consider the biblical critical movement. Inerrantists will reject the presuppositions and skepticism about the supernatural upon which it is based; however, we will gratefully accept and use the help it gives in getting at the human meaning of Scripture through which we find Scripture's divine message. Sectarian isolationism will not be the way to go. Critical selection, grateful reception of such truth and wisdom and helpfulness as may be found outside our own narrow evangelical circles, is very much a matter of duty for inerrantists as we move into the future.

A third point that Barr makes is that the practice of simplistic theology is evil. We must be careful not to do our theological thinking in terms of sterotypes, lest we be guilty of misstating a situation or position. There are different sorts of liberalism and different sorts of conservatism. Simplistic theology is never good enough. A rationalistic theology that attempts to turn faith into sight will not do. Barr accuses fundamentalists of doing so, and perhaps some of us every now and then have given that impression. But inerrantists know that it is not our business to prove the Bible true and thus turn faith into demonstration. It is our business, rather, to acknowledge that there is more in Scripture than ever we can grasp. There is mystery in theology, and the reverent thing to do is to acknowledge this fact. It is the responsibility of those of us who teach and preach to model these proper attitudes of hard and open and biblically shaped but inquiring thought.

With that as background, I would argue that the implications of biblical inerrancy for the Christian mission are positive, even dramatic, in their strength. Those who maintain the inerrancy of the Bible have an enormous advantage as they take in hand the work to which God calls His church, the work of the Christian mission. This mission may be defined or formulated, in terms, first, of evangelism and church planting, converting sinners, and establishing communities of the saints. I define it, second, in terms of serving the needs of all people of all levels so far as possible, thus giving credibility to the gospel by manifesting its power to create compassion in hearts. And, thirdly the Christian mission involves bringing the judgment of God to bear prophetically on human society so that sin is detected and the righteousness and repentance that are needed are made plain.

This is the mission. A belief in biblical inerrancy undergirds Christians as they take this mission in hand. First, biblical inerrancy secures for us the content of belief, the content that which we are called to proclaim and share with an unbelieving world. As we have already seen, the methodological significance of belief in biblical inerrancy is that all biblical teaching without exception would be maintained will full seriousness. This makes possible a consistent Christian supernaturalism on which all Christians in the church would agree. It will command unanimity on all that is essential, because the Bible is clear and explicit, full and exact, on all that is essential. In the world of liberal theology that sort of agreement is impossible, but in the world of evangelical theology, it is most certainly possible and the proof of that is that it has in fact been achieved.

When one studies the confessions of the historical Protestant denominations, one will find that though there are a wide number of different patterns of church government, different practices in relation to some of the secondary matters of church life in the Protestant world, the substance of faith is confessed with marvelous unanimity. That is no accident. Those who trust the Bible to guide them into the substance and content of the faith, those who are prepared to believe absolutely without qualification what they find the Bible teaching, end up in the same place with regard to things like Trinity, Incarnation, creation, providence and grace, atonement, resurrection, the reign and return of Jesus, the reality of the church as the new society, God's new Creation, the fellowship of the faithful, and the body of Christ. Evangelicals agree on all these basic things because the Bible teaches them so clearly. Thus, it is demonstrated historically that belief in the total trustworthiness of the Scripture does bring agreement on the substance of the faith which we have to proclaim to the world.

The second point is that belief in biblical inerrancy clarifies the ground of belief. That is, we believe what we believe because the Scripture teaches it, for all Bible teaching is God's teaching. Those who do not hold this view will sooner or later be found holding tenets that lack exegetical warrant, either on speculative grounds (i.e., because their reason concludes so) or on illuminist grounds (i.e., because something has triggered thoughts that they believe to be direct monitions from the Holy Spirit). In either case, an element of arbitrariness will have crept into their position. The authority of Scripture is the only proper ground of belief about God, both because Scripture is His own Word of instruction and because we sinners dare not trust our own thoughts about God, or our experiences of Him, where Scripture teaching does not provide confirmation of our intuitions. Where this principle is not observed, the church is weakened through resulting confusions and uncertainties, and the mission suffers.

Thirdly, belief in biblical inerrancy will determine your method of preaching. Christian preaching is a prolonging of the ministry of the Old Testament prophets. Where the prophets received directly from God the oracle that they were to deliver, we have from God His inspired Scripture which, properly interpreted, is His message to us today. As the business of the Old Testament prophet was to let the oracle of God come out in faithfulness and purity via his lips, so it's the business of the Christian preacher to let the message of God in the text come out purely and precisely via his lips in its application to those whom he addresses. In that sense, Christian preaching is prophetic and ought to be celebrated as prophetic.

Christian preaching's authority depends not on the emphasis with which the speaker speaks. Authority comes to the preacher and is mediated through the preacher when those listening perceive that this man is allowing God's Word to speak through him. In that sense, expository preaching is not one of many permissible forms of preaching, it is rather the only preaching. One allows the Bible to speak its message through him, and the business of sermon preparation is very largely a matter of ensuring that one does not get in the Bible's way. This sort of preaching communicates the force of the Bible in a way unlike any other human activity and carries the authority of God, which is mediated through the Bible and not any other way. The preacher whose commitment to biblical authority is not absolute will have a consequent loss of authority and power, for he will be perceived as a man enforcing his own thoughts rather then echoing Gods. The preacher who has the single purpose of letting the Bible speak through his lips, because of his unqualified faith in its authoritative truth at every point, will have a God-given, Spirit-sustained authority that other pulpiteers, no matter how accomplished in technique and emphatic in style, cannot match. For fruitful ministry and mission, this is essential.

A fourth way in which belief in biblical inerrancy furthers Christian mission is that it determines the method of pastoral counseling. The only right way to counsel individuals on spiritual questions (i.e., questions about their relation to God and their service to God) is to instruct their consciences from Scripture, as the Word of God, coming from His heart to their hearts, with a reply expected. Otherwise, the counseling relationship will produce dependence on the counselors rather than on the Lord, and will thus come under the just condemnation of "priestcraft." Ministry and mission require constant counseling of individuals, and counseling from Scripture will not be well done where absolute confidence in its truth, wisdom, and adequacy is to any extent lacking.

Fifth, belief in biblical inerrancy will determine our method of vindicating Christianity in apologetics. The central task of apologetics as I understand it is not to turn faith into sight, but rather to demonstrate the reasonableness of Christianity as against the unreasonableness of all alternative views. A pitfall in apologetics, however, is the *concessive* approach, whereby one gives up some elements of biblical supernaturalism in the belief that the less you have to defend, the easier will be the defense. Any such concession enfeebles apologetics and makes defense of the rest of supernatural Christianity harder, not easier. Thus, it is harder to defend a version of Christianity that avoids commitment to the New Testament teaching on the nature of Scripture than to defend one that accepts it. The only consistent and convincing stance is that of the apologist who disclaims all right to disagree with Scripture and therefore declines to allow anyone else in the discussion any such right.

Sixth, inerrancy as an embraced belief furthers the Christian mission by determining the method of integrating Christian faith with secular knowledge. The root issue is this: either one is going to let secular knowledge treat itself as an absolute to which Bible teaching must be relativized, or one is going to treat Bible teaching as an absolute to which the whole of secular knowledge must be relativized, relativized in the sense that the Bible is allowed to stand above secular knowledge, to interpret it, and to challenge it when it commits itself to views of man and human life that are anti-Scriptural. Only the latter option will enable the Christian mission to be carried out with conviction and meaningfully in a secularized culture like our own.

In conclusion, a belief in the inerrancy of Holy Scripture is beneficial to the mission of the church for all of the reasons discussed. Furthermore, any position other than inerrancy is incapable of sustaining and informing the Christian mission. May we go forth on mission, trusting God's Scripture unreservedly.

RESPONSE: Gene Williams

I. AGENDA: Dr. Packer says that the doctrine of Biblical inerrancy is beneficial.
   A. Not only is the belief in inerrancy beneficial in the sense of Augustine; it is also beneficial in Pauline sense. *(ophelimos)*. Paul used the word *Ophelimos* in II Tim. 3:16 translated "profitable."
   B. Dr. Packer indicated that the real issue is authority. He says Biblical Relativism (when the Bible doesn't get the last word) destroys authority. He mentioned that those who accepted a partly naturalistic view of Scripture will lack spiritual authority. I agree: When my son Randy was a pre-teen, I used to instruct him to tell his brother (eight years his junior) to do something. If he said, "Tim, you be sure to do this!" Tim would probably feel he could do it if he wanted to. However, if Randy said, *"Our Daddy* said do this!" then Randy would be speaking with authority, and Tim would more likely do what Randy asked. The difference was who said it. Errantists say: "Our authority is Jesus, the Living Word."

250

1. If the Bible is errant, how do we know Jesus said what He said?
2. How do we know He was the Son of God, Virgin Born, Crucified, Raised?
3. How do we know He ever really lived?
4. What about the Great Commission?
   a. We are to "make disciples" on the basis of the authority of Christ!
   b. But if the Bible is errant, how do we know Jesus said it?
   c. How do we know Matthew quoted Him correctly?
   d. Why study the Greek language?
      (1) What difference does it make that the word *teach* in vs. 19 is *Matheteuo* from *mathetes,* and the word *teach* in vs. 20 in *didasko?*
   e. Errantists say that they accept the Great Commission.
      (1) But who determines what to accept and what not to accept?
      (2) When will some of them cease to accept the Great Commission, also?
5. Our Authority is the Word!
   a. We are doing what He said to do and we know what He said.
   b. We are preaching what He said to preach and we know it is true.
   c. Our authority is the Word of God!
   d. God rules over us by His Word and He authorizes us by His Word.

II. Dr. Packer says that we sustain the mission of the church by Biblical inerrancy.
   A. He says inerrancy secures the content of belief.
      1. I'm sure Dr. Packer leaves open the possibility of different interpretations.
         a. Inerrantists do not expect everyone to interpret the Bible the same way!
         b. We don't expect everyone to come to the same conclusions.
            (1) One doesn't have to be a dispensationalist, a pre-millenialist, a Calvinist, or a seven-day creationist to believe in inerrancy. This is interpretation.
            (2) We do not have a creed. This is why we need to understand and accept Biblical inerrancy, which is more important for a non-creedal denomination (as Baptists are) than one that is creedal.
            (3) I hold dearly to the doctrine of the priesthood of the believer (a doctrine that came from an inerrant Bible).
            (4) This truth gives the believer the right to read and interpret the Bible for himself. It does not give him the right to deny the veracity of the Scriptures.
            (5) I would die to protect an agnostic's right to believe what he wishes; but I would not pay his salary to teach his agnosticism to our young preachers!

251

c. The issue here is not interpretation, but a rejection that God really said it.
  (1) The first thing Satan ever said to a human, was, "Yea, hath God said. . . ?"
  (2) At first, he didn't say God is a liar. He merely cast a doubt concerning God's word.
  (3) This is exactly what Satan tries to say to us individually in our ministries, to professors, to writers, to students, and to entire denominations!
  (4) I don't believe we should look under every log and rock to see if we can find a professor who is a heretic; however, we should not be totally shocked when we find one, since Satan is still asking that same question, and all of us have an impertect nature. We should deal with these teachers fairly, scripturally, and firmly. If a few be there, they can still teach, but teach someplace where we don't pay them to teach our young preachers.
d. We hear much about being on a pilgrimage seeking for some authority. We are all on a pilgrimage seeking God's will in our lives, seeking to grow and mature. None of us have arrived at perfection. But I am not still seeking for authority.
  (1) I've found it. I hope the pilgrimage of others won't be away from Biblical authority.
  (2) True maturity does come from feasting on the Word of God.
  (3) Inerrantists don't want authority coming from a Pope, a king, a pastor of a super-church, a creed, a professor, or the so-called Historical Critical Method. We want it to come down from God through His inerrant word.
B. Dr. Packer says our ground of belief should be the Authority of Scriptures.
  1. The major problem inerrants have is not that some disagree about finer points of inerrancy but that the Historical Critical Method denies the supernatural in Scripture. This method is not scholarly, because it is not neutral. It has radical, sub-Christian presuppositions and, therefore, hinders us from understanding the gospel and presenting it, because the Historical Critical Method casts doubt about the only source of the gospel.
  2. But they say, "It is just the unimportant matters of the Bible which are in error." How do we know what are important? This is how: the Historical Critical Method proceeds to say that the Bible merely contains the Word of God.
  3. Inerrantists have been criticized for our lengthy statement on inerrancy.
    a. One of the reasons for the length of the definition, is the sad fact that Neo-orthodoxy has tended to redefine every term we use.

252

(1) Inspiration (2) Infallability, now (3) Inerrancy (strict, extreme, militant, hard-core).

b. A second reason is that errantists imply we believe that which we do not: like the KJV is inerrant or the Textus Receptus is inerrant.

c. My short definition is as follows: (How) God used men of different ages, different backgrounds, with different vocabularies and different literary styles. He not only inspired the thought, but worked (inspired) through these men and controlled them so that He, without changing their styles or vocabularies, saw to it *(result)* that every word that the man put on the original manuscript was what God wanted and not one word got there that God did not want there. Therefore, all that is written down in the original manuscripts was "truth without mixture of (with) error."

d. This leaves room for Matthew to gather material or do research.

e. It also leaves room for God to use one Isaiah at three different periods in his life, so that three different styles show up in Isaiah with an increase in vocabulary.

f. I am not arguing for the word *inerrancy*. You don't have to use the word to believe the Bible. I am advocating a concept, which is: *the Bible is truth without mixture of (with) error.*

C. He spoke of the method of preaching.

1. There are three words in the New Testament for preach.

2. I would like to talk about the kind of preaching that translates *euaggelidzomai* (to proclaim the good message).

a. It is imperative that we as Baptists fulfill the Great Commission.

(1) This is the result of obedience to Christ and compassion for the lost.

(2) This is necessary for Baptist preservation.

(a) If we don't evangelize, we will finally die.

(b) As Joel Gregory said, "The Bible is indestructable, will last forever . . . it will not die." We believe that about the church. However, Southern Baptists could die.

(c) It would take only two generations.

(1) The first would reject the truth of the Great Commission.

(2) The second would fail to obey it.

b. I agree with Dr. Noll, when he said that errancy produces less concern for evangelism.

(1) The reason is that errancy causes many to lack confidence in the authority of the Bible.

(2) Inerrancy puts a man under the authority of the Bible.

(a) Belief in the inerrancy of Scripture compels me to evangelism.

(b) When I'm doing mission evangelism in the jungles, with no water, no electricity, with plenty of mosquitoes, my flesh wishes that Jesus had said, "I am *a* way, *a* truth, *a* life, there are many ways to be saved as long as one is sincere." Or that there was no hell.

(c) I had rather (in my flesh) be on tour of the Holy Land, or on a cruise, or at home with my wife. At those times my flesh might rather believe that all men will go to heaven or just be annihilated. It would be *so easy* just to believe Hinduism could be just as right as the Bible and that God gave enough truth in every religion, so that, if they sincerely followed their religious belief with all their hearts and treated their fellow men with love, they would be saved.

(d) Inerrancy causes me to believe that men are going to hell, that Christ can save them, that He is the only one who can, and that He wants me to carry that good message to the lost both at home and abroad.

(3) That is the reason those who believe in Biblical Inerrancy are leaders in:

(a) Church growth

(b) Sunday School attendance

(c) Baptisms

(d) Evangelistic and missionary activity

(e) Soul-winning promotion and training

I'm not saying only inerrants do this, nor that all inerrantists do this. And I'm not saying that all inerrants will have great success in growing churches. Many factors are involved in church growth, such as location of the church.

(4) That errancy seems to dull evangelism can be seen by any survey similar to scientific surveys of today. For instance, research proves that:

(a) Smoking produces cancer, more lilely.

(b) Cocaine use produces addiction, usually.

(c) Adultery produces divorce, more likely.

(d) The evidence is: acceptance of an errant Bible produces evangelistic lethargy, almost always. Many are saying, "Let's get back to missions and evangelism." The Biblical inerrantists are still doing it. We never quit. Look at the records!!! Examine any state annual. Every place Baptists are growing—it is where they believe the Bible without Historical Critical Method. Look at Russia, The Philippines, Nigeria, Korea and Brazil.

III. In his conclusion

A. Dr. Packer mentioned *deja vu*

1. He mentioned the Church of England.

2. He said, "The grandchildren of the first liberal evangelicals became radicals or unbelievers." We could mention others who have left evangelism because they left a view of Biblical inerrancy.
3. We could mention the University of Chicago.
4. It could be the same in our beloved Southern Baptist Convention.

B. I've heard it said that there are no liberals in the Southern Baptists Convention. I don't intend to call names, even though I heard a man at this conference call inerrancy close to Gnosticism, and another responder say that inerrancy bordered on heresy! I don't believe we have anyone who would identify with classical German Liberalism. However, we must ask what the word "liberal" means. It means: "moving away from an established position." If that is the meaning, and if we have those who have moved away from Biblical inerrancy, then we do have those who could be called liberal. Moving away is good in many areas, like from racism, but not from Biblical inerrancy.

C. I've heard that this is all a political movement. It was reported in an Asheville paper that one of the organizers of this Conference said, "The problem is political, not theological." I believe that is what he believes, and I'm sure he is sincere, but it is not purely political. It isn't for me! I'm not stupid enough to be "led by the nose" by some strong leader to vote a certain way just because I'm told to do so. Sure, it has become political, but only after twenty years of "jaw-boning." We begged for something to be done, but we received only promises, no action.

If a daughter keeps telling her mother that there is a "lion in the street," and the mother says, "Yes, darling," but doesn't seem to be listening, the daughter probably will do something to get the mother's attention. The inerrantists have gotten the attention of the leadership. We'll never solve the political problem until we solve the theological problem. Please, please solve it.

D. I've heard there is a place for both errantists and inerrantists! Yet there is no place for an inerrantist in our seminary faculties. They are not considered scholars, they are ridiculed if they are appointed.

If we re-define inerrancy so that all of us can be one, why won't some accept the concept.

E. We need a "mid-course" correction.
1. Every sailor and pilot understands this
2. We started out believing the Bible is "true without error," now let us come back to that for a "mid-course" correction. Let us keep doing this from time to time, and we'll still be evangelizing when Jesus comes (We all believe He will)! I believe the vast majority of inerrantists love our denomination. I don't believe they will allow a few who might be extremists to destroy anything. Let us love each other and listen to each other. I believe in five years, the political upheaval will be over.

F. I love all of you! I love our blessed denomination! I love the lost! I love

255

Jesus most. I believe you do too. Let us all obey the Word the God: to study, to witness, to win, to baptize, to teach, to grow, but mostly to honor Christ as our Lord, by obeying those words He gave just before He went to sit beside the Father: "All authority is given unto me . . . Go ye, therefore, and make disciples of every nation, baptizing. . . , teaching . . . and behold I am with you always unto the end of the age." Mt. 28:18-20

RESPONSE: Frank Pollard

My response is by no means critical of Dr. Packer's paper. I agree with it. I am totally convinced that to lose the authority of the Bible would be to lose our mission. What I am about to say is not confrontational to any among us. It is not an "either/or" assertion. It is a "both/and" matter. I feel it is where we all are, but it must be affirmed as an implication of biblical inerrancy on our mission. My major concern about the whole issue of inerrancy is that it can center on the inerrancy of the Bible and not on the message of the Bible. It can divert front line officers in God's army to spending an inordinate amount of time defending the authority of the Commander's Orders and to at least some degree prohibit the carrying out of those orders.

Now, if in the ranks there are those who dispute those orders and question them, the defense is necessary even though detrimental to the effectiveness of the army. So the question is: are the orders really being doubted or has the field officer invented or imagined an issue to enhance his own command position or perhaps to keep from fighting the real battle?

These are not judgments. They are only questions I must ask myself as pastor of a local church. To switch metaphors in mid-stream, it is far too easy for us to be like the farmer who worked so hard on his barn and machinery he had no time to go to the field to plant, cultivate, or reap a harvest.

I. I am only saying that along with our conviction about the inerrancy of biblical matter, we must remember the message of the Bible is not the Bible itself.

The preachers I admire and whose ministries are most effective are those who preach from the Word and not about it. To the Thessalonians, Paul speaks a word to all who are called to the ministry of God's Word: "We speak as men approved by God to be entrusted with the Gospel" (I Thessalonians 2:4).

When Henry Ward Beecher began his ministry, the results were underwhelming. There was no response, no growth, no signs of awakening. The indifferent remained indifferent. The lost remained unreached. One day a thought grabbed him and shook him awake. "There was a reason why, when the Apostles preached, they succeeded, and I will find it out if it is to be found out." What sound strategy. How immediate was the reward. Would to our Lord all of us would be driven back to the New Testament to seek the secret of the success of that early band of bold ministers of our Lord. They had a message which consumed them like a flame and through them set the world afire.

Their message was no theory, not something they had simply learned. It was no propaganda of beautiful ideas of the brotherhood of men. It was not an argument but an announcement! It was not a debate but a declaration! It was an infecting, contagious proclamation of the mighty acts of God. It's keynote was: "That which we have seen and heard declare we unto you, that you might have fellowship with us. And truly our fellowship is with the Father and with His Son, Jesus Christ" (I John 1:3).

Their declaration majored on relationship, not creed, on a person, not a plan. What did they declare? Two events which were really not two but one. "Christ died for our sins and He rose again on the third day." The book of Acts records that they preached "Jesus and the Resurrection." Paul reminded the Corinthians: "I determined to know nothing among you save Jesus Christ and Him crucified."

When He came to Thessalonica, Acts 17:2 records that Paul went straight to the Synagogue and "reasoned with them from the Scriptures, explaining and giving evidence that the Christ had to suffer and rise again from the dead and saying, 'This Jesus whom I am proclaiming to you is the Christ.'"

Dear people, I speak to my own cold heart as well as to you. We will never make an impact on our world unless we are sold out to Jesus Christ. It is not the teachings of and about Christ we share; it is the life of our Lord Christ we preach. Of Him Dorothy Sayers wrote: "From the beginning of time until now, this is the only thing that has ever really happened. When you understand this you will understand all prophesies and all history" *(Man Born To Be King).*

How easy to lose grip on our purpose. Denominations do not die because first they embrace faulty doctrine. They begin to die when they let the fire of compassion go out. Then they argue over lesser things. They engage in the dangerous sport of mountain climbing over molehills. When Paul wrote the Corinthian church, he addressed a church committing suicide. They were divided because they magnified leaders instead of the Lord. Having strayed away from their passion for Christ, their passions found less desirable avenues of expression. Some paraded their spiritual gifts rather than employ them for the good of the body. After leading them out of the boggy marshland of these pitfalls, Paul set them again on the solid foundation. He brought them back to the only cure for division. Chapter fifteen begins with a plea: "Remember the Gospel. This is of first importance. Christ died for our sins according to the Scripture. They buried Him and He rose again the third day just as the Scripture said He would." For more than fifty verses, he declares the life that is ours in knowing the living Christ and closes by saying: "Thanks be to God who gives us the victory through our Lord Jesus Christ. Therefore my beloved brethren, be steadfast, immovable, always abounding in the work of the Lord, knowing that your toil is not in vain in the Lord."

II. We are called to clearly declare that the ultimate Word of God is Jesus Christ.

257

The New Testament speaks often of "the word of the Lord" (i.e. Thessalonians 1:8). It is always "the word" (little "w") of the Lord (capital "L"). Exaggerated emphasis on the Bible itself with lessening emphasis on our Lord Christ makes it seem at times we have changed the phrase to "the Word (capital "W") of the "lord" (little "l").

Now you know I believe the Bible is the word of God. It is divinely inspired, God-breathed, it is everything it says it is. "It has God for its author, salvation for its end, and truth without any mixture of error for its matter" ("The Baptist Faith and Message," p. 7). I am an inerrantist. If you go from this meeting saying I don't believe in the Bible, I hope a yellow wart grows on the end of your nose! The Bible is God's Word. But it is not God.

The ultimate Word of God is Jesus Christ. John I asserts: "In the beginning was the Word and the Word was with God and the Word was God . . . and the Word was made flesh and dwelt among us . . ." (John 1:1, 14).

From His great heart of love, God wanted to reveal Himself to us. He wanted to speak a word. Not just a word in a language so a few people could understand, but a word in a person so everyone could understand. God wants us to know Him, not just His will, or He would simply have given us a book with laws in it—not just to know His power or He would have shown that in nature, in flashing bolts of lightning or in the blowing of hurricanes—not just to show us His love of beauty or He would have given us a rose or a bird or a mountain. He wanted us to know Him, so He gave us Himself in Jesus Christ. The Bible is the Word of God because behind the Bible is a voice and that voice is that of Jesus Christ.

The Bible never claims to be the way. It points us to the way. (Psalm 119:9, 11, 105). Jesus Christ is the way (John 14:6). The Bible makes no claims of ability to give eternal life. The Scripture points to Jesus Christ and He gives eternal life (John 5:39).

The plea here is for balance. The Bible is the Word of God. We preach only the Bible or we are not preaching, we're only making speeches. But the message of the Bible is not the Bible itself but Jesus Christ. Its clear word is that people will see God in Christ or they will not see Him. They will know God through Jesus Christ or they will not know Him.

My grandfather was named McDuff Boone. He was a direct descendant of Daniel Boone. My granddad was a village blacksmith. Perhaps for that reason, as well as its apparent truth, this snatch of poetry struck my fancy:

> "Last 'eve I paused beside the blacksmith's door
> And heard the anvil ring the vesper chimes.
> Then, looking in, I saw upon the floor
> Old hammers worn out with beating years of
>   time.
> 'How many anvils have you had," said I
> 'To wear and batter all those hammers so?'
> 'Just one,' said he, And with twinkling eye,
> 'The anvil wears the hammers out, you know.'
> So I thought, the anvil of God's Word

For ages skeptics blows have beat upon.
And yet, though the noise of falling blows was
    heard,
The anvil is unharmed. The hammers are
    gone!"

I think Dr. Packer is appealing to us not to become one of those hammers. The Word of God is durable and indestructible.

But maintaining and defending the anvil was not the business of my grandfather. Nothing could hurt the anvil and no one could steal it because they could not lift it. The anvil was by far the most important tool in the shop. McDuff Boone used the heat of the fire and the unrelenting solidity of that anvil to shape useless iron into usable tools or restore objects bent out of shape to their original condition.

Our Heavenly Father uses the convicting fire of His Holy Spirit to melt us and He shapes us around the solidity of the infallible matter of the Word of God.

This is my sincere reaction to the issue of biblical inerrancy as it has been trust on Southern Baptists: we have spent far too much time inspecting and authenticating the foundation. We ought to go ahead and build the house.

For our Lord's sake, for the sake of the people we are here to reach with the Gospel, let's not be only hearers, defenders, and watchdogs of the Word. God help us to be doers of the Word!

13

JAMES ORR AND THE QUESTION OF INERRANCY

Alan Neely

When I was a young pastor in Texas, I came across a news story describing an experience of a U.S. Congressman from Pennsylvania, William Moorehead. It seems that the congressman had given a rousing speech on a very controversial issue after which a woman rushed up to him and exclaimed:

"Oh, Mr. Congressman, your speech was *superfluous*, absolutely *superfluous!*"

Moorehead was momentarily stunned by the remark, but he quickly recovered and said, "Why, thank you madam. I am thinking of having it published *posthumously.*"

"Wonderful!" she said. "The sooner the better!" Not surprisingly, this anecdote seems strangely appropriate to me at this time. My modest contribution to this conference will be, I suspect, superfluous, but I sincerely hope it will not be published posthumously.

One is tempted in a setting such as this to approach the subject ranging far and wide, speaking in generalities—and wherever possible in ambiguities—so as to give the appearance of dealing with the subject without ever addressing the real issue. I hope that I can successfully resist that temptation and limit my remarks as much as possible to the infelicitous though fundamental question of inerrancy.

Let me say at the outset that I am aware that the theme is what James Orr thought and wrote about inerrancy, not what I may think or write about it. At the same time, I freely confess that my own perspective affects and colors how I interpret what Orr wrote, and that I find it impossible not to include some perspectives of my own.

This brings me to the point of stating initially one of my major misgivings about the theme assigned to me, namely, that James Orr (1844-1913) lived at a different time and in a different cultural and theological setting and that he was confronted with different challenges from those we face in our world today. What he thought about the matter of inerrancy, therefore, may provoke our curiosity or be of academic significance, but it is, at best, only marginally related to the questions that now deeply divide us in the Southern Baptist Convention.

Frankly, I would wish it otherwise, if for no other reason than what Orr said about the Bible and about inerrancy more than seventy-five years ago is essentially what the vast majority of Southern Baptists I know have said and are saying about the Bible and inerrancy today. For James Orr stood in that line of Protestant divines and professors who, since the advent of modern critical studies of the Bible (as well as of comparative religions), have defended fervently and ably a reverence for the Scriptures, "the Christian Scriptures" Orr called them.

Along with other conservative scholars, Orr viewed the Bible as uniquely revelatory in content, structure, purpose, and spiritual quality, for to him the Bible manifested a divine uniqueness which the advance of critical and historical biblical studies could not diminish, much less discredit.

In a phrase, Orr believed in the ultimate trustworthiness of the Bible and was during the late nineteenth and early twentieth centuries a leading spokesperson of those who are best described as enlightened, competent, and progressive theological conservatives. Theirs was, however, a conservativism that should be carefully defined, and Orr's conservativism, not unlike the "conservatism" or "liberalism" of others, can best be understood in the light of his times.

Before turning to a very abbreviated resume of his life and the historical context in which Orr lived and worked, allow me to make one further observation. I agree with Orr's overall view of the Bible. I think he is correct in what he says about inerrancy. But I am not insisting that either of us is, without question or qualification, right.

Orr's Life and Times

James Orr was not a Southern Baptist; he was a Scottish Presbyterian. As far as I have been able to determine, he never had any direct contact with or personal knowledge of Southern Baptists. He makes no references to Southern Baptists in any of his writings, and I have found no evidence that he was acquainted with our forebears, our traditions, or our eccentricities. The only occasion that he ever traveled into the southern part of the United States, where he may in fact have encountered some Southern Baptists, he had the misfortune of having his pocket picked of several hundred dollars and had to work his way back to New York by lecturing and preaching.[1] Thus, what he would say were he here and knew something about us, I could only conjecture.

Lacking seven months, James Orr lived the biblical span of three score and ten years. His was a period in the history of European theological development that was as momentous as it was turbulent. For it was a time when hardly a single tenet of the Christian faith was not called into question, when in divinity schools and universities alike the traditional Christian view of the world and of the Bible was questioned and sometimes rejected. This rejection of the traditional Christian world view, however, incited a singularly unfortunate response, especially in the United States, a response of religious obscurantism, anti-intellectualism, and fundamentalism represented by persons and groups who held tenaciously to traditional church dogmas, who stubbornly refused to subject their beliefs to the light of critical investigation, and who attacked swiftly and sometimes mercilessly anyone who did. Orr was clearly aware of both of these extremes, and he carefully, painstakingly sought to steer a middle course between them.

In the Scottish Presbyterianism of Orr's day, heresy charges and trials were not infrequent. Two of Orr's friends, a respected pastor and also one of his teaching colleagues, were formally accused of heresy. Their separate cases were front page news and widely discussed and debated as they proceeded laboriously through the various levels of the ecclesiastical judicial system of the Scottish Presbyterian Church.

Given the vulnerability of his own position as a professor in one of the Church's theological schools, Orr could have easily and understandably remained aloof from these doctrinal controversies, especially in light of the fact that his theological views were generally regarded as more conservative than those of the accused. This was not, however, Orr's nature. In both cases he chose not to ignore the difficulties of his two friends, though, I reiterate, Orr did not agree completely with either of them theologically. He opted, nonetheless, and at some personal risk, to defend them publicly.

One of those of whom I speak was the highly respected professor of Old Testament in Glasgow, Dr. George Adam Smith. The accusations against Smith arose from a series of lectures given and later published under the title *Modern Criticism and the Preaching of the Old Testament* (1901). In the public trial Orr was the final person designated to speak in Smith's defense, and he began by insisting that the real issue was not the merits of Smith's book but the attitude which the Church should take toward the modern critical movement as a whole. Modern biblical criticism, Orr declared, whether one agreed with its conclusions or not, was not going to recede or fade away. Better then that one deal with it responsibly and honestly than to decry its excesses or deny its legitimacy. The contributions of sound biblical criticism, Orr contended, should be utilized and its errors refuted. But whether one were inclined to accept or reject the methodology, it would be, Orr declared, as senseless as it would be "futile to attempt to deal with a movement of this character and magnitude" by seeking "to dispose of it by any vote of the Assembly, or decision of an Assembly Committee."[2] Matters of this sort were not best decided by majority vote.

Orr continued by stating that he had no patience with the charges being brought against his colleague because they were unfounded and unjustified. George Adam Smith, Orr said, was attempting to deal responsibly with the modern biblical criticism of the Old Testament, and as far as Orr was concerned, the attacks being made were by individuals who obviously were suspicious of any view or book that bore the mark of modern critical (analytical) study, and their trumped-up accusations were fueled by attributing to Professor Smith views that were not his at all.

Fortunately, George Adam Smith was acquitted of all charges against him, and he continued his distinguished career without further incident, despite the fact that some of his views continued to be criticized—even by Orr himself.

Orr's championing of persons whom he believed were unfairly treated may have stemmed from his deep sense of moral integrity. But I believe it may be traced in part at least to the very difficult circumstances he overcame in his own life. Orr was not the recipient either of financial or class advantages. His father was a working engineer, a technician, who died early in Orr's boyhood, only to be followed in death a short time later by Orr's mother. Like many orphans of that period, young James was left to live with relatives who soon apprenticed him to be a bookbinder. As it developed, however, Orr would eventually write books for others to bind. Somehow he managed to overcome his disadvantages as well as his grief and loneliness, and at great cost he secured his education. At the University of Glasgow Orr distinguished himself as a gifted and outstanding student, and upon graduation, he was licensed and then ordained as a minister in the United Free Church (Presbyterian) of Scotland.

For seventeen years he served as pastor of a single congregation while preparing himself and being prepared for appointment in 1891 as a professor of church history in the United Presbyterian College in Edinburgh.[3] His prodigious output of books, articles, book reviews, and sermons both as a pastor and professor is hardly matched by anyone of his era—writings, it should be noted, that were for the most part addressed not only to scholars but also to the rank and file of the Christian church.

Following his distinguished pastorate, Orr served as a theological professor for twenty-three years, first in Edinburgh, and then from 1900 until his death in Glasgow. Together with his lecturing and writing—not only in Scotland but also in the United States—Orr preached virtually every Sunday, a labor which added considerably to his already heavy load of responsibilities. At the same time the weekly preaching appointments served to keep him in direct contact with the life and the people of his Church.

Like most Scottish philosophical and theological students of his day, Orr was exposed to the school of thought usually referred to as "common sense realism," the philosophy of Thomas Reid and his successors who had reacted strongly to the skepticism of David Hume. The primary emphasis of the common sense approach was the insistence on the trustworthiness of human observation and intuition, both intellectually and morally. "It was," to quote Glen Scorgie, "a system with a highly democratic epistemology."[4] Experience as well as education probably account for Orr's "populist instincts and common sense convictions" that resulted in "a strong sense of responsibility for the religious welfare of the general Christian public,"[5] especially for the laity of his own Church.

As already indicated, the era during which Orr received his education and served as a pastor and theological professor was one of the most tumultuous in theological history. It was a time in which the very foundations of the Christian faith were under withering, sustained attack. Supernaturalism was challenged and widely disbelieved, and thus divine inspiration was denied. The nature and structure of the Bible was called into question. Portions of Scripture long thought to be historically-based were dismissed as fabrications, as fiction, often in the name of biblical criticism.[6]

This kind of biblical criticism, so unsettling to Orr, began with a denial of supernatural revelation. Its underlying philosophical presupposition, Orr observed, was, in a word, anti-supernatural, and the net result was: the negation of the the Bible as anything more than the "fragmentary remains of an ancient Hebrew literature," the denial of the uniqueness of Israel's faith, and the elimination of any suggestion of the miraculous in Israel's or in the church's history.

These were indeed the positions of some of the "biblical critics" of Orr's day, and he regarded their approach to the study of the Bible not only as misguided but ultimately as catastrophic for the Christian faith. For not only was the nature of the Bible as a tangible part of God's supernatural witness to humanity disputed, but likewise the long-held Christian understanding of the structure of the Bible was jettisoned. The Bible's internal structure of "part fitting into part and leading on to part, making up a unity of the whole . . . ,"[7] had seemed undeniable to Christians for centuries. But to some of the newer critics, the Old Testament documents were viewed as an invention of post-exilic priests and scribes who, it was said, constructed the books from the various legends and fragments of Jewish lore and literature. The canonical questions and the overall arrangement of the books, it was contended, were decided very late in the Old Testament era. And finally, the presentation of the documents by the post-exilic redactors was so skillfully done that the community, only recently returned from Babylonian captivity, was persuaded to accept these newly constructed documents as the very writings of Moses and the early prophets.

Something of the same criticism approach eventually came to be applied to the documents known as the New Testament,[8] but what Orr regarded as "destructive" biblical criticism concentrated in his day primarily on the Old Testament. Orr was unwilling to concede many of these points, and much of his professional career was given to disproving them.

I have intentionally sought to highlight the nature of the attacks upon the Bible during Orr's lifetime to accentuate the radical distinction between what was happening then in his theological milieu and what has been and what is the approach to the Bible in Southern Baptist seminaries. In our institutions, there is not the slightest evidence of an anti-supernatural bias. There is no denial of the uniqueness of Israel's faith. The miraculous is not disputed or ridiculed. The divine inspiration of the Scriptures not only is assumed, it is continually affirmed. Thus, to imply or charge that what is being taught in our seminaries is "liberalism" reflects either a lamentable manifestation of ignorance or a designed and willful attempt to discredit by association and innuendo those who attempt to use reverently and responsibly the historical-critical approach to the study of the Scripture.

Orr's Fundamental Assertion

The approach James Orr took to refute what he regarded as hazardous approach to the Bible, or what he regarded as a philosophical blunder and a theological mistake, could prove to be relevant to us. But let it be noted in this regard that James Orr grounded his defense against "destructive" biblical criticism not as a theory of the inerrancy of the Bible, but on the *evidence of the divine inspiration* of the Bible. The one (divine inspiration), however, did not for him necessarily presuppose the other (inerrancy), for repeatedly in his writings Orr insists that he will not be drawn into the debate as to *how* the Bible was inspired, nor into the argument over the inerrancy of the Bible in *every* aspect or in *every* detail.

In one of the last things he wrote before he died, in *The Fundamentals*, he repeated what he had said before, namely, that he would not enter into the question regarding theories of inspiration, nor would he attempt to defend the Bible as completely "errorless." These issues, he said, have long "divided good men." But then he added, "I want to get away from these things at the circumference" (theories of inspiration and inerrancy debates) in order to deal with the issues at "the center."[9] What was the central issue according to Orr? It was not how the Bible was inspired, nor was it whether the original texts were without error. The issue at the center of him was whether the Bible gives evidences of being inspired by God.

Though Orr returned to this fundamental assertion throughout his writings, the most comprehensive and detailed discussion can be found in his book *Revelation and Inspiration*, first published in 1910. He stated that he wrote the volume under the conviction that revelation and inspiration can only be defended on three bases: (1) the evidence of God's revelation in history, (2) the evidence of the inspiration of the records of that revelation, and (3) the evidence of the structural integrity of that record as found in the Bible. He rejected, thereby, what he called "the religious-naturalistic tendency" of higher criticism wherein the distinction between "natural" and "supernatural" is obliterated, but he did not reject biblical criticism or analysis as such. Rather he manifested an appreciation for the method which he called "believing-criticism." "Higher criticism," he said, has not been wholly destructive. As a matter of fact, it has resulted in several benefits, one of which is demonstrable, Orr contended: namely, that despite the application of the strictest historical and critical methods, "the absolutely unique and extraordinary character of the religion of Israel" has not been undermined.[10] As he wrote in an earlier work:

> With the best will in the world to explain the religious development of Israel out of natural factors, the efforts of the critics have resulted, in the view of many of themselves, in a magnificent demonstration of the immense and, on natural principles, inexplicable difference between the religion of this obscure people and every other.[11]

(Incidentally, Orr remarked in a footnote that "this is the argument pursued, on critical lines, in Lecture IV., on 'The Proof of a Divine Revelation in the Old Testament'" by George Adam Smith in his book alluded to earlier, *Modern Criticism and Preaching in the Old Testament*.)

It would be a mistake to conclude from this paragraph lifted out of *Revelation and Inspiration* that Orr saw the benefits of the critical approach to the Bible as accidental and unintentional. This was not his position. He was quite prepared to accord modern biblical study its rightful place.

> Let purely literary questions about the Bible receive full and fair discussion. Let the structure of Books be impartially examined. If a reverent science has light to throw on the composition or authority or age of these books, let its voice be heard. . . . No fright need to taken of the mere word, "Criticism."[12]

It was Orr's conclusion and conviction, however, that once the critics had examined and compared the text of the Bible with other literature, religious and non-religious, the results would be supportive of the traditional Christian belief about the nature and trustworthiness of the Scripture. I am satisfied that Orr was in this regard correct.

Orr and the Question of Inerrancy

As to the question of inerrancy, Orr had the following to say.

1. One could be confident in the *reliableness* of the historical content of the Old Testament [as well as the New] "without insisting on any overstrained theory of 'inerrancy' in historical detail."[13]

2. One could believe in the inspiration of the Bible without making the doctrine of inspiration depend on a theory of inerrancy, i.e., without holding to an inerrancy of historical, geographical, and scientific detail, that is, without making the doctrine of inspiration depend on a theory of inerrancy.[14] Curiously, Orr always put the word "inerrancy" in quotation marks, because, it would appear, he had a reservation about the use of the term in reference to the Scriptures.

3. One could believe in the inspiration of all of the Bible without holding to a theory of dictation, a theory, Orr contended, that simply is untenable.[15]

4. One could believe in the trustworthiness of the Bible and maintain a distinction between revelation and inspiration.

Orr did not develop this distinction between revelation and inspiration as he might were he alive today. I say this because the study of the science of communications is of rather recent origin. In light of such study, I would, however, infer the following: the argument that divine revelation must, because of its very nature, be inerrant—for God would not reveal or "inspire" error, and therefore the record of God's revelation would be necessity be inerrant since a perfect God would issue a perfect revelation—sounds quite logical and on the surface appealing. But I believe that Orr was implying something that is now generally accepted, namely, that what is communicated or "transmitted" by a sender is not necessarily what is understood by a receiver. In human communications there is always interference, static if you will, misunderstanding caused by a multitude of factors. And the argument that an infallible God could not inspire a fallible record confuses revelation (what is revealed) with inspiration (what is received). From what we know of human limitations, from what we know about communication, and from what we know from a careful study of the Bible, inerrancy is a highly questionable hypothesis.

I am of course aware of the fact that many of those who hold to a theory of the inerrancy of the Bible also hold to a theory of the "divine superintendence," that is, God protected and prevented the original authors from any species of error. I have no desire to denigrate this assumption regarding what God did or did not do. Those who hold this view may be correct, but the burden of proof is clearly upon them to offer more than they have to date to support this theory, especially if they expect many of us to accept it or to agree that it should or can be legitimately an authentic test of Christian orthodoxy.

It is not my wish, and it certainly is not my responsibility, to try to disprove the theory of biblical inerrancy since in the final analysis it is a philosophical presupposition and not a matter of tangible evidence. At the same time, I would hope that those who hold to a view of inerrancy for whatever reason would accord me the privilege of saying, "This simply is not a crucial issue for me." The reason it is not crucial is that I had never heard of inerrancy when I became a Christian, and as a professing Christian I choose to put my faith in the God revealed in Jesus Christ, not in a theory of inspiration.

Here I quote Orr's own words in this regard: "Does the Bible itself claim, or inspiration necessitate, such an 'errorless' record, in matters of minor detail?" The answer clearly is "No."[16]

> Very commonly it is argued by upholders of this doctrine [of divine "superin-tendendence" or protection of the writers] that "inerrancy" in every minute particular is involved *in the very idea* of a book given by inspiration of God. This might be held to be true on a theory of verbal dictation, but it can scarcely be maintained on a just view of the actual historical genesis of the Bible. One may plead, indeed, for "a supernatural providential guidance" which has for its aim to exclude all, even the least, error or discrepancy in statement, even such as may inhere in the sources from which the informa-tion is obtained, or may arise from corruption of anterior documents. But this is a violent assumption which there is nothing in the Bible really to support. It is perilous, therefore, to seek to pin down faith to it as a matter of vital mo-ment.[17]

Note, if you will, these three arguments Orr proposed against the theory of inerrancy. First, an insistence that the Bible must be inerrant ignores what we now know about the "historical beginnings of the Bible." In the second place, it is a theory that has no support in the Bible itself. And finally, it is a very precari-ous assumption on which to "pin" one's faith.

Orr began his final chapter of *Revelation and Inspiration* saying:

> It will have been seen that it is sought in the preceding pages to approach the subject of inspiration through that of *revelation*. This seems the right method to pursue. The doctrine of inspiration grows out of that of revelation, and can only be made intelligible through the latter. The older method was to prove first the inspiration (by historical evidence, miracles, claims of writers), then through that establish the revelation. This view still finds an echo in the note sometimes heard—"If the inspiration of the Bible (commonly some *theory* of inspiration) be given up, what have we left to hold by?" It is urged, *e.g.*, that unless we can demonstrate what is called the "inerrancy" of the Biblical record, down even to its minutest details, the whole edifice of belief in re-vealed religion falls to the ground. This, on the face of it, is a most suicidal position for any defender of revelation to take up. It is certainly a much easier matter to prove the reality of a divine revelation in the history of Israel, or in Christ, than it is to prove the inerrant inspiration of every part of the record through which that revelation has come to us. Grant the Gospels to be only ordinary historical documents—trustworthy records of the life of Christ, apart from any special inspiration in their authors—we should still, one may con-tend, be shut up as much as *ever* to the belief that the Person whose words and works they narrate was One who made superhuman claims, and whose character, words, and deeds attested the truth of these claims.[1] It is assuredly

easier to believe that Jesus spoke and acted in the way the Gospels declare Him to have done, than to prove that Mark and Luke possessed an exceptional inspiration in the composition of their writings—though, as has been already stated, there is the best reason for believing that they did.[18]

One can believe in the trustworthiness of the biblical message without insisting on an "errorless" record.

Those who held to the theory of inerrancy in Orr's time, such as A. A. Hodge and B. B. Warfield, did so, Orr contended, by stretching the theory of inerrancy to the limits with "qualifications, admissions, and explanations, till there is *practically* little difference between the opposite views," i.e., between those who hold to inerrancy and those who maintain the tradition high view of Scripture.[19]

Likewise, Orr appeared to be mystified—in view of the concessions made by Hodge and Warfield, the recognized leaders and proponents of inerrancy, in their essay entitled "Inspiration," published in *The Presbyterian Review* in April 1881 [p. 256]—when they revert to a position of "inerrant" autographs. The following are the words of these two stalwart proponents of inerrancy:

> It is not claimed that the Scriptures any more than their authors are omniscient. The information they convey is in the forms of human thought, and limited on all sides. They were not designed to teach philosophy, science, or human history as such. They were not designed to furnish an infallible system of speculative theology. They are written in human languages, whose words, inflections, constructions, and idioms bear everywhere indelible traces of human error. The record itself furnishes evidence that the writers were in large measure dependent for their knowledge upon sources and methods in themselves fallible, and that their personal knowledge and judgments were in many matters hesitating and defective, or even wrong.[20]

While admitting that there are in the Bible these insignificant mistakes "in the *matter* of the record," why would these defenders of inerrancy, Orr puzzled, contend that "the *ipsissima verba* of the original autographs" were "free from the slightest taint of such error."[21] What is one to say to such an assertion? There is really nothing one can say in view of the fact that this is simply an example of an unprovable assumption, not something that can be substantiated one way or another.

On the other hand, Orr agreed with Hodge and Warfield in "affirming that *the sweeping assertions* of error and discrepancy in the Bible" that were being exposed in the name of "higher criticism" were for the most part without foundation.[22] For Orr, the unshakable fact was this: the Bible, when judged and interpreted "impartially," will be found to be "free from demonstrable error in its statements, and harmonious in its teachings, to a degree that of itself creates an irresistible impression of a supernatural factor in its origin."[23]

To expend time and energy debating " 'inerrancy' in the abstract," Orr concluded, "is of little profit." It will only serve to divide good people, not to unite them around the one fundamental truth that in the Scriptures God reveals himself, his purpose, and his love.[24]

James Orr held to the divine inspiration of the Bible, not to the inerrancy of the Bible. The evidence of that inspiration, he said, is not to be found in every minute or trivial detail, but in the Bible's "essential message . . . [and] in the lifegiving effects which that message has produced, wherever its word of truth has gone."[25] His argument for inspiration, therefore, was not based on philosophical wish-thinking, but on the inner-witness of the Holy Spirit. That inspiration, that witness is acknowledged as divine because it leads us "to God and to Christ; it gives light on the deepest emotions of life, death, and eternity; it discovers the way of deliverance from sin," and it makes those who accept Jesus Christ as Savior "new creatures."[26] We can without reservation affirm that the Bible is indeed "useful for teaching the truth, rebuking error, correcting faults, and giving instruction for right living, so that the person who serves God may be fully qualified and equipped to do every kind of good deed" (2 Tim. 3:16-17 TEV).

In the early 1960s, we left the state of Virginia to accept the pastorate of a Southern Baptist church in Boulder, Colorado. Broadway Baptist was, I believe, the third Southern Baptist church established in what is now the Colorado Baptist Convention.

The first Sunday night after we had arrived in Boulder, the pulpit committee along with the deacons gave a reception to honor and to introduce us to the leaders of the community. All the pastors and their wives in the city were invited, and many came; and that very night we began friendships with other Southern Baptist pastors, some who came from Denver, as well as with the American Baptist, the Seventh Day Baptist, the Congregational, and Presbyterian pastors there in Boulder. It was a memorable evening.

After an hour or so of meeting people and eating and drinking (punch, of course), most of the people had left. My wife had taken the children home to put them in bed, and I was talking with the chairman of the deacons while others were picking up plates, cups, and silverware, and carrying them to the kitchen. Suddenly a couple arrived who identified themselves as the pastor and wife of the Conservative Baptist Church in Boulder.

I had never met a Conservative Baptist, although I knew that they were in Colorado and that they had a seminary in Denver. In fact, Dr. John Newport with whom I studied at Southwestern Seminary, had told me of one of the New Testament professors at the Denver seminary and suggested that I try to meet him.

The Conservative Baptist pastor apologized for arriving late, and we began to converse about subjects one usually discusses with people one has just met but with whom there appear to be things in common.

After a few minutes of the conversation, I asked the pastor if he knew the professor at the Denver seminary whom Dr. Newport had mentioned to me. He said, "No, I don't believe I know him." This seemed strange to me in view of the fact that the Conservative Baptist work in Colorado was not large, their seminary was only twenty-five miles away, and the New Testament professor was, as I understood it, widely known.

We talked on for a while longer, and I asked a second question about the Denver seminary. The pastor responded rather penitently this time, saying that he did not know the answer. And then he added, "I suppose you are wondering why I know so little about the seminary."

I replied, "Well, yes. I am a little surprised."

"Well," he said, "we've split!"

"Split?" I exclaimed. "Conservative Baptists in Colorado have divided?"

"Yes. We've split."

"What was the issue?" I asked.

"Pre-Trib," he answered

"Pre-Trib? What is that? I'm sorry, but I don't know what you are talking about."

"The Tribulation! The Rapture!" he answered, now clearly on the offensive.

"Oh," I grunted, but then was momentarily speechless. Finally I sputtered, "You mean . . . you mean you would divide your convention, your churches, your work over the question of whether the Rapture comes before or after the Tribulation?"

"Of course we would," his wife interjected. "How can two walk together except they be agreed?'" They had me, or so it appeared.

"My wife and I have been doing it for ten years," I countered.

Now admittedly, what I said to this pastor's spouse was somewhat hyperbolic. But the fact is my wife and I have never agreed on all theological points. I don't even agree with myself at times. But I do agree with Soren Kierkegaard who pointed out more than a hundred years ago that "there is truth that matters and there is truth that doesn't matter." And it matters not a fig whether Christians agree about every detail of eschatology or whether they agree on the subtleties related to most any subject so long as we trust in God, submit ourselves to the Lordship of Jesus Christ, and steadfastly reverence, study, and live by God's word as our "only sufficient, certain and authoritative rule of all saving knowledge, faith and obedience."[27]

Inerrancy, true or false, is for me one of those subjects that simply does not matter.

Notes

1. Alan Neely, "James Orr: A Study in Conservative Christian Apologetics." (Th.D. dissertation, Southwestern Baptist Theological Seminary, 1960), pp. 94-95.

2. United Free Church of Scotland Proceedings and Debates, 1902 (Edinburgh: Lorimer & Chalmers, 1902), p. 97.

3. Neely (1960), pp. 79-80.

4. "James Orr: Defender of the Church's Faith," Crux 2 (September 1986):23-24.

5. Ibid., p. 24.

6. I have intentionally avoided here the word myth primarily because of the un-

happy misunderstandings associated with the English word. But it should be noted that the limitations of any language are known to those who are bilingual, viz., that there are simply some things you cannot say as succinctly or as clearly when attempting to translate from one language to another. Moreover, there are times when a word or expression in a language has no precise equivalent in the second language. The basic idea usually can be approximated but not exactly translated for a lack of word-equivalents. The Greek terms *kairos* and *agape* are well known N.T. examples.

Modern biblical scholars sometimes use the word *myth* in reference to certain biblical passages. Pragmatically, it has proved to be less than satisfactory as a choice of terms primarily because it suggests to many hearers, to quote Walter Russell Bowie, an "ancient fairy tale, a haunting mirage conjured up in men's imaginations and dissolving into nothing when it collides with actual fact." Those who thus understand *myth* to mean fable are thus left to ask, "What becomes of the authority of the Bible if any part of it can be described as myth?" Yet, I like very much Bowie's comment when he says that *myth* as used by biblical scholars is not meant to convey the idea of fiction, but rather *myth* represents the "efforts of men to put truth into pictures." Cf. "Expositon of Genesis" *The Interpreter's Bible* 1 (Abingdon, 1952):463.

7. James Orr, "Holy Scripture and Modern Negations," *The Fundamentals* 9 (Chicago: Testimony Publishing Co., n.d.):39.

8. Cf. James Orr, "The Gospel and Modern Criticism," *The Faith of a Modern Christian* (London: Hodder & Stoughton, 1910), pp. 39-57.

9. Orr, "Holy Scripture and Modern Negations," p. 46.

10. *Revelation and Inspiration* (New York: Charles Scribner's Sons, 1910), p. 13.

11. *The Problem of the Old Testament* (London: James Nisbet & Co., 1907), p. 10.

12. "Holy Scripture and Modern Negations," p. 33.

13. *Revelation and Inspiration* (1910), p. 73.

14. Ibid., p. 199.

15. Ibid., p. 121.

16. Ibid., p. 213.

17. Ibid., pp. 213-4. Orr continues by saying: "Inspiration, in sanctioning the incorporation of an old genealogy, or of an historic document in some respects defective, no more makes itself responsible for these defects than it does for the speeches of Job's friends in the Book of Job, or for the sentiments of many parts of the Book of Ecclesiastes, or for the imperfect translation of the Old Testament passages in quotations from the Septuagint" (Ibid., p. 214).

18. Ibid., pp. 197-98.

19. Ibid., p. 214.

20. Cited by Orr, ibid., p. 215.

21. Ibid.

22. Ibid.

23. Ibid., p. 216.

24. Ibid., pp. 216-17.

25. Ibid., p. 217.

26. Ibid., p. 218.

27. Article I, "Scriptures" from the *Articles of Faith*, Southeastern Baptist Theological Seminary.

14

THE ROOTS OF CONSERVATIVE PERSPECTIVES ON INERRANCY (WARFIELD)

L. Russ Bush

In this brief essay I hope to do two things, both of which are relevant to the study of biblical inerrancy in general. I also believe they are relevant to the Southern Baptist dialogue today in the late 1980s.

First, I want to summarize fairly B. B. Warfield's views on biblical inspiration and inerrancy (though I must not pause to do much more than outline them and try to provide adequate documentation for each reader to pursue any further details needed for clarification). I am addressing Warfield because my assignment specifically instructed me to do so, but I am also happy to do so for he is undoubtedly one of the most significant figures in the recent history of evangelical discussions on the subject of biblical inspiration and authority.

Second, I want to interact with the hypothesis that Warfield was a theological innovator where inerrancy is concerned. In my view the so-called Warfield-Orr alternatives that I was taught in school and that stand as the obvious premise of this designated seminar are not particularly germane to the Southern Baptist debate today;[1] the Sandeen proposal[2] and the Rogers/McKim proposal[3] are relevant to our debate; and thus I hope to at least take note of them and again offer adequate documentation for a concerned reader to pursue if further study is desired.

B. B. Warfield and Biblical Inerrancy

Benjamin Breckinridge Warfield was born in Kentucky in 1851. He graduated from the College of New Jersey (now Princeton University) at the age of twenty and from there went to study in both Edinburgh and Heidelberg. Returning to the States he entered Princeton Theological Seminary and graduated with the class of 1876. He did a further year of study at Leipzig, and then returned to a pastorate in Baltimore. Before long, however, he was appointed as an instructor and then professor of New Testament language and literature at Western Theological Seminary in Pittsburg. In 1886 Archibald Alexander Hodge died and B. B. Warfield was named to succeed him as professor of systematic theology at Princeton Theological Seminary.

During his distinguished career he received a Doctor of Divinity degree from the College of New Jersey (1880), a Doctor of Laws from both the College of New Jersey and Davidson College (1892), a Doctor of Letters from Lafayette College (1911), and a Sacrae Theologiae Doctor from the University of Utrecht in 1913. He served as editor of the distinguished *Presbyterian and Reformed Review* from 1890 to 1903.

After his death in 1921 his voluminous writings were collected and published in a 10 volume set by Oxford University Press. Warfield is quite generally recognized among Evangelical scholars today as one of the most distinguished and intellectually gifted exponents of the so-called "Old Princeton" theology, and his writings on the subject of biblical inspiration are perhaps the most extensive and exegetically intensive ever produced on this theme.[4]

Sovereignty and Epistemology

Warfield defended the view of Scripture presented in the Westminster Confession.[5] His concern, however, was not simply to defend a confessional statement as such but rather (1) to defend the doctrine of divine sovereignty and (2) to defend the very possibility of having a source of knowledge from which a valid confession could be produced.

The "doctrine" of Scripture, for Warfield, is not so much a doctrine itself as it is the epistemological base for doctrine; that is, Scripture is the foundational basis by which true doctrine can be known. Scripture can serve as this epistemological foundation because it is divine revelation. Furthermore, if God could not or even if He had not exercised sovereignty over His own revelation of Himself to men, then we would have little (if any) reason to believe or expect His sovereignty to rule over the lives and the destinies of men.

Somehow the whole knowledge base for Christian doctrine seems to be tied up in the Scripture principle. This has always been so, but the rise of modern biblical criticism and theological liberalism forced evangelical theologians to be more explicit about some things that heretofore had more often been implicit (though not completely so).[6]

Sovereignty and Revelation

Warfield develops his view of divine revelation and biblical authority from the clearest New Testament passages on the subject: 2 Timothy 3:16 and 2 Peter 1:21. Paul states that "all Scripture" is *theopneustos* and therefore profitable. Peter declares that men spoke from God (when they delivered the prophecy of Scripture) as they were carried along by the Holy Spirit.

Theopneustos, Warfield explains, most definitely does not mean "inspiration" or even "inspired by God." This Greek term speaks not of *in*spiration but only of "spiration" or "breath," that which is "breathed *out*". The term, of course, is a figure of speech for God's "breath" being "breathed out" in the process of "speaking." As God "speaks," his "breath" comes "out" so as to communicate with others. This is quite different from the notion of God "breathing into" or inspiring humanly produced Scriptures.[7] Warfield, in a competently documented essay, demonstrates that Paul, by using *theopneustos,* clearly and without equivocation claims that Scripture originates with God not with man.[8]

Peter's phrase, "every prophecy of Scripture," is, according to Warfield, the exact equivalent of Paul's "every Scripture," and Peter is anxious to affirm that Scripture did not arise from "private interpretation." That is to say, "it is not the result of human investigation into the nature of things, the produce of its writer's own thinking. This is as much as to say it is of Divine gift."[9] To say that no prophecy ever came by the will of man is to say, according to Warfield, that prophecy (by which term Peter is referring to the whole of Scripture due to its divine origin) does not owe its existence, its content, its character, or its origin to human initiative. These human authors spoke from God as they were brought to their knowledge by the Holy Spirit.

Technically Peter speaks of the human authors as having been "borne by the Holy Spirit." Men wrote Scripture and thus spoke from God as they were borne by the Spirit. As Warfield elaborates the meaning:

> The term here used is a very specific one. It is not to be confounded with guiding, or directing, or controlling, or even leading in the full sense of that word. . . . What is "borne" is taken up by the "bearer," and conveyed by the "bearer's" power, not its own, to the "bearer's" goal, not its own. The men who spoke from God are here declared, therefore, to have been taken up by the Holy Spirit and brought by His Power to the goal of His choosing. The things which they spoke under this operation of the Spirit were therefore His things, not theirs. And that is the reason which is assigned why "the prophetic word" is so sure. . . . It will be observed that the proximate stress is laid here, not on the spiritual value of Scripture (though that, too, is seen in the background), but on the Divine trustworthiness of Scripture.[10]

While the 2 Timothy and 2 Peter passages are significant, Warfield also looks at numerous other passages that have a bearing on Divine sovereignty in revelation and inspiration. Warfield researches the usage of terms such as "Scripture" and "Scriptures," the phrase "the oracles of God," and the formula "It is written."[11] In each case he finds a consistent and a clear teaching. Scripture is the very Word of God.

For example, Old Testament passages quoted in the New are often introduced as having been spoken by God. Then, some passages in the Old Testament that are explicitly said to be directly from God are quoted only as "Scripture says." Some Old Testament passages quoted in the New are said to have been spoken by the Holy Spirit. Even verb tenses and minute details are sometimes quoted to make doctrinal points.[12] There is only one conclusion that can be drawn fairly from the collected evidence: Scripture is a divine product given through human mediation.[13]

Sovereignty and Human Authorship

In light of Warfield's strong emphasis on (actually it is simply an exegetical observation about) the divine character of Scripture, (that Scripture is not a human product breathed *into* by the Spirit but rather is a divine product breathed *out* by God through human instrumentality), the question that many immediately raise is, "Does the divine element exclude or even obscure the humanity of the Scripture and/or of its human authors?" According to Warfield the answer is decidedly negative.

In his Inaugural Address delivered upon the occasion of his induction into the Chair of New Testament Literature and Exegesis in the Western Theological

Seminary, Warfield strongly rejected the mechanical-dictation theory of Scripture production:

> It is to be remembered that we are not defending a mechanical theory of inspiration. Every word of the Bible is the word of God according to the doctrine we are discussing; but also and just as truly, every word is the word of a man. This at once sets aside as irrelevant a large number of the objections usually brought from the phenomena of the New Testament against its verbal inspiration. No finding of traces of human influence in the style, wording or forms of statement or argumentation touches the question. The book is throughout the work of human writers and is filled with the signs of their handiwork. This we admit on the threshold; we ask what is found inconsistent with its absolute accuracy and truth.[14]

Scripture sometimes refers to other Scriptures in terms of their human authors (for example: Matthew 22:24; Mark 12:19; John 12:39; Romans 11:9). Old Testament passages are at times quoted as being spoken by men (cf. Mark 12:36).[15] But more significant are the obvious marks of human authorship such as peculiarities of vocabulary and differences in style among the various biblical books.

For Warfield the Bible is simultaneously the divine utterance of God and the product of man's effort. Of every word of Scripture, Warfield affirms that it is God's Word and that it is man's word. As Warfield expresses it:

> . . . By a special, supernatural, extraordinary influence of the Holy Ghost, the sacred writers have been guided in their writing in such a way, as while their humanity was not superceded, it was yet so dominated that their words became at the same time the words of God, and thus, in every case and all alike, absolutely infallible.[16]

Sovereignty and Inspiration

At the risk of being overly tedious, perhaps a summary of Warfield's conception of the process of Scripture writing would be in order.[17] Consider a portion of sacred history such as Chronicles or the Gospel and Acts of Luke. First of all, Warfield points out, there must be the preparation of the history to be written. God leads the sequence of occurrences in order to teach his people. God also prepares a man by birth, training, experience, and gifts of grace; and if need be, God reveals truth, so that this divinely chosen man is not only capable but able and eager to appreciate the historical development and to clarify its meaning to others. When, then, by providence, this man sets out to write his history, will there not be a "spontaneous" desire to write what God wants written. Or consider a psalmist. Was he not prepared by his heredity, his home life, his environment, his experiences, his parental role models, etc., so that in him would be found just the right mind to express God's truth just as God would have it done.

Furthermore, if God's purpose were only to faithfully record sacred history or true religious experiences, nothing more than human intellect would be necessary. To produce books possessing powers beyond those humans might naturally possess would demand an additional divine operation, which we call inspiration. This further purpose is the Divine purpose. Thus the Spirit of God worked confluently along with and in the providentially and graciously determined work of men, "spontaneously producing under the Divine directions the writings appointed to them. . . ."[18]

Inspiration, then, gives the biblical books a superhuman trustworthiness, an authority, and a profound profitableness. Each reader, then, hears the word of God directly speaking in the voice of Scripture. According to Romans 15:4, those things written down in the past are for our learning. 1 Corinthians 10:11 also emphasizes how history occurred as it did in order to bear a message to us. Paul's conversion, a seemingly sudden event with no antecedents, is later seen by Paul as but one step in a long providentially guided process (Galatians 1:15-16).[19]

The analogy, then, upon which Warfield depends for his explanation of the production of a fully divine and yet fully human Scripture is the Protestant doctrine of grace. God's sovereignty is fully operative in salvation. God makes atonement for sin. God calls those whom He foreknew. He elects and thus predestinates and thus guarantees salvation. He renews the heart, He renews the will, He convicts us of sin and grants faith. So salvation is a work of God, a free gift of grace. It is not based on human works of any kind, and yet concursively, at the same time, it is we who repent and have faith. We hear and respond to a gospel message. We each have a testimony about how we came to know Christ. These testimonies often include circumstances, events, and relationships that we describe in human terms. We speak our testimony with our own personal vocabulary and in our own unique manner of speech. We are fully human throughout the whole of the conversion experience and yet the whole process is wholly divine providence and grace.

This then is the true meaning of the doctrine of plenary, verbal inspiration.[20] By virtue of their inspiration, the Scriptures are fully true, fully authoritative, fully infallible, and fully inerrant. Such affirmations, of course, refer to the proper meaning, the correct interpretation, of the biblical text. This proper meaning, according to Warfield, is set forth generally in the Westminster Confession and in the Reformed faith. Specific interpretations of controversial passages may not yet be finally settled, of course. For example, scholars must and do continually pour over the exegetical data. They gain new insight from archaeology and from historical and linguistic studies of all kinds. They constantly strive to interpret the Word of God correctly and thus relate its meaning faithfully to our day.

Sovereignty and Apologetics

Warfield reminds us of another aspect of this question that speaks to the common man as well as to the scholar:

> Let it suffice to say that to a plenarily inspired Bible, humbly trusted as
> such, we actually, and as a matter of fact, owe all that has blessed our lives

with hopes of an immortality of bliss, and with the present fruition of the love of God in Christ. This is not an exaggeration. We may say that without a Bible we might have had Christ and all that he stands for to our souls. Let us not say that this might not have been possible. But neither let us forget that, in point of fact, it is to the Bible that we owe it that we know Christ and are found in him. . . . Even with the Bible . . . after a millennium and a half the darkness had grown so deep that a Reformation was necessary if Christian truth was to persist. . . . Suppose there had been no Bible for Luther to rediscover . . .? Though Christ had come into the world and had lived and died for us, might it not be to us, —you and me, I mean, who are not learned historians but simple men and women, —might it not be to us as though he had not been? Or if some faint echo of a Son of God offering salvation to men could still be faintly heard even by such dull ears as ours, sounding down the ages, who would have ears to catch the fulness of the message of free grace which he brought into the world? who could assure our doubting souls that it was not all a pleasant dream? who could cleanse the message from the ever-gathering corruptions of the multiplying years? No: whatever might possibly have been had there been no Bible, it is actually to the Bible that you and I owe it that we have a Christ, —a Christ to love, to trust and to follow, a Christ without us the ground of our salvation, a Christ within us the hope of glory.[21]

The so-called "doctrine of inspiration" then has a very long history and the implications of the doctrine lie at the very heart of the Christian faith. Every belief has difficulties associated with it. Some keen mind can always raise numerous questions. These questions need to be heard, studied, and answered if possible. There are difficulties involved with the doctrine of the incarnation and with the doctrine of how Christ's death can save us. But the existence of difficulties does not destroy the truth of the doctrines. (There are "difficulties" that any beginning student of philosophy can recite even in believing in the existence of one's own self.) But Warfield returns over and over again to three impressive facts:

> . . . namely, that this doctrine has always been, and is still, the church-doctrine of inspiration, as well as the vital faith of the people of God as the formulated teaching of the official creeds; that it is undeniably the doctrine of inspiration held by Christ and his apostles, and commended to us as true by all the authority which we will allow to attach to their teaching; and that it is the foundation of our Christian thought and life, without which we could not, or could only with difficulty, maintain the confidence of our faith and the surety of our hope. On such grounds as these is not this doctrine commended to us as true?[22]

But, Dr. Warfield, if you were to be forced to the bottom line, to the most basic roots of your faith, why do you really believe in the inerrancy of Scripture? Do you simply presuppose this doctrine and fideistically resist all other views? Are you rationalistically trying to build a foundation in natural theology

278

to support your faith? Are you simply a scholastic who blindly follows Turretin[23] [though admittedly you rarely seem to quote or even refer to Turretin]? Warfield replies:

> We believe this doctrine of the plenary inspiration of the Scriptures primarily because it is the doctrine which Christ and his apostles believed, and which they have taught us. It may sometimes seem difficult to take our stand frankly by the side of Christ and his apostles. It will always be found safe.[24]

The Roots of Fundamentalism

W.A. Hoffecker, in *Piety and the Princeton Theologians*, has demonstrated the unity of Princeton's theology from Archibald Alexander through Charles Hodge to Benjamin Warfield.[25] Each of the Princeton theologians make distinctive contributions, and Warfield's contribution clearly was to the doctrine of Scripture. In fact some believe that Warfield made the greatest contribution to this subject of any Christian scholar before or since.[26]

Warfield's Critics

Some others, of course, contest the value of Warfield's work. The general trend of the complaint is that Warfield was an innovator, that he did not represent the historic Reformed faith at this point, that he misrepresented the theology of the Westminster divines, and that it is this new and seriously flawed doctrine of Scripture that produced Fundamentalism, a new brand of theology that is supposedly incapable of meeting the needs of the modern world.

In 1937 Emil Brunner, while lecturing at Princeton, attempted to defend his own view of inspiration by appealing to Charles Hodge over against Warfield, who, in Brunner's opinion, drove the historic Princeton orthodoxy to the extreme of verbal inerrancy.[27] J. J. Markarian, in his Drew University Ph.D. Dissertation in 1963, "The Calvinistic Concept of the Biblical Revelation in the Theology of Benjamin Breckenridge Warfield," argues that his theory fails because it makes the truth of the Christian faith depend upon "the ability of the scholar to beat back the attacks against Jesus' historicity."[28]

The two most serious and (among evangelical scholarship) the most influential critiques of Warfield come from Jack Rogers and Ernest Sandeen. Rogers claims that Warfield misrepresented the view of the Westminster divines and thus created a new doctrine,[29] and Sandeen believes that the whole of the Princeton theology deviated from that of Westminster.[30] However, neither Rogers nor Sandeen seem to have an adequate grasp of the historical facts at this point. They isogete rather than exegete their historical sources.[31]

The Sandeen Proposal

Sandeen's treatment of historical theology presupposes a misconstrued version of the history of the doctrine of biblical infallibility and full authority in the Reformed tradition by claiming that only scholastics held such views prior to their creation anew by late nineteenth century Princeton theology. However,

279

neither Cambridge professor William Whitaker (1547-1595) nor William Ames (1576-1633) were scholastics, yet both defended full biblical infallibility. Whitaker's *Disputation on Holy Scripture* (1588) is easily "the most extensive Protestant book on biblical authority in Elizabeth's England."[32] Likewise, the Puritan William Ames in his *Marrow of Sacred Divinity* (1624, 1627, 1629), a Harvard textbook in the seventeenth century, wrote of the Scriptures as being "free from all error," the writers as being "instruments of the Spirit," and the versions as not being "fully authentic except as they express the sources, by which they are also to be weighed. . . ." The writer's "manner of speaking," however, was that "which most suited his person and condition."[33] This by any fair reading is the same as Warfield's view: plenary inspiration and thus biblical infallibility in the original autographs.

Sandeen's proposal, furthermore, misrepresents the development of the doctrine at Princeton. As John H. Gerstner[34] so aptly points out, the Westminster confession itself (despite Sandeen's misrepresentation) does recite "proofs" whereby the Bible "doth abundantly evidence itself to be the Word of God." Sandeen overlooks the evidence element in the Confession and thus finds Hodge's evidence to be a misrepresentation of the Confessional faith. But this only shows that Sandeen misread the history.

Equally serious is Sandeen's (unintentional?) creation of theological differences between Warfield and both Charles Hodge and Archibald Alexander. For example, Sandeen quotes Alexander as saying, "In the narration of well-known facts, the writer did not need a continual suggestion of every idea but only to be so superintended as to be preserved from error." Incredibly Sandeen concludes from this that Alexander did not believe in verbal inspiration (showing that he does not understand the doctrine at all), and Sandeen seems to be unaware of statements almost exactly like that in Warfield.[35]

Sandeen's thesis is simply false. The Princeton theologians did not originate the doctrine of inerrancy, they perpetuated it. Their faith was more elaborate yet continuous with that of the Westminster Assembly. The so-called roots of theological fundamentalism[36] are simply the roots of historic orthodoxy.

Conclusion

B. B. Warfield was one of the most able expositors of the historic, orthodox view of biblical inspiration, authority, and interpretation. Warfield, however, is *not* the *source* of the doctrine of inerrancy nor of theological fundamentalism. He is a gifted expositor of the doctrine of Scripture in the Reformed tradition. His Westminster Confession tradition is independently paralleled in Baptist life due to the influence of the Second London Confession of 1677.

Warfield taught the doctrine of plenary inspiration and biblical infallibility. This was for him an aspect of the doctrine of God's sovereignty. Inspiration was explained as a concursive work of God. Just as divine grace and human repentance and faith are concursive acts, so Scripture is fully divine and yet at the same time fully human by a concursive work of God commonly called inspiration.

Inerrancy is still a crucial doctrine of the orthodox church despite the problems associated with it. To lose the strict doctrine of inerrancy would not be to lose Christianity, as Warfield admits and as Orr clearly demonstrates, but it would be a departure from traditional orthodoxy.[37]

Orr reminds us to keep the doctrine of inerrancy in perspective. Orr was quite properly concerned lest someone mistakenly identify Christianity with inerrancy and thus have their faith shaken by some minor irresolvable discrepancy or by some misinterpretation of a factual claim. But it is still true that if the Bible turns out to be untrustworthy in its "minor" claims and teachings, that it would then be more than difficult to claim its complete reliability on matters of greater consequence such as the life and teachings of Jesus, his historical existence, death, and resurrection. To the extent that we don't have a Bible that we can trust, we don't have a Jesus that we can know.

Popular Baptist preachers have sometimes referred to Gaussen or Urquhart, and by some Warfield was known and admired.[38] Yet it is extremely difficult to find Baptist theologians who refer to Warfield at all.[39] As we have shown in *Baptists and the Bible*, however, Baptists have an independent tradition not unlike the Presbyterian tradition in content. We can profit by studying Warfield because the Princeton tradition (through Boyce) is the founding tradition of Southern Baptist theological education at the seminary level. Warfield is a compatible figure but not a direct source of Baptist views of the subject of Scripture. Baptists have been taught and do generally believe in the infallibility of Scripture despite the fact that most have never read or even heard of Warfield.

Far more relevant for Southern Baptists has been the influence of men like Basil Manly, Jr., B. H. Carroll,[40] J. R. Graves,[41] Charles Haddon Spurgeon, John A. Broadus, A. T. Robertson, R. G. Lee, W. A. Criswell, Herschel Hobbs, and evangelists such as Billy Graham, Eddie Martin and Angel Martinez, and a host of others who have steadfastly taught the pastors and the laity to trust the Bible as the very Word of God.

John Woodbridge correctly comments:

> Strange as it may seem for us who have been influenced by the recent heavy press given to the Princetonians, the writings of Archibald Alexander, Charles Hodge, and others were frequently not noted in the works of Baptists, Methodists, Lutherans, and others who spoke about the Bible's absolute infallibility. These Christians had their own denominational spokesmen to quote on the subject; they did not need to seek specific Princetonian guidance. Or they could refer to the works of Gaussen, Lee, Robert Haldane, David Dyer, Eleazar Lord, and a host of other writers. The well known Baptist A. J. Gordon advocated a doctrine of biblical inerrancy, citing Gaussen and Lee, and doing so with the "almost complete lack of reference to the Princeton men."[42]

Baptist leaders in the nineteenth century were usually strong advocates of plenary inspiration and biblical inerrancy. Modern Baptists, in my judgment, are divided between those who maintain historic, orthodox roots regarding biblical authority, and those who have accepted modern philosophical models of truth and who have often adopted modern critical methods of biblical interpretation. The laity remain for the most part as common (as opposed to scholarly) inerrantists. Theological disputes are often misunderstood by "the faithful in the pews," but Baptists in the pew expect their leaders to affirm biblical inerrancy in its true sense, because they intuitively recognize the significance of the loss of a sure word from God.

Semantic debates, however, can be destructive and should be resisted. Nevertheless doctrinal disputes are not all semantic (cf. 1 Timothy 1:3-7; 4:7; 6:3-5, 20-21). Baptist educators have the task of maintaining freedom of research and academic dialog while at the same time reaffirming and confirming with evidence the authenticity of the Scriptures, the historicity of the Gospel accounts, and the Lordship of Christ over all things. As devout scholars we must devote our lives to the pursuit of truth, remembering the unequivocal statement of Christ when speaking in prayer to His glorious Father, "Thy Word is Truth!"

Notes

1. James Orr, a fine conservative theologian from Scotland, may fairly be distinguished from Warfield in some technical ways, but to identify Orr with Southern Baptist "moderates" in the academic realm and to identify Warfield with anti-intellectual (capital F) Fundamentalists (as some may have imagined the case to be) is to seriously misread both the past and the present. Warfield was an academician of the highest order, devoted to careful exegesis and theological scholarship. (To find comparable quantity, quality, and influence, Baptists have to look to the writings of men like A. T. Robertson and perhaps A. H. Strong.) Whatever their differences, Orr asked Warfield to write the articles on "Inspiration," "Revelation," "Godhead," "Person of Christ," and "Trinity" in the widely read, influential, and theologically conservative *International Standard Bible Encyclopedia* (1915) which Orr edited (generally referred to as ISBE). Furthermore, Orr's own *The Problem of the Old Testament* (1922) remains a stunningly perceptive (unanswered) critique of the critical methodology still employed by some modern biblical scholars. Orr was not an exponent of modernistic theology. His *David Hume and His Influence on Philosophy and Theology* (1903) and *The Christian View of God and the World as Centering in the Incarnation* (1893) seem strangely relevant in light of recent talk about "the myth of God incarnate." Moreover Orr's treatment of *The Virgin Birth* (1907) and *The Resurrection of Jesus* (1908) are classic evangelical statements that would not endear him to modern neo-orthodox or existentialist theologians. Admittedly, Orr's *Revelation and Inspiration* (1910) does not affirm the concept of "verbal inerrancy," but as Addison H. Leitch comments in the "Introduction" to the 1969 reprinting by Baker Book House, "he is so close to it that it is hard to see the distinction." Warfield does not deny the existence of the textual phenomena to which Orr points, thus Warfield and Orr, in my opinion, differ semantically more than they do substantially. In fact on p. 217 Orr concludes his discussion of inerrancy (after making some technical comments regarding his belief that certain types of "errors" might exist in the biblical text in small, inconsequential details) by saying: " On this broad, general ground the advocates of 'inerrancy' [by which he clearly means Hodge and Warfield] may always feel that they have a *strong position*, whenever assaults may be made on them in matters of lesser detail. They stand undeniably, in their main contention, in the line of apostolic belief, and of the general faith of the Church, regarding Holy Scripture. The most searching inquiry still leaves them with a Scripture, supernaturally inspired to be

an infallible guide in the great matters for which it was given—the knowledge of the will of God for their salvation in Christ Jesus, instruction in the way of holiness, and the 'hope of eternal life, which God, who cannot lie, promised before times eternal' (Titus 1:2)."

2. Ernest Sandeen's *The Roots of Fundamentalism: British and American Millenarianism 1800-1930* (Chicago: University of Chicago Press, 1970; reprint ed., Grand Rapids: Baker, 1978) was a major contribution to the scholarly literature about fundamentalism. Sandeen found the "roots" primarily in John Darby's Dispensationalism and in Old School Presbyterian teachers at Princeton Theological Seminary. These two groups joined forces, so to speak, and developed what Sandeen thinks was a "new" defense of the high view of biblical authority. It is worth noting (since Sandeen did not) that if these "roots" are the blend that produces Fundamentalism in the Northeast, the dispensationalism of J. R. Graves (1820-1893) and the Old Princeton theology of J. P. Boyce (1827-1888) are arguably two of the more important theological influences on late 19th and early 20th century Southern Baptists. (Boyce entered Princeton in September 1847 and was most profoundly influenced by his Princeton professor of theology, Charles Hodge.) Southern Baptists are not simply a blend of Boyce and Graves, however. While I see merit in Sandeen's thesis in many respects I would want to note that I am more impressed with the general analysis offered by George Marsden, *Fundamentalism and American Culture: The Shaping of Twentieth-Century Evangelicalism: 1870-1925* (New York: Oxford, 1980). Marsden corrects Sandeen in several ways (though he too fails to offer an account adequate to explain the Baptist phenomenon). However, the Sandeen proposal that I find most confusing and thus worthy of comment in the latter part of this paper is the notion that Princetonians Hodge and Warfield engaged in a theological innovation when they proposed the doctrine of the "inerrancy of Scripture in the original autographs."

3. In Jack B. Rogers and Donald K. McKim, *The Authority and Interpretation of the Bible* (New York: Harper & Row, 1979), Sandeen's proposal about Warfield's supposed innovation has been rather uncritically incorporated into their discussion of the Princetonians. Rogers and McKim are convinced that inerrancy is an intellectually impossible position and thus they reconstruct historical theology in order to "save" orthodoxy from the "evils" of inerrancy. That this reconstruction is seriously misleading and arbitrary has been rather effectively demonstrated by John D. Woodbridge, *Biblical Authority: A Critique of the Rogers/McKim Proposal* (Grand Rapids: Zondervan, 1982).

4. Major bibliographical sources for Warfield's work on inspiration include B. B. Warfield, *The Inspiration and Authority of the Bible* (Philadelphia: Presbyterian & Reformed Publishing Co., 1948) [page numbers used in this paper come from the sixth printing, 1970], *Selected Shorter Writings of Benjamin B. Warfield*, ed. John E. Meeter, vol. 2 (Nutley: Presbyterian & Reformed Publishing Co., 1973), and Mark A. Noll, Jr., *The Princeton Theology: 1812-1921: Scripture, Science, and Theological Method from Archibald Alexander to B. B. Warfield* (Grand Rapids: Baker Book House, 1983).

5. The relevance of this for Baptists is obvious when we remember that the Baptist Second London Confession (1677; 1689) is almost verbatim the Westminster Confession (1646). In fact the article on Scripture is identical except for the addition of the first sentence which reads: "The Holy Scripture is the only sufficient, certain, and infallible rule of all saving Knowledge, Faith, and Obedience." This sentence was added by the Baptists to make crystal clear their acceptance of nothing less than the full import of the rest of the affirmations of the confessional statement. In my published study of this confession and of the scripture principle in general among Baptists (see *Baptists and the*

Bible co-authored with Tom J. Nettles, [Chicago: Moody Press, 1980], pp. 59-72) we point out that the term "certain" is the equivalent of the modern scholarly usage of "inerrancy" (meaning "without errors"), and the term "infallible" extends this meaning even further so as to claim Scripture to be incapable of teaching or affirming an error as if it were the truth. (An error might be described or reported, of course: as when it is said that Jesus cast out demons by the power of Beelzebub [Mark 3:22]: but such errors are not taught or affirmed by the biblical writer as being the truth.) These adjectives, "certain" and "infallible," are used in the Confession to describe the "rule" which is Scripture itself. This 1677 confession (officially adopted in 1689) is, moreover, the basis of American Baptists' famous Philadelphia Confession (printed by Ben Franklin in 1743) (see *Baptists and the Bible*, pp. 374-76).

6. Reference to the "autographs" becomes more explicit with Warfield, but the idea is not new. "Inerrancy" may be a 19th century semantic innovation but by no means is it a 19th century conceptual innovation. Note, for example, the references to both "inerrancy" and "autographs" in the earliest explicitly Baptist affirmation about Scripture, the declaration of John Smyth (early 17th century): "The holy Scriptures viz. the Originalls Hebrew and Greek are given by Divine Inspiration and in their first donation were without error most perfect and therefore Canonicall" (quoted in *Baptists and the Bible*, p. 28). In fact Thomas Grantham (1634-1692) a General Baptist minister from Lincolnshire published in 1678 an extensive defense of the so-called "autograph theory" in *Christianismus Primitivus* (cf. *Baptists and the Bible*, pp. 38-44). He writes as if he is explaining and defending the traditional view, not as if he is teaching a new idea. He is responding to an accumulation of objections to his view. Warfield is no innovator conceptually, though his scholarly expertise is uniquely focused on the defense of this traditional view.

7. Warfield's exegetical research shows clearly that the idea behind the term *theopneustos* is *not* that men testify and/or witness to their experiences and thus write Scripture and *then* that God breathes "life" and "value" into the words as they are read by others who are spiritually sensitive. Quite to the contrary, the Pauline teaching here is that God's revelatory activity (God's out-flowing breath, His communication of truth) is the *source* of Scripture. What Scripture says, God says. It must be clearly stated, however, that this is a figure of speech, and no claim is being made here that divine revelation was always expressed in human language directly. The ultimate product, Scripture, is, of course, human language, words and sentences, but the revelatory activity was not always itself verbal (as to the process by which it was given). So called mechanical dictation theories confuse the doctrines of inspiration and revelation. Inspiration is a "Scripture producing" work of God's spirit and thus its *result* is necessarily verbal. Revelation is sometimes but not always overtly verbal. God acts in history, works miracles, makes Himself known in visions or dreams, or reveals His will in various other ways. In fact, Warfield suggests that there are three biblical modes of revelation that he believes can be set forth "not with perfect discrimination . . . but not misleadingly, (1) external manifestations, (2) internal suggestion, and (3) concursive operation." (Cf. "Revelation" in ISBE and "The Biblical Idea of Revelation" in *Inspiration and Authority*, pp. 71-102, see especially p. 83ff.)

8. "God-inspired Scripture" was first published in *The Presbyterian and Reformed Review* but is more accessible in Warfield, *Inspiration and Authority*, pp. 245-96. This is probably the most thorough study of the meaning and usage of *theopneustos* ever done. See also the ISBE article "Inspiration" or the reprinted version, "The Biblical Doctrine of Inspiration" in *Inspiration and Authority*, pp. 131-66.

9. Warfield, *Inspiration and Authority*, p. 136.

10. Ibid., p. 137. The obvious "objection" that Peter may only have been referring to the technically prophetic portions of Scripture is answered simply by saying that even if that were so, the affirmations apply to large tracts of Scripture; and to the further comment that Peter (and Paul) speak only about the Old Testament, Warfield would remind the reader that Peter and Paul both apply their affirmations to *all Scripture*. The question then becomes whether or not the New Testament is a valid canon of *Scripture*.

11. See "The Terms 'Scripture' and 'Scriptures' As Employed in the New Testament" in *Inspiration and Authority*, pp. 229-41; "'It Says:' 'Scripture Says:' 'God Says,'" in *Inspiration and Authority*, pp. 229-348; and "The Oracles of God," in *Inspiration and Authority*, pp. 351-407.

12. A brief summary of Warfield's evidence is collected and listed by Henry Krabbendam, "B. B. Warfield vs. G. C. Berkhower on Scripture" in *Inerrancy*, edited by Norman L. Geisler (Grand Rapids: Zondervan Publishing House, 1979, pp. 416-20, 426-30. Krabbendam is careful to remind us that Warfield argued that the New Testament writings are in the same category as the Old. 2 Peter 3:16 shows that Peter regarded Paul's writings as being on a par with the other (Old Testament) Scriptures. 1 Timothy 5:18 quotes Old *and* New as having the same authority. The prophets claim to have God's authority in their writings (e.g. 1 Corinthians 14:37). Paul insists that the church listen and follow New Testament teachings even if an angel tries to persuade otherwise (Galatians 1:7-8).

13. See ibid., p. 420.

14. Warfield, "Inspiration and Criticism," reprinted in *Inspiration and Authority*, pp. 419-22. This quote and Warfield's further related discussion is from p. 437ff. Because this charge of mechanical-dictation is so often raised, it is perhaps not overly redundant to quote one other relevant passage from *Inspiration and Authority*, p. 421f.: "It is by no means to be imagined that it is meant to proclaim a mechanical theory of inspiration. The Reformed Churches have never held such a theory: though dishonest, careless, ignorant or over eager controverters of its doctrine have often brought the charge. Even those special theologians in whose teeth such an accusation has been oftenest thrown (e.g., Gaussen) are explicit in teaching that the human element is never absent. The Reformed Churches hold, indeed, that every word of the Scriptures, without exception, is the word of God; but, alongside of that, they hold equally explicitly that every word is the word of man. And, therefore, though strong and uncompromising in resisting the attribution to the Scriptures of any failure in absolute truth and infallibility, they are before all others seeking, and finding, and gazing on in loving rapture, the marks of the fervid impetuosity of a Paul—the tender saintliness of a John—the practical genius of a James, in the writings which through them the Holy Ghost has given for our guidance. Though strong and uncompromising in resisting all effort to separate the human and divine, they distance all competitors in giving honor alike to both by proclaiming in one breath that all is divine and all is human. As Gaussen so well expresses it, 'We all hold that every verse, without exception, is from men, and every verse, without exception, is from God"; "every word of the Bible is as really from man as it is from God.'"

15. See *Inspiration and Authority*, pp. 151-152 where Warfield notes that in Mark 12:36 our Lord emphasizes that the words of Psalm 110 are David's own words that were spoken as he was borne by the Holy Spirit. See also Warfield, *Selected Shorter Writings*, pp. 542-45.

16. *Inspiration and Authority*, p. 422.

17. The examples that follow are paraphrased from *Inspiration and Authority*, pp. 156-58.

285

18. Ibid., p. 158.

19. After discussing the opening verses of 2 Corinthians in this light, Warfield (*Inspiration and Authority*, p. 160) makes this important observation: "It is beyond question, therefore, that the New Testament writers, when they declare the Scriptures to be the product of the Divine breath, and explain this as meaning that the writers of these Scriptures wrote them only as borne by the Holy Spirit in such a fashion that they spoke, not out of themselves, but 'from God,' are thinking of this operation of the Spirit only as the final act of God in the production of the Scriptures, superinduced upon a long series of processes, providential, gracious, miraculous, by which the matter of Scripture had been prepared for writing, and the men for writing it, and the writing of it had been actually brought to pass. It is this final act in the production of Scripture which is technically called 'inspiration'; and inspiration is thus brought before us as, in the minds of the writers of the New Testament, that particular operation of God in the production of Scripture which takes effect at the very point of the writing of Scripture—understanding the term 'writing' here as inclusive of all the processes of the actual composition of Scripture, the investigation of documents, the collection of facts, the excogitation of conclusions, the adaptation of exhortations as means to ends and the like—with the effect of giving to the resultant Scripture a specifically supernatural character, and constituting it a Divine, as well as human, book. Obviously the mode of operation of this Divine activity moving to this result is conceived, in full accord with the analogy of the Divine operations in other spheres of its activity, in providence and in grace alike, as confluent with the human activities operative in the case; as, in a word, of the nature of what has come to be known as 'immanent action.'"

20. See ibid., pp. 108, 116-19.

21. Ibid., pp. 126-27.

22. Ibid., p. 127. Perhaps it is relevant at this point to note that Baptists have never deviated from this view confessionally, that Warfield's three facts are affirmed again and again by Baptists long before Warfield's writings, and thus that Baptists traditionally have affirmed this doctrine quite independently from the Old Princeton formulations. See *Baptists and the Bible* for primary source documentation of this claim.

23. Francis Turretin (1623-1687) was a city pastor and a professor of theology at Geneva from 1648 until his death. His *Institutio Theologiae Elencticae* was exceedingly influential and by some accounts is directly perpetuated by Charles and A. A. Hodge and thus would have been mediated into American evangelicalism by Warfield. See Francis Turretin, *The Doctrine of Scripture*, edited and translated by John W. Beardslee III (Grand Rapids: Baker Book House, 1981).

24. *Inspiration and Authority*, p. 128.

25. See W. A. Hoffecker, *Piety and the Princeton Theologians* (Grand Rapids: Baker Book House, 1981).

26. See for example John R. Mackay, "B. B. Warfield—A Bibliography," *The Expositor*, Eighth Series, 24 (July 1922):37.

27. Southern Baptist Theological Seminary founder and first President, J. P. Boyce, one of Hodge's students, would likely have been surprised to find that he had so misinterpreted Hodge as to express his own theological views in ways that sound much more similar to Warfield than to Brunner. Cf. J. P. Boyce, *Abstract of Systematic Theology*. Philadelphia: American Baptist Publication Society, 1887. See also Basil Manly, Jr., *The Baptist Doctrine of Inspiration* (New York: A. C. Armstrong & Son, 1888). Manly, one of the first four professors at the newly formed Southern Baptist Seminary, authored the famous *Abstract of Principles* still in use as the Seminary's Statement of Faith. There is no question what Manly intended by the article on Scripture. His book is a

major statement of the doctrine of full inerrancy as Evangelicals generally understand it today. If Baptists had a theological tradition that was as generally and as academically influential as the Presbyterian tradition, undoubtedly Manly's name would stand equal with if not above Warfield's. At any rate, Manly's book (recently brought back into print by Gano Books, 1985) clearly defends inerrancy and plenary inspiration. Perhaps the most accessible summary of these Baptist views is in *Baptists and the Bible*, pp. 201-19. See also Tom J. Nettles, "Baptists and Scripture" in *Inerrancy and the Church*, edited by John D. Hannah (Chicago: Moody Press, 1984), pp. 323-57, especially p. 353f. Manly's views, like Warfield's, are not innovative, however. Baptist theologian John L. Dagg's *The Evidences of Christianity* clearly affirms the necessity of biblical inerrancy as early as 1869. His *The Origin and Authority of the Bible* defended the same view in 1853. Abel Morgan defended this view in the late 1700's (cf. A. D. Gillette, *Minutes of the Philadelphia Baptist Association* (Philadelphia: American Baptist Publication Society, 1851), pp. 146, 170-71). As noted earlier, Thomas Grantham in 1678 published a lengthy defense of biblical infallibility including a rather full discussion of the problem of not having the autographs. John Gill in the early eighteenth century developed many of the same points in his defense of biblical infallibility in his famous *Body of Divinity*. Warfield's view does not seem to represent any sort of major departure from mainline, established, Baptist writings on the subject of inspiration and authority.

28. J. J. Markarian, p. 75. This comment seems strangely relevant in light of the recent "Myth of God Incarnate" debates, but Markarian's able exposition seems in this instance to have missed a vital point in Warfield's apologetic, namely the centrality of the doctrine of sovereign grace.

29. Jack Rogers, in *Scripture in the Westminster Confession* (Grand Rapids: William B. Eerdmans Publishing Co., 1967), contends that the confession offered a person, not proofs, to persuade us, whereas Warfield supposedly does the opposite. But Warfield does no such thing. Nor can any fair reading of the Confession fail to see the list of "proofs" offered there.

30. See Sandeen, *Roots of Fundamentalism*, especially chapter 5.

31. Documentation of this rather significant charge is abundant. See for example John D. Woodbridge and Randall H. Balmer, "The Princetonians, and Biblical Authority: An Assessment of the Ernest Sandeen Proposal," in *Scripture and Truth*, edited by D. A. Carson and John D. Woodbridge (Grand Rapids: Zondervan Publishing House, 1983), pp. 251-79.

32. Ibid., p. 255.

33. Ibid., pp. 256-57.

34. See John H. Gerstner, "The Contributions of Charles Hodge, B. B. Warfield, and J. Gresham Machen to the Doctrine of Inspiration" in *Challenges to Inerrancy: A Theological Response*, edited by Gordon Lewis and Bruce Demarest (Chicago: Moody Press, 1984), pp. 347-81.

35. See for example, *Inspiration and Authority*, p. 95, quoted in this context by Gerstner, "Contributions," p. 363. Gerstner adds that Sandeen ". . . charges that Princeton, by championing inerrancy, 'in a sense seemed to risk the *whole Christian faith* upon one proved error.' This is so dreadful a misrepresentation that while one is wondering how anyone who knows anything about the Princeton theologians could write it, Sandeen immediately goes on to mention that Warfield most certainly did distinguish between the Christian religion and the inerrancy of the Bible; but then Sandeen has the audacity to call that a 'compromise' by which Warfield was able to have his cake and eat it too. That Sandeen really meant this slanderous and utterly unsubstantiated remark is seen in the still more slanderous statement about the whole school several pages later

(p. 130): they manifested a 'continuing tendency to treat every opponent of the Princeton theology as an atheist or a non-Christian.'" Surely the most that could be said is that *one proven error* in Scripture would only prove Warfield's understanding of infallibility to be wrong (in the sense of being a slight overstatement). That is quite different from proving Christianity to be wrong (in the sense of being false), and both Hodge and Warfield acknowledged that. As to the last charge, it is so ludicrous as to be unworthy of further comment. The characterization is not only false, but surely maliciously so.

36. I use this term "theological fundamentalism" to distinguish it from the belligerent, anti-intellectualism that has sometimes adopted the "Fundamentalist" name in the 20th century. "Fundamentalism," however, in this unusual modern sense may grow out of extreme literalism, but it does not grow out of inerrancy as such. Personally, I do not think extreme literalism is a "cause" as much as it is a "symptom" of this dogmatic "personality type." Fundamentalism as a theological movement, however, had the support of E. Y. Mullins, James Orr, and numerous other well known, respected scholars. See *The Fundamentals,* edited by R. A. Torrey, A. C. Dixon, and others, 4 vols. (The Bible Institute of Los Angeles, 1915; reprint edition, Grand Rapids: Baker Book House, 1970).

37. A proven, undoubted error in Scripture would only prove "inerrancy" to be an overstatement. The thrust of the doctrine remains until substantial biblical claims and affirmations are proven false.

38. See for example the introductory material in W. A. Criswell, *Why I Preach That the Bible Is Literally True* (Nashville: Broadman Press, 1969), p. 7. Louis Gaussen's *Theopneustia, or the Plenary Inspiration of the Holy Scriptures* was translated from the French as early as 1841, and was widely circulated. Gaussen (1790-1863) was a Swiss Reformed preacher and founder of the Evangelical Society of Geneva. John Urquhart's *The Inspiration and Accuracy of the Holy Scriptures* (1895, 3rd ed., 1930) is a masterpiece defending full biblical truthfulness. Urquhart was an Associate of Great Britain's Victoria Institute.

39. W. T. Conner (1877-1952) long time professor of theology at Southwestern Baptist Theological Seminary, in *Revelation and God: an Introduction to Christian Doctrine* (Nashville: Broadman Press, 1936) did mention Warfield as being "probably correct" when he interprets 2 Timothy 3:16 to say that God produced or caused the Scriptures. This is only a passing reference, however, and such references are not typically found in Baptist literature.

40. See B. H. Carroll's *Inspiration of the Bible* (New York: Revell, 1930). There is no doubt about Carroll's views, and George W. Truett identifies himself with Carroll's stance in a special Introduction.

41. See J. R. Graves, *The Work of Christ in the Covenant of Redemption Developed in Seven Dispensations* (Memphis: Baptist Book House, 1883).

42. John D. Woodbridge, *Biblical Authority,* p. 139f. The reference to Lee is William Lee's *Inspiration of Holy Scriptures, Its Nature and Proof* (1854).

15

THE TEACHING OF RECENT SOUTHERN BAPTIST THEOLOGIANS ON THE BIBLE

James Leo Garrett

In the outset the assigned title of this paper and the accompanying method-ology to be used in this paper should be carefully defined. The term *theolo-gians* is not to be confined to those who have been or are professors of systematic theology in the seminaries operated by the Southern Baptist Con-vention (SBC). Nor is it to be confined to those who have been or are profes-sors in any discipline in any of these aforementioned seminaries or professors of Bible or religion in colleges and universities supported by Baptist state con-ventions related to the SBC. Rather, *theologians* is to be construed as those "recent" Southern Baptists who have been authors of books or portions of books or journal articles that focus upon or pertain to the Bible.

In clarification of *teaching*, it should be noted that the research has been limited to published works and hence has not included cassette tapes and un-published addresses and typescripts. Curriculum materials have also not been included in the research.

The term *recent* has been generally construed to mean the twentieth cen-tury. From the first half of the century Edgar Young Mullins (1860-1928) and Walter Thomas Conner (1877-1952) will be studied as representative South-ern Baptist theological spokesmen concerning the nature and authority of the Bible. Such methodology is predicated on the widespread and generally ac-knowledged influence of these two professors of systematic theology.[1] Al-though other Southern Baptists did write significantly about the Bible prior to Conner's death in 1952,[2] only Mullins and Conner from that earlier period will be studied in this paper. For the thirty-five years since 1952, all the available books and journal articles by Southern Baptist authors have been gathered, examined, and interpreted on a topical basis. Biographical data on such au-thors are not being included, but all have been Southern Baptists during all or part of the period being studied.

The words *on the Bible* have been interpreted to include the inspiration, the canon, the interpretation, the authority, and the dependability or inerrancy of the Old and the New Testaments.

Edgar Young Mullins

E. Y. Mullins did not write any book about the Bible. He did treat the Bible succinctly in *Baptist Beliefs* (1912), at some length in *Freedom and Authority in Religion* (1913), again rather briefly in *The Christian Religion in Its Doctrinal Expression* (1917), in one chapter of *Christianity at the Cross Roads* (1924), and occasionally elsewhere. As to why Mullins did not write more on this subject one may speculate that he, as a theologian and apologist, may have left the topic to those engaged in teaching Old Testament and/or New Testament interpretation. He may have been more concerned to explicate the role of Christian experience, or controversy about the Bible among Southern Baptists may have become substantive after the major writings of Mullins had been written. The Southern Seminary president did write something concerning each of the categories chosen for this paper.

General Teaching

Some of Mullins's teaching about the Bible was of a general nature. He twice ascribed to the Bible three basic qualities: sufficiency, certainty, and authoritativeness.[3] The Bible, according to Mullins, is sufficient even though divine revelation also comes via "nature," "conscience," and "the religious struggles and beliefs of men." For Mullins

> none of these other sources of religious knowledge, nor all of them combined, are sufficient for our needs. The Bible gives the additional truth about God. . . . In and through the Bible God reveals himself to man. . . . In Jesus Christ, God spoke finally to makind. The Bible is God's record of his gradual revelation leading up to the final revelation in Christ. No element of truth is wanting for our religious needs when we have really obtained the message of the Bible.[4]

What is the certainty of the Bible? The laws of nature cannot "save the soul" of man, and philosophy "does not yield certainty in religions," but the "Bible tells us how to find God and by following its directions we actually find him."[5] When the term "certainty" is "applied to the Bible, . . . it means permanent dependability."

> Christ's appeal to men does not leave them wavering and uncertain. When he comes into the heart and life, he satisfies. Men at once recognize the certainty and finality of his word, and his person as the revelation of God to man.[6]

In what sense is the Bible authoritative? "The Scriptures speak with authority, as does no other literature in the world." The Bible's "authoritative note" does not derive from any "external" authority such as council or pope.[7] This is even true of the councils which pronounced on the canon of the New Testament. The writers of books in both testaments "claimed to speak for God" and "declared that they were moved by the Holy Spirit." Jesus endorsed "the Old Testament revelation" and "promised the presence and the guidance of the Holy Spirit to his disciples."[8]

Mullins variously defined the Bible, sometimes more from the divine side, sometimes more from the human. It "is God's message to man given to supply the needs of his religious life."[9] It is "the outward literary expression of the truths acquired in man's interaction with the spiritual universe."[10] Furthermore, Mullins was particularly interested in the proper relation of biblical "literature" to the "life-process" (i.e., "life-adjustments" and "life-experiences") of which the literature is "the record" (i.e., "its interpretation and explanation"). Mullins insisted that life and literature not be confused, that the life not be "exalted as if the literature were nothing," and that the literature not be "exploited as if the life were nothing." The "life preceded the literature historically," but "the literature is indispensable to the life," for tradition and reason cannot reliably preserve the life and truth. He who levels the charge of bibliolatry has "severed the literature from the life which gives it significance, and has judged the literature thus isolated from its true context in the life, and apart from its function." On the other hand, ecclesiastical and rationalistic rejection of the literature "in the interest of the life" and efforts "to maintain the life apart from the literature" also fail.[11]

The seminary president spelled out in some detail certain "distinguishing marks" of the "biblical revelation." It is both "historical and experiential," is "regenerative and morally transforming" (and not merely "communication of supernatural truth"), is "genetic" in that "the parts are vitally related to each other," is "gradual and progressive" (but not in the sense of natural evolution), is "unitary and purposive," does not impede the work of science, philosophy, and other disciplines, and is "supernatural."[12]

Biblical Inspiration

In 1912 Mullins wrote as if human beings cannot "determine precisely" the method or manner of the "process" of the divine inspiration of the Bible, but he seemed more confident about the "result of such inspiration, i.e., the serving of "all our practical religious needs and ends."[13]

In 1913 Mullins asserted that all the modern theories of biblical inspiration "take their departure from the person and work of Christ" in the sense that they hinge on whether Jesus is the "prince of saints" or the "divine Redeemer and Lord." Then he proceeded to discuss three types of theories. The "radical view"[14] rejects the authority of Jesus and hence of the Bible, which is fully comparable with other sacred books, and emphasizes immanence in a pantheistic way to the exclusion of transcendence. The "conservative view" is found in two distinct varieties, labelled by William Sanday as the "traditional" view (holding to divine inspiration of the Hebrew vowel points, dictation of the Bible by the Holy Spirit to passive human penmen, and complete scientific accuracy of the Bible) and the "inductive view"[15] (rejection of an a priori starting-point concerning the Bible, and emphasis on the Bible's own testimony to inspiration, its use of common human language and various literary forms, its being primarily a religious book, and its "core and center" as Jesus Christ. Mullins insisted that both varieties agree on the "reality" of the Bible's "supernatural revelation," "its sufficiency for our religious needs," and its "finality and authoritativeness." The "compromise view," of which Auguste Sabatier and William Newton Clarke have been somewhat different exponents, subordinates the Bible to the higher authority of "the Christian consciousness" and, for clarke at least, accepts only the "Christian element" in the Bible, which element centers in Jesus' teaching about God as Father. Mullins faulted Clarke for trying to hold both a high Christology and a low view of the Scriptures. Mullins by implications showed his sympathy with the "inductive" variety of "the conservative view."[16]

In 1917 Mullins in a briefer treatment identified the two "approaches" to inspiration ("processes" and "results") and four theories of inspiration: the "naturalistic," the "illumination" (without "infallible guidance into truth"), the "plenary verbal" (which Mullins identified with the Holy Spirit's dictation), and the "plenary"-"dynamical" (the inspiration of thought rather than language, but declaration of "truth unmixed with error"). The Louisville theologian clearly favored working on the "results" more than on the "processes" and espoused an inductive method but stopped short of an endorsement of the "plenary"-"dynamical" theory.[17]

Biblical Canon and Relation of the Testaments

Mullins regarded the New Testament as "continuous with the Old" Testament and the fulfilment of the Old Testament. "Jesus is the crown and goal of the Old Testament and the center of the New." He is "the keystone in the arch" that unites the testaments and unifies the Bible.[18]

The role of the councils in the patristic age which made decisions as to the canon of the New Testament is played down by Mullins. Such decisions do not bind the consciences of modern Christians; those councils "simply registered the common convictions of the Christian community," and the books finally canonized "were homogeneous books expressive of the spiritual life-exxperiences of the Christian community." Mullins recognized two criteria for the canonization of New Testament books: "apostolicity" (i.e., "derived from apostles or apostolic men, eye-witnesses or the associates of the eye-witnesses of Jesus in his earthly life") and "spiritual congruity or agreement with the Christian experience." Doubt as to Second Peter, Esther, Ecclesiastes, or the Song of Solomon do "not affect the larger fact of a homogeneous Bible." "If the present canon of Scripture should be disintegrated, no doubt the parts would coalesce again into the living unity of the Bible, since they are parts of a congruous whole."[19]

Biblical Interpretation

Mullins did not publish any detailed treatment of biblical hermeneutics or examine the various hermeneutical methods used throughout the post-biblical history of Christianity. He did provide a few incisive comments pertaining to interpretation. Illumination by the Holy Spirit is available for interpretation, and Christ is "the crown" of the Bible.

> Christ . . . is God's message to us and we are to understand the whole Bible simply and solely in its relations to Jesus Christ, the Son of God and Savior of the world.[20]

Mullins identified as a Baptist conviction the "right of private and individual interpretation" of the Bible but went on to call upon Baptists to "seek to produce the best scholarship and the greatest possible intelligence among the people in order that they may understand the Bible." "Its real message is obtained only by carefully, wise, sympathetic, and patient toil under the guidance of God's Spirit."[21]

Biblical criticism is a legitimate endeavor not only because criticism "is an inalienable intellectual right of man" but because it has clarified the progressive nature of revelation, underscored the unity of the Bible, showed "a superhuman power" to be active among the people who produced the Bible, manifested "the close connection between the literature and the life," and emphasized the human factor in revelation. Certain "counter-criticism," recognizing man's religious life, has curbed the rationalistic employment of biblical criticism.[22] Indeed "destructive critical theories grow out of world-views and are not based upon the science of criticism itself."[23] Contrary to Wilhelm Hermann, Mullins insisted that faith "is not dependent upon a bare historical judgment" and "yet the historical judgment is indispensable to faith." Mullins concluded that the Christian experience and the biblical literature are both distinguishable and interdependent.[24]

In 1924 the Louisville president addressed in greater detail the methods and validity of historical criticism of the New Testament in its search for facts, "combined with spiritual appreciation of its contents." He accepted such criticism, thus pursued, but he rejected (1) the anti-miraculous extraction of the moral and spiritual teachings from all the rest so that they become intuitions (James Martineau, Adolf Harnack); (2) the removal of supernatural events (e.g., virginal conception, miracles, resurrection) from the purview of historical research on the ground that these are verifiable only by faith (Friedrich Loofs, James Moffatt), when indeed "facts of any and all kinds in the realm of history are to be accepted if the evidence is sufficient"; (3) an a priori rejection of the supernatural; (4) an agnostic rejection of Jesus Christ and the New Testament; (5) the thoroughgoing apocalyptic view of the New Testament (Albert Schweitzer); and (6) the history of religion approach to the New Testament with its heavy influence of mystery religions. Such views are both unscientific and "out of touch with the religious spirit."[25]

Biblical Dependability

Mullins did not explicate or defend the infallibility or inerrancy of the Bible and treated the subject only when dealing with the Bible and science. The Bible is "the book of religion," not "a text-book on science or any other subject except religion." But the Bible's "statements conform broadly and generally to the teachings of science," even though the biblical writers used "the language of appearances." Job could hardly have been helped by knowing "the Newtonian law of gravitation," and the twentiety-century Christian should not stake "the integrity and authoritativeness of the Bible on its exact agreement with "such Newtonian law or the Copernican astronomy."[26] At the end of his career Mullins acknowledged that his book, *Christianity at the Cross Roads*, had been criticized by "[s]ome fundamentalists" because in it he had not developed and taught "a doctrine of an 'infallible and authoritative' Scripture." Indeed "[s]ome modernists" had also criticized it "because, as they allege, it does appeal to authority." Mullins as "an evangelical Christian" preferred to predicate the acceptance of the gospel rather upon "the facts of the gospel," i.e., an inductive approach to biblical authority.[27]

Biblical Authority

Mullins identified the two major Protestant expressions of religious authority in his day as the heritage of "Protestant Scholasticism," which "has wrought out elaborate rationalistic schemes to prove the authority of the Bible," and the Christian consciousness view of authority as represented in Auguste Sabatier's *Religions of Authority and the Religion of the Spirit*. Mullins accepted neither the rationalistic nor the subjectivist extreme and found "the true view . . . by taking into account the apartness and the interdependence of the literature and the life." Examining the teaching of Martin Luther and of John Calvin about the Scriptures, Mullins found both Reformers teaching in coordinate fashion the Word and the Spirit so as to avoid either of the modern extremes. Even some change in the New Testament canon "would not undermine the authority of the Bible."

Moreover, Protestant subjectivists were wrong in alleging that the concept of an authoritative Bible means capitulation to the Roman Catholic conception of authority. Roman Catholicism "has to do with institutionalized grace," whereas Protestantism "has to do with personalized grace." Corollary to the latter is the view that the "function of the Scriptures . . . is to correlate the soul with the living Redeemer." Likewise, Roman Catholicism "suppresses" the individual, whereas Protestantism "exalts" the individual. Consequently "the judicial quality in the individual" recognized in Protestantism not only can reject Scripture but also can "approve and accept" Scripture. The Bible's "truth and authoritativeness" have been "discovered." "The soul knows that in it God speaks. To bow to his authority as thus revealed is the supreme joy of life."[28]

Mullins specifically treated the authority of the Old Testament. It "is authoritative as God's preparatory revelation" even as the "New Testament is authoritative as God's completed revelation." "All that is permanent in the Old Testament is carried over into the New," and its mandates are "written on the heart."[29]

According to Mullins, the Bible "is final in all questions of doctrine, polity, and Christian living" and the only true basis for Christian or church unity.[30] But how does Mullins relate the Bible's authority to the authority of Christ? He does so by joining the lordship of Christ to biblical authority[31] and by making Christ to be the "seat of authority."

> . . . Christ, as Revealer of God and Redeemer of men, is the seat of authority in religion and absolutely final for human needs. . . . The Scriptures do not and cannot take the place of Jesus Christ. We are not saved by belief in the Scriptures, but by a living faith in Christ. . . . The authority of Scripture is that simply of an inspired literature which interprets a life. . . . The Bible is authoritative for the determinative ideas, but Christ is determinative for power. . . .

294

In short, Christ . . . is the seat of authority in religion and above and under-neath and before the Bible. But the Bible is the authoritative literature which leads us to Christ.[32]

In summary, Mullins affirmed the "sufficiency" of the Bible (as the book of revelation), its "certainty" (or "permanent dependability"), and its "authorita-tiveness." The biblical literature and the life-events and life-experiences out of which it arose, though different, must be kept integrated. Stressing the results of inspiration more than its processes, Mullins first identified the theories of inspiration as "radical," "traditional," "inductive," and subordination to Christian consciousness—with inductive as his choice—and later identified the theories as "naturalistic," "illumination," "plenary verbal," and "plenary"-"dynamical"—with no avowed preference stated. Christ is the "crown" of the Bible and the "key" to its interpretation. The homogeneity of the canonical books is more important than conciliar decisions about the canon. The Louisville theologian found the historical criticism of the New Testament to be legitimate when rightly used, but he could cite six contemporary patterns of misuse. As a book of religion the Bible is in "broad general" agreement with natural science. The Old Testament is authoritative as preparatory revelation, and the New Testament as completed. The Word and the Spirit are correlatives. True authority is not au-thoritarian. Christ is the "seat of [final] authority in religion," and "the Bible is the authoritative literature that leads" to Christ.

Walter Thomas Conner[33]

Conner as a systematic theologian made more specific use of biblical materi-als than many of the more speculative theologians, and his theology was framed under the supreme authority of the Bible. In his later years his use of biblical materials was even more pronounced, as a comparison of *The Gospel of Redemption* (1945) with *Revelation and God* (1936) will demonstrate. He wrote a major volume on New Testament theology: *The Faith of the New Testa-ment* (1940). His views concerning the Bible itself were expressed most fully in his systematic theological writings, especially *A System of Christian Doctrine*[34] and *Revelation and God*.[35]

The Nature of the Bible

The Bible, according to Conner, is essentially a book dealing with religion, not a book on science or mathematics. It was written in popular language rather than in "the language of the cloister or the laboratory." As a book of religion its teachings "are not invalidated by a change in scientific views."[36] Scientific ques-tions "have nothing to do with the substance of biblical teachings,"[37] and "the only science that ever raises a real issue with the Bible and its teachings is a science that is not science," but instead "an anti-theistic metaphysics."[38]

Unlike many of his theological predecessors who equated divine revelation and the Bible, Conner differentiated the two. The Bible is "the product of reve-lation," for "revelation preceded the Bible," and the Bible "now has revelation value for us." "God gave to men of biblical times experience with himself and they wrote down their thoughts and experiences." Modern Christians ought not to regard the biblical writers as mere "amanuenses or stenographers" whose primary function was the transmission of messages from God for future generations. Biblical revelation does not come to modern Christians "immediately, but through the biblical writers and their situation." Biblical events were not "a kind of stage show put on for effect." They have present-day revelation value because they had revelaton value for the original recipients.[39] The Bible, therefore, is the record of God's special or historical self-revelation.

Revelation under the Two Testaments

Conner taught that the Bible bears witness to a general revelation of God through nature (Ps. 19:1; Matt. 6;25ff.; Rom. 1:20) and through man's rational, moral, and religious being, which revelation is also attested by the universal human consciousness of God. This revelation manifests the deity and power of the one God[40] but does not show God's saving grace, afford "satisfactory religious assurance" of a right relation with God, or provide any "present victory over sin and evil." It served as the "foundation" for the special or historical revelation of God. Other religions may be said to be revelations from God "in the sense that they are an expression of man's religious nature," but Christianity is "the completion of all other religions." Other religions "represent man's groping in the dark after God; Christianty represents God's finding of man in Christ."[41]

Israel was the "organ or medium of God's revelation to the world." Israel, with whom Yahweh had entered a covenant relation, was Yahweh's own people, "not to the exclusion of others, but looking ultimately to the inclusion of the Gentile nations." God's "purpose of making Israel God's missionary to the nations was realized through the coming of Christ and the establishment of his universal religion, although . . . realized in spite of Israel's disobedience and her national pride and exclusiveness."[42] Revelation, as recorded in the Old Testament, was "the coming of God himself into the life of the people rather than the communication of a doctrine about God."[43] Such revelation to and through Israel came during various periods (Abrahamic, Mosaic, monarchial, later prophetic, captivity, restoration), especially in times of national crisis marked by divine intervention,[44] and through various means (dreams, visions, audible voices).[45]

Conner faced squarely an issue of importance to Old Testament scholars in the twentiety century: wehther the uniqueness of Old Testament religion lay in a unique history or in a unique prophetic interpretation of its history. While recognizing God's sovereignty over all nations, the biblical writers declared God's dealings with Israel to be special. Indeed, "the power to see God in history is itself the gift of God," and hence this power "is a differentiating factor in Israel's history." But, Conner contended, the uniqueness of Israel's religion rested not only on prophetic insight but also on "a series of unique events," indeed God's self-revelation.[46]

The Fort Worth theologian interpreted God's revelation under the New Testament through the centrality of the divine-human Jesus Christ. Revelation in

Jesus Christ has both an objective, historical aspect and a subjective, experiential aspect. Objectively, it brought to humankind a new consciousness of God through Jesus' own consciousness of God the Father, through his teaching about God, through is character and deeds, and through his saving death. Subjectively, it awakens in human beings a knowledge of God and his will through the work of the Holy Spirit and the response of faith—faith both as venture and as spiritual vision. God's revelation and God's redemption in Jesus Christ, inseparable as they are, have the character of finality or ultimacy.[47]

Revelation, the Bible, and Inspiration

Conner affirmed the fact of the divine inspiration of the Bible but, like E. Y. Mullins, he set forth no theory as to its method or process. In the New Testament writings God is regarded "as the author of Old Testament sayings and teachings."

> The Scriptures, then, are God's work. He produced the Scriptures. He was in the events of history and experience out of which the scripture records grew and he was in the producing of the records. . . . The Scriptures, then, are the product of revelation and inspiration. . . .[48]

Whereas revelation and inspiration can be differentiated, their interrelation is such that no "absolute distinction can be maintained." Inspiration did not restrict or suppress the writers but liberated each writer "to be himself, think his own thoughts, and speak and write in his own way."[49]

Interpretation of the Bible

Conner held that the Bible as a historical book should be interpreted in relation to his historical setting, for "in producing the Bible God did not work *in abstracto*." God was limited by the human beings through whom he worked and by "the whole historical and social situation with which he was dealing." Because the Bible "is the record of a revelation historically mediated and conditioned," in its interpretation and application it is necessary to distinguish between "form" and "substance." Conner cited the Pauline exhortation relative to a holy kiss and Jesus' washing of his disciples' feet as illustrations of biblical events the substance or attitude of which are to be followed, but not the form. Conner deplored the Bible's being made "a book of rules to which one can go to find specific direction for every particular situation that may arise."

The Southwestern theologian utilized a carefully defined concept of "progressive revelation" as a hermeneutical principle. It was not to be identified with the "naturalistic evolution" of Israel's religion but could serve to relieve "certain moral difficulties" in the Bible, such as the destruction of enemies. Coner often said to his classes, "The Bible does not mean what it says; it means what it means," thereby asserting that a literal interpretation will not suffice for every passage. All parts of the Bible are not of equal value to the Christian. Even as the nail on one's finger is of less importance than one's heart, so an Old Testament genealogical table is not of equal importance with John 3:16.[50]

297

Centralities of the Bible

As a book of religion recording a historically mediated revelation of God and consisting of two testaments, the Bible must be understood in light of its centralities. Its "central interest" is the divine redemption of man through the works of God (Exodus, death of Jesus). Its personal and thematic center is Jesus Christ. The Bible is "the literary means" of our knowing him. The partial and preparatory revelation under the Old Testament, including the Messianic hope, was fulfilled in Jesus, as the New Testament writers testify. While referring to typical persons, typical events, and typical institutions in the religions of Israel, Conner avoided the excesses of typology. The Gospels provide a "record of his life, death, resurrection, and ascension," while the remainder of the New Testament has as its theme the glorified Christ. The Bible's central function "is to awaken faith in man," and the Bible cannot be properly understood and appreciated apart from a "response of faith."[51]

Authority of the Bible

Conner was concerned to relate the Bible's authority to the authority of God and of Jesus Christ. The authority of the Bible is the authority of a sovereign and holy God "who speaks to men by way of command." The seat of authority in Christianity is not dual, but singular, for "the authority of the Bible is the authority of [Jesus] Christ." The Scirptures serve as the "medium" of the "revelation of the mind and will of Christ." Such authority does not enslave human beings or violate legitimate human freedom, for paradoxically "by submission to the spiritual authority of Christ man finds his spiritual freedom." Biblical authority, rightly understood, is the authority of God's redeeming grace, of God's holy love. In the Protestant Reformation, Conner affirmed, not only the locus of authority was changed but also its nature. But those today who want a religion without authority can find no solace in Conner. He clearly rejected the thesis of the liberal French Protestant, Auguste Sabatier, that "a spiritual religion is one that excludes authority and that an authoritative religion is unspiritual."[52]

In summary, Conner as a theologian sought to clarify the nature of revelation, both general and special, of inspiration, and of the Bible with its two testaments as the record of special or historical revelation. He affirmed divine inspiration without articulating any theory as to its mode, sought a balanced hermeneutical method without spelling out its details, correlated the two testaments without excessive typology, and held the Bible to be trustworthy without adopting an ideology of inerrancy. For Conner the authority of the Bible was to be understood as the literary dimension of the authority of God in Jesus Christ.

Southern Baptist Author-Theologians Since 1952

Biblical Inspriation

Some Southern Baptist authors, but not all, who since 1952 have written concerning the inspiration of the Holy Scriptures have followed E. Y. Mullins and W. T. Conner in their reluctance to attempt to define, choose, or opt for a specific theory of the method of inspiration. R. Edgar Glaze, Jr., noted that the leading Baptist confessions of faith (e.g., the 1651 General Baptist, the 1833 New Hampshire, and the 1925 SBC) had not specified a method or mode and that Baptist leaders (e.g., James Madison Pendleton, J. McKee Adams, William Richardson White) had been content to affirm the fact of inspiration (Pendleton), to see the Bible as the "inspired record of revelation" (White), and to major on the results of inspiration (Adams). Glaze reported that John Clyde Turner had embraced the "dynamical" theory, opposing "plenary, verbal inspiration," and that Wallie Amos Criswell inclined to the mechanical dictation theory.[53] Some ambiguity, however, is attached to Criswell's own theory of biblical inspiration. In 1965 and again in 1982 he clearly rejected the "*rational* or radical," the "*fractional* or partial," and "the *mechanical*" theories and espoused what he described as "a *dynamic, plenary, verbal, supernatural*" theory.[54] But in 1969 he wrote:

> On the original parchment every sentence, word, line, mark, point, pen stroke, jot, and tittle were put there by inspiration of God. There is no question of anything else. . . . This is called the verbal theory of inspiration, which is vehemently denied by many modern theologians. They say it is too mechanical. They say it degrades the writers to the level of machines. They say it has a tendency to make skeptics and unbelievers . . . . But I am insisting upon, and presenting, no theory except that which is found in the Bible.[55]

The present author interpreted in some detail the diverse views of biblical inspiration which had been held by Basil Manly, Jr., Augustus Hopkins Strong, William Newton Clarke, and Henry Wheeler Robinson, all of whom were Baptists.[56]

Clifton Judson Allen in the *Broadman Bible Commentary* espoused the "dynamic" theory, clearly bypassing the "verbal" and the "plenary" theories and disclaiming that "inerrancy" which "can allow no error of fact or substance."[57] but Richard P. Belcher later faulted Allen's view for downplaying the words of the Bible and for "existential fuzziness."[58] Preceded by the affirmations of "plenary verbal" inspiration made by Wendell H. Rone, Sr.,[59] and by Larry L. Lewis,[60] Leighton Paige Patterson in the *Criswell Study Bible* declared:

> Historically the Church has given unmistakable testimony to the plenary verbal inspiration of the Bible. . . . This does not mean that the entire Bible was dictated word by word.[61]

Gene Russell insisted that Josiah Blake Tidwell had held to the verbal theory.[62]

On the other hand, Glaze, following Wayne Eugene Ward and Joseph Franklin Green, Jr.,[63] asserted:

> Any survey of what Baptists have said and are saying about the Bible reveals that men equally committed to the authority and trustowrthiness of the Bible may differ in their understanding of inspiration and the exact relationship of the human and divine elements in the Bible.[64]

Such expected diversity among Baptists, including Southern Baptists, led Glaze to observe:

> One who has a full appreciation for the greatness of the Bible, its divine inspiration, and trustworthiness knows that attempts at description are never adequate. . . . Part of the evidence for the divine inspiration of the Bible is its ability to speak in different ways to individuals according to their varying needs. Therefore, no one person is able to formulate a theory that is completely satisfactory for all others.[65]

According to H. Stephen Shoemaker, the inspiration of the Bible is the basis for its trustworthiness.[66] John Moore Lewis examined carefully the major New Testament texts relative to inspiration, 2 Timothy 3:14-17 and 2 Peter 1:20-21, and treated other passages summarily. Lewis then defined and stated the strengths and weaknesses of the major theories of inspiration (intuitional, illumination, mechanical dictation, verbal-plenary, and dynaimc). He did not opt for one of these theories, explaining that none "has universal acceptance," but his treatment of "the evidences of inspiration" so focuses upon the Bible's "purpose" rather than on "the process of inspiration" as to suggest his greater sympathy for the dynamic view.[67] According to Dale Moody,

> A biblical view of inspiration must be broad enough to include the truth in all the historic theories and adequate for a constructive theology in dialogue with the sacred writings of other world religions, the contributions of great systems of philosophy, and the discoveries of modern science.[68]

Biblical Canon

Few Southern Baptist authors since 1952 have seriously addressed the subject of the canon of the Bible. One notable exception has been Marvin E. Tate, Jr., who, after recounting the five major Protestant arguments[69] for rejection as noncanonical the books of the Old Testament Apocrypha, reviewed favorably Albert C. Sudberg, Jr.'s critical rejection of the theory of a distinct Alexandrian canon of Jewish sacred writings and Sundberg's own conclusion that before A.D. 70 Judaism had a "closed canon" consisting only of Law and Prophets plus "a third group of writings of 'undetermined proportions'"—which canon was appropirated by Jesus and the early Christians, despite the Jewish decision of Jamnia ca. A.D. 90 for canonization of the Writings. Tate, concluding that the Proestant Reformers failed "on historical grounds" to get back "to the canon of Jesus and the Apostles," argued for the return of the Old Testament Apocrypha to the Protestant canon so as to enhance "the understanding of Judaism and the background of the" New Testament, to assist in interpreting the existing Old Testament, and to make more available the "'bridge between the Testaments.'"[70]

Dale Moody suggested that Marcion's second-century canon of the New Testament "perhaps began in the Lycus Valley" during the first century and asked whether today "it would be possibie to add [to the New Testament canon], say the letter Paul mentioned in 1 Cor. 5:9, 11 if it should be found." "Perhaps, since it would have no influence on years of tradition, such a writing should be as an appendix."[71] J. Morris Ashcraft held that the process of canonization of the New Testament books "was practically complete by A.D. 200" and that there were three principal criteria for canonization: association "with the name of an apostle," "faithfulness to Jesus and his teaching," and acceptance through reading in public worship.[72]

Biblical Interperetation

Southern Baptist authors since 1952 have given increasing attention to the history of biblical interpretation. In 1960 William L. Hendricks noted that the Alexandrian and the Antiochene schols of interpretation in the patristic era, the one allegorical and the other literal, represent the hermeneutical extremes.[73] In 1969 in the *Broadman Bible Commentary* John P. Newport cited allegorization (or "the search for hidden meanings"), hyperliteralism, and "Church-controlled" interpretation as historic "examples of the misuse and distortion of the Bible." He then described the "grammatical-historical-theological "method of the Protestant Reformers, the historical critical method of the Enlightenment and the nineteenth century, and the more theological interpretation of the post-World War I era. The "historical critics" "rejected the dogmatic presuppositions of the Protestant Scholastics" and "replaced them with the new dogmatic premises of a theology determined by idealism, romanticism, and the Enlightenment." They "succeeded in textual work, grammar, literary history, and archaeology; but they missed the meaning of the Bible."[74] In 1974 John J. Kiwiet identified three major hermeneutical controversies in the history of Christianity under the captions "Hermeneutics Is Interpretation," "Hermeneutics Is Proclamation," and "Hermeneutics Is Translation." These were the controversy between the schools of Alexandria and of Antioch, the differences between the Christocentric and soteriological hermeneutic of Martin Luther and the pneumatic approach of the Anabaptists (especially the Southern German Anabaptists), and the modern efforts from Schleiermacher to the post-Bultmannians to translate "the intention of the original author" across the centuries and the cultures "into the understanding of the contemporary reader." According to Kiwiet, "[h]ermeneutical principles, like theological doctrines, are born in the agony of controversy."[75] In 1986 Newport reviewed the history of biblical hermeneutics from the Patristic age to the twentieth century.[76]

In a series of parallel articles on Southern Baptist biblical interpretation from 1845 to 1945, Edward Glenn Hinson examined "the liberal tradition" and found as exponents only Crawford Howell Toy after he ceased to be a Southern Baptist and William Louis Poteat, a biologist,[77] Richard D. Land investigated "the fundamentalist tradition," focusing on biblical inerrancy, and found as clear example only James Marion Frost;[78] and Claude L. Howe, Jr., studied "the moderate tradition" and located E. Y. Mullins and W. T. Conner.[79]

The question as to the proper hermeneutical principles also has drawn the attention of Southern Baptist authors. In 1961 John P. Newport asserted that there was "a general consensus" that the linguistic or grammatical, the historical (background), the theological (Christocentrism, analogy of faith), and the homiletical or practical principles are "the basic exegetical principles."[80] Eight years later in the *Broadman Bible Commentary* Newport explicated these four principles in greater detail. The linguistic or grammatical principle was subdivided into lexical, syntactical, thought method, rhetorical, and contextual factors. These principles, according to Newport, "should not be looked at as rigid and mechanical rules" but rather "should be helpful guidelines."[81] In his revision of H. E. Dana's book on biblical hermeneutics, R. Edgar Glaze, Jr. retained Dana's "objectives" and "principles" or interpretatin.[82] In 1964 Dallas M. Roark identified and explained three principles of biblical interpretation: "the historico-grammatical," or what grammatical rules and historical facts require, "the Christological" or Christocentric, and "the existential" or the posture of hearing and appropriating the message.[83] Fred L. Fisher wrote in 1966 a monograph explaining a nine-step method of New Testament interpretation: "general understanding of the book," "the true text," "a satisfactory translation," religious and cultural background, word meanings, forms (literary, rhetorical, etc.), grammar and syntax, theological motifs, and "application to life."[84] In 1979 in the *Criswell Study Bible,* L. Paige Patterson cited four principles: illumination by the Holy Spirit, context, clarity (i.e., difficult passages interpreted in the light of clear passages), and "grammatical-historical."[85]

Should biblical interpretation be dependent upon biblical criticism, and, if so, how? In an article in 1953 on biblical theology Eric Charles Rust contended that biblical criticism had brought too many "positive gains" for mid-century Christian scholars to seek to return to pre-critical era. Yet he also warned that biblical criticism "can never be unconditioned or objective," admitted that it had often been made captive to "modern naturalism or humanism," and insited that "[c]ommitment to Christ . . . should govern our use of the historio-critical method."[86] Ray Summers wrote in 1969 in the *Broadman Bible Commentary:* "Basic to all competent approaches in New Testament study is the historiocritical method. . . . It is the only method which keeps the exegete in continuous dialogue with the text he seeks to understand."[87] John D. W. Watts in 1974 traced the usage of the historical-critical method from the Protestant Reformation to the middle of the twentiety century and explained the use of significance of "source analysis" (or literary criticism), "form-criticism," "tradition history," and "redaction criticism."[88] In 1986 Charles H. Talbert insisted that biblical criticism "aims to deal only with" "what the Bible meant in its original context," not with what it "means to its current readers."[89] In 1987 Marvin E. Tate reported that some have of late concluded that the historical-critical method is "'bankrupt'" and in serious need of transformation. Tate has alleged that "fundamentalist inerrancy's" attack on the method has delayed its internal transformation, and he has contended that "fundamentalist inerrancy does not offer an acceptable alternative to historical-critical study."[90]

Southern Baptists have likewise written with a view to arriving at and utlizing a valid contemporary method of biblical interpretation. In 1974 Carl Ferdinand Howard Henry delineated a detailed critique of the hermeneutical methods of Karl Barth, Rudolf Bultmann, Hans-Georg Gadamer, Gerhard Ebeling, Ernst Fuchs, and Richard E. Palmer, warned of the danger of "hermeneutical nihilism," and commended the criticism of these recent trends made by E. D. Hirsch, Jr., and Emilio Betti.[91] John P. Newport in 1986 surveyed such contemporary hermeneutical movements as "structuralism," which, seeing the text as a literary phenomenon, separates it from the intended meaning of the author; the "reading-response" approach of Gadamer, which with its "fusion of horizons" tends to confuse meaning and significance; and "canonical criticism," which majors on a biblical book when it has been given its final form and when passages may be compared with passages in other canonical books.[92] Marvin E. Tate similarly has reviewed such methods as "historical analysis," genre study, sociological-economic method, canonical criticism, and reader-hearer response, and he has concluded that structuralism and "Narrative criticism" "are arid as a desert."[93] In the pursuit of the most acceptable model, Newport in 1961 proposed the "eschatological-holy history" method, drawn from Johann Albrecht Bengel, Johann Christian Konrad Hofmann, Geehardus Vos, Otto A. Piper, Oscar Cullmann, and others. According to this method "a certain sequence of persons and events is related and infused with special signficiance because in them God was acting uniquely."[94] Eric C. Rust,[95] R. Edgar Glaze, Jr.,[96] and Morris Ashcraft[97] in their own ways espoused a Christocentric model of interpretation not alien to what Newport proposed. Peter Rhea Jones in 1975 proposed an integration of the "existential, historical [i.e., historical-critical], literary, and theological aspects of scripture" into a "post-critical" hermeneutical method. According to Jones, the goal of hermenutics "is to arrive at a) the conscious intention of the writer, b) the unconcsious intention of the writer, and c) the intention of the text as it stands."[98] According to Tate the interpreter needs to seek the guidance of the Holy Spirit, to take the Bible as a whole, to recognize biblical diversity, and to treat the Bible as "a book of the church."[99]

Biblical Authority

Since 1952 Southern Baptist treatments of biblical authority have tended either to review the Baptist past as to such authority or to explicate the nature of biblical authority. The present author in a study of Baptist confessions of faith differentiated the "functional" infallibiity of the Scriptures according to the Second London Confession of Particular Baptists (1677) and the "modal" infallibility of twentieth-century Landmark and fundamentalist confessions.[100] R. Edgar Glaze, Jr.,[101] William L. Hendricks,[102] and Roy Lee Honeycutt[103] reviewed statements about biblical authority in Baptist confessions of faith from the mid-seventeenth century to the latter twentieth century. Glaze also cited statements by E. Y. Mullins, B. H. Carroll, and J. Clyde Turner. Hendricks treated the 1979 Southern Baptist convention resolution concerning biblical authority. Honeycutt gave attention to the Abstract of Principles of Southern Baptist Theological Seminary. William R. Estep, Jr., interpreted the fact that the lengthy first article of the Second London Confession of Particular Baptists (1677) and hence of the Philadelphia Confession (1742), derived from the Westminster Confession, a dominantly Presbyterian document, dealt with the Bible in great detail in a fashion uncommon to earlier Baptist confessions to mean that such an order of topics was a step toward "biblioatry." Estep acknowledged that the New Hampshire, the 1925 SBC, and the 1963 SBC confessions also commence with articles on the Bible.[104] John E. Steely emphasized the probable influence of Alexander Campbell, of Landmarkism, and of controversy over evolution upon Southern Baptist attitudes toward the Bible.[105] Tom J. Nettles contended in 1985 that a cirsis on biblical authority among Southern Baptists had been building up for twenty-five years. Neither the Elliott controversy nor the *Broadman Bible Commentary* controversy according to Nettles, "terminated in a satisfactory settlement. Instead, each left the theological issue of authority poorly defined and even more poorly defended."[106]

Wayne E. Ward expounded the supremacy of the authority of the Bible above that of the Church and of the Inner Light and found this view to be held by Baptists. "The Scriptures are that indispensable link between the revelation of God in Jesus Christ and the community of believers today."[107] J. Morris Ashcraft set forth a restatement of the nature of biblical authority. It embraces both testaments. "Jesus recognized the authority of the Old Testament," but the early Christians appealed to the authority of Jesus. Biblical authority is not synonymous with "power," and ultimate authority rests in God. Rightly conceived, the authority of the Bible is "the *companion, not the foe of freedom.*" The authority is necessarily personal and persuasive in nature, and yet "the *acceptance of authority is necessary in nurture and teaching.*" *Sola Scriptura* as used during the Reformation era meant that "the Bible alone had more authority than the Church or the creeds of the Church if these differed," but Ashcraft was inclined to *supreme Scriptura.*[108]

Perhaps many Southern Baptists would identify with Glaze's statement:

> The world needs the *message* of the Bible, not its defense. . . . When God is heard in the Bible men know it is God's Word, are confident of its trustworthiness, and are submissive to its authority.[109]

Biblical Inerrancy

The inerrancy or infallibility of the Scriptures, especially in respect to historical, geographical, and scientific considerations, did not become a major subject for Southern Baptist authors until the 1970s and the 1980s as the scarcity of materials from the 1950s and the 1960s will testify. Clark H. Pinnock's pamphlet, *A New Reformation* (1968)[110] and William E. Hull's sermon, *Shall We Call the Bible Infallible?* (1970),[111] probably contributed significantly to the heightening of this subject as a theological issue for Southern Baptists.

Pinnock issued a militant call to grassroots Southern Baptists to resist the theological, evangelistic, and ecclesial decline which Pinnock associated with the abandonment of the doctrine of biblical infallibility, of a high Christology, and of a literal interpretation of the Scriptures. Pinnock laid the blame for such abandonment on college and seminary professors, but he had almost nothing to say about historical, geographical, and scientific matters.[112] Hull, writing soon after the 1970 session of the Southern Baptist Convention, undertook a brief biblical, historical, theological, and practical analysis of the concept of the infallibility of the Bible. The autogrpahs have not survived. If they had, they would have to be translated and to be "explained by fallible interpreters." "The central conviction of the New Testament is that the eternal has entered into time, the infinite has invaded the finite, the infallible has appeared in the midst of the fallible." Hull concluded:

> The cumulative force of the evidence is overwhelming: No, it is not wise to call the Bible "infallible." That term is subject to too many problems to become a controlling concept in our witness to Scripture. Let us say . . . that here is not the decisive place for our denomination to take a stand, nor is this an issue worthy of splitting our ranks.[113]

During the 1970s a series of Southern Baptist authors, especially in the *Southern Baptist Journal,* espoused the strict or complete or unqualified inerrancy of the Scriptures. Wendell H. Rone, Sr., applied the term "infallible," "inerrant," and "veracious" to the autographs of the Bible,[114] and James M. Bulman, finding "infallibility," or the Bible's being "incapable of containing error," to be a stronger term than "inerrancy," contended that E. Y. Mullins's own views should not be taken as normative for understanding what the 1925 SBC Baptist Faith and Message Statement's phrase "without any mixture of error" was intended to mean.[115] M. O. Owens, Jr., holding that inspiration and errancy "are incompatible," declared: "An inerrant, infallible autograph is the only view of the original Scripture which accords with the nature of the God we worship."[116] Fred C. Metts defended complete inerrancy on the basis of the Bible's own claims, the testimony of Jesus, the teaching of church fathers and of John Calvin, the testimony of Charles Haddon Spurgeon, E. J. Young, and A. W. Pink, and the Bible's speaking "to my heart like no oher book."[117] Lary L. Lewis explicated the doctrine in the following terms:

> Although the Bible is not primarily a book on science, it does not contain any scientific errors. . . . Although it is not primarily a history book, it does not contain any historical errors. Since God is its author, and God does all things perfectly, we can be sure that the Bible, in its Original Manuscripts, contained no mistakes.[118]

According to L. Paige Patterson, "The Bible claims in many places to be inerrant, i.e., without error . . . ."[119] L. Russ Bush, III, and Tom J. Nettles in their massive study, *Baptists and the Bible* (1980), mined a vast amount of data concerning Baptist teachings on the inspiration, authority, and infallibility of the Bible from the seventeenth century to the twentieth, but specific data about the modern question of biblical inerrancy in respect to scienttific, geographical, and chronological matters does not arise until the treatment of A. H. Strong, who was not, of course, a Southern Baptist.[120]

Another group of Southern Baptist authors espoused the religio-ethical inerrancy of the Bible. Eric C. rust affirmed that the biblical writers *"did not think about their world in the way that we do,"* for they *"were living in a pre-scientific age."*

305

They were unfamiliar with the developed understanding of the form of the physical universe and the developing movement of living things which modern science has made possible. They had no knowledge of modern psychology . . . . Hence the disclosure of God which came to them was expressed within the thought forms of their time and not those of ours. . . . The people who wrote our Bible were not twentieth century men! Yet they did have a disclosure of God, of God's purpose for and relationship to man, of man's true nature as made in God's image, and of man's estrangement from God and his fellows. That revelation is as true for our time as theirs. Men's models for the understanding of their world and of their own personal structures may change, but the divine Word that came those cnturies ago still comes to us, as fresh as when it was first given by God in our human history.[121]

After analyzing both the contributions and the "limitations" of modern science, Rust concluded that there is "no real conflict between the essential biblical disclosure and what modern science is saying."[122]

Howard P. Colson insisted that the Bible presents "religious truth" and contains no religious error, is "not an authority on" mathematics or science, and uses phenomenal language.[123] According to T. C. Smith, the revelation of God in Jesus Christ must be the basis for evaluating the various portions of the Bible, and Christians today need to allow for "human imperfections."[124] William L. Hendricks proposed as preferable the use of the biblical term *inspired* in place of *inerrant,* contended that ther term *inerrancy* is wrongly used if and when it should be joined with one particular hermeneutical method, and asserted that inerrancy should not become "a test of fellowship in any Baptist institution."[125] According to William P. Tuck, Jesus did not use the term *inerrancy,* there are unresolved difficulties in the Bible, and the "danger of a verbal infallibility or inerrancy doctrine is that it often leads to what is called bibliolatry."[126] Robinson B. James alleged that "militant inerrancy" is a "heresy" in that it "insists [that] anyone who wishes to pursue a ministry of teaching or leadership in an SBC institution must submit to the inerrantist view of the Bible as supreme over the Bible, rather than submitting directly to the Bible as supreme, *if* such a person wishes to avoid rejection, intimidation, suspicion or removal." Thus "'biblical inerrancy" has replaced "biblical authority as the controlling standard."[127] Charles H. Talbert took the position that the Bible

speaks with authority on relational and soteriological matters, not matters of fact. . . . This [relational] data . . . is [sic] validated by my experience with God. Matters of history and science I check against other sources to determine their accuracy. Inaccuracies in matters of fact do not detract from relational truth which is validated in experience.

Moreover, to say that when Jesus spoke on matters of fact he must be speaking as the Son of God is Christological heresy of the Apollinarian-Monophysite type.[128] According to R. Alan Culpepper, Jesus said nothing about inerrancy in the modern sense, and Matthew 5:18 "cannot be used to support the theory of inerrancy without taking it in isolation from Matthew 5:21-28, which it introduces."[129]

A few authors have offered criticisms of the *Criswell Study Bible* or of the statements of the Internattional Council on Biblical Inerrancy (ICBI). Raymond H. Bailey, examining the *Criswell Study Bible,* found a naturalistic view concerning Exodus 7:20 (river turned to blood), inconsistency as to giants (Gen. 6:4; Deut. 2:20), frequent resolution of difficulties by ascribing them to scribal "carelessness" or "inadvertence," its handling of Mark 16:9-20 as other than "the original ending" of Mark's Gospel, and its handling of John 5:3b-4, John 8:3-12, and 1 John 5:7. Bailey charged that those who produced this study Bible had accused others of "practices in which they themselves also engage."[130] Gordon James identified and discussed forty-two different aspects of the *Criswell Study Bible* in which he allegedly found liberal or anti-supernatural interpretations, acknowledgement of historical errors, or failure to acknowledge biblical variations.[131] Robert M. Price, analyzing the two Chicago statements of the ICBI (1978, 1982), found that they are ambiguous as to mechanical dictation of the Bible and in reference to progessive revelation, they unnecessarily reject form criticism and genre criticism and they "are essentially Catholocizing documents" in that they "subordinate exegesis . . . to prior doctrine" and move toward creedalism.[132]

A group of Southern Baptist authors who hold to the language of inerrancy as desirable, if not absolutely necessary, have written so as to qualify or refine the strict or complete inerrancy posture. William E. Bell, Jr., defined inerancy as the teaching that the Scriptures "contain exactly what God intended for them to contain and that, properly interpreted, they will lead no one astray." He affirmed that liberal scholars such as H. J. Cadbury, F. C. Grant, John Knox, Adolf Harnack, and Rudolf Bultmann "have acknowledged that Jesus accepted the common Jewish view of His day that the scriptures were absolutely infallible," but the same scholars concluded that Jesus was wrong on such a view. Then Bell proceeded to declare that inerrancy does not call for or demand mechanical dictation of the Bible; the sinlessness of its human writers; verbatim quotations of Old Testament texts by New Testament writers; an invariable use of conventional grammar and syntax; the denial of figures of speech, poetry, and phenomenal language; modern standards for the composition of genealogies and chronologies; verbal identity among parallel accounts; or the inerrancy of copyists or translators. Bell concluded that by the Bible

> we will not be deceived—theologically, historically or scientifically. We will
> continue to work with the problems, but our view of Scripture, taken from
> Christ Himself, does not await the solution.[133]

L. Russ Bush, III, in discussing inerrancy, focused almost completely upon crucial historico-theological issues—whether there was an historical fall of Adam and Eve, whether the Gospels are theologically but not historically reliable, whether the resurrection of Jesus was based on more than existential faith, and whether the different theologies of the New Testament are harmonizable—with the inference that scientific, geographical, and chronological matters are not serious.[134] Carl F. H. Henry stressed the "reliability of the present texts of the Bible," noting that the prophets and apostles did not have the autographs. For Henry the authority and the inspiration of the Scriptures are prior to or above inerrancy in importance, but inerrancy, though inferred from the Bible, "is a necessary correlate and logical deduction from its divine inspiration." Henry issued a twofold warning: "no movement can long impact influentially if its leaders constantly question the integrity of that movement's charter documents," and "no movement can significantly impinge upon society if its spokesmen exhaust their energies in defending the inerrancy of the Bible instead of directing its message to the runaway world for which it is divinely intended."[135] David S. Dockery offered a definition of what he called "criticial inerrancy": "When all the facts are known, the Bible in its original autographs, properly interpreted, will be found to be truthful and faithful in all that it affirms concerning all areas of life, faith and practice." The Bible is not a book of "history, geology, biology, or . . . psychology," but when it "speaks to such matters, it does so in a faithful way."[136] Dockery also surveyed nine contemporary views of biblical inerrancy, listing representative non-Southern Baptist exponents of such views: "mechanical dictation" (John R. Rice); "absolute inerrancy" (Harold Lindsell); "critical inerrancy" (Roger Nicole, J. Ramsey Micahels, D. A. Carson, John Woodbridge); "limited inerrancy" (i.e., doctrine, ethics) (Howard Marshall); "qualified inerrancy" (Donald G. Bloesch); "nuanced inerrancy" (Clark Pinnock); "functional inerrancy" (G. C. Berkouwer, Jack Rogers, Donald McKim); irrelevance of inerrancy (David A. Hubbard); and errancy of the Bible, which points to trustworthy encounters with God (William Countryman).[137]

The present state of the Southern Baptist controversy over biblial inerrancy has been most completely summarized and analyzed by Fisher Humphreys. He stated some eleven qualifications which inerrantists have made in reference to inerrancy. Then he identified eight defenses which have been set forth by inerrantists in behalf of inerrancy: (1) teaching by Jesus; (2) claimed by biblical writers; (3) traditional church teaching; (4) deduction from God's own inerrancy; (5) induction by resolution of so-called "errors"' (6) loss of inerrancy as danger to other doctrines—domino theory; (7) loss of inerrancy as danger to evangelism and missions; and (8) necessity for inerrancy on the basis that criteria for differentiating truth from error in the Bible cannot be established. Next the New Orleans professor listed four "concerns" of inerrantists: (1) a supernatural view of the Christian faith and of the Bible; (2) divine revelation, not human discovery; (3) revealed truth as cognitive and propositional; and (4) the Bible as the authoritative guide for Christians and for the church. Humphreys also identified ten "concerns" of non-inerrantists: (1) determining the residue of qualified inerrancy; (2) desire for reliability of Bibles as translated today; (3) inerrancy's preoccupation with details to the neglect of the Bible's "great message"; (4) uneasiness as to cognitive, propositional truth; (5) inerrancy's distraction from larger issues of revelation, canon, interpretation, guidance of the Holy Spirit; (6) greater importance of obedience to biblical teaching; (7) inerrancy of the autographs a teaching of recent origin; (8) whether inerrancy in all that the Bible intends to teach means the human author or God; (9) inerrancy as eroding the priesthood of all believers and the duty of private interpretation of the Bible; and (10) the divisive results of controversy over inerrancy. Humphreys concluded that he cannot "detect any substantial differences between" qualified inerrancy and "the high view of Scripture offered by many non-inerrantists."[138]

Southern Baptist author-theologians have taken one of three postures as to the inspiration of the Bible: the absence of the need for a specific theory, the espousal of the dynamic theory, or the espousal of the plenary verbal theory. Little attention has been given to the canon except for one major proposal that the Old Testament Apocrypha be restored to the Protestant canon of the Old Testatment. Mindful of the long history of biblical hermeneutics, these writers have sought to restate the principles needed for such interpretation. The majority has seemed to think that biblical criticism needs to be transformed but not laid aside and that most of its methods are legitimate. Among the models advanced for contemporary interpretation have been the salvation-history and the Christocentric. Conscious of how past Baptists had expressed their concepts of biblical authority, these authors have had little difficulty in affirming *suprema Scriptura* but may have been less agreed on the precise nature of biblical authority itself. Since 1970 Southern Baptist author-theologians who have treated biblical inerrancy have tended to be strict or complete inerrantists, inerrantists as to doctrine and ethics, or inerrantists in a qualified sense. The second and third of these groups have been moving toward each other.

The teaching of Mullins and the teaching of Conner concerning the Bible have more in common with each other than either of these has in common with the major trends among Southern Baptist authors since 1952. Neither Mullins nor Conner felt it necessary to embrace and teach a particular theory as to the method of biblical inspiration, preferring rather to emphasize the fact and the results of inspiration. Since 1952 the espousal of either the dynamic theory or the plenary verbal theory has become common. On biblical hermeneutics there are fewer observable differences between Mullins and Conner and their successors. Mullins's stress on Christ as the "crown" of the Bible and the key to its interpretation was matched by the revision of article 1 in the 1963 SBC Statement of the Baptist Faith and Message, though the latter has had some critics. Both Mullins and Conner and their successors agreed that biblical criticism had both its abuse and its proper use. Both Mullins and Conner sought specifically to correlate the authority of the Bible and the authority of Jesus Christ. Since 1952 the question as to whether the Bible is the "sole" standard or the "supreme" standard has taken on new significance, whereas on the nature of biblical authority differences have surfaced. Whereas Mullins and Conner affirmed the trustworthiness of the Scriptures without elaborating a doctrine of inerrancy, since 1970 Southern Baptist authors have been drawn increasingly into a vortex of controversy in which the issue of biblical inerrancy has become dominant and in which strict or complete, religio-ethical, and qualified views have become pronounced.[139]

309

Notes

1. The influence of Mullins was due to his roles as president of the Southern Baptist Convention (1921-1924) and president of the Baptist World Alliance (1923-1928) as well as to his presidency of Southern Baptist Theological Seminary (1899-1928).

2. Benjah Harvey Carroll (1843-1914), *The Inspiration of the Bible: A Discussion of the Origin, the Authenticity and the Sanctity of the Oracles of God*, comp. and ed. J. B. Cranfill (New York, Chicago: Fleming H. Revell Company, 1930); Edwin Charles Dargan (1852-1930), *Doctrines of Our Faith* (Nashville: Sunday School Board of the Southern Baptist Convention, 1905; rev. ed., 1920), ch. 1; *The Bible Our Heritage* (New York: Doran Company, 1924); Archibald Thomas Robertson (1863-1934), *An Introduction to the Textual Criticism of the New Testament* (Nashville; Sunday School Baord of the Southern Baptist Convention, 1925); and Harvey Eugene Dana (1888-1945), *The Authenticity of the Holy Scriptures: A Brief Story of the Problems of Biblical Criticism* (Nashville: Sunday School Board of the Southern Baptist Convention, 1923); *New Testament Criticism: A Brief Summary of the Nature and Necessity, History, Sources, and Results of New Testament Criticism* (Fort Worth: World Company, Inc., 1924); *An Introduction to the Critical Interpretation of the New Testament* (Fort Worth: Taliaferro Printing Co., 1924); *The Science of New Testament Interpretation* (Forth Worth: Southwestern Press, 1930); *A Neglected Predicate in New Testament Criticism* (Chicago: Blessing Book Stores, Inc., 1934); *Searching the Scriptures: A Handbook of New Testament Hermeneutics* (New Orleans: Bible Institute Memorial Press, 1936).

3. *Baptist Beliefs* (Philadelphia: American Baptist Publication Society, 1912), pp. 10-12; "Baptists and the Bible," *Encyclopedia of Southern Baptists*, 4 vols. (Nashville: Broadman Press, 1958-82), 1:141-42. The latter article was first published as a tract by the Sunday School Board of the Southern Baptist Convention in 1916 or 1917. See SBC *Annual* 1916, Appendix C, p. 10; 1917, p. 372; 1923, p. 227. I am indebted to A. Ronald Tonks for the dating of this tract.

4. "Baptists and the Bible," p. 142. Mullins's describing the Bible as the "record" of divine revelation preceded the rise of Neo-Orthodoxy. See *The Christian Religion in Its Doctrinal Expression* (Philadelphia: Judson Press, 1917), p. 142.

5. *Baptist Beliefs*, pp. 11-12.

6. "Baptists and the Bible," p. 142.

7. *Baptists Beliefs*, p. 12.

8. "Baptists and the Bible," p. 142.

9. *Baptist Beliefs*, p. 13.

10. *Freedom and Authority in Religion* (Philadelphia: Griffith and Rowland Press, 1913), p. 342.

11. Ibid., pp. 347-54.

12. *The Christian Religion in Its Doctrinal Expression*, pp. 145-51.

13. *Baptist Beliefs*, p. 13. A similar hesitation as to the adequacy of the theories is found in "Baptists and the Bible," p. 142.

14. Mullins identified this view with James Martineau, George Burman Foster, and Wilhelm Bousset.

15. Mullins identified this view with James Orr, William Sanday, and Marcus Dods.

16. *Freedom and Authority in Religion*, pp. 375-93.

17. *The Christian Religion in Its Doctrinal Expression*, pp. 142-44.

18. *Freedom and Authority in Religion,* pp. 346-47.

19. Ibid., pp. 354-58.

20. *Baptist Beliefs,* pp. 15, 16.

21. "Baptists and the Bible," pp. 142-43.

22. *Freedom and Authority in Religion,* pp. 358-61.

23. *Faith in Modern World* (Nashville: Sunday School Board of the Southern Baptist Convention, 1930), p. 30.

24. *Freedom and Authority in Religion,* pp. 361-64.

25. *Christianity at the Cross Roads* (Nashville: Sunday School Board of the Southern Baptist Convention), pp. 176-209, esp. 185, 183, 206.

26. *Baptist Beliefs,* pp. 13-15; cf. "Baptists and the Bible," p. 142.

27. *Faith in the Modern World,* pp. 25-26.

28. *Freedom and Authority in Religion,* pp. 364-75.

29. "Baptists and the Bible," p. 142.

30. Ibid., p. 143.

31. Ibid.

32. *Freedom and Authority in Religion,* pp. 393-94.

33. The following material originally appeared in the October 1986 issue of *Baptist History and Heritage* in the article by James Leo Garrett, Jr., entitled "The Bible at Southwestern Seminary during Its Formative Years: A Study of H. E. Dana and W. T. Conner" and is used here by permission of the Historical Commission of the Southern Baptist Convention. The article itself constituted a rewriting of portions of the same author's Th.D. dissertation, "The Theology of Walter Thomas Conner" (Southwestern Baptist Theological Seminary, 1954).

34. (Nashville: Sunday School Board of the Southern Baptist Convention, 1924).

35. (Nashville: Broadman Press).

36. *A System of Christian Doctrine,* pp. 115-16.

37. *Revelation and God,* p. 87.

38. *A System of Christian Doctrine,* p. 117.

39. *Revelation and God,* pp. 78-80.

40. A System of Christian Doctrine, pp. 75-80.

41. *Revelation and God,* pp. 72-74.

42. Ibid., p. 80.

43. *A System of Christian Doctrine,* p. 72.

44. *Revelation and God,* pp. 80-81.

45. *A System of Christian Doctrine,* p. 73.

46. *Revelation and God,* pp. 81-83.

47. Ibid., pp. 120-22, 111-17, 122-39.

48. Ibid., p. 84.

49. Ibid., pp. 84, 86.

50. Ibid., 85-90.

51. Ibid., pp. 90-95, 99-100.

52. Ibid., pp. 95-99; Conner, "The Nature of the Authority of The Bible," *Southwestern Journal of Theology* 2 o.s. (October 1918): 11-17.

53. "Southern Baptists and the Scriptures," *Theological Educator* 1 (October 1970): 9, 11, 14-17.

54. *The Bible for Today's World* (Grand Rapids: Zondervan Publishing House, 1965), pp. 47-53; *Great Doctrines of the Bible,* vol. 1, *Bibliology,* ed. Paige Patterson (Grand Rapids: Zondervan Publishing House, 1982), pp. 99-102. In 1982 Criswell omitted the term "dynamic."

55. *Why I Preach That the Bible Is Literally True* (Nashville: Broadman Press), p. 26.

56. James Leo Garrett, Jr., "Representative Modern Baptist Understandings of Biblical Inspiration," *Review and Expositor* 71 (Spring 1974); 179-95.

57. "The Book of the Christian Faith," in *Broadman Bible Commentary*, vol. 1 (Nashville: Broadman Press, 1969), pp. 5-9. Eric C. Rust, "The Authority of the Scripture: The Word of God and the Bible," *Review and Expositor* 57 (Janaury 1960); 51, had espoused the dynamic view.

58. "The Nature of the Bible according to the Broadman Commentary," *Southern Baptist Journal*, January 1974, p. 6.

59. "Bible Basics for Baptists," *Southern Baptist Journal*, January 1974, p. 6.

60. "What I Believe about Inspiration," *Southern Baptist Journal*, January 1978, pp. 3, 10.

61. (Nashville: Thomas Nelson, 1979), p. xix.

62. "Tidwell and Verbal Inspiration," *Southern Baptist Advocate*, August 1980, p. 8.

63. "Preface," to Ward and Green, eds., *Is the Bible a Human Book?* (Nashville: Broadman Press, 1970), pp. 5-6.

64. Ibid., p. 17.

65. Ibid., pp. 17, 18.

66. "Affirming the Scriptures," *SBC Today*, January 1984, pp. 14-15.

67. *Revelation, Inspiration, Scripture,* Layman's Library of Christian Doctrine (Nashville: Broadman Press, 1985), pp. 52-61.

68. *The Word of Truth: A Summary of Christian Doctrine Based on Biblical Revelation* (Grand Rapids: Eerdmans, 1981), p. 47.

69. I.e., "theological incompatibility," pre-1546 dissent among Christians as to the canonicity, Hebrew linguistic studies, the New Testament's "direct citation" of Old Testament books but not of the Apocrypha, and instrinsic insufficiency.

70. "The Old Testament Apocrypha and the Old Testament Canon," *Review andExpositor* 65 (Summer 1968); 339-56.

71. *The Word of Truth,* p. 45.

72. *Christian Faith and Beliefs* (Nashville: Broadman Press, 1984), pp. 80-81.

73. "Biblical Interpretation, the Pastor and the Contemporary Scene," *Southwestern Journal of Theology* 2 n.s. (April 1960): 20-22.

74. "Interpreting the Bible," *The Broadman Bible Commentary, vol. 1 (Nashville: Broadman Press), pp. 25-27.*

75. *"Hermeneutics in Historical Perspective,"* Southwestern Journal of Theology* 16 n.s. (Spring 1974): 1-14.

76. "Representative Historical and Contemporary Approaches to Biblical Interpretation," *Faith and Mission* 3 (Spring 1986): 32-29.

77. "Southern Baptists and the Liberal Tradition in Biblical Interpretation, 1845-1945," *Baptist History and Heritage* 19 (July 1984): 16-20.

78. "Southern Baptists and the Fundamentalist Tradition in Biblical Interpretation, 1845-1945," *Baptist History and Heritage* 19 (July 1984): 29-32.

79. "Southern Baptists and the Moderate Tradition in Biblical Interpretation, 1845-1945," *Baptist History and Heritage* 19 (July 1984): 21-28. It is noteworhty that none of these authors treated Archibald Thomas Robertson, John Ricahrd Sampey, or Harvey Eugene Dana.

80. "Biblical Interpretation and Eschatological-Holy History," *Southwestern Journal of Theology* 4 n.s. (October 1961): 83-86, 109-10.

81. "Interpreting the Bible," pp. 27-33.

82. H. E. Dana and R. E. Glaze, Jr., *Interpreting the New Testament* (Nashville: Broadman Press, 1961), pp. 122-39.

83. "Emphases in Hermeneutics," *Southwestern Journal of Theology* 7 n.s. (October 1964): 63-71.

84. *How to Interpet the New Testament* (Philadelphia: Westminster Press).

85. " The Bible: A Book of Desinty," *Criswell Study Bible* (Nashville: Thomas Nelson, 1979), pp. xvii-xxi.

86. "The Nature and Problems of Biblical Theology," *Review and Expositor* 50 (October 1953): 563-64, 471-72.

87. "Contemporary Approaches in New Testament Study," *The Broadman Bible Commentary,* vol. 8 (Nashville: Broadman Press), p. 48.

88. "The Historical Approach to the Bible," *Review and Expositor* (71 (Spring 1974): 169-77, 164-67. "Historical criticism in itself is neither liberal, radical, or conservative, but is a method for all who seek the truth" (p. 164).

89. "Biblical Criticism's Role," *SBC Today,* November 1986, p. 9.

90. "Confronting the Bible: New Openings for Authority," *SBC Today,* March 1987, p. 6.

91. "The Interpretation of the Scriptures: Are We Doomed to Hermeneutical Nihililsm?" *Review and Expositor* 71 (Spring 1974): 197-215. In reply to Henry, Morris Ashcraft, "Response to Carl F. H. Henry, 'Are We Doomed to Hermeneutical Nihilism?'" *Review and Expositor* 71 (Spring 1974): 221, contended that Henry's "presuppositions about revelation and the Bible [esp. propositional revelation] push us away from a stance in which genuine interpretation is possible."

92. "Representative Historical and Contemporary Approaches to Biblical Interpretation," pp. 39-44.

93. "Confronting the Bible: New Openings for Authority," pp. 7-8.

94. "Biblical Interpretation and Eschatological-Holy History," pp. 86-109.

95. "The Nature and Problems of Biblical Theology, pp. 472, 474, 479.

96. "Southern Baptists and the Scriptures," pp. 14, 15, 16.

97. "Response to Carl F. H. Henry, 'Are We Doomed to Hermeneutical Nihilism?'" p. 221.

98. "Biblical Hermeneutics," *Review and Expositor* 72 (Spring 1975): 139-47. Jones also declared: (1) "The historical-critical mehtod is both indispensable and inadequate for New Testament study." (2) "The hermeneutical process by its very nature requires the engagement of the intuition as well as the historical reason." (3) "An adequate hermeneutic maintains an historico-ontological tension."

99. "Confronting the Bible: New Openings for Authority," pp. 7-8.

100. James Leo Garrett, Jr. "Biblical Authority according to Baptist Confessions of Faith," *Review and Expositor* 76 (Winter 1979): 43-54.

101. "Southern Baptists and the Scriputres," pp. 9-16.

102. "Scripture: A Southern Baptist Perspective," *Review and Expositor* 79 (Spring 1982): 246-49.

103. "Biblical Authority: A Treasured Heritage!" *Review and Expositor* 83 (Spring 1986): 613-16.

104, Confronting the Bible: The Bible in Confessions," *SBC Today*, April 1987, pp. 6-7, 10-11.

105. "Biblical Authority and Baptists in Historical Perspective," *Baptists History and Heritage* 19 (July 1984): 14-15.

313

106. "SBC Crisis Rooted in Theology," *Southern Baptist Advocate*, Summer 1985, p. 7.

107. "The Authority of the Bible," *Review and Expositor* 56 (April 1959): 166-73. See also Richard A. Spencer, "The Role of Biblical Study in Preparation for Ministry," *Faith and Mission* 3 (Spring 1986): 12.

108 "The Issue of Biblical Authority," *Faith and Mission* 1 (Spring 1984): 26-30, 32-33. For a historical study of *sola Scriptura* and *suprema Scriptura* among Baptists, see James Leo Garrett, Jr., "Sources of Authority in Baptist Thought," *Baptist History and Heritage* (July 1978): 41-49. See also H. Stephen Shoemaker, "Affirming the Scriptures," p. 15.

109 "Southern Baptists and the Scriptures," p. 15.

110 (Tigerville, S.C.: Jewel Books).

111 "Crescent Hill Sermons," Crescent Hill Baptist Church, Louisville, Kentucky, 16 August 1970.

112 *A New Reformation*, pp. 7-9, 11-14, 18.

113 *Shall We Call the Bible Infallible?* pp. 1-7.

114 "Bible Basics for Baptists," p. 6.

115 "'Without Any Mixture of Error,'" *Southern Baptist Journal*, January 1974, p. 9.

116 "The Bible: Inerrant or Irrelevant," ibid., September 1974, p. 7.

117 "The Infallible Word," ibid., January 1978, pp. 1, 10.

118 "What I Believe about Inspiration," p. 3.

119. "The Bible: A Book of Destiny," *Criswell Study Bible, p. xviii.*

120. *(Chicago: Moody Press), esp. p. f273.*

121. "The Biblical Faith and Modern Science," *Review and Expositor* 71 (Spring 1974): 231.

122. Ibid., pp. 237-41.

123. "Truth without Any Mixture of Error," *Southern Baptist Journal*, June 1974, p. 6.

124. "The Canon and Authority of the Bible," ibid., March-April 1975, pp. 4-5.

125. "Henrick's [sic] Answers," ibid., September 1980, pp. 8-9.

126. "Was Jesus an Inerrantist?" *SBC Today*, March 1985, pp. 17-18.

127. "Biblical Authority or Inerrancy?" ibid., November 1985, pp. 8-9.

128. "Inerrancy: The Central Question," ibid., February 1986, p. 14.

129. "Jesus' View of the Scripture," ibid., December 1986, pp. 6-7.

130. "Using a Double Standard," ibid., June 1986, pp. 4-5.

131. *Innerancy and the Southern Baptist Convention* (Dallas: Southern Baptist Heritage Press, 1986), pp. 119-67. Twelve of James's items pertain to Genesis, twenty to the remainder of the Old Testament, and ten to the New Testament.

132. "Inerrancy: The New Catholicism?" *SBC Today*, August-September 1986, pp. 4-5.

133. "The Case for Biblical Inerrancy," *Southern Baptist Journal*, April 1978, pp. 1, 11-12; "The Doctrine of Scripture," ibid., June 1978, pp. 7-11; July 1978, pp. 5-9.

134. "Should Inerrancy Be an Issue?" *Southern Baptist Advocate*, November 1980, pp. 9-10.

135. "Is the Bible an Errant Book?" ibid., Spring 1982, pp. 8-9.

136. "Can Baptists Affirm the Reliability and Authority of the Bible?" *SBC Today*, March 1985, pp. 17-19.

137. "Variations on Inerrancy," ibid., May 1986, pp. 10-11.

314

138. "Biblical Inerrancy: A Guide for the Perplexed," ibid., February 1¹⁄₃97, pp. 6-7, 13.

139. I am indebted to my secretary, Mrs. Susie Sanders, for her expertise in computer technology and her diligent faithfulness in bringing this typescript to completion.

16

THE BAPTIST FAITH AND MESSAGE AND THE CHICAGO STATEMENT ON BIBLICAL INERRANCY

Fisher Humphreys

My purpose is to compare what two documents say about the Bible. They are The Baptist Faith and Message and The Chicago Statement on Biblical Inerrancy. I will begin by briefly stating the general background of each of them.

The Baptist Faith and Message is a confession of faith adopted by the Southern Baptist Convention in 1963. Baptists have always said that they are not a creedal people, but they also have always been willing to provide statements or confessions of their faith for those who would like to read them. The Southern Baptist Convention was formed in 1845, and it existed for eighty years without adopting a confession. In 1925 the Convention adopted its first confession and called it The Baptist Faith and Message. That document was a revision of an earlier Baptist confession, the New Hampshire Confession of Faith, which had become well known throughout the South because it was actively promoted by Landmark Baptist leaders.

In 1925 the Convention was involved in a controversy concerning evolution; though some Baptist leaders opposed the adoption of a confession, the majority felt that one was needed in order to respond appropriately to the controversy. The committee which prepared the confession was chaired by Dr. E. Y. Mullins who was President of the Convention and also President of Southern Baptist Theological Seminary.

In 1963 the Convention adopted a revised form of The Baptist Faith and Message, keeping the same title, in response to a controversy regarding the interpretation of Genesis. The chairman of the committee which prepared this revised document was Dr. Herschel H. Hobbs, who was pastor of the First Baptist Church of Oklahoma City and president of the Convention.

The Chicago Statement on Biblical Inerrancy was prepared at a three-day meeting in October, 1978, of 284 scholars who are committed to biblical inerrancy. The meeting was sponsored by the International Council on Biblical Inerrancy, and most of the scholars were Americans. Interestingly, this group also was responding to a controversy which was occurring in American evangelicalism. Evangelicalism is a loose coalition of churches and other conservative Protestant institutions. It includes leaders such as Carl F. H. Henry and Billy Graham, and institutions such as Wheaton College, Trinity Evangelical Divinity School, Fuller Theological Seminary, *Christianity Today,* and the Evangelical Theology Society. The controversy among evangelicals concerned whether or not institutions such as Fuller Seminary and individuals in the Evangelical Theology Society and other groups, were betraying their evangelical heritage if

317

they failed to affirm the inerrancy of the Bible. The Council was formed to support inerrancy, and the 1978 statement was its first major achievement. The statement has received careful attention from friends and opponents alike and is an outstanding example of a thoughtful, responsible affirmation of the inerrancy of the Bible. (The same group issued an additional statement on biblical hermeneutics in 1982 and another on biblical application in 1986). The Statement consists of four parts, a Preface, a Short Statement, Articles of Affirmation and Denial, and an Exposition.

We will compare what these two documents say about the Bible by asking and answering a series of twelve questions.

Is the Bible a Supernatural Book?

Both documents agree that the Bible is a supernatural book, and both emphasize that this is an important fact. The Baptist Faith and Message says: "Christianity is supernatural in its origin and history. We repudiate every theory of religion which denies the supernatural elements in our faith" (4), and the Bible "has God for its author" (7). The Chicago Statement says, "We deny that inspiration can be reduced to human insight, or to heightened states of consciousness" (Article VII).

These two documents clearly agree that the Bible is a supernatural book.

Is the Bible a Divine Revelation?

Both of our documents affirm that the Bible is a revelation which God has given of himself. The Baptist Faith and Message says, "It reveals the principles" (7), and it refers to "Jesus Christ whose will is revealed in the Holy Scriptures" (5).

The Chicago Statement says, "We affirm that the written Word in its entirety is revelation given by God" (III).

In the Baptist controversy over the past few years, a distinction has often been made between the Bible as revelation and the Bible as a record of revelation. Neither of our texts emphasizes this distinction or insists that these two concepts are imcompatible. The Baptist Faith and Message says that the Bible "is the record of God's revelation of himself" (7). The Chicago Statement says that God "has inspired Holy Scripture in order thereby to reveal himself to lost mankind through Jesus Christ" (Short Statement 1), which seems compatible with the idea of the Bible as a record of the revelation given in Christ. It also denies "that the Bible is merely a witness to revelation " (III).

These two texts agree that the Bible is itself a divine self-disclosure, and they do not deny that it also is a record of revelations given to people in the past.

Does the Bible Provide Cognitive Revelation?

The issue here concerns what is given in revelation. Does the Bible give us a helpful, formative influence only? Or does it also give us genuine knowledge about God?

Neither document stresses this issue very much, yet both seem to assume that what is given is not only an influence but also real knowledge. The Baptist

Faith and Message refers to the Bible as "a perfect treasure of divine instruction" and says that "it reveals the principles by which God judges us" (7). The Chicago Statement denies that the Bible "only becomes revelation in encounter" (III).

Neither document makes its case for cognitive knowledge at the expense of other functions of the Bible. But both documents teach that in the Bible God has provided genuine knowledge about himself.

Is the Bible Uniquely Inspired?

Both documents affirm the inspiration of the Bible. The Baptist Faith and Message says that "the Holy Bible was written by men divinely inspired," (7) and that the Holy Spirit "inspired holy men of old to write the Scriptures" (9). The Chicago Statement says that "God . . . has inspired Holy Scriptures" (SS 1) and "that the whole of Scripture and all its parts . . . were given by divine inspiration" (VI).

Neither document claims to understand how inspiration works. The Chicago Statement says that "the mode of inspiration remains largely a mystery to us." It also denies "that inspiration can be reduced to human insight, or to heightened states of consciousness" (VII). It affirms "that God in His work of inspiration utilized the distinctive personalities and literary styles of the writers whom He had chosen and prepared," and it denies that God "overrode their personalities" (VIII).

Even though The Chicago Statement says that the process of inspiration is a mystery, it is much more specific about that process than The Baptist Faith and Message is. For example, The Baptist Faith and Message avoids the question of whether it is the teachings of the Bible which are inspired, or the very words themselves. The Chicago Statement makes it clear that it is the words themselves: "We affirm that the whole of Scripture and all its parts, down to the very words of the original, were given by divine inspiration" (VI). The Chicago Statement is a sophisticated presentation of the theory which is usually called plenary (full) verbal inspiration.

In summary, both documents teach that the Bible is uniquely inspired by God. The Baptist Faith and Message offers no additional insights into the mystery of inspiration, but The Chicago Statement specifies that the inspiration is verbal.

Is the Bible a Human Book?

Neither document suggests that the Bible was dropped out of heaven ready-made. Both affirm unique divine revelation, but neither allows the fact to cancel out the humanity of the writers or of the language of the Bible. The Baptist Faith and Message says that "the Holy Bible was written by men" (7). The Chicago Statement is fuller in its acknowledgement of the humanity of the Bible. "God by His Spirit, through human writers, gave us His Word" (VII). He "utilized the distinctive personalities and literary sytles of the writers whom he had chosen and prepared" (VIII). His use of them did not confer omniscience on them (IX). They were finite and fallen men (IX). Yet, human language is adequate "as a vehicle for divine revelation" (IV), and The Statement denies "that the corruption of human culture and language through sin has thwarted God's work of inspiration" (IV). The finitude and fallenness of the writers did not introduce distortion or falsehood into God's Word (IX).

Is the Bible Authoritative and Normative?

Both documents teach that the Bible carries the authority of God. The Baptist Faith and Message says "that the sole authority for faith and practice among Baptists is the Scriptures of the Old and New Testaments" (4). The Chicago Statement opens with these words: "The authority of Scripture is a key issue for the Christian Church," and it goes on to say that we today need "a full grasp and adequate confession of its authority" (Preface). It refers to the "infallible authority" of the Bible (Preface) and to its "infallible divine authority" (SS 2). It associates authority with inerrancy, and says that "the authority of Scripture is inescapably impaired if this total divine inerrancy is in any way limited or disregarded" (SS 5). It specifies that Scripture receives its authority from God (I).

The Baptist Faith and Message indicates that the Bible is authoritative "for faith and practice." The Chicago Statement goes beyond this and says that the Bible is an "infallible divine authority in all matters upon which it touches" (SS 2).

Both documents affirm that the Bible is a norm or standard. The Baptist Faith and Message says that it is "the supreme standard by which all human conduct, creeds, and religous opinions should be tried" (7).

The Chicago Statement makes a similar affirmation. It says that "the Scriptures are the supreme written norm by which God binds the conscience" (II).

In summary, both documents affirm the authority of Scripture, and both associate its authority with its divine authorship. The Chicago Statement further associates authority with inerrancy. The Baptist Faith and Message explicitly affirms the authority of the Bible only in faith and practice, but The Chicago Statement says that the Bible's authority extends to all matters on which it touches. Both documents regard the Bible as normative for Christian faith.

How Is the Holy Spirit Related to the Bible?

Both documents affirm that the Holy Spirit inspired the writing of Scripture. The Baptist Faith and Message says: "He [the Spirit] inspired holy men of old to write the Scriptures" (9). The Chicago Statement says that the Bible was "written by men prepared and superintended by His Spirit" (SS 2).

Both documents also affirm that the Spirit assists those who read the Bible, to understand it. The Baptist Faith and Message says: "Through illumination He [the Spirit] enables men to understand truth" (9). The Chicago Statement says that the Spirit "opens our minds to understand its [the Bible's] meaning" (SS 3).

The Chicago Statement adds a third item, one not found in The Baptist Faith and Message. It says that "the Holy Spirit bears witness to the Scriptures, assuring believers of the truthfulness of God's written Word" (XVII). It also says that the Spirit "authenticates it [the Bible] to us by His inward witness" (SS 3). This particular work of the Spirit was emphasized by John Calvin.

In summary, both documents emphasize that the Spirit worked in the past to inspire the Bible and continues to work in the present to make the Bible's message a living truth, not a dead, scholastic text.

What May Be Said about the Bible's Great, General Message?

The Baptist Faith and Message presents a full picture of the Bible's great, general message; The Chicago Statement does not do so because it concentrates more specifically upon the Bible, yet it is possible to infer what the authors felt is the Bible's great, general message.

In both documents, the great, general message is the same. It is the Bible's revelation of a transcendent, personal Creator God, who is Father, Son, and Spirit, whose Son became incarnate as Jesus of Nazareth, who died and rose again for the sins of the world, who poured his Spirit into the hearts of believers forming a new people of God and equipping them for their world mission, and who in the future will complete his redemptive work. This great, general biblical message is the good news which the world needs, and it is to be proclaimed faithfully by all of God's people. In short, the great, general message of the Bible is the message which all Christians hold in common, together with an emphasis on evangelism and missions which is sometimes associated historically with the revivalist movement.

The Baptist Faith and Message says that the Bible "has God for its author, salvation for its end, and truth, without any mixture of error, for its matter" (7). The word "matter" refers to the Bible's great, general message, which is vigorously affirmed as "truth, without any mixture of error." Presumably the Bible's truth is associated with the other two facts mentioned in this sentence, namely, that God is the author of the Bible and that God's purpose is that men who hear the Bible will be saved.

The Chicago Statement goes byond The Baptist Faith and Message. It ties the great biblical message not only to God and to salvation, but to each individual teaching of Scripture, every detail of which is said to be true. Where The Baptist Faith and Message emphasizes the truth of the whole message, The Chicago Statement shifts the emphasis so as to include the truth of each part. "We deny that the inspiration of Scripture can rightly be affirmed of the whole without the parts" (VI). Further, "we deny that Biblical infallibility and inerrancy are limited to spiritual, religious, or redemptive themes, exclusive of assertions in the fields of history and science" (XII). Clearly the authors feel that unless the truth of each biblical teaching is affirmed, the great, general biblical message is jeopardized. "We affirm that a confession of the full authority, infallibility, and inerrancy of Scripture is vital to a sound understanding of the whole of the Christian faith" (XIX). This commitment to the truth of individual teachings does not, however, cause the authors to lose sight of the great, general biblical message.

In summary, both documents vigorously affirm the truth of the Bible's great

321

message and also the priority of that general mesage over the individual teachings. The Chicago Statement couples the truthfulness of the general biblical message to the inerrancy of individual biblical teachings, and The Baptist Faith and Message does not.

What Is Biblical Inerrancy?

We have come now to the question which will indicate the great difference in the two documents.

We have seen their similarities. Both affirm that the Bible is a supernatural revelation of cognitive truth. Both affirm that, although its authors and its language are human, it is a God-given authority for Christians, a norm for faith and life. Both affirm that the Spirit inspired its writing and makes its message come alive for people today. Both affirm that its great, general message is truth without error.

Is there anything else which must be emphasized about the content of the Bible? For The Baptist Faith and Message, there is not. For The Chicago Statement, there most certainly is.

At this point, it is no longer possible to compare the two documents. The Chicago Statement has an agenda which is not shared by The Baptist Faith and Message. In fact, this is the principal agenda of The Chicago Statement; the title of the document makes this clear: "The Chicago Statement on Biblical Inerrancy." The article in The Baptist Faith and Message is entitled simply, "The Scriptures." The Baptist Faith and Message does not use the words "inerrant" or "infallible." It does not couple the truth of the Bible's general message to the inerrancy of its specific teachings.

If we cannot at this point compare the two as we have been doing, how shall we proceed? I will attempt to present the teaching of The Chicago Statement by a series of three questions: What is biblical inerrancy? How is biblical inerrancy qualified? How is biblical inerrancy defended?

I hope to provide helpful resources for understanding The Chicago Statement's sophisticated, technical teaching about inerrancy. Therefore I will not restrict myself to answering these three questions, but also will attempt to identify the problems which technical inerrancy creates for some people today.

Before I begin with the technical teaching about inerrancy, let me mention two outstanding characteristics of The Chicago Statement. First, The Chicago Statement does not condemn non-inerrantists either as non-Christians or as non-Evangelicals. It does warn of the dangers of non-inerrancy, but it acknowledges that inerrancy is an issue on which serious, thoughtful, evangelical Christians disagree. Second, the tone and spirit of The Chicago Statement are very praiseworthy. This document is non mean-spirited, and it is not intended to be divisive. "We offer this Statement in a spirit, not of contention, but of humility and love, which we purpose by God's grace to maintain in any future dialogue arising out of what we have said" (Preface).

Now, the first question is, what is biblical inerrancy? The word is negative; it means "without error." The meaning, however, is positive; it is an affirmation that everything that the Bible teaches, is error-free. "Scripture is without error or fault in all its teaching" (SS 4). This includes its assertions in the fields of history and science as well as religion and spiritual matters (XII). Inerrancy and infallibility mean more or less the same thing (XI). Inerrancy begins with "God, who is Himself Truth and speaks truth only" (SS 1). Inerrancy is a product of inspiration: "the doctrine of inerrancy is grounded in the teaching of the Bible about inspiration" (XV). It is inerrancy which renders the Bible authoritiative and normative, and these qualities will be jeopardized if inerrancy is disregarded (SS 5).

How Is Biblical Inerrancy Qualified?

The Chicago Statement provides a list of careful qualifications of the affirmation of biblical inerrancy.

I will present them in the sequence which appears in the Articles.

First, God's revelation in Scripture is progressive (V). Later revelations may be greater than earlier ones and may fulfill them, but they cannot correct them, because there are no errors to be corrected.

Second, inerrancy applies only to the "autographic text" of the Bible, that is, the original, now no longer existent, Hebrew, Aramaic, and Greek manuscritps (X).

This is easily the most important qualification of inerrancy. It means that no modern text or translation is inerrant. This means that the difference between The Baptist Faith and Message and The Chicago Statement does not concern any text or translation of the Bible we have today.

Of course, The Chicago Statement affirms a high view of today's copies and translations. But it does not say that they are inerrant.

To be strictly accurate, The Statement should be re-named "The Chicago Statement on the Inerrancy of Non-Extant Ancient Hebrew, Aramaic, and Greek Manuscripts of the Bible."

What is even more important is this, that The Statement's concern for the autographs leads it to say something less about the Bible which we have today than The Baptist Faith and Message says. The Statement says: "We affirm that inspiration, strictly speaking, applies only to the autographic text of Scripture" (X). The Baptist Faith and Message does not restrict inspiration to the autographs; its affirmation of inspiration applies to the Bible we have today. Further, The Chicago Statement says "that copies and translations of Scripture are the Word of God to the extent that they are faithfully represent the original" (X). The Baptist Faith and Message does not need or employ phrases such as "to the extent that." For The Baptist Faith and Message, the Bible we have today is God's inspired revelation.

In summary, the two documents differ as follows: The Baptist Faith and Message uses general language to affirm the Bible we have today as God's inspired, trustworthy, authoritative revelation, and The Chicago Statement uses very technical language to affirm that non-existent Hebrew, Aramaic, and Greek manuscripts were God's inerrant and therefore trustworthy, authoritiative revelation. However, as different as the emphases of the two documents are, on the Bible as we have it today they are close together, with The Baptist Faith and Message holding a higher view than The Chicago Statement.

Third, the inerrancy of Scripture must be understood in terms of the standards of truth and error which are consistent with its usage (XIII).

This is a puzzling qualification. We tend to respond by saying: "We thought that by inerrant you meant 'true' in the ordinary sense, but now you are leaving open the possibility that another 'usage' may be intended." What that usage is may or may not be spelled out in what follows, but this is a curious and troubling qualification. To put it bluntly: Could not anyone rightfully claim to be inerrant provided he is allowed to define what truth and error are?

Fourth, the Chicago Statement says that inerrancy is to be understood in terms of the purpose of Scripture (XIII).

This is a very important qualification, and it raises some extremely complex issues. Purpose or intentionality ought strictly to be attributed to persons rather than to documents; people have purposes or intentions, texts do not. Usually we can refer loosely to the purpose of a text without confusion, because everyone understands that we mean the purpose or intention of the author of the text. But in the case of technical discussions about the Bible, this will not do, because the Bible has human authors but it also has God for its author. So, when in our technical discussions we refer to the purpose of the Bible, we should specify whether we mean the purpose of, say, Paul, or the purpose of God.

The importance of this can be made clear as follows. Suppose we emphasized this qualification more fully than The Chicago Statement does. Suppose we put it as follows: "Whatever God intends to teach in Scripture, is inerrant." Would non-inerrantists disagree with that? I think not. Nor would non-irrenatists disagree if we presed it a bit further and said, "Whatever God intends to teach on any subject, including science and history, in Scripture, is inerrant." I expect that this would be acceptable to most of the Christians who ordinarily do not use the word "inerrant."

Not let us reverse things, and ask a really hard question. Suppose an inerrantist hears this qualification and rejects it. Imagine someone saying this: "It is not enough for me to say that whatever God intends to teach in Scripture is inerrant; I insist that we say that Scripture itself is inerrant." Is there not a risk here of caring more about Scripture than about what God intends to teach in Scipture?

Let me be clear about something. I am not suggesting only that what God uses Scripture to teach to people today is inerrant; I am not talking about a functional understanding of inerrancy at all (that is an important topic, but it is not a debated one). I am talking, as The Chiago Statement is, about a cognitive understanding of revelation. What God intended to teach, cognitively, as his Spirit inspired the writers of the Bible, is inerrant. I recognize, of course, that The Chicago Statement does not emphasize this qualification as much as I am doing. I am only suggesting that if it had done so, it could have built bridges to many other people.

324

I can imagine an inerrantist offering this objection: "You are making it too hard for me to get at what is inerrant. I don't know how to tell what God intends." But don't we all have to accept this difficulty? For example, when our Roman Catholic friends (who, of course, believe in biblical inerrancy) tell us that God intends Matthew 16:16-19 to authorize the papal system, don't we all have to do the hard work of interpretation to show that in this passage God has not taught that? I do not think that any of us can avoid the hard work of studying the Bible to find what God is intentionally teaching in it. I do not think we should try to evade this responsibility.

Fifth, The Chicago Statement provides a list of phenomena which, when (or if) they appear in the Bible, do not negate inerrancy. There are ten items. They are (1) lack of modern technical precision, (2) irregularities of grammar, (3) irregularities of spelling, (4) observational descriptions of nature, (5) reporting of falsehoods, (6) use of hyperbole, (7) use of round numbers, (8) topical arrangement of material, (9) variant selection of materials in parallel accounts, and (10) use of free citations (XIII).

The meaning of most of these is self-evident, but I will comment on one or two. "Observational descriptions of nature" means that the Bible reports things as they appeared to the authors, not as they would be described by a scientist. If the Bible said that the sun rose rather than that the earth rotated on its axis, that is not an error. The reporting of falsehoods would be as in Ps. 14:1, where it is reported that some fool said that there is no God. Topical arrangement of materials would be an alternative to chronological arrangement, which means, for example, that no error is involved if stories about Jesus are told in different sequences in the various gospels. The use of free citations means that the New Testament writers do not err if they choose to paraphrase an Old Testament passage rather than to quote it precisely.

What are we to make of these ten qualifications of inerrancy? I concur with Clark Pinnock who wrote of Article XIII: "This comment is so generous, in fact, that some strict inerrantists will live to regret it simply because it allows a large degree of critical freedom. It is difficult to think of a liberal critical opinion that could not be worded to fit into their specification" (*The Scripture Principle*, p. 234). I do not think Pinnock has exaggerated at all; this list of qualifications would allow an inerrantist to hold to almost any critical interpretation of the Bible. I believe that this fact would come as a shock to, for example, many in the secular press who attempt to report on evanglicalism.

Sixth, The Chicago Statement acknoledges that there are "alleged errors and discrepancies" (XIV) in the Bible. The Statement does not claim that the Bible looks inerrant, only that it is inerrant—in spite of passages which do not appear to be inerrant.

Thoughtful inerrantists have always acknoledged that such passages do appear in the Bible. In his book *Why I Preach that the Bible is Literally True*, Dr. W. A. Criswell referred to these passages as "problems," and the Criswell Study Bible refers to them as "inadvertences." By whatever name, they exist, and those who read the Bible sensitively are aware of them. The Chicago Statement makes no effort to conceal them, which is wise.

Seventh, the writers of the Bible employed "literary forms and devices" (XVIII). The Statement does not say what these are, though it does hint that they would not include pseudonymous writings or what is sometimes called saga, that is, writings whose author used a name other than his own, or writings which appear to be history but are actually parables. Here is The Statement's denial: "We deny the legitimacy of any treatment of the text or quest for sources lying behind it that leads to relativizing, dehistoricizing, or discounting its teaching, or rejecting its claims to authorship" (XVIII). It is fair to say, I think, that this very important qualification is worded in such a guarded way that it can be fairly interpreted in support of any one of severally mutually contradictory views. It does not cleary settle, for example, whether the book of Jonah was a history or a parable.

This concludes the list of qualifications of inerrancy to be found in The Chicago Statement. Other inerrantists have sometimes included other qualifications, and I will mention two. One is an acknowledgement that the language of the Bible is not always literal but includes metaphors and figurative forms; a second is that the Bible is not all written in narrative or didactic prose, but includes other genres such as songs, prayers, laws, promises, apocalypses, and so on. These things are not mentioned in The Statement, but given the generous qualifications that have been included, I feel confident that the authors would be open to these as well. This is confirmed by the Exposition of The Chicago Statement. The Exposition says the following: "So history must be treated as history, poetry as poetry, hyperbole and metaphor as hyperbole and metaphor."

Now I want to offer a comment on these qualifications of inerrancy. The qualifications are frustrating to inerrantists and non-inerrantists, for different reasons. Inerrantists feel frustrated because they believe that they have qualified inerrancy so carefully that no Bible-believing Christian ought any longer to resist inerrancy. On the other hand, non-inerrantist feel frustrated because they cannot see why they should be asked to accept a view which seems problematic, only to be forced to qualify it extensively in order to avoid the problems which it unnecessarily created. Why not just bypass the problem and speak of theBible as God's uniquely-inspired, trustworhty, authoritative revelation?

That, of course, is what The Baptist Faith and Message does.

How Is Biblical Inerrancy Defended?

The Chicago Statement is a document which asserts rather than defends biblical inerrancy. Yet throughout the document, one can discern the kind of warrants which are called upon to support the position of inerrancy. I will mention six of them.

First, God's character is such that his Word will be truthful. "God, who is Himself Truth and speaks truth only, has inpsired Holy Scripture" (SS 1).

Second, Jesus taught inerrancy. This is hinted at rather than stated: "We deny that Jesus' teaching about Scripture may be dismissed by appeals to accommodation or to any natural limitation of His humanity" (XV).

Third, the Spirit gives Christians an internal witness to inerrancy. "The Holy

Spirit bears witness to the Scriptures, assuring believers of the truthfulness of God's written Word" (XVII).

Fourth, the Bible teaches that it is inspired and this leads to the conclusion that it is inerrant. "We affirm that the doctrine of inerrancy is grounded in the teaching of the Bible about inspiration" (XV). Inerrancy is usually defended as a direct teaching of the Bible itself, so I expect that it is significant that The Statement does not say that the Bible teaches that it is inerrant, only that it is inspired; this must represent an effort to stay on the most defensible ground possible.

Fifth, The Statement includes several warnings, in a kind spirit but quite firm, that to reject inerrancy is to put at risk the church's work and the rest of its theology. "We further deny that inerrancy can be rejected without grave consequences, both to the individual and to the Church" (XIX).

Finally, inerrancy is said to be the historic position of the church and not a doctrine invented by Protestant scholasticism or merely a reaction to biblical criticism (XVI).

My first response to these defenses is to note the absence of one defense which is frequently used, namely, the argument that unless a non-inerrantist can provide criteria for sorting out the Bible's truths from its alleged errors, then non-inerrancy has forfeited the credibility of the entire Bible, which clearly is a major disaster. The Chicago Statement is wise, in my judgment, to avoid this line of defense, since its own appeal to the autographs entails that inerrantists too need criteria for sorting out the truths of the Bible we now have from the errors which it, unlike the autographs, may contain.

What The Statement does not come to grips with, in my judgment, is the fact that its appeal to the autographs also undermines its argument that to forfeit inerrancy is to put at risk the entire theology and mission of the church. For the church's theology and mission today cannot, of course, be guided by inerrant autographs which do not exist but only by existing texts and translations for which no claim of inerrancy is being made. This argument, which is sometimes called the slippery slide argument or the domino effect, can be employed properly only by inerrantists who affirm that we today have an inerrant text or translation. There are such persons, but their view did not prevail at Chicago in 1978, nor have the exerted much influence, so far as I know, in the controversy in the Southern Baptist Convention.

In fact, the Chicago Statement's appeal to the autographs effectively undermines no fewer than four of its six lines of defense. Jesus did not appeal to autographs; the Bible never appeals to autographs when it speaks of itself; historically the church has not appealed to the autographs (until recently); and the argument that only the possession of an inerrant Bible can keep the Church faithful, falters on the fact that the inerrent autographs no longer exist.

My second response is that the defense which says that the biblical teachings about inspiration entail inerrancy does not hold up very well. This is certainly the case if we examine the only text which specifically affirms inspiration, namely, II Timothy 3:16: "All Scripture is given by inspiration of God, and is profitable for doctrine, for reproof, for correction, for instruction in righteous-

327

ness: That the man of God may be perfect, thoroughly furnished unto all good works." This is a very high view of Scripture as God-breathed and profitable, but it does not emphasize inerrancy.

I think that the same might be shown even if one widened the meaning of inspiration, but there is no way to be sure without examining the biblical texts one by one, and since The Chicago Statement does not tell us what text it means, we are not in a position to do that.

Third, the truthfulness of God does not logically entail that the Bible must be inerrant. Presumably God could, if he chose to do so, communicate his truth to us through a book which is not inerrant. Most Christians believe that God successfully communicates his truth through sermons which are not inerrant. We also believe that God may speak truthfully to us through a voice in our hearts, but we do not claim this inner voice is always inerrant. It is one thing to affirm that God is completely truthful, which he surely is; it is another to affirm that he can communicate his truth only by technically inerrant means, which does not necessarily logically follow.

Many people feel that it is wiser to describe the Bible as it actually appears rather than to deduce what the Bible ought to be from general principles. Needless to say, all Christians agree that God is truthful and that the Bible is God's Word, but all do not agree that it follows that the Bible must be inerrant. The flaw in the logic may be seen in a parallel example. We all agree that Jesus was God and that God cannot die, but from this we do not conclude that Jesus could not die. To know whether or not Jesus could die, we must read the Bible; to know whether or not the Bible must be technically inerrant, we must read the Bible, too.

Fourth, a simple comment can be made on the defense which says that the Spirit bears witness in our hearts that the Bible is inerrant. Clearly this is the case for many Christians; but for many others, the Spirit bears witness that the Bible is the inspired, trustworthy, authoritiative Word of God rather than that the Bible is technically inerrant.

In summary, the defense of inerrancy is a difficult task, and the lines of defense adopted by The Chicago Statement are not secure. This is especially true because The Statement appeals to the autographs, and this appeal is not found in the Bible itself, in the teaching of Jesus about the Bible, or in the church's historic view of the Bible. In my judgment, The Chicago Statement is a sophisticated, balanced, thoughtful, responsible affirmation of biblical inerrancy, but its defense of inerrancy does not succeed.

How Shall We Compare the Baptist Faith and Message with Biblical Inerrancy?

Let me acknowledge that in these concluding comments, the position taken is my own, and I am aware that it does not represent the view of many other Christians who are well-informed and who sincerely believe differently than I do. I offer my views with the full awareness that I could be mistaken.

First, I believe that the differences between The Baptist Faith and Message and The Chicago Statement on Biblical Inerrancy are very small. I realize that

The Statement's affirmation and defense of inerrancy seem to offer a higher view of the Bible than The Baptist Faith and Message; but I am convinced that when The Chicago Statement has provided its generous qualifications of inerrancy, nothing has been added to the very high view of Scripture found in The Baptist Faith and Message.

Second, I believe that, probably unintentionally, the authors of The Chicago Statement have forfeited something valuable about Scripture. They have eroded our confidence that the Bible which we now have is itself the very Word of God. All modern texts and all responsible translations of the Bible are, I believe, completely and fully inspired, authoritative, normative, and revelatory. The Chicago Statement's appeal to the autographs is unbiblical, unhistorical, and unwise. I favor doing what Jesus and the apostles and the whole church (until very recently) have done, which is to believe in the Bible which we hold in our hands as the very Word of God.

Third, The Baptist Faith and Message is a text around which people can naturally unite; The Chicago Statement, in spite of its authors' intentions, is a text which is naturally divisive. By emphasizing technical matters, it puts on the agenda the very issues on which sincere and informed Christians disagree. Concerning the Bible, The Baptist Faith and Message is a consensus document for all Bible-believing Christians; The Chicago Statement is not.

Fourth, if The Chicago Statement had traced out the implications of its single allusion to the purpose of God in Scripture, it might have managed to build a bridge to those who have not traditionally spoken of inerrancy. I am convinced that many people would agree with a statement such as, "Whatever God intends to teach in the Bible on any subject, is truth without any mixture of error." I deeply regret, however, that some inerrantists are suspicious of phrases such as this, and I wish that The Chicago Statement had enthusiastically embraced such a phrase.

Finally, perhaps in the end we do well to use the Bible's own language about itself, for when we do so, we find ourselves at peace. We can all agree with the psalmist who said (Ps. 119): "Thy word have I hid in mine heart; I will delight myself in thy statutes; Open thou mine eyes, that I may behold wondrous things out of thy law; teach my thy statutes; I will meditate in thy percepts; Give me understanding, and I shall keep thy law; thy statutes have ben my songs; the law of thy mouth is better unto me than thousands of gold and silver; thy word is a lamp unto my feet, and a light unto my path; thy testimonies have I taken as a heritage forever; for they are the rejoicing of my heart; Thy law do I love."

17

THE BACKGROUND AND MEANING OF THE 1963 SOUTHERN BAPTIST ARTICLES OF FAITH ON THE BIBLE

G. Hugh Wamble

The purpose of this seminar is to explore the background and meaning of statements respecting the Scriptures in the Baptist Faith and Message Statement adopted by the Southern Baptist Convention in 1963.[1]

This paper deals with these topics: (1) Provisions respecting the Scriptures, (2) background of the 1963 confession, (3) text, and (4) meaning. The latter topic receives major attention. When exploring the meaning, I will refer to statements in other Baptist confessions of faith.[2]

Provisions

The 1963 confession contains three provisions respecting the Scriptures.

First, according to the preamble, "the sole authority for faith and practice among Baptists is the Scripture of the Old and New Testaments" (No. 4). Confessions of faith, such as the 1963 Statement, "are statements of religious convictions, drawn from the Scriptures" (No. 5) and "are only guides in interpretation, having no authority over the conscience" (No. 4). Thus, confessions of faith neither supplant the Scriptures nor override them. This point bears emphasis at the outset. Any confessional statement is subordinate to Scripture; it must not usurp the authoritative position reserved for the Scriptures.

Second, Article I, entitled "Of the Scriptures," defines the doctrine of Scripture. It contains four sentences which I break down in numbered parts for future reference, as follows:

> [1] The Holy Bible [2] was written by men divinely inspired and [3] is the record of God's revelation of Himself to man. [4] It is a perfect treasure of divine instruction. It has [5] God for its author, [6] salvation for its end, and [7] truth, without any mixture of error, for its matter. [8] It reveals the principles by which god judges us; and [9] therefore is, and will remain to the end of the world, the true center of Christian union, and [10] the supreme standard by which all [11] human conduct, [12] creeds, and [13] religious opinions should be tried. [14] The criterion by which the Bible is to be interpreted is Jesus Christ.[3]

Third, the article on "Education" (XII) states:

> The freedom of a teacher in a Christian school, college, or seminary is limited by the pre-eminence of Jesus Christ, by the authoritative nature of the Scriptures, and by the distinct purpose for which the school exists.[4]

Why did the convention adopt such language? Where did particular words and phrases originate? Where did the ideas originate? What does the language mean? Even if historical evidence may be insufficient to provide a full answer to such questions, it at least offers some guidance for understanding what the 1963 confession means.

Background

In 1963 the Southern Baptist Convention adopted the confession during a controversy. The purpose of the entire confession was to ameliorate the controversy.

For about a year prior to the 1962 annual meeting of the Convention there had been an escalating controversy centering on Ralph H. Elliott's *The Message of Genesis,* published in mid-1961 by Broadman Press of the Convention's Sunday School Board. Elliot was the first professor of Old Testament at Midwestern Baptist Theological Seminary, created in 1957.[5] The school opened in Kansas City, Missouri, in 1958. During its first two years there was some criticism of the new seminary, primarily focussing on Elliott but not limited to him. Criticism diminished for a year or so. The publication of Elliott's book in mid-1961 occasioned a revival of criticism, coming originally from Kansas and Missouri.

By Fall 1961 controversy had spread to other places. K. Owen White, pastor of the First Baptist Church, Houston, Texas, became a leading figure in the expanding controversy. In late-November 1961 a special committee of Midwestern's Board of Trustees conducted a two-day hearing of criticisms against Elliott, plus Elliott's response. The committee voted to recommend that the full Board sustain Elliott. Before the year was out, the Board, by divided vote, approved the special committee's recommendation. Dissenting trustees stated that they opposed the recommendation because they thought that it was too early to act on the matter. My impression at the time, and one which has remained with me, was that political considerations figured into the dissent, for the controversy was still escalating.

Board action did not end the controversy. In fact, by Spring 1962 it had intensified. Criticism of Elliott's book focussed on his interpretation of chapter 1-11 of Genesis. There was little criticism of his interpretation of other chapters, with two exceptions—namely, the passage about Melchizedek, and the passage about the aborted sacrifice of Isaac. Critics also called for removal of trustees who had supported Elliott, for election of trustees committed to stopping biblical interpretation deemed offensive or heretical, and for financial boycott and designation of funds so as to exert pressure against Midwestern if other efforts proved ineffectual.

The heart of the controversy was the so-called "historical-critical method" of biblical interpretation. Opponents of Elliott tended to favor pre-critical interpretation and some seemed wedded to the chronology proposed by Bishop Usher of Ireland in the mid-seventeenth century and carried marginally in some printings of the King James Version.

Convention leaders became anxious over the intensifying controversy in

332

Spring 1962, for it threatened to become the major issue at the 1962 annual meeting in San Francisco, the first time the Convention had met outside the South.

The idea of restudying the Convention's confession, as a means of defusing a volatile situation, arose among Herschel H. Hobbs, Convention president and pastor of the First Baptist Church, Oklahoma City, and Porter W. Routh and Albert McClellan of the Convention's Executive Committee.[6] This idea came beofre the Executive Committee in San Francisco just before the opening of the annual meeting. The Executive Committee recommended, and the Convention approved, that the Convention president, as chairman, and state convention presidents serve as a committee "to present to the Convention in Kansas City [in 1963] some . . . statement which shall serve as information to the churches, and which may serve as guidelines" to SBC agencies, the statement to be similar to the Convention's 1925 confession and designed to be "helpful at this time"[7] Hobbs regarded "the grass roots flavor" as one of the committee's "greatest strengths."[8] In contrast to the 1924-25 committee which included several educators and theologians, the 1962-63 committee included persons meeting the qualification of popular election by Baptist conventions.

The creation of this special committee failed to prevent the "Elliott controversy" from coming before the Convention in San Francisco. K. Owen White, perhaps the best-known critic of Elliott, introduced a long motion which the chair subsequently ruled to be two motions: (1) That the Convention "reaffirm . . . faith in the *entire* Bible as the authoritative, authentic, infallible Word of God," (2) that the Convention

> express our abiding and unchanging objection to the dissemination of theological views in any of our seminaries which would undermine such faith in the historical accuracy and doctrinal integrity of the Bible

and

> courteously instruct the trustees and administrative officers of our institutions and other agencies to take such steps as shall be necessary to remedy at once those situations where such views now threaten our historic position.[9]

Both of White's motion's subsequently passed.[10]
Another motion called for the Convention to

> instruct the Sunday School Board to cease from publication and printing the book, *The Message of Genesis*, by Dr. Elliott, and . . . recall from all sales this book which contradicts Baptist conviction.[11]

When this motion came up for consideration, the sponsor withdrew the motion in response to a public request.[12] Later, however, another messenger introduced a motion "to instruct the Sunday School Board to cease publishing and to recall from all distribution channels, the book, *The Message of Genesis*, by

333

Dr. Ralph Elliott."[13] When this motion came up for action, the Convention defeated it.[14]

In Fall 1962 Midwestern's Board dismissed Elliott on the stated ground that he had not complied with an administrative request that he not permit another publisher to reprint his book. Though Elliott's name continued to figure in discussions, Elliott became less and less controversial in the next few months

The 1962-63 committee chaired by Hobbs organized soon after the San Francisco Convention and laid out its work. It decided to undertake a revision of the Convention's 1925 Statement on Baptist Faith and Message. By late-November 1962 it had prepared a basic draft for the circulation among personnel of the six seminaries and Sunday School Board for the purpose of eliciting reactions to assist the committee in finalizing its recommendations. The original preamble lacked the five introductory points of 1925 respecting the place of confessions of faith in Baptist life, but it contained a modified version of them. The draft went to seminary and Sunday School Board officials in December 1962. In January 1963 two members of the committee went to each of the seminaries to discuss with representatives any reactions to the draft. Following these visits, there was a meeting of the entire committee in February, at which there was the finalizing of the draft confession, including an introduction which included the five introductory points of 1925.[15]

In its report to the Convention in 1963 the committee stated that "[t]hroughout its work your committee has been conscious of the contribution" of the Convention's 1925 confession. It quoted, with concurrence, some statements made by the 1925 committee, including the five-point introduction on "the historic Baptist conception of the nature and function of confessions of faith in our religious and denominational life." As the 1925 committee used the New Hampshire Confession (1853 version) as its norm, "revised at certain points, and with some additional articles growing out of certain needs," so the 1962-63 committee basically followed the 1925 confession, sometimes without change, sometimes with slight revision in the interest of "clarity," "emphasis," and conciseness. "In no case," said the committee, "has it sought to delete from or to add to the basic contents of the 1925 statement."[16]

Thus, the confession purports to be a restatement of doctrine set forth in the 1925 confession which was, in its own way, a restatement of the New Hampshire Confession, each made in its own theological climate.

When acting on the committee's report in 1963, the Convention made no substantive change whatever. It defeated three motions: (1) To strike from the committee's report everything "except the Scripture references,"[17] (2) to receive (not to adopt) the confession and to "commend it to our churches and agencies for guidance,"[18] and (3) to strike from Article VI the last paragraph pertaining to the New Testament's references to "the church as the body of Christ which includes all of the redeemed of all the ages."[19]

One other action by the convention of 1963 bears notice because it pertains to the background out of which the confession came. After adopting the confession, the Convention approved a motion authorizing the printing, in its minutes, of the "entire statement" presented by the chairman of Midwestern's

Board to the Convention.[20] The chairman's statement included "nine principles of academic procedure" respecting the teaching of the Bible. This Board-approved statement recognized "the Historical-Critical approach. . . as a valid approach to Old Testament studies," acknowledged "[d]ifferences of opinion on interpretations of biblical passages," and asserted the teacher's obligation "to teach within the framework of the fundamentals of the Baptist faith."[21] The Convention did not approve these "nine principles" *per se*. However, the Convention's authorizing that these "nine principles" be printed in its minutes indicates the Convention's awareness of the matter with which they deal.

Text

The text of the 1963 article on the Scriptures derived from the New Hampshire Confession (1833), as revised by the Convention in 1925, and as further revised by the convention in 1963. Article I of the New Hampshire Confession reads as follows:

> We believe [that] the Holy Bible was written by men divinely inspired, and is a perfect treasure of heavenly instruction; that it has God for its author, salvation for its end, and truth, without any mixture of error, for its matter; and that it reveals the principles by which God will judge us; and therefore is, and shall remain to the end of the world, the true centre of Christian union, and the supreme standard by which all human conduct, creeds, and opinions should be tried.[22]

Southern Baptists' confession of 1925 retained the New Hampshire Confession's wording of Article I except for three changes: (1) Deletion of "and" before "it reveals"; (2) substitution of "will remain" for "shall remain'"; and (3) addition of the adjective "religious" as a qualifier of "opinions." Of these three changes, only the last altered meaning.

Though it appeared during the height of the Modernist-Fundamentalist controversy, the 1925 confession refrained from asserting that the Bible is the "supreme standard" for judging all opinions, as in the New Hampshire Confession. The 1925 confession stated that the Bible is the "supreme standard" for judging "all religious opinions." The 1925 preamble stated that confessions of faith "are religious convictions, drawn from the Scriptures, and are not to hamper freedom of thought or investigation into other realms of life" (Point 5). More importantly, the 1925 article on "'Education" began with the following:

> Christianity is the religion of enlightenment and intelligence. In Jesus Christ are hidden all the treasures of wisdom and knowledge. All sound learning is therefore a part of our Chrisitian heritage. The new birth opens all human faculties and creates a thirst for knowledge.

It seems clear, therefore, that the drafters of the 1925 confession and the five-point introduction desired to protect the educational enterprise from dogmatic restraints.

The 1963 confession accepted the 1925 statement on the Scriptures, except

335

for three changes, plus changes in style and punctuation: (1) Addition of the phrase "and is the record of God's revelation of Himself to man," (2) substitution of "divine instruction" for "heavenly instruction." and (3) addition of a new sentence: "The criterion by which the Bible is to be interpreted is Jesus Christ."

The preamble of the 1963 confession says:

> Baptists emphasize the soul's competency before God, freedom in religion, and the priesthood of the believer. However this emphasis should not be interpreted to mean that there is an absence of certain definite doctrines that Baptists believe, cherish, and with which they have been and are now closely identified.
>
> It is the purpose of this statement of faith and message to set forth certain teachings which we believe.

Though the original draft of the 1962-63 committee retained the language pertaining to "Education," quoted above,[23] the final version did not. It appears, therefore, that the 1962-63 committee desired to protect "certain definite doctrines."

Hobbs, as chairman, drafted the final version of the 1963 confession, but it was "the product of much sharing of opinions."[24]

Meaning

As Hobbs has pointed out, there is no official explanation or interpretation of the 1963 confession.[25] Any interpretation is exactly that—only an interpretation of the person offering it.

Therefore, there is nothing authoritative about the explanation which follows. However, I have read the records of the 1962-63 committee deposited with the Historical Commission (SBC). I have studied preceding confessions of faith with a view to determining how the 1963 language agrees with and differs from language appearing in prior confessions. I cite sources to support my suggestions. I encourage anyone to make his or her own study. Though the following is not authoritative, it, I trust, is informative and instructive.

1. Holy Bible

Most Baptist confessions prior to the New Hampshire Confession did not use the term "Bible" or "Holy Bible." Most used terms like "Scripture," "Scriptures," "sacred scripture," "canonical Scripture," or some variation, as a review of confessions will readily confirm.[26] Some used the term"Word,"[27] but the term "Word" or "Word of God" means various things in Baptist confessions—for example, Scripture, Jesus Christ, and gospel. Evangelicals or Protestants, including Baptists, customarily used "Scripture" for generations because the term is itself scriptural (cf. 2 Tim. 3:16). The Bible is a bound book containing the Scriptures. Indeed, "Bible" comes from a word meaning "book."

The first Baptist confession to use the words "the bible" was the Articles of Religion (1770) of the New Connection of General Baptists in England, but this confession also referred to "the scriptures."[28] One will find in Baptist literature of the eighteenth century references to "Bible"—for example, in the oft-reprinted writings of John Gill (d. 1769)—but the term "Scriptures" remained the preferred term among Baptists. The term "Bible" became increasingly popular in the nineteenth century, due at least in part to the wide distribution of Bibles, in connection with the modern mission movement, through such agencies as the British and Foreign Bible Society (1804) and the American Bible Society (1816).

The New Hampshire Confession was the first Baptist confession in America to use the term "Holy Bible" in an article on authority in religion, but the article's name, "Of the Scriptures,"[29] followed the older nomenclature favored by Baptists. The 1963 confession followed the New Hampshire Confession in this regard.

2. Written

Many Baptist confessions prior to the New Hampshire Confession gave no attention to the manner by which the Scriptures came to be written.[30] Others referred to this matter in a general way, without detailing any method of inspiration. For example, a General Baptist confession of 1651 referred to that "which was given by inspiration of the holy Ghost."[31] A confession of 1655 simply stated that "the Holy Scriptures. . . are given by inspiration of God."[32] Another confession (of 1656) stated that Jesus, in his role as prophet (the other roles being priest and king), "hath given us the scriptures, the Old and New Testament, as a rule and direction unto us both for faith and practice."[33] Even the influential Particular Baptist confession of 1677/1689, best known in America as the Philadelphia Confession (1742) and its many derivatives, simple stated that the books of the Old and New Testaments "are given by inspiration of God, to be the rule of Faith and Life."[34] General Baptists' confession of 1678 used the same language.[35]

I have not found in early Baptist confessions the kind of views of inspiration held by some, but not all, Reformed (Calvinistic) scholars of the seventeenth century. Cocceius (d.1669) held that "men of God. . . were God's assistants and amanuenses, who wrote exactly as they spoke, not by their own will but driven by the H. Spirit."[36] Voetius (d. 1676) taught that New Testament writers thought and wrote in Greek "by the inspiration and dictation of the H. Spirit."[37] The *Formula consensus ecclesiarum Helveticarum* (1675) of Switzerland said that the Hebrew text of the Old Testament was "God-inspired" as to "the vowels (whether the very points or at least the power of the points) and regarding things as well as words."[38] The manner of inspiration, so far as I can tell, was not a major concern of seventeenth century Baptists.

The New Hampshire Confession was the first Baptist confession in America to attempt to explain *how* the "Holy Bible" came into existence—namely, "written by men divinely inspired."[39] The Southern Baptist confessions of 1925 and 1963 retained this explanation. By way of contrast, the Articles of Faith of 1923 of the Baptist Bible Union, a fundamentalist group among Northern Baptists, said that the Bible was "written by men supernaturally inspired," "in such definite way that their writings were supernaturally inspired and free from errors, as no other writings have been or ever will be inspired."[40] Two Landmark Baptist confessions of the mid-twentieth century affirmed, respectively, "the infallible verbal inspiration of the whole Bible"[41] and "[t]he infallibility and plenary verbal inspiration of the Scriptures."[42]

The Southern Baptist confessions have gone no further than to say "[t]he Holy Bible was written by men divinely inspired." The emphasis, it seems to me, falls on inspired persons who did the writing.

3. Records of Revelation

The 1963 confession added to the 1925 article that the Bible "is the record of God's revelation of Himself to man." Though the phrase was new to Southern Baptists' confession of 1963, the idea was not new.

General Baptists' confession of 1651 mentioned "the record of God" but related it to inspriation, not to revelation.[43] Particular Baptists' confession of 1677, borrowing from Presbyterians' Westminster Confession (1647),[44] said that God's revelation "at sundry times, and in divers manners," was "afterward" committed to writing "for the better preserving and propagating of the Truth, and for the more sure Establishment and Comfort of the church," thus making "the Holy Scriptures to be most necessary, those former ways of Gods revealing his will unto his people being now ceased."[45] Such language, of hoary use among Baptists, suggests that Baptists have viewed the Scriptures as the record of God's revelation.

In 1946 the Southern Baptist Convention adopted a Statement of Principles, recommended by a special committee, which stated that

> the one and only authority in faith and practice is the New Testament as the divinely inspired record and interpretation of the supreme revelation of God through Jesus Christ as Redeemer, Savior and Lord.[46]

This statement, of course, focuses on the New Testament as the record of God's "supreme revelation" through Jesus Christ. It reflects an emphasis of modern scholarship that New Testament writings are interpretive documents written from the perspective of faith (see John 20:30-31).

E. Y. Mullins (1860-1928), president of Southern Baptist Theological Seminary, professor of theology there, and chairman of the committee which drafted the confession adoped by the Southern Baptist Convention in 1925, said: "We have in the Scriptures of the Old and New Testaments the record of God's revelation of himself to his people."[47] This language is virtually the same as what later appeared in the 1963 confession. It is possible, even likely, I think that Mullins's phraseology was the basis of what appears in the 1963 confession. Hobbs used similar language in books published in 1960 and 1964.[48] In his exposition of the 1963 confession, Hobbs cited Mullins on other points,[49] so it is possible, even probable, that Mullins influenced Hobbs at this point as well.

Hobbs's manuscript notes on the original draft for the 1962-63 committee's consideration indicates that he was the author of this language.[50] The purpose of adding this language, according to Hobbs, was to spell out the *purpose* of the divine inspiration. We felt that the reading of the 1925 statement, while true, was incomplete. It was our purpose to spell out the purpose so that anyone could understand it.[51]

4. Divine Instruction

The New Hampshire Confession was the first Baptist confession to refer to the Bible as "a perfect treasure of heavenly instruction." language which the Southern Baptist Convention retained in 1925. The idea that the Scriptures were written for "instruction" appears in various Baptist confessions—e.g., in the Helwys congregation's Declaration of 1611.[52] It is possible that the 1677/Philadephia Confession's phrase "the heavenliness of the matter"[53] may have been the basis of the New Hampshire phrase "heavenly instruction."

The reason why the 1962-63 committee changed "heavenly" to "divine" was "to focus upon God, not some heavenly being, as the one who revealed and inspired the Scriptures."[54]

5-7. Author-End-Matter

The New Hampshire Confession was the first Baptist confession to say that the Bible "has God for its author, salvation for its end, and truth, without any mixture of error, for its matter,"[55] language which the Southern Baptist Convention retained in 1925 and 1963. J. Newton Brown acknowledged about two decades after the New Hampshire Confession appeared that he was the chief drafter of this confession.[56] How Brown came by this language pertaining to author-end-matter I have not been able to document. That it originated with John Locke (1632-1704), English philosopher and an Anglican sympathetic with Protestant non-conformists, is clear, it seems to me. Brown could have gotten the phrase directly form Locke's writings, oft reprinted in the first half of the nineteenth century; he could have gotten it indirectly.

The first occurrence of such language known to me appears in a letter of August 25, 1703, from Locke to an Anglican clergyman, Richard King. This minister had asked Locke "what is the shortest and surest way, for a young gentleman to attain a true knowledge of the christian religion, in the full and just extent of it." Locke responded:

> . . . to this I have a short and plain answer. "Let him study the holy scripture, especially the New Testament." Therein are contained the words of eternal life. *It has God for its author; salvation for its end; and truth, without any mixture of error, for its matter.* So that it is a wonder to me, how any one professing christianity, that would seriously set himself to know his religion, should be in doubt where to employ his search, and lay out his information; when he knows a book, where it is all contained, pure and entire; and whither, at last, every one must have recourse, to verify that of it, which he finds any-where else.[57]

If Locke borrowed this language, he failed to identify his source. My impression is that Locke coined it. It is easity demonstrated that Locke was careful to indicate when he quoted others, as a cursory review of his writings will confirm.

He did not use quotation marks for his author-end-matter statement. His letter, I might add, provided guidance for young persons interested in gaining knowledge of "the christian religion" morality, "good breeding," and politics and government. He cited writers and books which he deemed helpful for one investigating each topic. To understand Christianity, he suggested, one should look to Scripture, especially the New Testament, not to other sources. He concluded: "The knowledge of the bible, and the business of his calling, is enough for an ordinary man; a gentleman ought to go farther."[58]

5. Author

The idea that god is the author of Scripture was common to English Puritanism. Particular Baptists' 1677 confession, following both Presbyterians' Westminster Confession (1647) and Congregationalists' Savoy Declaration, said:

> The authority of Holy Scripture for which it ought to be believed dependeth not upon the testimony of any man or church; but wholly upon God (who is truth it self) the author thereof; therefore it is to be received, because it is the Word of God.[59]

This language spread in America by virtue of the Philadelphia Confession and several other Baptist confessions based on it. General Baptists' confession of 1678 did not directly quote the Westminster Confession on this point, but it said that God "hath delivered and revealed his mind" in Holy Scripture,[60] thus implying God's authorship. In a similar vein, the Kehukee Association's Ariticles of Faith (1777), in North Carolina, affirmed that "Almighty God has made known his mind and will to the children of men in His word. . . comprehended or contained in the Books of the Old and New Testaments.[61]

6. End

Perhaps nothing about the Scriptures appears more clearly in English confessions than the idea that the "end" or purpose of Scripture is "salvation," even though the term "end" first appeared in the New Hampshire Confession.

The Thirty-Nine Articles (1571) of the Church of England, of which Locke was a member, said:

> Holy Scripture conteyneth all thinges necessarie to salvation: so that whatsoeuer is not read therein, nor may be proued therby, is not to be required of anye man, that it should be beleued as an article of the fayth, or be though requisite [as] necessarie to saluation.[62]

Presbyterians' Westminster Confession said:

> The whole counsel of God, concerning all things necessary for his own glory, man's salvation, faith, and life, is either expressly set down in Scripture, or by good and necessary consequence may be deduced from Scripture.[63]

All things in Scripture are not alike plain in themselves, nor alike clear unto all; yet those things which are necesary to be known, believed, and observed, for salvation, are so clearly propounded and opened in some place of Scripture or other, that not only the learned, but the unlearned, in a due use of the ordinary means, may attaiin unto a sufficient understanding of them.[64]

Particular Baptists borrowed the foregoing language except the phrase "or by good and necessary consequence may be deduced from Scripture" which these Baptists omitted[65]—perhaps because they regarded infant baptism as something "deduced" from Scripture.[66] The 1677 confession began with a sentence not appearing in the Westminster Confession: "The Holy Scripture is the only sufficient, certain, and infallible rule of all *saving* Knowledge, Faith, and Obedience."[67] In two instances, it may be noted, this confession used the adjective "infallible" to qualify the noun "rule"—as in the preceding quotation and as in this sentence: "The infallible rule of interpretation of Scripture is the Scripture it self."[68]

Particular Baptists' Midland Confession (1655) said that "the Holy Scriptures. . . are able to make men wise unto salvation" and, in general relied on Paul's phrasing in 2 Timothy 3:15-17.[69] General Baptists' Standard Confession (1660) stated:

That the holy Scriptures is the rule whereby Saints both in matters of Faith, and conversation [conduct] are to be regulated, they being able to make men wise unto salvation, through Faith in Christ Jesus, profitable for Doctrine, for reproof, for instruction in righteousness.[70]

General Baptist' *An Orthodox Creed* of 1678 drew from both Anglican and Presbyterian confessions for the views (a) that Holy Scripture "containeth all things necessary for salvation; and (b) that anything not "read therein, nor. . . proued thereby" is not an article of the Christian faith or requisite for salvation; this confession affirmed that "the holy scriptures are necessary to instruct all men into the way of salvation, and eternal life."[71]

Thus, Locke, when coining the phrase "salvation for its end," was simply distilling into an epigram a widely-held view in English Christianity of his day. Such view also prevailed in English colonies in the New World, and the Philadelphia Confession and its derivatives popularized it among American Baptists.

7. Matter
The New Hampshire Confession was the first Baptist confession to use Locke's wording that Scripture "has. . . truth, without any mixture of error, for its matter," and Southern Baptists' confessions of 1925 and 1963 retained this wording.

The term "matter" appears in the 1677/Philadelphia confession of Particular Baptists, which the New Hampshire Confession's drafters certainly knew. The 1677 confession, borrowing from Presbyterians' Westminster Confession, named eight factors as "arguments whereby it [Scripture] doth abundantly evidence it self to be the Word of God." The first of these is "the heavenliness of the matter." Notwithstanding these eight factors, according to the 1677 confession, "our full perswasion, and assurance of the infallible truth, and divine authority thereof, is from the inward work of the Holy Spirit, bearing witness by and with the Word in our Hearts."[72]

In his letter of 1703, Locke did not explain what he meant by "matter." My impression is that he used it in the sense of English idiom of the time—namely, in the sense of essence or substance, as distinguished from form or other factors. In the 1677 confession's phrase "heavenliness of the matter," "matter'" seems to be different from "'Doctrine," "stile," etc., mentioned in the other seven factors. An example of how Englishmen differentiated "matter" from other qualities appears in the statement of John Smyth in 1607, who inaugurated believer's baptism among Englishmen two years later, that the three requisites of the "true visible church" are "1. True matter, 2. true forme. 3. true properties." "The true matter of a visible church," he said, "are Saints"; the true form is both inward (Spirit, faith, and love) and outward ("a vowe, promise oath, or covenant betwixt God and the Saints"); and the true properties are the powers of self-government.[73]

If Locke's letter of 1703 fails to specify the meaning of "matter," as he used the term, his *The Reasonableness of Christianity, as delivered in the Scriptures* (1695) leaves no confusion about how he approached New Testament epistles in order to extract the truth. He said:

> [T]he epistles are written upon several occasions; and he that will read them as he ought, must observe what it is in them, which is principally aimed at; find what is the argument in hand, and how managed; if he will understand them right, and profit by them. The observing of this will best help us to the true meaning and mind of the writer; for that is the truth which is to be received and believed; and not scattered sentences in scripture-language, accommodated to our notions and prejudices. We must look into the drift of the discourse, observe the coherence and connexion of the parts, and see how it is consistenst with itself and other parts of scripture; if we will conceive it right. We must not cull out, as best suits our system, here and there a period or verse; as if they were all distinct and independent aphorisms; and make these the fundamental articles of the christian faith, and necessary to salvation; unless God has made them so. There be many truths in the bible, which a good christian may be wholly ignorant of, and so not believe . . .[74]

Noting that the epistles went to persons who were already Christians, Locke reasoned that

> every sentence of theirs must not be taken up, and looked on as a fundamental article, necessary to salvation; without an explicit belief whereof, no-body could be a member of Christ's church here, nor admitted into his eternal kingdom hereafter.[75]

Locke distinguished between the truth of Scripture dealing with Jesus Christ, as essential for salvation, on the one hand, and the truths of Scripture or, differ-

342

ently phrased, doctrinal propositions derived from Scripture, on the other hand.[76]

Such a view was not known among Baptists of the seventeenth century. Thomas Collier, leading Baptist in western England for several decades and one whose theology positionized him between Particular and General Baptists, made a distinction in *A General Epistle to the Universal Church of the First-Born* (1652) between the "truth" of Scripture, on the one hand, and letter, word, and circumstance of Scripture on the other hand. He said that Scripture is

> a Declaration of God who is Truth: Not that I minde every letter or circumstance in it, but for the substance of it, as it declares purely the God of Truth, so its without question to me a word of Truth. . . .
>
> I can look upon the Scripture, and see . . . that it is Truth: not that it is any Article of my Faith to believe every word or circumstance there written; but what Truth God hath made known in me, that I must acknowledge.[77]

Five years before Collier wrote, Presbyterians' Westminster Confession had identified the "authentical" Scriptures to be the Old Testament in Hebrew and the New Testament in Greek—"being immediately inspired by God, and by his singular care and providence kept pure in all ages"—to which final appeal must be made.[78] Collier perceived such emphasis to belong to scholars and teachers who contend that "Englishmen never reade the Scripture, because they never reade it in the Original, that is, in Greek and Hebrew." Collier rejected such view and insisted that God's truth comes through the vernacular as well as through Hebrew and Greek texts. "The greatest Scholars," he said, "are as far from seeing the Original Copies of Scriptures, as any English Man."[79]

Baptist writers distinguished between the matter and the words (form) of Scriputre, as exampled by the oft-reprinted *A Complete Body of Doctrinal and Practical Divinity* (1769) of John Gill (1697-1771), perhaps Baptists' most-quoted theologian for almost a century (1750-1850). Gill said:

> Let it be observed, that not the matter of the Scripture only, but the very words in which they are written, are of God. Some who are not for organical inspiration, as they call it, think that the sacred writers were only furnished of God with matter, and had general ideas of things given them, and were left to clothe them with their own words, and to use their own style, which they suppose accounts for the difference of style to be observed in them: but if this was the case, as it sometimes is with men, that they have clear and satisfactory ideas of things in their own minds, and yet are at a loss for proper words to express and convey the sense of them to others; so it might be with the sacred writers, if words were not suggested to them, as well as matter, and then we should be left at an uncertainty about the real sense of the Holy Spirit, if not led into a wrong one; it seems, therefore, most agreeable that words also, as well as matter, were given of divine inspiration; and as for differences of style, as it was easy with God to direct to the use of proper words, so he could accomodate himself to the style such persons were wont

to use, and which was natural to them, and agreeable to their genius and circumstances.[80]

The New Hampshire confession, while setting forth moderate Calvinism,[81] was a reaction to hyper-calvinism, of which Gillism was the best-known expression among Baptists. It is likely, therefore, that the drafters of this confession understood "matter" to mean essence or substance, as distinguished from form or word. In Calvinism, it may be noted, there was a distinction between "matter" and "sign" the former referring to the essence, the later referring to what points to the essence. For example, John Calvin (1509-1564) distinguished between the "matter" and the "sign" of a sacrament and was careful "not [to] transfer to the one what belongs to the other."[82]

The distinction between "matter" and "form" continued into the present century. For example, E. Y. Mullins, whose *The Christian Religion in Its Doctrinal Expression* (1917) was a textbook for several generations of seminary students, said:

> The meaning of theology has often been expressed in terms of its material and its formal principles. By material principle is meant its vital and essential content; by formal principle is meant the form or medium through which the meaning is apprehended. We may say then that as here presented, the material principle of theology is man's fellowship with God as mediated through Jesus Christ. The formal principle is the Scriptures spiritually interpreted.[83]

8. Basis of Judgment

The New Hampshire Confession was the first Baptist confession to state that the Bible "reveals the principles by which God will judge us." However, the concept that the Scripture sets forth the basis of judgment was not new with the New Hampshire Confession. For example, the 1677/Philadelphia confession, with respect to saving obedience, said that

> those things which are necessary to be known, believed, and observed for Salvation, are so clearly propounded, and opened in some place of Scripture or other, that not only the learned, but the unlearned, in a due use of ordinary means, may attain to a sufficient understanding of them.[84]

Thus, one must not only know and believe correctly; one must also obey and observe correctly.

The missionary theology of Andrew Fuller (1754-1815) and William Carey (1761-1834) made much of "obligation." A Christian, according to Fuller, is obligated to share the gospel with non-Christians; when non-Christians hear the gospel, they have an obligation to respond to it. Carey's proposal that Baptists organize a society for foreign missions grew out of his sense of the "obligation" of Christians to use "means" to carry the gospel to non-Christians, called heathens.

The New Hampshire Confession mentions "duty" in several connections— e.g., with respect to accepting salvation's blessings, repentance, and faith.[85]

Hobbs, chairman of the 1962-63 committee, said that the "principle of judgment" runs throughout the Bible—as to individuals, nations, races, etc.[86]

The point is that one has guidance with respect to the basis of judgment which awaits persons. It appears in the Scriptures which reveal "the principles by which God will judge us."

9. Center of Christian Union

The New Hampshire Confession was also the first Baptist confession to state that the Bible "shall remain to the end of the world, the true centre of Christian union." The first third of the nineteenth century witnessed much discussion about united Christians and the basis of such unity. The movement associated with Thomas and Alexander Campbell called for the dissolution of existing denominations and for a new union of Christians based on their interpretation of Scripture. But their interpretation, especially in the 1820s and early-1830s, opposed most of the "means" then being developed among American Christians, especially among Baptists. The same period saw Christians of several denominations working together to accomplish specific ends, perhaps the best known and most successful being the distribution of Bibles through the American Bible Society.

In such context, the New Hampshire Confession stated the *sine quo non* of unified Christian activity—namely, the centrality and authority of Scripture. The Scripture itself, not interpretations of Scripture, is the "true centre" of Christian union.

The spirit captured by the New Hampshire Confession's phraseology was not new. One will find it in the preamble of the 1677 confession. Particular Baptists said that they had "no itch to clog religion with new words," that they could "readily acquiesce in that form of sound words which hath been, in consent with the holy scriptures, used by others before us," and that they could declare "our hearty agreement" with Presbyterians and Congregationalists "in that wholesome protestant doctrine, which, with so clear evidence of scriptures they have asserted." They indicated, however, that where they differed from Presbyterians and Congregationalists, they would express themselves "with all candour and plainness," and affix "texts of scripture in the margin, for the confirmation of each article in our Confession." They expressed the hope that

> the liberty of an ingenuous unfolding our principles and opening our hearts unto our brethren, with the scripture-grounds on which our faith and practice leans, will by none of them be either denied to us, or taken ill from us.[87]

One purpose of the 1677 confession was to show wherein Particular Baptists agreed with Presbyterians (Westminster Confession) and Congregationalists (Savoy Declaration, 1658), or "wherein our faith and doctrine is the same with theirs"; the other was to show wherein Particular Baptists differed from them.[88]

Hobbs said that the Bible "reveals the fellowship which believers have in Christ" and furnishes "the one rallying point" for all of God's people.[89]

Scripture as "the true centre of Christian union" is a necessary corollary of the fundamental Protestant principle that Scripture is the supreme authority in religious matters. If Scripture be such authority, Christians cannot unite on some other basis—such as doctrine, worship, church government, etc.—for, in such event, the other basis would supplant Scripture.

11-13. Supreme Standard

The concept set forth in the statement that the Bible is "the supreme standard by which all human conduct, creeds, and religious opinions should be tried" (1925 and 1963 confessions) is common to Baptist confessions, variously stated.

11. Conduct

"Conduct" refers to behavior or what seventeenth-century English Christians referred to as "conversation." It relates to what a person does, as distinguished from what one cognitively knows or inwardly believes. It pertains to what John Bunyan, in *The Pilgrim's Progress* (1678), referred to as the "practick part" or "soul of religion."

With respect to the two terms "faith and practice'" used by Baptists, "conduct" relates more to "practice" than to "faith." However, "conduct" has a moral dimension which"practice" does not always connote, especially when it focusses on ecclesiology.

12. Creeds

"Creeds" refers to doctrinal formulations. As used in the New Hampshire Confession, it refers to more than the historic creeds like the Apostles' Creed, Nicene Creed, and Athanasian Creed, which General Baptists included in their 1678 confession.[90] As used in the New Hampshire Confession, "creeds" also comprehended confessions of faith.

13. Religious Opinions

Where the New Hampshire Confession said "opinions," the Southern Baptist confessions of 1925 and 1963 said "religious opinions," a term which, as I understand it, includes interpretations, understandings, and views which have not yet attained the status of fixed doctrinal formulations. By inserting the term "religious" before the word "opinions," the Southern Baptist Convention clarified in 1925 that Scriptures' status as a "supreme standard" applies to religious opinions, not to opinions broadly classified. When deliberating the confessional statement in 1925, the Convention defeated, by a vote of 950 ays and 2,013 noes, a motion to affirm, in the article on "fall of Man," that "man came into this world by direct creation of God and not by evolution,"[91] an action subsequently explained to mean that it was not an endorsement of evolution.[92] The Southern Baptist Convention's action of 1925 differs noticeably from the Baptist Bible Union's retention of "opinions" in 1923 and its affirmance of "the Genesis account of creation . . . to be accepted literally, and not allegorically or figuratively."[93] In similar vein, two Landmark Baptist groups later affirmed faith in "[t]he Genesis Account of Creation"[94] and "[t]he biblical account of creation."[95]

The original draft of the 1962-63 committee, sent to seminaries and the Sunday School Board, used the New Hampshire Confession's version, "opinions," not the 1925 confession's version, "religious opinions."[96] My impression is that this was an inadvertent oversight.

The phrase "the supreme standard by which all human conduct, creeds, and religious opinions should be tried" conveys a concept common to Baptist confessions. A General Baptist confession of 1651 rejected any doctrine (creed) not set forth in "the records of God."[97] By the Holy Scriptures, said the Midland Confession of 1655, "we are (in the strength of Christ) to try all things whatsoever are brought to us, under the pretence of truth."[98] According to General Baptists' Standard Confession (1660), "the holy Scriptures is [sic] the rule whereby Saints both in matters of Faith [creed], and conversation [conduct], are to be regulated."[99]

The fullest expression of this idea, basically borrowed from Presbyterians' Westminster confession, appears in the 1677/Philadelphia confession, undoubtedly the most influential Baptist confession in America prior to the Civil War:

> The supream judge by which all controversies of Religion are to be determined, and all Decrees of Councels, opinions of antient Writers, Doctrines of men, and private Spirits, are to be examined, and in whose sentence we are to rest, can be no other but the Holy Scripture delivered by the Spirit, into which Scripture so delivered, our faith is finally resolved.[100]

"Since we have the scriptures" according to General Baptists' confession of 1678, Christians ought not "to depend upon, hearken to, or regard the pretended immediate inspirations, dreams, or prophetical predictions, by or from any person whatsoever, lest we be deluded by them"[101]—a statement consciously reacting to the Quakers' view of "immediate revelation"[102] which surfaced after the Westminster confession appeared. All people, these General Baptists said, should "endeavor to frame their lives, according to the direction of God's word, both in faith and practice"; "no decrees of popes, or councils, or writings of any person whatsoever, are of equal authority with the sacred scriptures."[103]

A homiletical expression of this theme appears in a sermon of 1750:

> The scriptures are the only external guide in matters of religion; they are the way-posts we should look up unto, and take our direction from, and should steer our course accordingly. . . . trial should be made according to the word of God.[104]

Point by point this sermon lists the subjects on which one is to look to Scripture for guidance: Salvation, doctrines, Trinity, Jesus Christ's satifisfaction for man's sins, extent of Christ's death, justification, free-will or free-grace, perseverance, resurrection of the dead and judgment, worship, nature of the church, and the ordinances—all of which pertain to religious matters.

In view of the statements in the prefaces of the 1925 and 1963 confessions that "the sole authority for faith and practice among Baptists is the Scriptures of the Old and New Testaments," it is fitting to show that this is a historic Baptist concept. In the preamble of a confession issued in 1654, General Baptists said that it is " the Scriptures of the Prophets and Apostles that we square our faith and practice by" and called on readers to "[l]et the Scripture . . . be the rule of thy faith and practice."[105] This appeal was an antidote to current Quaker agitation about the "Light within" or "immediate revelation." Particular Baptists' Somerset Confession of 1656 called the Scriptures "a rule and direction unto us both for faith and practice."[106] The 1677/Philadelphia confession[107] and General Baptists Orthodox Creed (1678),[108] borrowing from Presbyterians' Westminster confession, referred to Scripture as "the rule of Faith and Life." When Regular and Separate Baptists in Kentucky united under the Terms of Union (1801), thereafter calling themselves United Baptists, they called the Scriptures "the only rule of faith and practice."[109] The Sandy Creek Association's Articles of Faith (1816) employed the identical phrase.[110] In short, the phrase "faith and practice" is one of the most common expressions in the Baptist idiom.

Southern Baptists' insertion of "religious" before "opinions" was a way to affirm the Bible's authority in religious matters, on which Southern Baptists were in agreement, and to refrain from asserting its authority in other matters, on which Southern Baptists were not in agreement. As Hobbs said, "the Bible is primarily a book of religion," and it "lays no claim to being a textbook of history, literature, philosophy, psychology, or science," even though it "contains true elements of all these and more."[111]

14. Criterion

The 1963 addition that "[t]he criterion by which the Bible is to be interpreted is Jesus Christ" is unique to the 1963 confession. I have run across such language in no other Baptist confession.

However, this Christological emphasis has affinities with some earlier confessional statement. For example, the Helwys group's Declaration of 1611 said that "wee ought to search them [Scriptures] for they testifie off Christ" and to use them "withall reverence, as conteyning the Holie Word off God, which onelie is our direction in al thinges whatsoever."[112] Borrowing from Congregationalists' confession of 1596,[113] seven "baptized" congregations in London said in 1644 that, in the "written Word" ("contained in the Canonicall Scriptures"), God revealed everything "needful for us to know, beleeve and acknowledge, touching the Nature and Office of Christ."[114]

Hobbs regards this criterion-sentence as the "most important change" which the 1962-63 committee made in Article 1. The committee believed that "this added sentence would prove helpful" in "the historicial context of the controversy" involving Elliott's *The Message of Genesis*, especially as it concerned Christ's priesthood "after the order of Melchizedek." Hobbs said:

> God's full, complete revelation of Himself is in Jesus Christ. Any interpretation which is in any way contrary to that revelation is incorrect. The final

word, especially in Christology and redemption, should be as to how an interpretation fits God's revelation in his Son.[115]

Writing about Jesus Christ as the "Criterion of Interpretation," Hobbs said:

> The Bible is the written Word about the living Word. Therefore, any interpretation of a given passage must be made in the light of God's revelation in Jesus Christ and his teachings and redemptive work. Indeed, the Bible is its own best interpreter as one discovers its meaning in any particular in the light of the whole.[116]

The idea of Scripture interpreting Scripture is one long held by Baptists. The 1677/Philadelphia confession said:

> The infallible rule of interpretation of Scripture is the Scripture itself: And therefore when there is a question about the true and full sense of any Scripture (which is not manifold but one) it must be searched by other places that speak more clearly.[117]

As General Baptists' confession of 1678 expressed it, Scripture "is the best interpreter of itself."[118]

The germ of the idea of Jesus Christ as the criterion of interpretation appears in the Convention's Statement of Principles of 1946:

> [T]he one and only authority in faith and practice is the New Testament as the divinely inspired record and interpretation of the supreme revelation of God through Jesus Christ as Redeemer, Saviour and Lord.[119]

As Hobbs has written, Jesus is "the final authority"; "[t]he Bible points forward to Christ, backward to Christ, and again forward to Christ in his glorious return and reign."[120]

The basic meaning of the 1963 criterion-statement is that Jesus Christ is the clue to understanding the Scriptures, for God's ultimate revelation has come through Jesus Christ and the Scriptures are "the record of God's revelation of Himself to man." Therefore, the central truth derived from Scripture by interpretation is that God supremely revealed Himself in Jesus Christ

Conclusion

As the foregoing has demonstrated, I trust, the language appearing in Article I of Southern Baptist' confession of 1963 largely derives from the New Hampshire Confession (1833), supplemented by a major clarification in 1925 ("religious opinions") and by two major additions in 1963: "the record of God's revelation of Himself to man" and "[t]he criterion by which the Bible is to be interpreted is Jesus Christ." But the concepts conveyed by this language have been common in the English-American Baptist tradition since the seventeenth century.

349

In 1981 the Southern Baptist Convention adopted a motion introduced by Hobbs, affirming that

> we reaffirm our historic baptist position that the Holy Bible which has truth without any mixture of error for its matter, is our adequate rule of faith and practice and that we reaffirm our belief in "the Baptist Faith and Message" adopted in 1963, including all seventeen articles, plus the preamble which protects the conscience of the individual and guards us from a creedal faith.[121]

Explaining his motion, Hobbs made a statement, written into the record at the request of Adrian Rogers, pastor, Bellevue Baptist Church, Memphis, Tennessee, that his motion was designed "to emphasize that the preamble is as much a part of the statement voted by the Convention as any other part" and that the confession "*shall* serve as information to the churches and *may*— notice the difference—not shall, *may* serve as guidelines for agencies of the Convention."[122] With respect to the phrase "truth without any mixture of error for its matter," he said that all Scripture is "God-breathed" and that "a God of truth does not breathe error."[123] In 1985 the Convention defeated a motion to amend the 1963 confession "by removing the words 'mixture of'" from Article I, a motion against which Hobbs spoke.[124] There has been no change in the 1963 confession since its adoption almost a quarter century ago.

Notes

1. See Southern Baptist Convention, Annual, 1963, items 112-124, p. 63, for the legislative history, and pp. 269-281, for the special committee's report including the texts of the 1925 and 1963 confessions in parallel columns. Hereinafter SBC Annual.

2. William L. Lumpkin (ed.), *Baptist Confessions of Faith* (Philadelphia: The Judson Press, 1959; rev. ed., 1969), contains numerous Baptist confessions of faith. I will cite article numbers in parentheses to aid in locating.

3. SBC, Annual, 1963, p. 270; Lumpkin, *Confessions* (rev. ed.), p. 393.

4. SBC, Annual, 1963, p. 278; Lumpkin, *Confessions* (rev. ed.), p. 398.

5. SBC, Annual, 1957, items 17-24, pp. 45-47, 408-417.

6. Herschel H. Hobbs, *The Baptist Faith and Message* (Nashivlle, Tenn.: Convention Press, 1971), p. 14. Hereinafter Hobbs, *BFM*.

7. SBC, Annual, 1962, item 44, p. 64.

8. Letter, Herschel H. Hobbs to Dotson M. Nelson, Jr., Birmingham, Ala., July 26, 1962, in Historical Commission (SBC), Baptist Faith and Message Committee Files 1962-1963, No. 115. Hereinafter cited as Comm. Files, followed by number of item. These records are availabile on microfilm as the Historical Commission's Publication No. 1991.

I have gone through these records which consist largely of correspondence. There are minutes of some meetings of the comittee (Nos. 243 and 404), but they do not provide information about comitteemen's discussion of specific articles.

9. SBC, Annual, 1962, items 57, 83, 84, 86, pp. 65, 68; emphasis in motion.

10. *Ibid.*, items 84 and 86, p. 68.

11. *Ibid.*, item 60, p. 65.

12. *Ibid.*, item 91, p. 69.

13. *Ibid.*, item 109, p. 71.

14. *Ibid.*, item 126, p. 73. The Board later decided not to reprint the book.

15. Comm. Files, Nos. 84, 85, 89, 199, 200, 202, 203, 211, 231, 234-239, 243, 283, 310, 317, 320, 326, 330, 350, 351, 404.

16. SBC, Annual, 1963, pp. 269-270. Answering a letter in Fall 1962, Hobbs said that any changes in the 1925 statement "will not be toward liberalism" and that "the tone of the thinking of the brethren" is conservative (Hobbs to W. Marion Lewter, Waynesboro, Tenn., October 5, 1962; Comm. Files, No. 194). Answering another letter in early-1963, Hobbs said that "the recommended statement is not a change in the theology of the 1925 Statement" (Hobbs to Reverend Wayland Boyd, First Baptist Church, Eunice, New Mexico, February 15, 1963; Comm. Files, No. 333).

17. SBC, Annual, 1963, items 113, p. 63.

18. *Ibid.*, item 114, p. 63.

19. *Ibid.*, item 115, p. 63; see text of article, p. 275.

20. *Ibid.*, item 159, p. 67.

21. *Ibid.*, item 161, p. 68. In a pre-convention article entitled "Kansas City—A Prospectus," Hobbs listed "nine points of agreement reached by the trustees of Midwestern Seminary: e. g. the historical-critical approach in Bible research; the possibility of varying conclusions in such study; the balance between academic freedom and academic responsibility" as one of the five developments between the 1962 and 1963 annual meetings which he classified as "progress" (Comm. Files, No. 335, pp. 3-4).

22. Lumpkin, *Confessions,* pp. 361-362.

23. Comm. Files, No. 203, p. 5.

24. Letter, Herschel H. Hobbs to Hugh Wamble, February 20, 1987, p. 1. This letter is in my possession. I forwarded a copy to the Historical Commission to file with Comm. Files.

25. Hobbs, *BFM,* p. iv.

26. Lumpkin, *Confessions,* pp. 102 (art. 1) 107 (art. 27); 122 (art. 23); 125, 135-136 (cf. arts. 4, 60, 61, 63, 68); 158 (art. 7); 192; 198 (art. 3); 207 (art. 18); 232 (art. 23); 248-252 (ch. 1); 324-325 (art. 37); 358 (art. 2); 359 (art. 1).

27. *Ibid.*, p. 355 (art. 2).

28. *Ibid.*, p. 343 (arts. 2 and 5).

29. *Ibid.*, pp. 361-362 (art. 1).

30. For example, see *ibid.*, pp. 109 (art. 27); 135-136 (arts. 60, 61, 63, 68); 158 (art. 7); 232 (art. 23).

31. *Ibid.*, p. 182 (art. 46).

32. *Ibid.*, p. 198 (art. 3).

33. *Ibid.*, p. 207 (art. 18).

34. *Ibid.*, p. 249 (art. 1.2).

35. *Ibid.*, p. 326 (art. 37).

36. Quoted in Heinrich L. S. Heppe, *Reformed Dogmatics,* trans. G. T. Thomson (London: Allen & Unwin, 1950), p. 17.

37. Quoted in *ibid.*, p. 19.

38. Quoted in *ibid.*, p. 19.

39. Lumpkin, *Confessions,* p. 361 (art. 1).

40. *Ibid.*, p. 385 (art. 1).

41. *Ibid.*, p. 378 (art. 1).

42. *Ibid.*, p. 380 (art. 2).

43. *Ibid.*, p. 182 (art. 46).

44. See text of ch. 1.1, in Philip Schaff (ed.), *The Creeds of Christendon (3 vols., New York: Harper & Brothers, c. 1919), 3:601-602.

45. Lumpkin, *Confessions*, pp. 248-249 (ch. 1.1).

46. SBC, Annual, 1946, item 27, p. 38.

47. Edgar Young Mullins, *The Christian Religion in Its Doctrinal Expression* (Nashville,Tenn.: Broadman Press, 1917), p. 142.

48. See Herschel H. Hobbs, *Fundamentals of Our Faith* (Nashville, Tenn.: Broadman Press, 1960), p. 8; Herschel H. Hobbs, *What Baptists Believe* (Nashville, Tenn.: Broadman Press, 1964), p. 63.

49. See Hobbs, *BFM*, pp. 8-9.

50. Comm. Files, No. 330, p. 1.

51. Hobbs to Wamble, February 20, 1987, p. 2.

52. Lumpkin, *Confessions*, p. 122 (art. 23).

53. *Ibid.*, p. 250 (ch. 1.5).

54. Hobbs to Wamble, February 20, 1987, p. 2.

55. Lumpkin, *Confessions*, pp. 361-362 (art. 1).

56. Henry S. Burrage, *A History of the Baptists of New England* (Philadelphia: American Baptist Publication Society, 1894), p. 286.

57. Leter, Locke to Richard King, August 25, 1703, in *The Words of John Locke, in Ten Volumes* (11th ed., London: W. Otridge and Son, 1812), 10:306; emphasis added.

58. See *ibid.*, 10:305-309, for the entire letter.

59. Lumpkin, *Confessions*, p. 250 (ch. 1.4).

60. *Ibid.*, p. 325 (art. 37).

61. *Ibid.*, p. 355 (art. 2).

62. Schaff, *Creeds*, 3:489 (art. 6).

63. *Ibid.*, 3:603 (ch. 1.6).

64. *Ibid.*, 3:604 (ch. 1.7).

65. Lumpkin, *Confessions*, p. 250 (ch. 1.6).

66. See William J. McGlothlin (ed.), *Baptist Confessions of Faith* (Philadelphia: American Baptist Publication Society, 1911), pp. 274-289, for the confession's lengthy appendix on believer's baptism.

67. Lumpkin, *Confessions*, p. 248 (ch. 1.1); emphasis added.

68. *Ibid.*, pp. 251-252 (ch. 1.9).

69. *Ibid.*, p. 198 (art. 3).

70. *Ibid.*, p. 232 (art. 23).

71. *Ibid.*, p. 325 (art. 37).

72. *Ibid.*, p. 250 (ch. 1.5).

73. John Smyth, *Principles and inferences concerning the visible Church* (1607), in W. T. Whitley (ed.), *The Words of John Smyth* (2 vols., Cambridge: At the University Press, 1915), 1:253-254.

74. Locke's *Works*, 7:152.

75. *Ibid.*, 7:155.

76. See *ibid.*, 7:152-156, for Locke's full discussion of this matter.

77. Quoted in H. Leon McBeth, *The Baptist Heritage* (Nashivlle, Tenn.: Broadman Press, 1987), p. 72.

78. Schaff, *Creeds*, 3:604-605 (ch. 1.8).

79. Quoted in McBeth, *Heritage*, p. 72.

80. John Gill, *A Complete Body of Doctrinal and Practical Divinity* (1769) (new ed., 2 vols. London: Thomas Tegg. 1839), 1:17-18; see John Gill, *The Word and*

Works of God (New York: Edward H. Fletcher, 1857), pp. 62-63, for a similar statement.

81. Lumpkin, *Confessions,* p. 360.

82. John Calvin, *Institutes of the Christian Religion* (1559 ed.), 4.15.15, in *The Library of Christian Classics,* ed. by John T. McNeill (26 vols., Philadelphia: The Westminster Press, 1960), 21:1290.

83. Mullins, *Christian Religion,* p. 28.

84. Lumpkin, *Confessions,* p. 251 (ch. 1.7).

85. *Ibid.,* p. 364 (art. 8).

86. Hobbs, *BFM,* pp. 26-27; cf. Hobbs, *Fundamentals,* pp. 7-8.

87. Lumpkin, *Confessions,* p. 246. See pp. 244-248 for the lengthy preamble in which Particular Baptists explained their approach and spirit.

88. *Ibid.,* pp. 245-246.

89. Hobbs, *BFM,* p. 27.

90. Lumpkin, *Confessions,* pp. 326-327 (art. 38).

91. SBC, Annual, 1925, item 53, p. 76.

92. *Ibid.,* item 77, p. 87.

93. Lumpkin, *Confessions,* p. 386 (art. 5).

94. *Ibid.,* p. 378 (art. 2).

95. *Ibid.,* p. 380 (art. 3).

96. Comm. Files, No. 203, p. 1.

97. Lumpkin, *Confessions,* p. 182 (art. 46).

98. *Ibid.,* p. 198 (art. 3).

99. *Ibid.,* p. 232 (art. 23).

100. *Ibid.,* p. 252 (ch. 1.10). See Schaff, *Creeds,* 3:605-606, for ch. 1.10 of the Westminster Confession.

101. Lumpkin, *Confessions,* p., 325 (art. 37).

102. See Robert Barclay, *Apology* (1676), Prop. 2, in Schaff, *Creeds,* 3:790-791, for a confession-like statement of the Quaker view.

103. Lumpkin, *Confessions,* p. 325 (art. 37).

104. *The Scripture the Only Guide in Matters of Religion, Being a Sermon Preached at the Baptism of Several Persons in Barbican,* November 2, 1750 (Wilmington: Bonsal & Niles, 1803), in *Sermons on Various Occasions by several Eminent Divines* (Philadelphia, 1817). This volume is in the library of Southern Baptist Theological Seminary, Louisville, Kentucky. The Barbican church was in London.

105. Lumpkin, *Confessions,* p. 191 (preamble).

106. *Ibid.,* p. 207 (art. 18).

107. *Ibid.,* p. 249 (ch. 1.2).

108. *Ibid.,* p. 326 (art. 37).

109. *Ibid.,* p. 359 (art. 1).

110. *Ibid.,* p. 358 (art. 2).

111. Hobbs. *BFM,* p. 26; cf. Hobbs, *Fundamentals,* pp. 6-7.

112. Lumpkin, *Confessions,* p. 122 (art. 23).

113. *Ibid.,* p. 84 (arts. 7-8).

114. *Ibid.,* p. 158 (arts. 7-8).

115. Letter, Hobbs to Wamble, February 20, 1987, pp. 3-4.

116. Hobbs, *BFM,* p. 30.

117. Lumpkin, *Confessions,* pp. 251-252 (ch. 1.9).

118. *Ibid.,* p. 325 (art. 37).

119. SBC, Annual, 1946, item 27, p. 88.

120. Hobbs, *BFM*, pp. 25-26.

121. SBC, Annual, 1981, items 51 and 118, pp. 35, 45.

122. *Ibid.*, item, p. 45.

123. *Ibid.*

124. SBC, Annual, 1985, items 146 and 253, pp. 73, 87. The motion said "Article 2."

18

THE RELATIONSHIP OF THE BIBLE TO NATURAL SCIENCE

by J. Kenneth Eakins

Since most of you who hear or read this paper do not know me, I believe it is appropriate to share with you some of my personal background that is relevant to the topic under consideration.

I completed undergraduate studies at Wheaton, a major Christian school, which is a highly-respected college in Illinois. My major there was General Science (pre-med), with extensive studies in chemistry, physics, and zoology. Following this, I earned an M.D. degree from the University of Illinois College of Medicine, in Chicago, and then spent four years in internship and residency programs in Ohio. I am a diplomate of the American Board of Pediatrics, and served as a pediatrician for two years in the Army, stationed at Redstone Arsenal in Huntsville, Alabama. Later, while engaged in the private practice of pediatrics in Thomasville, Georgia, the Lord called me into the Christian ministry. Since 1977, I have been the osteologist (bone specialist) for the Joint Archaeological Expedition to Tell el-Hesi, Israel, and have been responsible for the excavation and study of a large Bedouin cemetery located at the site. For many years, my chief hobby has been astronomy.

These items in the scientific area have been recorded as much to reveal my limitations as to suggest any qualifications. I do not claim real expertise in any field of science outside of two small areas: ambulatory pediatrics, which I continue to practice in a limited way at a hospital in California, and osteology, restricted to the recent historical period. I have, however, tried to remain generally knowledgeable in a wide range of scientific disciplines—a task made difficult because of the rapidity of change occurring in all areas of scientific knowledge.

My biblical and theological studies began at Wheaton, but developed seriously at the Southern Baptist Theological Seminary in Kentucky, beginning in 1963, when I was called into the ministry. I earned the B.D. and Ph.D. degrees, at Southern Seminary, majoring in Old Testament studies. Since 1970, I have taught archaeology and Old Testament at Golden Gate Baptist Theological Seminary in California.

It may also be good to relate some of my basic convictions, which do, of course, help shape my remarks. I am a Southern Baptist—taught, converted, baptized, nurtured, and married in a Southern Baptist Church in Missouri, and licensed to preach and ordained by a Southern Baptist Church in Georgia. I have served two Southern Baptist congregations in Kentucky, one as pastor and the other as minister of education. Currently, I teach a Sunday School class in a Southern Baptist Church in California and, as previously noted, teach at Golden Gate, a Southern Baptist Seminary.

It is my conviction that the entire Bible is the inspired word of God and that its message is wholly true. I fully concur with the summary of beliefs commonly held by Southern Baptists contained in the *Baptist Faith and Message*. It is also my conviction that God reveals Himself in the natural world, and that certain categories of truth are appropriate for scientific inquiry. I reject the idea that truth revealed in the Bible and truth discovered through scientific methodology can be in conflict. Truth is truth, whether discovered by a pastor in the study, a layperson at prayer, or a scientist in the laboratory. The potential for conflict arises whenever error is embraced as truth, whether as Christian dogma or scientific pronouncement. God's revelation is true, both in the Bible and in the natural order. Human beings, however, are often fallible in their apprehension and interpretation of the truth.

The question of the relationship between the Bible and natural science has been a topic of interest, and sometimes bitter debate, for many years. Challenges posed long ago to traditional beliefs about the nature of the physical universe by persons such as Copernicus (1473-1543) and Galileo (1564-1642), and to cherished views in the biological realm by men such as Darwin (1809-1882), have continued at an accelerated rate into modern times. Emotions have often run high, and the Church at times took positions that could not be sustained. For example, the banning of Copernicus' book, *Concerning the Revolution of Celestial Spheres,* did not prevent the earth from making its annual trip around the sun. Galileo, who supported the theory of Copernicus, was branded as a heretic by the Inquisition and lived his last several years under house arrest. Not until 1980 did the Roman Catholic Church officially begin to take action to reverse the unjust verdict reached against Galileo about 350 years earlier, although the validity of his views had long been acknowledged.

The purpose of this seminar is the explore briefly, in a rational and dispassionate manner, a few of the major issues that are of concern to the Christian as he or she attempts to understand, and evaluate in the light of the biblical revelation, the plethora of new information being disseminated by scientists at work in the numerous branches of natural science. Many topics will have to be omitted, and none can be discussed in detail. It will be helpful to note different positions taken, particularly by those persons who hold the trustworthiness of Scripture in high regard. I will quote from and refer to many works written by evangelicial scholars of the past and present. Perhaps some of the parameters appropriate for Christian belief in dialogue with current, and sometimes frightening, scientific thought can be traced. An attempt will be made throughout to use non-technical language whenever possible. Quotations of Scripture are from the *New American Standard Bible.*

Discerning and Expressing Truth

Theological truth is revealed truth. We could know nothing about God unless He chose to reveal Himself. In many ways, however, including through nature, through history—especially as interpreted by the prophets—through the still small voice speaking to the receptive heart, and supremely through Jesus Christ, God has revealed Himself and His truth. Such subjective truth is not open to the usual methods of empirical verification—it cannot be "proved." But the Christian knows that the truth he or she has apprehended, or that has apprehended him or her, is nevertheless certain.

For example, I cannot prove objectively that it was God who spoke to me as I prayed to Him beneath the Live Oak trees in that beautiful park in Georgia and sought His will concerning closing my medical practice and going to seminary. The voice was inward, heard by no human ear, but nevertheless it was definitely the voice of God to me. Twenty-four years later I am even more certain about this, and countless numbers of Christians will understand because they, too, know the absolute certainty of God's presence in their lives. The Christian must always reject the kind of strict empiricism that insists one can know nothing unless it can be discerned by the senses, unless it can be "proved."

A major way that God has chosen to reveal Himself is through the Bible. The Bible not only records God's revelation to persons in the past, it continues to be our major source of revelation today. Its religious teachings, the major tehological themes it develops, are precise and clear and authoritative. The Holy Spirit helps us in our study of the Bible so that we can understand more fully the truth that God seeks to communicate.

The Bible is not, however, as all will agree, a science book. One should not turn to the Bible as a textbook for the study of physics or biology. Nor should students learn their science at church, although this sometimes happens, as a professor of geology at Wheaton College recently lamented.[1] The Bible is simply silent about most items of science.

Christians have often noted that statements in the Bible about the natural order are frequently observational in nature and do not claim to be otherwise. Absolute precision was not intended in many cases. In Article XIII of *The Chicago Statement on Biblical Inerrancy,* formulated in 1978 by leading evangelical Christians, one reads "We further deny that inerrancy is negated by biblical phenomena such as a *lack of modern technical precision,* irregularities of grammar or spelling, *observational descriptions of nature. . . .*[2]

When Jesus, as related in Mark 4:31, spoke of the mustard seed as the smallest seed on earth, He was speaking in observational terms. The mustard seed was the smallest seed the disciples had seen. The fact that smaller seeds do exist does not convict the Bible of error. Mark 4:30-32 is a parable, not a botany lesson. The prophet, in Isaiah 40:15, was quite correct in noting that dust on a scales was entirely inconsequential. Certainly the balances of that time would not have been affected by its presence. The fact that some delicate balances today might be renedered inaccurate by dust does not indicate that the prophet was mistaken. Isaiah 40:12-20 is an outpouring of praise to an incomparable God, not a statement about precision scientific tools.

There are, however, as we shall see, some very important statements in the Bible about the natural order which *are* quite definite and universally true. The Christian cannot surrender these realities to any scientific theory.

The scientific approach to truth is different from that employed by the theologian. The scientific method is not easy to define, but the general components are clear. The first step is frequently an *observation* of some pheomenon in nature. The scientist reflects upon what has been detected by the senses and constructs an *hypothesis* that might explain what has been observed. The hypothesis is then tested by additional observations and, if possible, by experimentation. If the hypothesis appears to be supported by this investigation, it may come to be regarded as a *theory*. A theory is subject to continued scrutiny over a long period of time and by many investigators. Refinements and modifications are usually made. The accumulation of evidence may necessitate a theory being abandoned, or it may lead to a general acceptance of the theory. In some cases a theory may gain the status of a natural *law;* for example, the law of gravity.

Central to the scientific method is a willingness to consider new data and to modify or abandon a view if indicated. The work of a scientist is never finished. Even the most secure concepts are always subject to revision. In general, scientists have done a good job in detecting and correcting their mistakes.

In theory, the scientific method precludes metaphysical speculation. In reality, scientists have historically succumbed to the temptation to venture outside the limits imposed by their method. A recent article in *Astronomy* by Tony Rothman and George Ellis is entitled "Has Cosmology Become Metaphysical?" The article closes with the statement ". . . there can also be no argument that cosmology is approaching the frontier when science is no longer based on experimental evidence and makes no testable predictions. Once this border is crossed, we have left the world of physics behind and have entered the realm of metaphysics."[3] Although it is an over-simplification, the questions of *how* and *when* the universe was created have always been considered appropriate for scientific study, but questions concerning *who* created the universe and *why,* have been reserved for theological and philosophical discussion. These boundaries, never absolute, are now even less distinct.

Cosmology—the Heavens and the Earth

"The Cosmos is all that is or ever was or ever will be."[4] This is the opening statement in *Cosmos,* a book which has become a best-seller, by astronomer Carl Sagan. A Christian who takes the Bible seriously must dissent. A parameter has been reached which cannot be crossed without departing from the clear teaching of the Bible, beginning with the statement in Genesis 1:1, "In the beginning God created the heavens and the earth," and reaffirmed in numerous other portions of Scripture. God was before the cosmos and He created the cosmos. He alone is the One "who is and who was and who is to come, the Almighty."[5] The Bible makes no provision for dualism, much less for the existence of matter before God, or in place of God.

The Origin of the Universe

The most widely accepted scientific theory of the origin of the universe today is the Big Bang theory (sometimes referred to as the "cosmic singularity" view), which won out over the competing Steady State theory some years ago. According to the Big Bang theory, at the beginning of time the entire universe was packed toether in an infinitely small space. An explosion occurred which resulted in the matter and energy content of the universe being dispersed rapidly and uniformly in all directions. Scientific observation indicates that this process is still going on and that we live in a rapidly expanding universe. Eventually, hot gasses and dust condensed to form such bodies as the stars and smaller objects, including planets and moons.

According to some scientists, the universe is actually in a perpetual state of oscillation. The present expansion, they say, will eventually slow down and stop due to gravitational force, which will then pull the constituents of the universe back together into another super-dense state, which will be followed by a new explosion, and the process will begin all over once more. Present evidence, however, suggests to most scientists that there is not enough matter in the universe for the force of gravity to prevent the present expansion from continuing forever.

Scientists recognize that the Big Bang model is imperfect and is associated with a number of problems. Thought is now being given to a modificiation of this theory, and an "Inflation" model has been proposed. A good discussion of this is contained in the article by Rothman and Ellis, referred to earlier, and also in an article by David H. Smith, "The Inflationary Universe Lives?" in *Sky and Telescope*.[6]

A number of new and daring speculations about the origin of the universe are now current. Many of these grow out of the study of quantum mechanics, a branch of physics which concentrates on the investigation of subatomic particles. For example, one reads about the possibility of the creation of matter *ex nihilo* (out of nothing) through purely natural processes,[7] the likelihood of multiple universes,[8] the suggestion that human beings actually create the universe,[9] and the apparent disorder of the universe at the sub-atomic level.[10]

How should the Christian react? What are the parameters? For one thing, we can concur that creation was *ex nihilo*. We can also admit that *we do not know how* the universe began. We can listen with interest to any new theory. But we must deny that the universe came into being by chance or through any impersonal law of physics. The Bible teaches that God is the creator of the cosmos. We must affirm not only Genesis 1:1, but also John 1:1-3, "In the beginning was the Word, and the Word was with God, and the Word was God. He was in the beginning with God. All things came into being through Him; and apart from Him nothing came into being that has come into being." We also, I believe, can confidently expect that future discoveries will indicate that the order observed in the universe, a predictability that scientists especially must depend on in their work, extends into the subatomic realm.

The Age of the Universe

Scientists commonly agree that the age of the universe is about 13 to 20 billion years and that the solar system, including the earth, is about 3.5 to 5.0 billions years old. The evidence comes from a number of different sources, including astronomy, chemistry, geology, and physics. General concurrence regarding this matter, derived from different avenues of investigation, compels the Christian to take seriously the claim that we live in an ancient universe. But is this compatible with the teaching of the Bible? Some do not believe it is and hold to a belief that the earth is no more than about 10,000 years old.[11] They can cite evidence to support their claim, and their viewpoint should be respected. I suspect most Christians, however, doubt that the Bible denies the great antiquity of the earth.

It is certainly true that the Bible no where says when the heavens and the earth were created. "In the beginning" is undated. At one time, in certain Christian circles, it was common to believe that a gap, long enough to accommodate any length of time, existed between Genesis 1:1 and 1:2. This view is less widely held today.

Many Christians believe that the "days" in Genesis 1 should be understood as long periods of time. I cannot examine here the numerous components of this view, with its several variations, but good discussions of the concept can be found in Bernard Ramm's *The Christian View of Science and Scripture*[12] and in Gleason Archer's *A Survey of Old Testament Introduction*.[13] Archer is one of many conservative Christian scholars who believes that a "day" (Hebrew *yom*) most likely represents a long period, a stage, in the process of creation. Ramm at one time held to this "age-day" theory, but later rejected it in favor of the idea that the days were *revelatory* days. According to this concept, God created the universe over a long period, but He revealed the account of His creative activity in six 24-hour days.

Many scholars, however, continue to argue that the "days" in Genesis 1 are 24-hour days. An example is H. C. Leupold, as can be seen by referring to his commentary on Genesis.[14]

Although any view that one may take about the length of time present in Genesis 1 has associated difficulties, it appears that one can accept a long period without being outside the parameter of orthodox Christian faith. An editorial in a 1982 issue of *Christianity Today* states, "even the most loyal defenders of biblical inerrancy can find no hard data pinpointing the chronology of 'in the beginning'. It is important that we refrain from going beyond what the text demands. We cannot set dates for creation on the basis of the biblical data."[15] In an earlier issue of *Christianity Today,* an editorial says, "the creation scientists who defend a recent earth may well be carrying on the battle at too broad a front. It is not essential to firm commitment to an infallible or inerrant Bible that one must also deny the validity of the entire geological timetable. Or insist that the universe is of recent origin."[16]

The Nature of the Universe

The ancient psalmist looked at the night sky, undimmed by the light pollution that plagues an observer today, and was moved to say, "When I consider Thy heavens, the work of Thy fingers, The moon and the stars, which Thou has ordained; What is man, that Thou doest take thought of him? And the son of man, that Thou doest care for him?"[17]

How much greater should be our awe today! The psalmist could see only

5,000-6,000 stars. We now know that there are billions of stars in our own galaxy, the Milky Way, and that there are billions of other galaxies. We also are informed that our own star, the sun, is a rather average star and is located out toward the edge of our galaxy.

The size of the universe is almost beyond comprehension. But Christians have adjusted, not always easily, to its vastness and to the apparent insignificance of our location in space. We know that the earth is a sphere and that it does indeed, as Copernicus believed, carry us in orbit around the sun. We also can turn from our telescopes and spectrographs and look the other way, through light microscopes, electron microscopes, and theories of atomic and sub-atomic physics, and discover a complexity and a vastness that defies our imagination.

Persons in an earlier period, including those whom God chose and inspired to write the Bible, did not have telescopes and microscopes. They described the world as they observed it to be through their own eyes. God did not reveal the marvels of modern science to His chosen authors. But there is nothing in the Bible that demands a belief in a flat earth, or a solar system with the earth at its center, or a small universe.

The Bible does clearly teach, however, that God not only created the universe, but that He also continues to be closely associated with His creation. He sustains that which He made. Behind the natural laws that govern the complex mechanisms, both macroscopic and microscopic, of this universe is the omniscience and omnipotence of a personal being, Almighty God, who became incarnate in Jesus Christ. Thus we read in Colossians 1:15-17 "And He is the image of the invisible God, the first-born of all creation. For in Him all things were created, both in the heavens and on earth, visible and invisible, whether thrones or dominions or rulers or authorities—all things have been created through Him and for Him. And He is before all things, and in Him all things hold together."

People have always been impressed by the orderly character of the observable universe. Its workings are precise and predictable. For example, astronomers tell us far in advance about an eclipse of the moon or of the sun, and it occurs right on schedule. Much of scientific theory and method depends upon the reliability of nature. Building upon this, a British geolgoist, Charles Lyell (1797-1875), advanced the theory of *uniformitarianism*. By this, he meant that geological and meteorological processes affecting the surface of the earth today operated in a similar, uniform manner throughout the past. Geologists today still accept this principle, though they do recognize that catastrophic and unpredictable events, such as vulcanic eruptions, earthquakes, and floods do occur and may have profound consequences.

Christians have often stressed the role of *catastrophe* in the history of the earth, primarily in terms of the great flood described in Genesis 6-8. Although some Christians believe that the deluge can be understood as a symbol of God's judgment, without the need for belief in a literal flood of water, most of us have not understood it in that way.

One science writer has said "the Great Deluge is the Grand Delusion of creationism, an albatross hung about their necks by the ancient Hebrew scribes who adapted an already-ancient Middle Eastern Flood myth and recorded it in Genesis."[18] This verdict must be rejected. It is true that there are Mesopotamian flood stories more ancient than the Genesis account and that these stories are, in some ways, very similar to what one reads in the Bible. There are also significant differences between these Mesopotamian flood traditions and what one reads in Scripture. A logical position is to recognize that each reflects memory of an ancient event. In one case, the memory, distorted at many points, is enshrined in Sumerian and Babylonian mythology. In the other case, the memory has been preserved under the care of God and written by God's inspired author. The Great Flood is not a Grand Delusion; it is the story of a Great Tragedy.

There is a difference of opinion, however, among conservative Christians about the extent, and to some degree the date, of the Genesis flood. Joseph P. Free has written, "There are two main views among fundamentalists as to the area covered by the flood: 1. It covered the inhabited earth, that is, Mesopotamia, and perhaps some of the surrounding lands, but not the whole earth. . . . 2. The flood covered the *entire* earth."[19] Many, like Free, believe that the Biblical account definitely describes a universal, world-wide deluge.[20] Others believe that an extensive, but local flood, involving all humankind, or, according to some, only the line of Seth, was more likely.[21]

A conservative scholar, Edward J. Young, has written, "The acount of the flood is told in terms of universality. This does not necessarily mean that the flood covered the entire face of the globe. Rather, it was universal in that it destroyed all flesh. If the habitations of mankind were limited to the Euphrates valley, it is quite possible that the flood was also limited."[22]

Whichever view one accepts has its own set of problems, involving anthropology, geology, biblical interpretation, language, and common sense. This is an issue over which Christians should exercise tolerance toward one another. I recommend reading the relevant portions of the books by Archer and Ramm, referred to earlier, for a good discussion of the problem.

The Fate of the Universe

A recent and excellent scientific textbook on astronomy concludes a section dealing with the fate of the universe with the words of Mark Twain, found in *Life on the Mississippi*, "There is something fascinating about science. One gets such a wholesale return of conjecture out of such a trifling investment of fact."[23] Scientists differ on how they believe the universe will end, or what state it will exist in if it lasts forever. Most acknowledge that present data and theory do not provide an adequate basis for any firm conclusions. There are more questions than answers. As scientists probe further and further toward either the origin of the universe or its ultimate fate, they reach a boundary beyond which speculation becomes metaphysical in nature.

Christians recognize that the Bible is relatively silent concerning the End Time. As Section X of *The Baptist Faith and Message* puts it, "God, in His own time and in His own way, will bring the world to its appropriate end." Whatever may happen, Christians confidently await the fulfillment of John's vision, "And I saw a new heaven and a new earth; for the first heaven and the first earth passed away, and there is no longer any sea."[24]

The Phenomenon of Life

The world teems with life—in the air, on the land, and in the sea. The microscope reveals a myriad of life forms unknown to the ancients. To this point life has been detected only on the earth, but many scientists confidently expect to find life, even intelligent life, many places in the universe. While this may occur, and I believe there is nothing in the Bible to deny its possibility, my hunch is that life, particularly intelligent life, is limited to this planet.

How did life begin? Scientists believe that it began in the primeval sea, called an "acquatic Garden of Eden," by one writer.[25] Atoms and molecules in the warm water are said to have joined together to form progressively more complex compounds, including amino acids, basic building blocks of physical life. Eventually, through ways not fully defined, self-reproducing cells developed, and primitive plant and animal life emerged. Many, but not all scientists, believe this happened through purely natural chemical and physical processes.

Life forms, we are told, became more and more complex, and certain types eventually left the sea and established themselves on land. Fossils of marine plants and animals become abundant in strata dating to about 600 million years ago. Land forms, first plant and then animal, are abundant in fossils dating from 400 to 250 million years ago.

According to present scientific thought, complex life forms progressively emerged from simpler forms. This is not the place to discuss the details of current evolutionary concepts, but these can be found in almost any college textbook of biology. A book entitled *Humankind Emerging*, edited by Bernard G. Campbell, presents a lucid view of human evolution as commonly understood by many scientists.[26] It is probably correct to say that most scientists now consider evolution to be a fact. They use the word "theory" only to describe various ideas about the mechanisms of the process.

How should a Christian respond? First of all, it is obvious that we must deny any concept of evolution which teaches that life originated and evolved apart from the active will and action of God. Just as He created the physical universe, so He created life. The One who is Life is the source of all life. To believe otherwise would place one outside the parameter of orthodox belief drawn from Genesis 1-2 and other portions of the Bible. Also, one cannot accept any type of evolutionary scheme that would deny such basic Biblical themes as the special nature of human life created in the image of God, the sin of all persons and the need for redemption.

On the other hand, many persons, including some conservative scholars, have noted that the story of creation in Genesis 1 could fit roughly into an evolutionary pattern. George F. Wright wrote in Volume IV of *The Fundamentals*, published by The Bible Institute of Los Angeles, in 1917, that "the word evolution is in itself innocent enough, and has a large range of legitimate use. The Bible, indeed, teaches a system of evolution. The world was not made in an instant, or even in one day (whatever period day may signify) but in six days. Throughout the whole process there was an orderly progress from lower to higher forms of matter and life. In short there is an established *order* in all the Creator's work."[27]

James Orr wrote in his book *The Christian View of God and the World,* "On the general hypothesis of evolution, as applied to the organic world, I have nothing to say, except that, within certain limits, it seems to me extremely probable, and supported by a large body of evidence. This, however, only refers to the fact of a genetic relationship of some kind between the different species of plants and animals, and does not affect the means by which this development may be supposed to be brought about."[28]

The respected conservative scholar, Benjamin Warfield, believed that evolution "cannot act as a substitute for creation, but at best can supply only a theory of the method of the divine providence."[29]

Today, although numerous Christians strongly deny the validity of almost any kind of evolutionary concept, many other Christians accept the idea that God, in one way or another, utilized a process of evoution in His creative activity. Generally, such thought can be divided into the two categories of theistic evolution and progessive creation. The one who is interested can read further about these concepts in such sources as Ramm's *The Christian View of Science and Scripture*, referred to earlier (Ramm accepts the view of progressive creation), and in *Scientific Creationism*, edited by Henry M. Morris (Morris denies the validity of both concepts).[30] Although it is a bit out-of-date, I recommend the book, *Evolution and Christian Thought Today,* edited by Russell L. Mixter, for a discussion of the numerous facets of evolutionary thought.[31]

Most Christians recognize that theories raised by evolutionist become particularly troublesome when applied to human life. An editorial in a 1982 issue of *Christianity Today* states, "On purely exegetical grounds it would be difficult to rule out the possibility that God created all plant and animal species by a divinely guided process that would include an unspecified amount of evolution— short of Genesis man, whom God made uniquely in his own image."[32] A bit later, in the same editorial we read, "Moreover, the Christian who takes his Bible seriously can scarcely bring Scripture into harmony with an unbroken evolution even when that process is guided by God. At the very least the believer must introduce sheer supernatural miracle at two points in the process: original creation and the origin of man."[33] My own judgment is that, in addition to the two points mentioned, a direct act of God must also at least be present at the origin of animal life, and probably at the beginning of plant life.

I believe it may be instructive that the Hebrew word *bara* (create) occurs only in three verses of Genesis 1. In verse one, God created *(bara)* the heavens and the earth. The beginning of animal life is marked by the use of *bara* (verse 21). Verse 27 is striking in that *bara* occurs not one time, but *three* times, "And God created man in His own image, in the image of God He created him; male and female He created them." From the first, the special status of human life is stressed. While human beings may qualify for classification as an animal from a biological point of view, they are obviously created by God to be uniquely different from other life forms.

Many believe that this special act of God included the formation of the physical body at that point in time. Others, however, hold that God took a biological form that He had been preparing and, as Albertus Pieters said, "made him the first human being, by endowing him with a human soul and a morally responsible nature."[34] Pieters made clear that he did not believe that this was necessarily what God did, but that it was a possibility.

David L. Dye, a repsected scientist and Christian, wrote "At some point in time, perhaps 20,000 years ago, perhaps earlier, one of the primate products of the God-designed biological processes had a body somewhat similar to the body of today. . . . God took this primate, and made a man of him."[35] Although many Christians doubt that it happened that way, all of us need to be careful to respect the views of others, and to realize how precaious it is, when, in the absence of unequivocal Biblical teaching, we insist that God could not have done something in a particular way.

What about the antiquity of human life? Obviously, Christians who sincerely believe in a recent origin of the earth will also reject any idea that human beings came into being hundreds of thousands years ago. Some Christians who accept a very old earth may still believe that human life has a history of only a few thousand years. Other Christians, including many conservatives, have accepted the antiquity of both the earth and human life.

Long ago Warfield wrote "The question of the antiquity of man has of itself no theological significance. . . . The Bible does not assign a brief span to human history: this is done only by a particular mode of interpreting the Biblical data, which is found on examination to rest on no solid basis."[36] Byron Nelson has stated, "No proved or imagined antiquity of man can be too great to be accepted by Christians, since no fundamental doctrine is in any way involved."[37]

David Young, a Christian geologist, believes that man is at least 50,000 years old "inasmuch as religious burial practices and highly developed art indicate that Neanderthal remains are genuinely human."[38]

Currently, anthropologists date the earliest forms of *homo erectus*, the first fossil man securely ascribed to the genus *homo*, to about 1.5 million years ago. *Homo sapiens*, modern man's designation, possibly began as early as 300,000 years ago. Forms of genus *Australopitheous*, found in some abundance, begin at least as early as 3 million years ago.

These great ages certainly stagger one's imagination. Personally, I find it difficult to accept the earliest fossil forms, such as various special of *Australopitheous*, as being truly human in the Biblical sense. I am more comfortable with an editorial comment in *Christianity Today* which states, "Most anthropologists, including those who make a full commitment to biblical inerrancy and a biblical view of man, place Cro-Magnon man (roughtly 10 to 30 thousand years ago) and Neanderthal man (roughly 30 to 70 thousand years ago) as clear examples of *homo sapiens* and fully human in the modern sense. Data for them go far beyond mere physical structure to include drawings and artifacts that suggest a worshiping creature. Here, then, we have biblical man."[39]

Sincere Christians who take their Bibles seriously certainly differ concerning many of the questions about life, including human life, which have been raised by modern science. No attempt has been made here to resolve those differences—indeed it would be arrogant to suppose that this could be accomplished in this paper. It is hoped, however, that parameters have been located within which we all can function, with tolerance and respect for one another, while we continue to weigh the evidence from science and Scripture under the tutelage of the Holy Spirit.

The Reality of Miracle

The word "miracle" is used with various shades of meaning by both Christians and non-Christians. A check in my office dictionary informs me that miracle is "an extraordinary event manifesting divine intervention in human affairs," and also "an extremely outstanding event, thing, or accomplishment."[40] C. S. Lewis, in a good book entitled: *Miracles: A Preliminary Study*, wrote, "I use the word *Miracle* to mean an interference with Nature by supernatural power."[41] He admitted that this was a "popular" and somewhat crude definition.

J. S. Lawton suggested that "a miracle is an event or situation which is so designed by God as to be recognized as a special revelation of His personal activity in the world, and which contributes in some recognizable way to the fulfillment of His purpose for mankind."[42] This definition, I believe, has much to commend it. Definitions that stress the "interference" of God in the natural order are not wholly adequate.

For those of us, scientists, or non-scientists, who believe in God, the question of His relationship to the natural world is important. I have already expressed my conviction that God who created the natural world continues to maintain a dynamic relationship to His creation. This does not mean, however, that He is a capricious Deity who is always interfering with natural processes and human history. One would expect this type of activity to be unusual.

Scientists have historically worked on the basis that nature is orderly and predictable. The essential correctness of this view has been validated time and time again. Christians may well insist that miracle, in one sense of the world, has been built into the very process of nature and history. A "miraculous" cure resulting from the use of penicillin, for example, is possible because of a gift from God, discovered, developed, and employed through human instrumentality.

There are, however, numerous examples in the Bible where God does seem to have acted in more direct, unique, and supernatural ways. Miracle stories tend to be concentrated in two main periods of Biblical history. They occur in profusion at the time of the Exodus and Wilderness Period, when the nation of Israel was being formed, and in the period of Jesus and the disciples when the Church was coming into being. Otherwise, perhaps apart from those associated with Elijah and Elisha, miracles are not mentioned very often in Scripture.

A number of the miracles recorded in Scripture do appear to exhibit divine power used directly in ways that modify natural processes, at least as we currently understand those processes. For example, we all remember that Jesus quieted the stormy Sea of Galilee by the authority of His command. We also remember the story of His ability to walk on the surface of the water. Some of the sick persons healed by Jesus may have been suffering from psychsomatic illnesses or disorders which could have been cured, at least theoretically, by others. But many of those who sought Him and were healed by Him had organic disease and defects which were clearly beyond the possibility of cure by the medical and surgical help available at that time. Also, on at least three occasions, He restored life to persons who had died.

How should one react to these miracle stories? Personally, I beileve they are all true. Those of us who accept, as I do, the supreme miracle of the Incarnation, who believe in the mystery of the Virgin Birth, who do not doubt the triumph of the Resurrection, and who are convinced of the omnipotence of God, surely would not dare to set any limits on His ability to act. He can do absolutely anything that is consistent with His nature and purpose. With Mary, we hear the angel say, "For nothing will be impossible with God."[43] We believe that God did perform great miracles in the past and can and does perform miracles in our day.

Scholars have often suggested that God used natural means to accomplish some of the miracles recorded in the Bible. Certainly there is nothing theologically wrong with this possibility. In the case of any particular miracle story, it is never a question of what God *could* have done, but rather one of what He *did* do. God used the wind to bring quail from the sea to feed the hungery Israelites, as we read in Numbers 11:31 and in Psalms 78:26-28. Natural law, as understood today, does not always have to be set aside for God to do His phenomenal work. Working through, or apart from, such law, He is able to impinge on human existence in ways that can only be described as miraculous. Often, it is only to eyes of faith that the miracle is visible at all.

Some scientists deny the existence of God and reject the possibility of the supernatural. Christians, including the many who are scientists, affirm the reality of a personal, miracle-working God who is both transcendent and immanent. We do not demand a daily miracle to sustain our faith, but rather we live daily in the miracle of His presence.

Observations and Suggestions

I have tried, in this paper, to indicate some of the unity and diversity of thought toward natural science and the Bible characteristic of evangelical Christians with an undoubtable loyalty to the integrity of Scripture. No attempt has been made to incorporate the concepts of what might be regarded as more liberal Christians thought, but the insights of these scholars, as well as those of Jewish authorities, would need to be investigated in a more exhaustive study of the subject.

Evangelical Christians, including most Southern Baptists, share a high degree of unity in their understanding of, and commitment to, the basic doctrines of the Christian faith, including the authority and truthfulness of Scripture. As far as Southern Baptists are concerned, there is little doubt that most are in agreement with the statements found in *The Baptist Faith and Message*.

Christians who hold firmly to the great historic affirmations of the Faith often differ, however, in their interpretation of specific passages of Scripture. This has been shown to be true in this study of the relationship of the Bible to natural science. The thrust of this paper has been toward determining where some of the boundaries of belief may be legitimately drawn. I am sure that I have not been entirely successful, and that the limits established by others might include greater or smaller space, but hopefully the differences would not be great.

I believe conservative Christians, including Southern Baptists, should be able to live and cooperate within the parameters indicated. V. Elving Anderson, in an article in *Christianity Today* has wisely observed, "We should identify and emphasize areas of agreement among evangelicals rather than points on which even strict creationists are divided: a young earth, a universal flood, the fixity of species, and the advisability of laws to teach creation."[44]

I would like to conclude by making several suggestions for those who wish to continue to explore the relationship between science and the Bible—and I hope there are many of you who will want to do this.

1. *Be knowledgeable about the issues.* Read widely, and don't just read those sources that support your position and attack opposite views. For example, don't be afraid to read a college textbook on biology. I have found *Biology: The Science of Life* by Wallace, King, and Sanders to be useful,[45] but there are many others. Read what Christian writers, past and present, have said about these issues. You may want to read two recent books: *The Genesis Debate: Persistent Questions about Creation and the Flood,* edited by Ronald Youngblood,[46] and *God and Nature,* edited by D. C. Limberg and R. L. Numbers.[47] The endnotes for this paper, which you have been given, should be useful in locating source materials.

2. *Be cautious as you evaluate new ideas.* Don't automatically embrace or reject what scientists and other scholars say. Exercise the Berean spirit mentioned in Acts 17:10-11. Examine the Scriptures carefully for yourself, praying for illumination from the Holy Spirit.

Be cautious also in any attempt to harmonize the Bible and science. Remember that the understanding of the natural order by science is always changing. Any harmony established today will likely have to be redone in the future. And, although the truth of Scripture is unchanging, our understanding of that truth may need to change with continued study.

Also be careful not to stake your faith upon, and to defend too tenaciously, some view of the natural order that is not absolutely supported by Scripture. And let your concept of what is "absolute" be informed by the insights of other Christians who have genuinely sought to understand the teaching of Scripture. The Church can ill afford to experience another debacle like it suffered concerning the teachings of Copernicus and Galileo.

3. *Be confident.* You need not be afraid that the message of the Bible will ever be proved to be false. You and I may indeed find that we must modify our

understanding of what the Bible teaches, but the truth itself, the actual doctrine, is eternally valid. As we read in Isaiah 40:8, "the word of our God stands forever."

Recognize that there does not have to be a state of hostility between science and religion. Many scientists are devout Christians. Most who do not profess the Christian faith are still not actively antagonistic toward those of us who do. Early in this paper, I quoted Carl Sagan. Now listen to these words by Tim Stafford contained in an interesting article entitled "Cease-fire in the Laboratory," found in the April 3, 1987 issue of *Christianity Today:* "Carl Sagan, when he interprets the cosmos, speaks as an amateur philosopher. He is not speaking for science; he is speaking for himself."[48]

Do not feel that you must debate those who hold views that differ from your own. God has done what He has done, is doing what He is doing, and will do what He will do, in spite of our attempts to tell Him how we should or should not act. He is not impressed with applause meters, swayed by the score cards of debate judges, or bound by the votes of any ecclesiastical body. Know what you believe, be willing and able to discuss your convictions with others, but do not feel that you have to defend God.

Our main task is not to solve all the problems that we may encounter in our Bible study, although we should work on these, but to share the good news of the Gospel. The message of redemption is clear and unambiguous. We can proclaim it with joy and confidence.

4. *Be humble*. Our attitude toward those with whom we differ, especially toward those who share with us the same basic convictions about the eternal validity of God's word, should be characterized by a generous, tolerant, and respectful spirit. There is just no room for a harsh and sarcastic disposition. Not one of us has a corner on the truth. Not one of us can say that he or she has never been mistaken. An interesting book by Robert Jastrow, entitled *God and the Astronomers,* expresses the belief that scientists can never successfully continue their pursuit of the past back beyond the point of creation. The main text of the book ends with this statement: "For the scientist who has lived by his faith in the power of reason, the story ends like a bad dream. He has scaled the mountains of ignorance; he is about to conquer the highest peak; and he pulls himself over the final rock, he is greeted by a band of theologians who have been sitting there for centuries."[49]

I would express the matter a bit differently. Although as Christians we have already arrived with assurance at the point of certain basic convictions, there is still much that we do not know about God and His activity in the natural world and in history. We do know that it was He who created the universe. With the prophet, we affirm that God is the One "who stretches out the heavens like a curtain."[50] But, like Job, we were not there when He "laid the foundation of the earth."[51] We must confess with Paul that "we see in a mirror dimly . . . (and) know in part."[52] We rejoice, however, in the truth that we do have a Guidebook and a Guide.

And so all of us, scientist and theologian alike, climb the mountain of ignorance. And one day all of us will scale the final peak, and we will find waiting for us the One who is the Truth, before whom we all will bow and confess that He is Lord.[53]

Notes

1. Jeffrey Greenberg, quoted by JoAnne Klein, "Taking Up Geology," *Wheaton Alumni* (February, 1987), 13.

2. Article XIII, *The Chicago Statement on Biblical Inerrancy*, published by the International Council on Biblical Inerrancy, 1978. (Italics mine.)

3. Tony Rothman and George Ellis, "Has Cosmology Become Metaphysical?" *Astronomy*, 15 (February, 1987), 22.

4. Carl Sagan, *Cosmos* (New York: Ballantine Books, 1980), p. 1.

5. Revelation 1:8

6. David H. Smith, "The Inflationary Universe Lives?" *Sky and Telescope*, 65 (March, 1983), 207-201; cf. Jay M. Pasachoff, *Contempoary Astronomy*, 3rd ed. (Philadelphia: Saunders College Publishing, 1985), 316-320.

7. Alan MacRobert, "Beyond the Big Bang," *Sky and Telescope*, 65 (March, 1983), 211-213.

8. Ann Finkbeiner, "A Universe in Our Own Image," *Sky and Telescope* 68 (August, 1984), 106-111.

9. ibid.

10. Allen Emerson, "A Disorienting View of God's Creation," *Christianity Today* 29 (February 1, 1985), 18-25.

11. Henry M. Morris, ed., *Scientific Creationism*, General Edition (San Diego: Creation-Life Publishers, 1974), p. 158; cf. Thomas G. Barnes, "Evidence Points to a Recent Creation," *Christianity Today* 26 (October 8, 1982), 34-36.

12. Bernard Ramm, *The Christian View of Science and Scripture* (Grand Rapids: Wm. B. Eerdmans Publishing Company, 1954), pp. 211-229.

13. Gleason L. Archer, Jr., *A Survey of Old Testament Introduction*, Rev. ed. (Chicago: Moody Press, 1974), pp. 181-188.

14. H. C. Leupold, *Exposition of Genesis*, vol. 1 (Grand Rapids, Baker Book House, 1950), pp. 57-58.

15. "Guideposts for the Current Debate over Origins," *Christianity Today* 26 (October 8, 1982), 24.

16. "Of Evolution and Creation and the Space Between," *Christianity Today* 26 (May 7, 1982), 13.

17. Psalm 8:3-4

18. Robert J. Schadewald, "The Evolution of Bible-Science," in *Scientists Confront Creationism*, ed. Laurie R. Godfrey (New York: W. W. Norton & Company, 1983), p. 288.

19. Joseph P. Free, *Archaeology and Bible History* (Wheaton: Van Kampen Press, 1950), p. 42.

20. For example, John C. Whitcomb, Jr. and Henry M. Morris, *The Genesis Flood* (Grand Rapids: Baker Book House, 1962); H. C. Leupold, *Exposition of Genesis*, vol. 1, pp. 301-304.

21. Bernard Ramm, *The Christian View of Science and Scripture*, pp. 229-249; cf. R. K. Harrison, *Introduction to the Old Testament* (Grand Rapids: Wm. B. Eerdmans Publishing Company, 1969), p. 558; Marcus Dods, "The Book of Genesis," in *The*

Expositor's Bible, W. R. Nicoll, ed. (New York: A. C. Armstrong and Son, 1905), pp. 55-57; David L. Dye, *Faith and the Physical World: A Comprehensive View* (Grand Rapids: Wm. B. Eerdmans Publishing Company, 1966), pp. 154-157; cf. William LaSor, "Does the Bible Teach a Universal Flood?" *Eternity* XI (December, 1960), pp. 11-13.

22. Edward J. Young, *An Introduction to the Old Testament* (Grand Rapids: Wm. B. Eerdmans Publishing Co., 1949), p. 60; cf. James Orr, "The Early Narratives of Genesis," *The Fundamentals,* vol. 1 (Los Angeles: The Bible Institute of Los Angeles, 1917), p. 240.

23. William J. Kaufman, III, *Universe* (New York: W. H. Freeman and Company, 1985), p. 560.

24. Revelation 21:1

25. E. Peter Volpe, *Understanding Evolution,* 2nd ed. (Dubuque: Wm. C. Brown Company Publishers, 1970), p. 142.

26. Bernard G. Campbell, ed., *Humankind Emerging* (Boston: Little, Brown and Company, 1976).

27. George F. Wright, "The Passing of Evolution," *The Fundamentals,* vol. IV (Los Angeles: The Bible Institute of Los Angeles, 1917), p. 72.

28. James Orr, *The Christian View of God and the World* (Grand Rapids: Wm. B. Eerdmans Publishing Company, 1948), p. 99 (The 1890-91 Kerr Lectures.)

29. Benjamin B. Warfield, *Biblical and Theological Studies* (Philadelphia: The Presbyterian and Reformed Publishing Company, 1952), p. 238. (Published thirty years after Warfield's death.)

30. Ramm, pp. 260-293; Morris, *Scientific Creationism,* pp. 215-221.

31. Russell L. Mixter, ed., *Evolution and Christian Thought Today* Grand Rapids: Wm. B. Eerdmans Publishing Company, 1959).

32. "Guideposts for the Current Debate over Origins," *Christianity Today* 265 (October 8, 1982), p. 62.

33. Ibid.

34. Albertus Pieters, *Notes on Genesis* (Grand Rapids: Wm. B. Eerdmans Publishing Company, 1954), p. 52.

35. David L. Dye, *Faith and the Physical World,* pp. 147-148.

36. Warfield, *Biblical and Theological Studies,* pp. 238-239.

37. Byron C. Nelson, *Before Abraham* (Minneapolis: Augsburg Publishing House, 1948), p. 16.

38. Davis A. Young, "An Ancient Earth Is Not a Problem; Evolutionary Man Is," *Christianity Today* 26 (October 8, 1982), p. 45.

39. Guideposts for the Current Debate over Origins," *Christianity Today* 26 (October 8, 1982), p. 25.

40. *Webster's New Collegiate Dictionary,* 1980.

41. C. S. Lewis, *Miracles: A Preliminary Study* (New York: The Macmillan Company, 1947), p. 10.

42. J. S. Lawton, *Miracles and Revelation* (New York: Association Press, n.d.), p. 253; cf. H. H. Farmer, *The World and God* (London: Nisbet & Co., 1936), pp. 107-127.

43. Luke 1:37

44. V. Elving Anderson, "Evolution Yes; but Creation Too," *Christianity Today,* 16 (October 8, 1982), p. 40.

45. Robert A. Wallace, Jack L. King, and Gerald P. Sanders, *Biology: the Science of Life* (Santa Monica: Goodyear Publishing Company, Inc., 1981).

46. Ronald Youngblood, ed., *The Genesis Debate: Persistent Questions About Creation and the Flood* (Nashville: Thomas Nelson Publishers, 1986).

47. David C. Lindberg and Ronald L. Numbers, eds., *God and Nature: Historical Essays on the Encounter between Christianity and Science* (Berkeley: University of California Press, 1986).

48. Tim Stafford, "Cease-fire in the Laboratory," *Christianity Today* 31 (April, 3, 1987), 19.

49. Robert Jastrow, *God and the Astronomers* (New York: W. W. Norton and Company, Inc., 1978), p. 116; but cf. Sten Odenwald, "To the Big Bang and Beyond," *Astronomy* 15 (May, 1987), pp. 90-95.

50. Isaiah 40:22

51. Job 38:4; cf. Isaiah 40:12-14

52. 1 Corinthians 13:12

53. Philippians 2:10-11

19

THE IMPORTANCE AND PROBLEM OF DISTINGUISHING BETWEEN BIBLICAL AUTHORITY AND BIBLICAL INTERPRETATION

Robert L. Cate

Before actually beginning the consideration of the subject, you need to know who I am and upon what basis I approach this subject. Several basic presuppositions are present in my life. These are spiritual convictions which shape my life and ministry. These are profoundly important, for they reveal who and what I really am. I state them here for you.

1. I believe in God. I believe that He is, that He exists, that He is alive. I believe that He is sovereign over people and nations, that all history is literally 'His-story', and that all truth of whatever nature ultimately has its foundation in Him.

2. I believe that God is love. This means that He loves all people. This, in turn, means that He loves you and me. I believe that His love is not some passive thing but that it is God's all-consuming nature and that it is active in the affairs of human life.

3. I believe that people are sinful, that all persons when they reach a time of spiritual awareness, consciously and willfully choose to rebel against their understanding of God's will, alienating themselves from Him. This means that I am such a sinner. It means that you are, too.

4. I believe that because of my sin, and also because of yours, God acted out of His love to send His Son, Jesus Christ, to die for me and for you, offering us cleansing from our sin and forgiveness of it. I believe that He was raised from the dead and through that resurrection gives me a new life, a life which can be lived in a loving relationship with Him. I believe that He is Lord, and that He will return again to effect the final redemption of this universe and that He will reign over all.

5. I believe that the redeemed have been given the task of carrying the Gospel, the good news of Jesus Christ, to all the peoples of the earth. That means that you and I bear that responsibility until Jesus comes again.

6. I believe in the church as God's established human institution for carrying out His Divine purposes. All other Christian and denominational institutions are subsidiary to this. Here is where God's work is expected to be centered and where loyal Christians are expected to be found. The local church must be the center from which all Christians carry out their part of God's great commission.

7. I believe in the Bible as God's inspired revelation of His will and purpose. It is intended, at the very least, to point people to the God who loves them, who has sent His Son to redeem them from their sin, and who sends His redeemed ones to bear this message to the ends of the earth. It is my authority

373

for life. I study it to understand it. But this study is no mere academic pursuit. Having discovered its meaning, I must obey the Bible as God's revelation to me.

These, then, are my basic presuppositions. They shape me and they shape my life and ministry. I became a Southern Baptist at the time of my baptism. It was a conscious choice. I have remained a Southern Baptist because I believe that we are seeking to live by those things which I consider basic to faith. I have served my Lord and my denomination as a pastor, professor, revival preacher, conference leader, curriculum writer, and author. I pray for us daily. I have unashamedly signed the 1963 Baptist Faith and Message Statement which was adopted by the Southern Baptist Convention. This, then, is who I am and from whence I come to address the subject of "The Importance and Problem of Distinguishing between Biblical Authority and Biblical Interpretation."

Basic Definitions

A number of very important terms will show up again and again in the development of this discussion. Everyone who deals with this subject uses these terms or some like them. However, not everyone uses the terms in the same way or with the same meanings. Therefore it is important that you at least know how I will use the terms and what they mean to me.

Revelation

The Baptist Faith and Message Statement on "The Scriptures" says: "The Holy Bible was written by men divinely inspired and is the record of God's revelation of Himself to man." God has revealed Himself in numerous ways, as the author of Hebrews tells us. (cf. Heb. 1:1-2) Amos asserted, "Surely the Lord God does nothing, without revealing his secret to his servants the prophets" (Amos 3:7). The last book of the Bible calls itself The Revelation (Rev. 1:1). Revelation literally means "unveiling," "uncovering." It is with this sense that we use it in referring to the Bible. In the Bible God uncovers Himself. He makes clear how He dealt with Israel in the Old Testament and with Christians in the New. Further, not only did God reveal Himself to them through His historical acts as recorded in the Bible, through the record of those acts He also reveals His will and purposes for all people of all time. Ultimately, *revelation is God's self-disclosure of Himself and His will to human kind*. For our purposes here today, we shall limit this definition to the Bible itself, although the Scripture is quite clear that God is revealed to everyone collectively through the world of nature and individually through His Holy Spirit. The very fact that the Bible is Divine revelation is perhaps its most significant aspect. It is because of this that we are involved in this particular discussion at all.

Inspiration

Closely related to and intimately involved with the idea of revelation is the fact that the Bible is inspired. To make this claim, however, is not as simple as it may sound. To understand what is meant by the claim that the Bible is inspired is a wholly different matter than simply making it. The word "inspiration" actually is found only twice in the Bible. Job was told, "There is a spirit in man, and the inspiration of the Almighty giveth them understanding." (Job 32:8, KJV) And Timothy was admonished, "All scripture is given by inspiration of God, and is profitable for doctrine, for reproof, for correction, for instruction in righteousness (2 Tim. 3:16), KJV)." Other versions translate these verses differently, but the meaning remains the same.

Inspiration literally means to have been breathed into. That the Bible has been inspired means that God has breathed into it. The background for this may go back to the creation account in Genesis, where we are told, "Then the Lord God formed man of dust from the ground, and breathed into his nostrils the breath of life, and man became a living being (Gen. 2:7)." Here we see that the breath of God gives life. This adds the dimension that God's breath makes the Bible a living book, unique in the world's literature.

However, the modern use of the term inspiration is far less precise. We speak of music, paintings, and literature as being inspired. We certainly do not mean that they are inspired in the same way the Bible is. We must be more precise than this.

The inspiration of the Bible is a fact: it has been breathed into by God. But the inspiration of the Bible is also a process.

First, the writers and speakers themselves were inspired. The Second Epistle of Peter plainly asserts that "men moved by the Holy Spirit spoke from God" (2 Pet. 2:21). Thus, any concept of biblical inspiration must go back to the original speakers and writers. However, we dare not stop there.

Second, the admonition made to Timothy insists that the words themselves are inspired, for he was told, "All scripture is given by inspiration of God." (2 Tim. 3:16) The word "scripture" literally refers to written words. It is not merely the ideas or concepts but the very words of the Bible which have been breathed into by God. The Holy Spirit fills them with life and uses them in bringing life to humans. It is at this point that many interpreters stop in their consideration of inspiration. However, it appears to me that the Bible goes one step farther.

Third, God's inspiration is also available to those who interpret the Bible. In an earlier passage, we noted that Elihu asserted to Job that the inspiration of God brings understanding to those who interpret His Word. (Job 32:8) This was underscored in the New Testament by the assertion that

> First of all you must understand this, that no prophecy of scripture is a matter
> of one's own interpretation, because no prophecy ever came by impulse of
> man, but men moved by the Holy Spirit spoke from God (2 Pet. 1:20-21).

Jesus even further underscored this when He told His disciples, that when the Holy Spirit came, He would "teach you all things, and bring to your remembrance all that I have said to you" (Jn. 14:26). He also asserted, "I have yet many things to say to you, but you cannot bear them now. When the Spirit of truth comes, he will guide you into all the truth (Jn. 16:12-13). Here, then, is the assertion that God's Holy Spirit is available and able to guide His people into truth.

Thus, the biblical understanding of inspiration moves from God through the speakers and writers into the Word itself and ultimately to the interpreter. Anything less than this is less than what the Bible asserts about itself.

Authority

Since we shall deal with the authority of the Bible in greater detail elsewhere in this paper, we may confine our discussion of authority at this point to a basic definition. The *Layman's Library of Christian Doctrine* defines authority by stating:

> With a wide range of meaning, our word *authority* comes from the Latin, *auctor,* meaning "originator, beginner, creator, source, author." The term *authority* directs our minds, therefore, to the source of the true reality of any matter under consideration.[1]

However, as the term is used in Bible and in contemporary life, it has come to include the idea of power, since one who creates or authors something controls it. It is that sense of power which comes to the fore as we speak of biblical authority. In this relationship, when we speak of authority,

> we mean that which provides sufficient grounds for belief and action and by its inner power is able to call forth faith and obedience based on the true knowledge of experience and reality.[2]

Further, the authority of the Bible is a derived authority, ultimately resting upon the authority of God.

Interpretation

Again, as we shall deal with interpretation in greater detail later, we shall also confine ourselves here to a basic definition of the term. Interpretation is that process by which we seek to arrive at an understanding of what any passage in the Bible means. It is here that we confront the basic problem which this paper seeks to address. Two persons may, and frequently do, agree totally on the authority of the Bible and disagree radically on what some specific passage of the Bible means.

It was precisely this problem, the disagreement over interpretation, which gave rise to the great Jerusalem conference which is recorded in Acts 15. There Paul and the leaders of the church in Jerusalem apparently agreed heartily on the authority of the Bible, yet disagreed vehemently on whether or not Gentiles could become Christians without becoming Jews. This was a matter of interpretation. We shall return to this issue later.

As we have defined it, interpretation is a process. But it is more. Interpretation also refers to the specific meaning which any interpreter believes that a particular passage has for him or for her. The fact that our interpretation may be in error has nothing to do with the authority which a passage has. The Bible is authoritative whether I interpret a passage properly or not. When my interpretation is wrong and I obey, I get in trouble. When my interpretation is wrong and others depend upon it, it may be a matter of life and death. Therefore, the very fact that I am both sinful and limited must make me consistently re-examine my interpretations. I can be wrong. So can you.

Application

The Bible contains many different kinds of literature. Its teachings are contained in direct commands, in historical narratives, in sermons and prayers, in psalms and hymns, in parables, and in numerous other forms. However, if, as we believe, these teachings are authoritative and demand obedience, then we must determine how this can be accomplished. The application of any passage is the way by which that passage and its teachings are related to the life of the interpreter. If the Bible is authoritative, then it must be applied to life. To claim to believe in the authority of the Bible and to fail to apply its teachings to life is to demonstrate that we do not really believe in the authority. On the other hand, different interpretations of a passage will certainly lead to different applications, even when both interpreters truly accept the Bible's authority.

With these definitions before us then, we are now ready to turn our attention to the first major section of this presentation. I shall seek to be consistent and use these terms as I have defined them and only as I have defined them.

The Nature of Biblical Authority

The Nature of the Bible

I have already indicated that the Bible is a unique book. Part of its uniqueness lies in its very nature, for it is both a Divine and a human book. The Divine nature is seen in the fact that it is God's revelation of Himself and that He has inspired it. The Bible comes from God. It has its origin in His nature, in His love, and in His will and purposes of redemption. He could have chosen and did choose other ways to reveal Himself to humanity. However, the Bible is His written revelation. Further, from the people of Israel comes the long-standing tradition and testimony that the Old Testament is the Word of God. Jesus Himself acknowledged and taught this, saying,

> truly I say to you, till heaven and earth pass away, not an iota, not a dot, will pass from the law until all is accomplished. Whoever then relaxes one of the least of these commandments and teaches men so, shall be called least in the kingdom of heaven: but he who does them and teaches them shall be called great in the kingdom of heaven. (Matt. 5:18-19)

Furthermore, the early Christians acknowledged this authority for the Old Testament, for they used it as the source of the texts from which they proclaimed the first Gospel messages. In addition, as soon as the early writings from the New Testament era began to circulate, certain of them were accepted by other churches and Christians as the authoritative Word of God. These eventually made up our New Testament.

377

The Bible is certainly a Divine book. On the other hand, the Bible is also clearly a human book. Its humanity can be seen in numerous evidences. It contains many different kinds of literature. Among these are poetry, sermons, parables, history, songs, prayers, proverbs, letters, and perhaps even drama and short stories. In addition, in each and all of these various literatures, a variety of characteristics of human authors are plainly seen. They use different languages (Hebrew, Aramaic, and Greek), different vocabularies, different styles of grammar and syntax, and reflect differing degrees of language skills and knowledge. It appears quite clear that while God inspired His human authors, He also left them free to be themselves.

The Bible also clearly reflects its humanity through the variety of cultural backgrounds which are seen therein. The culture of the patriarchs is quite different from that of the time of the monarchy, and that of the exile is different from that when Israel was under Persian domination. Even in the brief time span covered by the New Testament, we find different cultures. The Judaism of Jerusalem contrasts significantly with the more simple faith of the Galileans. And the philosophical erudition of Athens is strikingly different from the hustle and bustle of the Roman Empire centered in Ephesus or in Rome itself.

Yet this Divine-human nature of the Bible should not be thought surprising. We must remember that in God's ultimate self-revelation, this same combination is found. In fact, this combination is the very message of the incarnation, for in Jesus of Nazareth the Divine Son of God became a human being. In Jesus we find the ultimate Word of God, revealed in a unique Divine-human nature. In both Jesus and the Bible, the involvement of these two natures is not either/or but both/and.

The Source of Biblical Authority

Granted that the Bible is unique and has an authority, we must seek to identify what the source of that authority is. The basic question appears to be quite simple. Is the Bible's authority inherent within itself, or does it derive from some other source? Essentially, for the evangelical Christian, the authority of the Bible rests in the fact that it is the inspired revelation of the Triune God. The Christian becomes a Christian by accepting Jesus Christ as Lord. Jesus Himself claimed to have all authority given to Him, for just before He spoke the words of the so-called Great Commission, He said, "All authority in heaven and on earth has been given to me." (Mt. 28:18) Further, the commands of Jesus which He laid upon His disciples are found written in the Scriptures. The Holy Spirit also has an authority over the affairs of mankind. It is He who takes the words of the Bible and leads people to surrender to His lordship and to obey Him in faithfulness. Ultimately, all authority rests with God the Father, the Creator of all things. It is He who revealed the Scriptures and who inspired them for His people. Each Person of the Trinity has an authority which in some way is communicated through the words of the Bible.

Numerous books have been written to try to enlarge upon the basic nature of the authority of the Bible. All persons who submit themselves to the Lordship of Jesus Christ and to the sovereignty of God over humankind will find as a part of that submission that the Scriptures have an authority for them which is derived from the authority of God. The Bible is God's book. He imparts its authority to it.

The authority of the Scriptures, contrary to the belief of some, does not rest in the traditions or teachings of any church. Neither do they rest in any individual person, whether he be pope or television evangelist. Neither are they authoritative because you or I say they are.

The Bible is authoritative because God makes it so. It is that simple. It is also that profound.

The Absoluteness of Biblical Authority

The question is sometimes debated, particularly between Christians and unbelievers, as to whom the Bible is authoritative over. In essence, the issue is raised by asking: "Are the Scriptures authoritative over all people, or are they simple authoritative over Christians, over those who acknowledge the Lordship of Jesus?"

Again, for the Christian, the answer is usually quite simple. Jesus is Lord whether or not you or I or anyone else acknowledges Him to be so. He is Lord because God the Father established Him as such. If He as Lord acknowledged the authority of the Scriptures, then they have an authority whether I acknowledge it or not. The authority of the Bible is not dependent upon human acknowledgment of it.

The Kinds of Biblical Authority

We have already noted the fact that the Bible is composed of many different kinds of literature. This fact means that various passages in the Bible are possessed of one of at least two different kinds of authority. Some passages are propositional. They are specific commands and as such have a very explicit authority upon life. Most people recognize this kind of authority in the Ten Commandments: You shall not kill; You shall not commit adultery; You shall not steal; You shall not bear false witness against your neighbor; You shall not covet . . . (Ex. 20:13-17). Thus we recognize that we have explicit authority here, even though most of us have difficulty accepting the fact that the latter two should be taken as seriously as the first three. Equally as explicit in authority are some of the words of Jesus: "Come to me, all who labor and are heavy laden, and I will give you rest. Take my yoke upon you, and learn of me, . . . (Mt. 11:28-29)." We may choose to obey or to disobey such words, but we recognize them as commands which have an explicit authority over life.

On the other hand, most of the Bible is not so explicit in its teaching. The account of creation, the calls of the prophets, David's conflict with Goliath, the Twenty-third Psalm, the parables of Jesus, Paul's difficulties in Athens, and the symbols of Revelation are all quite different in nature. We would agree that, as part of the Bible, these passages have an authority. But we must also acknowledge that here the authority is implied. It is an implicit authority rather than an explicit authority. There is no way by which we can apply these passages, or others like them, without being involved in interpretation. This does not mean

379

they are without authority. However, it is clear, or should be so, that we are dealing with an entirely different kind of authority here. Therefore we face a problem of a different nature. Unfortunately, or perhaps it is not unfortunate, the overwhelming part of the Bible is of this latter nature. Its authority is implicit rather than explicit.

The Application of Biblical Authority

Since we acknowledged that the Bible has an authority over human life, we must raise the question as to how this authority is to be applied. We need to ask, "How is the Bible authoritative, in what measure, and in what relations?"[3]

First of all, we have already acknowledged that the Bible, as the inspired revelation of the Sovereign God of the universe, has an authority over all human life. On the other hand, the laws of the United States have an authority over everyone who lives here, but not everyone acknowledges that authority. In the same way, the Bible has an authority over everyone, but the unbelievers do not know or acknowledge it. The fact that some of them may even accept the Ten Commandments or the Golden Rule as having some kind of authority does not really alter the basic fact. Even when this limited authority is acknowledged by unbelievers, they are not doing so because they acknowledge the authority of the Bible.

On the other hand, when we consider the Christian's relationship to the Bible, we face a different situation. Here, at least, most of us acknowledge the authority of the Bible over our lives. Some have not accepted the Old Testament, but that heresy has been with us for centuries. On the other hand, differences do exist in the way by which different Christians deal with biblical authority.

Two of these approaches have at least been with us since the time of the Reformation. There the cry of the reformers was *sola scriptura,* "Scripture alone". They were rejecting the authority of pope and church and replacing it with the authority of the Bible. Yet even they disagreed as to how this authority was to be applied to the life of the believer. Luther approached the Bible by insisting that the Christians could do anything which was not forbidden by the Bible. Zwingli, on the other hand, was equally insistent that the Christian could only do what was commanded. (This approach, carried to its ultimate dimension, is the basis for the style of life lived by the so-called "plain people" of the Pennsylvania Dutch communities.) Obviously, these two reformers and their followers all took quite seriously the authority of the Bible. Just as obviously, they disagreed quite radically as to how that authority was to be dealt with by the individual believer. We still have a great deal of this kind of disagreement present with us.

A third approach to biblical authority has been with us at least since the latter part of the nineteenth century. Typical of this is the approach of James Barr, who clearly acknowledges the authority of the Bible but makes that authority subject to his understanding of the Scriptures.[4] I maintain that if the Bible has an authority, it has that authority regardless of what I believe about it.

On the other hand, biblical authority apparently does have two basic ways of working. There is a subjective side to it. Here we find the Holy Spirit working with power upon the heart and life of the believer to convince and convict so that the human response to the Bible is an act of faith, commitment, and obedience. However, "on the objective side, Scripture becomes the basis of appeal in all matters pertaining to the content of faith and the practice of Christian living."[5] By this I mean that we turn to the Bible for guidance for all of life.

For the contemporary twentieth-century Christian, I think that we must find some middle ground between the positions of Luther and Zwingli, while avoiding the wholly subjective, rationalistic approach of interpreters like James Barr. In doing this, I believe that we must assert that the Bible has an inherent authority over all of life. At the same time, we must acknowledge Jesus' teaching that the Holy Spirit will guide us into all truth (John 16:13). Biblical authority rests in God, is present in the Scriptures (in whatever version or translation you use), and is binding, whether accepted or not, upon all human life.

The Nature of Biblical Interpretation

However, acknowledging the authority of the Bible and knowing what any particular passage of the Bible means are two decidedly different things. It is at this point that we come face to face with the nature of biblical interpretation.

The Importance of and Necessity for Biblical Interpretation

Let us begin by considering the episode of Philip and the eunuch who served Candace, Queen of Ethiopia. The eunuch was returning home from Jerusalem, reading the Old Testament. He was literally searching the Scriptures. Philip asked, "Do you understand what you are reading?"

The eunuch responded with a question of his own, "How can I, unless someone guides me?"

After reading the passage together, the eunuch then asked Philip, "About whom, pray, does the prophet say this, about himself or someone else?"

Philip then interpreted the passage for him, pointing him to Jesus. Finally, they drew near to some water, probably an oasis, and the eunuch asked, "What is to prevent my being baptized?" (Acts 8:29-38).

It is worth noting here that the eunuch implicitly acknowledged the authority of the Bible. Yet, that in itself did not help him until the passage was interpreted for him. He needed to understand it before he could act properly upon it. Further, a case can be made for the proposition that not any of this would have happened if they had not been asking questions of each other and of the Bible. If there had been no questions, there would have been no understanding. If there had been no questions, there would have been no answer, no interpretation.

Every week, millions of people are engaged in Bible study. Singly and in groups, people are seeking to understand what the Bible means, what God is revealing to them through its pages. It would be bad enough to think of how much time might be wasted by poorly guided Bible study. It is even worse to have poor interpretation when you believe that the Bible is God's Word of redemption to humankind. That being so, bad biblical interpretation can be death-dealing. It was Jesus Himself who admonished us to search the Scriptures. (John 5:39) The intent of that admonition was that we would come to an understanding of their meaning, not that we would simply compound our ignorance.

The need for good biblical interpretation is as great as any other human need. If the Bible is what we believe it to be, God's Word to sinful humanity, then we must take it seriously. We can rejoice in the fact that God can succeed in spite of our frailties and failures. On the other hand, that is no excuse for not doing our very best in the task of interpreting His Word. We should offer our best skills and thought to biblical interpretation, with the prayer that God's Holy Spirit will guide us in our task.

Additional Definitions

Before proceeding further with our discussion of biblical interpretation, some additional terms need to be defined. Each of these is involved in or with the process of interpretation.

1. *Exegesis.* Made up of two Greek words, exegesis means to bring out of any passages all of the meaning which it contains. This includes the cultural references, the implications, the attitudes, the assumptions, the teachings, etc., which both the human author and the Divine Author intended. J. I. Packer says,

> This gives the "literal" sense . . . . I call it the "natural" or "literary" sense, whereby the exegete seeks to put himself in the writer's linguistic, cultural, historical, and religious shoes.[6]

This process is practiced, as far as I have been able to determine, by all serious contemporary biblical interpreters.

2. *Eisegesis.* Also made up of two Greek words, eisegesis means to read or carry into a passage a meaning which is not actually present. This is generally done by interpreters who approach a passage with preconceived notions of what it means or teaches. This normally occurs when the interpreter does not do serious, detailed linguistic, historical, and cultural studies of the passage in question. It results from overconfidence mixed with poor biblical scholarship. Unfortunately, this term is sometimes used by persons who disagree on interpretations in accusing one another of sloppy or improper biblical scholarship.

3. *Apogesis.* Less common than the two preceding terms, apogesis is also make up of two Greek words and means to read or take away from a passage a meaning which is actually present. This is sometimes done by interpreters whose mind is so made up in advance that they fail to see a meaning which the passage actually has. It is more often done in an attempt to appear intellectual by ignoring the generally obvious meaning of a passage.

4. *Hermeneutics.* Among the gods in ancient Greek mythology, Hermes was considered to be the messenger of the gods. From his name, the term hermeneutics has been created to describe the technique of interpreting any passage and applying it to specific situations in contemporary life. It is the pro-

cess of discovering the message from God which is contained in the passage. It can be described both as a science and an art. The term is intended to describe the process or technique by which any ancient passage of the Bible is made relevant to the reader.

Different interpreters may and do disagree as to the techniques of hermeneutics. On the other hand, there is no disagreement as to the goal of hermeneutics, — a relevant and accurate interpretation, — or as to the necessity of it. If the Bible is God's Word, then that Word has a meaning, a revelation for us. Therefore it needs to be heard, understood, applied, and obeyed.

Kinds of Biblical Interpretation

With these definitions before us, we are now ready to consider different kinds of biblical interpretation. Each of these has had and still does have some followers among those people who seek to hear God speak through His Word. The 1963 "Baptist Faith and Message" statement says of the Scriptures, "The criterion by which the Bible is to be interpreted is Jesus Christ." While we all may, and probably do, agree with that assertion, the statement still leaves a great deal of room for diversity in approaching the Bible to interpret it. With that statement as a foundation, we must still ask as a basic question: "How do we interpret the Bible?" We can identify at least six different ways by which the Bible has been interpreted.

1. *The path of allegory*. Allegory was a method of interpretation originally developed by the Greek philosophers. It was first applied to the Old Testament by the rabbis just before the time of Jesus. The method was also applied by some early Christians to the entire Bible. This method begins with the assumption that behind the obvious meaning of any passage, a "real or spiritual meaning is found."[7] Using this method, the rabbis interpreted the Song of Songs as teaching about God's love for Israel, His bride, and about her responsive love for Him. Numerous early Christians, as well as some later ones, saw it as teaching Christ's love for His bride, the church, and vice versa. Yet any contemporary teen-ager who has read the book realizes that it deals with physical love between a man and a woman. Its apparent message appears to be that God's gift of human sexuality is something wonderful, something to be enjoyed and appreciated as a gift from God. It may also teach that if physical love is this wonderful, then spiritual love is to be treasured and appreciated even more.

Starting with the allegorical approach to interpretation, the search for hidden and unusual meanings became quite bizarre. "Augustine, in the fifth century A.D., found interpretations fruitful in proportion to their difficulty."[8] When this approach is used, any given passage can be made to mean anything which the interpreter wishes it to. There are no limits except human fancy and imagination. Furthermore, using this method, there is and can be no agreement among interpreters as to what any specific passage means. The allegorical method of interpretation leads to a passage meaning anything, and thus ultimately meaning nothing.

2. *The path of dogmatism*. The interpretative method which I call "dogmatic" approaches the Bible with the concept that it is little or nothing more

than a series of propositions which can be directly applied to life in any age and in any culture. That material which cannot be so handled is generally considered to be informational only and generally irrelevant or immaterial. Essentially, this approach assumes that the Bible really needs no interpretation. The major weakness of this approach is that it ignores the fact that very little of the Bible is truly propositional. It also ignores all the cultural difficulties, for few of us have ever seen a Girgashite or Hivite or sacrificed an animal upon an altar recently. Even fewer care. Finally, this approach totally ignores the example of Jesus in the Sermon on the Mount. There He took the basic propositions of the Ten Commandments and sought the principles behind them, carrying their thrust farther into a larger application.

3. *The path of extreme literalism.* Similar to the interpretative method of extreme dogmatism is the path of extreme literalism. This was developed among the early rabbis. As they applied it, getting involved even with the shapes of letters and the numbers of times particular letters occurred in a passage, they became so bogged down in minor details and trivialities that they missed the obvious meaning of a passage.[9] It was also adopted and modified as a method of interpretation by some early reformation preachers and some of the early frontier preachers of America. In more recent times it has been utilized by Jehovah's Witnesses and some other cultic groups. Like the approach of dogmatism, it too ignores the basic example of Jesus.

4. *The path of church or tradition control.* From the time of Augustine, the Roman Catholic Church became the authority upon which biblical interpretation was to be based. No passage could mean anything other than what the church councils or the pope had said. It was partially as a blow against this concept that the Protestant Reformation occurred. However, it was not long after that event until some of the followers of the Reformation began to substitute tradition as the authority upon which biblical interpretation was to be based. To counteract the former approach, John Calvin "called for religious discussion of obscure and difficult passages among Christian scholars. Lacking this, said Calvin, there would be no liberty or opportunity for new light to break forth from the Bible."[10] Calvin's approach is just as effective in breaking the stranglehold of tradition-bound interpretation as it was in breaking the hold of church-controlled interpretation. It is a corrective to those who seek to control the minds and hearts of Christians by controlling their understanding of what the Bible teaches.

5. *The path of contextual interpretation.* Beginning primarily with the Protestant Reformation, although some feeble steps had been taken earlier, an approach to biblical interpretation was made which sought to base the understanding and interpretation of a passage upon its canonical context. This method seeks to discover linguistic, grammatical, historical, and literary characteristics. Upon this basis, a passage is to be understood in the light of its plain meaning and then applied to life.

This approach to interpretation clearly rejects the allegorical approach, as well as that of dogmatism, extreme literalism, and church or tradition control. On the other hand, this approach has also led to abuses. The nineteenth-century literary-historical critics applied these techniques, but were unfortunately frequently guided by philosophical and theological presuppositions alien to the Bible and hostile to Christianity. This led to abuses which sometimes included the rejection of ideas of revelation, inspiration, and biblical authority. While not a necessary result of the use of this method, these abuses occurred often enough to cause many people to question the use of the method itself.

6. *The method of Jesus.* Jesus Himself set us an example for biblical interpretation. In the Sermon on the Mount, He began by dealing with a passage in the light of its obvious meaning in the Old Testament context. Then He sought for a principle or meaning which underlay each passage. Finally, based upon His own authority and His understanding of human life, He sought for the thrust of the passage and applied it with an enlarged meaning to contemporary life. In so doing, He carried it farther in the direction in which it was already headed. This hermeneutic of Jesus incorporates the best of the other hermeneutics. Furthermore, it also takes seriously the Lordship of Jesus Christ and the authority of the Bible, offering a genuine basis for developing a satisfactory method of biblical interpretation.

Steps to Effective Interpretation

The interpretation of the Bible is both an art and a science. Much interpretation fails because the interpreter does not recognize that it is a science. There is a method to doing it which can be repeated over and over again, and when applied to the same passage should yield similar results each time. If we ignore the scientific side of interpretation, we may occasionally stumble across the proper interpretation of a passage. More often than not we shall merely stumble.

On the other hand, there is an art side to interpretation which is ignored equally as often by interpreters. The art side of interpretation is rooted in our relationship to God, in His gifts to us, and in our openness to His will and to the leadership of His Holy Spirit. This dimension of interpretation is quite personal and varies significantly from individual to individual. We can only accept and use the gifts which God bestows. However, we can develop our techniques and skills in the use of those gifts as we seek to interpret His Word. Obviously, we cannot develop gifts we do not have.

The art side of interpretation can be enhanced. On the other hand, the science side of interpretation can be learned. It involves a process which includes several basic steps which we can follow and in which we can gain significant skill.

1. First, we must determine what a text says. People who have spent their lifetime studying the actual text of the Bible are called textual critics. They have engaged in the study of ancient manuscripts and versions in order to try to get as close as possible to the original text of any particular passage. As a result of these studies, although we do not have the original autograph of any biblical book, we can at least approximate it in most instances in the New Testament and in many instances in the Old. This allows us to approach most verses of the Bible with a high degree of confidence.

Obviously, most of us cannot do this kind of textual study. Therefore we need to choose and use the best translations available, those based upon the work of experts in the field. (This does not mean choosing the translation with which we agree.) Further, in making such choices, we should not normally confine ourselves to just one translation. Comparing a variety of translations will help us better to understand what the original text said. Until we are sure what a text really says, we cannot have much confidence in our understanding of it.

However, merely knowing the words of a text is not enough. We must also seek to know what those words mean. Few ancient Hebrew and Greek words can be translated into English with precision. Here again, this is where multiple translations may help us, as translators grapple with the problems of accurate translation of foreign terms and concepts. This attempt to understand words and their usage and meaning is the science of linguistics. Furthermore, we must also seek to understand how words relate to one another in the passage. This is grammar and syntax. It is extremely important that we know both what words mean and how they relate if we are going to interpret the Bible accurately. All of this is a part of determining what a text says, but there is still more. We must also seek to identify historical, geographical, cultural, and literary references. Only after we have done this can we have any real confidence that we truly understand what a text says.

2. At this point we are ready for the second step, which is determining what a passage meant. We actually need to know what it meant both to the original speaker or writer and to the audience who heard or read it. At this point, therefore, we need to identify the literary category of the passage. Prose and poetry are used differently and should be interpreted differently. Parables are different from historical references. Ritual laws are different from prophetic sermons and both are different from the New Testament letters. Until we know the literary category and how to deal with it, we shall be groping in the dark as we seek to interpret any passage. The canonical context also influences our interpretation. Consider the words of the Old Testament, "the just shall live by his faith" (Hab. 2:4). It is quoted three times in the New Testament, and in each instance, although the same words are used, the passage meant something slightly different. Romans says, "The *just* shall live by faith;" Galatians says, "The just *shall live* by faith;" and Hebrews says, "The just shall live *by faith*" (Rom. 1:17; Gal. 3:11; Heb. 10:38;.KJV;.italics mine).

In addition, the context sometimes indicates that what was being said was wrong. We cannot trust the words of Amaziah in Amos nor those of Hananiah in Jeremiah, for each was in direct opposition to a prophet of God (Am. 7:10-16; Jer. 28:1-4). And in the infamous confrontation between Job and his friends, although much of what the friends said sounds good, the book concludes with God proclaiming to Eliphaz, "My wrath is kindled against you and against your two friends; for you have not spoken of me what is right, as my servant Job has (Job 42:7). All of this should point up the extreme importance of knowing what a passage really meant as a basic and fundamental step in the science of interpretation.

3. The third step in interpretation is that of determining what a passage means. The contemporary meaning of a passage should be related to and flow from its ancient meaning. Jesus sought for underlying principles and the forward thrust of a passage in order to apply it to His day. We, following His example, should seek to do the same. We have not completed the task of interpretation until, under the leadership of God's Spirit, we have found the forward thrust of any passage and seen how it applies to us in our contemporary society.

In performing each and all of these basic steps leading to the interpretation of a passage, we need to get and to use the best tools which we can obtain to help us to do the job. We have already noted that an interpreter should have several good translations. We also need a good Bible concordance in order to see how words in one passage are used elsewhere. In addition to this, a good Bible history is helpful and a good set of maps is essential. We frequently discover that a knowledge of geography will make a difficult passage clear. To these we can add biblical introductions, commentaries, and books on archaeology. Obviously, such resources are expensive. Yet, with patience, over the years we can build a good library for the enhancement of biblical study. At the same time, we must always do the very best with the resources which we have and which we can afford. However, we need to avoid the danger of becoming a pawn in the hands of those who have written the books for us. Let us remember that we, as well as they, have the Holy Spirit available to guide us in the interpretation of His Word. We read them for their background knowledge, not for their superior access to God. Let us offer to Him for His glory the best skills, resources, and preparation which we have.

Distinguishing the Difference Between Authority and Interpretation

I have sought to define and describe the nature of biblical authority. I have also sought to describe biblical interpretation and to identify the process by which any specific passage of the Bible should be interpreted. However, it is in the consideration of these two separate concepts that we arrive at the crux of our concern here. The fact that many people, many Christian people, and many Southern Baptists do not appear adequately to distinguish between these is the source of major difficulties.

The Importance of Distinguishing the Difference

It is obvious that not only do present-day Christians disagree on what the Bible teaches on many subjects, present-day Southern Baptists do as well. One church decides to ordain women and another seeks to have the first one removed from membership in the local association. One pastor insists that all church members be premillenialists and another insists that millenialism should be no test for membership or of orthodoxy. One church will not have a deacon who has been divorced while another makes no issue of the matter. At first glance, it appears that there is a major disagreement among these (and us) over the authority of the Bible.

First of all, we have already noted that there may be genuine commitment to the authority of the Scriptures and yet still be disagreement as to the actual nature of that authority. Consider Luther and Zwingli, for example. On the other hand, it appears that the kinds of differences which I have described here are not based upon this kind of issue. To the contrary, these kinds of disagreements rest on differences in interpretations rather than upon differences in commitment to biblical authority. It is precisely here, then, that we need to become sensitive to one another's problems, as well as to our own. Let us become aware that we can have identical commitments to biblical authority or to biblical inerrancy and still have honest disagreement over interpretations. Unless we carefully distinguish between these things, we shall argue, debate, and perhaps even break fellowship for the wrong reasons.

The Problems in Distinguishing the Difference

It is precisely as we confront the need of distinguishing the differences between disagreeing over biblical authority and disagreeing over biblical interpretation that we need to hear and heed Jesus' words.

> Judge not, that you be not judged. For with what judgment you pronounce you will be judged, and the measure you give will be the measure you get. Why do you see the speck that is in your brother's eye, but do not notice the log that is in your own eye? (Matt. 7:1-3)

We need to recognize and openly acknowledge that most of us have a problem in distinguishing between interpretation and authority. Unless we recognize this, we shall constantly be faced with two other problems. Carson and Woodbridge point out that the first of these

> is pugnaciousness. The line between contending for the faith and being contentious about the faith is extremely thin. A Christian can almost unknowingly develop a boisterous rhetoric and a caustic spirit, neither of which are helpful for the advance of the kingdom. The evangelical community suffers when its members lack humility and grace.[11]

What they applied to the larger evangelical community can clearly be applied to the Southern Baptist Convention as well.

On the other hand, facing this problem can give rise to the second. This is that we may become so cautious that we become proudly apathetic. We can become so content with divergent interpretations, so wrapped up in the search for truth that we fail to recognize, accept, and act upon truth when we confront it or are confronted by it. We cannot proclaim truth unless we have truth to proclaim. It is my opinion, however, that while the second problem may confront many evangelical Christians, the first is more present with most of us Southern Baptists at this point in our history.

Opportunities

At this point, most of us have major opportunities for doing good as we minister in our churches, our communities, our institutions, and our denomination. These opportunities rest with our communication of the truth that there is a difference, a major difference, which exists between biblical interpretation and biblical authority. We need to acknowledge that we can honestly disagree over many interpretations without disagreeing over authority. Let us help one another to at least listen to each other with more sensitive ears and hearts.

Conclusions

My conclusions have really been given throughout the paper. However, perhaps some of the more significant of these should be repeated here.

1. The Bible is a unique book, being both Divine and human. It is the revelation of God, being inspired by Him while being written by human beings.

2. The Bible has an authority over the lives of all people.

3. Christians acknowledge the authority of the Scriptures, finding that this authority rests upon the Lordship of Jesus Christ and the sovereignty of God.

4. The Bible, as an ancient book but a living Scripture, needs to be interpreted and applied to life as it is for people as they are. To acknowledge its authority and to fail to interpret it carefully, to apply it diligently, and to obey it devotedly is the height of folly.

5. We need to take seriously the responsibility of developing the skills and gifts bestowed by God as we work on the techniques of biblical interpretation.

6. We have a major opportunity to recognize, acknowledge, and communicate the fact that biblical authority and biblical interpretation are different issues. Let us seize this opportunity as the gift of God.

Notes

1. John M. Lewis, *Revelation, Inspiration, and Scripture,* p. 127.
2. Ibid., p. 129.
3. James Barr, *The Scope and Authority of the Bible,* p. 52.
4. Ibid., pp. 52 ff.
5. Dewey M. Beegle, *Scripture, Tradition, and Infallibility,* p. 301.
6. J. I. Packer, "The Infallibility of Scripture," *Scripture and Truth,* D. A. Carson and John D. Woodbridge, eds., p. 345.
7. John Newport, "Interpreting the Bible," BBC, vol. 1, rev., p. 25.
8. Ibid., p. 25.
9. Ibid., p. 26.
10. Ibid., p. 26.
11. D. A. Carson and John D. Woodbridge, eds. *Scripture and Truth,* p. 9.

20

THE RELATIONSHIP BETWEEN BIBLICAL INERRANCY AND BIBLICAL AUTHORITY

J. Terry Young

Let me introduce myself. I have been more than casually involved with the Bible virtually all my life. I had the good fortune of being born into a fine Baptist home. My earliest memories of my mother are of her holding me on her lap, telling me Bible stories, and leading me in a time of prayer. When I was a little older, she read the Bible to me and led me to pray. It was in one of those daily devotional times that she led me to a personal profession of faith in Jesus as my Savior and Lord. My earliest memories of my father are of him standing in the First Baptist Church of Houston, leading in prayer with his big Scofield Bible tucked under his arm. Our home life was built around the church and church activities.

About the time I entered college, I felt the strong call of God into the ministry. The Lord made it possible for me to get the best possible education for ministry in one of our fine Baptist colleges. Then I was blessed with the opportunity of earning two degrees from one of our fine Southern Baptist seminaries. Through all of those years the Bible was my devotional altar and was the subject of my scholarly study. Never was I not conscious of being in touch with the living God through his inspired written word.

I have had the opportunity to serve as pastor to three fine Baptist churches. My brethren in the associations and the state convention where I served expressed their confidence in me by electing me to a variety of offices, including a position as an officer of the state pastors conference and the state convention's executive board. After these years of proven service, I became editor of a state Baptist paper and now for the past sixteen years I have had the opportunity to teach at New Orleans Baptist Theological Seminary. The Bible is the basic textbook for each of my classes. I keep reminding my students that while it may matter what Carroll, Conner, Mullins, and Strong said, and while it may matter what Barth, Brunner, Bultmann, or Tillich said, it matters much more what the Bible says.

It is in that same vein that I am coming to you today. I am coming to you with reverence and respect for the Bible as the Word of God, and with a commitment to study it, teach it, and preach it with all of the intensity and expertise that I have.

I would like to begin with a discussion of biblical authority and then move to a discussion of biblical inerrancy and its relationship to biblical authority.

391

Biblical Authority

There is no more important question, in any discussion, than the question of authority. The question of authority is the most basic question that can be asked of one's system of belief, life style, or expression of hope for the future.

Definition of Authority

From a doctrinal or religious point of view, what is authority? Religious authority is the right to prescribe religious belief and behavior, or doctrine and ethics. Behind every system of belief there is an authority of some sort. Something, or some one, has the right to tell us how to shape our religious thought, our doctrines. This authority goes beyond the conceptual or doctrinal. Religious authority equally has the right to prescribe what actions are required of us. The question of authority is all determinative.

One's authority may be clearly understood, openly stated, and carefully followed. On the other hand authority may be more assumed than stated. One may assume that he is operating from one source of authority when in fact he is operating under an entirely different authority, following some other agenda.

Clearly perceived, clearly defined authority is critically important. In Christianity, we profess to have a theocentric faith, that is, a faith centered upon God. If that is the case, we must have a source of authority centered in God himself, lest we be guilty of making God in our own image and shaping our religious thought and practice to suit our own pleasures.

Possible Sources of Authority

If one does not agree with Baptists that the Bible is authoritative for our faith and practice, what then is his source of authority? Let us look briefly at four commonly accepted sources of authority.

Reason is a widely held source of authority not only in religion but in other matters as well. The human mind, following carefully developed processes of thought, can reach remarkable insights and conclusions. Many of these positions reached through the careful use of human reason have greatly benefited all mankind. Surely no one questions the power of human reason as a tool with which to work. But, very few, if any, among Baptists would want to make reason the final authority in matters of Christian belief and practice because it is so easily influenced by subjective factors.

Intuition is a second source of authority. Intuition is the ability to perceive truth apart from rational processes, on the one hand, and apart from empirical experience on the other hand. Intuitive ideas, ideas that seem to arise in the mind apart from our having consciously developed them, are very powerful. But are they always right? Only the most naive would want to assign authority to intuition, due to its subjective nature.

A third source of authority is tradition. In one sense, tradition is simply another name for history. We can ignore the insights of history, of our tradition, only at great peril to ourselves. But can we endow tradition with authority? Can the present generation go no farther than the previous one? Tradition, slavishly followed, effectively limits us to trying to reproduce the past in a society which advances ever farther from us. While tradition may help to keep alive the faith once delivered to the saints, it may also pass on to us all the failures and mistakes prompted by Satan himself and cause us to lose touch with the reality of our day. Tradition may be a good tool, but it makes a poor master. For when tradition becomes authoritative, we are absolutizing human insight and human wisdom.

Revelation is the fourth possible source of authority. And it is clearly the one selected by virtually all Baptists. Religious thought and action must be ordered by God himself, not by human insight, not even human insight at its best. The contours of Christian belief and service are given to us by God himself. The revelation that God has given of himself, of his saving work through Jesus Christ, and of what he expects of us as believers has become for us the authority in religious matters. Responding to God's revelation takes priority over all other ways of thinking or acting. The God who is said to be at the center of our Christian faith is also the ultimate authority in determining how we shall think of him and how we shall serve him. His revelation comes to us as a demand that clearly transcends all other ways of thinking about him. But how does this authority confront us?

How Authority Functions

There are several ways of understanding how authority works. Let us look at them briefly.

One model of authority is the institutional model. Authority, whatever its source, is invested in an institution. An obvious example here is the Roman Catholic Church. The system, the institution, is considered all-important and all else is secondary. Authority administered through an institution, takes on a rather impersonal, mechanical face.

A second model of authority is the legal model. Here authority is invested in a set of laws or fixed ideas. The laws and precepts may have been given originally to express the will of the one who stands above and behind them, but they have now become an end in themselves. A good example of the legal model of authority is what Jesus saw in the Pharisaic interpretation of the Law in his day.

The third model of authority is the personal. Authority rests in a person. In this case, the authority of the Bible is seen to be the authority of God himself. The authority of the Bible is seen to be not so much in what it says as in who said it. And the authority we sense when we read the Bible is not so much the authority of the information contained in the Bible as it is the authority of the one who inspired the Bible and continues to speak through it.

Surely, when we talk about religious authority, or biblical authority, we are talking primarily about the personal authority of God himself. Let us examine more fully how the authority of the Bible is the personal authority of God himself.

A Pattern of Authority

Baptists are a people who have given the highest possible emphasis to the authority of the Bible in our faith and practice. Indeed, one who does not know us better might conclude that we are making the Bible to be God, since we use such strong language about the authority of the Bible.

Perhaps we need to clarify what we are saying here, lest we be misunderstood. The Bible has an unsurpassed authority, but it is a derived authority, not an authority of its own. It is supremely authoritative for us because it draws its authority from God who inspired it. We must always beware the temptation to let something take the place of God.

For the sake of clarity and simplicity, we are prone to reduce complex matters to their lowest common denominator. We want to reduce the question of religious authority to a simple, single source of authority. If we say the Bible is our ultimate authority, what happens to God? Does he have no authority? Or, if we say that God is our ultimate authority, what happens to the Bible? And to Jesus Christ? And, to the Holy Spirit?

Can we reduce the question of authority to a single source? Or, must we conclude that religious authority exists in a pattern of authority, a complex structure of shared authority, heading up in God himself. Merely to raise these questions is to answer them, at least in part. As long as we believe that the Bible is authoritative and that God is sovereign, we will be forced to understand that authority exists in a pattern or complex of shared authority.

The real world is made up of complexities, no matter how much we may like to reduce things to simplicities. We seek the one and only true God, and when we find him we discover that he exists only in the mystery of the trinity. We seek the one and only authority to tell us about God and what he expects of us. But when we find that authority in the Bible, we discover that it is a derived authority which exists only in a complex pattern of authority that heads up in God himself.

God is the ultimate authority, not only in religious matters, but in all things. His sovereignty extends to all of reality. (Even the political authority of this world is derived from the authority of God himself, according to Paul in Romans 13:1-6.) His authority is without parallel.

God himself is the ultimate, supreme authority, but he shares that authority in order to accomplish his will. The ultimate authority of God the Father is shared in a pattern or complex of authority that flows down from him. Jesus Christ shares the authority of God, his Father. He is the beloved Son of God, sent as the Savior of a lost world, and as the full personal revelation of God.

The Holy Spirit also shares in the authority of God the Father. He represents the personal presence of both God and Jesus with the people of God, the disciples of Jesus. Because the Holy Spirit is the third person of the trinity, and therefore shares in the ultimate authority of God, he can guide the church, give boldness and power to believers, convict the lost, and produce the miracle of the new birth or conversion for those who are dead in their sins.

Where is the authority of the Bible in this pattern of authority? It certainly is

394

not in fourth place, counting downward in an organizational chart. The authority of the Scriptures is certainly not a secondary authority. But the authority of the Scriptures is a derived authority, an authority which comes from God himself. Saying that the authority of the Bible is a derived authority, an authority imparted by God, does not at all diminish the significance of the authority of the Bible. Rather, this stresses the significance of the authority of the Bible, because in the Bible we are confronted with the authority of God himself.

The Bible is critically important to us, from the standpoint of authority, because it is our primary window through which to understand the workings of the Holy Spirit, see Jesus and what he did, and to know of God the Father in whom all authority rests and from whom all authority flows. It is only through the Bible, which God has made authoritative, that we can gain information about God, about salvation, and about what God expects of us in this life. What does the Bible itself say about its authority?

The Authority of the Bible as Attested in Scripture

The authority of the Bible is more assumed than taught in the Scriptures. The authority of the word of God is more praised than explained by the various authors of Scripture. That is not so surprising when you remember that nowhere does the Bible prove the existence of God; it simply assumes the existence of God and proceeds to talk about him. (Note how Genesis 1:1 begins.) Hundreds, if not thousands, of Scripture passages indirectly suggest the authority of the Bible. These are casual statements made in the process of developing some other point.

There are many references praising the authority, power, beauty, or some other aspect of the Bible. A good example of this is the 119th Psalm. This entire Psalm is a beautifully crafted poem concerning the Scriptures. It begins with the declaration of profound confidence in the word of God to guide one in life, "Blessed are those whose way is blameless, who walk in the law of the Lord!" (Psalm 119:1). "For ever, O Lord, thy word is firmly fixed in the heavens" (Psalm 119:89). "Thy word is a lamp to my feet and a light to my path" (Psalm 119:105). These are all exclamations of praise rather than carefully developed statements or arguments to prove the authority of the Scriptures.

The Bible does go beyond mere praise of the authority of the Scriptures, however. In a few passages, the authority of the Bible is stated rather explicitly. For instance, 2 Peter 1:20-21 declares that though there is a human element in Scripture, what is in Scripture is initiated by God and comes from God: "First of all you must understand this, that no prophecy of Scripture is a matter of one's own interpretation, because no prophecy ever came by the impulse of man, but men moved by the Holy Spirit spoke from God."

A much earlier passage in the Old Testament makes a strong case for recognizing the authority and sanctity of the Scripture. "You shall not add to the word which I command you, nor take from it; that you may keep the commandments of the Lord your God which I command you" (Deuteronomy 4:2). This same teaching is repeated in Deuteronomy 12:32, in Joshua 1:7-8, and in Revelation 22:18-19. The Scriptures are to be reverenced and followed in obedience, letting the teaching of Scripture saturate all of life for the people of God.

Perhaps the most important passage in all of the Bible concerning the Scriptures is found in 2 Timothy 3:14-17. This is the only passage in the whole Bible that directly declares that the Scriptures are inspired. Here Paul declared to Timothy, "All Scripture is inspired by God . . ." (2 Timothy 3:16). The word translated inspired here is the Greek word *theopneustos*. It comes from two words, *theos* (which means God) and *pneuma* (which means breath or spirit). Literally, the word *theopneustos* means God-breathed. Nothing is said as to how inspiration works or how the Scriptures are God breathed. No theory of inspiration is suggested. But what is said here is crucially important. Note that the International Conference on Biblical Inerrancy declared in its 1978 Chicago Statement on Biblical Inerrancy that the mode of inspiration remains a mystery that we cannot penetrate, and that we can do no more than declare that the Bible is inspired.

The idea of the Scriptures being God-breathed suggests that the Holy Spirit was directly involved in the process of God giving the Scriptures through the various writers. This figure of God-breathed also calls to mind the account of the creation of man in Genesis 2:7. God created man from the dust of the ground and breathed his own breath into the man's nostrils so that he became a living being.

Scriptures are *theopneustos,* God-breathed. That is, they draw their life and vitality, their worth, from God who has breathed life into them just as he did into Adam. We can speak of the Scriptures being a living word of God precisely because they are God-breathed, not just one more piece of dead literature.

We must not take away from the meaning of this profound declaration that the Scriptures are God-breathed. But we must also be careful that we do not add to what is being said. It is enough to say that they are God-breathed, or inspired. If that does not command our respect for the Scriptures, no amount of speculative theorizing on our part will suffice. The most compelling argument that can be given for the authority of the Bible is the simple declaration that the Scriptures are God-breathed. The Scriptures draw their life, their authority from God himself.

Why are the Scriptures God-breathed, inspired? Paul answers that for us in this same passage where he declares that the Scriptures are inspired. He told Timothy that the Scriptures "are able to instruct you for salvation through faith in Christ Jesus" (2 Timothy 3:15). The purpose of the Scriptures is redemptive, to bring us to salvation in Jesus. There is a scarlet thread of redemption running all the way through the Bible, from the first to last. We dare not lose sight of that redemptive theme or let it be transformed into something else.

Paul expanded on this theme of redemption as he dealt with the inspiration and authority of the Bible in this passage addressed to Timothy. "All Scripture is inspired by God and profitable for teaching, for reproof, for correction, and for training in righteousness, that the man of God may be complete, equipped for every good work." The inspired Bible is therefore our basic textbook for teaching in the church. It is in the Bible that we can learn about God, about ourselves, about how God has chosen to save us, and what it means for us to be born-again children of God.

The Bible is authoritative for us for training in righteousness, for rebuking and correcting us in our sins. The Christian life is meant to be a life born of the Spirit of God and developed to maturity in Christlikeness. The Bible is the norm or standard by which we are to order our conduct.

The Bible is authoritative for us to use in equipping God's people for every good work. We have been saved to serve God, not just to get a free trip to heaven sometime out in the future. God expects that every Christian will be a serving Christian in some way or another. And the Bible is the manual of instruction we should use in equipping believers for obedient service to God and man.

While there may be relatively few passages of Scripture such as 2 Timothy 3:14-17 and 2 Peter 1:20-21, which teach us explicitly concerning the authority of the Bible, there are hundreds, if not thousands, of references which assume the integrity, validity, and authority of the Bible as the word of God. Isaiah was certainly convinced that his own message was a message from God as he addressed Judah, "Hear the word of the Lord, you rulers of Sodom! Give ear to the teaching of our God, you people of Gomorrah!" (Isaiah 1:10). Jeremiah directly attributed his message to God as he said, "Now the word of the Lord came to me, saying . . ." (Jeremiah 1:4). Ezekiel was convinced that his message came from God and that he was but the human spokesman. "Moreover he said to me, 'Son of man, all my words that I shall speak to you, receive in your heart, and hear with your ears. And go, get you to the exiles, to your people and say to them, "Thus says the Lord God . . ."'" (Ezekiel 3:10-11). Instances like these could be given almost indefinitely. How many times we find a biblical writer or preacher saying, "Thus says the Lord," or "the word of the Lord came unto me," or "Hear the word of the Lord." Clearly they understood that something was being given to them in inspiration from God, and what they were given was packed with authority, God's own authority. But the writers of sacred Scripture never tell us *how* the word came to them.

Jesus clearly reverenced the Scriptures. Hear him in the Sermon on the Mount, "Think not that I have come to abolish the law and the prophets; I have come not to abolish them but to fulfill them. For truly, I say to you, till heaven and earth pass away, not an iota, not a dot, will pass from the law until all is accomplished" (Matthew 5:17-18). But note also that Jesus did not hesitate to build upon what was already given in the Old Testament Scriptures and bring forth new dimensions and deeper meanings than had been apparent prior to his day. (See Matthew 5:21-22, 27-28.)

Jesus found that his own life and ministry here upon the earth was grounded in the Scriptures of the Old Testament. His first public sermon, according to Luke, was to announce that he had come to fulfill what was written in Isaiah 61 (Luke 4:16-21). The word of God, treasured in his heart, gave him courage and direction when he was confronted with temptation. Each of the three times Satan tried to tempt him when he was in the wilderness, Satan was rebuked with a quotation of Scripture from Jesus' lips. Jesus found that the Scriptures were authoritative not only for us ordinary people but for himself also (Luke 4:4, 8, 12).

Jesus repeatedly used Scripture to interpret to his disciples who he was and what was going to happen to him (Luke 18:31-33, 24:27). These are but a few of the many instances that could be cited where Jesus showed his respect for the authority of the Scriptures.

Characteristics of Biblical Authority

How can we best describe the authority of the Bible? Earlier, I suggested that there are three models of authority, institutional, legal, and personal. Surely, the personal model best serves as the model of biblical authority. If we view the authority of the Bible as either institutional or legal, we lose the personal sense of God speaking through the Scriptures to us.

The authority of the Bible is derived from God who is the ultimate authority. The authority of the Bible is the personal authority of God himself speaking through Scripture to us. This is not at all to play down the significance of the Bible and what it teaches. It is to play up the authority of almighty God who was the source of this message when it was first written and who speaks through it to us today. The authority that confronts us in the Bible is none other than the authority of God himself.

The authority of the Bible is a living authority. The Bible is not just a dead letter or book which records important ideas and events from a remote past. The Bible is a living book, alive with the personal presence and authority of God still revealing himself through its teachings. We may not always sense the presence and power of God when we read the pages of the Bible. But the fault is with us, not with God or the authority of the Bible. Very likely, most of us here have had many experiences when we felt God speaking through the Scriptures to us to comfort, or guide or convict, or enlighten us. The authority of the Bible is the authority of the Holy Spirit sent by both the Father and the Son to be our constant companion and guide.

The authority of the Bible is dynamic, powerful. The Bible is the primary means by which God has chosen to reveal himself to us today. Therefore, he seeks to speak through it powerfully and persuasively, God is not a detached, disinterested God far removed from us. He is at work, seeking the lost and nurturing the saved. That is why God has declared, "For as the rain and the snow come down from heaven, and return not thither but water the earth, making it bring forth and sprout, giving seed to the sower and bread to the eater, so shall my word be that goes forth from my mouth; it shall not return to me empty, but it shall accomplish that which I purpose, and prosper in the thing for which I sent it" (Isaiah 55:10-11). God was not content merely to inspire a book of truth about himself and his will for us. God has made the written word a living word, speaking through it wherever it is read, if the reader is listening for the voice of God. "For the word of God is living and active, sharper than any two-edged sword, piercing to the division of soul and spirit, of joints and marrow, and discerning the thoughts and intentions of the heart" (Hebrews 4:12).

This conception of the Bible as dynamic is closely related to our understanding of the Holy Spirit. Jesus told his disciples that one of the functions of the Holy Spirit is to convince persons concerning sin, righteousness, and judgment (John 16:8-11). The Holy Spirit in the world convicts, converts, equips, guides, and comforts people. In doing all of these things, the Holy Spirit is intimately involved with Scripture. The authority and power of the Bible is the authority of the Holy Spirit working through the Bible wherever it is preached, taught, or studied.

The authority of the Bible is purposive. God has sent forth his written word to reveal what he is like and what he wants for and from us. It is much more than just a collection of historical memorabilia. The purpose of the Bible in its authoritative address to us is to make God known to us and help us realize that we are lost in sin without the salvation offered through Jesus Christ. The Bible's purpose is to bring us to salvation and nurture us into stalwart Christians who gladly and joyfully become servants of God.

The authority of the Bible is the authority of redemption. From the beginning right on through to the end, the Bible unfolds for us the redemptive nature of God and his work of redemption which was worked out patiently and lovingly until it was most fully revealed in the death, burial, and resurrection of his Son, Jesus Christ. The power which once brought Jesus back from the dead now calls persons from spiritual death to the vitality of new birth and new life. Any view of the authority of the Bible which does not see it as the authority of redemption misses the true nature of the Bible and misunderstands the purpose of God.

The authority of the Bible is dependable and trustworthy, because the authority of the Bible is the authority of God himself. We need never fear that the Bible will lead us astray at any point. It is God's purpose to lead, not mislead, us when we come to the pages of sacred Scripture. In addition to the many verses of Scripture which assure us of the dependability of the Bible, all of the passages which assure us of the dependability of God himself can be applied to the authority of the Bible.

The authority of the Bible is unchanging. It does not gradually diminish with the passing of time. The fact that we are getting ever farther away in time from the days when Jesus walked this earth does not at all diminish the authority of the Bible. As Isaiah said, "The grass withers, the flower fades; but the word of our God will stand forever" (Isaiah 40:8).

The authority of the Bible demands our serious attention. It is not a neutral or indifferent authority. The authority of the Bible is an insistent authority. It confronts us with urgency. "He who despises the word bring destruction on himself, but he who respects the commandment will be rewarded" (Proverbs 13:13). The purposes of God are urgent and important. That is why the authority of the Bible, derived from God's own authority, is so urgent and demanding.

399

The authority of the Bible is the authority of the holiness of God. It is the authority that confronted Moses when he stood before the burning bush in the wilderness. The voice of God confronted him, saying, "Put off your shoes from your feet, for the place on which you are standing is holy ground" (Exodus 3:5). When we stand before the Bible, we are confronted by the holiness, the authority of God, which demands our utmost respect, reverence, and obedience. It is not accidental that the Scriptures are called The Holy Bible.

At the same time, the authority of the Bible is gentle as it confronts us. It works through inner persuasion, rather than external compulsion, trying to draw the proper response from us in personal faith and commitment. The authority of the Bible works through the inner pleading of the Holy Spirit rather than through some form of coercion or compulsion. God is God and can use any means he so chooses, but he has chosen to respect our free wills, leaving us to make intelligent, personal decisions as we relate to him or to his word. To be sure, all power belongs to God, but he does not always use all of the power available to him as he relates to us. The authority of the Bible, while it is awesome in its potential power, moves in quiet, persuasive, yet gentle ways as it convicts, nurtures, and leads us. "Not by might, nor by power, but by my Spirit, says the Lord of hosts" (Zechariah 4:6). There are unlimited powers undergirding the authority of the Bible. But they operate in controlled restraint, speaking in the persuasive still small voice (See 1 Kings 19:11-12).

The authority of the Bible is the authority of grace and peace. These two important biblical concepts are so much at the heart of the gospel of Jesus Christ that the Apostle Paul used them in the introduction to each of the letters that he wrote in our New Testament. (See Romans 1:7, 1 Corinthians 1:3, 2 Corinthians 1:2, Galatians 1:3, etc.). These were not empty words for Paul. Rather they were his badge of authority, his mark of identification. These words were more than a friendly greeting with a religious sound. Grace and peace were the very reason why the persons who received Paul's letters should read them and pay close attention to what was said. God's grace is that unmerited favor which God offers to us. It is God's love and power in action, forgiving our sins and granting us new life in Christ Jesus. Grace is the blessing of God reaching down to us to meet our needs, not only for forgiveness and salvation, but also for the development of the Christian life. Through grace God establishes a bond of peace between himself and us, a bond of peace so strong that no outside power can break it. God seeks to nurture that bond of peace so that we grow closer to him in an ever deeper, ever richer relationship to him.

The authority of the Bible is the authority of love, God's love. Perhaps this is the most important statement that can be made about the authority of the Bible. For, the most important thing that can be said about God is that he is love (see 1 John 4:8, 16). The whole Bible summed up in one verse is built on the foundation of love, "For God so loved the world that he gave his only Son, that whosoever believes in him should not perish but have eternal life" (John 3:16). This love is the authority that confronts us in the word of God. This love has all the characteristics described by Paul in 1 Corinthians 13. So important and

400

powerful is this love which comes to us that it kindles a fire of love in us (1 John 4:19). And Jesus insisted that our highest priority in life is to love God with a total love that knows no restrictions, and that we are also to love our fellow human beings with at least as much concern as we have for our own best interests (Matthew 22:36-40). We have not really understood the authority of the Bible until we see it as the authority of God's love reaching down to us. We have not really understood that authority until we fully live in love for God and love for each other.

The Proof of Biblical Authority

How can we really know that the Bible has the authority that we have been describing? There is no proof that the Bible has any authority whatsoever, unless we resort to quoting verses from the Bible itself to prove that it is authoritative, and that is a circular argument. In the final analysis, we know that the Bible is authoritative only by faith. This does not put the Bible on a shaky foundation, or cast shadows of doubt upon it. Remember that we cannot prove the existence of God, either. We know God only by faith; no one can prove that God exists and then use the proof to compel others to believe in him. Nor can we prove the authority of the Bible and then use that proof to make it impossible for others to disbelieve.

We can know the authority of the Bible only by approaching it reverently, in sincerity, in faith, allowing it to speak to us. When we come to the Bible in faith, then we will perceive its authority, an authority that seems to grow stronger the better we become acquainted with the Bible.

Some are not content to say that the authority of the Bible can be known only by faith. They want carefully devised proofs of the authority of God's word. However, those who demand external proofs never really trust the authority of the Scriptures. They rely on human arguments about the Bible rather than hear God in the heart through faith. You cannot establish the authority of the Bible in an argument, or in a court of law, or in a scholar's study. You can only establish the authority of the Bible on your knees in prayer.

Biblical Inerrancy

Several observations are in order as we turn to the topic of inerrancy. As Baptists we are universally agreed on the authority of the Bible as the unalterable standard for Christian faith and practice. This is made perfectly clear in the Baptist Faith and Message. Baptists are also universally agreed that the Bible is fully inspired.

When we turn, however, to the topic of biblical inerrancy we find that Baptists are deeply divided over this question. This is not due to a lack of confidence in the Bible on the part of some. It is due, partly, to the difficulty of defining what is meant by inerrancy. It is due, partly, to the fact that the term inerrancy is not a biblical term. And it is due, in part, to the fact that Baptists have come to the discussion of inerrancy relatively recently.

401

Historical Perspective

While there are strong affirmations of the truthfulness and reliability of the Bible in every age, dating all the way back to the New Testament, the subject of biblical inerrancy is of more recent origin. Many scholars believe that the discussion of inerrancy as such arose during the post-Reformation era. The subject of infallibility and inerrancy arose in the period just after the Reformation known as Protestant Scholasticism, a time when Protestant scholars sought to fix doctrinal thought just as it was then and preserve it intact forevermore. Every doctrine was hedged about with a rational defense.

The discussion of inerrancy did not enter the language of Southern Baptists until the last decade or two. Most of our confessions of faith make strong affirmations of the reliability, trustworthiness, authority, and inspiration of the Bible, but they do not use the terminology that some are insisting on today.

The theologians who have most influenced Southern Baptists in the 20th century are Edgar Young Mullins, Walter Thomas Conner, and Augustus Hopkins Strong. In their basic systematic theology books, which have been the textbooks of thousands of us, they did not use the language of inerrancy/infallibility and they showed that they were keenly aware of the issues of inerrancy. Strong argued against inerrancy in one place, although developing a major argument for the authority and reliability of the Bible. Mullins and Conner, writing in the heat of the modernist-fundamentalist controversy, argued for a strong position concerning the authority and reliability of the Bible but refused to accept the inerrancy position. They showed that they were well aware of the issue and chose to uphold the authority of the Bible apart from the position of inerrancy. When the Baptist Faith and Message was drafted in 1925, and revised in 1963, the authors chose to follow the New Hampshire Confession of Faith, which deliberately avoids the inerrancy position, instead of following the Philadelphia Confession of Faith which uses the term infallible. Inerrancy has not been part of our Southern Baptist heritage. We have only lately come to this discussion.

The discussion of inerrancy among Southern Baptists during recent years is a classic example of misunderstanding. It represents an almost total breakdown in communication because when examined closely the subject is much more complex than it appears. We have contended over labels and slogans without honestly examining issues.

Biblical Perspective

The inerrantist quickly admits that the term inerrancy does not appear in Scripture. But he is just as quick to assert that the Scripture writers are teaching inerrancy, even though the term is not used. This is a logical implication, a rational conclusion based upon study of the Scriptures. The inerrantist holds that nearly any statement in Scripture concerning the trustworthiness and dependability of the Bible is a statement in support of the idea of inerrancy. To reject inerrancy is to reject the trustworthiness and reliability of the Bible.

The non-inerrantist, at least among Baptists, has equal confidence in the

402

trustworthiness and reliability of the Scriptures; there is nothing to debate here. But the non-inerrantist feels that the teaching of inerrancy, with its technical implications, is imposed on the Scriptures rather than found in them. The non-inerrantist feels that he is being more faithful to the Bible by not going beyond what the Bible says about itself.

Clearly, in the Bible there are many assertions of the trustworthiness of Scripture. No one among Baptists would argue that. But affirming the inerrancy of the Bible goes far beyond affirming the complete reliability and trustworthiness of the Bible. Inerrancy, as used by most writers, is a specialized, technical statement about the reliability of the Bible. It is very important to recognize this technical aspect of inerrancy. The inerrantist must be asked here, "What do you mean by the term inerrancy?" It is here that we discover that there are many forms of inerrancy with very considerable differences of meaning between some of them. And, there are many forms of non-inerrancy. The discussion is much more complex than is readily apparent.

Different Levels of Discussion

Among Southern Baptists, discussions of the Bible are actually moving on two different levels. The popular and the scholarly, or the technical and the non-technical. It is one thing to affirm, at the popular level, that the Bible is fully reliable and will not mislead us in any way in our Christian belief and practice. But, it is quite another matter to declare that the Bible is technically perfect in every way.

Many among us are using the term inerrancy to signify support for the trustworthiness and reliability of the Bible in a popular or non-technical way. This is the language of common speech, of the pulpit, where we simply affirm the Bible as the word of God and declare it totally reliable. Which one of us does not use ordinary, popular, non-technical language for the major portion of our talk with loved ones and friends? As I hear many Baptists using the terms inerrancy and infallible, I hear them using these terms in just this non-technical way.

At the same time, the scholar is functioning at a very technical and sophisticated level. Here words are rarely used in an everyday or common way. Words here can have specialized meanings and carry very significant implications that are foreign to everyday talk. This is why many refuse to use the terms inerrant and infallible with reference to the Bible. They have no doubts about the integrity and validity of the Bible. But they are acutely aware of the connotations that inerrancy and infallibility carry. They are unwilling to accept all of the baggage that comes with the terms on the technical level. The scholar then searches for more acceptable language.

The inerrantists and the non-inerrantists may be much closer together than is readily apparent. Unfortunately they can't communicate because they do not seem to realize that they are functioning at two different levels, each of which certainly has its place.

403

Different Approaches to the Bible

The confusion over discussions of inerrancy is further compounded by two very different approaches to study of the Bible. This makes the debate even more difficult to resolve.

Inerrantists use a deductive approach to the Bible. They begin, apart from the Bible, with the premise that God is perfect and reach a conclusion through logic that the Bible is totally without error of any kind since it is the word of God. Then, in turning to the Bible, that conclusion is quickly limited to the original manuscript, since it very obviously does not fit the Bible we have today.

The non-inerrantists use an inductive approach to the Bible, beginning with the Bible itself, and discover through reading the Bible that the Bibles we have today cannot be called inerrant. Everyone is quite aware, including inerrantists, that the Bible we use today has many minor discrepancies and variations in it, none of which affect any teaching. The Bible is perfectly reliable in terms of its purpose, for it will not lead us astray at any point of Christian belief or practice. But we cannot use the term inerrant since there are many superficial flaws in our present texts.

In essence, the inerrantists and the non-inerrantists are not even talking about the same thing. The inerrantists are only talking about the original manuscripts of the Bible, and the non-inerrantists are only talking about the Bible we have to use today.

It is no wonder that there is misunderstanding and confusion and deep division. We are dealing with a very delicate matter where feelings are very sensitive. We are functioning at two different levels, the popular and the technical. And we are operating with two different methodologies, the deductive and the inductive. One group is talking about original manuscripts, and the other group is talking about the Bible we use today.

The problem is further compounded by the fact that there are many varieties of inerrancy and non-inerrancy.

Varieties of Non-Inerrancy

Non-inerrantists are not all alike. There is no one position of non-inerrancy. They do not all believe the same thing about the Bible. They can range from very conservative to quite liberal.

Some non-inerrantists deny that the Bible is either inspired or authoritative. They see the Bible simply as one more human document. There are the radical biblical critics. Very likely there are no Southern Baptists among this group.

Some non-inerrantists strongly insist that the Bible is fully inspired and supremely authoritative. They see it as the word of God. They respect the Bible and seek to understand it and teach it faithfully and responsibly. Southern Baptist non-inerrantists are almost certainly in this group. They are as serious about the Bible as the inerrantists are.

Varieties of Inerrancy

There are many varieties of inerrancy. The mere fact that one accepts the label of inerrantist does not tell you much about his position with regard to the

Bible. There are numerous kinds of inerrancy, with subtle and not-so-subtle differences. Virtually every inerrantist has some qualification that he makes to define his position. Almost no one teaches an absolute, total inerrancy of the Bible, with no qualifications or reservations. The popular perception may be that this is what is being defended courageously and vigorously, but such a position is only put forth at the popular level.

When the inerrantist works out his view at a more serious or scholarly level, he inevitably makes numbers of concessions or qualifications in order to describe more accurately what he is talking about.

Very important qualifications of inerrancy are made by virtually all of the leading scholars contending for inerrancy. The International Conference on Biblical Inerrancy, composed of several hundred inerrantists, made 19 statements defining what is meant by inerrancy, and 19 statements defining what is not meant by inerrancy (See the Chicago Statement on Biblical Inerrancy, 1978).

A quick review of some of the qualifications that various inerrantists introduce into their statements concerning inerrancy reveals that inerrancy is not what is appears to be to the casual observer.

1. Only the autographs (original manuscripts) are inerrant/infallible.
2. The Scripture writers used phenomenological language, the non-technical language of common appearances.
3. Inerrancy/infallibility does not apply to grammatical errors.
4. Inerrancy/infallibility is limited to what the author intended to teach, and does not include circumstantial, casual references.
5. Standards of modern technical precision do not apply to these ancient writings.
6. Reporting of falsehoods is recognized.
7. Use of hyperbole is recognized.
8. The topical arrangement of material is recognized.
9. Variant selections of material in parallel accounts does not negate inerrancy/infallibility.
10. The use of free citations is recognized.
11. The unresolved difficulties with problem passages do not negate inerrancy/infallibility since these may yet be resolved.

After all of the qualifications are made, the inerrantist position is virtually identical to the position of the non-inerrantist. For the inerrantist has openly identified and set aside most, if not all, of the problems which prevent the non-inerrantist from using the term inerrancy. Perhaps a term which has to have so many qualifications is not the best term to use. It may hide rather than reveal the true nature of the Bible. At best it is misleading, the non-inerrantist will say.

The non-inerrantist feels that a major weakness of inerrancy is that it seems to cast doubt on the Bible we use today. The non-inerrantist is unhappy with the position of inerrancy, not because it claims too much for the Bible, but because it claims too little for it. Saying that inerrancy applies only to the original manuscripts automatically implies that the Bibles we have today are faulty, unreliable. The serious non-inerrantist among Baptists would never make such an assertion.

Search for Common Ground

In Baptist circles, there is not as much difference between the inerrantist and the non-inerrantist as it might appear. When all of the qualifications of inerrancy are made by the inerrantist, his position is virtually identical to that of the non-inerrantist.

Is there common ground, a basis for some productive discussions that might bring us back together? Surely there is. Professor David S. Dockery of Criswell College has identified nine possible positions held by various scholars with regard to inerrancy, suggesting that somewhere in these nine positions we might be able to find common ground. (See his "Variations on Inerrancy" in *SBC Today*, May, 1986, pages 10-11). Let's look briefly at these nine possible positions.

1. Mechanical dictation—God dictated every word of the Bible. This view simply ignores style differences as well as differing historical and cultural contexts.
2. Absolute inerrancy—The Bible is true and accurate in all matters. This view uses the plenary-verbal view of inspiration, attempting to separate itself from the dictation view while assuring that the Bible is the written word of God. It does not take seriously the human aspect, or the historical contexts, in trying to harmonize the apparent differences and difficulties in Scripture.
3. Critical inerrancy—This view says that the Bible is completely true in all that the Bible affirms to the degree of precision intended by the original author. It does not seek to harmonize every detail. Scientific matters are considered to be treated with phenomenological language rather than technical or scientific thinking. This view allows cautious use of critical methodologies in interpretation. It takes seriously both the human and divine elements.
4. Limited inerrancy—The Bible is inerrant in all matters of salvation and ethics, faith and practice, and matters which can be empirically validated. It is inerrant only in matters for which the Bible was given. It seeks to be empirical.
5. Qualified inerrancy—This view is similar to the previous position but starts with a faith statement concerning inerrancy. It attempts to take seriously the human and the divine elements. The view is difficult to articulate.
6. Nuanced-inerrancy—This view takes into account the various kinds of literature in the Bible recognizing that some passages require dictation in inspiration while others, as in poetry or stories or proverbs, may require only dynamic inspiration. It takes seriously the human and the divine elements.
7. Functional inerrancy—The Bible is inerrant in its purpose or function. It is inerrant in bringing people to salvation and growth in the Christian life.
8. Inerrancy is irrelevant—This view neither affirms nor denies inerrancy.

406

Inerrancy is pointless, irrelevant, concerned only with theological minutiae.

9. Biblical authority—This view suggests that the Bible is authoritative only to point one to an encounter with God. It does not take seriously the divine element in the words of the Bible. It freely admits human errors and finds them of no consequence.

Several of the views of inerrancy identified by Dr. Dockery might prove to be acceptable to both inerrantists and non-inerrantists in our present Baptist fellowship.

Relationship of Authority and Inerrancy

Baptists are unanimous in affirming the authority of the Bible. Inerrantists and non-inerrantists alike affirm the full authority of the Bible for Christian faith and practice. Baptists differ only on the question of inerrancy, and we are probably much closer together on this question than is apparent.

What is the relationship between biblical authority and biblical inerrancy? And where are Baptists on this comparative question? Perhaps there are four possible positions concerning the relationship of authority and inerrancy.

1. The question of authority and the question of inerrancy are identical questions; they only use different terminology to signify the same concept. One might hold this position but he would find very little support for this view. Historically, they have almost always been treated as separate questions.

2. The question of authority and the question of inerrancy are totally unrelated questions. Neither depends upon the other, and neither necessarily leads to the other.

3. Biblical inerrancy is the primary question and biblical authority is the secondary question. This would mean that authority, which is an important biblical teaching, is made dependent upon inerrancy which at most is only an implication drawn from Scripture.

4. Biblical authority is the primary question and biblical inerrancy is the secondary question. Biblical authority is much more forcefully established in Scripture and furnishes a secure foundation upon which a case for inerrancy can be made.

Most Baptists probably support either the second or the fourth options. The first option cannot be substantiated. The third option would leave biblical authority in a vulnerable position of lesser importance.

Some inerrantists feel that inerrancy is the necessary companion of biblical authority. They feel that biblical authority is seriously weakened, if not destroyed, if inerrancy is not maintained. Some inerrantists do not understand an authority which does not include inerrancy, because for them biblical authority is the authority of rational truth.

Non-inerrantists feel that biblical authority stands independent of any theory of inerrancy. Even if biblical inerrancy could be proved, the non-inerrantist feels that it would add nothing to the idea of biblical authority, for the authority of the Bible is the personal authority of God himself. Furthermore, biblical authority is

407

a major teaching of the Bible whereas biblical inerrancy is only an implication, if it is taught at all. The non-inerrancy points out that there is a long tradition of biblical authority, while inerrancy is a relatively recent idea. at least as far as the term itself is concerned.

Neither biblical inerrancy nor biblical authority necessarily leads to the other. The question of authority is of a higher priority than the question of inerrancy, and it has received much more attention in the history of Christian thought. Biblical authority is not made stronger by a doctrine of inerrancy, nor is it necessarily made weaker by the lack of a doctrine of inerrancy. For the authority of the Bible is the authority of God. How can we add anything to the authority of God, or take anything away from the authority of God?

Conclusion

Let us take our bearings and see where we are after sailing some stormy seas for nearly a decade now. Several things might well be noted here.

1. We have had more division than debate or discussion. It is at least a step in the right direction that we have met this week to discuss issues.

2. We are solidly united in terms of support of biblical authority. There is no division in the Baptist family concerning the authority of the Bible.

3. We are divided on the question of inerrancy, partly because the two groups among us are approaching the Bible at different levels and with different methodologies, and partly because the position of inerrancy has not been defined carefully by those who favor inerrancy.

4. We may be much closer together as Baptists concerning the Bible than is immediately apparent. For, the non-inerrantists and the inerrantists are saying virtually the same thing after the inerrantists make their qualifications of inerrancy.

There are at least three unresolved issues that need to be noted.

1. Biblical Interpretation: As I have heard and read much of what has been said and written concerning Baptists and inerrancy in recent years, I have had a growing conviction that inerrancy is not the real issue at all. The underlying issue is the issue of interpretation. How the Bible is interpreted is of much greater significance than is a theory concerning inerrancy. It is good that we are meeting in 1988 for a conference on biblical interpretation, and again in 1989 to discuss biblical imperatives or biblical application.

2. Biblical Application: It is also crucially important that we apply the Bible carefully and faithfully. Biblical authority and biblical inerrancy are rendered meaningless if we do not translate the biblical teachings into both belief and practice. Biblical inerrancy, or any other affirmation of the Scriptures, is no more than an empty shibboleth if we do not apply the teachings of the Bible to our relationships to each other in our denomination and in our churches. Perhaps the ultimate irony is a group of brethren fighting over what word to use in describing the Bible.

3. Overt Political Activity: Without passing judgment upon anyone, let us recognize that we are now confronted with an enormous escalation of overt political activity which was unheard of and unthought of in Baptist work only a

few years ago. Can we ever return to the days when fellowship and inspiration and the challenge of our convention programs were more important than elections and political parties and strategies? What can we now do to restore trust and cooperation and bring our convention sessions back to their historic purpose?

There is a paramount need for some meaningful discussion among us. Here are several suggestions.

1. Isn't it time that we begin to talk *to* each other, *with* each other, not *about* each other? Better yet, let's try *listening* to each other.

2. Let's tone down the rhetoric. Harsh words and bitter attitudes can only drive us farther apart. Let's begin to respond to each other in humility, respect and love.

3. Let's try to understand each other rather than react to each other. Let's look at issues carefully, analytically, in a genuine attempt to understand all sides of the issues, not merely defend a favorite position.

4. Let's take the format of this national conference back to every state convention, to every region, and engage in meaningful, sincere examination of the issues we have discussed here, carefully examining both sides with an open mind and warm heart.

If we cannot do these things as brothers and sisters in Christ, then we do not deserve to occupy positions of leadership as pastors or professors or whatever.

21

HISTORICAL-LITERARY CRITICISM—AFTER TWO HUNDRED YEARS: ORIGINS, ABERRATIONS, CONTRIBUTIONS, LIMITATIONS

E. Earle Ellis

Origins

Two centuries ago this year two events occurred that may serve to mark the beginning of the discipline of "higher" criticism in biblical studies. One was the publication of the second edition of J. G. Eichhorn's *Introduction to the Old Testament* in which, apparently, the term 'higher criticism' was first applied to the study of scripture.[1] The term was identified by Eichhorn with an analysis of "the inner constitution" of the biblical books, that is, their sources, literary composition and historical origins as determined by their internal characteristics. In time this approach came to be known as historical-literary criticism or the historical-critical method.

A second event of 1787 relevant for our topic was the inaugural lecture of Eichhorn's pupil, J. P. Gabler, on the "distinction between biblical and dogmatic theology."[2] Gabler argued that the original meaning of scripture, with its mix of cultural and trans-cultural teachings, could be discerned by a careful linguistic, historical and literary analysis (181, 187f.) and this "biblical theology" be classified into "those things which . . . refer most immediately to their own times and . . . those pure notions which divine providence wished to be characteristic of all times . . ." (185). While the former were "merely premises," the latter were intended to be "a part of Christian doctrine" (189). We "must so build upon these firmly established foundations of biblical theology . . . a dogmatic theology adapted to our own times, [teaching] the harmony of divine dogmatics and the principles of human reason" (193). "Only from these [exegetical] methods can those certain and undoubted universal ideas be singled out, those ideas which alone are useful in dogmatic theology" (192).

Gabler anticipated a number of developments in later criticism: (1) a canon within a canon, (2) the identification of abiding revelation with universal ideas rather than with historically conditioned events and teachings and (3) a conviction that careful historical-literary criticism was an objective science that would produce a consensus about the original meaning of a particular biblical passage if not about its meaning today. His optimism regarding the outcome of this approach was doubtless shared by his mentor, J. G. Eichhorn.

Of course, Eichhorn and Gabler had predecessors in the use of an historical method both in Germany[3] and even earlier in Deistic circles in England.[4] But they provided the programmatic framework for subsequent biblical criticism, and their work may be regarded as the bench-mark for the beginning of the discipline.

Although an historical approach to the Bible has been useful in numerous respects, the high hopes of these two pioneers and a myriad others like them can now be seen, in the light of two centuries of effort, to have failed. Not only is there no consensus about the reconstruction of the various events in biblical history, there is also no agreement among critical scholars about the meaning of even one passage in the whole Bible. When a majority of scholarly opinion is claimed for this or that viewpoint, about the most one can say in light of the history of research is that the majority is probably wrong. For there is more than a little truth in the fictional obituary notice of one scholar which stated that he was the leading authority on the Gospel of John from March to December 1938. Scholarly majorities are a transient and often localized phenomenon in the world of biblical criticism.

In this state of affairs, while most have continued to pursue the traditional critical method,[5] at least one scholar has declared the method to be bankrupt and another regards it as moribund and near to its end.[6] Still others have moved to various kinds of language analysis[7] or to symbolic and psychological exegesis reminiscent of allegorical and other non-historical methods in the patristic and medieval church.[8] Moreover, many in the pews and among the pastors of the churches regard historical criticism as either irrelevant or detrimental to the true understanding of scripture. These disaffections seem to arise not only from the lack of any assured or abiding results in the use of the method but also from the seeming abstraction or hostility of many critical studies for the meaning of the Bible in the church. How is it that a method which began with so much promise could have reached such a confused and disordered state?

Aberrations

The historical analysis of scripture is subject, of course, to the same errors in its use as the analysis of any other historical documents. However, the problems and disagreements that have plagued the use of historical criticism may, I believe, be largely attributed to two mistaken assumptions, one concerning the nature of historical knowledge and the other concerning the competence and role of human reason. Let us consider these factors in turn.

First, in the nineteenth century it was widely believed that history-writing was a science which could recreate the past "as it actually occurred" *(wie es eigentlich gewesen),* to use the oft repeated phrase of Leopold von Ranke.[9] Certainly Ranke towered above contemporary historians in his effort "to divorce the study of the past from the passions of the present" and in his insistence on the use of primary and contemporary sources in the writing of history.[10] But it is doubtful that he gave his phrase the objective ring that was given it by others or regarded his work as disinterested science since, as he put it, it was philosophic and religious interest and the hope to come nearer to God that drove him to history.[11]

In fact, modern history-writing has often been highly subjective and, intentionally or not, has served the national, economic or ideological interest of the particular historian. In general terms this can be seen in the Prussian School[12] and in various British historians including both those who sought to write "scientific history" and those who viewed "history as literature."[13] More specifically, it was evident quite early for those of us from the American South who were weaned on oral family traditions of the War between the States and on such books as Jefferson Davis' *The Rise and Fall of the Confederate Government* and who later experienced in school the interpretations of, say, the historian Charles A. Beard.[14]

The myth of the objective critical historian was shattered above all by the devastating critique of Carl Becker.[15] For the modern historian, he wrote,

> it is the concept that determines the facts, not the facts the concept . . . Instead of "sticking to the facts," the facts stick to him, if he has any ideas to attract them (534) . . .

> [He] is detached from any fixed idea of religion, placing himself "too far off— for espousing the cause of either good or evil." But he knows well that he must espouse, with fine enthusiasm, the cause of not espousing any cause (534f.) . . .

> But it is difficult not to take sides if sharp contrasts and impassable gulfs are permitted to appear. If one could serve neither God nor Mammon, it is necessary to dispense with both. The modern historian has therefore a concept, a preconcept, of continuity and evolution, with "natural law" at the back of things . . . Facts which do not contribute to establish these concepts will not be selected; they may be unique, but they are judged not important (535).

Becker's observations bring to mind a story about Georg W. F. Hegel's lectures on the philosophy of history at the University of Berlin. At some point a student protested, "But, Herr Professor, the facts are otherwise." Hegel replied, "So much the worse for the facts." His point, I suppose, was that historical "facts" take on meaning only in the context of interpretation and that interpretation, therefore, is the more important component of historical knowledge.

In nineteenth and twentieth-century biblical studies the historical-critical method was assumed to have an objectivity, a "scientific" character, that endowed it with an almost irresistible authority. It was thought to give us the "historical facts" in contrast to the dogmatic pictures of the biblical story traditional in the church. Unfortunately, it only substituted one dogma for another, philosophical for theological. One may illustrate this briefly by three examples, the reconstruction of Old Testament history popularized by J. Wellhausen, the Quest for the "historical" Jesus, and the Baurian reconstruction of early Christian history.

The Wellhausen theory of the origin and composition of the Pentateuch, which determined his own understanding of Old Testament history and continues in a modified way to influence contemporary reconstructions,[16] could have been produced and found acceptable only in the late nineteenth century when the then dominant evolutionary ideas of progress and Hegelian theories of history provided the conceptual magnet to which Wellhausen's selected facts could stick.[17] Likewise, the "Quest of the historical Jesus" from H. S. Reimarus to W. Wrede, brilliantly reviewed by Albert Schweitzer,[18] sought to recover a

413

Jesus freed from theological dogma but only succeeded in finding a "liberal" Jesus congenial to its own interests. The original Quest ended in failure,[19] and subsequent "quests" that produced an "apocalyptic" or "existentialist" or "revolutionary Jesus," also carried the brand-marks of their times and their authors.[20] The "historical" Jesus was inevitably the historian's Jesus. All such reconstructions are necessarily interpretations since history, in this sense, is itself interpretation.[21] For the church they will succeed only to the degree to which they accord with and explain the "historical" Jesus presented by the Evangelists, those prophetically inspired interpreters who provide the church's standard by which all other works are to be measured, and they have often failed because they set their interpretations over against the Gospels and wrongly supposed that their own constructions carried an "objectivity" that was lacking in others.

In the mid-nineteenth century F. C. Baur carried out a thoroughgoing reconstruction of early Christian history that imposed a diachronic pattern upon the relationship of the New Testament documents based, like Wellhausen's views, upon a Hegelian philosophy of history.[22] He interpreted the whole of early Christian history on a supposedly enduring conflict between Peter ("thesis") and Paul ("antithesis") which was slowly reconciled in later generations ("synthesis") and on this basis dated most of the New Testament books to a post-apostolic period. His largely theoretical reconstruction, which in fact was not only philosophically determined but also misunderstood the nature of the conflicts reflected in the New Testament, became a dominant factor in the criticism of both the Gospels and the New Testament letters and continues to be influential in New Testament scholarship today.[23] Nevertheless, while he freed New Testament exegesis from some mistaken traditional models and demonstrated the importance of early Christian conflicts for understanding its history, he did so only to lead New Testament study into a Hegelian captivity from which it has not even yet escaped. And primarily for this reason he was, as a historian, much less reliable than, say, his counterpart in the British Isles, J. B. Lightfoot.[24]

A second factor that has been detrimental to the contribution of historical criticism has been the assumption that human reason in itself was competent to determine the meaning, at least the historical meaning, of scripture. In part it was the product of what Karl Barth has called the eighteenth century's "absolute man," who may also be termed "autonomous man,"[25] filled with the self-confidence not to say the hubris associated with the scientific and political enlightenment of "man come of age."

In part it derived from a Cartesian and earlier rationalism that affected in diverse ways the approach to the Bible of both traditional Protestant "high orthodoxy" as well as Deistic-influenced scholarship.[26] In biblical criticism from J. P. Gabler to the present, it expressed a confidence that method was master of scripture and that if the right tools were rightly applied the historical meaning of the text would become apparent.[27] This assumption about the competence of human reason, which flew in the face of Paul's indictment of secular reason in I Cor 1:18-3:20, led to a dismissal of the Holy Spirit from the task of historical criticism even if, in orthodox circles, a *pro forma* nod to the illumination of the

Spirit was still given. Among theologians who worked within a naturalistic world view, criticism became even more narrowly anthropocentric.

A mythological interpretation of biblical accounts of miracles, which pushed out an earlier rationalism,[28] is usually associated with the name of Rudolf Bultmann although "the myth school" has roots going back to D. F. Strauss and J. P. Gabler.[29] For Bultmann it rested upon a philosophical dogma and determined his understanding of historical-literary criticism. In one article[30] he wrote,

> The historical method includes the presupposition that history is a unity in the sense of a closed continuum of effects in which individual events are connected by the succession of cause and effect . . .

> This closedness means that the continuum of historical happenings can not be rent by the interference of supernatural powers and that therefore there is no "miracle" in this sense of the world. Such a miracle would be an event whose cause did not lie within history . . . [Historical science] cannot perceive such an act . . . [but] understands in terms of that event's immanent historical causes.

> It is in accordance with such a method as this that the science of history goes to work on all historical documents. And there cannot be any exceptions in the case of biblical texts . . .

One observes here how Bultmann's confessional commitment to a particular philosophical dogma determined his understanding of history and thus of historical criticism. It had particularly perverse effects for understanding the biblical documents because it imposed a confessional norm and world view that succeeded in silencing the very affirmation that the biblical writers wished to make, that is, their conviction and experience of the redemptive action—including miraculous action—of God in time and history.

Nevertheless, historical criticism as such should not be identified with the rationalistic assumptions on which it has sometimes been pursued. There are encouraging signs today that it is moving beyond the "closed" world view of rationalism toward a renewal of theistic assumptions and an openness to transcendence in its analysis and interpretation of the scriptures.[31]

Errors in historical criticism are also due, of course, to a faulty use of the method. They may include mistakes in understanding the words, grammar and syntax, in identifying the literary genre, and in perceiving the historical origins, context and relationships of a given passage or document. It is important to remember, however, that such errors are common to all historical and literary analysis and that they can be corrected only by a better use of the method.

The Necessity And Contribution Of Historical Criticism

In the light of the uncertainties of the art of historical reconstructions and the variety and subjectivity of interpretation, we may be tempted to the cynical remark of Voltaire that history, after all, is only a pack of tricks that the living play on the dead. However, as Christians we can never forget that ours is a historical faith, our salvation a salvation in history, and the written Word of God

415

a collection of documents composed by prophets in specific times and places. The historical analysis of scripture is for us, therefore, not an option but a necessity, a necessity that has become more urgent because of the heightened historical consciousness and enterprise of the world in which we live. Pursued properly, it is also a part of the Christian's responsibility to "love the Lord your God . . . with all your mind" (Mt 22:36) and, if we are called to do so, to fail to pursue this avenue of mental endeavor is to sin.

To paraphrase Winston Churchill's comment about democracy, historical-literary criticism is the worst method of interpretation ever devised by man, except for all the others that have been tried. This is perhaps an exaggeration since the Apostle Paul, using the rabbinic methods, brought forth the Word of God from the scriptures more abundantly than anything modern historical studies have been able to produce. Nevertheless, for our time and place in the church historical criticism, as a method, has offered more in term of explanation, clarification and heuristic probing of the biblical texts than other approaches, traditional or speculative. From the exegetical-historical work of, say, a J. B. Lightfoot or an Adolf Schlatter I am fully persuaded of that.[32]

It has two virtues that set it apart: it is falsifiable and it is self-corrective. (1) If as a method it can not identify the certain and true meaning of a passage, it can set out various options and in some cases show that a given interpretation is erroneous. (2) When it is misused, others are able to point out what went wrong and to offer a more defensible interpretation of the matter. This may be illustrated in New Testament criticism by two issues, the form criticism of the Gospels and the authorship of certain New Testament letters.

The classical form criticism of the Gospels and the nineteenth-century criticism of the Pauline letters rested, respectively, on historical and literary assumptions that can now be shown to have been mistaken. Consequently earlier conclusions in these disciplines must now be revised. The early form criticism assumed *inter alia* that Jesus' acts and teachings were first transmitted exclusively in an oral manner and, like folk traditions, were freely transformed by any jackleg preacher who cared to do so. This "oral transmission" theory was thought to be supported from the early Christians' expectation of a near-term end of the world. It received a considerable shock, therefore, with the discovery of the library of the Qumran sect, a Jewish group contemporaneous with earliest Christianity, that combined intense apocalyptic anticipation with prolific writing. It also encountered other historical objections. (1) Education was widespread and had a long tradition in Palestinian Judaism,[33] and teaching children to read and write was, according to Josephus, commanded by the Law.[34] (2) The occasion that necessitated written transmission of Christian traditions was the separation of believers from the teaching leadership, as the Apostolic Decree and the letters of Paul show, but this was already the situation in the earthly ministry of Jesus, who had groups of followers in various towns and villages of both Galilee and Judea.[35] (3) Even the first-century rabbinical schools, who prided themselves on oral memorization, apparently used some written materials in their teachings.[36] There was, in fact, no pre-literary stage in

416

early Christianity. The theory of an "oral period" propounded by the classical form criticism had its background not in the practices of first-century Judaism but in J. G. Herder's eighteen-century conception of the Gospel traditions as "oral saga."[37]

The theory of a folk-tradition type transmission of Jesus traditions has even less historical bases.[38] It also had its background in Herder's romanticism, evidenced little knowledge of first century Jewish practice, and was at odds with the cultivated and controlled "receiving" and "delivering" of religious tradition characteristic of early Christianity[39] and of rabbinic Judaism, as O. Cullmann, H. Riesenfeld, B. Gerhardsson and R. Riesner have shown.[40]

Historical criticism enables us today to correct these previous errors and to set forth a better form criticism showing that the traditions of Jesus were carefully cultivated, transmitted by an authorized leadership and fixed in writing much earlier than was formerly supposed.

The self-correcting character of historical-literary criticism may also be illustrated in the question of the authorship of certain New Testament letters. Nineteenth-century scholars observed that some Pauline letters, for example, differed from others in vocabulary, style and theological expression. Some of these scholars, in particular F. C. Baur, rejecting the Pauline ascriptions in the letters and the testimony of the patristic church, concluded that Paul could not have authored them. Under the influence of Hegelian dialectic they dated them to a time long after Paul's' death.[41] A major assumption underlying this viewpoint, an assumption shared by traditional and speculative scholars alike, was that Paul either sat down on a Sunday afternoon and wrote his letters or that he dictated them verbatim to a secretary. On this view of the matter it could be argued that a different style, vocabulary and theological expression meant a different author. However, historical and literary criticism has now shown that the assumption was mistaken.

In antiquity, expert amanuenses or secretaries were regularly employed to write letters and other documents of any length, and they exercised a variable degree of freedom in their composition. Thy also would include, as the author might direct, previously written materials that were pertinent to the topic.[42]

Paul also employed secretaries in the writing of his letters, persons who in accordance with the practice of the day exercised some influence on the letters' style and vocabulary.[43] Even more important, a considerable number of preformed traditions are included in Paul's letters. In I Timothy and in Titus they make up over 40% of each letter, and in I Corinthians about 15-20%.[44] Some of the preformed pieces were authored by Paul, but others were composed by prophets and inspired teachers in his and allied apostolic circles. In the light of the role of the amanuenses and the presence of preformed traditions one can no longer use in any precise way internal criteria of style, vocabulary and theological expression to make judgments about the authorship of the letters ascribed to Paul. Thus, nineteenth-century objections to Paul's authorship of some of them can now be seen to be without historical basis.

Limitations

In the nature of the case, "method" is a limited instrumentality for understanding scripture. It may be refined and utilized to the highest degree possible for human reason and still miss the meaning, even the historical meaning, of the text. There are at least two reasons for this, the limitations and frailties of historical knowledge, which we have observed above, and the nature of scripture.

The essential nature of scripture, also in its historical and literary dimension, is revelation. It is truth that may be hidden from the reader or revealed to him, but it is never merely truth available like pebbles on the beach. In our Lord's temptation both he and Satan can quote scripture (Mt 4:3-10). The churchmen and theologians of Jesus' day knew the scripture virtually by heart, but according to Jesus they made the Word of God null and void by wrong interpretations (Mt 15:6). There are two conditions in which one reads scripture, with a veiled mind or an unveiled one. The veiled mind may be, as in II Cor 3, the result of unbelief, the absence of glasses that only Christ can supply. For believers it may be because of God's purpose, as in Dan 12:8-9 or Lk 9:44-45.

The unveiling of the meaning of scripture is not achieved by man's effort or wisdom but by God's act. When Peter understood that the scripture identified Jesus as Messiah, Jesus replied, "Flesh and blood has not revealed this to you but my father in heaven" (Mt 16:15-17). It is in this context that we can understand the words with which Jesus sometimes concluded a sermon: "He who has ears to hear, let him hear" (Mt 11:15). Only the Holy Spirit can provide the ears by which the truth of scripture will be received.

As is the case in other aspects of Christianity, for example, the command to love, there is a paradoxical element in the understanding of scripture. When the Word of God hidden in scripture in unveiled, it is a divine disclosure, not a truth that one achieves but a truth that one receives from God. Nevertheless one is not to remain passive in receiving it. One is commanded to pray, to study, to listen and to meditate on the words of the prophets and apostles. It is in this frame of reference that God is pleased to unveil his prophetic word to the seeker of his truth.

We historical-literary critics are, like all ministers, servants of the Word of God, not masters of it. We come to scripture to listen. Only in the context of listening in the Spirit, even as we do our historical-literary analysis, will the mysteries of the scripture both in its historical and present meaning be unveiled. Using the Bible apart from the Spirit, whether in the pulpit or study, will inevitably lead to aberrations, if not the ones discussed above, then to others. The Reformation symbol of the Spirit-Dove above the open scriptures should always be emblematic of our study.

Notes

1. J. G. Eichhorn, *Einleitung in das Neue Testament*, Leipzig ²1787, Preface: "I have been obliged to bestow the greatest amount of labour on a hitherto unworked field, the investigation of the inner constitution of the individual books of the Old Testament by the aid of the higher criticism—a new name to no humanist" (tr. and cited in F. F. Bruce, "Biblical Criticism," *The Illustrated Bible Dictionary*, 3 vols., ed. N. Hillyer, I, 197).

2. J. P. Gabler, "On the Proper Distinction between Biblical and Dogmatic Theology and the Specific Objections of Each" (30 March 1787), tr. J. Sandys-Wunch and L. Eldredge, *SJT* 33 (1980), 134-144, from J. P. Gabler, *Kleinere Theologische Schriften*, Ulm 1831, 179-198.

3. For example, J. A. Ernesti, C. G. Heyne and G. T. Zachariae.

4. For example, Edward Herbert (Lord Cherbury), John Locke and Matthew Tindal. Cf. W. G. Kümmel, *The New Testament: . . . Investigation of its Problems*, Nashville 1972, 52-107; Sandys-Wunch and Eldredge (note 2), 144-158; H. G. Reventlow, *The Authority of the Bible and the Rise of the Modern World*, Philadelphia 1985, passim; A. Richardson, *History Sacred and Profane*, London 1964, 17-53.

5. Cf. E. Krentz, *The Historical Critical Method*, Philadelphia 1975.

6. W. Wink, *The Bible in Human Transformation*, Philadelphia 1973, 1: "Historical biblical criticism is bankrupt;" G. Maier, *The End of the Historical-Critical Method*, St. Louis 1977. For Roman Catholic objections, reactions and suggested new directions in biblical criticism cf. R. E. Brown, "All Gaul is Divided," *Union Seminary Quarterly Review* 40 (1985), 99-103 (a critique of three French Catholic scholars: J. Carmignac, C. Trestemont and R. Laurentin); D. Farkasfalvy, "In Search of a 'Post-Critical' Method . . ." and I. de la Potterie, "Reading Holy Scripture 'in the Spirit' . . . ," *Communio* [USA] 4 (1986), 288-325.

7. For example, "Structuralism." Cf. D. Patte, *What is Structural Exegesis*, Philadelphia 1976; R. M. Polzin, *Biblical Structuralism*, Philadelphia 1977; J. Calloud, *Structural Analysis of Narrative*, Philadelphia 1976, 46-108 (Mt 4:1-11).

8. For example, Wink (note 6), 19-83. Cf. G. Aichele, *Limits of Story*, Philadelphia 1985, 36-46, 121-128. The affinity in certain respects of the "dehistoricizing" existentialist hermeneutic of R. Bultmann with second-century Gnosticism has been noted by W. Rordorf, "The Theology of Rudolf Bultmann and Second-Century Gnosis," *NTS* 13 (1966-67), 357-362. Cf. also O. Cullmann, *Salvation in History*, London 1967, 24-28 (GT: 6-10).

9. According to Richardson (note 4, 104n.) the phrase occurred in L. v. Ranke, *Geschichte der romantischen und germanischen Völker von 1494-1514*, Frankfurt 1824, preface.

10. G. P. Gooch, *History and History Writing in the Nineteenth Century*, London 1928, 101f.

11. Gooch (note 8), 77.

12. Gooch (note 8), 130-155 (discussing, among others, G. Droysen and H. v. Treitschke).

13. Cf. John Kenyon, *The History Men: The Historical Profession in England Since the Renaissance*, London and Pittsburgh PA 1984 (from Sr. Walter Raleigh to G. R. Trevor-Roper). Further, on the problem, C. K. Mueller-vollmer, *The Hermeneutics Reader*, New York 1985, 1-53; H. S. Commager, *The Study of History*, Columbus OH 1966, 53-60.

419

14. J. Davis, *The Rise and Fall of the Confederate Government*, 2 vols., London and Cranbury NJ 1958 (1881). Cf. the discussion in D. H. Fischer, *Historians' Fallacies*, New York 1970, 24-31.

15. C. Becker, "Detachment and the Writing of History," *Atlantic Monthly* 106 (1910), 524-536 = *Detachment and the Writing of History: Essays and Letters* . . . , Ithaca NY 1958, 3-28. For an opposing view cf. Fischer (note 14), 41ff.

16. Cf. B. S. Childs, *The Old Testament as Scripture*, Philadelphia 1979, 119-124; O. Kaiser, *Introduction to the Old Testament*, Oxford 1975, 39f.; O. Eissfeldt, *The Old Testament: An Introduction*, Oxford 1966, 164-170.

17. Cf. R. Smend, Jr., "De Wette und das Verhältnis zwischen historischer Bibelkritik und philosophischem System im 19. Jahrhundert," *TZ* 14 (1958), 107-119; W. F. Albright, *History, Archeology and Christian Humanism*, London 1965, 136-140.

18. A. Schweitzer, *Geschichte der Leben-Jesu Forschung*, 2 vols., Hamburg 1966 (1906); partial English translation in *ibid.*, *The Quest of the Historical Jesus*, New York 1968 (1910).

19. Cf. G. Bornkamm, *Jesus of Nazareth*, New York 1960, 13: "Albert Schweitzer . . . has erected its memorial, but at the same time has delivered its funeral oration. Why have these attempts failed? Perhaps only because it became alarmingly and terrifyingly evident how inevitably each author brought the spirit of his own age into his presentation of the figure of Jesus."

20. Cf. J. W. Bowman, *Which Jesus?* Philadelphia 1970.

21. Cf. B. Lonergan, *Method in Theology*, New York 1972, 175-234; "The word, history, is employed in two senses. There is history (1) that is written about, and there is history (2) that is written. History (2) aims at expressing knowledge of history (1)" (175).

22. Cf. especially F. C. Baur, *Paul*, 2 vol., London ^{2}1876 (1845); *ibid.*, *The Church History of the First Three Centuries*, 2 vols., London 1878 (1853); *ibid.*, *Ausgewählte Werke*, 4 vols., Stuttgart 1963-1970.

23. Cf. E. E. Ellis, "Gospel According to Luke," *International Standard Bible Encyclopedia*, 4 vols., ed. G. W. Bromiley, Grand Rapids 1979-1987, III (1986), 181f.; *ibid.*, "Dating the New Testament," NTS 26 (1980), 492-296; *ibid.*, *Prophecy and Hermeneutic*, Tübingen 1978, 86-95, 100-105; *ibid.*, *Paul and His Recent Interpreters*, Grand Rapids ^{5}1979, 18ff.

24. Cf. S. Neill, *The Interpretation of the New Testament, 1861-1961*, London 1964, 19-60; Ellis, *Prophecy* (note 23), 89-95.

25. Cf. K. Barth, *Protestant Theology in the Nineteenth Century*, London 1972, 33-79, 37 (absolutistische Mensch): "the man of the eighteenth century approaches even Christianity with the belief in the omnipotence of human capability" (83); H. Thielicke, *The Evangelical Faith*, 3 vols., Grand Rapids 1974-1982, I, 49-53.

26. Cf. J. B. Rogers and D. K. McKim, *The Authority and Interpretation of the Bible*, San Francisco 1979, 187f., 247f.

27. Cf. K. Stendahl, "Method in the Study of Biblical Theology," *The Bible in Modern Scholarship*, ed. J. P. Hyatt, Nashville TN 1965, 196-205, and the (quite convincing) response of A. Dulles in the same volume (210-216). Stendahl's essay stands in the tradition of J. P. Gabler.

28. For example, as espoused by H. E. G. Paulus (*Das Leben Jesu als Grundlage einer reiner Geschichte des Urchristentums*, 4 vols., Heidelberg 1828), Gue explained miracles as the onlookers' misunderstanding of natural events. This approach had its background in David Hume's, "Of Miracles," *An Inquiry Concerning Human Understanding*, London 1748, Section 10. It died of its own weight, partly because it was easier to believe the miracles than the fantastic rationalistic explanations of them.

29. On its background in German theology cf. C. Hartlich and W. Sachs, *Der Ursprung des Mythosbegriffes in der Moderne Wissenschaft*, Tübingen 1952. For its most notorious representative piece cf. D. F. Strauss, *The Life of Jesus Critically Examined*, Philadelphia 1972 ([4]1840).

30. R. Bultmann, "Is Exegesis Without Presuppositions Possible?" *Existence and Faith*, New York 1960, 291f. (GT: *TZ* 13 (1957), 11). For a critique of Bultmann's point of view cf. Richardson (note 4), 139-147; T. F. Torrance, *Theological Science*, London 1969, 312-337.

31. For example, in the work of P. Stuhlmacher, *Historical Criticism and Theological Interpretation of Scripture*, Philadelphia 1977, 61-91. Cf. E. E. Ellis, "Forward" to L. Goppelt, *Typos: The Typological Interpretation of the Old Testament in the New*, Grand Rapids 1982, ix-xix.

32. For example, the oft-reprinted J. B. Lightfoot, *St. Paul's Epistle to the Galatians*, London [10]1892, and A. Schlatter, *Der Evangelist Matthäus*, Stuttgart 1959 ([2]1933).

33. R. Riesner, *Jesus als Lehrer*, Tübingen 1981, 97-206.

34. Josephus, *Against Apion* 2, 204; cf. *ibid.*, *Antiquities* 4, 211. Cf. Testament of Levi 13, 2; Philo, *Embassy to Gaius* 115; 210.

35. Ellis, (note 23), 242-247.

36. Cf. J. Neusner in *Journal for the Study of Judaism*, 4 (1973), 56-65; B. Gerhardsson, *The Origins of the Gospel Traditions*, Philadelphia 1979, 22-24.

37. Cf. Kümmel (note 4), 80-83.

38. Cf. E. E. Ellis, "Gospels Criticism," *Das Evangelium und die Evangelien*, ed. P. Stuhlmacher, Tübingen 1983, 42f.

39. Cf. Lk 1:2; Acts 16:4; Rom 6:14; I Cor 11:2, 23; 15:1-3; Col 2:6ff.; II Pet 2:21; E. E. Ellis, "Traditions in 1 Corinthians," *NTS* 32 (1986), 481f., 486-490.

40. O. Cullmann, "The Tradition," *The Early Church*, London 1956, 57-99; H. Riesenfeld, *The Gospel Tradition*, Philadelphia 1970, 1-29; B. Gerhardsson, *Memory and Manuscript*, Uppsala 1961; Riesner (note 10), 353-502.

41. Cf. Ellis, "Dating" (note 23), 487-502 (French tr., *Communio [Paris]* 7, 1 *(1982), 75-89;* German tr., *TZ* 42 (1986), 409-430).

42. This has been demonstrated in the case of Josephus by H. St. John Thackeray (*Josephus*, 9 vols., London 1926-1965, II, xvf., xx-xxiv) and for *The Letters of Pliny* (Oxford 1966, 538-546) by A. N. Sherwin-White.

43. Rom 16:22; Gal 6:11; II Thess 3:17; Plm 19; cf. O. Roller, *Das Formular der paulinischen Briefe*, Stuttgart 1933.

44. Cf. E. E. Ellis, "Traditions in the Pastoral Epistles," *Early Jewish and Christian Exegesis: Studies in Memory of William Hugh Brownlee*, ed. C. A. Evans, Decatur GA 1987, 237-253; *ibid.*, "Traditions in 1 Corinthians," (note 39), 481-502.

22

THE CONTRIBUTIONS AND WEAKNESSES OF KARL BARTH'S VIEW OF THE BIBLE

David L. Mueller

Dedicated to my father and theological mentor, William A. Mueller, who introduced me to the theology of Karl Barth, on the occasion of his eighty-fifth birthday, May 8, 1987.

The Doctrine Of The Word Of God: The Norm Of Evangelical Theology

Barth introduces his *Church Dogmatics* with an exposition of "The Doctrine of the Word of God" which is the norm of all Christian theology and preaching. The Word of God is threefold: the revealed Word, the written Word and the proclaimed Word. The proclaimed Word must conform to the written Word, Holy Scripture, and Scripture attests the revealed Word which is the foundation of both the proclaimed and the written Word. Like the persons of the Trinity, the three forms of the one Word of God are inextricably interrelated. Since the Word of God has to do with the revelation of God, Barth unfolds the next major chapter, "The Revelation of God," in terms of "The Triune God" who makes himself known as Father, Son and Holy Spirit thereby distinguishing himself from all other purported deities. There follows the analysis of "The Incarnation of the Word," the self-revelation of God in Jesus Christ, and "The Outpouring of the Holy Spirit."[1] It is within this comprehensive understanding of the Word of God and the revelation of God that Barth develops the doctrine of Holy Scripture.[2]

The Revealed Word of God

The sole foundation for rightly interpreting Scripture as the written Word of God is to see that it always has to do with God's revelation of himself. The Word of God is God's action and speech by which he makes himself known. "The Word of God is the Word that God *spoke, speaks,* and *will speak* in the midst of all men."[3] This speaking and action of God is attested in the old and new covenants with their center in Jesus Christ, the Word made flesh, who unites the two covenants. The Old Testament anticipates Jesus Christ while the New Testament recalls his first coming and anticipates his final coming. Following Calvin, Barth teaches that "all true knowledge of God is born out of obedience" to God's revelation of himself in his Word.[4]

The Written Word of God: Holy Scripture

In developing his doctrine of Holy Scripture in terms of its primary authority as "The Word of God for the Church," Barth consciously seeks to reassert the primacy of the Reformers' Scripture principle. This approach necessitates Barth's continuing criticism both of Roman Catholicism and Protestant liberalism. The Catholics elevated Church tradition to a place of equal (or superior) authority alongside Holy Scripture and liberals surrendered the primary authority of Holy Scripture in the Church by focusing on the revelation of God immanent in nature, history, and supremely in the self-consciousness of Christian believers. In Barth's view, the anthropocentrism characteristic of liberalism in the train of Schleiermacher always leads to subjectivism and theological relativism. Its dominant twentieth century expression is Christian existentialism.

Barth reintroduces the primacy of Holy Scripture and its authority as "The Word of God for the Church" in the following summary thesis:

> The Word of God is God Himself in Holy Scriptures. For God once spoke as Lord to Moses and the prophets, to the Evangelists and apostles. And now through their written Word He speaks as the same Lord to His Church. Scripture is holy and the Word of God, because by the Holy Spirit it became and will become to the Church a witness to divine revelation.[5]

It is significant that Barth regards the authority of the Bible to be axiomatic for all Protestants standing in the Reformation tradition. The Bible's authority for the Church is not based finally on external proofs or argument but on the fact that the Bible has vindicated itself by revealing God to us and calling us to salvation through him.[6] Ultimately, the affirmation of the Bible's authority is beyond the need of human justification. Barth observes that it would be inappropriate to ask a child: "Why is *this* woman your mother?" This child could only reply: "She *is* my mother!" Analogously, the Bible's authority is not problematic for the Church whose life and witness have been determined by it. The Bible again and again authenticates itself as the Word of God and thus is acknowledged in obedience as authoritative for the Church and the believers. In sum, it is through the Bible that the saving revelation of the triune God is made known. No argumentation or theories about the Bible's authority can take the place of God's authentication of himself through the Bible.

The Word of God Preached

The preached Word is the third form of the Word of God. In the tradition of the Reformers, Barth states: "The Word of God is God Himself in the proclamation of the Church of Jesus Christ. In so far as God gives the Church the commission to speak about Him, and the Church discharges this commission, it is God Himself who declares His revelation in His witness."[7] Since preaching is divinely commissioned, it is central in the Church's witness. True preaching is subservient to the Word of God attested in Holy Scripture and to nothing and no one else. Through God's grace, the preacher's human witness, based on Scripture, becomes the living Word of God to the hearer.

The Word of God therefore meets us in these three forms, but it is the one Word of God. The revealed Word gives rise to the written and preached Word, but we never know the revealed Word apart from Scripture and proclamation. Barth summarizes the relationships of the three forms of the Word of God as follows:

424

The revealed Word of God we know only from the Scriptures adopted by Church proclamation or the proclamation of the church based on Scripture. The written Word of God we know only through the revelation which fulfills proclamation or through the proclamation fulfilled by revelation. The preached Word of God we know only through the revelation attested in Scripture or the Scripture which attests revelation.[8]

The Doctrine Of Holy Scripture

Barth's thesis that Holy Scripture is the primary "witness of divine revelation" is based "simply on the fact that the Bible has in fact answered our question about the revelation of God, bringing before us the lordship of the triune God."[9]

Scripture as Witness to Divine Revelation

Scripture as witness may be likened to the figure of John the Baptist. Standing midway between the covenants, John was "sent from God . . . for testimony, to bear witness to the light . . . ," namely, to Jesus Christ (Jh. 1:6-7). Barth repeatedly refers to Grüenwald's painting of Jesus' crucifixion in which John the Baptist—with his "prodigious index finger"—points away from himself to the Crucified. John witnesses to Christ in saying, "He must increase but I must decrease" (Jh. 3:30). This stance is the essence of what constitutes a biblical witness to revelation.[10]

Biblical witnesses are not directly identical with God's revelation of himself. For this reason, the Bible in and of itself cannot be equated with the Word of God which it attests. This distinction between the Bible and the revelation of God himself constitutes the Bible's limitation: "We distinguish the Bible as such from revelation. A witness is not absolutely identical with that to which it witnesses."[11] Barth obviously does not use the concept of "witness" in a weak sense, but in terms of the way in which prophets and apostles function in the Bible. Jesus says of his twelve disciples, "He who receives you receives me . . ." (Mt. 10:40).

Bromiley notes that Barth relies on the way in which Jesus depicts the Old Testament Scriptures as "they that bear witness of me . . ." (Jh. 5:39). To speak of the Bible as witness does not diminish the Bible's significance, but enhances it. Indeed the limitation of the Bible as witness in no way denies its uniqueness as revelatory for us. Barth states:

> In this limitation the Bible is not distinguished from revelation. It is simply revelation as it comes to us, mediating and therefore accommodating itself to us—to us who are not ourselves prophets and apostles, and therefore not the immediate and direct recipients of the one revelation, witnesses of the resurrection of Jesus Christ.[12]

Biblical Authority and Inspiration

How does Barth account for the special authority of the biblical witnesses whose testimony is recorded in Holy Scripture? His answer is clear and unequivocal: they are unique by virtue of being divinely inspired, appointed, elected and commissioned as the primary witnesses of God's deeds and word.

These men are the *biblical witnesses of the Word,* the prophetic men of the
Old Testament and the apostolic men of the New . . . the prophets and apostles became and existed as eyewitnesses of those deeds done in their time,
and *hearers of the Word* spoken in their time. They were destined, appointed, and elected for this cause by God, not by themselves; they were
also commanded and empowered by him to speak of what they had seen
and heard. They speak as men who in this qualified senses were *there.*[13]

We have in these prophets and apostles our only access to the knowledge of
God's reconciling deeds fulfilled in Jesus Christ. For this reason Barth holds
that ". . . though [evangelical] theology has no direct information about the
Logos, it nevertheless has, with utmost certainty, this indirect information [i.e.,
through the biblical witnesses.]"[14] Inasmuch as the human testimony of the
biblical witnesses is inspired and empowered as the true testimony to the "lordship of the triune God," its acceptance in faith means that God has become
contemporary to us as "an actual presence and event."[15] Barth rejects both
liberalism's interpretation of the Bible as the record of the evolution of the human religious consciousness and Bultmann's contention that the theme of the
apostle's witness is their new self-understanding. It is evident that from the time
of Barth's break with liberalism beginning about 1914, his hermeneutical axiom
was that all biblical texts intend to attest the word and acts of God.

Barth's view of the intention of the apostolic witness contrasts sharply with
much modern biblical interpretation:

The subject and strength of their commission were neither their impressions
of Jesus, their estimation of his person and his work, nor their faith in him.
Instead, their theme was God's mighty Word spoken in Jesus' resurrection
from the dead which imputed to his life and death power and control over all
creatures of all times. The apostles spoke, told, wrote, and preached about
Jesus as men who were in this way directly illumined and instructed. They
spoke as men who had behind them the empty tomb and before them the
living Jesus.[16]

Inspiration and Verbal Inspiration

In the preface to his commentary on *Romans* in 1919, Barth states that his
own method of biblical interpretation was indebted to the Reformation emphasis on the divine inspiration of the biblical witnesses and the corollary doctrine
of verbal inspiration. Throughout the *Church Dogmatics* the distinctiveness of
the biblical witness by virtue of its divine inspiration is emphasized. Thus Barth
affirms: "If God speaks to man, He really speaks the languages of this concrete
human word of man. That is the right and necessary truth in the concept of
verbal inspiration."[17] It is by virtue of this divine inspiration that biblical testimony is distinguished from all others. On this basis, Holy Scriptures is the
preeminent authority above both the preached Word and the sacrament. Indeed, all post-biblical human witness in the Church is true witness only insofar
as it accords with Scripture.

426

On the basis of his exegesis of the classic texts often cited as fundamental to a doctrine of biblical and verbal inspiration, namely, 2 Tim. 3:14-17 and 2 Pet. 1:19-21, Barth makes several comments. First, the major emphasis of both texts is that the "Holy Spirit . . . is described as the real author of what is . . . written in Scripture. . . . [The] witnesses to revelation . . . speak in the place and under the commission of Him who sent them, that is, Yahweh or Jesus Christ. They speak as *auctores secundarii* [secondary authors]."[18] Barth interprets Paul's statement in 2 Tim. 3:16, "all scripture is inspired by God," to mean:

> all, that is the whole Scripture is—literally: "of the Spirit of God," i.e., given and filled and ruled by the Spirit of God and actively outbreathing and spreading abroad and making known the Spirit of God. It is clear that this statement is decisive for the whole. It is because of this, i.e., in the power of the truth of the fact that the Spirit of God is before and above and in Scripture, that it was able and will be able for what is said of it both before and after. But it is equally clear that at the center of the passage a statement is made about the relationship between God and Scripture, which can be understood only as a disposing act and decision of God Himself, which cannot therefore be expounded but to which only—a necessarily brief—reference can be made. At the decisive point all that we have to say about it can consist only in an underlining and delimiting of the inaccessible mystery of the free grace in which the Spirit of God is present and active before and above and in the Bible.[19]

Commenting on 2 Pet. 1:21 and its affirmation that the prophecy of Scripture has its source in that "men moved by the Holy Spirit spoke from God," Barth states: "*Theopneustia* in the bounds of biblical thinking cannot mean anything but the special attitude of obedience in those who are elected and called to this obviously special service."[20] Though they write as "secondary authors" beneath the primary authorship of God and his Spirit, they did not cease to be human authors. Their "direct relationship to divine revelation" and the obedience to which they were moved by the Holy Spirit makes their inspiration unique. Barth opposes the view that the Spirit's inspiration of the biblical witnesses is restricted to their prophetic experience, their thinking or speaking apart from their writing, or to their writing apart from the fact that they were uniquely inspired human beings.[21] Rather, they confront us as God's chosen witnesses in what they have written. The "voice of God" is heard only through their voices. And that is their *theopneustia*."[22]

It is not the case that an absolute identification can be made between the biblical witnesses and God's historical revelation itself. The stance of the believing Church and Christian is the recollection that in the past the biblical witness has reproduced the "voice of God," and leads us "to expect that it will be so again." Hence the believer approaches the Bible in the confidence that Scripture will be the Word of God today—in our present.[23]

427

The Humanity of the Biblical Witness

In affirming the divine inspiration of the biblical witnesses, Barth recognizes their humanity and therewith that the interpretation is also a human book. It is therefore necessary that the "Bible should be read and understood and expounded historically. . . ."[24] It should be recalled that in the preface to the first edition of his commentary on *Romans,* Barth acknowledged that historical-critical study of the Bible "has its rightful place." His dissatisfaction with much historical-critical biblical interpretation was due to its failure to move beyond the consideration of the human and historical issues related to the biblical texts to their true subject-matter and theme, namely, God and his revelation of himself. Thus Barth's fundamental hermeneutical axiom for all biblical interpretation is to listen for the Word of revelation within the words of Scripture.

This rules out interpreting Scripture with what was once thought to be a legitimate "scientific" detachment or engaging in interpretations which focus on the human words without regard to the revelation they attest. Such exegesis is not true listening to the Bible and therefore is not true historical understanding in terms of what the Bible itself teaches. Moreover, the exegete takes the text seriously not in by-passing its humanity or its literary form, but in submitting to it as the sole place in which God mediates his presence. Barth could not say it more clearly: "We are tied to these texts. And we can only ask about revelation when we surrender to the expectation and recollection attested in these texts."[25]

Barth's approach is not to be confused with the method of modern historicism which seeks to reconstruct a history purportedly lying behind the biblical texts.[26] A humanly determined and reconstructed history lying behind the biblical texts is not the theme of the Bible. Honest biblical interpretation recognizes that "we cannot have revelation except through this witness. We cannot have revelation 'in itself.'"[27] Hence Barth's repeated call is for "more attentiveness, accuracy and love to the texts as such."[28] In response to the charge that this transforms Christianity into a book-religion, Barth responds that "strangely enough Christianity has always been and only been a living religion when it is not ashamed to be actually and seriously a book-religion."[29]

Nevertheless, the Bible is a human book which is like many other books in terms of its human dimensions. Its uniqueness derives from its divine inspiration and therewith in its witness through which the saving activity and nature of the triune God may be known and confessed. Hence the Evangelical Scripture principle in no way absolutized or divinized the Bible so as to undermine the "single absolute fundamental and indestructible priority . . . of God as Creator over the totality of His creatures and each of them without exception."[30] The divine and human coexist in the Bible in a manner analogous to their coexistence in the person of Christ. In the incarnation, however, there is a direct unity of God and man whereas this is not the case in the relationship of God (the divine) to the humanity of the prophets and apostles. Moreover, the human witness of prophets and apostles has no capacity to reveal God independently: it always attests the revelation in the "humanity of Jesus Christ."[31] It is therefore evident that the Bible cannot be equated with the incarnation itself. Yet it is by virtue of the Word having become flesh that these witnesses are empowered to mediate his presence. Their human word, however, is neither absolutized nor does it become divine in and of itself. This is always due to a divine decision.

> As the Word of God in the sign of this prophetic-apostolic word of man Holy Scripture is like the unity of God and man in Jesus Christ. It is neither divine only nor human only. Nor is it a mixture of the two nor a *tertium quid* between them. But in its own way and degree it is very God and very man, i.e., a witness of revelation which itself belongs to revelation, and historically a very human literary document.[32]

Barth's frank recognition of the full humanity of Scripture does not mean that the Word of God is to be located apart from its witness. No! It is precisely through exegesis of biblical texts that confrontation with the Word of God is to be expected. Contrary to many evangelical critiques of Barth as subjectivistic in his biblical interpretations, he insists on careful attention to the biblical texts themselves. The Word of God cannot be known apart from engagement with Holy Scripture through which his Word is made known to faith. "The door of the Bible texts can only be opened from within."[33] On being banned from Germany by Hitler in 1935, Barth's parting counsel to his Bonn students was loud and clear: "Do exegesis, exegesis, exegesis!"

Barth rejects any attempt to discount the humanity of the biblical witnesses by regarding their testimony as infallible in all respects. Since all of God's dealing with Israel and the Church and humanity as a whole involve God's accommodation of himself to finite, mortal, erring and sinful human beings, there is no reason to deny the full humanity of the biblical witnesses. The offense occasioned by their humanity is "grounded like the overcoming of it in the mercy of God."[34]

What does Barth mean by speaking of the fallibility of the human witness in Scripture? First and most obvious is "that we cannot expect or demand a compendium of solomonic or even divine knowledge of all things in heaven and earth" from the biblical witnesses seeking to make them "inerrant proclaimers of all and every truth. They did not in fact possess any such compendium."[35] They were not exempt from the limitations which mark all human perspectives in all times and places. On the other hand, recalling Bultmann's zeal for making the modern world-view normative for interpreting what can be affirmed in the Bible, Barth warns that we have no right to presume that the latter alone contains "solomonic" wisdom! However, given the relativity of the knowledge of the biblical witnesses, one must allow for "their 'capacity for errors.'"[36] Second, biblical literature shares antiquity's perspective for which there was "no distinction of fact and value which is so important to us, [or] between history [*Historie*] on the one hand, and saga and legend on the other."[37] This lack of distinction must simply be accepted as part of their human perspective and should not lead us to presume that God can mediate his Word to us only on the basis of what moderns might accept as an "historical" occurrence.[38] Third, in Barth's view "the vulnerability of the Bible, i.e., its capacity for error, also extends to its religious or theological content."[39] Though some evangelicals find this point offensive, Barth contends that one cannot exempt what at times is their limited and conditioned theological viewpoint. Honest acceptance of this limitation would be seen in the willingness to concede that the Old and much of the New Testament is a product of the "Israelitish, or to put it more clearly, the Jewish spirit."[40] The long anti-semitic tradition in Christianity is indicative of the offense occasioned by the Jewish humanity of the biblical witnesses with the result that the Church often closed itself off from allowing the Old Testament to become the Word of God to be heard in faith.[41]

Barth's point about the fallibility of the Bible's witnesses and their capacity for error does not mean that we should attempt to distinguish between the divine and human, the central and peripheral in their witness. Since no New Testament writers provide us with a "thorough-going theological system," even to determine humanly speaking what is central for a single witness requires hard theological work. More importantly, Barth stresses repeatedly that we are not permitted to distinguish in advance between what is human and divine in Scripture, between form and content, letter and spirit. "Always in the Bible . . . we shall be met with both." Our human determination is not equatable with God's determination concerning where and when he will speak through his witnesses.

> Verbal inspiration does not mean the infallibility of the biblical word in its linguistic, historical and theological character as a human word. It means that the fallible and faulty human word is as such used by God and has to be received and heard in spite of its human fallibility.[42]

Barth chooses his words very carefully in stressing that God justifies and sanctifies the human and fallible witness of his prophets and apostles.

> . . . every time we turn the Word of God into an infallible biblical word of man or the biblical word of man into an infallible Word of God we resist that which we ought never to resist, i.e., the truth of the miracle that here fallible men speak the Word of God in fallible human words—and we therefore resist the sovereignty of grace, with which God Himself became man in Christ, to glorify Himself in His humanity.[43]

Hence the miracle with which we are confronted in the human witness of the prophets and apostles is that God has spoken, speaks now, and will speak through them.

> That the lame walk, that the blind see, that the dead are raised, that sinful and erring men as such speak the Word of God: that is the miracle of which we speak when we say that the Bible is the Word of God.[44]

The Bible and the Witness of the Holy Spirit

Everything said to this point underlines Barth's view that true knowledge of God is always dependent upon the divine initiative through which God makes himself known. The climax of his self-revelation in his Son, Jesus Christ, is attested in Holy Scripture, true preaching, and Christian witness. The issue is how it is possible for us to appropriate God's saving revelation of himself? Barth's single and consistent answer is: through the Holy Spirit. Barth's favorite Pauline text is "no one can say 'Jesus is Lord' except by the Holy Spirit" (1 Cor. 12:3).

Barth's thesis may be put simply: only through God's initiative in his historical revelation fulfilled in Jesus Christ, attested in Scripture and continually made alive through Scripture in the present through his Holy Spirit, does knowledge of God become actual for us. Against liberalism Barth maintains that the effects of human sin are so great that only God through his Spirit can bridge the gap between him and us caused by our sin. Against some forms of orthodoxy, Barth contends that faith is neither merely intellectual acceptance of the Bible as the Word of God nor intellectual assent to certain doctrines. Furthermore, Barth opposes all views which treat faith as a human capacity which can be turned on at will. "Through God alone may God be known."

Following the Reformers, and especially Calvin, Barth sees an inextricable unity between Jesus Christ, the revealed Word, the testimony of Holy Scripture, and the work of the Holy Spirit as the "Teacher of the Word," who illumines the written Word.

> As God, the Holy Spirit is a unique person. But He is not an independent divinity side by side with the unique Word of God. He is simply the Teacher of the Word: of the Word which is never without its Teacher. . . . It is God Himself who opens our eyes and ears for Himself. . . . and is so doing He tells us that we could not do it ourselves, that of ourselves we are blind and deaf.[45]

Scripture and preaching are not in and of themselves—that is, in terms of their humanity—identical with God himself and his self-revelation. Yet through God's gracious presence and condescension in his Spirit, he indwells the human witness of Scripture (and preaching) so that they become his living Word. "Scripture is holy and the Word of God, because of the Holy Spirit it became and will become to the Church a witness to divine revelation."[46] God always remains the Lord of the Bible. "If the Church lives by the Bible because it is the Word of God, that means that it lives by the fact that Christ is revealed in the Bible by the work of the Holy Spirit."[47] It is by means of the miracle of God's gracious approach in his Spirit that the words of Scripture become the Word of God heard in faith. Thus God's immediate presence is mediated to us through the written word. We never control God. No theory about revelation or the Bible can control—or should seek to control—the free grace of God. Hearing the Word of God in the words of Holy Scripture—like our justification—is due wholly to God's grace. The way to the knowledge of God is always from God to us, from above to below. The eternal God makes himself present through the inner testimony of the Holy Spirit in the human words of his biblical witnesses. That is why we confess in faith that the Bible is the Word of God. Yet—contrary to the way Barth is often branded as a subjectivist and existentialist

who contends that the Bible becomes the Word of God because of our faith—
he says: "It [the Bible] does not become God's Word because we accord it faith
but in the fact that it becomes revelation to us."[48]

Scripture as the Word of God: the Canon

Barth delineates what it means to hear and confess the witness of Holy Scripture as the Word of God. First, it means that with the Church we confess and
acknowledge Holy Scripture to be the Canon. Contrary to a widespread view,
Barth contends that it was only on the basis of God's authentication of himself
through his chosen witnesses and their writings that the Church was led in faith
to acknowledge the Canon. "The Church can only confirm or establish it as
something which has already been formed and given."[49] While recognizing that
the present Canon cannot be closed absolutely by virtue of the possibility that
lost letters may receive divine validation in the Church, it remains true that all
our knowledge of revelation is dependent upon the acknowledgement of the
Canon of Scripture as holy in and with the Church.[50]

Second, to accept the witness of Holy Scripture as witness to divine revelation means to acknowledge both testaments in relationship to Jesus Christ who
unites them. The Old Testament as a witness or expectation and the New Testament as the witness of recollection in their differences and unity are binding on
the Church as the total witness to the revelation of the triune God.[51] Third,
Holy Scripture is acknowledged to be the Word of God because it alone is the
authentic and primary testimony of divinely inspired witnesses to God's revelatory activity fulfilled in the incarnate Son of God raised from the dead. "To look
on him, as we are requested to do in Ac. 3:4, always means to look on Him
who has sent them."[52] Fourth, to confess Holy Scripture as the Word of God is
the acknowledgement "that we cannot have revelation except through this witness. We cannot have revelation 'in itself.'"[53] There can be no division between
the content of revelation and the witness of Scripture. Fifth, the Scripture is not
unique by virtue of the surpassing excellence of its human qualities, but
because—paralleling the incarnation—it has pleased God that it stand "in that
indirect identity of human existence with God Himself . . . brought about by the
decision and act of God."[54] Hence Scripture is "the Word of God in the sign of
the word of man. . . ."[55] Sixth, Scripture is confessed as the preeminent authority in the Church and as the Word of God over all secondary sources because
God, through his Spirit, has authenticated himself to prophets and apostles
empowered to testify of him and has ratified their testimony to him through his
Spirit again and again.[56]

Throughout his entire exposition of the doctrine of Scripture, Barth reasserts
the Reformation's emphasis on Holy Scripture as the Word of God through
which the Church is created, nurtured, and sustained. This receives strong
emphasis in a lengthy section on "Authority in the Church" developed in terms
of "The Authority of the Word." Whenever some human authority replaces
Holy Scripture as the preeminent authority over the Church, it loses its sure
foundation. It is reduced to talking with itself. Barth thus contends that the
"Church does not claim direct and absolute authority and material authority for

432

itself but for Holy Scripture as the Word of God."[57] Barth affirms: "Under the Word, which means Holy Scripture, the Church must and can live, whereas beyond or beside the Word it can only die. It is this its salvation from death which it attests when it makes, not the Catholic or Neo-Protestant [Liberal], but the Evangelical decision."[58]

When Barth discusses "Freedom in the Church," it is necessary to speak in terms of the responsible freedom of those engaged in interpreting Holy Scripture—and thus of their "Freedom under the Word." This requires mutual submission to the written Word of God and the willingness "to listen to one another in expounding and applying it."[59] In the Protestant tradition, no possibility exists for the elevation of a person, group, or communion to a place of authority in competition with the given authority of Holy Scripture. "Freedom in the Church is limited as an indirect, relative and formal freedom by the freedom of Holy Scripture in which is it grounded."[60]

Evangelical Criticisms Of Barth's View Of Scripture

1. Barth overemphasized that revelation was incapable of being verified by historical proofs, rational argumentation and proofs from Scripture by focusing too much on the realm of faith.[61] He should have developed a Christian apologetic to prove the superiority of Christianity.

2. Barth did not go far enough in speaking about Scripture as witness to God's revelation. He should have spoken of the Bible as "inscripturated revelation" and therefore of the "objective truth of the inspired teaching of Scripture."[62] Bromiley always commends Barth for his commitment to biblical authority, but finds his emphasis on Scripture as witness to revelation inadequate. It may lead to viewing Scripture in "an inferior role except in so far as the Holy Spirit empowers it in sovereign freedom."[63]

3. While applauding Barth's recovery of the biblical emphasis on revelation in terms of God's mighty acts or the dynamic dimension of God's revelation, Runia states: "Alongside this dynamic aspect and inseparably linked with it there is [in the Bible] also the static, that is, revelation in the sense of revealedness. The Bible knows nothing of a fundamental contrast between the dynamic and static, between the personal and conceptual."[64]

4. Barth is wrong to regard the equation of the Bible with the Word of God or with God's revelation as denying the freedom of God. God bound himself in covenant to Israel, but remained the free Lord. That God wills the Scriptures to be his written Word neither jeopardizes his freedom nor makes faith incidental. It is only through faith that God's revelation of himself in the Bible is acknowledged and confessed.[65]

5. Barth is correct to stress the role of the Holy Spirit in faith's appropriation of the Bible's witness as the Word of God thereby recognizing a weakness in Protestant Orthodoxy at this point. However, in emphasizing the present role of the Spirit, he seems at times to undermine the objectivity of the Bible as the Word of God apart from, and prior to, faith. In this way, Barth moves toward subjectivism and robs Scripture of its objective and absolute authority whereby it provides certainty in the knowledge of God.[66]

433

6. Is the Bible only authoritative and inspired when God inspires it from time to time? Barth's exegesis of 2 Tim. 3:14-17 and 2 Pet. 1:19-21 along these lines is not convincing. That is, he does not make his case versus the objective inspiredness of the Scriptures as they stand.[67]

7. Barth wrongly limits inspiration to the obedience of the biblical witnesses whereas it refers primarily to their inspired transmission of God's Word in writing.[68] The work of the Holy Spirit in the present is better understood as illumination.

8. The basis of Barth's critique of the doctrine of verbal inerrancy is that it appears to provide control over God. Hence he identifies it as a naturalistic doctrine. It goes contrary to Barth's basic axiom that God is always sovereign and free in his revelation and its corollary that man can never control God's revelation.[69] Though this is a needed warning against all attempts to manipulate the revelation of God, it is erroneous to regard the equation of the Bible with the written revelation of God in this way. Jesus and the apostles equated the Old Testament with the inspired Word of God and as authoritative in itself.[70]

9. Inasmuch as Barth did not accept absolute biblical inerrancy, evangelicals ask how the Bible can exercise direct, absolute and substantive authority? If there are incorrect statements in the Bible, and if events like Jesus' resurrection lie beyond the bounds of ordinary historical verification, is not the material authority of the Bible surrendered? Does this not lead to doubt concerning the adequacy and reliability of the Bible's testimony?

10. Though Barth speaks of the "capacity for error" on the part of the biblical witnesses, he does not provide examples of the type of error involved. It is further not helpful to equate being human with error. Though the witnesses were fallible, God's action preserved them from error. Only if this is in fact the case can Barth establish the absolute authority of Scripture in all doctrinal matters. Furthermore Bromiley maintains against Barth that it is not only the form of the Bible as an expression of its humanity which is offensive to unregenerate reason, but also its total message. Could it be that Barth's talk about the offense which resides in the humanity of the biblical message is the expression of his reason still warring with his faith?[71]

11. Barth's view of the Bible is faulty because he allows for errors in the Bible thereby rejecting biblical inerrancy. Henry even says that Barth emphasizes the fallibility of the Scriptures more than their divine inspiration.[72]

12. Barth's basic problem is that he operates with two incompatible axioms in his theology. First, that the Bible contains errors; second, the biblical writings are the Word of God. These are irreconcilable. "By respecting the law of contradiction he would have avoided irrationalist tendencies. The difficulties of Barth's expositions can be overcome only by closing the gap, as Scripture itself does, between divine revelation and the prophetic-apostolic writings, between the Word of God and the Bible."[73]

13. Barth intended to stress the divine authorship and therewith the authority of Scripture, but he did not feel it warranted regarding inerrancy as a necessary implication of this view. It would have been more consistent with Barth's view that Scripture testifies "to its own total reliability and truthfulness" if he had

gone on to stress its infallibility as the Word of God. Since he does not, there is a certain inconsistency in his making the shift from fallible documents to the infallible Word of God.[74]

14. Barth's stress on the limitation of human language does not preclude that language can convey what is "unchangingly and universally true."[75]

15. Barth is wrong to maintain that the Protestant orthodox view of inspiration requires a theory of dictation. It is also false to say that a high view of inspiration leads to bibliolatry. No orthodox believer ever taught that the Bible replaces Christ![76] He further errs in failing to see that the Bible puts more stress on the inspiration of the words of the prophets and apostles than on the inspiration of the prophets and apostles themselves.[77] Barth redefines inspiration by making it refer more to sporadic communications from God rather than to the "inspiredness" of Scripture.[78]

16. Henry notes that contemporary evangelicals teach that the inspiration of the prophets and apostles does not suspend or violate their humanity. Barth would certainly welcome this modification of 17th century Protestant orthodoxy's viewpoint.[79]

17. Barth is wrong to charge that orthodoxy is docetic in denying the witnesses' "vulnerability to error." The fact that the Holy Spirit kept them from error does not deny their humanity. The fact that they were shaped by their culture can be affirmed. They were infallible in transmitting God's message: they did not transmit the fallible views of their culture.[80]

Barth's Major Theses on Scripture as the Word of God

In light of the foregoing composite of evangelical critiques of Barth's doctrine of Scripture, it may be well by way of conclusion to summarize some of his dominant emphases set forth above.

1. First and fundamental is the recognition that the Bible is *God's* own Word. He is the Lord of Scripture and never comes under our control. "When we have the Bible as the Word of God, and accept its witness, we are summoned to remember the Lord of the Bible and to give Him the glory."[81] To confess the Bible as the Word of God involves our repeated praise and acknowledgement of the sovereign Lord "whose Word the Bible is." In so doing, we again and again know of its inspiration.

2. The "Word of God" is always the act or "*Work* of God" and therefore not to be identified with a fixed state or object like other objects in the world. Since God's Word is God's presence himself, he cannot be identified with any-thing. That the Bible is present to us as the Word of God "reminds us of the act of God achieved once and for all."[82] Our knowledge of the Bible as the Word of God entails the recollection that God has spoken to us through the written Word in times past and the expectation, anticipation and prayer that he will speak through it again in the future.

3. The "Word of God" always has to do with the "*miracle* of God." The content of the Word of God attested and mediated through Holy Scripture is nothing other than "the grace of God." "If we allow the Bible to say this to us, and in so doing to speak the Word of God, how else can we think of the Word

of God in the Bible except as a miracle?"[83] We do not honor the Bible as God's own Word if we in any way domesticate it by identifying it with that which is natural and therefore under our control.

4. The miracle involved in the event when the Bible is and becomes the Word of God does not do away with its humanity which may always be an offense removable only "by the power of the Word of God."[84] To deny the humanity and fallibility of the biblical witnesses by making their words infallible misplaces the miracle which is nothing other than "the miracle of the grace of God to sinners. . . ."[85]

5. Inasmuch as the Bible's becoming the Word of God is always an event—a miracle of God's condescension—it follows that *"the presence of the Word of God itself"* in the Bible "is not identical with the existence of the book as such."[86] In God's freedom in his Spirit, some Bible text "is taken and used as an instrument in the hand of God, i.e., it speaks to and is heard by us as the authentic witness of divine revelation and is therefore present as the Word of God."[87]

6. This act of God through which the written Word becomes the living Word of God to the Church and to us leads to clinging to the Scriptures and searching them in expectation and with prayer. Lack of faith and indolence toward God's written Word is as inappropriate as the attempt to coerce God to speak. Nor is it appropriate to presume that we can distinguish in advance what is divine and human in Scripture—between the real content of the Word of God to be found there and the form in which it is expressed. Nor are we to be satisfied that God has spoken through his witnesses to the Church and to us in the past. Rather we are called to move "from faith to faith" (Rom. 1:17) in thankfulness and in hope and in reliance on the faithfulness of God.

7. The grace of God through which the Bible becomes the Word of God involves a "twofold reality." First, a specific biblical text claims our attention and study. Second, when the text becomes the Word of God heard in faith, it means that "*God* Himself now says what the text says. The *work* of God is done through this text. . . . By the *decision* of God this text is now taken and used."[88] Thus even though Barth does not like to speak of "verbal inspiredness" or of the infallibility of the text, he strongly emphasizes that the content of the Scriptures or the Word of God is inseparable from the words of Scripture, or the matter from the words. The correct and true meaning of verbal inspiration always to be affirmed is that "the hearing of the Word of God [occurs] only in the concrete form of the *biblical* word."[89] Barth's warning is appropriate:

> If the biblical text in its *literalness* [*Wörtlichkeit*] as a text does not force itself upon us, or if we have the freedom word by word to shake ourselves loose from it, what meaning is there in our protestation that the Bible is inspired and the Word of God: To say, "Lord, Lord" is not enough. What matters is to do the will of God if we are to know His grace and truth—for that is the inspiration of the Bible.[90]

8. Finally, Barth underlines once again the objective nature of the inspiration of the Bible over against the misinterpretation that faith and experience

cause the Bible to be the Word of God. Indeed, Barth follows Calvin in contending that no logical, rational or other proofs can establish that the Bible is the Word of God. The Bible authenticates itself as the Word of God through God's self-witness in it. No secondary proofs can be the final basis of this certainty. Calvin's appeal to the inner witness of the Holy Spirit which convicts one that the Bible is the Word of God is not an appeal to a subjective proof from experience, but rather to the objective activity of God in his Spirit. When we say "by the Holy Spirit," we confess that God who was revealed to, attested by, his prophets and apostles graciously speaks to us through their witness to him. "When we say 'by the Holy Spirit' we say that in the doctrine of Holy Scripture we are content to give the glory to God and not to ourselves."[91]

A Final Statement

It is hoped that my analysis of Karl Barth's doctrine of Scripture has indicated the faithful way he reasserted the significance of the doctrine of Holy Scripture and its preeminent authority for any theology which regards itself as evangelical in the tradition of the Reformers. It is generally admitted that Barth played a dominant role in the reassertion of the Reformation's Scripture principle in the face of its gradual erosion in modern liberal theology beginning about the year 1800. In addition, the renaissance of biblical theology in mid twentieth century following Barth was strongly influenced both by his doctrine of Scripture and mode of biblical interpretation.

Contemporary American evangelical theology has profited immensely from Barth's interpretation of Holy Scripture. Indeed, evangelical theology would be greatly impoverished without the contributions which Barth made to it. Although there are significant points of disagreement, it is my opinion that evangelical theology will be enriched by continuing to engage in dialogue with both his doctrine of Scripture and his interpretation of the major doctrines of evangelical theology in the tradition of the Reformers. The most important anglo-saxon evangelical theologians have been immensely enriched by their interaction with Barth's theology. In order to improve on it, evangelical theology must faithfully engage the total witness of Holy Scripture and the significance of its fulfillment in Jesus Christ, the incarnate Son of God, through whom God reconciled the world unto himself. This is an ongoing task which requires not only a doctrine of Scripture but also its unceasing exposition to the end of faithful proclamation and teaching of the Gospel to the glory of God and so "that the man of God may be complete, equipped for every good work" (2 Tim. 3:17).

In attempting to assess Barth's doctrine of Scripture and his mode of biblical interpretation, I am in agreement with the conclusion of Bernard Ramm, a leading American evangelical and careful interpreter of Barth. Ramm's thesis is that Barth's doctrine of Scripture and his mode of exegesis provides the best model for evangelical theology today. He supports his thesis as follows: First, Barth reasserts the full, absolute, and material authority of Holy Scripture in the tradition of the Reformers in opposition to the undermining of the Scripture principle in the Enlightenment and in liberal theology. Second, he affirms the authority of Scripture in accord with Scripture's testimony regarding itself. However, Barth did not deny the full humanity of the Scriptures. In this way he was able to incorporate the historical study of the Scriptures developed in modern biblical studies. Thus the affirmation of the Bible's divinity should not be at the expense of asserting its full humanity. Both must be affirmed—and together. Third, in contrast to the theory of the absolute inerrancy of the Bible in its autographs or present copies, Barth locates infallibility in God and his self-revelation alone. Fourth, the inspired biblical witness is the indispensable medium through which God makes himself known today through his Spirit which also inspired the original biblical witness. In this way persons are brought to a saving knowledge of Jesus Christ.[92]

Though he does not cite Barth's position often, Pinnock's conclusions on the inspiration and authority of Scripture are quite compatible with the main lines of Barth's position. In summarizing his treatment thereof, he states that the "practical purpose of the Bible as a book [is] that it testifies to salvation in Jesus Christ." He continues:

> The Bible is basically a covenant document designed to lead people to know and love God. As such, it has a focused purpose and concentration. This is the kind of truth it urges us to seek in it, and this is the context in which its truth claims ought to be measured.[93]

Barth's reaffirmation of the authority of Holy Scripture and of Jesus Christ whom it attests as the Lord of Scripture was of decisive influence in the German Church struggle occasioned by Hitler's rise to power in 1933. Along with a small minority in the German Evangelical Church, Barth stood strongly opposed to the "German Christians" who regarded German National Socialism as a legitimate second source of revelation alongside of the revelation of Jesus Christ attested in Holy Scripture. As the leading theological spokesman of the "Confessing Church," Barth was representative of those opposed to the pernicious synthesis of the Gospel of Jesus Christ and the Nazi political ideology. In declaring their opposition to this illicit merger, the Confessing Church met at Barmen, Germany, on May 29-31, 1934. Fifty-three years ago, the Church was called upon to make its witness clear. Virtually all Christians in Germany had adopted the Nazi ideology and were sympathetic with the German Christian movement. Only the small and courageous minority in the Confession Church were faithful to the authority of Scripture and its witness to the Lordship of Jesus Christ in the face of that radical threat.

It was Barth who drafted the initial text of the Barmen Declaration. In its final form, it bears his unmistakable imprint. More importantly, the Confessing Church was reaffirming its traditional Confession: "The inviolable foundation of the German Evangelical Church is the gospel of Jesus Christ as it is attested for us in Holy Scripture and brought to light again in the Confessions of the Reformation."[94]

Following this affirmation, the first article of the Barmen Declaration confesses the following fundamental evangelical truth:

Jesus Christ, as he is attested for us in Holy Scripture, is the one Word of God which we have to hear and which we have to trust and obey in life and death. We reject the false doctrine, as though the Church could and would have to acknowledge as a source of its proclamation, apart from and besides this one Word of God, still other events and powers, figures and truths, as God's revelation.[95]

If one makes this Confession as one's own, one confesses the Lordship of Jesus Christ in the tradition of the biblical witnesses and of the Evangelical Church of the Reformation. If the Church, the Body of Christ, lives out this Confession, it will be faithful to its commission and will glorify God. Barmen's third article points us today to the way we are called to be faithful to Jesus Christ as "the way, and the truth, and the life" (Jh. 14:6).

As the Church of pardoned sinners, it has to testify in the midst of a sinful world, with its faith as with its obedience, with its message as with its order, that it is solely his [Jesus Christ's] property, and that it lives and wants to live solely from his comfort and from his direction in the expectation of his appearance.[96]

Notes

1. Karl Barth, *Church Dogmatics* (Edinburgh: Clark, 1932-68), cf. CD I/1, I/2. The official translation cited hereafter as CD with volume: the German original as KD.
2. CD I/1, par. 19-21.
3. Karl Barth, *Evangelical Theology* (Grand Rapids: Eerdmans, 1963), p. 18. Hereafter cited at ET.
4. ET, p. 18, citing Calvin.
5. CD I/2, p. 457.
6. CD I/2, pp. 457 ff.
7. CD I/2, p. 473.
8. CD I/1, second edition, p. 121. Citations from CD I/1 will be from the second edition unless otherwise noted.
9. CD I/2, p. 462.
10. CD I/1, pp. 112 ff. Cf. CD I/2, pp. 441 ff.
11. CD I/2, p. 463; cf. CD I/1, p. 111.
12. CD I/2, p. 463.
13. ET, p. 26.
14. ET, pp. 26-27.
15. CD I/2, p. 463.
16. ET, p. 29. Barth provides an excellent summary of his doctrine of Holy Scripture and his view of Scripture as witness in ET, ch. 3.
17. CD I/2, p. 532.
18. CD I/2, p. 505.
19. CD I/2, p. 504.
20. CD I/2, p. 505.
21. CD I/2, p. 505.
22. CD I/2, pp. 506.

23. CD I/2, p. 506. Barth interprets 2 Cor. 3:14-18 and 1 Cor. 2:6-16 along the same lines, CD I/2, pp. 514-517.

24. CD I/2, p. 464. On this issue, cf. pp. 463-472.

25. CD I/2, p. 49.

26. CD I/2, p. 492.

27. CD I/2, p. 492.

28. CD I/2, p. 494.

29. CD I/2, pp. 494-495.

30. CD I/2, pp. 497-498.

31. CD I/2, p. 500.

32. CD I/2, p. 501.

33. CD I/2, p. 533.

34. CD I/2, p. 529. The parallel is the offense of the cross.

35. CD I/2, p. 508.

36. CD I/2, p. 508.

37. CD I/2, p. 509.

38. The reader is referred to Barth's interpretation of the Genesis creation accounts, CD III/1, as indicative of his approach in this regard.

39. CD I/2, p. 509.

40. CD I/2, p. 510.

41. CD I/2, pp. 510-511.

42. CD I/2, p. 533.

43. CD I/2, p. 529.

44. CD I/2, p. 529.

45. CD I/2, pp. 243-244. Cf. references to Calvin, pp. 240-242. Cf. IV/1, p. 648. See the entire section, "The Ourpouring of the Holy Spirit, CD I/2, par. 16, pp. 203-279, and pp. 512 ff. and parallels in the CD. Calvin introduces his treatment of the authority of Holy Scripture (*Institutes,* BK I, ch. 7, 4) thus: "If, then, we would consult most effectually for our consciences, and save them from being driven about in a whirl of uncertainty, our conviction of the truth of Scripture must be derived from a higher source than human conjectures, judgments, or reasons; namely, the secret testimony of the Spirit." He concludes: "Let it therefore be held as fixed, that those who are inwardly taught by the Holy Spirit acquiesce implicitly in Scripture; that Scripture, carrying its own evidence [*esse autopiston*] along with it, deigns not to submit to proofs and arguments, but owes the full conviction with which we ought to receive it to the testimony of the Spirit." (*Institutes,* I, 7, 5.) For full bibliographic note, see below, note 15. For a critical analysis of Calvin's doctrine of Scripture as the written Word of God authenticated through the inner witness of the Holy Spirit—which concurs with Barth's reading of Calvin—cf. Ronald W. Wallace, *Calvin's Doctrine of the Word and Sacrament* (Grand Rapids: Eerdmans, 1957), esp. ch. 8. For Calvin, cf. *Institutes,* Bk. I, chps. 7-9).

46. CD I/2, p. 457.

47. CD I/2, p. 513.

48. CD I/1, p. 110. This discussion is based on Barth's analysis of the Word of God as the "Speech of God," and "Act of God," and the "Mystery of God" in CD I/1, pp. 125-186 and pp. 187-247. Cf. CD I/2, pp. 512 ff. For Barth's rejection of all natural theology which speaks of a knowledge of God apart from Jesus Christ and his Spirit, cf. David L. Mueller, *Karl Barth* (Waco: Word, 1972), pp. 86-93.

49. CD I/2, p. 473. Cf. the parallel discussion, CD I/1, pp. 101 ff.

50. CD I/2, pp. 473-481.

51. CD I/2, pp. 481-485.

52. CD I/2, p. 492; cf. pp. 485-492.

53. CD I/2, p. 492.

54. CD I/2, p. 500.

55. CD I/2, p. 500.

56. CD I/2, pp. 502 ff. Cf. the parallel discussion in CD I/1, pp. 104 ff.

57. CD I/2, p. 538. Cf. the entire section.

58. CD I/2, p. 585.

59. CD I/2, p. 538.

60. CD I/2, p. 661. Cf. the section, par. 21, pp. 661-740.

61. Carl F. H. Henry, *God, Revelation and Authority* (Waco: Word, 1979), III, pp. 100ff. Cited hereafter as GRA and volume. For a good introduction to Henry, see: Bob E. Patterson, *Carl F. H. Henry* (Waco: Word, 1983).

62. Henry, GRA, IV, p. 97.

63. Geoffrey W. Bromiley, "The Authority of Scripture in Karl Barth," in *Hermeneutics, Authority, and Canon,* ed. by D. A. Carson and John D. Woodbridge (Grand Rapids: Zondervan, 1986), p. 290. Cited hereafter as ASKB.

64. Klass Runia, *Karl Barth's Doctrine of Holy Scripture* (Grand Rapids: Eerdmans, 1962), p. 202. Cited hereafter as DHS.

65. Runia, DHS, pp. 203 ff.

66. Henry, GRA, IV, p. 97 ff.

67. Bromiley, ASKB, p. 291.

68. Henry, GRA, III.

69. Runia, DHS, pp. 189 ff.

70. Runia, DHS, pp. 196 ff.

71. Bromiley, ASKB, pp. 291-292.

72. Henry, GRA, III.

73. Henry, GRA, IV, p. 200.

74. Bromiley, ASKB, p. 293.

75. Henry, GRA, IV, p. 14.

76. Henry, GRA, IV, pp. 138 ff.

77. Henry, following Gordon Clark, GRA, IV, p. 143.

78. Henry, GRA, IV, p. 148.

79. Henry, GRA, IV, p. 148.

80. Henry, GRA, IV, p. 152.

81. CD I/2, p. 527.

82. CD I/2, p. 527.

83. CD I/2, p. 528.

84. CD I/2, p. 529.

85. CD I/2, p. 530.

86. CD I/2, p. 530.

87. CD I/2, p. 530.

88. CD I/2, p. 532.

89. CD I/2, pp. 532-533.

90. CD I/2, pp. 533-534.

91. CD I/2, p. 537.

92. Bernard Ramm, *After Fundamentalism: The Future of Evangelical Theology* (San Francisco: Harper, 1983), pp. 88-134.

93. Clark H. Pinnock, *The Scripture Principle* (San Francisco: Harper, 1984), pp. 54-55.

94. *The Book of Confessions,* Part I, Second Edition (Philadelphia: The General Assembly of The United Presbyterian Church, 1970), cf. section 8.05-.07.

95. *Ibid.,* 8.08-.19.

96. *Ibid.*

Appendix

The History Of The Doctrine Of The Authority And Inspiration Of The Bible

The Early Church

Barth regards developments in the interpretation of inspiration in the early church to be expressive of a "rather naive secularization of the whole conception of revelation."[1] First, while not denying the crucial significance of the stress on the initial inspiration of the biblical witnesses, Barth regards the limitation of inspiration to the "emergence of the spoken or written prophetic and apostolic word as such" to be representative of an apologetic tendency to render the supernatural miracle of God in such a way that it becomes more readily intelligible.[2] Here nothing is said about the need of the Holy Spirit in order to comprehend the revelation of which they testified. Second, there was a "tendency to insist that the operation of the Holy Spirit in the inspiration of the biblical writers extended to the individual phraseology used by them in the grammatical sense of the concept."[3] Barth does not take issue with the emphasis on "*verbal* inspiration," but rather that it was construed apart from the need of the continuing work of the Holy Spirit. The question is "whether it [i.e., the interpretation of verbal inspiration] has not been taken out of the circle and regarded as verbal-*inspiredness,* something for which we give thanks to the grace of God, but which is itself no longer understood as grace but as a bit of higher nature?"[4] Finally, there is a tendency so to magnify the divinity of the inspired words of the Bible—certainly, in Barth's view a worthy motive—that the "real humanity" of the "real human word" of the biblical writers is surrendered. The mystery that a human word could be the Word of God then and there and here and now is secularized when the theory of dictation becomes prominent. "Where there is this idea of a 'dictation' of Holy Scripture through Christ or the Holy Spirit, is not the doctrine of inspiration slipping into Docetism?"[5]

The Protestant Reformers

The Reformation of the sixteenth century led to a true reform of the Church grounded on "the restoration of the authority and lordship of the Bible in the Church" which in turn led to a "new reading and understanding and expounding of Scripture in accordance with this authority and lordship."[6] The resultant "new doctrine of Scripture, and especially of the inspiration of Scripture," in Barth's view was in accordance with the teaching of "Scripture itself."[7] The Reformers' distinctive contributions are threefold. First, on the basis of the aforementioned Pauline passages they unapologetically spoke of inspiration, verbal inspiration, and of the divine authorship of the Bible and even made use of the concept of dictation. The intention was to accentuate "with greater and more

442

radical seriousness . . . the subjection of the Church to the Bible as the Word of God and its authority as such."[8] Barth contends, however, that despite the use of the foregoing concepts they adopted "neither a mantico-mechanical nor a docetic conception of biblical inspiration. . . ."[9] Second, the Reformers saw the Bible's inspiration as *sui generis* and not to be compared with any other inspiration: it had to do with a unique and incomparable miracle. The inspiration of the biblical witnesses is inextricably determined by the content inspiring them, namely, the mystery of the revelation of God, and supremely, Jesus Christ. Barth concludes:

> Therefore for the Reformer the question as to the inspired Word was as such always the question of that which inspires and controls the Word. For them the literally inspired Bible was not at all a revealed book of oracles, but a witness to revelation, to be interpreted from the standpoint of and with a view to its theme, and in conformity with that theme.[10]

Finally, the Reformers restored in a powerful way the view that the same Spirit who originally inspired the biblical witnesses inspires and illumines their witness so that it becomes a living Word of God to us in the present. Along these lines Barth credits the Reformers for having recovered a "doctrine of inspiration" which is "an honouring of God, and of the free grace of God." He continues:

> The statement that the Bible is the Word of God is on this view no limitation, but an unfolding of the perception of the sovereignty in which the Word of God condescended to become flesh for us in Jesus Christ, and a human word in the witness of the prophets and apostles as witnesses to His incarnation. On their lips and understanding this is the true statement concerning the Bible which is always indispensable in the Church.[11]

Protestant Orthodoxy

In Barth's estimate, seventeenth century Protestant Orthodoxy's view of inspiration was a departure from that of the Reformers. It lost appreciation for their view that faith's confession that the Bible is the Word of God confesses God's sovereignty and his mysterious working through his Spirit enabling the human word of the biblical witnesses to mediate his presence. Barth identifies several problematic features of the orthodox view of inspiration. First, he regards Orthodoxy as a precursor of modern Protestantism in that it began to experience the loss of certainty of salvation and of the judgment and grace of God. There was simultaneously a gradual influx of natural theology. Rather than viewing these two trends as antithetical as might appear warranted, Barth sees Orthodoxy's hardening of the doctrine of inspiration as a sign of a "process of secularisation" or of the inroads of natural theology. Thus in spite of the "supranaturalistic character" of the language used by the Orthodox to depict the absolute and total infallibility of the Scriptures by virtue of its total divine inspiration, Barth is not impressed! He anticipates his critical disagreement with this perspective as follows:

This new understanding of biblical inspiration meant simply that the statement that the Bible is the Word of God was now transformed (following the doubtful tendencies we have already met in the early Church) from a statement about the free grace of God into a statement about the nature of the Bible as exposed to human inquiry [and] brought under human control. The Bible as the Word of God surreptitiously became a part of natural knowledge of God, i.e., of that knowledge of God which man can have without the free grace of God, by his own power, and with direct insight and assurance.[12]

Second, Barth substantiates his thesis with several arguments. He concurs with Orthodoxy that the Reformers affirmed that God or his Spirit is the "primary author" of Scripture. Problematic is the way Orthodoxy increasingly viewed the biblical writers as *amanuenses* (clerks, secretaries) or *actuarii* (shorthand writers) who wrote only what was dictated to them by God. The interpretation of divine inspiration in terms of a theory of divine dictation led G. Voetius to include the pointing of the Hebrew text as inspired. Barth observes a marked departure from Calvin's description of the biblical witnesses as *ministres* (servants, helpers). The "legal preciseness' of this dictation theory required that everything in Scripture be directly attributable to the Spirit's inspiration and dictation. The idea of biblical witnesses as "mere flute players" recurs.[13] Barth asks: "Why must the humanity of the biblical witnesses and the humanity of their language be nullified?"

This leads us in the third place to Barth's answer to his question and to the heart of his critique. The unexamined postulate giving rise to a theory of inspiration which would assure a wholly inerrant Bible was that "Holy Scripture must be for us a *divina et infallibilis historia* [a divine and infallible history]."[14] The entire doctrine of biblical authority is restricted to this partial view of inspiration with this particular goal. The sole concern is with the origin of inspiration: now the Bible's divinity can be asserted without reference to its theme. Moreover, the Reformation emphasis on the inner witness of the Spirit authenticating Holy Scripture to the believer appears insignificant even while the Spirit is "brought into a no less remarkable relationship to all kinds of other convincing qualities of the Bible."[15]

Instead of attacking the Orthodox doctrine of inspiration for its excessive supranaturalism, Barth opposes it for not being supranaturalistic enough!

The intention behind it was ultimately only a single and in its own way very "naturalisitic" postulate: that the Bible must offer us a *divina et infallibilis historia;* that it must not contain human error in any of its verses; that in all its parts and the totality of its words and letters as they are before us it must express divine truth in a form in which it can be established and understood; that under the human words it must speak to us the Word of God in such a way that we can at once hear and read it as such with the same obviousness and directness with which we can hear and read other human words; that it must be a codex of axioms which can be seen as such with the same formal dignity as those of philosophy and mathematics. The secular nature of this postulate showed itself plainly in the assumption that we may freely reproach

444

This Protestant orthodox doctrine of inspiration represents the systematization of the questionable tendencies in this direction in the early Church alluded to above. While not decrying the "desire for certainty" regarding the authority of Scripture felt by post-Reformation Orthodoxy in its fight against Rome on the right and the sectarians on the left, Barth laments that instead of speaking of "spiritual" certainty along the lines of the Reformers it went another way. "What was wanted was a *tangible* certainty, not one that is given and has constantly to be given again, a *human* certainty and not a divine, a certainty of *work* and not solely of faith."[17]

This is what precipitated a "docetic dissolving or a mantico-mechanical materialising of the concept of the Bible's witness to revelation" in Orthodoxy. Barth's dissatisfaction with Orthodoxy's departure from its Reformation heritage in this arbitrary theory of inspiration is unequivocal. The mystery of the origin of the divine inspiration and of God's continuing decision to mediate his saving presence repeatedly through the human witness of Holy Scripture is lost to view.

The Bible was now grounded upon itself apart from the mystery of Christ and the Holy Ghost. It became a "paper Pope," and unlike the living Pope in Rome it was wholly given up into the hands of its interpreters. It was no longer a free and spiritual force, but an instrument of human power.[18]

In the last analysis, the claims made for Holy Scripture by the Orthodox were not essentially different from claims made by other religions for their sacred texts. Hence instead of staving off historical relativism by means of this seemingly impregnable theory of inspiration and biblical infallibility, Orthodoxy actually paved the way for its rise in the eighteenth and nineteenth centuries.

Further consequences necessarily followed from Orthodoxy's deficient view of inspiration because it "asserted things which cannot be maintained in the face of a serious reading and exposition of what the Bible says about itself, and in face of an honest appreciation of the facts of its origin and [transmission]."[19] It not only proved itself "incapable of fulfillment," but also more importantly "was believed only for a short time."

That it remained for many ages, and still is to some extent at the present time, a kind of theological bogeyman, the [supposedly] logically necessary intention of the statement that the Bible is the Word of God, . . . has prevented whole generations and innumerable individual theologians and believers from seeing the true, spiritual[,] biblical and Reformation meaning of the

445

statement, causing them to go past Luther and Calvin and even Paul in order to accompany Voetius and Calov.[20]

A final historical consequence is important. The Enlightenment critique of Orthodoxy's view of inspiration and its adoption by liberalism involved reasserting the human dimensions of the biblical witness and witnesses thereby providing a necessary corrective to Orthodoxy's denial of the same. In Barth's analysis, however, subsequent liberal and conservative attempts to locate and establish a "God in history" ascertainable through historical-critical reconstruction denied the divinity of the Scriptures and totally lost the Reformation understanding of the Bible as the Word of God. "The knowledge of the free grace of God as the unity of Scripture and revelation had been lost. No wonder that the statement that the Bible is the Word of God was now dismissed [by modern criticism] as 'untrue.'"[21]

Notes

1. CD I/2, p. 519.
2. CD I/2, p. 517.
3. CD I/2, p. 517.
4. CD I/2, p. 518. Italics from original, KD I/2, p. 575.
5. CD I/2, p. 518.
6. CD I/2, p. 519.
7. CD I/2, p. 519.
8. CD I/2, p. 520.
9. CD I/2, p. 520.
10. CD I/2, p. 521.
11. CD I/2, p. 522.
12. CD I/2, pp. 522-523. Italics and bracketed material from the original, KD I/2, p. 500.
13. CD I/2, pp. 523-524.
14. CD I/2, p. 524; cf. pp. 523-524.
15. CD I/2, p. 523. Barth views orthodoxy's tendency to treat what Calvin regarded as the "secondary" evidences/testimonies to the divinity of Scripture on virtually the same level as God's authentication of Scripture through his Spirit giving rise to faith as a bad omen. These secondary proofs include the Bible's antiquity, its prophecies and miracles, its role in church history, etc. See CD I, 2, pp. 536-537. For Calvin, cf. *Institutes*, Bk. I, ch. 8, esp. sections 1 and 13. Calvin's major point—which Barth applauds—is "These [secondary helps], however, cannot of themselves produce a firm faith in Scripture until our heavenly Father manifest his presence in it, and thereby secure implicit reverence for it. Then only, therefore, does Scripture suffice to give a saving knowledge of God when its certainty is founded on the inward persuasion of the Holy Spirit . . . it is foolish to attempt to prove to [unbelievers] that the Scripture is the Word of God. This it cannot be known to be, except by faith." John Calvin, *Institutes of the Christian Religion* (Grand Rapids: Eerdmans, 1957), Tr. by H. Beveridge, Vol. I, Bk. I, 8, 13, p. 83.
16. CD I/2, p. 525. Italics in original, KD I/2, p. 583.
17. CD I/2, p. 524. Italics in original, KD I/2, p. 581.
18. CD I/2, p. 525.

19. CD I/2, p. 526. I am translating *"Überlieferung"* as "transmission" rather than as "tradition." Cf. KD I/2, p. 584.

20. CD I/2, p. 526. Italics in original, KD I/2, p. 584; also bracketed material.

21. CD I/2, p. 526.

23

BIBLICAL TEACHING ON INSPIRATION
AND INERRANCY

Bruce Corley

God has spoken. This affirmation—that God has revealed himself to mankind—lies at the heart of the Christian faith. The acting God who appears to us in mighty deed is also the speaking God who communicates to us in personal utterance. Revelation is both event and word.[1] The majestic declaration which opens the Book of Hebrews makes this plain: "When in former times God spoke to the forefathers, he spoke in fragmentary and varied fashion through the prophets. But in this final age he has spoken to us in the Son . . ." (Heb. 1:1-2a, NEB).

God's speaking is here described in two stages, corresponding to the old and new covenants, which are contrasted in terms of eras, recipients, spokesmen, and messages. In the former era revelation came through the prophets in "fragmentary and varied fashion"; bit by bit, this way and that, (the force of the two Greek adverbs *polymerōs* and *polytropōs*) the prophets heard God and announced the word. But in this final era of history, God has spoken distinctively "in a Son-way," i.e., a revelation mediated not by the prophets but through one who by nature is God's Son.[2] The careful parallelism leads us to supply the contrasting feature of the Son's mediation when compared to the "fragmentary and varied fashion" of the prophets. How are we to understand it? The message of Hebrews (and for that matter the rest of the New Testament) develops the answer we seek: God has spoken in his Son completely and finally ("once for all," Gk. *hapax,* cf. Heb. 9:26).[3] The ancient word was fully true but not truly full; the complete and final word is the personal, incarnate one. Christ, the Word of God (John 1:1), embodies the fullness of divine being and speaking (Col. 2:9); thus revelation as deed and revelation as word are inseparably bound in him. God has spoken, his word is Jesus Christ. Jesus Christ—his presence and work, deeds and words—is the supreme criterion for understanding all the revelation of God.[4]

Such a confession does not mean that the words spoken by Jesus are no longer important. To drive a wedge between the *fact* of the incarnation and the *words* of Jesus is a mistaken notion. Those who heard him could not receive his person and disregard his words: "He who rejects me and does not receive my sayings has a judge; the word that I have spoken will be his judge on the last day" (John 12:48, RSV, cf. Mark 8:38).[5] The Incarnation as the highest modality of the divine speaking means that the words of Jesus have eternal validity. Although heaven and earth pass away, his words never will (Matt. 24:35). This conviction underlies Jesus' intention to fulfill the Old Testament

(Matt. 5:17-18) because it has a similar abiding character. It also provides the rationale and impetus for a proclaimed witness to Jesus in the apostolic preaching and, concurrently, the written New Testament enshrining his words. What the apostles saw and heard, they proclaimed and wrote not as an exercise of historical recall but as the manifestation of eternal life (1 John 1:1-4). "In a word, the *written* witness of the life of Christ (cf. Luke 1:1-4) is the extension of the *spoken* word, and just as Christ offered himself in the words which he spoke (John 4:24), so Christ is now offered by the written word of special revelation."[6]

We can now summarize what has been said to this point: (1) divine revelation includes event and word, (2) the supreme revelation is Jesus Christ, and (3) a primary product of revelation is the written word, the Scriptures, which are uniquely related to Christ, both the Old and the New. We will not labor the discussion of these assumptions any further but turn to the primary focus of this study.

How are we to understand the Scriptures as the written word of God? When the assertion is made, "The Bible is the Word of God," what does "is" mean? Our inquiry must now deal with the term *inspiration,* which in the history of theology refers to the divine activity involved in the human production of the Scriptures.[7] A related question hangs upon the answer concerning inspiration. The assertion, "the Bible is true," assumes the Bible's inspiration, i.e., as a product of divine activity its trustworthiness is safeguarded. Here the term *inerrancy* calls for consideration as a proper description of the truthfulness of Scriptures. As we will see below, inerrancy is a difficult concept to define because it must be broad enough to cover the phenomena of the Bible yet narrow enough to satisfy the sense "free from error." From the biblical perspective the heart of the matter is whether inspiration implies the concept of inerrancy (whatever the appropriate term might be) and, if so, how this concept is to be defined. The warrants for and against inerrancy terminology from historical, theological, and philosophical perspectives are numerous and weighty; although they are compelling and interesting, our concern is more modest in scope yet ultimately more crucial: what does the Bible say about this? I propose to first describe what the Bible says about itself, concentrating on a classical passage and biblical terms, then second, in light of this evidence, suggest what we should say about the Bible.

The procedure I have taken up is vexed at the outset by the problem of method. We might begin with the formal statements of the Bible, doctrinal passages which testify to inspiration, and proceed deductively to demonstrate how the phenomena in the rest of the Bible square with this testimony. Or, we could marshal the particulars of the Bible inductively, those which illustrate inspiration, and attempt to make a generalization which adequately represents the formal testimony. Although some argue that the method chosen determines the logical outcome, in actual practice both deduction and induction must be employed.[8] "A paradigm, or conceptual model, is formulated through an informed and creative thinking process, generally involving the data to be explained, and is then brought back, adduced, or tested against the data for 'fit', or accuracy."[9] This procedure of checks and balances permits the meaning of formal statements about the Scriptures to be informed by the particulars of the biblical texts and prevents improper abstraction and speculation. And in like manner, the phenomena of difficult texts can be clarified through the interpretive grid of the formal concept. While attempting to observe these constraints, we will turn to the classical passage which is usually treated in discussions of inspiration: 2 Tim. 3:16.

In the Latin Vulgate the verb *inspiro*, "to inspire," (Gen. 2:7; Wis. 15:11; Ecclus. 4:12; 2 Tim. 3:16; 2 Pet. 1:21) and the noun *inspiratio*, "inspiration" (2 Sam. 22:16, Job 32:8; Psa. 17:25) occur nine times. In the English Bible the AV retains only the noun *inspiration* for Job 32:8, "But there is a spirit in man: and the inspiration of the Almighty giveth them understanding"; and 2 Tim. 3:16, "All Scripture is given by inspiration of God, and is profitable for doctrine, for reproof, for correction, for instruction in righteousness." The former passage need not concern us because it does not directly relate to the Scriptures. The translation, however, of 2 Tim. 3:16 is of decisive importance; the alternative translation favored by some, "Every scripture inspired of God is also profitable" (RV, ASV), raises the issues. The interpretation of the passage involves three related questions.

1. Does *pasa graphē* mean "all Scripture" (AV, RSV, Moffatt, Goodspeed, GNB) or "every Scripture" (RV, ASV, TCNT, NEB)? The adjective *pas* regularly means "all" when it occurs with the article and "every" when the article is missing, as it is here. In certain technical phrases and proper names this rule seems to be suspended, e.g., *pas Israēl* means "all Israel" (Rom. 11:26; cf. Acts 2:36; Eph. 2:21; 3:15; Col. 4:12).[10] It may be that these are not exceptions at all but simply draw attention to the "partitive aspect of the expression, and, if that is so, the present phrase many mean Scripture as viewed in each separate part of it."[11]

The use of the word *graphē* supports this conclusion. It is used more than fifty times in the New Testament and invariably refers to the Old Testament. In the New Testament the singular form *graphē* can denote the Scripture as a whole (e.g., Gal. 3:8, 22; Rom. 11:32; 1 Pet. 2:6) or individual passages of Scripture (e.g., Mark 12:10; Luke 4:21; Gal. 4:30; Jas. 2:23).[12] There is no major difference, when all is said, between the collective and distributive renderings. To say that *every* passage of Scripture is inspired is to say that the *whole* is inspired; however, the balance of argument favors the translation, "every Scripture."[13]

2. Where should the verb "is" (Gk. *estin*) be supplied in the sentence order? Because Greek commonly omits the linking verb, as it does here, we must insert it before or after "and" (the Gk. conjunction *kai*). If before *kai*, the adjective *theopneustos*, "inspired of God," is a predicate, and we translate "Scripture is inspired of God and profitable" (AV, RSV). If after *kai*, *theopneustos* is attributive, and the meaning of the sentence is "Scripture, inspired of God, is also profitable" (RV, ASV), with *kai* taking the ascensive force "also."

Several considerations should be taken into account.[14] (1) It would be more natural for the adjective, if attributive, to precede the noun, i.e., "inspired

451

Scripture" rather than the sequence in our text "Scripture inspired." (2) In the absence of a verb, it seems more natural to construe both adjectives (*theopneustos* and *ōphelimos,* "profitable") in the same way, making them predicates on analogy with the parallel construction in 1 Tim. 4:14. (3) It is difficult to see why Paul should need to assure Timothy that inspired Scripture is also profitable; this seems to be a "curious specimen of anticlimax."[15] Nevertheless, the "also" may take up and expand the thought of v. 15, which we could paraphrase as follows: "The sacred writings (*hiera grammata*) make one wise to salvation; indeed every Scripture, seeing that it is God-breathed, is also profitable."[16] Paul's object on this view, since presumably the inspiration of the sacred writings is taken for granted, would be to stress the usefulness of the Scripture for Christian faith and practice.

It is sometimes suggested that the attributive view leaves open the possibility of non-inspired Scripture, viz. "every inspired Scripture" (NEB) means some are not.[17] Such an implication is not necessary. If *graphē* means a religious writing in the general sense of the term, which it never does in the rest of the New Testament, then it is clearly reasonable for Paul to insist that only the inspired writings are profitable. If *graphē* means Scripture in the canonical sense, which it surely does, the attributive "inspired" is a defining characteristic of each part of the whole. The phrase "inspired Scripture" no more means some of the Scripture is uninspired than "sacred writings" means some of them are profane. Therefore, there is no objection to the attributive view on the grounds that it weakens the view of inspiration for the totality of Scripture.

It is noteworthy that on this point B. B. Warfield and James Orr concur: there is little to choose between the attributive and predicate renderings. Orr states, "On this it is to be remarked that, whichever form is adopted, the sense is not essentially altered. The form, 'Every Scripture inspired of God is also profitable' may be a broader, but it is certain that it is not intended to be a *narrower,* form of the statement than the other."[18] Warfield considers the question interesting but of no moment and settles for the attributive view: "On the whole, the preferable construction would seem to be, 'Every Scripture, seeing that it is God-breathed, is as well profitable.'"[19]

While not ruling out this interpretation, it seems less likely on the grounds of syntax and Pauline usage. Thus, we favor the rendering "Every Scripture is inspired and profitable."

3. What does the adjective *theopneustos,* "inspired by God" (NASB), mean when used of the Scripture? The usual translation "inspired" or "inspiration" conveys the idea "breathed into by God," and this meaning is supported by the standard lexicons and commentators.[20] This can be taken to mean that the Scripture is the product of divinely inspired authors or that the Scripture itself is infused with the presence of God, hence it breathes out God. Whatever may be taught elsewhere about the Scripture as the product of inspired religious experience or as the vehicle of gripping, inspiring power, these specific points are not made in the use of *theopneustos.* The Greek word is properly understood not as *in*-spiration, breathing into something, but as *ex*-piration, something breathed out.

452

This assertion, widely accepted in evangelical discussions of inspiration, has three bases of support. (1) The word *theopneustos* is a compound of *theos*, "God," and the verb *pneō*, "breathe," with the suffix *-tos*. The terms formed by adding *-tos* belong to a group called verbal adjectives (some 150 occur in the New Testament), which may be active or passive, depending on the verb involved. The majority of the *-tos* class is passive, e.g., *theodidaktos* means "God-taught" not "God-teaching"; cf. "you yourselves are taught by God [*theodidaktoi*] to love one another" (1 Thess. 4:9, NASB).[21]

(2) The occurrences of *theopneustos* in extrabiblical literature (it occurs only once in Scripture) and the use of analogous compounds of *theos* plus *-tos* in classical and patristic writings argue for the passive meaning. This is demonstrated in the painstakingly careful and unsurpassed survey by Warfield, some fifty pages long. He concludes: "If analogy is to count for anything its whole weight is thrown thus in favor of the interpretation which sees in *theopneustos*, quite simply, the sense of "God-breathed," i.e., produced by God's creative breath."[22]

(3) That the Scripture is breathed out by God fully accords with Paul's understanding of the Old Testament. The Scripture can be personified and speak the words of God (Gal. 3:22); or the totality of Scripture is the oracle of God (Rom. 3:2). Paul introduces Old Testament passages with recurrent formulas of saying, e.g., "Scripture says" (Rom. 4:3; 11:2; Gal. 4:30), "God says" (2 Cor. 6:16; Rom. 9:15; 11:4), and "Isaiah says" (Rom. 10:16, 20; 15:12). These formulas are particularly important for showing Paul's attitude toward the divine origin of the Scripture. "'The Scripture says', 'God says', and 'Isaiah says' are for Paul only different ways of expressing the same thing."[23] The Scripture is the product of the divine speaking, whether through a human spokesman or the written word.

We may conclude that *theopneustos* emphasizes the creative act of God in producing the Scripture. No better definition of the word has been penned than Warfield's own summary:

> The Greek term has, however, nothing to say of *in*spiring or of *in*spiration: it speaks only of a "spiring" or "spiration." What it says of Scripture is, not that it is "breathed into by God" or is the product of the Divine "inbreathing" into its human authors, but that it is breathed out by God, "God-breathed," the product of the creative breath of God. In a word, what is declared by this fundamental passage is simply that the Scriptures are a Divine product, without any indication of how God has operated in producing them.[24]

The "breath of God" is a metaphorical description of God's creative fiat, his power to create by saying, "Let it be so!" "By the word of the Lord," the psalmist says, "the heavens were made, and by the breath of His mouth all their host." (Psa. 33:6, NASB).[25] We can little imagine a more expressive term to describe the divine origin of the Scripture.

The implications of 2 Tim. 3:16 for our understanding of biblical inspiration deserve careful attention. We note the following:

453

1. *Scope of inspiration*. Each part of Scripture, whether it seems to us central to the Bible's message or rather incidental, is equally inspired. Since the whole originates with God, even that which appears to be mundane and casual has a divine purpose. How much inspiration, then, will we claim for a common request like "When you come, bring the cloak that I left with Carpus at Troas, and my scrolls, especially the parchments" (2 Tim. 4:13)? Surely the same measure we claim for "Here is a trustworthy saying: If we died with him, we will also live with him" (2 Tim. 2:11, NIV).[26]

2. *Means of inspiration*. Inspiration denotes Scripture as a product of divine activity; it does not prescribe a single or specific means by which this occurred. Different circumstances of writing, forms of literature, and human authors of Scripture are clearly reflected in how the sixty-six books of the Bible came to be written. Solomon's proverbs were written down after two centuries by the men of Hezekiah's reign (Prov. 25:1); the disciples of Isaiah were instructed to preserve his testimony (Isa. 8:16); only once does the psalmist call for a written praise to guide the worship of God (Psa. 102:18); Jeremiah used a secretary named Baruch, a practice followed by Paul (Tertius, Rom. 16:22) and Peter (Silas, 1 Pet. 5:12) after him, to write down on a scroll what the Lord had spoken (Jer. 36:2, 4) and to produce a second, supplemented edition (Jer. 36:27-28, 32); Luke's acknowledged method in writing his gospel (Luke 1:1-4) was historical research dependent upon careful investigation and sources of information (personal and written). The Bible's own witness marshals a complex of human situations which God used to produce the written word; therefore, each kind of literary process indicated in the Bible is a legitimate vehicle of inspiration. Inspiration assumes the activity of God in all the historical processes which produced the Scripture.[27]

3. *Purpose of inspiration*. To postulate the divine origin of Scripture relates directly to its usefulness for a particular end, namely, to give the "wisdom that leads to salvation through faith which is in Christ Jesus" (2 Tim. 3:15, NASB). If Scripture as inspired points to the idea "divinely given," then Scripture as profitable points to "divinely intended." Because Scripture is stamped with divine character, it bears divine authority expressly located in four spheres: (1) for faith, the Scripture provides "teaching," positive doctrine, and "reproof," the negative aspect of teaching; and (2) for practice, the Scripture gives "correction" of faults on the ethical plane and, its positive counterpart, "training" in right behavior. Here we enter a caution: we must not suppose that only those parts of Scripture related to our faith and practice are profitable (and thus, inspired); on the contrary, we should understand that *every* part of Scripture is profitable for faith and practice because it is inspired.

4. *Character of inspiration*. The word-of-God character of the Scripture constitutes its claim to be true. When a prophet or apostle spoke the word of God, they believed it to be reliable and trustworthy because one could place absolute confidence in the God who spoke it. The dominant biblical description of God's word is the concept of truth, featured primarily in the word groups for "true and trustworthy" (Heb. *'emet* and Gk. *alētheia* and *pistos*).[28] Inspiration leads us to make the highest claim for the Scripture, "The Bible is the Word of

454

God." It follows from this that we make a related and dependent claim, "The Bible is true." Although truth as a category must be defined, it has the merit of being a strong biblical term, encompassing both knowledge—the sum of the divine word is truth (Psa. 119:60)—and power—the truth will liberate the one who knows it (John 8:32). To sum up, when we assert the inspired character of the Scripture, we also claim that it is true.

Notes

1. I am in full agreement with James Barr on this point (*Old and New in Interpretation: A Study of the Two Testaments* [New York: Harper and Rowe, 1966], p. 22): "What then of this speaking of God to particular men? Surely we over-rationalize the phenomenon of prophecy, as it was understood at the time and as this understanding has been recovered in modern scholarship, if we picture it as if the prophets were unusually discerning interpreters of the contemporary historical scene, so that from it they drew their consequences of divine judgment and mercy? A good newspaper columnist can do this. But the prophetic consciousness is one of hearing what God says to the prophet, not of diagnosing the forces and probabilities inherent in the historical situation." See also George E. Ladd, *The New Testament and Criticism* (Grand Rapids: Eerdmans, 1967), p. 27: "Here is the biblical mode of revelation: the revealing acts of God in history, accompanied by the interpreting prophetic word which explains the divine source and character of the divine acts"; and I. Howard Marshall, *Biblical Inspiration* (Grand Rapids: Eerdmans, 1983), pp. 12-15.

2. On the absence of the article from the phrase "in a Son" (Gk. *en huiō*) see B. F. Westcott, *The Epistle to the Hebrews: The Greek Text with Notes and Essays* (London: Macmillan, 1892), p. 7.

3. For the rhetorical analysis see William L. Lane, *Hebrews*, Word Biblical Commentary, vol. 47 (Waco: Word Books, forthcoming). The theological implications of this passage are elaborated in J. I. Packer, *God Has Spoken* (Downers Grove, Ill.: InterVarsity, 1979), esp. 45-46, 65-66, 84-85.

4. "But in the last days," says Philip Hughes, "which are the days of the fulfillment of the ancient promise and prophecies, God has spoken his final word, and he has done so in the single person of the Son, who is himself the divine Word (John 1:1) and as such the supreme, the ultimate, and the absolute Prophet" ("The Christology of Hebrews," *Southwestern Journal of Theology* 28 [1985]: 19).

5. The Gk. construction, a single article with two participles ("one rejecting me and not receiving my words"), indicates that rejection of Jesus entails his words and vice versa. The argument I am making assumes the credibility of the gospel reports. I find it highly difficult to explain the interests of the evangelists to preserve the words of Jesus if the fact of the incarnation is discounted. See C. F. D. Moule, *The Birth of the New Testament*, 3d rev. ed. (New York: Harper & Rowe, 1982), pp. 9-18.

6. Bernard Ramm, *Special Revelation and the Word of God* (Grand Rapids: Eerdmans, 1961), p. 116.

7. See the chapter "Inspiration in the Christian Tradition" in Clark H. Pinnock, *Biblical Revelation—The Foundation of Christian Theology* (Chicago: Moody Press, 1971), pp. 147-74; and the historical essays in *Scripture and Truth*, eds. D. A. Carson and John D. Woodbridge (Grand Rapids: Zondervan, 1983), pp. 173-279.

8. The Orr-inductivist school, leading to limited inerrancy, is often pitted against the Warfield-deductivist school, leading to total inerrancy (see Dewey M. Beegle, *Scripture, Tradition and Infallibility* [Grand Rapids: Eerdmans, 1973], pp. 175-224; and J. Barton Payne, "Higher Criticism and Biblical Inerrancy," in *Inerrancy*, ed. Norman L. Geisler [Grand Rapids: Zondervan, 1980], p. 95). The need for both approaches surfaces in the exchange between Arthur F. Holmes, "Ordinary Language Analysis and Theological Method," *Bulletin of the Evangelical Theological Society* 11 (1968): 131-38; and Norman L. Geisler, "Theological Method and Inerrancy: A Reply to Professor Holmes," *Bulletin of the Evangelical Theological Society* 11 (1968): 139-46. The retreat of Clark Pinnock from his previous position illustrates how slippery the methodological issue is. See *The Scripture Principle* (New York: Harper & Row, 1984), pp. 58-59.

9. Paul D. Feinberg, "The Meaning of Inerrancy," in *Inerrancy*, ed. Norman L. Geisler (Grand Rapids: Zondervan, 1980), p. 273. Feinberg's description of the problem is levelheaded, and his proposal is appealing.

10. See the discussion in C. F. D. Moule, *An Idiom Book of New Testament Greek*, 2d ed. (Cambridge: At the University, 1959), pp. 95-97; A. T. Robertson, A Grammar of the Greek New Testament in the Light of Historical Research (Nashville: Broadman, 1934), p. 772; and Nigel Turner, *A Grammar of New Testament Greek*, vol. 3: *Syntax* (Edinburgh: T. & T. Clark, 1963), pp. 199-200. Moule prefers the "whole of Scripture"; Turner, "whatever is Scripture"; and Robertson is ambivalent.

11. Donald Guthrie, *The Pastoral Epistles*, Tyndale New Testament Commentaries (Grand Rapids: Eerdmans, 1957), p. 163.

12. See Gottlob Schrenk, *"graphē,"* *Theological Dictionary of the New Testament*, 4:751-55, for a full discussion; on our passage, Schrenk comments: "[2 Tim. 3:16] obviously means every passage of Scripture" (p. 754).

13. Besides Guthrie, for this view see the commentaries of J. N. D. Kelly, *A Commentary on the Pastoral Epistles*, Harper's New Testament Commentaries (New York: Harper & Row, 1963),p. 202; and J. H. Bernard, *The Pastoral Epistles*, Cambridge Greek Testament for Schools and Colleges (Cambridge: At the University, 1899), pp. 136-37. The other view is defended by E. K. Simpson, *The Pastoral Epistles: The Greek Text with Introduction and Commentary* (London: Tyndale Press, 1954), p. 150.

14. For the details see A. T. Robertson, *Word Pictures in the New Testament*, vol. 4: *The Epistles of Paul* (Nashville: Broadman, 1931), p. 627; Guthrie, *The Pastoral Epistles*, pp. 163-64; and Kelly, *The Pastoral Epistles*, pp. 202-3.

15. Simpson, *The Pastoral Epistles*, p. 150.

16. Many older commentaries advance this explanation, e.g., Bernard, *The Pastoral Epistles*, p. 137; cf. the similar paraphrase suggested but not adopted by Gordon D. Fee, *1 and 2 Timothy, Titus*, Good News Commentary (New York: Harper & Row, 1984), p. 229.

17. E.g., Edwin A. Blum, "The Apostle's View of Scripture," in *Inerrancy*, ed. Norman L. Geisler (Grand Rapids: Zondervan, 1980), p. 46; Ronald A. Ward, *A Commentary on 1 & 2 Timothy and Titus* (Waco, Tx: Word Books, 1974), p. 200; and Kelly, *The Pastoral Epistles*, p. 203.

18. James Orr, *Revelation and Inspiration* (London: Duckworth, 19190), p. 160.

19. B. B. Warfield, *Inspiration and Authority of the Bible*, ed. Samuel G. Craig (Philadelphia: Presbyterian and Reformed, 1948), p. 134.

20. Cf. Edward Schweizer, *"theopneustos,"* *Theological Dictionary of the New Testament*, 6:454; *A Greek-English Lexicon of the New Testament and Other Early Chris-*

tian Literature, 2d ed. (1979), s. v. *"theopneustos,"* by Walter Bauer et. al.; and Kelly, *The Pastoral Epistles,* p. 203.

21. See Friedrich Blass and Albert Debrunner, *A Greek Grammar of the New Testament and Other Early Christian Literature,* trans. and rev. by Robert W. Funk (Chicago: University of Chicago, 1961), pp. 61-63; and note the separate comments by J. H. Moulton, W. F. Howard, and Nigel Turner, *A Grammar of New Testament Greek,* 1:121-22; 2:370-71; and 3:150-65.

22. Warfield, *Inspiration and Authority,* p. 283.

23. E. Earle Ellis, *Paul's Use of the Old Testament* (Grand Rapids: Eerdmans, 1957), p. 23.

24. Warfield, *Inspiration and Authority,* p. 133.

25. The *word* and the *Word* of God create and sustain the visible universe; cf. the divine word in Gen. 1:3 ff., "God said," with the creator role of Christ, Col. 1:16-17; Heb. 1:3; and John 1:1. For the biblical motifs see Edmond Jacob, *Theology of the Old Testament* (New York: Harper & Row, 1958), pp. 132-34; Bertold Klappert, "Word," in *New International Dictionary of New Testament Theology,* ed. Colin Brown, 3 vols. (Grand Rapids: Zondervan, 1979), 3:1087-117; and Donald Guthrie, *New Testament Theology* (Downers Grove, Ill.: Inter-Varsity, 1981), pp. 321-30.

26. In principle the inspiration of the Old Testament Scripture extends to the New. The extension is hinted at in the New Testament itself: (1) apostolic faith places the words of Jesus on a par with the Old Testament Scripture (John 2:22; 5:47); (2) the writings of Paul are classed as authoritative alongside the "rest of the Scriptures" (2 Pet. 3:16); and (3) Paul quotes Deut. 25:4 together with a saying of Jesus from Luke 10:7 under the heading, "For the Scripture says" (1 Tim. 5:18). Interpreters are divided over whether or not the quotation comes from the written gospel: (a) earliest citation of a gospel (Jeremias, Spicq, Simpson), (b) a saying of Jesus either from a written collection (Guthrie) or oral tradition (Barrett, Hanson), or (c) a current proverb commonly used by Jesus and Paul (Kelly, Bernard). For a review of the evidence see Ceslaus Spicq, *Les Épîtres Pastorales,* Études bibliques, 4th ed., 2 vols. (Paris: J. Gabalda, 1969), 1:543-44.

27. A basic model for understanding the historical processes can be derived from 2 Pet. 1:21, a testimony to the veracity of prophecy: "No prophecy ever came [Gk. *pherō,* "carry")] by the impulse of man, but men moved [Gk. *pherō* again] by the Holy Spirit spoke from God" (RSV). The wordplay on the verb "to carry" *(pherō),* which is difficult to reproduce in English, recalls Acts 27:15, 17, where the same word is used of Paul's ship being driven by the wind. "The prophets raised their sails, so to speak," suggests Michael Green, "(they were obedient and receptive), and the Holy Spirit filled them and carried their craft along in the direction He wished" (*The Second Epistle General of Peter and the General Epistle of Jude,* Tyndale New Testament Commentaries [Grand Rapids: Eerdmans, 1968], p. 91). This metaphor "impelled," or "borne along" is the key thought in Warfield's oft-quoted "concursive operation" whereby the Spirit works "confluently" with the human personality, both preserving and elevating it under divine sanction (see *Inspiration and Authority,* pp. 94-95).

28. There are more than three hundred fifty references in the Bible to the truthfulness of the word of God. Admittedly, the concept has to be defined (what biblical concept doesn't?), but what term can lay claim to be a better *biblical* description of God's word? For the terminology and semantic considerations, see Otto Procksch, "The Word of God in the Old Testament," s. v. *"lego," Theological Dictionary of the New Testament,* 4:91-100, esp. p. 93; Anthony C. Thiselton, "Truth," *New International Dictionary of*

New Testament Theology, ed. Colin Brown, 3 vols. (Grand Rapids: Zondervan, 1979), 3:874-902; Roger Nicole, "The Biblical Concept of Truth," in *Scripture and Truth,* eds. D. A. Carson and John D. Woodbridge (Grand Rapids: Zondervan, 1983), pp. 287-98; and Ramm, *Special Revelation,* pp. 152-54.

[Editor's note: The present essay is an abbreviated version of the seminar presentation which included a lengthy discussion of truth and inerrancy.]

24

THE PLACE OF THE BIBLE IN THE BIBLICAL PATTERN OF AUTHORITY

M. Vernon Davis

What is the nature of authority as it is understood in the Scriptures? How is religious authority known by people in the context of their contemporary experience? These questions provide the focus of this study. The subject of the paper itself includes two significant clues for understanding the issues that are involved. Comprehending the role of the Bible is essential for Christians who address the questions. The title also implies that knowledge of religious authority is to be understood in terms of a complex or pattern of realities.

The title of this study is suggested by the work of Bernard Ramm, *The Pattern of Religious Authority,* which was first published in 1957. Other evangelical scholars have more recently focused upon the relationship of the Bible to the total pattern of phenomena in which the authority of God is made known to the believer. Notable among these is *The Scripture Principle* by Clark H. Pinnock.[1] Bernard Ramm provides a basic definition of authority per se with which there is wide concurrence. He states: "Authority itself means that right or power to command action or compliance, or to determine belief or custom, expecting obedience from those under authority, and in turn giving responsible account for the claim or right to power."[2]

People experience different kinds of authority in their lives. Persons, communities, government, and documents come to their "right to rule" from varied bases. Each has its own foundation and limitations. Imperial authority comes because of the possession of superior power or status. The one who possesses such right and power to command may delegate it to another, so that delegated authority becomes a form in which people possess and relate to authority. Stipulative authority is another common kind of rule with which persons live. This authority is that which is accepted by a society as the structure in which they will live and govern their lives. Constitutions, rules of order, and established historical precedents illustrate this form of authority.

The authority of truth itself has been called by Ramm and others veracious authority. This authority is mediated in varied forms—by eye witnesses to events, by persons, books, and principles which carry the truth to us. This kind of authority is compelling because it "issues form superior knowledge or first hand experience. It is the authority of the expert, the professional, the participant, the eye witness."[3] These means are compelling in implementing their function of mediating authentic truth which has impact for life.

The Bible partakes of this kind of compelling, veracious authority. The role of eyewitnesses to the events of redemptive significance is of essential importance in its pages. The significance of the historical proximity of writings to events themselves was a major concern in the process of canonization of the New Testament.

In its ultimate sense authority belongs to God alone. This statement is the foundational assumption of all religion. Christianity is not unique in making this affirmation, but rather shares the claim with the other religions of mankind. The personal character of religious authority, however, is especially emphasized in the Christian faith.

The basic New Testament word for authority is *exousia*. The term denotes a right to decide and a power to carry out the decision. As applied to God, this authority grows out of His own being, as the etymology of the word suggests. The authority of God in the Bible is all-inclusive, being characterized by the freedom and power to command both persons and the entire created order.

The crucial issue for Christians lies in the question: How is the authority of God known to us? Because authority belongs ultimately to the infinite God, how can it be experienced by the finite human being, whose limitations in creation are compounded by the distortions of his or her sin? The affirmation of the Bible is that the people of God know His authority only through His self-revelation. Revelation and authority are bound together in the Christian understanding of God.

In the Christian faith authority is understood in personal terms. The Old Testament bears witness to the living God who is active in history. He interacts with human beings, especially those with whom he has established a covenant relationship. His power and right to rule are experienced in terms of who He is. People are called to obey Him in light of what He has done for them. He is the Lord who brought His people out of Egypt. He is faithful to His covenant with Israel, and He calls His people to be faithful.

God is known in the Scriptures not simply in terms of power, but as power in the service of love, truth, and justice. Because He is God, the inevitable response to His revelation is that of awe, fear, and reverence. Because He is the God whose character is revealed in His mighty acts of redemption and in the covenant, the appropriate response includes love for Him and commitment to become like Him.

The meaning of authority, like that of all the basic concepts in Christian theology, is definitely revealed in the person of Jesus, the Christ. His right to rule became evident in His deeds and teachings. It was confirmed in His resurrection. In His ministry people were amazed at His teaching, because "He taught them as one who had authority, and not as the scribes" (Mark 1:22). The *exousia* which belongs ultimately to God alone is given to me" (Matthew 28:19). In the presence and power of the risen Christ, the early church experienced the authority of God. The Scriptures mediate that experience to all generations which follow.

The full expression of God's authority in His self-revelation is a complex reality. Ramm emphasizes the necessity of finding "the pattern through which it expresses itself concretely and practically."[4] Clark Pinnock also contends that we must speak of a pattern of revelation to do any justice to it. We will find as we look into it that God acts in human history, gives some understanding of his will to prophets and apostles, becomes flesh in the person of Jesus, moves in power in the Spirit of Pentecost, and provides written Scriptures for the church.[5]

Thus, awareness of the authority of God involves a pattern and a process. Event, interpretation, preservation, and understanding are essential. Each phase or part of the pattern is vital. Without appropriate recognition of each one's understanding of revelation, authority will inevitably be distorted. An analysis of this pattern of biblical authority and the significance of each part of it is the focus of this study.

The Authority of God Is Expressed in His Acts in History

While God is revealed in creation and universal human experience, He is known most clearly in the special history recorded in the Bible. This history finds its fulfillment in the life and ministry of Jesus and the community that forms around Him.

Christianity is an historical religion. This assertion means far more than the fact that its story can be traced historically. Rather, its primary meaning lies in the assertion that its truth is revealed in historical events. In the common events of ordinary life for ordinary people God revealed Himself. History is the medium of His self-disclosure.

Yahweh made a covenant which He remembered through many generations. He delivered His people from bondage in the definitive act of grace. He gave them the Law to enable them to experience the life of grace fully and freely. He did not abandon His people, even when they were unfaithful to Him. In many ways at various times He spoke to them by the prophets. God revealed Himself in the history of a people to whom He had bound Himself in covenant love.

The climax and definitive expression of God's revelation and authority came in a person, His Son. "The word became flesh and dwelled among us, full of grace and truth; and we beheld His glory—the glory as of the only Son from the Father" (John 1:14). The witness of Paul to this central revelation is clear: "God was in Christ reconciling the world unto himself, not counting their trespasses against them, and entrusting to us the message of reconciliation" (2 Corinthians 5:19).

In a profound text that declares the unity of God in the act of creation and the history of redemption Paul states:

> For it is the god who said, "Let the light shine out of darkness" who has shone in our hearts to give the light of the knowledge of the glory of God in the face of Christ. But we have this treasure in earthen vessels, to show that the transcendent power belongs to God and not to us (2 Corinthians 4:6-7).

The revelation of God continued to be made known in the history of the early church. As the early believers searched their covenant history and reflected on their personal experience, God revealed to them what He had done and was doing with them. A characteristic of that revelation was the truth that God was sovereign of their past and of their future. They were His people— living from the decisive redemptive event in Jesus Christ and living toward the culmination of God's purpose for them and for the world. They lived, as Christians continue to do, between the time of the "already" of their redemption and the "not yet" of their final experience of salvation.

The Authority of God Is Expressed in the Scriptures

The events recorded in the Scriptures were inadequate for human salvation apart from the inspired interpretation of faith. Events plus interpretation form the heart of the biblical witness. Without the appropriate understanding of faith the meaning of history can be missed in much the same way that people fail to see the presence and purpose of God through his handiwork in creation.

John Calvin made a strong case for the reality of revelation in nature, but he said that people nevertheless fail to understand God in creation. The Bible, according to Calvin, can be compared to spectacles which people need in order to see and comprehend the reality that is actually there.[6] In a comparable way the Scriptures provide the means through which the meaning of the events of special history they record can be grasped. The inspiration of the Scriptures involves the faithful recording of events, appropriate theological interpretations of the events, and pertinent application of those events and interpretations in the lives of the people of God. Such applications are both corporate and individual.

The inspiration of Scripture is essential in the biblical pattern of authority. The written word of God does not come by accident of history nor simply by the heightened sensitivity of religious persons to what was happening in the world. Rather, the Scriptures are authoritative because God has provided them as an authentic record of what He has done and an effective instrument for what He is doing among people in every age.

Obviously, the data on which our understanding of the essentials of faith is grounded can be obtained in no other place. In the words of E. Y. Mullins:

> Scripture as a record of original experience cannot be transcended, nor can it lose its authority; for the sufficient reason that to discard Scripture is to discard the only means of understanding the historic Christ who emancipates man and imparts to him spiritual autonomy.[7]

In a similar statement Hans Kung has said:

> The New Testament has continually proved its irreplaceable normative authority and significance. And we are thrown back on this norm as long as we remain authentic Christians and do not want to be anything else. The New Testament as the original written Christian testimony remains (fortunately) the unchangeable norm for all later proclamation and theology in the church and provides protection against subjective whims and all kinds of fanaticism.[8]

The Scriptures, thus, provide the trustworthy understanding of people in the past for the sake of people in the future. In them is the authentic expression of the authority of God in a special history that becomes the basis on which persons can experience his authority in every time and place. W. T. Conner said:

> The Bible records events in which God was revealing himself to men. As the record of such events, it enables us also to know God. As we read about God's dealings with men, we too are enabled to come to fellowship with him. In that sense the Bible is God's revelation to us.[9]

The bible thus mediates God's word to us. It is the authority that is compelling because it is veracious. It is functional in that it brings the truth of salvation to us and through us to others. It is the unique word that enables us to have an authentic understanding of God Himself through His self-revelation.

The Bible functions as it is intended to do when persons look confidently *through* it rather than merely *at* it. When faith in its reliability is shaken, people tend to look at it, becoming preoccupied with questions of the mechanics of its inspiration and the truth of its message. The situation is very much like that of those who wear glasses when a lens cracks or the frames become bent. In such circumstances the instrument which is intended to enable us to see more clearly the reality around us becomes instead the focus of our vision.

A college student and I were discussing his plans for his Christmas vacation. He described a family tradition in which his extended family gathered at his grandparents' home to celebrate Christmas. "The part I hate," he said, "is when my two uncles break out their slides and set up the projector to show us pictures of the annual trip they take together. It's not that the slides are bad—both of them are really quite good photographers and they always go to interesting places. But every time they engage in a continuing argument over who used the best angles, had the best lens settings, or had the superior equipment. We end up with nobody really looking at the pictures."

The Bible is the way by which we come to know the authoritative God who in the beginning said, "Let light shine in the darkness," and who in the person of Jesus gave us "the light of the knowledge of the glory of God." It is the trustworthy means by which persons are enabled to see God and meet Him in the transforming encounter of faith. How unfortunate it is when the Bible itself becomes the focus of attention as a "problem" rather than the dependable way of mediating the realities of faith. In such circumstances we become like the persons who preferred to argue over the camera rather than look at the pictures it had taken.

One day I stood in the British Museum where I had gone primarily to see the Codex Sinaiticus, that rare and important biblical manuscript. I had been in awe of it since studying its significance for our understanding the biblical text and hearing the fascinating story of its recovery by Tischendorf. After standing before it for a long time, I turned to look around the room at other famous manuscripts which were there. Most of them were important works by famous British authors. In one case there was the original score of Handel's *Messiah*. I

463

began to reflect on the remarkable process by which music is heard in the mind of the composer, orchestrated for existing instruments and voices, and reduced to symbols on a page. Before me were the notes and rests, the key signatures and the time, the accidentals and the interpretive words. In the mystery of music, those symbols can be understood by those who study them faithfully and commit themselves to the disciplines of mastering their meaning. In this way the music can come to life again. The symbols can become the means of experiencing reality.

As I left that room, I began to reflect on my experience of those two manuscripts. They began to come together for me. I began to see Codex Sinaiticus in something of the same terms I pondered the score of the *Messiah*. The "word became flesh." And the word made flesh became words of witness and understanding. All of that was done in order that in a real sense the Word might become flesh again and again. The symbols on the page make possible the personal, saving experience of the self-revealing God.

The Authority of God Is Experienced in the Scriptures Through the Inner Witness of God's Spirit

The biblical pattern of authority involves not only the historical disclosure and the authentic interpretation and preservation. Authority is experienced through the illumination of the Holy Spirit.

Early Baptist Confessions reflect the influence of a Puritan heritage in which the Bible was believed to be confirmed and authenticated by the witness of the Spirit. The Westminster Confession stated: "Our full persuasion and assurance of the infallible truth and divine authority [of the Bible] is from the inward work of the Holy Spirit, bearing witness by and with the Word in our hearts." In 1677 this language was included in the Second London Confession of Baptists. William Lumpkin in noting the Puritan influence upon this Baptist statement of faith said that "the Puritan found his authority in the Spirit-prompted response of his mind and heart to the Word. The Spirit who inspired the writer also spoke within the Puritan as he read."[10]

The recognition of the authority of the revelation of God for us is not ultimately based upon rational proofs and evidence. While these can open persons to the possibility of the authority of the Scriptures, in the final analysis they do not provide it to their satisfaction. The God to whose authority the Bible bears witness in authenticity and truth continues to speak in human hearts and minds through His word. As Donald Bloesch has said:

> The authority of the Bible is based on the One whom it attests and the one who speaks through it in every age with the word of regenerating power. We here concur with Calvin: "The highest proof of Scripture derives in general from the fact that God in person speaks in it." This by no means implies that the biblical witness is fallible or untrustworthy. Instead we hold that this witness does not carry the force of infallible authority apart from the Holy Spirit who acts in and through it.[11]

464

The recovery of a strong emphasis upon the inner witness of the Holy Spirit in the understanding of the Scriptures can be a key to avoiding a rationalistic doctrine of Biblical authority. At the same time, it is not to be identified with a subjectivism which leaves theology with no objective norm. According to Bloesch:

> Revelation is truly given in and through the words of Scripture, and this means intelligible content as well as spiritual presence (cf. Romans 16:25,26; Colossians 1:25-28). The action of disclosing God's will and purpose not only entails revelation through Scripture but also revelation as Scripture . . . . Scripture embodies the truth that god desires us to hear. The unity between the revealed Word, Jesus Christ, and the written word lies both in the inspiration of the Spirit who guarantees a trustworthy witness to Christ and in revelatory action in which the Spirit speaks through this witness to people of every age (I Corinthians 2:10-13).[12]

In the history of Protestant theology the pattern of authority and revelation has been developed in varied ways. The significant role of disclosure, inspiration, and illumination is basic to an adequate doctrine of humanity's knowledge of God. In the twentieth century Karl Barth has clearly sounded his understanding of the Word of God in a threefold manner: the word incarnate, the word written, and the word proclaimed. This is a significant witness to the pattern through which God has spoken and continues to speak with authority to His people.

J. I. Packer has said,

> Revelation signifies the whole work of God communicating with sinners redemptively to bring them to saving knowledge of himself. It embraces three levels of activity: (i) historical saving action (redemption obtained); (ii) inscripturation (redemption recorded, attested, celebrated); (iii) illumination (redemption understood and received).[13]

Recognizing the pattern through which the authority inherent in God Himself is known to human beings provides the theologian with a structure through which to address significant issues—such as the relationship of the infinite to the finite, the true and perfect to the sinful, the past to the present, the objective nature of revelation and its subjective recognition. Appropriate attention to the place of the Bible in the pattern of authority can enable theology to avoid being torn from its historical grounding as well as dissolving into mere pietistic subjectivism or scholastic rationalism.

Notes

1. Bernard Ramm, *The Pattern of Religious Authority,* (Grand Rapids: Eerdmans, 1957), and Clark H. Pinnock, *The Scripture Principle,* (San Francisco: Harper and Row, 1984).

2. Ramm, *op. cit.*, p. 10.

3. Robert G. Bratcher, "Toward a Definition of the Authority of the Bible," *Perspectives in Biblical Studies*, vol. 6, no. 2, Summer, 1979, p. 113.

4. Ramm, *op. cit.*, p. 18.

5. Pinnock, *op. cit.*, p. 4.

6. John Calvin, *Institutes*.

7. Address by E. Y. Mullins, July 14, 1905, quoted by John Steely.

8. Hans Kung, *On Being a Christian*, p. 466

9. W. T. Conner, *Revelation and God*, (Nashville: Broadman, 1936), pp. 79-80.

10. William L. Lumpkin, "The Bible in Early Baptist Confessions of Faith," *Baptist History and Heritage*, vol. XIX, no. 3, July, 1984, p. 35.

11. Donald Bloesch, "Crisis in Biblical Authority," *Theology Today*, vol. 35, no. 4, January, 1979, p. 456.

12. Ibid., pp. 457-8.

13. J. I. Packer, "The Divinity and the Humanity of the Bible," address to the Conference on Biblical Inerrancy, Ridgecrest, North Carolina, May 6, 1987.

25

THE ROLE OF THE HOLY SPIRIT IN RELATION TO THE AUTHORITY OF THE BIBLE

Wayne Ward

The authority of the Bible rests firmly upon the conviction that the Holy Spirit of God is vitally active in the process of inspiring, recording, preserving, and interpreting Holy Scripture from the beginning to the end. Preoccupation with the theory of infallible and inerrant original manuscripts betrays a seriously deficient doctrine of scripture, because it suggests that God gave us a perfect Bible in the beginning and then left us to struggle on our own with the crucial problems of recognizing and accepting these texts as authoritative scripture. Even worse, the obsession with inerrant autographs completely ignores the essential role of the Holy Spirit in copying, transmitting, translating, and interpreting the biblical text.

If God the Holy Spirit is not active in this entire process a thousand inerrant autographs will not give us a reliable and authoritative Bible today. This does not mean that the Holy Spirit must inspire human beings to produce an absolutely inerrant manuscript, canon, or translation. Rather, if the Holy Spirit is active in the entire process, God can use a translation which is not perfect, read by a person with limited education, to bring His Word infallibly and inerrantly into the mind and heart of the earnest believer!

A Solid Foundation

A sound doctrine of Holy Scripture includes the conviction that God was active in the events which the bible records and in the prophets and apostles who observed and participated in those events. It affirms that the Holy Spirit not only inspired the writers who recorded the scripture but also continued to be active in the process of preserving, interpreting, and living that Word. The purpose of this study is to trace the dynamic activity of the Holy Spirit in the original creation, through God's redemptive acts in history, and throughout the writing, preserving, interpreting, and living of authoritative Holy Scripture today. Anything less would be an incomplete and inadequate doctrine of scripture.

A Shaky Foundation

For any thoughtful believer, a doctrine which emphasizes "inerrant autographs" and then admits that we do not have them, leaves the disturbing question, "Can we trust the Bible we have today?" From my conversations with fellow-believers, all across the land, I am convinced that they are disturbed more by continuous emphasis on non-existent inerrant autographs than by all the so-called "liberal professors" put together. Conservative believers do not pay much attention to those whom they consider "liberals." They do not trust them. But they want to trust those who call themselves "inerrantists," because they believe that they are stout defenders of the Word of God. Imagine their shock when they hear self-styled inerrantists proclaiming: "We once had inerrant original manuscripts of the Bible, but we don't have them any more"; or, "Probably about ninety-seven per cent of our biblical text is authentic!" No wonder such statements have disturbed many devout believers.

Why have they not been told that not one of the manuscript variants among 10,000 manuscripts affects any fundamental Christian doctrine? Why have they not been informed that those "scary" variants in our present biblical texts are simply matters of word order, spelling, duplicate texts, and collation of multiple texts, which make no difference at all to the biblical message? Why have they not been assured that even in those cases where there are ungrammatical constructions or variant historical references, which grammarians and historians may call "errors," God still communicates His Word infallibly to the devout reader? In fact, if the reader speaks incorrect grammar, he might understand ungrammatical language better!

God can use all our fallible words and thoughts for His infallible purpose. As grandfather said, "Wayne, offer God the best you have. It may not be perfect, but it will be enough. God can hit a straight lick with a crooked stick!" It is good that God can use our imperfect lives. It is the only kind we have to give Him.

God did not disappear after He inspired the original writings. The Holy Spirit did not go away and abandon the scriptures or the faithful reader. He has gone right on using His Holy Word in hundreds of translations, none of them perfect, through thousands of interpreters, none of them infallible, doing His perfect work of convicting sinners, redeeming them, sanctifying, and sealing them for all eternity.

The Sin of Eden

It is time we called again for people to put their absolute trust in God and not in some theory of the scripture, constructed by human beings, about original documents, which we do not have. We must resist that fatal tendency in humankind to want a religious idol which they can hold in their hands. We must condemn that ancient longing to escape our human finitude and grasp the knowledge of truth as infallibly as God.

Our problem is not the claim that God's Word is infallible. No genuine believer will deny that. Our problem is the subtle assumption by some of us that we have grasped infallible truth and anyone opposing our view is opposing God's truth. In fact, we may automatically assume that since we see it the way God sees it, anyone who differs must be in league with Satan and fighting against God. It is a sin as old as Eden and as contemporary as this conference.

This sin afflicts "liberals" as pervasively as it afflicts "fundamentalist." It is the sin of Genesis, chapter three: the longing to remove any significant distinction between our knowledge and God's knowledge, between ourselves and God. We still want to "be like God, knowing good and evil" (Genesis 3:5). When a

468

person assumes that his viewpoint is absolutely right and that anyone who differs is contradicting God's truth, that person is demonstrating the sin of Eden: the inability to accept any significant distinction between themselves and God. We must all bear witness to God's infallible truth as we see it; but we must never forget that our perception of that truth is fallible, imperfect, distorted by our sin, and often self-serving.

Our witness to God's truth may involve passionate proclamation, reasoned argument, and gentle persuasion. Unless one assumes omniscience, he will be anxious to learn from his fellow-believer as to persuade him. After all, we need the witness and the correction of other committed believers as we seek to understand to share the biblical message. What is absolutely forbidden is to forget our fallible humanity, identify ourselves completely with the truth of God, and try to do what even God Himself will never do: impose our perception of divine truth upon a fellow-believer.

God is Spirit

Fundamental to all Christian theology is the conviction that Ultimate Reality is spiritual, not material. People who describe the Bible with such expressions as "the inscripturated Word," or the "objectivity of the Written Word," are often unwittingly betraying their subtle contamination by the humanistic materialism of our age: something which we can see, something which is physical and "objective," is somehow more real, and therefore more trustworthy, than the Spiritual Reality which they cannot see. It is, in fact, a subtle form of unbelief in God Who is Spirit. Those who hold this view of Ultimate Reality, while at the same time denying it, usually demand a eucharistic sacrament in which the bread becomes the literal, physical body of Christ; the cup contains His literal blood; the waters of baptism literally remove sin; and the Sacred Book is the literal Word of God. In this material view of reality, matter is dependable, ultimate, and absolutely real. Spirit is "subjective," unreal, elusive, and even dangerous.

Material Reality

If a Christian theologian argues that humanists have a point, that material things are real, too, he is quite right, up to a point: material things are real only as long as the creator God continues to give them temporal reality. Without the sustaining Creator Spirit of God, this universe, and everything in it, would collapse instantly. Spirit does not depend upon matter, but matter depends absolutely upon God Who is Spirit for its temporary reality.

When the first Russian cosmonauts were circling the earth in their manned space vehicle, they could hardly resist taunting their American competitors who were still earthbound. They were understandably proud to be "up there" first! You remember they radioed from space a message something like this: "Dear American comrades, we have circled planet earth seven times; and we have not bumped into any angels up here or seen any god!" It is a good thing I am not God. I would have been tempted to remind them of my presence by snatching the breath with which they mocked me and releasing the gravity

469

which kept their little ship in orbit, slinging them forever past moon and sun into endless space. But the patient, loving, Creator God continued to give them life and breath, supported their tiny efforts with His dependable natural order, and waited for them to respond to His revealing love in nature and in gospel witness.

When one applies this spiritual view of Ultimate Reality to the Bible, it means that the Spirit of God is the Source of the letter of scripture. Indeed, we need the letter of Holy Scripture, because we are also physical-spiritual creatures in a physical universe; but the Spirit comes first, inspires the writer and the written word, and inspires the earnest believers who seek to understand the scriptures. The letter of scripture depends upon the Spirit, but the Spirit does not depend upon the letter. There was, is, and always will be the Spirit of God whether we ever had the Holy Scripture or not! But the alternative is not true: we could never have the Holy Scripture without the Holy Spirit.

Strange Gods

There is no way to exaggerate the fundamental importance of this basic Christian understanding of Ultimate Reality: God is omnipresent, omnipotent, independent, Personal Spirit. He cannot be reduced to any material object, any restricted location in a box, sanctuary, sacred talisman, or book. It comes down to this: does one put his faith ultimately in the Living God Who is Spirit, or in a doctrinal system, an ecclesiastical institution, a sacramental means of saving grace, or an infallible book? When it is put this bluntly, it seems ridiculous. But I meet it every day!

Recently, when I opened my systematic theology class, as I often do, with an interpretation of our seminary seal (the Dove hovering over the open Bible), a student came to me and said, "Professor, that seal is wrong" It shows the Holy Spirit hovering over the open Bible like He did when He inspired it. But now He is *in* the Bible, not hovering over it."

While I was trying to fathom this amazing statement, it brought back to my memory the shocking admonition from a Christian brother with whom I was engaged in earnest theological discussion: "Wayne, quit appealing to the Holy Spirit so much. God gave His Holy Spirit to guide people before we had a Bible. Now we have the Sword of the Spirit, the Bible; we don't need the Holy Spirit like they did before the Bible came. We have the sure word of Holy Scripture to guide us; we do not have to depend on some subjective idea of the spirit." Hear his testimony: something he can hold in his hand is more reliable and trustworthy than the Holy Spirit Who dwells in the temple of our bodies. We can dispense with the Holy Spirit because we have the Book! Whole Christian denominations have been founded upon that strange "trinity": God the Creator; God the Man Jesus; and God the Book. They reject totally the presence, power, and reality of the Holy Spirit. In the Bible there is a specific name for this kind of faith: the word is *Idolatry!*

When the New Testament portion of the Revised Standard Version appeared in the late 1940's, one of my most faithful churchmembers reacted strongly to my public reading from that version. She came to me in great distress and said, "Brother Ward, you are destroying my faith. I put my faith in the King James Version and my faith is gone. Better to change the moon and stars than to change the deal Old Word!" How could I tell her that if her faith was really placed in any version of the Bible, rather than in the Living God to Whom the scriptures lead us, that she was actually trusting a false god. Like so many of our churchmembers, she had probably not really thought about what she was saying. Because I had just come to know a devout Muslim whose faith was in the infallible, inerrant, and unchanging Koran, I thought: "There is a man who would really understand her. He also told me his faith was in the infallible Koran." The urge toward idolatry is relentless. We are afraid to trust the Invisible God. We must reduce Him to something we can handle, hold, and see. Remember the word of Jesus to Thomas: "Thomas, because you have seen me, you have believed; blessed are they that have not seen, and yet have believed" (John 20:39). Even Thomas could not be saved by believing in the physical body of Jesus; Thomas had to see in Him the Eternal Word of God in order to receive eternal life.

Testing the Spirits

To be sure, many spirits have gone forth into the world; and we must "test the spirits, whether they be of God" (I John 4:1). The testing requires the words of Holy Scripture, the crucible of our own experience, the witness of the believing church community, the corrective of church history, and the reasoning of our minds. God uses all of these, and more, to guide us in our Christian lives; but "all is vain unless the Spirit of the Holy One come down!"[1]

We are utterly dependent upon the Holy Spirit to lead us to the conviction that the Bible is the authoritative word of God. Rational argument cannot compel reasonable minds to accept the authority of the Bible. Many "Christian evidences" can be amassed to argue persuasively for the value, the influence, and the self-authenticating truth of the Bible. But only the Spirit of God could lead early Christian communities to accept these writings, and, after centuries of struggle, no others, as authoritative Holy Scripture. No council could decree this and compel the hearts and minds of Christian believers to accept them. The history of the canonization of the Old and New Testament scriptures was exactly the reverse: the councils could only affirm what Christians had actually accepted as authoritative Holy Scripture in their personal lives and in their corporate worship. If the Holy Spirit did not act decisively to authenticate the proper writings as authoritative scripture in the early Christian communities around the Mediterranean Sea, in their ongoing experience with these writings, in their personal lives and in the worship experience in their churches, then we have no authoritative scripture today. Because God cared about people beyond the apostolic generation, we can believe that He cared enough to bring His saving Word to use through the pages of Holy Scripture, empowered by the inspiring, preserving, interpreting Holy Spirit.

The Role of the Spirit in Creation

When we read in Genesis 1:1 that "in beginning God created the heavens and the earth," we understand that God the Creator was bringing into being and sustaining all things through His creative Word and by His creative Spirit. When we read that the "Spirit of God was brooding over the face of the waters" (like a nesting bird), we understand that God was bringing out of His original creation life, order, and, ultimately, human personality, a process which still continues. When God said, "Let there be light," we know that His Word, borne by His Spirit, is the Originator and Sustainer of all creation: CREATOR SPIRITUS in Whom we live and move and have our being (Acts 17:28).[2]

The biblical text tells us that the climax of God's creative activity was the creation of human personality. Whatever else the *imago Dei* means, it certainly means that human beings were created for a special relationship with God. No other creatures have His image, and no other creatures have this special relationship. God is related to all His creatures by making them and sustaining them in ordered and instinctive relationships. But only to human beings, made in His image, does God give Himself in personal relationship. Only from them does He require personal obedience. It is this distinctive nature of human beings which makes possible and necessary the next level of the Spirit's activity.

The Holy Spirit in Revelatory Historical Events

If God made all of creation for the purpose of reaching the goal in creating persons for fellowship with Himself, it follows that His Spirit Who sustains the creation must work in all of nature and in all of human life and history to bring about this relationship for which human beings were created. It is one and the same God Who creates persons, reveals Himself to them, and redeems them unto Himself. While the activity of God's Spirit in the redemptive events of human history may differ in many ways from His activity in nature, the same Holy Spirit uses both nature and human personality to accomplish His divine purpose of revelation and redemption.

There is freedom and indeterminacy in nature, and there is even more freedom in human mind and will. The old science of the eighteenth and nineteenth centuries, in which the universe was viewed as a closed mechanical system of natural law, has long since been discredited. Modern nuclear physicists know that there is random and unpredictable behavior in the tiniest particles of the atom. Even if scientists later discover some patterns of behavior which they do not now understand, they already know that there is, and will always be, a frontier beyond which their rational explanations cannot go. It is the self-limited nature of scientific method.

For me, this is the fundamental presupposition of all human freedom. If every atom of every element in nature were locked into a pre-determined system, there would be no "room" for the freedom of human mental processes or moral decision. A full knowledge of all our genes and all our environmental influences could predict our behavior perfectly. We have freedom because the

472

Creator left "room" for undetermined behavior in nature, especially that part of nature which we call human mind. But, in non-human nature and in human decision-making, this freedom is contingent and severely limited. Nature is free only within divinely established limits. Human beings are free only within the boundaries of God's creative and redemptive purpose.

While God is preserving His creation in all of human history and in all of nature, there have been certain points at which He discloses Himself to people of faith in powerful redemptive activity. God does not have to invade His *Kosmos* in order to work a miracle or reveal Himself. God the Creator Spirit is already working in nature and in human living, thinking, and willing. He does not pull levers and make everything happen mechanically. He certainly gives the freedom for His creation in nature and in human history to behave in unprogrammed and unpredictable ways. But God can work through nature and through human history to reveal Himself to those creatures whom He made in His image.

From nature we can infer some things about the Creator. We do not actually see God in nature, but we see His "handiwork" (Psalm 19:1). His "handiwork" tells us, at least, that the Creator must be powerful and dependable, and that He loves order, beauty, and extravagance. In the events of our lives and in our encounters with God through the medium of worship, prayer, and the reading of His Written Word, we come to know Him in a far more personal way. We can walk with Him in the garden in the "breeze time" of the day (Genesis 3:8), and we can see His "hand" in the east wind that blew the waters back and opened a pathway to freedom through the Red Sea.

Inspiring the Witnesses of Revelatory Events

No event of history would have been revelatory of God, and none would have been recorded in the Bible, if there had been no devout believers who saw, by faith, the working of their Redeemer God in those events. When the children of Israel saw the strong east wind come up and blow the waters back under the outstretched arm of Moses, they realized, by faith, that God was acting to deliver them from Pharaoh. If Pharaoh had believed what Israel believed, he might have fallen down and worshipped Yahweh. But Pharaoh was probably non-plussed by this astounding phenomenon of nature and decided that he had better act quickly or his slaves would get away. All of the scientific, philosophical, historical, and meteorological evidence in the world could never prove that the Living God wrought this miracle. Only the Holy Spirit of God could lead the Israelites to the faith that He had acted to deliver them. Only the Holy Spirit can convince us that God acted in this dramatic historical event or in any other redemptive miracle, whether it is the Virgin Birth of Jesus, His atoning death on Calvary's cross, His victorious resurrection from the grave, or His certain coming again to bring history to its close.

People do not strengthen, but actually weaken, their argument when they try to prove a miracle by scientific, philosophical, or historical evidence. If they could prove it by any of these means, it would not be a miracle. It would be a

473

rationally comprehensible natural happening. Such people betray their addiction to the materialism of our age, which trusts the physical sciences more than it trusts the Living God.

It is pathetic to hear theologians and preachers trying to compel people to believe a miracle because of scientific and historical evidence. No one who does not believe in God, or come to believe in God, will ever see or accept His miraculous working in nature or in human history. The historical evidence can be important for believers, because it can clarify and inform faith. But the evidence for God's redemptive acts in history comes from the witness of people who already believed that God wrought His saving miracles for them. If modern theologians try to prove any of these miracles by the ambiguous and inconsistent "scientific" evidence, they will reap the result they deserve: multiple naturalistic "explanations" and theories, all of which will undermine faith instead of strengthening it.

Inspiring the Biblical Writers

Since the Protestant Reformation, some evangelical Christians have been so preoccupied with the effort to replace an infallible Pope with an infallible Book that they have weakened their doctrine of Holy Scripture. They have concentrated on trying to guarantee an inerrant original text, right down to the inspiration of the Hebrew vowel points, which were added by the Jewish Massoretes in the tenth century A. D.! Admittedly, the Holy Spirit was active in these Massoretic scholars, preserving and sustaining their lives and, perhaps, even guiding these devout Jewish believers as they preserved and vowel-pointed the biblical text for all Christians, Jews, and others who accept the Hebrew Bible as Holy Scripture. But the most extreme Christian inerrantist would be unlikely to attribute infallibility or inerrancy to these tenth century Jewish scholars. They were the theological leaders of a community that was violently opposed to the central claims of the Christian faith: that Jesus was both Messiah and Lord, *Jesus Christos Kurios*. Even though their decisions were often grammatical and linguistic, hundreds of decisions turned upon theological presuppositions. It would be inconsistent to call such scholars infallible when their whole theology was marshalled to reject the messiahship and deity of Jesus, even when they made judgments about the Hebrew texts which bore witness to Him.

Some of the theories of inspiration of the Bible focus upon the writers, and some focus upon their product, the Written Word. Any adequate theory of inspiration must deal with both the writers and their written texts. If you are talking about an authoritative Bible, you cannot stop with inspired people and not carry through to the words they left for all their contemporary and future readers. "Dynamic inspiration," so popular among more liberal scholars a general ago, is fatally flawed at this point. It makes no real confessional claim regarding the Bible itself, and it is therefore seriously deficient in a doctrine of Holy Scripture. Dictation theories, and many plenary verbal theories (but not all!), are seriously flawed in the opposite direction. They override the humanity of the writers and make them passive puppets on the strings of the Spirit. Theories that speculate about intuition or exceptional illumination are simply that:

474

speculations about religious states of consciousness which fail to deal with the basic question: was the Holy Spirit of God active in the Biblical writers in such a way that the scriptures they wrote were the absolutely reliable and authoritative Written Word of God, infallibly accomplishing the purpose for which God inspired them?

All of these inspiration theories founder upon the same deadly shoal: the attempt to give a rational explanation for what is clearly perceived as a miracle by people who receive the Bible as authoritative Written Word. It is the same misguided attempt to give a rational explanation for a divine miracle. The more rational and logical the theory becomes, the more it wanders into flagrant heresy, denying the mystery of God's miraculous power and substituting a rationally plausible explanation.

This theorizing about the manner or method of inspiration is quite similar to the almost endless debates of early Christians about the way of defining, in rational terms, the unity of Christ's Person with the distinction of His two natures: fully human and fully divine at the same time. As Arius, Nestorius, or the monophysites came closer to their rationally satisfying explanations of the Person of Christ, the church recognized them as further and further from the biblical witness which the church proclaimed. The same has happened with all theories of inspiration of the bible. Like most creedal propositions, the theories of inspiration are most helpful when they clarify, defend, and proclaim the inspiration and authority of Holy Scripture, without going into the wasteland of rational explanation. The moment a theory of inspiration yields to the rational straightjacket of human comprehension it becomes a naturalistic human achievement and no longer a miracle of God, Whose thoughts are above our thoughts as the heavens are high above the earth!

The biblical writers were not left to write what became scripture within the limits of their own ability, even though they might be exceptionally brilliant or talented religious geniuses, as some theories of inspiration have maintained. God empowered them to do what they could never have done even by human genius; but God used all their talent, experience, knowledge, and personality to accomplish His purpose: bring His Word truly and authoritatively through their human instrumentality. Exactly because God is able to use fallible and imperfect human beings to accomplish His infallible purpose, believers can be sure that the finished product, the Holy Scriptures, were preserved by God Himself from any effort which would interfere with that holy purpose for the scriptures.

God did not require the biblical writers to become perfect or sinless; nor did they become omniscient. God did not require them to give up their humanity or elevate them to deity in order to write His Holy Word. It is the glory of our Redeeming God that He could use His faithful servants, in all their humanity, to accomplish His purpose for the scriptures: to reveal Himself to humankind through the scriptures, inspired and interpreted by the Holy Spirit, in order to lead humankind back to fellowship with Himself through faith in His Son Jesus Christ.

When people argue that God inspired the biblical writers to record inerrant twentieth century science, philosophy, or history according to the canons of modern historical research, they forget that all contemporary science, philosophy, and history will be revised, rejected, or transcended by future generations, as all these disciplines have been revised by past generations. To tie inerrant manuscripts to these fallible human disciplines is to hang a deadly millstone around the neck of the biblical text. When those disciplines are revised or rejected, the biblical authority goes with them!

God used imperfect human languages, Hebrew, Aramaic, and Greek, to communicate His divine Word. World views, scientific theories, and philosophical assumptions were part of the language and culture of the biblical writers. To deny their humanity by placing incomprehensible words and future world views in their minds or on the biblical parchments on which they wrote would be an outrageous destruction of the image of God in them as human beings, limited in time, place, and knowledge. It would turn them into mechanical puppets. It is the dictation theory with a vengeance, and it will destroy a sound and viable doctrine of Holy Scripture and leave us with a strange irrelevant Bible. Surely genuine believers can trust God to use the people who responded to His call and surrendered to His Spirit to accomplish His unerring purpose in the divine-human Holy Scripture!

Receiving and Preserving the Written Word

Most theories of the inspiration of scripture absolutely ignore the role of the Holy Spirit in the indispensable task of canonizing and transmitting, down through the centuries, the text of the Bible. The Hebrew Bible, our Old Testament, was defined, limited, and canonized as authoritative scripture over a long period of use and testing in the worship of the covenant community of Israel. Not until the Council of Jamnia, about 90 A. D., did the Jewish leaders finally close their Hebrew canon.

It is disturbing to some Christians to learn that the greater portion of their Bible was defined and canonized by the scholars of the Jewish community, just a generation or so after the crucifixion of Jesus. Although some Christians may be reluctant to allow the possibility of divine guidance for these Hebrew scholars who were so diametrically opposed to the Christian gospel, it was certainly true that their criteria for accepting or rejecting the various religious texts leaves room for the working of the Holy Spirit in their community of faith as they selected and preserved the writings which became our Bible. The rabbis of Jamnia rejected those books which they believed were written originally in Greek, rather than their "sacred language" of Hebrew; and, more important, they accepted as canonical only those writings which had been consistently used in the worship and instruction of the covenant community over an extended period of time. Because God cared about the generations of people who came after the time of the biblical events, as well as those who were widely removed geographically from those events, we should be confident that God protected the collection, preservation, and transmission of the biblical writings which carried His redemptive message.

476

Translating the Bible

When we come to the situation of the later translators of the Bible, we see the continuing activity of the Spirit in a new dimension. For later translators, the extent of the canon had usually been fairly well determined. Where there were still outstanding questions of the proper text, they could at least, present the alternative texts and leave the interpreter to make his own decision.

But another shift in their situation presented a very serious problem for the translators. A theological and liturgical tradition had grown up alongside the scriptures, and the translators were often cramped by the weight of their tradition as they tried to make an accurate translation. The distress of the King James translators is evident from the records which survive and, even more, from a careful observation of the English text which they created. Although they had no trouble translating, or transliterating, *diakonos*as "deacon" in most places, they balked at translating it when they came to Romans 16:1. In a biblical context which almost demands the use of a ministerial title for Paul's Christian sister and co-worker, Phoebe, in the church in Cenchrea, the Anglican priests who dominated the translation committee refused to let her be a *deacon* as Paul actually wrote.

They went back to the root meaning of the word, apparently to avoid the official title. After all, each of them had first been a deacon, and then a priest, of the Anglican Church. Their letters and translation notes suggest that they were not about to launch Phoebe on the road to the priesthood, even though the Greek text said plainly that she was a deacon.

Equally indefensible was their deliberate disguising of the meaning of *baptidzo* by refusing to translate this word which contradicted their Anglican practice. They also deliberately excluded the ministry of "the women" in 1 Timothy 3:11, by inserting the words "must their," which are not in the Greek text, and by gratuitously substituting the word "wives" in the place of "the women," thereby precluding the most natural reading: that a ministry of "the women" is being designated and described in terms parallel to *episcopoi* and *diakonoi*. It is obvious that their duties are carefully enunciated in chapter five.[3]

Can the Spirit of God have anything to do with such deliberate or careless acts which protect unbiblical practices by making the translation inaccurate or ambiguous? Obviously, we have paid a heavy price in confusion and misunderstanding, growing out of inadequate or misleading translations. Even with the very best of human scholarship and the most complete dedication to accuracy, translations always involve compromise and approximation. There will always be disagreement among translators, and no translation can claim to be "correct." There are always tradeoffs, compromises, and accommodations in any translation.

We have maintained that God used the biblical writers for His purpose in spite of their human imperfections. God has to use translators that are also sinners; no sinless ones are available. God, in all His divine purposes, has to work around, over through, or under human limitations and deliberate sin. He would not be the Sovereign God of this universe if He did not have the power, however long it may take, to accomplish His ultimate purpose with, through, and in spite of, human sin and limitations. Human translators will inevitably use their translations to support their own biases on some occasions; no matter how hard they try to avoid it, they will do it unconsciously. If God cannot use us in spite of our sinfulness, God has no human ministers on this earth.

Although the activity of the Holy Spirit in authenticating and translating the Holy Scripture may differ somewhat from His activity in the original authors of scripture, there would be no trustworthy definition of the canon of scripture and no reliable translation of scripture without the continuing activity of the Spirit in these processes.

Interpreting, Applying, and Living the Biblical Message

No link in the entire doctrine of Holy Scripture is more important than this last one which fulfills the purpose of scripture: that is, rightly interpreting the authoritative Word of God, applying it to our lives, and living in obedience to it. It is unthinkable that God would inspire "holy men of God" (2 Peter:1:21) to write the sacred scriptures and then be unconcerned about the ultimate step in this process: the bringing of His word accurately and authoritatively into the lives of faithful believers.

Just as God used all the gifts, knowledge, and experience of the biblical writers to accomplish the task of writing the scriptural text, so He uses all the linguistic, archaeological, historical, and hermeneutical skills of the interpreter to bring that biblical Word into the lives of believers today. The skills associated with the interpretation of any writing may be employed in the task of interpreting the Bible, but an authoritative and accurate interpretation of the text could never be attained without the guidance of the Holy Spirit.

We may bring this brief essay to a close with the reminder that we must not rest our doctrine of scripture upon the deistic concept that the Holy Spirit created a perfect Book and then departed, leaving the covenant community of Israel or the Christian Church to wrestle with the problems of canon, preservation, translation, and interpretation, unaided by divine guidance. The Omnipresent Creator Spirit is not only sustaining the whole of creation, including those who received, preserved, translated, and interpreted the Bible; He is also fulfilling the divine purpose of communicating God's Word to earnest readers and hearers, in order that He may call them to saving faith in Jesus Christ, to whom the scriptures bear witness (John 5:39, 40). This is the ultimate purpose of Holy Scripture, guaranteed by the continuing activity of the Holy Spirit from the creation to the consummation of the age.

Notes

1. The American folk hymn, *Brethren We have Met to Worship.*
2. See especially Martin Luther's concept of the Holy Spirit in Regin Prenter, *Spiritus Creator* (Philadelphia: Muhlenberg Press, 1953).

3. For a full discussion of the interesting records from the translators of the King James Version, see Gustavus S. Paine, *The Men Behind the King James Version* (Grand Rapids, Michigan: Baker Book House, 1959, 1977). The bibliography collected by this author leads to an exciting trove of information on the agonies and joys of the translators of our most influential English version of the Bible.

26

THE DIFFERENCE BETWEEN SUBSTANCE (MATTER) AND FORM IN RELATIONSHIP TO BIBLICAL INERRANCY

William L. Hendricks

Where did it all begin? This discussion all began with Plato and Aristotle. It certainly did not have its origins in Scripture. Analytical discourse is the primary way western civilization has described reality. By tortuous and possibly unrecognized paths, the analytical division of form and matter wound its way through western philosophy and came into more functional uses in statements of faith in Protestant communions. Since Kant and the Enlightenment the discussion has suffered the slings of outrageous precision and has been filtered through the Kantian split (objective-subjective). Currently form and matter are divided, and that in different ways, by the physical sciences and the humanities. Our present discussion about the Bible is very much the step-child of this intellectual pilgrimage, and it behooves us to unpack and trace it to the present, even though, in my opinion, the discussion is largely extraneous to modes of biblical thinking. A simplistic outline will serve: (1) Where did it all begin? the philosophical background; (2) How it continued, the theological discussion; (3) Where it is now, a contemporary survey; and (4) An alternative approach, a parable toward resolution.

Where Did It All Begin?

Plato

Rationalist patterns of Western thought began with Plato. I agree with Gilbert Ryle.[1] (1) That Plato developed this theory of forms in discussing general ideas or concepts which according to Plato's new doctrine were "immutable, timeless, one over many, intellectually apprehensible and capable of precise definition at the end of a piece of pure ratiocination." This theory made the forms existing entities. (2) Plato patterned this definition of forms after mathematical models to give scientific, "objective" validation to these forms. It is my thesis that early on this theory of forms and their "validation" by mathematical analogies served as a model for Protestant scholasticism in which ideas about "inspiration," "truth," and "form" serve as Platonic forms analogous to mathematical laws to validate the authority of Scripture. It is my opinion that neither the apostles (including Paul) nor the prophets made use of this type of discourse or model. Their reference was to the word of God given in a specific context in order to establish a redemptive relationship and inform a way of life. When defense and appeals for corroboration were made, they were made to the world of nature ("can a leopard change his spots") to the ways of humankind ("no man has ever hated his own body") or to the traditions "of our fathers" which may have been used causistically, as in Rabbinic exegesis, but which were never analytical or the products of "ratiocination."

The allegations above do not imply that biblical revelation cannot be translated into and defended by Platonic categories, for indeed it has been as evidenced by Clement, Origen, and Augustine in whose thinking Greek Philosophy was seen to be (almost on a par with the Old Testament) a preparation for the gospel. In the Middle Ages Platonism and its offspring pseudo-Dionysius were used as a philosophical ballast for revelation by John Scotus Erigena, Bonaventure, and Nicholas of Cusa. In the seventeenth century the Cambridge Platonists, Cudworth, Whichcote, Henry More, and John Smith undergirded their defense of religion with Platonism as did Hare, Maurice, Westcott, Inge, and Jowett in the eighteenth and nineteenth centuries. In Germany Schleiermacher and Hegel bore the Platonic standard. My point is not to deny the contribution of these thinkers. My point is to illustrate that our current discussion owes its idea of forms to Plato and may be expressed in philosophies as diverse as those of Anglican neo-platonists, mystics, Whitehead, and Wittgenstein. Are the intellectual traditions of the Greeks all bad? On principle I tend to agree with Vergils Lacöon, who said: *Timeo Danaos donates ferentes.* (I fear the Greeks even when bearing gifts). If one were obliged to select a Greek to defend and describe revelation, a luxury I am not sure we can afford, Platonism would be my choice. Plato is the first but by no means the most prominent source of where it all began. The predominant figure in the philosophical background of the form and matter discussion is Aristotle.

Aristotle

Aristotle inverted Plato's hierarchy of form and matter. Matter became the substrate or the abiding thing which persisted through change. The forms of things changed by way of privation or from potentiality to actuality, but the matter (substrate) did not. The phenomenon of change is explained by the four causes: material, formal, efficient, and final. Although the four causes are discussed in both the *Physics* and the *Metaphysics,* it is probably that the first discussion was in the *Physics,* on which the subsequent discussion in the *Metaphysics* depends. As in Plato mathematics is the corroboration of form, so in Aristotle's *Physics* natural science (in a pre-modern sense) is the paradigm for determining the discussion of metaphysics. The distinction between matter and form is the first Aristotelian contribution to our discussion. The second contribution is Aristotle's logic, or as he styled it "analytics," especially the syllogism. For Aristotle logic was not one of the sciences. It was the prolegomenon to all branches of knowledge. Kerford is correct in asserting that Aristotle's "treatment of syllogistic argument . . . provided the basis of the teaching of traditional formal logic until the beginning of the twentieth century."[2] In Western medieval thought Aristotelian empiricism was the dominant philosophical underpinning for Catholic scholasticism via Thomas Aquinas. Catholic Scholasticism transposed the Aristotelian categories of matter, form, and substance into such altered terms as nature, essence, and quiddity. What was crucial to the discussion is the acknowledgment of substances which "are recognized as being constantly what they are over the whole span of their existence."[3]

I believe that this is, to use a double entendre, substantially what is meant by the earliest Baptist confessions in their expressions about matter and substance, i.e. that God's word is constantly and continuously what it is, the word of God, and has truth as it matter or substance.

The purpose of this philosophical discussion was to secure an objective reference to the universal while avoiding commitment to the details of the realist demands. It seems to me that this is analogous to inerrancy discussions in which a theory of the autographs is secured by definition regardless of details of textual variants and canonical processes. In nuce, the Bible becomes a universal and as such is secured by definition against realist demands and historical particularities. This way of postulating biblical authority does not take into account modern (since Kant) philosophical discussions. Nor, in my opinion, is it commensurate nor readily explicable to the contemporary mind. Assuredly it is not what the average layperson nor the average proponent of inerrancy has in mind when affirming biblical inerrancy. It is to me problematic as to whether this philosophical position can readily be correlated with biblical self-awareness which seems more direct, less esoteric, and simple than the scholastic categories used to defend Scripture. The strict scholastic discussion of matter, form, and substance required precise and exact meanings and did not acknowledge the loose texture or ordinary use of language recognized by Anselm.

It is this Anselmian awareness of the necessity of clarifying the difficulties raised by the technical language of Scripture and ordinary language that gave rise to the historico-linguistic principles of biblical interpretation used by early Christian humanists including Calvin. Ockham's preference for the common use of language and his eschewing of scholastic distinctions was reinforced by Renaissance philology and gave way to Hobbes and Locke's empirical thought. Distinctions of form and matter began with Plato and Aristotle and played out a very involved scenario on their way to the sixteenth century. It is elemental to say that Plato was for the universal idea which he called form and Aristotle was for in-formed matter. Plato utilized abstract mathematics, and Aristotle found his paradigm in the realities of pre-scientific physics described by syllogistic logic. In the Middle Ages Aristotle's pre-scientific empiricism won the day as the predominant philosophy for describing all reality. And with Aquinas' synthesis of Aristotle and Christianity even God and all things pertaining to God were described in transformed Aristotelian thought.

How It Continued

In Protestant scholasticism the meaning of substance as matter was applied primarily to literary content, authorial intention, and subject matter. Form was applied to style, grammar, literary genre via Reformed humanism á la Cop and Calvin. Substance, in apologetic use, retained the older philosophical purpose of securing an objective reference to the universal while avoiding commitment to the details of realist demands.

As used in Baptist confessions "matter or substance" took on the more liter-

483

ary Reformed meaning and, by and large, the scholastic, apologetic meaning was ignored.

The Reformed tradition, influenced in English speaking lands by Scottish realism (J. T. Reid), continued the literary use of matter or substance as distinct from form. Form was examined rigorously and quite diversely by the historico-linguistic schools in settings as divergent as German criticism, spurred on by the rationalism of the Enlightenment and the exegetical works of Calvin, Beza, and Gill. The former suggested the "matter or substance" of Scripture was to be subject to rigorous historical critique in the light of other ancient near Eastern records and the diversities of the form were to be highlighted. The latter (Calvin, Beza, Gill) considered "matter and substance" as the content, intent, and purpose of Scripture, which was held inviolable and the form as text, style, grammar, and genre, about which diverse opinions might or even must be established. In discussions of form both conservative and radical schools shared comparable tools related to the text, the grammar, the style of Scripture.

As pertaining to "matter or substance" the biblical materials were treated differently because of the presuppositions of the exegetes. With the rise and emphasis on items delineated as higher criticism (style, *Gattungen*, literary relationships) Reformed theologians either disallowed the "results" of higher criticism or moderated these studies while further contributing to their findings in more moderate and conservative ways. The preponderant tendency of Southern Baptist educators was to use both higher and lower criticism in a moderating conservative fashion. Baptist confessions persisted in the dichotomy of the literary distinction between form and matter or substance.

There are no separate articles on Scripture in the forerunner confessions (1524-1644) to the Baptist confessions reproduced by Lumpkin.[4] Of the confessions listed from 1644-1955 twenty-one have separate articles on Scripture and all but three recent confessions (The American Baptist Association 1944, The North America Baptist Association 1955, and the Baptist Union of Victoria 1908) make some functional distinction between form and matter. The usual phrase indicating the intent of matter of Scripture is "in matters of faith and practice of life." Baptist confessions before 1944 (The London Confession) were intensely biblical and used extensive biblical citations as a funding for all of their articles and affirmations. There were, however, no separate articles of faith about Scripture in these early confessions. The London Confession mentions Scripture in article VIII with a Christological hermeneutic. The Second London Confession (1677) has the first full—and the most extensive—article on Scripture of all the confessions Lumpkin cites. The confession begins with the article on Scripture signalling a departure from the traditional order which placed the articles on God first. The Second London Confession confesses the Scriptures as infallible and that "the whole councel of God concerning all things necessary for his own Glory, Man's Salvation, Faith, and life is either expressly set down or necessarily contained in the Holy Scriptures . . ."[5]

At the time Baptist confessions of faith began to differentiate form and matter a major philosophical shift took place in the definition of form and substance in the work of Thomas Hobbes (1588-1678).[6] Form and substance were redefined by Hobbes so as to apply both to all reality and to affirm that all reality was corporeal and involved with motion. In Hobbes what has classically been called form is named "accident." An accident is "the manner by which any body is conceived. Most accidents can be absent from the substance of a thing without the destruction of the body (substance or matter of a thing)." It is a tendentious and tenuous argument to relate Hobbes' insights directly to the bifurcation of form and matter. It is, however, a part of Western intellectual history since Hobbes to distinguish form (accidents) and body (matter and substance). This distinction has been made in literary contexts in a way that is divorced from Hobbes' physicalism, corporeality, and motion theories.

Such are the torturous and tortuous ways in which philosophers and Baptist Confessions have dealt with form and matter. At this juncture, if not long before, the simple Christian and pious believer must be shaking his or her head and quoting Balthasar Friedberger's affirmation that "all teachings that are not of God are in vain and shall be rooted up. Here perish the disciples of Aristotle, as well as the Thomists, the Scotists, Bonaventure and Occam, and all teaching that does not proceed from God's word."[7]

Where We Are

Current Baptist discussion of inerrancy heralds a return to the earlier, scholastic philosophical ideas of securing an a priori objective ground for substance. This is the primary purpose of speaking of the inerrancy of the original autographs. As such those theories and claims are addressing a philosophical, apologetic purpose not basically addressed or intended in Baptist confessions. This inerrancy position is a priori, analogous to mathematical proofs, deductive, and established by formal logic. In Kantian terms it is derived from the first argument, *The Critique of Pure Reason*. The majority of Southern Baptist biblical scholarship, utilizing all critical theories has assumed an inductive, practical, relational purpose for biblical exegesis which in Kantian terms is derived from the second argument, *The Critique of Practical Reason*. Such scholarship has sought to be true to Scripture by expressing its contents in terms of fidelity of purpose and applicability of contents. It is my opinion that these scholarly treatments are as orthodox, as conservative, as biblically based as exegesis predicated on the inerrantist a priori view of Scripture, which predetermines what kinds of questions may be addressed to and addressed by Scripture. Inerrancy so defined and built on the presuppositions suggested has dilemmas with the canonization, preservation, analogous literary relationships, and internal tensions of Scripture. These dilemmas are seen in the caveats and conditions expressed in articles X, XIII, XIV, XVI, XVIII of the affirmations and denials accompanying the Chicago Inerrancy Statement.

The reference to the Chicago Statement is germane because it is presupposed that the Reformed evangelical and "independent" sources which framed the Chicago Inerrancy statement are more influential on Southern Baptist inerrantists than are the Baptist confessions and denominational scholarship of the Southern Baptist Convention. Attempts to coalesce our heritage with that of informed sources of the Reformed community are not convincing because: (1) Such attempts do not give full weight to the diverse streams which have informed our heritage. Calvin is not our only church father. (2) Such attempts tend to give static, unchanging meaning to terms which have a more dynamic and fluid meaning within the time frame of 150 years. (3) Such attempts tend to read the fulness of current discussions back into the previous use of terms. (4) Such attempts tend to conflate infallibility and inerrancy and to assume that they are identical and inseparable.

It is obvious that we are at a turning point in our heritage. There is one group which feels that Scripture is best understood inductively. This group desires to use the full range of tools the better to understand the word of God. These tools include comparing, exploring, and translating texts; studying historical backgrounds, expressing a variety of hermeneutical styles, and being aware of and candid about one's presuppositions. There is another group which prefers to begin with an a priori theory of what the Bible is and limits exploration of Scripture to textual, grammatical matters so as to discover the one revealed body of doctrines presupposed to be in them. To the best of my knowledge there is no intellectual resolution of these two disparate ways of viewing Scripture. There is a third group among us. It is the largest group, our sizeable majority who do not understand the technical philosophical issues expressed here. It is with them and with the beleaguered structures of our denomination that my personal sympathies lie, as will be evident in the concluding paragraph of this paper. When a logical and philosophical impasse is reached, it is time to approach the questions in a new way.

An Alternative Proposal

Is there another way of looking at Scripture besides the two models or paradigms we have discussed? There are: (1) the *a priori* rational theories about Scripture and the way it must be interpreted (Kant's first argument) espoused in Aristotelian form by scholasticiam and (2) that model which looks as Scripture first and foremost in an inductive manner to discuss its parts (Kant's second argument). This second model is used by all critical studies whether textual-grammatical or historico-critical. I believe there is a third way. It is the aesthetic approach (Kant's third argument, the Critique of Judgment) which is committed to seeing matter as primary and form as auxillary to the substance of Scripture. This aesthetic hermeneutic is convinced that the subject/object split is a false dichotomy. Gadamer and the phenomenologists are right. We see as we see, and no amount of a priori logic or sophisticated methodology is going to forestall that. The "we" of the Bible is the "we" of the people of the Bible, and the "we" of today is persons in our context. To suppose that even divine words are not perceived by various "We's" in their circumstances is not feasible. What is essential is to be as self critical as possible about who "we" and all other "we's," including the "we's" of Scripture, are.

It might be argued that this preference for the aesthetic approach—which takes the Bible on its own terms and is critical of the reader of Scripture and that reader's place in the divine economy and in human history—is derived from

Gadamer, Ricoeur, phenemonology, etc. I would certainly want to acknowledge that these philosophical insights are helpful in expressing and giving philosophical ballast to this aesthetic way of dealing with Scripture. But I want formally and very forcefully to assert that I did not come to Scripture via these sources. Rather I feel that these insights have come first from Scripture itself to which all of these later Western philosophical theories are "foreign." The question is one of how "foreign." It is my perspective that scholastic arguments and even some historico-critical methods of dealing with Scripture are more foreign to Scripture than the approach I am suggesting. It seems to me that the correspondence of symbols between the biblical persons' and simple believers' first naivete and Paul Ricoeur's second naivete is closer than scholastic discussions about securing a universal truth against the vagaries of all historical accidents or than computer analysis of word frequency to determine biblical authorship. It seems to me that this aesthetic model relates to the substance of the Bible while acknowledging the various forms in which it is expressed. The aesthetic approach does not make a fetish of form nor does it hedge the Bible about with a theory of what it must be so as to prevent a full revelatory exploration of substance and form.

I will acknowledge that the aesthetic approach recognizes the inductive approach and its sundry methods as an ally in discovering the text, discerning its form, and exploring ways to interpret it. It seems to me that the deductive approach is non-essential to an explanation of biblical faith and that it is inimical to what the Bible says about itself and to current ways of relating to reality.

The aesthetic approach stresses that revelation is more than verbal, not less. Behind words lie the realities they describe. Through words we image reality. Beyond words we are apprehended by ultimate reality. God burned the bush (manifestation), Moses perceived, was given, and interpreted God's purpose (inspiration). We are convinced of the reality behind the account, embodied in the account, and which energizes us by divine initiative (illumination). To reduce revelation to only one of its necessary components is a truncation of the process. To express, explain, theorize, or perceive revelation only in words is an unfortunate reductionism. Beauty embodied in the world, captured by all of the arts, expressed in a variety of ways can be revelatory. Verbalism must give way to linguisticality. Linguisticality can account for both incarnation and inscripturation. Linguisticality can account for both the song of Miriam and the sound of music among all the people of God. Linguisticality can see the Glory of God in a natural sunset and a Turner painting of a sunset. These analogues of life suffer enormous loss when reduced to verbalism.

There is not time enough to convey the full program of an aesthetic hermeneutic or to supply the biblical analogues which make it convincing to me. I am convinced that we must begin to perceive the Bible differently—in the direction of the way in which the biblical authors and simple believers perceive it. This new perception will require all of us to step away from our carefully designated lines and our cherished shibboleths. Our explanations of Scripture and beliefs about Scripture must begin to be expressed in narratives, in music, in drama, in painting, in stained glass, in ethics, and also in words, but not only in words.

When we cannot agree upon truth with rational discursive ways, then it is time to lean into goodness and to learn from beauty so that we can approach truth in a different way.

Now let me devise a parable which, put in the idiom of a painting, may help us "see ourselves as others see us."

Let me tell you a story. It is a parable of a painting. There is an original painting. The painting is fact. It is given. It is what it is. The painting embodies beauty, goodness, and truth. The style of the painting is classic, old style. The story of the painting is universal. Most who see the painting come, behold, are transformed. They go away inspired. They come again in awe. The painting is compelling. There are guides to explain the painting. Many are persuasive and helpful pointing out nuances and details the average viewer might never have seen. There are many guides. Their interpretations differ. Often it seems as though they reconstruct the painting by their descriptions, but the painting itself remains the same. The various interpretations and explanations of the painting say more about the interpreters than they say about the painting. There are restorers. They work diligently to repair, reconstitute, reconstruct what seems fading or eroded or damaged. So long as their work brings out the obvious and well set designs of the painting their work is helpful and invaluable. Those parts of the painting less discernible are given their contours by the plainly perceived elements of the picture. There are conservers who would preserve the picture by placing it under glass and/or putting on coats of sealer. The glare of the glass often prohibits a full view of the richness of color. The coats of sealer mask and can even discolor the original hues. There are those technicians who seek to discern how the paint was mixed, applied, and the number of layers neces- sary to every nuanced reticule. They shed much light. Their information is interesting. There are those who would destroy the painting because its evoca- tive image haunts them and their passions are for the preservation of a self which admits no reconsiderations such as an open view of the painting re- quires. But the painting endures. The Painter smiles. Here ends the parable.

When the believing layman asks me: "Are there mistakes in my Bible, are there errors that would make this book less than the Word of God? Are these Scriptures full of contradictions so that there is no word from the Lord?" My answer is a simple unambiguous no! no! no! But when scholars ask: Do we have imprecisions of number, dates, details, incorrect technical scientific infor- mation according to recent cosmology? Do not matters of style and customs of quotation give us inconsistancies? Must not the canons of secular criticism be made ultimate in determining *die Gattungen* of the Bible? Ought we not to have an a priori, scientific (in the mathematical sense) model of Scripture to guarantee the objectivity of the universal? Then my reply is: you are probably barking up the wrong tree in order to grasp the full message of Scripture. You are barking up the tree of knowledge of good and evil, and the scenario of the fall is about to be replayed in the SBC. My plea is: trust God, believe the Bible, say about the Scriptures what they say about themselves. Use the Book for what it is intended. And above all keep your hearts and minds set above where, according to the substantial statement of inspired Scripture, Christ is sitting at the right hand of God.

Notes

1. "Plato" in *The Encyclopedia of Philosophy* edited by Paul Edwards, 8 vols. (New York: Maxmillan Publishing Co., Inc. & The Free Press, 1967), VI, 314-333; see p. 322.

2. "Aristotle," *The Encyclopedia of Philosophy,* I, 151-162, see p. 155.

3. "Medieval Philosophy," *The Encyclopedia of Philosophy,* V, 252-257.

4. William L. Lumpkin, *Baptist Confessions of Faith* (Chicago: The Judson Press, 1959).

5. Lumpkin, p. 250.

6. "Thomas Hobbes," *The Encyclopedia of Philosophy,* IV, 30-45.

7. Lumpkin, p. 21.

27

THE RELATIONSHIP BETWEEN VIEWS OF THE BIBLE AND MISSIONS AND EVANGELISM

Joe H. Cothen

The Book was a new, leather bound, gold edged, reference edition study Bible. I had bought it especially for the trip. At the end of that two week preaching/teaching tour of India, I felt a growing impression to give my new Bible to the bi-vocational Indian pastor who had translated for me. Not knowing protocol among these eastern people, I wondered how to give him the Book in a way that would not offend him. I chose my words very carefully as I presented it while the two of us were alone together. As I handed the Bible to him, a strange, incredulous look came over his face. Then he sat down in the nearest chair and began to weep. I wondered what to do or say next. I was afraid I had offended him in spite of my best efforts not to do so.

When he composed himself, he thanked me profusely and said, "I have a friend who owns a hard back copy of this Bible. I borrow it often to help me prepare my sermons. I have prayed that someday I might afford one. Thank you, this will help me so much in my work." The tearful, humble preacher held his new treasure reverently and looked at it with a sense of awe.

My heart wishes that every Christian could do the same, i.e. hold the Word of God as a treasure with reverence and genuine awe. What one feels for the Bible will determine whether he will do anything for God, what he will do for God, how much he will do for God, and with what spirit he will render his service. With a lost world at the doorsteps of the church growing ever greater in its numbers and needs, and with the Christian community shrinking in comparison, it behooves us not only to believe the Bible, treasure and reverence the Bible, but to utilize the Bible in missions and evangelism. To neglect it in this generation places us one generation away from a pagan world. To obey and use it in the power of the Spirit places us but one generation away from a changed world.

As he faces the demands of evangelism and missions, the state of the Christian's mind should be free from slavish fear and presumptuous confidence. He is authorized to entertain a confidence, because he had omnipotence for his support and the veracity of God pledged to supply him with all that he needs for his spiritual warfare.

He has need of fear also, because he is in the midst of temptation and has a deceitful heart ever ready to beguile him. In view of his privileges, he may rejoice, but in view of his dangers he should tremble. In a word, as the psalmist expressed it he should "rejoice with trembling." (Psalm 2:11).

As we look upon opportunity and feel responsibility for our world, we recognize the truth of the Indian preacher's words about the Bible, for it will indeed help us in the work. The help available from the Bible in the work of missions and evangelism is seven fold.

The Bible Authorizes Missions and Evangelism

To all evangelism the Bible gives authority, relevancy, color, vitality and irrefutable commands. The Bible is The Book from God and about God. It tells us who He is and what He is doing in the world and in history. It is the most powerful and understandable medium of the Holy Spirit. James Cox has noted,

> The Bible gives us authoritative information about our faith. . . . We test all other sources of faith, inspiration, and information by its fundamental, as well as enduring, standard.
>
> How does the Bible enjoy such authority? It witnesses to the revelation of God through a special history; it is the testimony of those who were closest to what God was revealing; and, by its fruits, it bears the stamp of divine inspiration.[1]

In speaking of Biblical authority over the church and its activities, J. I. Packer has said anything contrary to that authority is alien to the nature of Christianity.

> To deny the normative authority of Scripture over the Church is to misconceive the nature of Christianity, and, in effect, to deny the Lordship of Christ. If the teaching of Christ and the apostles is to rule the church, the church must be ruled by the Scripture . . . . Those who acknowledge the Lordship of Christ are bound to accept the principle of Biblical authority.[2]

E. Y. Mullins was more specific in relating the Bible to evangelism and to individual Christian growth and ministry. He felt it to be a "vital and living authority" and not just a mechanical and ecclesiological one.

> It is our authoritative source of information as to the historical revelation of God in Christ. It is regulative of Christian experience and Christian doctrine. It is the instrument of the Holy Spirit in His regenerative and sanctifying influences. As regulative and authoritative it saves us from subjectivism on the one hand and from a bare rationalism on the other. . . . It is final for us in all matters of our Christian faith and practice.[3]

Paul attests that "we have this treasure in earthen vessels, that the excellency of the power may be of God, and not of us." (II Corinthians 4:7). In our weak state He has given to us the ministry of reconciliation. We are authorized as His representatives, "Now then we are ambassadors for Christ, as though God did beseech you by us: we pray you in Christ's stead, be ye reconciled to God" (II Corinthians 5:18,20).

492

The Bible Empowers Us for Missions and Evangelism

The Scriptures are inspired—literally, *theopneustos* or "outbreathed"—by God. Inspiration is to be defined as the supernatural influence of God's Spirit upon the human writers which caused them to share God's revealed truth with us. The same Spirit empowers the reader through the inspired Word. The Word itself is given power, "For the Word of God is quick (alive), and powerful, and sharper than any two-edged sword, piercing even to the dividing asunder of soul and spirit, and joints and marrow, and is a discerner of the thoughts and intents of the heart.

The coming of the Holy Spirit upon the early church along with the preaching of the Word brought about life changing miracles that affected the whole course of history. In a matter of days God allowed His people to see how totally dependent they were upon strength greater than their own. The drama of Pentecost transformed a group of self-seekers into a set of self-givers such as the world has never known. Those who formerly looked out for number one suddenly found themselves deeply concerned for others. Those who had been told to "feed my sheep" became servants in the urgent work of the Shepherd of Israel who had promised to show His love and compassion for His flock through them.

> For thus says the Lord God, Behold, I myself will search for my sheep and seek them out. As a shepherd cares for his herd in the day when he is among his scattered sheep, so I will care for my sheep and will deliver them from all the places to which they were scattered on a cloudy and gloomy day. And I will bring them out from the people and gather them from the countries and bring them to their own land; and I will feed them on the mountains of Israel, by the streams, and in all the inhabited places of the land. I will feed them in a good pasture, and their grazing ground will be on the mountain heights of Israel. There they will lie down in good grazing ground, and they will feed in the rich pasture on the mountains of Israel. I will feed my flock and I will lead them to rest, declares the Lord God. I will seek the lost, bring back the scattered, bind up the broken, and strengthen the sick. . . (Ezekiel 34:11-16 NASV).

The compassion of God to find and save the lost can only be manifested through those who serve in His name. He teaches us to care the same way He cares. The person who has been touched by the power of the Word will make every possible effort to be involved in missions and evangelism.

The Bible Validates the Need for Missions and Evangelism

The circumstances of people's lives may differ, but their spiritual needs are basically the same in every place and in every generation. I have been privileged to serve as pastor in the poorest of rural communities and in the most affluent suburban neighborhoods. The economic and social conditions were different, but the basic needs were the same.

493

Time, circumstances, frugality, hard work, good fortune, a reasonable degree of prosperity, and education may combine to keep people out of the slums, but affluence does not always keep the slums out of the people. People may not be concerned about their next meal, but this does not mean that they have no concerns. Some do not live in the confusion of a ghetto, but they do live in confusion. Need in a man's life is not determined by the condition of his stomach alone; emptiness describes more than the digestive system. Housing may be adequate or even luxurious while the home is falling apart. Income may be above average and morals still below par. The minister who watches human life and behavior is not long in realizing that destitution describes more than the condition of one's bank account or kitchen pantry. Neither place, prestige, nor property can solve the sin problem and ease the broken spirit.

Problems are real, and those who live with them need the message of the Scripture. Human nature is basically the same wherever and whenever it is found. Selfish ambition is just as real for the man in a stylish business suit as it was for Lot as he pitched his tent toward Sodom. Bitterness can be found in the life of an unwed mother today just as it was found in the heart of Hagar by the spring on the way to Shur. Fear is real whether it be found in the heart of a senior citizen in a modern city or in the mind of Elijah as he fled from the wrath of Jezebel. Hatred can blight the soul of an Arab refugee in this century just as it did the heart of a Jew as he looked at the Samaritan of the first century. Jealousy impedes growth in the life of a minister now in the same way that it darkened the minds of the twelve as they argued over who was to be first in the kingdom. Loneliness is just as real to a widow of the Vietnamese war as it was to Ruth in the fields of Boaz. Lust can destroy happiness for a college student at a pot party in the same way it did for David as he looked upon Bathsheba. Sickness is a stark reality for the cancer victim in a surgical suite just as it was for Naaman on the muddy banks of the Jordan. Futility can overcome whether one be in a ghetto without hope or a penthouse without purpose. With all the weaknesses, temptations, and personal trials of living, people are in need of spiritual help no matter where they live or when they come upon the scene.[4]

As we face the validated need for evangelism we must not allow ourselves to be discouraged by some of the fallacies of the age. First, is the mistaken idea that human nature cannot be changed. If this were true, there would be little point in preaching at all. God can change lives, and He does so through the preaching of His Word. Paul said, "For seeing that in the wisdom of God the world through its wisdom knew not God, it was God's good pleasure through the foolishness of preaching [literally, 'the thing preached'] to save them that believed (I Corinthians 1:21 ASV). Second, is the fallacy that people can change people. We can save no one, but we are the emissaries of Him who can make all things new. Realizing this, we are able to proclaim, "and my speech and my preaching were not in persuasive words of wisdom, but in demonstration of the Spirit and of power; that your faith should not stand in the wisdom of men, but in the power of God." (I Corinthians 2:4-5 ASV).

John F. Walvoord said it well,

To know God rightly man must renounce the sufficiency of his sinful, human reason and seek the ultimate ground of his faith in a divine reason, a fides divina. He came to recognize the Scripture to be the Word of God not merely upon the grounds of his own judgment but primarily on the grounds of God's perfect wisdom provided for man.[5]

The Bible validates the lostness of man, his deep and abiding spiritual needs, and the provision of God's grace to meet those needs. To have firm convictions about the Word of God places a burden for people on the heart of the true believer.

The Bible Assures the Purpose of God in Missions and Evangelism

The Baptist Faith and Message Statement on the Scripture is as follows:

> The Holy Bible was written by man divinely inspired and is the record of God's revelation of Himself to man. It is a perfect treasure of divine instruction. It has God for its author, salvation for its end, and truth, without any mixture of error, for its matter. It reveals the principles by which God judges us; and therefore is, and will remain to the end of the world, the true center of Christian union, and the supreme standard by which all human conduct, creeds, and religious opinions should be tried. The criterion by which the Bible is to be interpreted is Jesus Christ.

This and many other such affirmations show with what high regard we hold the Word of God. It is a marvelous book of sixty-six different books. It was written over the space of a millennium and a half by kings and farmers, soldiers and fishermen, tax collectors and doctors, shepherds and tentmakers. With such diverse human instrumentalities the Spirit of God worked to produce the super naturally inspired volume with a central theme—the King of Kings.

This wonderful work began in law and ends in grace; it started in Eden and ends in the New Jerusalem. It is God's Word—God's only written Word to the world. On it we build our churches, erect our hospitals, launch our mission programs and continue to assert God's claim on the hearts of men.

The Bible deserves no attack, but it requires no defense. It has lived to preside at the funerals of both its critics and defenders. It asks only to be known thoroughly and preached accurately and compassionately. There have been those who denied, decried, and burned the Bible, but nothing has ever hurt it as much as the dust of neglect falling upon it in the pastor's study.

The Bible assures us of its success in the purpose of God.

> For as the rain cometh down, and the snow from heaven, and returneth not thither, but watereth the earth, and maketh it bring forth and bud, that it may give seed to the sower, and bread to the eater:
>
> So shall my Word be that goeth forth out of my mouth: it shall not return unto me void, but it shall accomplish that which I please, and it shall prosper in the thing whereto I sent it. (Isaiah 55:10-11)

The Bible has something to say to every circumstance of life and it says it with divine power. It is a Book that came from the struggles of divine/human experience, and it remains the only Book that can bring the light of God to that scene of struggle.

The Bible Instructs in Missions and Evangelism

"The purpose of Scripture is identical with the purpose of revelation itself: to witness to Jesus as the Christ."[6] Clark Pinnock makes a good case of the intention of God in revelation and inspiration. Indeed, it was the purpose of a loving God to reveal Himself to all men. In that process He inspired the Biblical writers to share the message that the Spirit gave to them. In that process He providentially prepared the man, the language, the occasion, and the first recipients. It was His design to provide various works at different times—all of them meaningful in their own time—to be put together as a single, equally meaningful book in its due time. The product of all these efforts is our Bible.

Because of our faith in a perfect God, we believe those original documents—if still extant—to be without error. Because of His protective providence the Bible we have in hand today meets His purpose and intention with unerring faithfulness in all points of importance and reality. Instead of quibbling over terms and semantics, Christians should give attention to application. God has handled revelation and inspiration quite well. He expects us to get on with the business of instruction and implementation in the fields of missions and evangelism. Paul spoke to Timothy about his background in the second writing, "and how from childhood you have been acquainted with the sacred writings which are able to instruct you for salvation through faith in Christ Jesus." (II Timothy 3:15).

J. I. Packer has reminded us of the fact that Paul in writing Romans, "brings together and sets out in systematic relation all the great themes of the Bible— sin, law, judgment, faith, works, grace, justification, sanctification, election, the plan of salvation, the work of Christ, the work of the Spirit, the Christian hope, the nature and life of the Church, the place of Jew and Gentile in the purposes of God, the philosophy of the church and of world history, the meaning and mission of the Old Testament, the duties of Christian citizenship, the principles of personal piety and ethics."[7]

With this one compilation of doctrine one has sufficient instructional material to change the world. In addition to Romans, we have a wealth of Scripture throughout the New Testament that is waiting to be applied. Russell Dilday has well said, "Biblical authority is not so much a topic to be debated and defended as it is a truth to be applied."[8]

The Scripture is Christocentric in its purpose. Christ is the hub of its message and the realization of its hope. The Scripture is both Christological and soteriological. It is a part of God's divine plan of the ages to redeem sinners.

The current and historic debates over words to describe the Word may well stem from semantic differential among those debating. Bois says, "Semantics deals with words and their meanings (dictionary definitions); general semantics deals with our reactions to words, symbols, and to whatever happens to us."[9]

496

What Bois is saying is that both hearers and speakers assign their own meanings to words or verbal symbols used in the communication process. In so doing meaning becomes distorted and conflict ensues.

Not only should we use great care among ourselves to be accurately understood, but we should use painstaking care to be understood by those with whom we share our faith. Paul was of a different background from those in Thessalonica to whom he witnessed. In Acts 17:2-3 Luke writes of his struggle to be understood, "and Paul went in (at Thessalonica) as his custom was, and for three weeks he argued with them from the Scriptures, explaining and proving that it was necessary for the Christ to suffer and to rise from the dead and saying, 'This Jesus, whom I proclaim to you, is the Christ.'" He found, as we find, that those who do not have the same cultural or experiential background have more difficulty in communication of meaning.

The Scripture is clear, however, that we are under our Lord's mandate to keep on trying, "and Jesus came and spoke unto them, saying, All power is given unto me in heaven and in earth. Go ye therefore, and teach all nations, baptizing them in the name of the Father and of the Son and of the Holy Ghost; Teaching them to observe all things whatsoever I have commanded you: and, lo, I am with you alway, even unto the end of the world." (Matthew 28:18-20).

The Bible Equips the Believer for Missions and Evangelism

The Bible is the central message of missions and evangelism. Haddon Robinson observed that there is always the temptation to move in some other direction or to preach some other message than that of the Scripture. It may be to talk about a political system (either right wing or left wing), a theory of economics, a new religious philosophy, old religious slogans, a trend in psychology, or something else. A preacher can proclaim anything in a "stain-glass voice" at 11:30 on Sunday Morning. Yet where he fails to preach the Scripture, he abandons his authority . . . God speaks through the Bible.[10]

If a person is to be serious about missions and evangelism, he must begin with the Bible. Within its hallowed pages he finds the reason for reaching others for Christ. It is in the Bible that the fact of sin and rebellion is faced. It is therein that judgment is promised, grace is revealed, forgiveness is offered, repentance is required, faith is mandated, conviction of the Holy Spirit is experienced, the New birth is accomplished, sanctification and growth begin, and glory is assured. Without a strong, resolute conviction about the Word of God, there would be neither need nor desire for missions and evangelism.

As the adversary is faced we need to be "strong in the Lord and in the power of His might." We must turn to the spiritual arsenal of the Book to be able to "Put on the whole armor of God, that we may be able to stand against the wiles of the devil. . . . we wrestle not against flesh and blood, but against principalities, against powers, against the rulers of darkness of this world, against spiritual wickedness in high places . . . ." Because of the fierce nature of our antagonists we are admonished, " . . . take unto you the whole armor of God that you may be able to withstand in the evil day. . . . Stand therefore, having your loins girt about with truth, and having on the breastplate of righteousness;

and your feet shod with the preparation of the gospel of peace; above all, taking the shield of faith, wherewith ye shall be able to quench all the fiery darts of the wicked. And take the helmet of salvation, and the sword of the Spirit, which is the Word of God." (Ephesians 6:10-17).

In this list we see some powerful equipment inventoried. Truth, righteousness, gospel of peace, faith, salvation, and the Sword of the Spirit. Only in the Bible could we find such potent weapons of defense and offense. In the life of a Spirit dominated believer these tools can make a real difference in the conflict with sin and Satan.

Robert Speer has rightly written:

> The Word prevails when all else fails.
> The Bible is the solid fact of Christianity.
> What it is, is not affected by what men think of it.
> Changing opinions do not change this book.
> It is not men's thoughts about the Bible that judge it;
> It is the Bible that judges men and their thoughts.
> It has nothing to fear but ignorance and neglect.
> The Church need have no other fear on its
>   account.
> The Bible will take care of itself if—
> The Church will preach it and get it read.

The Bible Motivates Christians in Missions and Evangelism

It has been reported that Sir Walter Scott wrote the following lines on the fly leaf of his Bible.

> Within this awful volume lies
> The mystery of mystries!
> Happiest they of the human race
> to whom God has granted grace
> To read, to fear, to hope, to pray,
> To lift the latch and force the way;
> And better had they not been
>   born
> Who read to doubt or read to
>   scorn.

It is indeed a blessed Book that equips and spurs us on in a ministry to a lost world. We have perfect confidence in its adequacy: "All Scripture is given by inspiration of God, and is profitable for doctrine, for reproof, for correction, for instruction in righteousness, that the man of God may be perfect, thoroughly furnished unto all good works." (II Timothy 3:16-17).

The Word of God is what we need for it is perfect—converting the soul: "The testimony of the Lord is sure, making wise the simple. The statutes of the Lord are right rejoicing the heart. The commandment of the Lord is pure, enlightening the eyes. The fear of the Lord is clean, enduring forever: the judgments of the Lord are true and righteous altogether. More to be desired are they than gold, yea, than much fine gold: sweeter also than honey and the honeycomb." (Psalm 19:6-10).

When our youngest son was a teenager his aunt gave him a poster which said, "I know I'm O.K. because God made me and God don't make no messes." May I adapt that phrase? "I know My Bible is O.K. because God gave it, and God don't give no mess." It is my source book for life, for death, for this world and the next.

Notes

1. James W. Cox, *A Guide to Biblical Preaching,* (Nashville: Abingdon Press) p. 17.

2. J. I. Packer, *Fundamentalism and the Word of God,* (London: Inter-Varsity Fellowship) p. 68.

3. Edgar Young Mullins, *The Christian Religion in Its Doctrinal Expression.* (Philadelphia: The Judson Press) p. 153.

4. Joe H. Cothen, *Equipped for Good Work,* (Gretna, Louisiana: Pleican Publishing Company) pp. 80-81.

5. John F. Walvoord, ed. "Calvin and the Scripture," *Inspiration and Interpretation,* (Grand Rapids: Wm. B. Eerdman Publishing Co.) p. 127.

6. Clark H. Pinnock, *Biblical Revelation — The Foundation of Christian Theology,* (Chicago: Moody Press, 1971), p. 36.

7. Packer, *Fundamentalism and the Word of God.* p. 106.

8. Russell H. Dilday, *The Doctrine of Biblical Authority,* (Nashville: Convention Press, 1982) p. 130.

9. J. O. Samuel Bois, *The Art of Awareness: A Textbook on General Semantics,* (Dubuque, Iowa: Wm. C. Brown Publishers, 1966) p. 33.

10. Haddon W. Robinson, *Biblical Preaching,* (Grand Rapids: Baker Book House, 1980) p. 18.

28

THEOLOGICAL VIEWS ON THE NATURE OF THE BIBLE AND THE SUBSEQUENT IMPACT ON EVANGELISM AND MISSIONS: A HISTORICAL PERSPECTIVE

Lewis A. Drummond

Introduction

Patent is the fact that the mission of the Church has experienced both bleak and blessed times. For example, at the cessation of hostilities after the American Revolution, the churches of young America had their backs to the wall. As historian J. Edwin Orr has so graphically described the scene:

> In the wake of the American Revolution there was a moral slump. Drunkenness became epidemic. Out of a population of five million, 300 thousand were confirmed drunkards: they were burying 15 thousand of them each year. Profanity was of the most shocking kind. For the first time in the history of the American settlement, women were afraid to go out at night for fear of assault. Bank robberies were a daily occurrence. What of the churches? The Methodists were losing more members than they were gaining. The Baptists said they had their most wintery season. The Presbyterians and General Assembly deplored the nation's ungodliness. In a typical congregational church, the Rev. Samuel Sheperd of Lennox, Massachusetts, in 16 years had not taken one young person into fellowship. The Lutherans were so languishing they discussed uniting with Episcopalians, who were even worse off. In case this is thought to be the hysteria of the moment, Kenneth Scott Latourette, the great church historian, wrote: "It seemed as if Christianity were about to be ushered out the affairs of men."[1]

In the context of this bleak situation, Baptist historian Isaac Backus, with several other ministers—the total number being 24—called young America to a "Concert of Prayer" for spiritual awakening and revival. Picking up the "Concert of Prayer" motif of Jonathan Edwards used during the First Great Awakening, a letter was sent to every church and minister in the newly formed United States. They called for special prayer for a reviving of the work. In 1792 the first fruit of the concerted national prayer effort began to ripen. In the New England states the refreshing rain of revival began to fall. It soon spread up and down the East Coast until the Eastern Seaboard was deluged by what historians now call the Second Great Awakening. The "latter rains" had come.

The Western movement had begun at the turn of the 19th Century, and streaming through the Cumberland Gap and down the Ohio River came the revived frontiersmen. The Second Awakening broke out in the West in 1800 in Logan County, Kentucky under the ministry of James McGready. One year later, at the Cane Ridge Meeting House in Bourbon County, Kentucky, Pastor

Barton Stone saw the awakening phenomenon engulf the entire area. In excess of 20,000 people came for a weekend series of meetings at the small Cane Ridge Meeting House. It was a scene undreamed of. As a consequence of this Second Great Awakening, thousands upon thousands of new converts pressed into the Kingdom of God. The camp meeting motif of evangelization experienced its birth and the nation was spiritually and morally transformed. It became a blessed time for the people of God. The Second Great Awakening was seemingly God's answer to the serious decay that threatened the new nation. The highlight of the entire movement was the tremendous evangelistic ingathering that populated the churches at a phenomenal rate. For example, from 1800 to 1803 Baptists in Kentucky tripled; the Methodists quadrupled. Evangelism, outreach and missionary concern became the order of the day.

Illustrations of this nature can be multiplied over and over again in the course of church history. We can confidently conclude, there has rarely, if ever, been a true rejuvenating of the Church that has not culminated in fervent evangelism and significant missionary advance along with great social enrichment. One might even say that this is what an awakening is all about, viz. the church giving itself in a new way to the task of furthering God's Kingdom on earth through evangelistic-missionary activity.

The Basic Issue

Christians are always grateful for reviving, awakening times. The question naturally arises; what are the ingredients that precipitate such refreshing eras? Many things, of course! Prayer, new commitment, dedicated service, etc. all play their role as the Holy Spirit revives His people. It is also abundantly clear that the Word of God, the Holy Scriptures moves center stage as the drama of revival unfolds. The Bible is always "rediscovered" during revival times. That raises the basic issue of this paper, viz. *what views of the nature of the Bible normally arise (or are already there) in the context of the Church dynamically and dramatically fulfilling its evangelistic-missionary responsibilities,* as it does during the brighter days of a quickened people? Is there a *discernible pattern?* Obviously, we would be wise to find out.

Perhaps it is presumptuous to imply that such a pattern exists as suggested above, let alone can be discovered. Nonetheless, some feel they have found a definite correlation between view of the Bible and effective missionary-evangelism. For example, Arthur P. Johnston states:

> Pietistic (i.e. evangelical) evangelism was only possible because of the doctrine of an infallible Bible as defined by the Reformation Period. This one divinely given book was the only source of saving revelation, and it was the Judge of man and the world in which he lived. The scriptures defined all that is inherent in and related to salvation, past, present, and future. . . . The questions that arise concerning individual conversion, social work, and the conversion of man and his total international environment have their ultimate origins in the sources of revelation.[2]

Johnston clearly contends that one's views of the Bible profoundly affect one's views of evangelism and missionary activity; hence, the mission of the Church. But Johnston could obviously be wrong. It would be well to let history as a whole tell us the answer to our essential question. Thus we launch into a survey of approximately the past millenium and a half concerning biblical concepts and their impact on missions-evangelism leaving the New Testament era and the very early church fathers to other studies. Of course, this is a most presumptuous move, i.e. trying to transverse over 1500 years in such a short space. It will be necessary, therefore, to touch just the high points of the developing missionary-evangelistic activities of the Church in the light of biblical understandings. Nonetheless, we may hopefully find something of a discernible pattern if one is to be found. We begin with the church fathers.

Various Church Fathers

Justin Martyr (A.D. 100-165 approximately) was an early, able defender of the faith. In his apologetics, he argued for a very high view of the Scriptures. His work entitled *Apology,* reveals his view of inspiration. He strongly affirmed:

> But when you hear the utterances of the prophets spoken as it were personally, it was not supposed that they are spoken by the inspired themselves, but by the Divine Word who moves them . . . for they do not present to you artful discourses . . . but use with simplicity the words and expressions which offer themselves, and declare to you whatever the Holy Ghost, who descends upon them, chose to teach through them to those who are desirous to learn the true religion.[3]

This statement leaves little doubt in one's mind concerning the view of divine inspiration and authority of the Scriptures held by this well known apologist.

One of the strongest views of inspiration was projected by a brilliant convert to Christianity from Athens by the name of Athenagoras (125?-190?). He wrote an apology for Christians, addressing it to Emperor Marcus Aurelius. In that particular work he stated: "Lifted in ecstasy above the natural operations of their minds by the impulses of the Divine Spirit, (the biblical authors) uttered the things with which they were inspired, the Spirit making use of them as a flute player breathes into a flute."[4] This approach of Athenagoras is virtually tantamount to the so-called "dictation theory" of inspiration.

One of the best known of all church fathers was Irenaeus (135?-202). It was his conviction that the inspiration of the Scriptures, and hence their subsequent authority, dynamically involved both the inspired men and the moving of the Holy Spirit, thus making the writings the very Words of God. He did not take quite the extreme view of Athenagoras; yet, he always considered the inspiration of the Bible as far above that of the mere product of the enlightened human mind. Most scholars agree that Irenaeus held to what is often termed the "verbal plenary" view of inspiration, i.e. *all* the Scriptures are *totally* inspired by the Holy Spirit.

503

Tertullian (A.D. 150-230 approximately) was the well respected preacher of Carthage, North Africa. His view of inspiration is found in his words as follows:

> From the beginning He sent into the world men who because of their inno-
> cence and righteousness, were worthy to know God and make Him known
> to others. These men He filled with the Holy Spirit, that they might teach that
> there is but one God who made the universe and formed man from the
> earth.[5]

Tertullian was never hesitant to call the Scriptures "the writings of God," or "the words of God."

Perhaps the best known of all church fathers is the great Origen (185-254). He became one of the leading teachers in the Alexandrian School of Christian Theology. Origen, along with Clement—another well known church father— ministered in Alexandria. As can be surmised, they were under the influence of Philo. Following something of Philo's approach to biblical inspiration and au- thority, Origen declared: "Small wonder if every word spoken by the prophets produced the proper effect of a word. Nay, I hold that every wonderful letter written in the oracles of God has its effects. There is not one jot or one tittle written in the Scriptures which, for those who know how to use the part of the Scriptures, does not effect its proper work."[6]

Space forbids the mentioning of other important church fathers. But B. F. Westcott summarizes the views of the majority of the church fathers quite well with these comments:

> The unanimity of the early fathers in their views of holy scriptures is more
> remarkable when it is taken in connection with the great differences of char-
> acter and training and circumstances by which they were distinguished. In
> the midst of errors of judgement and error of detail they maintained firmly
> with one consent the great principles which invest the Bible with an interest
> most special and most universal, with the characteristics of the most vivid
> individuality and the most varied application. They teach us that inspiration is
> an operation of Holy Spirit acting through men, according to the laws of their
> constitution, which is not neutralized by his influence, but adapted as a vehi-
> cle for the full expression of divine message. . . . It cannot, I think, be denied
> that as a whole it lays open a view of the Bible which vindicates with the
> greatest clearness and consistency the claims which it makes to be considered
> as one harmonious message of God, spoken in many parts in many manners
> by men and two men—the distinct lessons of individual ages reaching from
> one time to all time.[7]

Thus we conclude, the earlier church fathers, as Westcott argues, saw clearly the great principles that the Bible declares for itself. For them, the Word of God was viewed as just that; a Word of God inspired by the Holy Spirit through human instrumentality to declare the authoritative truth of God. This calls for a brief look at the last of the patristic period.

Perhaps the two most famous later church fathers, who impacted the early centuries significantly, were Jerome (347-420) and Augustine (354-430).

Jerome will always be remembered for his Latin translation of the Bible, later known as a Vulgate. Augustine made his mark as the remarkable Bishop of Hippo in North Africa. In a letter written by Jerome to Augustine in A.D. 405 he stated,

> For, I admit to your charity that it is from those books alone of the Scriptures which are now called canonical, that I have learned to pay them such honor and respect as to believe most firmly that not one of their authors has erred in writing anything at all.[8]

It seems quite clear from this reference that Jerome firmly believed in what could be broadly termed the "inerrancy of the Scriptures." Concerning Augustine, Dewey M. Beegle states, "Augustine's formulation comes the closest to expressing the doctrine of inerrancy."[9]

Citations of this nature relative to other later church fathers can be multiplied. In summary, let it simply be said that the earlier and later fathers had an extremely high view of the Scriptures. The developing doctrine apparently came to its final culmination in a broad formulation of inerrancy as seen in Jerome and Augustine. Although some argumentation and exceptions may be given to this contention, the general run of history certainly moved in at least that general direction.

A word of caution is needed right here, however. Flag words like "inerrancy," "infallibility," etc. were used by theologians through the ages up until modern times, as shall be seen. But they had various shades of meaning to different thinkers. It seems wise, therefore, not to attach too much theological baggage to these terms, because of their various usages. Most theologians simply mean by these words that the Bible is wholly truthful and absolutely trustworthy; it is true in all it states. The use of these terms is an attempt to place as high a view of reliability on the Scriptures as is possible. They certainly had no "political" connotations. The writers simply wanted to communicate they see the Bible as utterly reliable and unequivocally truthful. Moreover, that approach to the nature of the Bible largely persisted for centuries. But were these early years evangelistic and missionary in impetus. Did these high views of the Bible give significant missionary thrust to the early Church? To that vital question we must obviously address ourselves, even if briefly.

Evangelistic and Missionary Endeavors in the Early Centuries

As early as A.D. 250 Barbarian tribes from northern and eastern Europe were moving south and establishing settlements along the Danube River, which formed something of a natural northern boundary for the Roman Empire. There was constant bloodshed between these invading Barbarians and Rome. In that fluid situation the nomadic marauders often took Roman captives as slaves. Christians were regularly taken. These believers often had a vibrant testimony for Jesus Christ. They engaged in considerable personal evangelism. As a consequence, many of the Barbarians came to Christian faith—one of whom was a certain Ulfilas. After his conversion, Ulfilas was immediately moved by a deep desire to win his people to faith in Jesus Christ. He became something of a self-appointed missionary. His work was tremendously successful. Consequently, he was encouraged by receiving official recognition by the Roman Church. He was ordained as Bishop of the Goths in 348. He was a fearless and tireless worker. Through his endeavors many Barbarians turned to the Christian faith. Ulfilas decisively declared his whole agenda of Christian beliefs and ministry in the following doctrine statement:

> I, Ulfilas, Bishop and Confessor, have ever believed thus and before my God and Lord do confess this true and only faith. I believe in one only unborn and invisible God, the Father, and in His only begotten Son, one Lord and God, the Creator of all creatures, to whom none is like but that He is God over all; and in the Holy Spirit, the power which enlightens and sanctifies, who . . . is a servant of Christ, subject and obedient to the Son in all things, as the Son is subject and obedient in all things to the Father, the blessed forever.[10]

One of the outstanding achievement of Ulfilas' ministry was his translation of a large part of the Bible into the Gothic tongue. His contribution here was tremendous. The final result was that multitudes were won to Jesus Christ. He was a *most* effective missionary-evangelist. At his death in 388, the Bishops of Constantinople raised a stone monument to his memory, exemplifying the tremendous service and influence that he created in the winning of thousands to faith in Jesus Christ.

During those dynamic days, Patrick of Ireland came on the scene. St. Patrick was certainly more than a man who drove the snakes from the country and eulogized the shamrock. Patrick (390?-370?) was a true apostle of Jesus Christ. A native of Scotland, in the providence of God, he was kidnapped by pirates and hauled off to Northern Ireland. There he was sold as a slave to an Irish chief. In his suffering circumstances, he recalled the Psalms and prayers of his mother. This led to a genuine salvation experience of Jesus Christ. After his conversion, Patrick developed a deep love and burden for the conversion of Ireland. He determined to master their language and learn their ways to the end that he might lead them to faith in Christ. After six years of captivity he made his escape and found passage on a ship bound for his homeland, Scotland. But eventually his burden for Ireland overwhelmed him and he determined to preach the Gospel of Jesus Christ to the Irish.

About 432 Patrick returned to Ireland, arriving in the spring of the year while the Druids were holding their pagan festival. Running right into the midst of the religious festivities, he began to proclaim salvation through Jesus Christ. Through a series of unusual circumstances, the king came to believe that Patrick was sent by God and that the Gospel was true. From this dramatic beginning, the influence of Patrick reached gigantic proportions. During his ensuing ministry, Patrick established no less than 365 churches and saw 120,000 converts come to faith in Christ. The Irish, as is well known, honor him as their patron saint.

The sixth century epitome of evangelistic Christianity in pagan Scotland was

Columbo (A.D. 521-97). Coming from Irish aristocracy on his father's side, his mother was a member of one of the oldest clans of Scotland. He was a very gifted young man and displayed unusual talent and aptitude. At the age of 21 he dedicated himself to Jesus Christ to become a proclaimer of the Gospel. In 562, Columbo and twelve brothers started their well known venture for the Lord. They sailed to the small island of Iona, an island off the coast of Scotland. There the center of the operation was established. Although Columbo experienced much opposition from the Druids (the pagan priests), the king of the area came to realize the power of the Gospel and through a miraculous healing in his own life embraced the Christian faith. This opened the door for the Gospel and people by multitudes began to be converted. Columbo was an ardent worker. He let no moment be lost. The doctrines he proclaimed were based on the Bible. God's Word was always the cornerstone of his faith and life. Through his vast evangelistic activities, many came to faith in Jesus Christ. He labored in the Iona community for 34 years. His final statement to his brethren just before his death was: "This is my last commandment to you, my children, that ye should love one another sincerely, be at peace, if ye follow the example of the good God, who strengthens such, he will surely be with you."[11] In June of 1587 he went to his reward, dying as he had always lived, sharing God's blessings with others.

In the dynamic years of the sixth century the great Augustine of Canterbury burst on the scene. He became the evangelist of the pagan Saxons of England. Since A.D. 450 the Barbarian tribes of the Angles and Saxons from Europe had been invading the British Isles. Simultaneously, Roman influence was declining and Rome began withdrawing its legions from Britain, thus giving the Saxons and Angles the opportunity they had sought. About this time, Gregory the Great conceived the idea of Christianizing the Anglo-Saxon tribes. The person chosen for the mission was Augustine (not Augustine of Hippo). He had been Gregory's earlier comrade in the monastery. Augustine was given the privilege of picking forty companions to assist him in the evangelization of the Britons. In 596 Augustine and his band headed for the British Isles. They landed on the south shore of England in 597, not far from Dover.

Augustine immediately made contact with Ethelbert, the ruling personality of that general area, and Ethelbert was won to faith in Jesus Christ. Augustine established a base of operations which became known as Canterbury. From this new base location, the missionaries began an itinerant evangelistic ministry. They demonstrated such love for the natives that soon many came to faith in Christ. The majority of the people of Kent, as the surrounding area was known, was brought into a vital relationship with Christ. At this point, Britain was divided into two ecclesiastical areas with an archbishop over each separate district. One bishop would reside in Canterbury and the other in London. Augustine became the first archbishop of Canterbury. By 605, the year of Augustine's death, the majority of the savage Angles and Saxons had been brought into subjection to Jesus Christ. It was a monumental tribute to the power of the Gospel and the fervent commitment and sacrificial services of Augustine and his fellow evangelists.

507

In these early centuries of the Christian mission, the Continent was not without its important personalities. The Eighth Century embodiment of evangelistic endeavor was personified in Boniface of England (760-854). Boniface, a Britisher, became known as the "Apostle of the Germans." After Britain had been quite thoroughly "Christianized," they began to look out and see the needs of others.

Young Boniface felt that burden. With a winsome personality and being an eloquent preacher, he received the honor of being appointed deputy to the Archbishop of Canterbury. But he refused that prominent ecclesiastical position, and offered his services to work for the conversion of the Germanic people. In the context of his commitment, he was given the name "Boniface." It's the root of the word "benefactor," and that he was. His commission came from Gregory II which read as follows:

> Knowing that thou hast from childhood been devoted to sacred letters, and that thou hast labored to reveal to unbelieving people the mystery of faith . . . we decree . . . that, since thou seemest to glow with salvation-bringing fire which our Lord came to descend upon the earth, thou shalt hasten to whatsoever tribes are lingering in the air of unbelief, and shall institute the rights of the kingdom of God.[12]

Boniface devoted himself to the propagation of the Gospel. He journeyed and ministered first in Friesland and next in Gaul. By 719 he was eager to penetrate areas that had never been touched by the Good News. He thus moved into the pagan portion of the Frankish empire, the Rapuarians and their neighbors the Thuringians. Boniface gave himself recklessly to the challenge and fearlessly preached the simple Gospel of Jesus Christ based on a typical high view of the Scriptures.

Boniface' labor of love ended prematurely by his martyrdom. During the preparation for a religious service, a hostile band of pagans learned of the plan and early on the morning of the appointed day the enemies invaded the service and Boniface was slain. He had been a rare instrument in God's hands and had seen thousands upon thousands come to faith in Jesus Christ.

Time fails to recount the tremendous experiences of a multitude of others who made similar contributions to the evangelization of the world in those dramatic early centuries of the Church. The entire course of early Church evangelism scintillated with life and dynamic. With few exceptions, these great evangelistic endeavors were undertaken in the context of an extremely high view of the Bible. There is no question whatsoever that along with the traditional high view of the Scriptures held by the church fathers there was an ardent missionary-evangelism. This does not necessarily mean one dictates the other; but the implication seems evident. A pattern does seemingly begin to emerge. The early evangelists followed the time honored views of inspiration that are rooted in the Old and New Testaments, which it must be granted even the Lord Jesus Christ Himself held.

That Jesus held a high view of the Scriptures is granted by most scholars. As Kenneth Kantzer has pointed out:

H. J. Cadbury, Harvard professor and one of the more extreme New Testament critics of the last generation, once declared that he was far more sure as a mere historical fact that Jesus held to the common Jewish view of an infallible Bible than that Jesus believed in His own messiahship. Adolf Harnack, greatest church historian of modern times, insists that Christ was one with his Apostles, the Jews and the entire early church, in complete commitment to the infallible authority of the Bible. John Knox, author of what is perhaps the most highly regarded recent view of Christ, states that there can be no question that his view of the Bible was taught by our Lord himself.[13]

And no one questions Jesus' evangelistic mission and commitment. Nor is there any doubt about the apostolic days.

Michael Green, in his classical work, *Evangelism in the Early Church*, puts it all together in the following statement:

> The writings that really evoked an abiding interest (in the early church) were the Scriptures. There is abundant evidence . . . to show that Christians, unlike Jews, did use the Scriptures evangelistically. From the Acts of the Apostles down to Gregory and Origen we find the same story repeated time and again. This stress on Scripture is a potent factor in bringing men to faith continued. Jerome tells us that in the third century of Pamphilus of Caesarea, "Readily provided Bibles not only to read, but to keep, not only for men but for any woman whom he saw addicted to reading. He would prepare a large number of volumes, so that, when any demand was made upon him, he might be in a position to gratify those who applied to him."[14]

Thus the pattern we have been seeking does seem to be developing; viz. that a high view of Scriptures normally precipitates fervent evangelism and missionary activity. But now we must look briefly at the next approximate one thousand years.

The Middle "Dark" Ages

The fact that the Church slowly slipped into what is commonly called the "Middle" or "Dark Ages" is one of the tragedies of the history of Christianity. Although some fervent evangelistic and evangelical activity took place during those bleak years, it required the Reformation to break the syndrome of the stagnated Church and once again release the simple Gospel.

Yet, even during this suppressed dark period, a high view of the Scriptures was held by the Roman church. This is common knowledge. The problem was that tradition had ascended to a place of equal (if not superior) authority with the holy Bible. The Scriptures were wrested from the hands of the common people and all authoritative pronouncements emanated from either the local pulpit or Rome itself. The consequences were that the Gospel became shrouded in a host of church traditions and few people grasped the simplicity of the Gospel.

One of the paradoxes of the Roman situation is that even during those bleak days there were individuals who came to grasp the kernel of the Gospel and launched into fervent evangelistic endeavors. And almost without exception, it occurred when they *rediscovered the Bible.* This is most noteworthy.

One of the best known personalities in that context was Bernard of Clairvaux (1091-1153). Although Bernard had been preceded by earlier evangelistic missionaries, e.g. Ansgar of France (800-865), Olaf Tryggvason of Norway (964-1000), etc. it was the mighty ministry of Bernard that became one of the bright spots before the Reformation. Bernard possessed a deep and profound zeal to come into a vital experience of Jesus Christ personally. Through a spiritual crises, he was brought to an all our surrender to the will of God. This radically changed his whole life and precipitated a dynamic experience of Jesus Christ. Immediately he set out as a preacher and minister of the simple Gospel. He was a man of devout love for God with a zeal to introduce others to Jesus Christ. Bernard was a man of God who knew the Lord Jesus Christ intimately and proclaimed His Gospel fearlessly. Multitudes came to faith in our Lord by the simple proclamation of the kernel of the Gospel that Bernard had gleaned from his scriptural knowledge.

No doubt the most singular personality of this whole period was the great St. Francis of Assisi (1182-1226). Born in Assisi, Italy, Francis' original name was Giovanni. His childhood companions nicknamed him Francesco, or the little Frenchman, because of his great love for French poetry. His nickname eventually became Francis, the name by which he has been known through the years. Countless adulations—and rightly so—have come his way.

In Francis' early manhood, he was always on the search for thrills and sensual pleasures. But after the disillusionment of an illness and a subsequent crises that crossed his path, he came to vital faith in Jesus Christ. Immediately he began a ministry of preaching. So often he is erroneously pictured as merely a man interested in birds and animals, but he was a man fervent in spirit, given to great benevolent work and a fearless preacher of the Gospel. A mystic of the first order, he preached Christ in His purity. Even though he soon sloughed off many of the trappings and traditions of Rome, he was actually given a commission by the Pope to carry on his itinerate evangelistic ministry. Disciples soon began to gather about him and an order was established. The disciples fanned out all over Italy and into other parts of the Roman empire to preach Christ.

The secret of Francis' fantastic ministry centered in the fact that he got a grip on the essence of the Gospel from the Word of God. Consequently, multitudes came to simple faith in the Lord Jesus Christ. The spirit of evangelism had so gripped all the disciples of the early Franciscan order that they learned the language of the people and traveled throughout the Empire singing the glad songs of the faith and sharing Christ. It was a glorious movement as the Gospel once again was brought to the common people.

Another outstanding personality of this period was the thundering Jerome Savonarola (1452-98). Savonarola will always stand as one of the great proclaimers of the Gospel. A native of Ferrara, Italy, he was born in the year 1452. He was the antithesis of Francis. Being a dour young man, he spent many hours in fasting and prayer, even as a teenager. In 1475 he left home and made his way to a monastery in Bologna and presented himself for holy orders. The

510

next seven years were devoted primarily to an intensive study of the Scriptures. In that setting he came to the conclusion, and historian Taylor put it: "The messages of this book, with their startling images, their awful denunciations of sin, their exalted and throbbing pity, could alone break up the corruption which abounded, and bring back to earth the peace of God and the recognition of the sovereignty of Jesus Christ."[15]

After the years in Bologna, Savonarola was sent to St. Marks monastery in Florence. There he was asked to give a series of Lenten sermons in the Church of San Lorenzo. In that setting he discovered the book of Revelation. He began to preach about the judgment of God that was certainly coming upon the Church and the infidels because of sin and corruption. He preached some 300 sermons from that last book of the Bible. As his fame began to spread and larger crowds gathered, he had to be moved to the famed St. Marks Cathedral. Soon the entire city of Florence was in the grips of a mighty spiritual awakening. Thousands upon thousands came to a new vibrant faith in Jesus Christ as a consequence of Savonarola's discovery of the Bible and the principle of salvation by grace through faith. He is often called a "pre-reformer" Reformer, and that is certainly an apt description of this man. So influential was his preaching, and so many were the multitudes that came to faith in Jesus Christ, that it was said of Florence "The Carnival was like Lent." Great was the revival and great were the number of converts. And it came about essentially by a rediscovery of the Scriptures. Savonarola sealed his ministry with his blood. Yet, he will always stand as one of the giants of the Middle Ages before the breaking in of the great Reformation era.

Space precludes the accounting of the evangelistic and missionary ministries of men like Tauler of Strassburg (1290-1361), the Waldenses, the Lollards and others, who coming to grips with the Scriptures, found the heart of the Gospel, and began to preach Christ. The whole period can be summed up in the words of George Duncan Berry, himself no believer in a high view of the Scriptures, when he said:

> The fact that for 15 centuries no attempt was made to formulate a definition of the doctrine of inspiration of the Bible, testifies to the universal belief of the Church that the Scriptures were the handiwork of the Holy Ghost . . . yet it was, to modern judgment, a mechanical and erroneous view of inspiration that was accepted and taught by the church of the first centuries, seeing that it ruled out all possibility of error in matters of either history and of doctrine. . . . The writers were used by Him as a workman uses his tools; in a word the Books, the actual words, rather than the writers, were inspired.[16]

Again, the pattern emerges, a high view of the rediscovered "Word of God" precipitates evangelistic-missionary commitment. This now leads to the Reformation era.

The Reformation Era

Little needs to be said concerning the views of the Bible held by the great Reformers. So much has been written in this particular vein that it would be redundant to retrace in detail those steps again. The fact that the Bible was rediscovered through the lives and ministries and influence of the Reformers is clear to all. A strong case can be made for a very high view of the Scriptures as formulated by Reformers such as Calvin, Luther, Zwingli, and others. And evangelism soon followed. It is quite incontestable that the Reformation "tool" in the new commitment to evangelization was the Scriptures. Johnston contends that the major Reformation truth was an infallible Bible: "The judge and critique of experience was not subjective but in subject to the Holy Scriptures . . . Voltzel says that the Reformed Church of the 17th Century recognized the authority of Scriptures, they alone possess an absolute and infallible character."[17] It seems that, generally speaking, the Reformation doctrine of the authority and inspiration of the Scriptures was basically a continuation of the teaching of the church fathers. The Reformers saw the Holy Spirit alone as the original author of the Bible and that He gave us an infallible rule of faith. John Calvin, in his *Commentary* on 2 Timothy 3:16 stated:

> Whoever then wishes to profit in the Scriptures, let him first of all lay down as a settled point this—that the Law and prophesies are not teaching (doctrinarm) delivered by the will of men, but dictated (dictatum) by the Holy Ghost . . . It was the mouth of the Lord that spoke . . . We owe to the Scriptures the same reverence which we owe to God, because it has proceeded from Him above, and has nothing of man mixed with it. (See also *Institutes,* VII.1.)

Martin Luther in like spirit said:

> I have learned to ascribe the honor of infallibility only to those books that are accepted as cannonical, I am profoundly convinced that none of these writers have erred.[18]

Martin Bucer (1491-1551) built his entire theology upon the Scriptures, which he considered infallible. Along with Luther, Zwingli, Calvin, and others, Bucer certainly did not consider his exegesis to be infallible; but he certainly saw the Bible in that light.

Further, the second Helvetic confession of 1566 talks about the Bible as "of the Holy Spirit being the true Word of God." The Westminster Confession of 1664 states very precisely that the Scriptures are the "Word of God written." Unquestionably, the Reformers stood in the general tradition of the fathers. With Romanist traditions now eliminated, and a high view of the Bible, the Reformers built all their theological structures on the principle of *scriptura sola.* The Bible alone was seen as totally inspired, inerrant, and hence the only authority for faith and practice. That approach gave us the Reformation doctrines of grace, and moved the Church into the fervent proclamation of the Gospel as multitudes come to faith in Christ. All historians of all theological stripes attest to this fact. Granted, there has been some dispute as to whether or not Calvin and Luther believed in the actual inerrancy of the Scriptures; but in the light of the above quotations, it seems evident that the burden of proof rests heavily upon those who would say otherwise. The strongest case by far, it seems to me, can be made that these Reformers held a very high view of the Scriptures, so high that they did not hesitate to say the Bible is the infallible Word of God.

Again space does not allow us to go into the various arguments of various historical theologians on this issue. But ample material and writings are in abundance on the book shelves of theological libraries for those who wish a further investigation of this issue. It is my contention that these men were essentially inerrantists and their high view of the Scriptures precipitated the great evangelistic thrust of the Reformation.

It must be said right here that a high view of the Scriptures does not *necessarily* and *always* bring about great evangelistic fervor. It is very easy to slip into a scholasticism that maintains proper doctrine and proper views of the Bible but stultifies in a rationalistic quest for orthodoxy. The latter part of the Reformation era is certainly a classic example of this problem. What became known as "Protestant scholasticism" invaded the reformed church as it gave itself to an inordinate search for orthodoxy. Creeds became so rigid that one could not bend either to the right or to the left. The Bible was approached in a wooden, rationalistic manner that allowed for no deviation or freedom whatsoever. There developed such a rigid view of inspiration that to disagree was to bring the charge of heresy and oftentimes ex-communication. That sort of tragedy took over certain sections of the reformed church. Faith became "intellectual" alone with little of any emphasis on personal experience. That was a tragedy, indeed. Actually, it looked as if a new Dark Age was about to descend upon the European Reformation scene. What Rome had done in stultifying the whole Christian faith by the rigid "school men's" views, segments of the Reformation church did the same thing in essence with a "scholastic" approach to their views of the Scriptures and their ensuing theologies. It was a rather dismal scene that was beginning to develop. But all that is not to imply that "liberal" views thus bring about fervent evangelism. If such flag terms are permissible, "fundamentalism" *and* "liberalism" can both become so rational and rigid that they kill fervent missionary-evangelism.

Just as the Reformation was seemingly bogging down, God suddenly did one of His marvelous acts of grace. A movement began that broke the rigidity of the Protestant "school men" and brought a new influx of spiritual life and vitality. With this there came a somewhat more relaxed view of the Bible, although it was held in highest authority and by most as infallible. This touch of God brought a fresh breeze of evangelistic fervor and missionary advance to the Church. It became known as the Puritan-Pietistic movement. A fascinating history lies back of this thrust, and actually brings us up to our modern contemporary scene.

The Significant Puritan-Pietistic Movement

The English Puritan movement and the Continental Pietistic movement must be grasped in the singular. Many modern historians contend this 17th-18th century movement is separated only by the geography of the English channel

513

and the temperament and politics of two different peoples. For example, Ernest Stoeffler of Temple University states emphatically in his book *The Rise of Evangelical Pietistic:*

> The fact is that essential differences between pietism and what we have called Pietistic Puritanism cannot be established because they are non existent. The pressure towards a certain pattern of piety within the Calvinistic tradition, regarded broadly, whether in England, the Low Countries, and Rineland, or elsewhere are basically the same.[19]

Having something of its early center at Cambridge University under leading professors like William Perkins, the Puritan-Pietistic movement made a tremendous impact, first in Britain and then later on the Continent. The prime point of the movement is projected in the German word *Herzenreligon,* i.e. "religion of the heart." The essential emphasis of the entire thrust became total *personal* involvement in the faith. For the Puritan-Pietist, faith was inward, experiential, and all consuming. This was clearly quite different from the "Protestant Scholasticism" of the day. Still, at the same time, heavy weight was laid on the objective Scriptures as the sources of faith and as a balance to the existential elements of Christian experience. But creeds, mere intellectual ascent, and theology were not seen as the real essence of Christianity. William Ames, one of the first systematic theologians of reformed Pietism, stated: "Faith is the resting of the heart in God." Jonathan Edwards, who must be included in this noble train, clearly distinguishes between what he termed a "speculative" and a "saving" faith. The former centers in the "ascent of the understanding," but saving faith demands "the consent of the heart." He said, "true religion consists so much in the affections that there can be no true religion without them."[20]

As implied above, the New Testament was of vital importance to the Puritan-Pietists. Because of this biblicism, the movement never degenerated into religious humanism or mere mysticism. Pietists insisted on the absolute authority of the Word of God, and that held the movement in balance. Further, they believed that the Holy Spirit is able to communicate the truth of the Scriptures to all sincere souls without the necessity of biblical professionals. The Puritan-Pietistic tradition would trust the opinions of theologically untrained but dedicated lay persons. This was tremendously important in rescuing the doctrine of the priesthood of believers from being no more than a reformed dogma. The approach finally moved the Pietists to the formation of conventicals, private meetings in homes, and Bible study groups where the Scriptures were studied in depth.

Phillip Spener, the Continental "Father of Pietism," upheld and applied the essential Reformation doctrine of Scriptures. He followed the traditional view that had been in dominance for a millenium and a half. He taught that the Scriptures possess the inherent power of God. Spener believed it is by the Word that the Holy Spirit works. He virtually united the work of the Holy Spirit and the work of the Scriptures. All true religious experience is measured in terms of God's written Word, according to Spener and most of his fellow Pietists. Of course, it must be emphasized, in traditional Pietistic thought the written Word of God needs the inspiration of the Holy Spirit to quicken people's understanding. But that in no way was meant to diminish or weaken their high view of the Scriptures.

By this approach to the Bible, the foundation for the great evangelism that flowed from the Puritan-Pietistic movement was laid. As Johnston states, "It was this type of Pietism as represented in Spener that must be considered the dominant spirit of the missionary movement . . . that followed for many years. The whole roots of Pietism are to be discovered in the Reformation doctrine of the Scriptures."[21] Being fully convinced that God has spoken through the Scriptures by his Son the Lord Jesus Christ, this doctrinal and biblical firmness seemed to bring about the Pietist's quest for personal conversion and the responsibility of witnessing on the part of all God's people. It was this thrust that eventually precipitated the great revivalism and evangelism of early America. It also precipitated the significant missionary impetus of men like William Carey (1761-1834). Virtually every church historian recognizes the prominent place of Puritan-Pietism is this phenomenal missionary-evangelism movement. Johnston again makes the point very emphatically: "This evangelistic zeal seems to be intimately related to the evangelical doctrine of the scriptures and the conversion and welfare of the individual."[22] Johnston finally goes so far as to state in *World Evangelism and the Word of God*, "Pietistic evangelism was only possible because of the doctrine of infallibility as defined by the reformation. This one divinely given book was the only source of saving revelation, it was the judge of man and the world in which he lived. The scripture defined all that is inherent and related to salvation past, present and future."[23]

It should be made clear, however, that pietistic biblicism was not legalistic. The spirit, not the mere letter of the word, was the constant pietistic quest. For Spener the authority of the Bible was a spiritual one. Thus it is easy to see why our modern missionary thrust began with Pietism. It is the rock from which our evangelistic missionary impetus is hewn. Actually, the movement gave birth to contemporary evangelicalism generally. To recognize this is most important. The Reformers, as is common knowledge, did not stress *world* missions and evangelism to the extent many would have wished. It took pietists like Zinzendorf, the father of the Moravian revival, to say, "My joy until I die . . . (is) to win souls for the Lamb."[24] If Pietism was anything, it was a deep and profound spiritual awakening to worldwide missionary-evangelism. All the way from its early beginnings around Cambridge, to the contemporary revivalism of Billy Graham, one thing is central; the heart cry of the movement has always been, as expressed by John Knox, "Give me Scotland or I die." The Puritan-Pietists had it right, and that deep concern and burden essentially grew out of and was controlled by their biblicism.

It is only correct—and fair—to point out one deviation to the pattern that has been emerging. Count Zinzendorf of the Moravian pietistic movement had a somewhat lower view of the Bible than some of his pietistic counterparts. He believed the Scriptures contained errors. This is somewhat remarkable in light of the fact that he was a Lutheran—remembering Luther's inerrantist position.

515

Perhaps he was in reaction to the scholasticism that had diminished the existential, evangelistic, spiritual elements of the faith in some Lutheran circles. Not only that, the strong emphasis on the inner work of the Spirit gave a *very* decided emotional flavor to the Moravian moment, even moving them to attempt to find God's will by "casting lots" and letting the Bible fall open at random. That approach no doubt, diminished the importance of the Bible—at least to a degree—in their practical theology. At any rate, Zinzendorf had a lower view of the Bible than many reformed Pietists; at the same time he and the Moravians had a great and fervent missionary-evangelistic commitment—a commitment to be commended. In some sense, the Moravians gave the real impetus to modern missions.

So one cannot say *invariably* that a person must be an "inerrantist" to be zealously evangelistic and mission minded; Zinzendorf puts the lie to that. Yet, it must still be admitted the Count had a quite high view of Scripture and saw it as the only final authority in faith and practice; pragmatically he used it as many so-called "inerrantists" do. Moreover, he is more of the exception than the rule among mature Pietists. Later, George Whitfield wrote *An Expostulatory Letter to Nicholas Louis, Count Zinzendorf* in which he refuted the Moravian's view of Scripture. It proved to be the jolt that moved the Moravians to depend less on inner experience and revelations, giving more stress on the objective Scriptures.

Out of the great Puritan-Pietistic awakening a noble history has flowed—our own history as Baptists. Again space precludes the telling of the marvelous ministry of the Continental Pietists as personified in men like John Arndt, Phillip Spener (1635-1705), his protege, Herman August Franke (1633-1727) and a host of other giants. Of course, the British counterpart was the great John Wesley and George Whitfield. There were other great personalities in Britain in that same general period, e.g. William McClullock, Howell Harris, etc. The tremendous Eighteenth Century Awakening occurred in and through their ministries. But these stories are all well known. All these men held high views of the Bible and strove to maintain the purity of the Gospel. As they preached Christ, literally hundreds of thousands came to faith in our Lord. America had its counterpart in the First Great Awakening of the 18th century. Most are conversant with the ministry of Jonathan Edwards, William and Gilbert Tennett, Theodore Freylinghusen, and the multitudes that made up the First Awakening in America. All these revival leaders strongly argued for very high concepts of the holy Scriptures.

We have already seen something of the deterioration of Church and spiritual life in America in the wake of the Revolutionary War, and then the advent of the Second Great Awakening that saw thousands upon thousands converted. Giants of the faith emerged in the Second Great Awakening, e.g. Lyman Beecher, Ashel Nettleton, and the great Charles G. Finney. Concerning the Bible, Finney stated it was "Infallibly secured from all error."[25] And with Finney, virtually all 19th century evangelists would agree.

But now we must move to more modern times, and to Southern Baptist life in particular. This brief historical survey of 1500 years plus has established the pattern reasonably well, it seems to me: high views of the Bible generally develop strong commitment to missions and evangelism. But what about our Southern Baptist history? Does the pattern hold there? To that we must turn.

Our Southern Baptist Heritage

It was in the context of the Second Great Awakening that Southern Baptists had their birth in 1845. Some of the backgrounds start with men like Isaac Backus, Baptist historian, who was converted in the First Great Awakening, and was, as previously seen, a key figure in precipitating the Second Awakening. Backus was an ardent evangelist. Also, in the revival setting Shuble Stearns and Daniel Marshall came to faith in Jesus Christ. In the heat of the Second Awakening, Stearns and Marshall moved from Enfield, Connecticut to the South. At Sandy Creek, North Carolina, Shuble Stearns planted his life and gave birth to the great missionary-evangelistic church planting zeal of Southern Baptists. All of these, and a host of others, essentially came out of the spirit of the Puritan-Pietistic awakening with its attending biblicism and missionary-evangelistic concern. It points up dramatically the corollary and the pattern we have been searching for between views of the Bible and their impact on missionary-evangelism. For example, Isaac Backus stated: "The Holy Scriptures of the Old and New Testaments, are the Word of God, which He hath given, as our only *perfect* rule of faith and practice."[26]

In the early years of the Southern Baptist Convention, the Reformation doctrine of the Bible was by and large held by all. Exceptions were few. Moreover, that view predominated for several decades.

One of the significant personalities of this period was John Albert Broadus (1827-1895). He was a very gifted man with an unusual combination of authentic personal piety, a winning personality, and superior intellectual ability. As is well known, he was a major contributor to the birth and early life of the Southern Baptist Theological Seminary, the Southern Baptist Convention, and the larger world of evangelical Christianity during the last half of the 19th century. He was highly respected by all of his contemporaries and still holds the undiminished esteem of those who know of his life and service. He therefore stands as something of a model for our early Southern Baptist history and heritage. A brief study of John Broadus should be quite helpful to our task.

The fact that Broadus was deeply and profoundly committed to evangelism is incontestable. Although he was not primarily known as a evangelist in the professional sense, he was certainly solidly committed to the priority of evangelism and was actually a fervent personal witness for Jesus Christ. Broadus' involvement in personal evangelism began immediately following his conversion. After he had come to faith in Christ, a preacher urged him to share his faith and witness to the unconverted. Young Broadus responded and one day approached a man. The man's name was Sandy, who was slightly mentally retarded. Broadus witnessed to Sandy and he was gloriously converted. Thereafter, whenever Sandy would see Broadus, he would run up to him and say: "Howdy, John? Thankee, John. Howdy, John? Thankee, John." A. T.

Robertson, great biblical scholar of Southern Baptist Seminary, said concerning this event:

> Dr. Broadus often told of this first effort at his soul winning and would add: "If I ever reach the heavenly home and walk the golden streets, I know the first person to meet me will be Sandy, coming and saying again: 'Howdy, John? Thankee, John.'"[27]

Another clear indication of Broadus' commitment to evangelism is found in one of his letters. While he served as professor in the early days of Southern Seminary, he preached on Sundays, and taught a large ladies' Bible class on Wednesday afternoon. To one of those ladies in his class, he wrote:

> Is it any harm for me to express the earnest desire that you should become a Christian, and *now?* We are friends, and I delight in it—I have been your teacher in the scriptures, and you have listened to me often as I preach the gospel—and I pray you, be reconciled to God. Seek the Lord while He may be found. Some people deceive themselves, but religion is not a deception. Oh, to be a Christian, to try to bring all you love to be Christians, too. Begin to pray, that you may pray for others as well as yourself. I am going to make daily prayer for you. Oh, pray for yourself—have mercy on yourself.[28]

In another letter to a college student Broadus wrote these words, "I envy those who are most directly concerned with saving souls."[29]

Broadus was deeply convinced that evangelism must be a central element in the life of the Church. For many years he was the pastor of the Charlottesville Baptist Church. In his last sermon to that great congregation he noted that he had preached 761 sermons, and that 241 people had been baptized, 112 of these being black. The very fact that he knew the number that had been converted and was able to present these in such glowing terms to his congregation indicates something of his concern for evangelism.

Not only that, Broadus was deeply committed to the ministry of two of the greatest contemporary evangelists of his day, viz. the pastor-evangelist Charles Haddon Spurgeon and the itinerate evangelist D. L. Moody. Broadus heard Spurgeon preach and made these comments: "The whole thing—house, congregation, order, worship, preaching, was as nearly up to my ideal as I ever expect to see in this life."[30] And most are quite aware of Spurgeon's deep evangelistic commitment—and success. The London pastor said:

> When I began to preach in the little thatched chapel at Waterbeach, my first concern was, Would God save any souls through me? . . . How my heart leaped for joy when I heard tidings of my first convert! I could never be satisfied with a full congregation, and the kind expressions of friends; I longed to hear that hearts had been broken, that tears had been streaming from the eyes of pentents.[31]

In the course of Spurgeon's thirty seven years in London, the small church of about 100 grew into the largest evangelical church in the world. If Broadus could say this about Spurgeon, he certainly had a deep profound commitment to evangelism.

Writing to another concerning the evangelist Moody, Broadus said, "I have never heard Mr. Moody speak without gaining fresh and wholesome impulses in the right direction. He is one of the most useful and justly honored Christian men of the age."[32] Not only did Broadus eulogize Moody, he was a regular and popular preacher at Moody's Northfield Baptist Conferences. Quite clearly, here was a man committed to evangelism and missions. But what were his views on the Bible?

It should perhaps first be pointed out that Broadus got embroiled in controversy concerning the nature of the Scriptures. In that regard, his time, in principle if not in degree, was little different from ours. Nevertheless, he did not see biblical controversy as necessarily totally negative. He said on one occasion:

> Wherever men care for Bible Christianity and are free, there is sure to be much controversy about the Bible. This should be welcomed as a token of interest. Controversy is much better than indifference, or dull, unthinking acquiescence in received opinion. Human life at present is in almost every direction the choice of evils, it is better than man should even quarrel over the Bible than that they should neglect it.[33]

What stand, therefore, did Broadus take in the light of the biblical controversy of his day? One of the clearest and most concise statements of his views concerning the nature of the Scriptures is found in a small volume entitled, *A Catechism of Bible Teaching*. In that work he raises and then answers a number of questions. They are as follows:

> Does the Bible contain any errors? The Bible records something said by uninspired men that were not true; but it is true and instructive that these men said them.

> What authority has the Bible for us? The Bible is our only and all-sufficient rule of faith.

> Do the inspired writers receive everything by direct revelation? The inspired writers learned many things by observation or inquiry, but they were preserved by the Holy Spirit from error, whether in learning or in writing these things.

> Has it been proven that the inspired writers stated anything as true that was not true? No; there is no proof that the inspired writers made any mistake of any kind.[34]

What did Broadus feel about the revelation of the Bible. He stated:

> I do not think it necessary to insist on any particular theory as to the nature and *modus operandi* of inspiration and I am not sure that it is wise to formulate any theory on that subject. The essential point is the fact that the scriptures are fully inspired, and speak truly throughout. Here, as in the case of the incarnation, it is not wise for those who agree in accepting the complete

and sublime fact to array themselves against each other regarding theories as to the nature and mode of the fact. Those who concede errors in the Scriptures as to matter of fact, in order to remove conflict with some scientific opinions of our time, may tell us that they have great satisfaction in being at peace with science. But there are two drawbacks upon such a peace. It is the peace of sheer submission, which, as many of us remember, is sometimes the best that people can do, and then they may yield satisfying results; but which is not commonly regarded as desirable for its own sake. And it is only a partial and temporary peace. Other scientific men at once make still further demands, tending ever toward the complete abandonment of the supernatural. If we assume that the inspiration of the Bible as only partial where are we to stop? Every man must then select *ad libitum* what portions of the Bible's teachings he will accept is true. It may be said that men often do this anyhow. But we answer, they do it as a result of human infirmity, and with earnest effort to guard against this tendency. But if inspiration be regarded as only partial it is every man's right and his duty to select for himself.[35]

Broadus can perhaps be best summarized in his own words: "Whatever these inspired writers meant to say, or whatever we learn from subsequent revelation that God meant to say through their words, though not by themselves fully understood, that we hold to be true, thoroughly true, not only in substance but in statement—unless the contrary can be shown."[36]

Therefore, it seems to say there is a central interplay between Broadus' views of Scripture and his evangelistic commitment and fervency. The pattern continues to develop that a high view of the Bible generally lends itself to a high view of commitment in evangelism and missions.

Another important early Baptist leader and educator was James P. Boyce. One of the founders of Southern Baptist Theological Seminary and also professor of systematic and polemic theology at Furman University, he made a very significant impact on Southern Baptist life. He too was sensitized to the theological battles that were beginning to manifest themselves in Southern Baptist beginnings. His statements on the Scriptures can be found initially in an inaugural address delivered before the board of trustees of the Furman University on July 31, 1856, at the annual commencement. In that sermon he said, "The Bible as a book (is) not to be interpreted in any way fancy may direct . . . (because of) believing equally in the verbal inspiration of its writers."[37] This gives the first clue concerning the view of Bible held by Boyce.

Boyce was the formulator, Manly the writer, of the so-called *Abstract of Principles* which became the guiding theological statement of The Southern Baptist Theological Seminary after its institution in 1859. That particular document was written for the purpose of forestalling, as Boyce put it,

A crises in Baptist doctrine (that) is evidently approaching. . . . Those of us who still cling to the doctrines which formally distinguished us, have the important duty to perform of equally contending for the faith once delivered to the Saints. Gentlemen, God will call us to judgement if we neglect it.[38]

Boyce wrote a rather extensive systematic theology based on the *Abstract of Principles*. In it he said many important things concerning the Scriptures. Some of his statements are as follows:

> With reverence for truth and especially for the truths taught in the word of God . . . we are brought face to face with the fact that our knowledge is bounded by God's revelation are led to acknowledge it as its source . . . we consequently warned not to admit any of the truths assigned from any source nor to add to it anything that properly embrace therein. A departure from this rule will lead to inevitable error.[39]

That Boyce considered the Bible to be revelational in itself is evident by the following statement, "By revelation, we mean the knowledge which God conveys by direct supernatural instruction, preeminently that given in the book known as the Bible."[40] In the latter part of Boyce's theological presentation of the *Abstract of Principles* he raises several questions concerning the Bible. He forthrightly states:

> How came it to be written? God inspired Holy men to write it; did they write it exactly as God wished? Yes. As much as if He had written every word Himself; Ought it, therefore, to be believed and obeyed? Yes; as much as though God had spoken directly to us.[41]

All this leaves little doubt in the mind of any objective reader what James Boyce, an early and most significant systematic theologian in Southern Baptist life, felt concerning the Word of God. The whole purpose of the *Abstract of Principles* was to throw up a bulwark against the encroaching concepts of Arminianism, Campbellitism, and German rationalistic thought that was beginning to manifest itself in the early days of Southern Baptists.

This latter problem, which will be discussed briefly in a moment, first manifested itself in the so-called "Toy incident." Professor Toy of Southern Seminary had imbibed a large portion of German rationalism that grew out of the Enlightenment. It led the professor in repudiating aspects of the *Abstract of Principles*. Subsequently, he was dismissed from his professorship. Toy's life ended rather tragically in that he finally became a Unitarian and repudiated all traditional evangelical doctrine. It was a double tragedy in the sense that he at one time had been engaged to none other than Lottie Moon.

So theological controversy over the nature of the Bible and its inevitable doctrinal formulations is not particularly new to Southern Baptist life. Boyce was much concerned about this. In his inaugural address to Furman University he stated:

> It has been felt as a sore evil, that we have been dependent on great part upon the criticism of Germany for all the more learned investigations in Biblical Criticism and Exegesis and that in the study of the development of the doctrine of the Church, as well as of its outward progress, we have been compelled to depend upon works in which much of error has been mingled with truth, owing to the defective stamp or occupied by their authors.[42]

521

Furthermore, it is certainly clear that Boyce was not negative towards "statements of faith." He stated:

> A crisis in Baptist doctrine is evidently approaching . . . the evil is one which calls for the adoption of a remedy by every Church and every Minister among us. It demands that every doctrine of Scripture be determined and expressed, and that all should see to it, the Churches which call and by the Presbyteries which ordain, that these set apart and preach the word "whose faith in the Churches may follow," "who take heed to themselves unto the doctrine" and "are not as many who corrupt the word of God."[43]

Boyce was very forthright concerning this principle in regards to theological institutions. Concerning professors signing an abstract of principles as a prerequisite to teaching he stated:

> If the summary of truth established be incorrect, it is the duty of the board (of the Trustees) to change it, if such be within their power; if not, let an appeal be made to those who have the power, and if there be none such, then far better it is that the whole endeavor be thrown aside than that the principle be adopted that the professor sign any abstract of doctrine which he does not agree, and in accordance with which he does not intend to teach. No professor should be allowed upon any such duties as are there undertaken, which he has been placed there to inculcate.[44]

Boyce was extremely sensitive to the key position that theological institutions hold and how important it is that their doctrinal integrity be held intact. He wrote:

> This it is that should make us tremble, when we think of our Theological Institutions. If there be any instrument of our denominational prosperity which we should guard at every point, it is this. The doctrinal sentiments of the Faculty are of far greater importance than the proper investment and expenditures of its funds, and the trusts devolved upon those who watch over its interests should in that respect, if in any, be sacredly guarded.[45]

Boyce was not duped by the mere statement that we have the New Testament for our only creed. He well recognized the fact that *interpretation* of Scripture is as vital as giving high marks to *believing* the Bible. He said, "It is not whether they believed the Bible, but whether believing it they deduce from it such doctrine as shown, according to the judgement of the Christian, that they have been so taught by the Spirit of God as should be guided into the knowledge of all truths."[46]

In the light of all of these statements it is quite evident that Boyce held a very high view of the Bible and demanded that believers, especially those who are in places of leadership, ought to develop a theology from their acceptance of the Scriptures as the very Word of God that was commensurate with the evangelical faith generally and the Baptist position particularly. Thus he formulated the *Abstract of Principles* and demanded that all professors sign it with integrity and absolute honesty. Moreover, Boyce had a deep commitment to evangelism and missions as evangelicals understood it—as did virtually all our early Southern Baptists.

Another early Baptist leader was the great B. H. Carroll, first president and founding father of Southwestern Baptist Theological Seminary. It was Carroll's absolute conviction that the Bible was the written revelation of God. This was foundational to Carroll's entire theology and biblical exegesis. Carroll went to lengths to define the inspiration of the Scriptures so as to distinguish inspiration from both revelation and illumination. He stated:

> Revelation is divine disclosure of hidden things. Inspiration is that gift of the Holy Spirit which enables one to select and arrange material to a definite end and inerrantly record it. Illumination, another gift of the Spirit, enables one to understand the revelation or to interpret the facts of the inspired revelation.[47]

Carroll was adamant in making his point that the Bible was verbally inspired. He did not accept the notion of "degrees of inspiration" or the idea of partial inspiration. He stated:

> When you hear the silly talk about the Bible "contains" the word of God and is not the word of God, you hear a fool's talk. I don't care if he is a Doctor of Divinity, a President of a university covered with medals from universities of Europe and the United States, it is fool talk. There can be no inspiration of the book without the inspiration of the words of the book.[48]

This leaves little doubt concerning B. H. Carroll's view of Scripture. And everyone knows the evangelistic fervor and commitment of Southwestern Baptist Theological Seminary from its very inception to the present moment.

No one epitomized the spirit of evangelism in Southern Baptist life more profoundly than President L. R. Scarborough of Southwestern Seminary. He created the "Chair of Fire," teaching evangelism through the many years of his presidency. Concerning the Bible he said:

> It is God-breathed and is the infallible will of God concerning man and binding in its authority upon the conscience and conduct of every man, that it will never fail, and on its truth alone the world is to be reconstructed.[49]

The spirit of missions and evangelism has permeated faculty and student body alike at Southwestern. The general pattern continues to build.

Another, yet not quite so renowned, early Southern Baptist leader, was professor Dagg. He served as president of Mercer University in Georgia. In the same general spirit of other Baptist leaders and theologians, he said:

> The question, whether inspiration extended to the very words of Revelation, as well as to the thoughts and reasonings, is answered by Paul: "We preach, not the words which man's wisdom teaches, but which the Holy Ghost teacheth" (1 Cor. 2:13). The thoughts and reasonings within the minds of the inspired writers were not a revelation to others until they were expressed in

523

words: and if the Holy Spirit's influence ceased before expression was given these thoughts and reasonings, he has not made a revelation to mankind.[50]

Baptist professor Basil Manly raised the question, "Is the Bible the word of God?" Manly answered the query in a letter dated January 4, 1882, to the Rev. Norman Fox, a prominent Baptist journalist of New York. Manly stated, "The Scriptures of the Old and New Testament were given by inspiration of God and are the only sufficient, certain and authoritative rule for all-saving knowledge, faith and obedience . . . In brief, then, the points are the Infallibility, the Divine Authority, and the Sufficiency of the Scriptures, as the Word of God." The statement could hardly be more explicit and forthright.

A more contemporary Baptist scholar was the great A. T. Robertson. Probably no man Southern Baptists have produced was more renowned nor developed a greater expertise in the Greek language than Robertson. His view of the Scriptures was very clear. In an address entitled *The Relative Authority of Scripture and Reason,* given at Philadelphia to the tenth Baptist Congress (May 21, 1892), Robertson stated that in the Bible, God "gave a revelation to make it free from errors. I believe He first made it inerrant as He made nature so. Hence, I boldly hold that the analogy of nature is in favor of inerrancy of God's original scriptures" (p. 6). Along with Boyce, Robertson was sensitized to the skeptical approach that was beginning to encroach into Baptist life from the Germanic rationalistic school of his day. In the same address he asked, "Why in the world is it that there is such a terrible contention by destructive higher critics? . . . I think I can tell. The school wants to change the whole order . . . they wish to get an entering wedge by having it admit that there were inaccuracies . . . in order to shift and change the order of the Word to suit themselves" (p. 6). Again we see something of the high view of Scriptures by an earlier, yet in many respects contemporary, New Testament scholar of Southern Baptist.

But does all of this really admit of a pattern between a high view of Scripture and evangelistic fervency in missionary involvement, as has been continually implied. Perhaps it would be helpful to spend a moment looking at this question from the negative perspective, viz. does a low view of Scripture tend to diminish evangelistic commitment and missionary involvement? To that question we briefly turn.

A Negative Approach

It has been made quite evident that 19th century evangelicals, Baptists and otherwise, by and large held a very high view of the Bible. That century also saw the advent of missionary and evangelistic activity unprecedented in the history of the Church, save in the early years of its life. That 100 year period became known, in the words of church historian Kenneth Scott Latourette, as "The Great Century." The giants of evangelistic and missionary grandeur that century produced is quite fantastic. Men like Charles Haddon Spurgeon, Charles Finney, D. L. Moody, Alexander McClaren, Joseph Parker, Hudson Taylor, C. T. Studd, and a host of other evangelists, pastors, and missionary leaders graced the scene. It looks like a parade of God's best. The "Great Century" culminated in the renowned Edinburgh Conference of 1910. That missionary Conference, spear-headed by John Mott and other missionary leaders, stood as the high water mark in commitment to world evangelization. Yet, it also became something of a turning point in the era of high views of the Scriptures—but more of that in a moment.

By the turn of the 20th Century new thought, given rise by the Enlightenment, precipitated in some evangelical circles Germanic rationalistic epistomologies. This particular philosophical-theological approach was personified in the philosopher Frederick Von Hegel. His dictum was, "The real is rational, the rational is real." That concept took root first among Continental thinkers. It was not long before rational epistemological presuppositions began to gain the ascendency in certain theological circles. Prior to this invasion of crass rationalism, traditional evangelicals built their epistemological theological base on four essential presuppositions:

1. God has revealed Himself primarily in the life, ministry, death, resurrection, ascension and continuing intercession of Jesus Christ, God's Son and the world's Savior.

2. God addresses us in propositional language about Jesus as well as in personal encounter with the person of Christ.

3. The propositional revelation of God is contained in the truthful, totally inspired Word of God, the Holy Scriptures.

4. Revelation is the supreme epistemological principle in formulating all Christian beliefs, i.e. reason is subject to revelation.

The entire evangelical concept of revelation and subsequent theology and doctrine was predicated upon those epistemological presuppositions.

The advent of the rationalistic epistemological system, however, virtually eliminated all the above evangelical presuppositions save one, i.e. Christ Jesus is God's supreme revelation. But even that idea was severely damaged. Why is that so? Because *rationalism* became the supreme epistemological presupposition in testing truth claims as over against *revelation*. Human reason, based on a rational-empirical critical basis, was crowned "king of the hill" in the epistemological game of attempting to derive truth and reality. This meant essentially that revelation was not the final word. These epistemologists did not deny that God gave revelations of himself, but the veracity of a claim to divine revelation must be tested by rational-empirical critical categories, the supreme epistemological presupposition. It meant, therefore, that the Scriptures were alleged to contain rational-empirical error. And because human rational reason is the arbitrator between what is true and what is false, the Scriptures therefore err. That opened the door to all sorts of theological formulations, some a far cry from evangelical categories.

Some critical thinkers went so far as to say that revelation is not propositional at all, nor can it be. They contend that revelation is *always* personal encounter and nothing more. Of course, this projected Christian experience into an existential never never land with no objectivity to keep it in bounds. That in turn opened the door to all sorts of theological deviations and also developed some rather strange concepts of religious experience itself. It further precipitated various concepts concerning how God addresses people. The end result for some was either a universalism or a syncretism or both. The "exclusiveness" of the Christian faith was lost, as were some of the essential doctrines of Christ's own person and mission. Obviously, that was quite destructive to evangelism as we who are evangelical have known it.

These basic ideas, based on a non-evangelical set of epistemological presuppositions had covered Europe by the end of the 19th century. The fact that the approach began to invade seriously the European Church is clearly seen, for example, in Britain by the middle of the 19th century. The theological battles that transpired are legendary. As an instance, it made its frontal attack in British Baptist life as manifested in the well known "Downgrade Controversy" in which Charles Haddon Spurgeon was involved. As a consequence of the tragic Downgrade Controversy, Spurgeon withdrew from the British Baptist Union. He died a broken and a crushed man. The devastating effect all this had on British Baptist life is quite obvious; most of the churches of Britain are virtually empty. There are some beautiful exceptions, but those few exceptions are normally churches that hold a high evangelical view of Scripture and fervently preach the Gospel. The British people can still be reached, but they are not reached by the destructive critical approach that decimated the Church at the end of the last century and the early decades of the twentieth.

The same basic controversy swept through the major denominations of the North in America in what was termed the "Modernist-Fundamentalist battles." We all are aware of what has happened to several main line protestant denominations as a consequence of that particular warfare.

It does seem quite correct to surmise that as the traditional high evangelical view of the Bible deteriorates, so does missionary-evangelism. Johnston put it quite succinctly when he stated, "Rationalism did not leave a heritage of evangelism. To the contrary, to the extent which the supernatural elements were stripped from the scriptures, the same extent the force of Protestanism seems to have been diverted from evangelism to activities of public utility."[51]

Johnston sees this phenomenon epitomized in the development of the International Missionary Council (IMC) that grew out of the Edinburgh Conference of 1910. The Edinburgh Conference still exalted the great missionary Watchword: "The evangelization of the world in our generation." But even at the Conference, in a rather insipient form, as Johnston states, "A more liberal theological position influenced the evangelistic foundations by questioning the Watchword."[52] As early as 1908, as Johnston points out, "A commission chaired by J. H. Oldham expressed concern that 'other activities' were crowding out evangelistic work."[53] Through the International Missionary Council, which in turn finally led to the well known ecumenical movement, there developed a softening of high views of the Bible. Edinburgh of 1910 was a watershed. New directions began there. Johnston is correct when he states: "the missionary movement of the 19th century left its pietist moorings at Edinburgh in 1910."[54] For example, there was considerable debate and disagreement concerning the idea of "verbal" inspiration. The theologies of Schleiermacher, Ritschl, Darwin and Harnack began to infiltrate the general scene. The theological presuppositions at Edinburgh, therefore, were mixed. It was decided that unimity could be found around the "person of Christ." Both the "evangelical" and the "social" Gospel could unite for world evangelization around the cross. That sounded like a solution, but Edinburgh admitted the higher criticism theologians into the missionary movement, and the deterioration of missionary-evangelism, as evangelicals understand it, began. The New York Conference of 1900 was thoroughly evangelical; but, Edinburgh represented a new theological shift. For this reason, Edinburgh was unable to come to a satisfactory and final decision on the nature of the Christian message to the non-Christian world, obviously a subject of great importance to evangelism.

The next great conference was held in Jerusalem in 1928, followed by a third significant conference in Madras, India, in 1938. The shift was rapidly developing towards a very broad based, non-theological stance in evangelism and missions. Johnston states,

> The 18 years between Edinburgh in 1910 and Jerusalem 1928 brought new developments in the theological scene. Although they were more apparent at Madras 1938 meeting, these changes were first apparent at Jerusalem. What was often implied at Edinburgh became evident at Jerusalem. The theological positions of Edinburgh influenced evangelism, the practical work of the IMC (International Missionary Council).[55]

A multitude of things can—and perhaps should—be said regarding the biblical shift begun in Edinburgh in 1910. It stands as a symbol of the beginning move towards rationalistic approaches to the Christian faith and mission. But obviously, space precludes it. Let it all be simply summarized by stating that a critical rationalism with its inevitably lower view of the Bible decidedly tends to diminish evangelistic activity, at least as evangelicals traditionally understand it. Moreover, since Edinburgh the "shift" has continued and deepened.

But where are Southern Baptists today? It is clear that Southern Baptists are at the contemporary moment in a quite fluid state. What the future holds, only our Lord knows with certainty. Nevertheless, some things can be said concerning the basic thrust of this paper.

Final Conclusions

It now appears to be quite evident that the pattern we have been seeking is reasonably well established. It seems relatively conclusive that whenever there is a high view of Scriptures as traditional evangelicalism has espoused, a commensurate commitment to evangelism and missionary activity generally emerges; and a low view of the Bible tends to arrest it. Granted, there have been exceptions, and there is always the danger of an extreme rigid rationalism invading one's approach to the Bible and stultifying evangelistic fervor. That holds for evangelicals and non-evangelicals alike. For evangelicals it happened in the Protestant scholasticism of the later Reformation days; for non-evangelicals it occurred in the crass rationalism of the Germanic school. We must beware and keep to our moorings. Still, the general pattern holds.

Thus, it appears most wise for us today, with the contemporary variety of views of the Bible we see, to contend for a high view of the Scriptures if we are concerned about propagating the Christian faith in a lost and dying world. That is a quite broad conclusion; but, history seems clearly to establish it. We Southern Baptist evangelicals have committed ourselves to the worldwide evangelistic task we call Bold Mission Thrust. We know that to fail in missionary-evangelism is finally to fail in all and eventually become a relic of history. Significant are the words of philosopher Santyana: "They who do not understand history are doomed to relive it." Therefore, may God move us by His grace to undertake great exploits in missions and evangelism in the power of the Holy Spirit based on God's own Word.

Notes

1. J. Edwin Orr, from a film produced by Campus Crusades for Christ International.

2. Arthur P. Johnston, *World Evangelism and the Word of God,* (Minneapolis, MN: Bethany Fellowship, Inc., 1974), pp. 16, 17.

3. Justin Martyr, *Apology I,* chapter 36, p. 38. From "The Writings of Justin Martyr and Athenagoras," Volume 2, Ante-Nicene Christian Library.

4. Athenagoras, chapter IX, ibid., p. 384.

5. Tertullian, *Apology,* chapter 18, paragraph 2, pp. 53-54, in Tertullian, *Apologetical Works,* volume 10, "The Fathers of the Church."

6. Origen, Homily XXXIV, in Jeremiah, p. 50., *Selections from the Commentaries and Homilies of Origen,* translated by R. B. Tollinton.

7. Westcott, "Appendix B. On the Primitive Doctrine of Inspiration PDI," p. 445-456, *An Introduction to the Study of Gospels.*

8. Augustine, Letter 82, p. 392, in *Augustine, Letters (1-82, volume 12), Fathers of the Church.*

9. Dewey M. Beegle, *Scripture, Tradition, and Infallibility,* (Grand Rapids, Michigan: William B. Eerdmans Publishing Co., 1973), p. 138.

10. H. F. Massman, *Ulfilas,* translated by Henry McCracken (New York: M. F. Barton Co., p. 72.)

11. Robert Scott and George Gilmore, *Selections from the World's Devotional Classics,* (New York: Funk and Wagnall's Company, 1916), II, p. 180.

12. Tauler, "Union with God," as quoted in Robert Scott and George Gilmore, *Selections from the World's Great Devotional Classics,* (New York: Funk and Wagnall's Co., 1916), III, p. 102.

13. Harold Lindsell, *God's Incomparable World, Conclusions of the Early Church Period,* (Minneapolis, MN: Worldwide Publications, 1977), p. 53.

14. Michael Green, *Evangelism in the Early Church,* (London: Hodder and Stoughton, 1970), pp. 133-134.

15. Mendell Taylor in *Exploring Evangelism* (Kansas City, MO: Beacon Hill Press, 1964), p. 124.

16. Harold Lindsell, op. cit., p. 53.

17. Arthur P. Johnston, *World Evangelism and the Word of God,* p. 29.

18. James Warrick Montgomery, ed. *God's Inerrant Word* (Minneapolis, MN: Bethany Fellowship, Inc., 1974), p. 90.

19. Ernest F. Stoeffler, *The Rise of Evangelical Pietism* (Leiden, Netherlands: E. J. Brill, 1971), p. 29.

20. Donald Bloesch, *The Evangelical Rennaisance* (Grand Rapids, MI: William B. Eerdmans Publishing co., 1973), p. 104.

21. Johnston, *World Evangelism and the Word of God,* p. 34.

22. Ibid., p. 37.

23. Ibid., p. 16.

24. Stoeffler, *The Rise of Evangelical Pietism,* p. 132.

25. Charles G. Finney, *The Heart of Truth* (Minneapolis, MN: Bethany Fellowship, Inc., 1976), pp. 19-20). All the leading personalities of Second Great Awakening would have agreed—and all were utterly committed to evangelism.

26. Olvah Honey, *A Memory of the Life and Times of the Rev. Isaac Backus* (Boston: Gould and Lincoln, 1859), p. 334.

27. Archibald Thomas Robertson, *Life and Letters of John Albert Broadus* (Philadelphia: American Baptist Publications Society, 1901), p. 35.

28. Ibid., p. 215.

29. Ibid., p. 382.

30. Ibid., p. 243.

31. The *Autobiography,* Vol. I (London, Alabaster and Passmore, 1895), p. 196.

32. Ibid., p. 429.

33. John A. Broadus, *Three Questions as to the Bible* (Philadelphia: American Baptist Publication Society, 1883), pp. 5-6.

34. John A. Broadus, *The Catechism of Bible Teaching* (Nashville: Sunday School Board of the Southern Baptist Convention, 1892), pp. 13-16.

35. John A. Broadus, *Three Questions as to the Bible* (Philadelphia: American Baptist Publication Society, 1883), pp. 26, 46.

36. Ibid., p. 26.

37. James P. Boyce, "Inaugural Address Delivered Before the Board of Trustees of Furman University," The Annual Commencement, July 31, 1856, p. 27.

38. Ibid., p. 34.

39. James Petigrew Boyce, *Abstract of Systematic Theology,* 1887, pp. 6-7.

40. Ibid., p. 47.

41. Ibid., appendix p. 1.

42. Ibid., p. 28.

43. Ibid., p. 34.

44. Ibid., p. 35.

45. Ibid., p. 37.

46. Ibid., p. 40.

47. B. H. Carroll, *Inspiration,* p. IV, 11.

48. Ibid., p. 85.

49. L. R. Scarborough, *With Christ After the Lost,* (Nashville: Sunday School Board of the Southern Baptist Convention, 1919), p. 36.

50. Dagg, *Evidences* Manual, p. 23.

529

51. Arthur P. Johnston, *World Evangelism and the Word of God*, p. 45.
52. Ibid., p. 78.
53. Ibid., p. 79.
54. Ibid., p. 127.
55. Ibid., p. 130.

29

THE STRENGTHS AND WEAKNESSES OF FUNDAMENTALISM

Morris Ashcraft

No other address or seminar title of this conference includes the term Fundamentalism. The inclusion of this title is obviously connected with the relationship of biblical inerrancy and Fundamentalism. To avoid some confusion it will be necessary for me to define Fundamentalism. This is not easy for there are many definitions of Fundamentalism, and there is great doctrinal diversity among those who are so identified.

Let me preface my observations with two remarks. First, those who planned this conference indicated that "The setting and sessions are designed for pastors, church staff, denominational leadership and lay persons who are interested in a scholarly study of inerrancy." For that reason, professionally trained theologians present may think my remarks elementary. I hope to be understood by those who have not had the opportunity of professional theological study, and, therefore, make no apology for the simplicity of this presentation. Second, I will later distinguish between Fundamentalists and Evangelicals or Conservatives and Evangelical Conservatives hoping not to be unnecessarily offensive to those who hold to a theological position often identified as Fundamentalism but innocent of the unpleasant connotations often associated with that term.

A Preliminary Definition of Fundamentalism

Webster defines Fundamentalism as "A recent development in American Protestantism re-emphasizing as fundamental to Christianity belief in the inerrancy of the Scriptures, Biblical miracles, especially the virgin birth and physical resurrection of Christ, etc."

Harold B. Kuhn stated in his article on "Fundamentalism" in the conservative *Baker's Dictionary of Theology,* published by the Baker Book House, that "The term denotes a movement in theology in recent decades designed to conserve the principles which lie at the foundation of the Christian system, and to resist what were considered dangerous theological tendencies in the movement calling itself Modernism."[1]

Van A. Harvey, from quite a different viewpoint, in *A Handbook of Theological Terms,* defined: "Fundamentalism is a name that was attached to the viewpoint of those who, shortly after the turn of the century, resisted all liberal attempts to modify orthodox Prot. belief or to question the infallibility of the Bible in any respect."[2]

The late Edward John Carnell, a champion of recent "Evangelical Conservative" theology, made a sharp distinction between Fundamentalism and Orthodox Theology (Conservative Theology). In his article on "Fundamentalism" in *A Handbook of Christian Theology* (in the Living Age Books series by Meridian Books, Inc.), Carnell distinguished as follows: "Fundamentalism is an extreme right element in Protestant orthodoxy. Orthodoxy is that branch of Christendom which limits the basis of authority to the Bible. Fundamentalism draws its distinctiveness from its attempt to maintain status by negation."[3]

James Barr, who is not an advocate of the position, pointed out in his book *Fundamentalism* in 1977 that the plain man's definition identified a Fundamentalist as one who "takes the Bible literally," but indicated the inadequacy of this simple view. Rather, he defined Fundamentalism as a set of characteristics: (1) the inerrancy of the Bible meaning absence of any kind of error; (2) hostility to modern theology and theological methods and the "implication of modern critical study of the Bible;" (3) and, the conviction that those who differ with their views are not true Christians.[4]

David Rausch writing on "Fundamentalist Origins" in the 1984 study *Fundamentalism Today What Makes It So Attractive!* justifiably protested the use of the word to describe Ayatollah Khomeni of Iran or Muslim fundamentalists.[5]

Perhaps the best way to understand Fundamentalism is to make a brief survey of the historical emergence of Fundamentalism in America.

A Brief Historical Summary

There are numerous sources available on the history of Fundamentalism.[6] Let me acknowledge a special indebtedness to Ernest R. Sandeen, James Barr, Stewart G. Cole, Norman F. Furniss and to Bill J. Leonard for his "The Origin and Character of Fundamentalism" in the Winter 1982 issue of the *Review and Expositor*.

The Fundamentals and "Fundamentalism"

Perhaps one should list as a primary source of Fundamentalism the twelve-volume work entitled *The Fundamentals: A Testimony To The Truth*. This series appeared in print between 1910 and 1915. Two brothers, Lyman and Milton Stewart both laymen, reportedly persuaded C. C. Dixon to edit the volumes and funded the publication and distribution of about 3,000,000 copies free to pastors, missionaries, other ministers etc. There have been several printings of *The Fundamentals*. Kregel of Grand Rapids published a two-volume edition in 1958 and a one-volume issue in 1961.

The "fundamentals" appear, of course, scattered through the series, but the diversity of the entire work makes it impossible to summarize. In Volume 7, George S. Bishop wrote "The Testimony of the Scriptures to Themselves." He stressed the basic tenet or foundation of Fundamentalism in these words:

> There must be a Standard and an Inspired Standard—for *Inspiration is the Essence of Authority,* and authority is in proportion to inspiration—the more inspired the greater the authority—the less, the less . . .
> Verbal and direct inspiration is, therefore, the "Thermopylae" of Biblical

and Scriptural faith. No breath, no syllable; no syllable, no word; no word, no Book; no Book, no religion.[7]

The term "Fundamentalist," and therefore, the name of the movement appears to have been used first by a Northern Baptist, Curtiss Lee Laws, who was editor of the *Watchman-Examiner*. He was writing of those who opposed modernism, held to the belief in the inerrancy of Scripture, and opposed the use of historical-critical methods in biblical study. He suggested that those who held to these fundamentals be called "Fundamentalists," and apparently was willing to be called by that name.[8] Although the name was not used until 1920, the Fundamentalist movement had, of course, begun decades earlier.

A Reaction to Modernism

The rapid changes of the 18th and 19th centuries constituted a major threat to traditional religious beliefs. The rise of the various sciences raised numerous and severe questions about traditional religious beliefs concerning creation, the age of the world, the length of the history of mankind, et cetera.

Many biblical scholars utilized the new historical and scientific methods in the study of the ancient texts, the religious ideas of those texts and similarities between the biblical texts and other writings of the ancient world. Friedrich Schleiermacher attempted to re-write Christian theology in light of these new insights of the modern world. He later became known as the Father of Liberalism.

Liberal Theology flourished in the latter 19th and early 20th centuries. The "Liberals" are as diverse and difficult to characterize as are the "Fundamentalists," but we must try. In general, Liberal Theologians held to ideas such as these. (1) They respected modern science and its methods and applied these methods to biblical study. (2) They tended to be skeptical about human claims of *certain* knowledge, even about God, and preferred to speak of our tentative knowledge. (3) They stressed the idea of continuity in history thereby finding little room for the miraculous. Hebrew and Christian religious beliefs were seen in relationship to other religions and not primarily as direct revelation from God. (4) Liberals held to a very optimistic view of humanity which tended to overlook the gravity of human sin and estrangement from God. (5) The Liberal thinkers tended to stress the immanence of God to the neglect of transcendence. Jesus became a friend, if not a chum. (6) Liberal Christians tended to stress social reform and idealism as a means of achieving the Kingdom of God. Although their theology appears to have been unsound, they contributed much to society.

Lest I be guilty of caricaturing Liberalism, let me point out that there was a distinction between Evangelical Liberals and Modernist Liberals. While I don't like the terms particularly, there were different kinds of Liberals. One group was composed of persons who were primarily oriented toward their Christian faith and wanted to incorporate as much of modern thought as they could. Those in the other group were primarily modern people who wanted to accept as much of Christian faith as their modern orientation would permit.

533

Fundamentalism arose to combat modernism. American Fundamentalism cannot be understood apart from this historical context. You noted in the definitions at the beginning this negative attitude or reactionary stance. Their opposition to the theory of evolution, the documentary hypothesis regarding the Pentateuch, and the use of historical-critical method continues today.

It would not be true to reduce Fundamentalism to this negative and reactionary definition. Positively, Fundamentalism was a re-statement of orthodox Protestant theology with a new emphasis and rigidity which made it distinctive.

A New Statement of Protestant Orthodoxy

After Luther, Calvin, Zwingli, Knox and others, a Protestant Orthodoxy (not uniformity by any means) developed. Only the summary can be sketched. (1) The Bible had an authority over church, theology and history. (2) Jesus Christ was the full revelation of God. (3) Salvation was by faith in Jesus Christ and a matter of the grace of God. (4) Human beings were hopelessly lost apart from the atoning work of Christ. (5) Views of the atonement were therefore very important. (6) God's transcendence was all-important and led to views regarding the seriousness of judgment and the beyond.

These great theological themes, and many others, were recaptured and restated by the Fundamentalists in very positive terms. They spoke of the inerrancy of the scriptures, the Virgin Birth of Jesus as the proof of his deity, the substitutionary view of the atonement, the bodily resurrection of Jesus, the personal and imminent return of Christ, and a literalness in the meaning of Scripture, the miracles, the historical return of Christ, heaven, hell et cetera.

The negative element, or combative element in Fundamentalism led to strong opposition to anything Liberal. Liberals spoke tentatively; Fundamentalists spoke exclusively and with finality. Liberals employed historical-critical methods; Fundamentalists were not only suspicious, but opposed. Liberals were often at least partially appreciative of the theory of evolution; the Fundamentalists hated the term and concept. Liberals were optimistic about human reason, achievement, and basic human goodness; the Fundamentalists stressed the degradation of humanity if not total depravity. Liberals could love Jesus while not being overly worried about the Virgin Birth; the Fundamentalists made the Virgin Birth the test of Christ's Deity.

A New Conservatism

The Fundamentalists produced a large number of very erudite scholars and should not be down-graded in that area. The movement of Fundamentalism, however, has been correctly characterized as being inappropriately belligerent and lacking a social concern.

After World War II a large number of brilliant theologians appeared on the scene championing the Orthodox theology but with a remarkable difference. Edward Carnell[9] who wrote the Westminster Press volume on *The Case For Orthodox Theology* was representative of this group. Perhaps Carl F. H. Henry was the best known for a decade or two, and Billy Graham the most popular preacher of the group. Carnell spoke of the older Fundamentalism as "intransi-

534

gent and inflexible" demanding "conformity," fearing "academic liberty" and believing that the "Liberals corrupt whatever they touch."[10] This was not the case with the new Orthodox Theologians (not to be confused with Neo-Orthodox), who prefer to be called Evangelicals, or Conservative Evangelicals.

These new Conservatives held to the theology of Fundamentalism, but without the belligerent attitude. They also developed a healthy social concern, employed lower criticism in biblical study especially the study of textual criticism.

For over two decades I carefully distinguished in my classes in Contemporary Theology between Fundamentalism and the New Evangelicalism. Students often reminded me that my distinction was not entirely correct, that I spoke only of the scholars in the movement. They reminded me that the militancy had not abated, and that the insistence that only they were right while all others were wrong was still quite alive. They were correct. Popular leaders and preachers revived or continued the Fundamentalist tradition.

We need to note again, lest we misunderstand, that the theology of Conservatism (or New Evangelicalism) is essentially the same as that of older Fundamentalism. The difference was a social concern, an irenic spirit instead of belligerency, and much more appreciation for modern learning and its methods.

The scholars of New Conservatism, including those who are giving the major lectures here this week, are almost always of this irenic spirit. On the popular and political levels, however, the more damaging aspects of older Fundamentalism often appear.

The Theology of Fundamentalism

In the Winter issue of the *Review and Expositor* of 1982, I published an article entitled "The Theology of Fundamentalism." The entire issue was devoted to the theme of "Fundamentalism and The Southern Baptist Convention." In my article I cited Ernest R. Sandeen's works on the subject who had argued on the basis of persuasive evidence that the theology of Fundamentalism was shaped in America by the Princeton Theologians Archibald Alexander, Charles Hodge and B. B. Warfield. Apparently, Hodge focused inspiration on the very words of Scripture (rather than on the ideas only, leaving the writers free reign in choosing the words), hence "verbal" inspiration. Warfield focused inspiration on the "inerrancy" of Scripture rather than on the term "infallible" previously used. Warfield, also, introduced and defended the concept that "inerrancy" applied only to the autographs of biblical writings (the original but non-existent copies).

These theologians were looking for certainty, proof—proof to withstand the implications coming from modern science and other learning which were threatening. Charles Hodge had developed a rationale employing a comparison of natural science—nature, theology—the Bible. The logic is:

> If natural science be concerned with the facts and laws of nature, theology is concerned with facts and principles of the Bible. If the object of the one be to arrange and systematize the facts of the external world, and to ascertain

the laws by which they are determined; the object of the other is to systematize the facts of the Bible, and ascertain the principles or general truths which those facts provide.[11]

As I read this, I detected a radical departure from the Westminster Confession in which "The authority of the holy Scripture, for which it ought to be believed and obeyed, dependeth not upon the testimony of any man or church, but wholly upon God (who is truth itself), the Author thereof; and therefore it is to be received, because it is the Word of God."[12]

Hodge's statement seems to move theology from the study of God to the study of the Bible. The parallel between the reality of nature which natural science seeks to know compares to the reality of the Bible which theology seeks to know. The word "theology" points to God and the discipline of study seeks to understand and make intelligible and coherent statements about God and his relationships. The Bible is the primary source book, of course, but the focus is God.

As previously indicated, there is no uniformity in the summaries of Fundamentalist beliefs. Some authorities insist on a strong dependence on premillennialism and the inclusion of those beliefs. Others do not. The most popular summary, the one most of us memorized in seminary, is the "Five Points."

The Five Points of Fundamentalism

These should be seen as the distinctive beliefs since the Fundamentalists held to the mainline Protestant Orthodoxy on other doctrines. The five points are: the inerrancy of the scripture; the virgin birth of Jesus; the substitutionary view of the atonement; the bodily resurrection of Jesus; and, the physical return of Christ.

Stewart G. Cole in *The History of Fundamentalism* of 1931 stated that the Niagara Bible Conference of 1895 had published five points: the inerrancy of the scriptures; the deity of Christ; the virgin birth of Jesus; the substitutionary atonement of Christ; and Christ's physical resurrection and return to earth.[13]

Norman Furniss in his history summarized the twelve volumes of *The Fundamentals* as: the infallibility of the Bible; Christ's virgin birth; the substitutionary atonement; his resurrection; and, his second coming.[14]

In these summaries, it is obvious that the inerrancy of the Bible is always the foundation. It is also obvious that the Fundamentalists insisted on a literalness about Christ's birth, death, resurrection and second coming. Also, they narrowed the views of atonement in the New Testament to the single view of substitutionary atonement. Vincent Taylor has identified fourteen important atonement ideas in the New Testament including sacrificial, vicarious, representative, et cetera.[15] Fundamentalists, and some Conservatives, to this day insist exclusively on the substitutionary view of the atonement.

It is significant that E. Y. Mullins (who wrote volume III of *The Fundamentals*) addressed the SBC in 1923 on the subject of "Science and Religion." He suggested to scientists that they remember the authority of the Bible, the virgin birth, the atonement, Christ's visible resurrection, and his physical return. It is

536

quite obvious that the "Five Points" are in the background, but it is also obvious that Mullins spoke of the authority rather than the inerrancy of the Bible, and the atonement rather than the specific substitutionary atonement.

The Fourteen Points of the Niagara Bible Conference of 1878

These included: the plenary verbal inspiration of scripture (did not use inerrancy or infallibility), the doctrine of the trinity, human creation and fall, universality of human sin, necessity of re-birth, salvation by the blood of Christ, salvation by faith alone, assurance of salvation, Christ is the center of the canon of scripture, universality and spirituality of the church, the Holy Spirit, Christian life, the literal reality of hell, and the joys of heaven and the premillennial coming of Christ.[16]

The One Point Theology of Fundamentalism

The theology of Fundamentalism comes to rest on one doctrine—the doctrine of the inerrancy of the biblical autographs. We noted earlier that George Bishop in *The Fundamentals* had referred to this view of inspiration as the Thermopylae concluding "No Book, no religion." This exclusivism is characteristic of Fundamentalist writings and of some of the statements being published today by New Conservative Evangelicals.

The Strengths and Contributions of Fundamentalism

The Fundamentalist movement and the New Evangelicalism which holds to the theological beliefs of Fundamentalism were and are very vigorous movements. In seeking to list their strengths and contributions, I will speak only illustratively, not exhaustively. The list could be much longer. I hope you will accept these as expressions of gratitude which I genuinely mean.

1. Fundamentalists *made a needed emphasis on the importance of the Bible*. They called people to read the Bible. They elevated respect for it. While many other factors may also have been involved, we need only look at the enormous sales of Bibles now translated or paraphrased, even taped, for wide and unlimited distribution. All Christian theologians and their followers depend heavily on the Bible, and I think, love it, but the Conservative Christians appear to place an emphasis here which is exemplary.

2. The theology of Fundamentalism and New Conservativism *correctly restored the concept of God's holiness or transcendence* which the Liberal understanding of Jesus Christ had temporarily obscured or eclipsed.

3. Fundamentalism, with its insistence on Virgin Birth and literal resurrection and return, made a *renewed emphasis on the deity of Christ*.

4. The stress on biblical faith required and achieved a serious *re-study of the other major doctrinal beliefs* found in the Bible.

5. Fundamentalist preaching and teaching always laid heavy emphasis on *individual human responsibility and accountability* not only in a future judgment but in present life. At times, this accountability appears to have been

537

achieved in a kind of individual salvation related to heaven and hell more than to the issues of today, but that is another matter.

6. Fundamentalist and Conservative preaching and teaching *called forth large numbers of devout Christians* who have shouldered the burden in the local churches and communities. Gratitude for these people and their faith and lives must include great appreciation for their preachers and teachers.

7. These theological movements have also *inspired many persons to be the missionaries, preachers, pastors and lay ministers* for the church. For these we are grateful.

The Weaknesses of Fundamentalism

Again, I will be illustrative, not comprehensive. I will mention and define or illustrate a few of the weaknesses as I see them.

1. *Is the doctrinal foundation of Fundamentalism true?* Actually, this is really the only question one need ask. In my judgment, the entire theological position rides on the doctrine of biblical inerrancy. Without that doctrine, their view of inspiration would be identical to that of moderate Christians.

B. B. Warfield moved this doctrine of inerrancy to the original writings of the Bible because he knew there were discrepancies in the details of the biblical manuscripts which have come to us. He won the debate because his opponents could hardly speak convincingly about manuscripts which do not exist. Of course, neither could he. The question is not who can win the debate, or get the most votes, but what is true.

Russell H. Dilday, conservative by most standards, listed eight different qualifications employed by the inerrantists.[17] Roy Honeycyutt of Southern Seminary in writing about the Chicago Statement on Inerrancy spoke with bafflement at all of the qualifications necessary to make the statement acceptable.[18]

What does it mean to speak of the inerrancy of the autographs if one must qualify: (1) no modern text or translation is inerrant, only the original manuscripts; (2) inerrancy does not apply to all of the statements in the Bible, just those in which the author was intentionally teaching a view; (3) human authors used their own languages, cultural terms and the like which were not inerrant; (4) "innocent errors" such as rounded-off numbers in historical sections are not errors; (5) when New Testament writers quoted incorrectly, or inexactly, from the Old Testament, these are not errors; (6) apparent errors will probably be clarified in the future; (7) grammatical errors are not errors; and, (8) an error would have to be an intentionally misleading statement.

2. *Is the claim of inerrancy of the scripture the accurate way to state the view of inspiration being described?* When I read the qualifications above, I wonder if they don't mean the truthworthiness of scripture, or the unfailingness of the scripture in matters of faith.

When I read a defense of the view by those who hold it, I find that they are actually portraying a high view of inspiration not unlike that of many of the rest of us who do not use the term. The Chicago Statement for instance, states

"Scripture is inerrant, not in the sense of being absolutely precise by modern standards, but in the sense of making good its claims and achieving that measure of focused truth at which its authors aimed."[19] Apart from the word inerrant, which I find has no meaning in this sentence, I find the rest of the statement quite in keeping with my own view and that of so-called moderates I know.

Clark Pinnock, for example, who taught theology, including a view of inerrancy, at New Orleans Baptist Seminary, now states that he had found that view in the Bible because he had wanted to find it there so as to "maintain a firm stand against religious liberalism."[20] Now, he acknowledges that it really isn't in the Bible, although he would retain the word with another meaning.

3. *Does not the Fundamentalist claim of inerrancy of scripture move the foundation of theology from the Incarnation to a theory of inspiration?* If so, of course, it is not intentional. The theologians of this group state very clearly their conservative views on the other doctrines of the faith. My question, however, has to do with the fact that a Fundamentalist makes everything else rest on this foundation—the inerrancy of the Bible. The Fundamentalist statement is "No Book, no religion!" The early Christians, of course, had the Old Testament or parts of it, but they had no New Testament for several decades. They did quite well in their Christian faith on the basis of their belief that God had come in Jesus Christ the Son who had died and rose again, and they were witnesses. My question has to do with the foundation of theology, or the norm by which all else is determined.

4. *Why are the biblical statements on inspiration inadequate?* Why do we need a word like inerrant which is not a biblical word? Is it not adequate to believe that "All scripture is inspired by God and profitable for teaching, for reproof, for correction, ..." (2 Tim. 3:15-16). Do we need more than "First of all you must understand this, that no prophecy of scripture is a matter of one's own interpretation, because no prophecy ever came by the impulse of man, but men moved by the Holy Spirit spoke from God" (2 Pet. 1:20-21).

5. *Does not this exclusive claim for the Bible suggest a subtle possibility of a hint tending toward idolatry?* I heard of a church whose outside bulletin board had on it these words: "The Bible is God in Print." Of course, the people responsible wanted to say something about the inspiration of the Bible, but does this not suggest an objectifying of God?

The Chicago Statement says, "What Scripture says, God says." I wish the order had been reversed. Indeed, God has spoken. The Bible is our inspired and trustworthy record of His Word. The quote above suggests to me that God is almost subordinate, or the scripture seems to be equated. I think God spoke before there was a Bible. It seems somewhat limiting to suggest that God may not speak again. Of course, if the Bible is accurate and trustworthy as we believe it is, we can assume that God would speak consistent with his own nature, but to my ear the quote has a counterfeit ring to it.

6. *Does not the militant, exclusivistic stance of Fundamentalism do something quite damaging to all expressions of biblical inspiration and authority dif-*

ferent from its own? The view is all-important to those who hold to it, so they find it difficult to acknowledge any truth in any other view, and often exhibit an unfriendly attitude toward those who suffer.

7. *Does not the narrowing tendency of Fundamentalism do damage to the beautiful diversity of the Christian faith and its doctrinal illustrations?* We have noted that Fundamentalism has rather uniformly demanded the substitutionary view of the atonement of Christ. The New Testament speaks of Christ's atoning work in a variety of ways, each one throwing light on the mystery which we can never explain. "Christ died for our sins" can mean "on behalf of," and probably does. Many competent New Testament scholars doubt if "huper" ever means "instead of" in the sense of substitution. The New Testament speaks of Christ's death for us as sacrificial, representative, vicarious, as a ransom, as a victory in which we participate. Why surrender the rich variety of the New Testament from which we receive inspiration? Why coerce all views into one theory? Can we not say the same for inspiration? The New Testament preserves variety.

Conclusion

In my judgment, Fundamentalism has made numerous contributions to the Christian movement, but its exclusive claim to the whole truth in the matter of inspiration has produced many results which appear to me to have been injurious to the whole Christian community.

I do not overlook that vast host of devout men, women and children who follow their teachers and who do not think these matters through for themselves, and therefore indirectly participate with their teachers in what I perceive to be error. Rather, I express gratitude for them and for the rightness of so many of their other views and witness.

I do not intend to label as Fundamentalists those conservative Christians of our day who, for the most part, hold to the basic doctrinal views of Fundamentalism. The Fundamentalist attitude, or stance, of exclusiveness, and belligerency is not a part of their nature, and I would not imply that it is. Perhaps we all need to be reminded not to make again the mistakes of generations past when our forebears learned through bitter controversy that in conflict on issues such as this there are no winners, only survivors.

I was asked to address this subject. I have done so insofar as my abilities and time permit. I close with the acknowledgment that, of course, I may be wrong.

Notes

1. Everett F. Harrison, ed., *Baker's Dictionary of Theology* (Grand Rapids: Baker Book House, 1960), "Fundamentalism."

2. Van A. Harvey, *A Handbook of Theological Terms* (New York: Macmillan Publishing Co. Inc.), p. 103.

3. Edward John Carnell, "Fundamentalism," in Marvin Halverson and Arthur A. Cohen, eds., *A Handbook of Christian Theology* (New York: Meridian Books, Inc. 1958), p. 142.

4. James Barr, *Fundamentalism* (Philadelphia: The Westminster Press, 1977), p. 1.

5. Marla J. Selvidge, ed., *Fundamentalism Today What Makes It So Attractive!* (Elgin, Illinois: Brethren Press, 1984), p. 11.

6. Stewart G. Cole, *The History of Fundamentalism* (New York: Richard R. Smith, Inc., 1931); Ernest R. Sandeen, *The Roots of Fundamentalism* (Chicago: The University of Chicago Press, 1970); Norman F. Furniss, *The Fundamentalist Controversy, 1918-1931* (Hamden, Conn.: Archon Books, 1963).

7. *The Fundamentals: A Testimony To The Truth* (12 vols.; Chicago: Testimony Publishing Company, 1910-15), VII, 39.

8. Bill J. Leonard, "The Origin and Character of Fundamentalism," *Review and Expositor*, LXXIX, No. 1, Winter 1982 (Louisville: Faculty of the Southern Baptist Theological Seminary), p. 13.

9. Edward John Carnell, *The Case for Orthodox Theology* (Philadelphia: The Westminster Press, 1959).

10. Carnell, "Fundamentalism," *Handbook of Christian Theology*.

11. Charles Hodge, *Systematic Theology, I* (1871 rpt.; Chicago: University of Chicago Press, 1970), p. 18.

12. Philip Schaff, *The Creeds of Christendom with a History and Critical Notes* (Grand Rapids: Baker Book House, 1977, III, 602f.

13. Cole, op. cit., p. 34.

14. Furniss, op. cit., p. 72.

15. Vincent Taylor, *The Atonement in New Testament Teaching* (London: Epworth Press, 1940).

16. Pamphlet "The Fundamentals of the Faith as Expressed in the Articles of Belief of the Niagara Bible Conference," published by the Great Commission Prayer League of Chicago, now republished in full in Appendix A of Sandeen's *Roots,* cited above.

17. Russell H. Dilday, Jr., *The Doctrine of Biblical Authority* (Nashville: Convention Press, 1982), pp. 97f.

18. Roy Lee Honeycutt, "Biblical Authority: A Treasured Heritage!" *Review and Expositor*, LXXXIII (Fall, 1986) p. 606f.

19. "The Chicago Statement On Biblical Inerrancy," *Journal of the Evangelical Theological Society,* (December, 1978), pp. 289-96.

20. Clark H. Pinnock, *The Scripture Principle* (San Francisco: Harper & Row, 1984, p. 58.

BIBLIOGRAPHIES

Some of the authors included bibliographies in their papers. These bibliographies were not included in the body of the text because they were not parts of the actual presentations at the Conference. Instead, the editors have chosen to gather the various bibliographies into one section at the end of the volume. There are four bibliographies, put together by L. Russ Bush, Robert L. Cate, James Leo Garrett, and H. Edwin Young. Each of these bibliographies is printed in the form chosen by the author.

L. Russ Bush

Baillie, John, *The Idea of Revelation in Recent Thought,* Columbia University Press, 1956.

Barclay, William, *By What Authority,* Richard Clay Ltd., 1974.

Beegle, Dewey M., *Scripture, Tradition and Infallibility,* Eerdmans Publishing Company, 1973.

Bloesch, Donald, *Essentials of Evangelical Theology,* Harper and Row, 1978.

Boice, James Montgomery, *The Foundation of Biblical Authority,* Zondervan, 1978.

Bush, L. Russ and Nettles, Tom J., *Baptists and the Bible,* Moody Press, 1980.

Campbell, Dennis M., *Authority and the Renewal of American Theology,* United Church Press, 1976.

Carroll, B. H., *Inspiration of the Bible,* Thomas Nelson Publishers, 1980.

Carson, D. A. and Woodbridge, John D., *Scripture and Truth,* Zondervan Publishing House, 1983.

Coleman, Richard J., *Issues of Theological Warfare: Evangelicals and Liberals,* Eerdmans, 1972.

Conner, Walter Thomas, *Christian Doctrine,* Broadman Press, 1937.

Conner, Walter Thomas, *Revelation and God: An Introduction to Christian Doctrine,* Broadman Press, 1936.

Davis, John Jefferson, *Foundations of Evangelical Theology,* Baker Book House, 1984.

Davis, Rupert E., *The Problem of Authority in the Continental Reformers,* Epworth Press.

Davis, Stephen T., *The Debate About the Bible,* Westminster Press, 1977.

Dilday, Russell H. Jr., *The Doctrine of Biblical Authority,* Convention Press, 1982.

Dodd, C. H., *The Authority of the Bible,* Mayflower Press, 1938.

Draper, James T., *Authority: The Critical Issue for Southern Baptists,* Fleming H. Revell, 1984.

Erickson, Millard J., *Christian Theology* Vol. 1, Baker Book House, 1983.

Geisler, Norman L., *Inerrancy,* Zondervan, 1979.

Geldenhuys, J. Norval, *Supreme Authority,* Marshall, Morgan and Scott, 1953.

543

Gnuse, Robert, *The Authority of the Bible,* Paulist Press, 1985.

Grant, Robert M., *The Bible in the Church,* Macmillan Company, 1954.

Hannah, John D., ed., *Inerrancy and the Church,* Moody Press, 1984.

Helm, Paul, *The Divine Revelation,* Crossway Books, 1982.

Henry, Carl F. H., ed., *Revelation and the Bible,* Baker Book House, 1985.

Hodge, Archibald A. and Warfield, Benjamin B., *Inspiration,* Baker Book House, 1979.

Leckie, J. H., *Authority in Religion,* T. & T. Clark, 1909.

Lewis, John M., *Revelation, Inspiration, Scripture,* Broadman Press, 1985.

Lindsell, Harold, *The Battle for the Bible,* Zondervan, 1976.

Marshall, I. Howard, *Biblical Inspiration,* Eerdmans Publishing Company, 1982.

May, Lynn E. Jr., ed., *Baptist History and Heritage,* Historical Commission, SBC, 1984.

McDonald, H. D., *Theories of Revelation,* Baker Book House, 1979.

McKim, Donald K., *The Authoritative Word,* Eerdmans Publishing Company, 1983.

Miller, Donald G., *The Authority of the Bible,* Eerdmans Publishing Company, 1972.

Montgomery, John Warick, *God's Inerrant Word,* Bethany Fellowship Inc., 1974.

Morris, Leon, *I Believe in Revelation,* Eerdmans Publishing Company, 1976.

Mullins, Edgar Young, *Freedom and Authority in Religion,* Griffith and Rowland Press, 1913.

Mullins, Edgar Young, *The Christian Religion in its Doctrinal Expression,* Judson Press, 1917.

Nash, Ronald H., *The Word of God and the Mind of Man,* Zondervan, 1982.

Nicole, Roger R., and Michaels, J. Ramsey, ed., *Inerrancy and Common Sense,* Baker Book House, 1980.

Pache, Rene, *The Inspiration and Authority of Scripture,* Moody Press, 1969.

Pinnock Clark H., *Biblical Revelation-The Foundation of Christian Theology,* Moody Press, 1971.

Pinnock, Clark H., *The Scripture Principle,* Harper and Row Publishers, 1984.

Radmacher, Earl D. and Preus, Robert D., ed., *Hermeneutics, Inerrancy, and the Bible,* Academie Books, 1984.

Ramm, Bernard, *The Pattern of Authority,* Eerdmans Publishing Company, 1957.

Ramm, Bernard, *Protestant Biblical Interpretation,* W. A. Wilde Company, 1950.

Ramm, Bernard, *Special Revelation and the Word of God,* Eerdmans Publishing Company, 1961.

Reid, J. K. S., *The Authority of Scripture,* Harper and Brothers Publishers.

Ridderbos, Herman, *Studies in Scripture and its Authority,* Eerdmans Publishing Company, 1978.

Rogers, Jack B., and McKim, Donald K., ed., *The Authority and Interpretation of the Bible,* Harper and Row Publishers, 1979.

Rogers, Jack ed., *Biblical Authority,* Word Books, 1977.

Sproul, R. C., *Explaining Inerrancy,* International Council on Biblical Inerrancy, 1980.

Strong, Augustus Hopkins, *Systematic Theology,* The Judson Press, 1907.

Ward, Wayne E. and Green Joseph F., ed., *Is the Bible a Human Book?* Broadman Press, 1970.

Warfield, Benjamin Breckinridge, *The Inspiration and Authority of the Bible,* Presbyterian and Reformed Publishing Company, 1948.

Williams, R. R., *Authority in the Apostolic Age,* SCM Press Ltd., 1950.

Woodbridge, John D., *Biblical Authority,* Zondervan Publishing House, 1982.

Robert L. Cate

Achtemeier, Paul J. *The Inspiration of Scripture: Problems and Proposals*. Philadelphia: The Westminster Press, 1980.

Allen, Clifton J. *The Broadman Bible Commentary* (vol. 1, rev.). Nashville: Broadman Press, 1973.

Barr, James. *Holy Scripture: Canon, Authority, Criticism*. Philadelphia: The Westminster Press, 1983.

————. *The Scope and Authority of the Bible*. Philadelphia: The Westminster Press, 1980.

Beegle, Dewey M. *Scripture, Tradition, and Infallibility*. Grand Rapids: William B. Eerdmans Publishing Company, 1973.

Boer, Harry R. *Above the Battle? The Bible and Its Critics*. Grand Rapids: William B. Eerdmans Publishing Company, 1975.

Boyce, James P. *Abstract of Systematic Theology*. Pompano Beach: Christian Gospel Foundation, 1887.

Bright, John. *The Authority of the Old Testament*. Grand Rapids: Baker Book House, 1967.

Bush, L. Russ, and Tom J. Nettles. *Baptists and the Bible*. Chicago: Moody Press, 1980.

Carson, D. A., and John D. Woodbridge, eds. *Scripture and Truth*. Grand Rapids: Zondervan Publishing House, 1983.

Cate, Robert L. *How to Interpret the Bible*. Nashville: Broadman Press, 1983.

————. *Old Testament Roots for New Testament Faith*. Nashville: Broadman Press, 1982.

Childs, Brevard S. *Old Testament Theology in a Canonical Context*. Philadelphia: Fortress Press, 1985.

Coats, George W., and Burke O. Long, eds. *Canon and Authority*. Philadelphia: Fortress Press, 1977.

Conner, William Thomas. *Christian Doctrine*. Nashville: Broadman Press, 1937.

————. *Revelation and God*. Nashville: Broadman Press, 1936.

Criswell, W. A. *Why I Preach that the Bible Is Literally True*. Nashville: Broadman Press, 1969.

Dilday, Russell H., Jr. *The Doctrine of Biblical Authority*. Nashville: Convention Press, 1982.

Dodd, C. H. *The Authority of the Bible*. London: Nisbet & Co. Ltd., 1952.

Draper, James T., Jr. *Foundations of Biblical Faith*. Nashville: Broadman Press, 1979.

Fee, Gordon D. and Douglas Stuart. *How to Read the Bible for All Its Worth*. Grand Rapids: Zondervan Publishing House, 1982.

Geisler, Norman L., ed. *Inerrancy*. Grand Rapids: Zondervan Publishing House, 1979.

Grant, R. M. *The Letter and the Spirit*. London: S.P.C.K., 1957.

Herbert, A. G. *The Authority of the Old Testament*. London: Faber and Faber Ltd, 1947.

Hobbs, Herschel. *The Baptist Faith and Message*. Nashville: Convention Press, 1971.

————. *Fundamentals of Our Faith*. Nashville: Broadman Press, 1960.

————. *What Baptists Believe*. Nashville: Broadman Press, 1964.

Kantzer, Kenneth S. ed. *Evangelical Roots*. Nashville: Thomas Nelson Inc., Publishers, 1978.

La Sor, William Sanford, David Allan Hubbard, and Frederic William Bush. *Old Testament Survey*. Grand Rapids: William B. Eerdmans Publishing Company, 1982.

Lewis, John M. *Revelation, Inspiration, Scripture*. Nashville: Broadman Press, 1985.

Lewis, Gordon, and Bruce Demarest, eds. *Challenges to Inerrancy: A Theological Response*. Chicago: Moody Press, 1984.

Lindsell, Harold. *The Battle for the Bible*. Grand Rapids: Zondervan Publishing House, 1976.

———. *The Bible in the Balance*. Grand Rapids: Zondervan Publishing House, 1979.

McKim, Donald K., ed. *The Authoritative Word; Essays on the Nature of Scripture*. Grand Rapids: Wm. B. Eerdmans Publishing Company, 1983.

———. *What Christians Believe About the Bible*. Nashville: Thomas Nelson Publishers, 1985.

Mickelsen, A. Berkeley. *Interpreting the Bible*. Grand Rapids: Wm. B. Eerdmans Publishing Co., 1956.

Montgomery, John Warwick, ed. *God's Inerrant Word*. Minneapolis: Bethany Fellowship, Inc., 1974.

Mowinckel, Sigmund. *The Old Testament as Word of God* (Reidar B. Bjornard, trans.). Oxford: Basil Blackwell, 1960.

Nettleton, David. *Our Infallible Bible*. Schaumburg: Regular Baptist Press, 1977.

Newport, John P., and William Cannon. *Why Christians Fight over the Bible*. Nashville: Thomas Nelson, Inc., 1974.

Packer, J. I. *Beyond the Battle for the Bible*. Westchester: Cornerstone Books, 1980.

Pinnock, Clark H. *Biblical Revelation – The Foundations of Christian Theology*. Chicago: Moody Press, 1971.

———. *The Scripture Principle*. San Francisco: Harper & Row, Publishers, 1984.

Robinson, H. Wheeler. *Inspiration and Revelation in the Old Testament*. Oxford: Clarendon Press, 1946.

Rogers, Jack, ed. *Biblical Authority*. Waco: Word Books, 1977.

——— and Donald K. McKim. *The Authority and Interpretation of the Bible: an Historical Approach*. San Francisco: Harper & Row, 1979.

Snaith, Norman H. *The Inspiration and Authority of the Bible*. London: The Epworth Press, 1956.

Stagg, Frank. *New Testament Theology*. Nashville: Broadman Press, 1962.

Young, Edward J. *Thy Word Is Truth*. Grand Rapids: Wm. B. Eerdmans Publishing Co., 1957.

Youngblood, Ronald. *Evangelicals and Inerrancy*. Nashville: Thomas Nelson Publishers, 1984.

James Leo Garrett

Allen, Clifton Judson. *Affirmations of Our Faith*. Nashville: Broadman Press, 1972, pp. 20-30.

———. "The Book of the Christian Faith," in *Broadman Bible Commentary*, vol. 1 (Nashville: Broadman Press, 1969), pp. 1-14.

Ashcraft, Jesse Morris. *Christian Faith and Beliefs*. Nashville: Broadman Press, 1984, pp. 78-88.

———. "The Issue of Biblical Authority." *Faith and Mission* 1 (Spring 1984): 25-35.

———. "Response to Carl F. H. Henry, 'Are We Doomed to Hermeneutical Nihilism?'" *Review and Expositor* 71 (Spring 1974): 217-23.

Bailey, Raymond H. "Using a Double Standard." *SBC Today*, June 1986, pp. 4-5.

Belcher, Richard P. "The Nature of the Bible according to the Broadman Commentary." *Southern Baptist Journal*, May 1976, pp. 1, 6, 9, 10.

Bell, William E., Jr. "The Case for Biblical Inerrancy." *Southern Baptist Journal,* April 1978, pp. 1, 11-12.

————. "The Doctrine of Scripture." *Southern Baptist Journal,* May 1978, pp. 5-8; June 1978, pp. 7-11; July 1978, pp. 5-9; August 1978, pp. 5-8, 11; Sept. ; October 1978, pp. 5-9; November 1978, pp. 5-8, 11; March-April 1979, pp. 5-8; September 1979, pp. 9-10.

Bulman, James M. "'Without Any Mixture of Error.'" *Southern Baptist Journal,* January 1974, p. 9.

Bush, Luther Russell, III, "Should Inerrancy Be an Issue?" *Southern Baptist Advocate,* November 1980, pp. 9-10.

Bush, Luther Russell, III, and Thomas J. Nettles. *Baptists and the Bible.* Chicago: Moody Press, 1980.

Campbell, J. Thomas. "Did Jesus Teach Inerrancy? Yes or No: A Dialogue with Dr. Alan Culpepper," *Southern Baptist Advocate,* April 1987, pp. 12-15.

Carroll, Benajah Harvey. *The Inspiration of the Bible: A Discussion of the Origin, the Authenticity and the Sanctity of the Oracles of God,* comp. and ed. J. B. Cranfill (New York, Chicago: Fleming H. Revell Co., 1930).

Carter, James Edward. "Guest Editorial: The Bible and 20th Century Baptist Confessions of Faith." *Baptist History and Heritage* 19 (July 1984): 2-3.

Colson, Howard P. "Truth without Any Mixture of Error." *Southern Baptist Journal,* June 1974, p. 6.

Conner, Walter Thomas. *Christian Doctrine.* Nashville: Broadman Press, 1937, pp. 35-43.

————. *The Faith of the New Testament.* Nashville: Broadman Press, 1940, pp. 13-15.

————. *Gospel Doctrines.* Nashville: Sunday School Board of the Southern Baptist Convention, 1925, pp. 13-23.

————. "The Nature of the Authority of the Bible." *Southwestern Journal of Theology* 2 (October 1918): 11-17.

————. *Revelation and God:* An Introduction to Christian Doctrine. Nashville: Broadman Press, 1936, pp. 27-28, 75-101.

————. Review of Benjamin Breckinridge Warfield, *The Inspiration and Authority of the Bible,* in *Baptist Standard,* 5 May 1949, p. 3.

————. Review of Benjamin Breckinridge Warfield, *Revelation and Inspiration,* in *Southwestern Evangel* 13 (November 1928): 59.

————. Review of Harry Emerson Fosdick, *A Guide to Understanding the Bible,* in *Baptist Standard,* 30 January 1941, p. 14.

————. *A System of Christian Doctrine.* Nashville: Sunday School Board of the Southern Baptist Convention, 1924, pp. 18, 105-26.

Criswell, Wallie Amos. *The Bible for Today's World.* Grand Rapids: Zondervan Publishing House, 1965.

————. *Great Doctrines of the Bible,* ed. Paige Patterson. 5 vols. Grand Rapids: Zondervan Publishing House, 1982ff. Vol. 1 on Bibliology.

————. "The Infallible Word of God," *Southern Baptist Journal,* June 1977, pp. 1, 6-7, 5.

————. "The Pattern of Death for a Denomination." *Southern Baptist Advocate,* Summer 1985, pp. 1, 18-22.

————. *These Issues We Must Face.* Grand Rapids: Zondervan Publishing House, 1953. Ch. 5, "The Preservation of the Word of God; ch. 6, "Whose Is the Bible?"

547

———. *Why I Preach That the Bible Is Literally True*. Nashville: Broadman Press, 1969.

Culpepper, R. Alan. "Jesus' View of the Scripture." *SBC Today*, December 1986, pp. 6-7.

Dana, Harvey Eugene. *The Authenticity of the Holy Scriptures: A Brief Story of the Problems of Biblical Criticism*. Nashville: Sunday School Board of the Southern Baptist Convention, 1923.

———. *An Introduction to the Critical Interpretation of the New Testament*. Fort Worth: Taliaferro Printing Co., 1924.

———. *A Neglected Predicate in New Testament Criticism*. Chicago: Blessing Book Stores, Inc., 1934.

———. *New Testament Criticism: A Brief Summary of the Nature and Necessity, History, Sources and Results of New Testament Criticism*. Fort Worth: World Company, Inc., 1924.

———. *The Science of New Testament Interpretation*. Fort Worth: Southwestern Press, 1930.

———. *Searching the Scriptures: A Handbook of New Testament Hermeneutics*. New Orleans: Bible Institute Memorial Press, 1936.

Dana, Harvey Eugene and R. Edgar Glaze, Jr. *Interpreting the New Testament*. Nashville: Broadman Press, 1961.

Dargan, Edwin Charles. *Doctrines of Our Faith*. Nashville: Sunday School Board of the Southern Baptist Convention, 1905; rev. ed., 1920. Ch. 2 (1905); ch. 1 (1920).

———. *The Bible Our Heritage*. New York: Doran Company, 1924.

Davis, Walter R. "The Bible Is Truth without Any Mixture of Error," *Southern Baptist Journal*, December 1975, p. 5.

Dilday, Russell Hooper, Jr. *The Doctrine of Biblical Authority*. Nashville: Convention Press, 1982.

Dockery, David S. "Can Baptists Affirm the Reliability and Authority of Bible?" *SBC Today*, March 1985, p. 16.

———. "Variations on Inerrancy." *SBC Today*, May 1986, pp. 10-11.

Downs, David W. "The Baptist Heritage: The Bible." *SBC Today*, November 1985, pp. 8-9.

Draper, James T., Jr. *Authority: The Critical Issue for Southern Baptists*. Old Tappan, N.J.: Fleming H. Revell Company, 1984.

Ellis, Edward Earle. "The Authority of Scripture: Critical Judgements in Biblical Perspective," *Evangelical Quarterly* 36 (1967): 196-204.

———. "Foreward" to Leonhard Goppelt, *Typos: The Typological Interpretation of the Old Testament in the New*. Transl. Donald H. Madvig. Grand Rapids: Eerdmans, 1982, pp. ix-xx.

Estep, William R., Jr. "Confronting the Bible: The Bible in Confessions." *SBC Today*, April 1987, pp. 6-7, 10-11.

Fisher, Fred Lewis. *How to Interpret the New Testament*. Philadelphia: Westminster Press, 1966.

———. "How You Can Understand the Bible," in Wayne E. Ward and Joseph F. Green, eds., *Is the Bible a Human Book?* Nashville: Broadman Press, 1970, pp. 83-92.

Flamming, Peter James. "Could God Trust Human Hands?" in Wayne E. Ward and Joseph F. Green, eds., *Is the Bible a Human Book?* Nashville: Broadman Press, 1970, pp. 9-18.

Freeman, Harold Vern. "Biblical Inerrancy, with Reference to American Conservative

Theology." Th.D. Dissertation, Southwestern Baptist Theological Seminary, 1968. 259 pp.

Gaddy, Curtis Weldon. Review of James T. Draper, Jr., *Authority: The Critical Issue for Southern Baptists,* in *SBC Today* March-April 1984, pp. 1, 7-9.

Gafford, Gene. "A Reply to 'Shall We Call the Bible Infallible?' *Southern Baptist Journal,* December 1974, p. 12.

Garrett, James Leo, Jr. "The Bible at Southwestern Seminary during Its Formative Years: A Study of H. E. Dana and W. T. Conner." *Baptist History and Heritage* 21 (October 1986): 29-43.

————. "Biblical Authority according to Baptist Confessions of Faith." *Review and Expositor* 76 (Winter 1979): 43-54.

————. "Biblical Infallibility and Inerrancy according to Baptist Confessions of Faith." *Search* 3 (Fall 1972): 42-45.

————. "Doctrinal Authority, 1925-1975: A Study in Four Representative Baptist Journals." *Foundations* 22 (January-March 1979): 3-12.

————. "Representative Modern Baptist Understandings of Biblical Inspiration." *Review and Expositor* 71 (Spring 1974): 179-95.

————. "Sources of Authority in Baptist Thought." *Baptist History and Heritage* 13 (July 1978): 41-49.

Glaze, R. Edgar, Jr. "Southern Baptists and the Scriptures." *The Theological Educator* 1 (October 1970): 8-20.

Grant, Worth C. Review of Harold Lindsell, *The Battle for the Bible,* in *Southern Baptist Journal,* November 1976, p. 5.

Groves, Richard. "What the Bible Means to Me." *SBC Today,* June 1986, pp. 26-27.

Hefley, James Carl. *The Truth in Crisis: The Controversy in the Southern Baptist Convention.* Dallas: Criterion Publications, 1986.

Hendricks, William Lawrence. "Biblical Interpretation, the Pastor, and the Contemporary Scene." *Southwestern Journal of Theology* 2 (April 1960): 17-26.

————. "Hendrick's [*sic*] Answers." *Southern Baptist Journal,* September 1980, pp. 8-9.

————. "Scripture: A Southern Baptist Perspective." *Review and Expositor* 79 (Spring 1982): 245-57.

————. "Southern Baptists and the Bible." *One in Christ: A Catholic Ecumenical Review* 17 (1981): 205-18.

————. *A Theology for Aging.* Nashville: Broadman Press, 1986, pp. 264-71, 287-94.

————. *A Theology for Children.* Nashville: Broadman Press, 1980, pp. 39-62.

Henry, Carl Ferdinand Howard. *God, Revelation and Authority.* Waco: Word Books, 1976-83. 6 vols.

————. "The Interpretation of the Scriptures: Are We Doomed to Hermeneutical Nihilism?" *Review and Expositor* 71 (Spring 1974): 197-215.

————. "Is the Bible an Errant Book?" *Southern Baptist Advocate,* Spring 1982, pp. 8-9.

————. "A Postscript: Reply to Morris Ashcraft." *Review and Expositor* 71 (Spring 1974): 225-27.

————. (ed). *Revelation and the Bible: Contemporary Evangelical Thought.* Grand Rapids: Baker Book House, 1958.

————. Review of James T. Draper, Jr., *Authority: The Critical Issue for Southern Baptists,* in *Southern Baptist Advocate,* January 1984, pp. 6, 13-14.

549

Hinson, Edward Glenn. "Southern Baptists and the Liberal Tradition in Biblical Interpretation, 1845-1945," *Baptist History and Heritage* 19 (July 1984): 16-20.

Honeycutt, Roy Lee. "Biblical Authority: A Treasured Heritage!" *Review and Expositor* 83 (Fall 1986): 605-22.

Howe, Claude L., Jr. "Learning from the Debate in the Lutheran Chruch [Mo. Synod]," *Theological Educator* 6 (Fall 1975): 11-14.

———. "Southern Baptists and the Moderate Tradition in Biblical Interpretation, 1845-1945," *Baptist History and Heritage* 19 (July 1984): 21-28.

Hull, William Edward. "The Nature of the Bible and Its Message." *Faith and Mission* 3 (Spring 1986): 3-10.

———. "Shall We Call the Bible Infallible?" *Crescent Hill Sermons*, Crescent Hill Baptist Church, Louisville, Kentucky, 16 August 1970.

Humphreys, Fisher. "Biblical Inerrancy: A Guide for the Perplexed." *SBC Today*, February 1987, pp. 6-7, 13.

———. *Thinking about God: An Introduction to Christian Theology*. New Orleans: Insight Press, Inc., 1974, pp. 37-52.

Hunt, William Boyd. "What Is Inspiration?" in Wayne E. Ward and Joseph F. Green, eds., *Is the Bible a Human Book?* Nashville: Broadman Press, 1970, pp. 120-29.

———. What Makes the Bible Authoritative?" in David K. Alexander and C. W. Junker, eds., *What Can You Believe?* Nashville: Broadman Press, 1966, pp. 70-74.

Hymers, R. L. "Ten Reasons Why You Believe in the Infallibility of the Bible," *Southern Baptist Journal* [May 1983], pp. 4-7; also in June 1983, pp. 8-11.

James, Gordon. *Inerrancy and the Southern Baptist Convention: A Historical and Theological Survey and Analysis*. Dallas: Southern Baptist Heritage Press, 1986.

James, Robison B. "BFM Statement: Best Answer." *SBC Today*, October 1986, pp. 8-9.

———. "Believing the Bible Biblically," *SBC Today*, January 1987, pp. 6-7.

———. "Biblical Authority or Inerrancy?" *SBC Today*, November 1985, pp. 1, 6-7.

———. "Inerrancy: To Divide or to United [sic] Us?" *SBC Today*, May 1986, p. 12.

———. "Pinnock's Discovery: A Way Out." *SBC Today*, May 1986, p. 1.

Jones, Peter Rhea. "Biblical Hermeneutics." *Review and Expositor* 72 (Spring 1975): 139-47.

Keiwiet, John J. "Hermeneutics in Historical Perspective." *Southwestern Journal of Theology* 16 (Spring 1974): 1-14.

Land, Richard D. "Southern Baptists and the Fundamentalist Tradition in Biblical Interpretation, 1845-1945." *Baptist History and Heritage* 19 (July 1984): 29-32.

Lewis, John Moore. "The Bible and Human Science," in Wayne E. Ward and Joseph F. Green, eds., *Is the Bible a Human Book?* Nashville: Broadman Press, 1970, pp. 93-102.

———. *Revelation, Inspiration, Scripture*. Layman's Library of Christian Doctrine. Nashville: Broadman Press, 1985.

Lewis, Larry L. "What I Believe about Inspiration." *Southern Baptist Journal*, January 1978, pp. 3, 10.

Lindsell, Harold. *The Battle for the Bible*. Grand Rapids: Zondervan Publishing House, 1976.

———. *The Bible in the Balance*. Grand Rapids: Zondervan Publishing House, 1979.

———. "Response to Eric C. Rust, 'The Biblical Faith and Modern Science,'" *Review and Expositor* 71 (Spring 1974): 243-48.

Lumpkin, William Latane. "The Bible in Early Baptist Confessions of Faith." *Baptist History and Heritage* 19 (July 1984): 33-41.

McKnight, Edgar V. "Confronting the Bible: All Were Fundamentalists?" The A. T. Robertson Case," *SBC Today*, June 1986, pp. 6-7, 18-19.

Metts, Fred C. "The Infallible Word." *Southern Baptist Journal*, January 1978, pp. 1, 10.

Miller, Eldridge L. "'If It's Not Broken." *Southern Baptist Advocate*, January-February 1983, pp. 4-5.

Moody, Dale. *The Word of Truth: A Summary of Christian Doctrine Based on Biblical Revelation*. Grand Rapids: Eerdmans, 1981, pp. 38-52.

Moody, Dwight Allan. "Doctrines of Inspiration in the Southern Baptist Theological Tradition." Ph.D. Dissertation, Southern Baptist Theological Seminary, 1982.

Mullins, Edgar Young. *Baptist Beliefs*. Philadelphia: American Baptist Publication Society, 1912, pp. 10-13.

———. "Baptists and the Bible." *Encyclopedia of Southern Baptists*. 4 vols. Nashville: Broadman Press, 1958-82. 1:141-43.

———. *The Christian Religion in Its Doctrinal Expression*. Philadelphia: Judson Press, 1917, pp. 142-53.

———. *Christianity at the Cross Roads*. Nashville: Sunday School Board of the Southern Baptist Convention, 1924, pp. 176-209.

———. "The Dangers and Duties of the Present Hour," Address, SBC, Kansas City, Mo., 16 May 1923.

———. *Faith in the Modern World*. Nashville: Sunday School Board of the Southern Baptist Convention, 1930, pp. 25-26.

———. *Freedom and Authority in Religion*. Philadelphia: Griffith and Rowland Press, 1913, pp. 346-94.

———. Review of Auguste Sabatier, *Religions of Authority and the Religion of the Spirit*, in *Review and Expositor* 1 (October 1904): 370-78.

Nettles, Tom J. "SBC Crisis Rooted in Theology," *Southern Baptist Advocate*, May 1985, pp. 6-8.

Newman, Stewart Albert. "Confronting the Bible: The Baptist Adventure; A Look at W. T. Conner, A Shaper of Baptists." *SBC Today*, May 1986, pp. 4-5.

Newport, John Paul. "Bible, The: The Authority of the Bible." *Encyclopedia of Southern Baptists*. 4 vols. Nashville: Broadman Press, 1958-62. 1:161-62.

———. "Biblical Interpretation and Eschatological-Holy History." *Southwestern Journal of Theology* 4 (October 1961): 83-110.

———. "Interpreting the Bible," in *Broadman Bible Commentary*, volume 1. Nashville: Broadman Press, 1969, pp. 25-33.

———. *The Lion and the Lamb: The Book of Revelation for Today*. Nashville: Broadman Press, 1986, pp. 23-77.

———. "Representative Historical and Contemporary Approaches to Biblical Interpretation." *Faith and Mission* 3 (Spring 1986): 32-48.

———. "The Unique Nature of the Bible in the Light of Recent Attacks." *Southwestern Journal of Theology* 6 (October 1963): 93-106.

———. *What Is Christian Doctrine?* Layman's Library of Christian Doctrine. Nashville: Broadman Press, 1984, pp. 14-73.

———. "Why Christians Argue over Biblical Interpretation.: *Southwestern Journal of Theology* 16 (Spring 1974): 15-29.

——— and William Cannon. *Why Christians Fight over the Bible*. Nashville: Thomas Nelson, 1974.

Owens, M. O., Jr. "The Bible: Inerrant or Irrelevant," *Southern Baptist Journal*, September 1974, p. 7.

551

Patterson, Leighton Paige. "The Bible: A Book of Destiny." *Criswell Study Bible*. Nashville: Thomas Nelson, 1979, pp. xvii-xxi.

———. Review of Russell H. Dilday, Jr., *The Doctrine of Biblical Authority*, in *Southern Baptist Advocate*, July-August 1983, pp. 11-14; September 1983, pp. 7, 10-13.

Pinnock, Clark H. "Acrimonious Debate on Inerrancy." *Southern Baptist Journal*, July-August 1976, pp. 6, 11. [Review of H. Lindsell, *The Battle for the Bible*].

———. *Biblical Revelation: The Foundation of Christian Theology*. Chicago: Moody Press, 1971.

———. *Defense of Biblical Infallibility*. Philadelphia: Presbyterian and Reformed Pub. Co., 1967.

———. *A New Reformation*. Tigerville, S.C.: Jewel Books, 1968.

———. Response to T. C. Smith's Review of *The Scripture Principle*, *SBC Today*, May 1986, pp. 6-7.

———. *The Scripture Principle*. San Francisco: Harper and Row, 1984.

———. "Transcending SBC Polarization." *SBC Today*, August-September 1986, pp. 10-11.

Powell, William A. "The Historical Critical Method." *Southern Baptist Journal*, November 1977, pp. 2-3.

———. *The SBC Issue and Question*. Buchanan, Ga.: Baptist Missionary Service, 1978 (?).

[———]. "Verbal Inspiration." *Southern Baptist Journal*, March 1978, pp. 5-6.

———. "The Verbal Inspiration of the Bible." *Southern Baptist Journal*, December 1975, pp. 2, 4, 5.

Price, Robert M. "Inerrancy: The New Catholicism?" *SBC Today*, August-September 1986, pp. 4-5.

Roark, Dallas M. "Emphases in Hermeneutics." *Southwestern Journal of Theology* 7 (October 1964): 63-71.

Robertson, Archibald Thomas. *An Introduction to the Textual Criticism of the New Testament*. Nashville: Sunday School Board of the Southern Baptist Convention, 1925.

Rone, Wendell H., Sr. "Bible Basics for Baptists." *Southern Baptist Journal*, January 1974, p. 6.

Russell, Gene. "Tidwell and Verbal Inspiration." *Southern Baptist Advocate*, August 1980, p. 8.

Rust, Eric Charles. "The Authority of the Scripture: The Word of God and the Bible." *Review and Expositor* 57 (January 1960): 26-57.

———. "The Biblical Faith and Modern Science." *Review and Expositor* 71 (Spring 1974): 229-42.

———. *Nature and Man in Biblical Thought*. London: Lutterworth Press, 1953, pp. 1-19.

———. "The Nature and Problems of Biblical Theology." *Review and Expositor* 50 (October 1953): 463-87.

———. "A Postscript: Reply to Harold Lindsell." *Review and Expositor* 71 (Spring 1974): 249-50.

———. *The Word and Words: Towards a Theology of Preaching*. Macon, Ga.: Mercer University Press, 1982, pp. 1-15.

Shoemaker, H. Stephen. "Affirming the Scriptures," *SBC Today*, January 1984, pp. 14-15.

552

Smith, Taylor Clarence. "The Canon and Authority of the Bible." *Southern Baptist Journal,* March-April 1975, pp. 4-5.

———. Review of Clark H. Pinnock, *The Scripture Principle, SBC Today,* May 1986, p. 6.

Spencer, Richard A. "The Role of Biblical Study in Preparation for Ministry." *Faith and Mission* 3 (Spring 1986): 11-22.

Shurden, Walter B. "'I Am the Bible in Baptist History.'" *Baptist History and Heritage* 19 (July 1984): 4-6.

———. "The Problem of Authority in the Southern Baptist Convention." *Review and Expositor* 75 (Spring 1978): 219-33.

Stagg, Frank. *New Testament Theology.* Nashville: Broadman Press, 1962, pp. 1-12.

Steely, John Edward. "Biblical Authority and Baptists in Historical Perspective." *Baptist History and Heritage* 19 (July 1984): 7-15.

Summers, Ray. "Contemporary Approaches in New Testament Study," in *Broadman Bible Commentary,* volume 8. Nashville: Broadman Press, 1969, pp. 48-58.

———. "God Has Spoken." *Baptist Standard,* 7 January 1970, pp. 12-13; "What God Has Said," ibid., 14 January 1970, pp. 8-9; "How God Said It: Part 1," ibid., 21 January 1970, pp. 12-13; "How God Said It: Part 2," ibid., 4 February 1970, pp. 12-13.

Talbert, Charles H. "Biblical Criticism's Role." *SBC Today,* November 1986, pp. 8-9.

———. "Inerrancy: The Central Question," *SBC Today,* February 1986, p. 14.

Tate, Marvin Embry, Jr. "Confronting the Bible: New Openings for Authority." *SBC Today,* March 1987, pp. 6-8.

———. "The Old Testament Apocrypha and the Old Testament Canon." *Review and Expositor* 65 (Summer 1968): 339-56.

———. "Old Testament Theology: The Current Situation." *Review and Expositor* 74 (Summer 1977): 279-300.

Tuck, William Powell. "Was Jesus an Inerrantist?" *SBC Today,* March 1985, pp. 17-19.

Vestal, Daniel G., Jr. "The Word of God: Isaiah 40:6-8." *Southern Baptist Advocate,* May-June 1981, pp. 8-10.

Vinson, Richard B. "Inerrancy Will Settle No Important Bible Questions for the SBC," *SBC Today,* June 1986, pp. 24-25.

Ward, Wayne Eugene. "The Authority of the Bible." *Review and Expositor* 56 (April 1959): 166-77.

———. "The Concept of Holy Scripture in Biblical Literature." Th.D. Dissertation, Southern Baptist Theological Seminary, 1952.

———. *The Drama of Redemption.* Nashville: Broadman Press, 1966, pp. 9-22.

———. "Preaching and the Word of God in the New Testament." *Review and Expositor* 56 (January 1959): 20-30.

———. "Stories That Teach," in Wayne E. Ward and Joseph F. Green, eds., *Is the Bible a Human Book?* Nashville: Broadman Press, 1970, pp. 71-82.

———. "Towards a Biblical Theology." *Review and Expositor* 74 (Summer 1977): 371-87.

———. *The Word Comes Alive.* Nashville: Broadman Press, 1969.

Watts, John D. W. "The Historical Approach to the Bible: Its Development." *Review and Expositor* 71 (Spring 1974): 163-78.

———. "The Methods and Purpose of Biblical Interpretation." *Southwestern Journal of Theology* 2 (April 1960): 7-16.

Westmoreland, N. J. "Will Southern Baptists Declare the Bible to Be Infallible?" *Southern Baptist Journal,* December 1973, pp. 9, 16.

H. Edwin Young

Archer, Gleason L. *Encyclopedia of Bible Difficulties*. Grand Rapids: Zondervan, 1982.

Barclay, William. *The Daily Study Bible, The Gospel of Mark*. Edinburgh: Saint Andrew Press, 1954.

Baxter, J. Sidlow. *Majesty, The God You Should Know*. San Bernardino: Here's Life, 1984.

Boice, James Montgomery. *Does Inerrancy Matter?* Oakland: International Council on Biblical Inerrancy, 1979.

————. *Standing on the Rock; The Importance of Biblical Inerrancy*. Wheaton: Tyndale, 1984.

————. ed. *The Foundation of Biblical Authority*. Grand Rapids: Zondervan, 1979.

Bush, L. Russ, and Nettles, Tom J. *Baptists and the Bible; The Baptist Doctrines of Biblical Inspiration and Religious Authority in Historical Perspective*. Chicago: Moody, 1980.

Buttrick, George Arthur, ed. *General Articles on the New Testament, The Gospel According to St. Matthew, The Gospel According to St. Mark*. Vol. 7 of *The Interpreter's Bible*. 12 Vols. Nashville: Abingdon, 1956.

————, ed. *General Articles on the New Testament, The Gospel According to St. Luke, The Gospel According to St. John*. Vol. 8 of *The Interpreter's Bible*. 12 Vols. Nashville: Abingdon, 1956.

Carroll, B. H. *Inspiration of the Bible*. Nashville: Nelson, 1980.

Criswell, W. A. *Why I Preach That the Bible is Literally True*. Nashville: Broadman, 1969.

Draper, Dr. James T., Jr. *Authority: The Critical Issue For Southern Baptists*. Tappan: Revell, 1984.

Geisler, Norman L., ed. *Biblical Errancy; An Analysis of Its Philosophical Roots*. Grand Rapids: Zondervan, 1981.

————, ed. *Inerrancy*. Grand Rapids: Zondervan, 1980.

Henry, Carl F. H. *God Who Speaks and Shows, Preliminary Considerations*. Vol. 1 of *God, Revelation and Authority*. 6 vols. Waco: Word, 1976.

Jones, Hywel. *The Doctrine of Scripture Today*. Choteau: Gospel Mission, 1980.

Kantzer, Kenneth S. "Evangelicals and the Inerrancy Question." *Christianity Today*.

Lindsell, Harold. *The Battle For the Bible*. Grand Rapids: Zondervan, 1976.

MacArthur, John F., Jr. *Why Believe the Bible?* Ventura: Regal, 1980.

McBeth, H. Leon. *The Baptist Heritage; Four Centuries of Baptist Witness*. Nashville: Broadman, 1987.

Mears, Henrietta. *What The Bible Is All About*. Ventura: Regal, 1982.

Packer, J. I. *Beyond the Battle For the Bible*. Westchester: Cornerstone, 1980.

————. *"Fundamentalism" And The Word of God; Some Evangelical Principles*. Grand Rapids: Eerdmans, 1958.

Pink, Arthur W. *The Divine Inspiration of the Bible*. Grand Rapids: Baker, 1976.

Ryle, J. C. *The Inspiration of the Scriptures*. Choteau: Gospel Mission, 1980.

Sproul, R. C. *Knowing Scripture*. Downers Grove: InterVarsity, 1977.

Stott, John R. W. *God's Book For God's People*. Downers Grove: InterVarsity, 1982.

Ward, Wayne, and Green, Joseph. *Is the Bible a Human Book?* Nashville: Broadman: 1970.

Warfield, Benjamin Breckinridge. *The Inspiration and Authority of the Bible*. Philadelphia: The Presbyterian and Reformed Publishing, 1970.

Young, J. Edward. *Thy Word is Truth; Some Thoughts on the Biblical Doctrine of Inspiration*. Grand Rapids: Eerdmans, 1957.

Notes

Notes

Notes

Notes

Notes

Notes

Notes

Notes

Notes

Notes